The Archaeology of Cathedrals

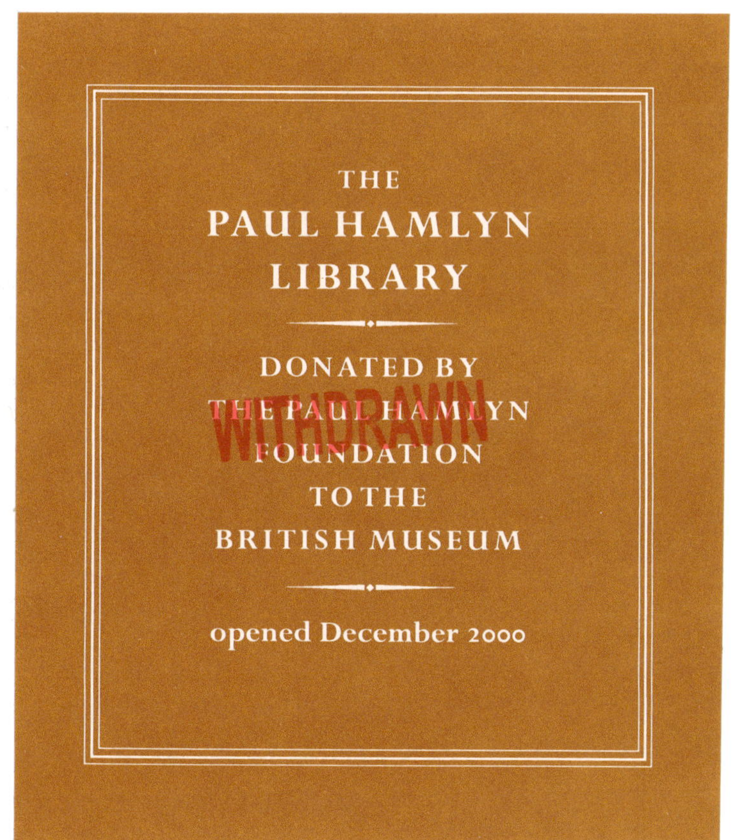

Oxford University Committee for Archaeology
Monograph No. 42

The Archaeology of Cathedrals

Edited by
Tim Tatton-Brown and Julian Munby

Oxford University Committee for Archaeology
1996

Published by the Oxford Committee for Archaeology
Institute of Archaeology
Beaumont Street
Oxford

Distributed by
Oxbow Books, Park End Place, Oxford OX1 1HN

ISBN 0 947816 42 9

Origination and Layout by Oxbow Books
Printed in Great Britain at
The Alden Press, Oxford

Contents

Preface

This volume contains the proceedings of a conference held at Rewley House, Oxford, in April 1989. It reflects the remarkable quality and amount of research in our greater churches and, despite subsequent discoveries, remains a valuable statement of current practice and potential. Cathedrals almost uniquely combine spiritual value with the wonderment at the achievement of past ages; their further study can surely be to the benefit of both.

It remains to thank those, from Rewley House and Oxbow Books, who have made this volume possible, and to apologise to the contributors who are not to be held responsible in any way for production delays that in large part are due to the editors.

Tim Tatton-Brown and Julian Munby
Martinmas 1996

The Archaeological Study of Cathedrals in England, 1800–2000: A Review and Speculation

Richard Morris

"Of all the artistic achievements of the English race" wrote Francis Bond in the introduction to his *Gothic Architecture in England*, published in 1905, "two make unchallenged claim to pre-eminence: our imaginative literature, and our medieval architecture."

Bond's career lies towards the midpoint of the span which is to be considered in this essay. His books on so many aspects of English medieval churches are still required reading, and the ideas and observations they contain make a convenient point from which to look back into the 19th century and forwards up to and beyond the present.

It would be instructive to consider Bond's work within the wider context of what was going on in the arts, academic, and political life in the early 1900s. That is too large a task to be properly undertaken here, but even a quick look at Bond's cultural surroundings raises issues of interest. For example, whereas England's "imaginative literature" had more than held its own through the 19th century, the best new music heard in Victoria's reign had been composed overseas. This was now changing. The first decade of the 20th century has been fairly described as a time of musical renaissance. In the years around the publication of *Gothic Architecture in England* some of its readers might have attended the first performance of Elgar's *The Kingdom*. Vaughan Williams and Holst were rising to prominence: both had immersed themselves in the study of English folksong; Vaughan Williams was working on his epic and visionary *A Sea Symphony*, and was shortly to explore the soundworld of Tudor music in furtherance of his quest for a distinctively national form of utterance. As for literature, 1906 was the year of the first novel of *The Forsyte Saga*. Authors like H. G. Wells and Arnold Bennett were productive; so too George Bernard Shaw, and, albeit from prison, Oscar Wilde. In London town, celebrated a few years before in Elgar's *Cockaigne*, and a few years later by Vaughan Williams's *A London Symphony*, the Bakerloo and Piccadilly tube lines opened.

There has been a tendency to depict much of this activity as a manifestation of Edwardian self-possession, and the rest of it as a naive pursuit of Englishness. But that is a superficial view. Elgar wrote music suffused as much by neurosis and doubt as by confidence. Likewise, although we might now suppose that *Gothic Architecture in England* represented a fulfilment of nearly a century of ecclesiological research, its author viewed the contemporary state of what we would call church archaeology not with pride, but with dismay. "Nowadays", he wrote, "architecture is outside the precincts of culture In this general neglect, medieval architecture beyond all is immersed. For a brief period interest in this supreme artistic achievement of our race was revived by Britton, Pugin, Wyatt, Petit, and Willis, greatest of all. That interest was not to endure" (Bond 1905, xvii-xviii).

Bond looked upon the second quarter of the 19th century as a golden age; his own, as an age of philistinism. Perceptions of golden ages are interesting, not least because of the factors which cause a need for them to be felt. Nevertheless, Bond had a point. He observed that there was no provision for students to study the subject; no Oxbridge chair; no dedicated periodical; no museum of medieval architectural antiquities. The distractions of an empire did not help, for priorities in archaeological excavation were upside down: "Immense sums are spent in excavating civilizations in far-away countries with which we have little concern; our own Byland, Rievaulx, Glastonbury remain lost beneath the soil."

Leaving aside the modern judgement that if only Byland, Rievaulx, and Glastonbury *could* have been left beneath the soil, protected from the sterilising hand of the Office of Works, it is worthwhile to consider the reasons that Bond adduced for the neglect of his subject.

First, Bond noted, medieval buildings are ideally to be studied *in situ*. They stand far apart. Only those endowed with private means and free time could commute between them. Time, rather than access, seems to have been the main problem, for the coming of the railways had revolutionized ecclesiology. After the 1840s journeys to study, compare and revisit churches were immensely easier than the expeditions on foot, by horse, or coach, which had been required previously. Railways and telegraphy also had intriguing side-effects. One of them was nationally consistent time-keeping. After *c*.1850 it was possible for cathedral clocks to be harmonized. Later, railway companies sometimes went to considerable lengths to market their services through the promotion of ecclesiology. In 1925, for instance, the Great Western Railway published a book entitled *Abbeys*. Following an earlier *Cathedrals* volume (1924) this was written by M. R. James, and contains a valuable essay on monastic life and buildings by A. Hamilton Thompson. The main drawback of these books is that their scope is limited to the region served by the GWR.

Second, failing opportunities for study on site, one must have access to accurate records. Bond listed the publications he admired: Brown & Crowther's *Churches of the Middle Ages*; Brandon's *Analysis* and book on timber roofs; Britton – the *Architectural* and *Cathedral Antiquities*; Collings's *Details*; Sharpe's *Parallels* – the rather grammatical character of these titles will be noticed – and of course the works of Willis, which Bond described as being "scattered about" in various sources.[1] Even in the 1900s most of these books were considered rare, costly, and inconveniently bulky. Such a collection was "entirely out of reach" except for residents of London or Oxbridge. So the basic apparatus required for popular study was unavailable. On the other hand, there were compensations: some of the older engravings were now out of copyright, and the advent of photography in publication offered a partial remedy.

Bond's third point lay in what he called the "Fragmentary and disconnected presentation" of the subject. He criticised the tendency of commentators to study the components of cathedrals by period, rather than following them with reference to functional development through time. He thought that aspects of the continuity of the subject were being lost.

And last, Bond attacked systems of periodization. Rickman's four periods, he argued, could be applied only to the development of fenestration. In cathedral planning there were not four periods, but two broad ones; for the development of vaults he argued five; for structural systems, all the main elements were present by 1200. Bond stressed the primacy not of periods but of continuous change. A deficiency of periods is that they have joins, which can acquire a status which may be unrealistic or irrelevant. Bond argued for study which paid due regard to metamorphosis.

So far, then, so bad. It is interesting that Bond reprimanded the provincial archaeological societies for failing in what he saw as their main duty: they had been founded, he said, "mainly" for the study of medieval architecture. Their "proper task" should be that of "analysing, describing, and classifying the churches of each district".

What Bond did not say, apparently because it seemed to him to be self-evident, was why cathedrals and allied buildings required to be analysed or described at all. In this he seems to have been unusual, for some of his contemporaries, and a good number of his predecessors, had tried very hard to define a theoretical basis for their subject.

Edmund Prior, for example, writing in his *Cathedral builders*, published in the same year as Bond's *Gothic architecture*, identified three reasons why cathedral archaeology was important. It mattered because it addressed the "ideals" of Christianity, the "ambitions" of medieval craftsmanship, and the "independence" of English feeling.

This last aspect is significant. As was suggested at the start, the contemporaneity between figures like Elgar and Vaughan Williams and Prior and Bond can be no more coincidental than that of Chaucer, Yeveley, and the world of the *Gawain* poet. If a cultural analogue is to be found for the Perpendicular style – an essentially *indigenous* style – it might well be looked for first in the extension of literacy which took place in 14th-century lay society, increasing the capacity of ordinary people to participate in intellectual matters which formerly had been a clerical preserve; and in the dissolution of linguistic barriers which hitherto had divided different orders of laypeople. What has been described as a "new homogeneity" in English society around 1400 (Cross 1976, 13–14) has an analogue in architecture (Harvey 1978).

Prior's theory of relationship between medieval cathedrals and medieval society followed a different line. It was, in a sense, socialist with a small "s". His concept of the process of artistic design was that it was a matter of common property. Whereas in the 19th century creativity had become a monopoly of individuals, medieval artists, sculptors, and builders were held to be "just folk generally". He discerned no "extraordinary personalities" – only the people. And this is why Prior regarded medieval cathedrals as important: in their art he saw the expression not of "the fancy of a wayward will, but a *revelation of human quality in the aggregate*." Following from this, he divided medieval society into two broad classes: one that took the cathedrals; the other that gave them. As for Christianity, Prior developed the 19th-century idea that Christian style was to be found in the shape of Gothic. The more perfect the building, the more Christian it was.

Prior's idea of cathedral building as the outcome of a lost propensity for collective invention was of course put to the sword by a succession of scholars in the 1920s and 30s, culminating in the research and writings of Dr John Harvey from the 1940s to the present. Harvey's elucidation of the role of individual artists in the design and construction of cathedrals will be known to all, and it is no longer an aspect that needs to be laboured. The romantic (although historically speaking it is *anti*-romantic) notion of collective creativity has been vanquished by the singularity of the controlling hand. Medieval master builders are less conspicuous than figures like William Burges or Richard Rogers not because they were less important or authoritative, but because of the nature and patterns in survival of the sources which document them.

Yet if Prior's vision of co-operative art now seems rather quaint, the basis of his approach stands further consideration. When Prior wrote about why and how cathedrals touch our deeper sensibilities, perhaps he was reaching out for a concept that he could not quite articulate:

> Hardly in the detail of their shaping can lie the source of appeal to the imagination, that stirring of the aesthetic sense which a genuine medieval church seldom fails to make in us. We conclude that the art of the middle ages was *not* this architectural dress, but something underneath it.

There are pre-echoes here of more recent thinking. The structuralism of the early 1980s suggested that every society expresses itself through symbols which signal the same meaning to every member of society. In one sense related to Prior's this is "co-operative", since a mason could only operate using the vocabulary of symbols familiar to his time. But then, there is the question of how such symbols could come to be modified, augmented, or discarded. Theories which have entered archaeological thinking within the last few years – most notably structuration theory – are more concerned with how individual "actors" within society maintain or change the existing social order. Today's theorists might not dispute the influence of individual expression, but they would see such expression as being subordinate to mechanisms of social change.

More akin to Prior's logic, especially his division of cathedral "givers" and "takers" (which exactly reverses what we might assume to have been the relationship between a medieval patron and builder), is the outlook of Marxist archaeologists who might see the cathedral as facilitating the maintenance or intensification of a *status quo*. Here the cathedral is not a manifestation of co-operative art, nor of a shared mentality, so much as an instrument for the enforcement of a single mentality. Visual impact, majesty and scale (apparent today, the belittling effect of a cathedral upon its surroundings was even more dramatic in the Middle Ages), liturgical use, the shrine-like tombs of courtier-bishops: all were used to bind the social order. Crudely put, the first view sees the cathedral as an image of social forces, whereas the second regards it as an instrument of cultural hegemony.

By comparison with Edwardian scholarship the efforts of today's archaeologists in assimilating the material remains of the later Middle Ages to their off-site theoretical reflections seem rather jejune. In result, the practice of archaeology within the medieval period tends more towards description than analysis, and the agenda of research is influenced as much by written sources as by the archaeological material with which the discipline must actually deal. But the themes of archaeology may differ from those of history, and a methodology for placing archaeological and historical records in dialogue has still to be formulated. The development of such an approach may best be introduced by a consideration of approaches which have been adopted in the past.

It is 1912. The Society of Antiquaries of London is sponsoring the first – and until the 1960s, the last – extensive campaign for the archaeological disinterment of a cathedral. The site is Old Sarum.

There were four main seasons of work, reported upon in successive issues of the Society's *Proceedings*. Work began in earnest on 13 May, although there had been some earlier rather basic quasi-remote sensing, involving a sharpened iron bar, and no doubt it was this that enabled Lt Col Hawley and his labourers almost immediately to come upon the south-western corner of the south transept of the lost cathedral. Pursuing this wall, Hawley explained, "we overran its line and found ourselves *inside* the building". Today, of course, this might well be where one would want to be, and taking Hawley's remark out of context it would be easy to depict the work at Old Sarum as pure old-fashioned wall-chasing. In fact, it was impure wall chasing. There was also a good deal of area clearance, leading among other things to the exposure of parts of the medieval cemeteries, some of their monuments still *in situ*, and neighbouring buildings.

The first season saw the recovery of the greater part of the cathedral plan, portions of the defences and precinct boundary, and houses to the west of the church. The 1913 campaign began with innovative zest. In order to remove spoil from the excavation to a large former chalk pit outside the defences, the excavators built a railway which ran across the ditch on a home-made bridge. The bridge cost £77.00, and at the end of the summer the Society appealed for more funds – although the University of Birmingham had already contributed £500 – and there was talk about the desirability of state support through a Minister for Fine Arts. All very prescient. So in its way was the excavation. Among the achievements of that year was the reconstruction of a robbed stone pavement, originally in contrasting colours, but realised anew through the careful brushing out of impressions left in the mortar, and planning of the distribution of stone chippings. The work was facilitated in damp conditions, when soil features became more legible. St John Hope, in his report to the Society of Antiquaries, defined his work as being "a critical science". Development of this science was curtailed by the Great War. Work continued into 1915 on a reduced scale, and then petered out. It might be revived: there is much more to learn.

Not the least of the lessons administered by Old Sarum is that cathedral archaeology is about more than churches. The plan published by RCHME which conflates the discoveries made between 1909 and 1915 reminds us that a cathedral complex of the Old Foundation was a substantial settlement in its own right. The bishop's palace, when occupied, supported a large household which included not only clergy but also knights, squires, yeomen, grooms, pages, and minor ancillaries. To this periodic population may be added the households of the capitular dignitaries (dean, chancellor, precentor, treasurer) and those of the canons who made up the rest of the chapter. It has been pointed out that the residence of a dignitary or canon resembled a manor house (Barley 1986, 64, 60–5). These were substantial establishments, any one of which might possess a gatehouse, courts, a grand hall, chapel, guest rooms, barns, and accommodation for servants, cooks, ostlers and other staff. Since a cathedral complex could contain up to a dozen of these magnate houses massed on or around a single site, the size of its population could equal or exceed that of a small town. The economic demands and influence of these elite enclaves must have been more forceful, akin to those of a city. The requirements in consumption of a cathedral community were both large and specialised. A cathedral, its population, and guests, created demand for luxury goods, garments, cloth, vellum, parchment, special foodstuffs, precious metals and pigments, timber, and other materials, as well as basic commodities.

The extension of cathedral archaeology to embrace considerations beyond those of building form and development is overdue. To what extent, for example, did the social make-up of a cathedral complex – a largely masculine community – resemble or depart from that of the town outside? Were cathedral communities (or parts of them) victualled through the town, or from their own landed resources? Was there in any sense a cathedral economy? If there was, did its development match that of the town, or were there periods when the two behaved differently or pulled in different directions? In what ways did the presence of a cathedral complex influence the development of the town in which it stood? No structured study of a cathedral community – its buildings, society, and economy – has yet taken place. Old Sarum might well be a site where the agenda for such a programme could be worked out.

Returning to our review, the ultimately abortive campaign on that draughty Wiltshire hilltop was to be the last great episode in cathedral archaeology until the 1960s. Of course, in the decades that followed there was constant scholarly attention being directed towards cathedrals, whether included in works of general synthesis, as in Clapham's book on Romanesque architecture (1934), or particularlistic inquiries into glass, or wallpainting, or liturgy, or sculpture. In 1925 came Alexander Hamilton Thompson's fine book – arguably the best general study until the second edition of Harvey's in the 1970s. But in all of this we find that cathedral architecture and, saving Harvey, archaeology, had somehow parted company. Causes of this estrangement, and of the subsequent reconciliation which began in the late 1960s, have been reviewed elsewhere and need not be repeated (e.g. Morris 1979; 1983; Rodwell 1989; Tatton-Brown 1989). Nevertheless, it will be useful to observe some of the consequences of the changing nature of the relationship. York is as good a cathedral as any at which to do this (Phillips 1985, 9–46).

Works characteristic of the doldrum period were carried out in 1930, when there was limited excavation within the eastern crypt. Sir Charles Peers published the results (Peers 1931). Peers was the Great Man who pronounced upon findings made by others. His contact with the site was limited to one or two visits. Other Great Men, including, on occasion, Willis and St John Hope, worked in the same way. The intention here is not to make anachronistic criticism of worthy predecessors who were simply operating within the conventions of their time. The aim is rather to draw attention to the fact that successive interpretations of the 11th-century cathedral at York failed to recognize that the layout departed from expected norms. Hence, Willis gave it aisles, whereas it had none. Peers did not even recognize it as being of the 11th century, but propagated a theory that what is the eastern arm of the 11th-century cathedral was a basilica built in the 8th. His idea lived on to be restated by Taylor & Taylor (1965, 700–709; corrected in Taylor 1978, 1086). Again, we must not abuse the gift of hindsight. But we might reflect that what is extraordinary about the discoveries made at York between 1967 and 1972 centres less upon the strange aisleless building that was gradually wrestled into focus through archaeology which was conducted, initially, in the teeth of official complacency (Phillips 1985, 38), but rather that York is the only cathedral at which such an opportunity for extensive study has yet arisen. What assumptions and oft-copied plans would have to be changed or redrawn if similar campaigns were to be undertaken at Lincoln, or Lichfield, and has recently been done at Canterbury? As Bond remarked: "No honest student can continue to work at this subject year after year without having his good opinion of his previous work considerably lowered".

The range of interests represented within current and future archaeological study of cathedrals is large. As a point of principle, it is good that we have recaptured the definition of archaeology from the sub-surface sense to which it was unfortunately narrowed in the middle years of the century. The rest of this book makes manifest that the archaeology of a cathedral concerns all of the building, above and below ground, while part of the aim of this introductory chapter is to stress that a medieval cathedral was more than a church.

Archaeology in the 1990s, reinforced and legitimized by the new *Care of Cathedrals Measure*, will tackle many questions. One of them concerns medieval technology – how buildings were designed, erected, and what ideas (both technical and metaphysical) could lie behind their structural systems. As a foundation we have the work of Professor Heyman (1966; 1967; 1967–8; 1968), or of Derek Phillips and his interpretation of the 11th-century substructure at York which contained some two miles of oak (Phillips 1985); or the photoelastic modelling of structural performance of vaults (Mark 1982). There is an archaeology of liturgy and ritual: how buildings and their spaces were used, and the changing character and emphasis of their ritual geography. The cult of saints, their influences upon the sites, layouts, and financing of cathedrals is being examined anew, from several perspectives. There is an archaeology of mentalities, witnessed in sculpture, adornment, and tombs. Beneath cathedral pavements are burials, with evidence for ecclesiastical status, funeral customs, palaeodemography. And beneath them there are buried landscapes: the sites as they were before cathedral builders got to work, sometimes distinguished by prominent structures of earlier ages, the presence, status, and final uses of which may have significances which have yet to be discerned. All these form part of the proper field of current and future inquiry.

Yet, to an extent, the cathedral church is a beguiling distraction from larger issues for which no strategy has yet emerged. Some of these have already been mentioned: for example, the size, housing, composition, and consumption of the cathedral community, all within the larger context of the cathedral town, and that within its hinterland. This broader approach is demanded not simply in order to rescue the cathedral church from its present position as a kind of disembodied art-object and return it to its former surroundings. It is required because the cathedral settlement represents a rare concentration of economic, temporal, and spiritual power within medieval society. Study of this convergence, which is amply represented in the physical remains with which archaeology has to deal, has scarcely begun. It calls for the establishment of research paths of a complexity which individual urban units, increasingly preoccupied with the exigencies of competitive tendering, may not be able to deliver.

Whence, then, should inspiration come? Should we leave it to individual initiative and chance? Or to the creative action of an appropriately located university department? Or to the instincts of English Heritage inspectors? It is certainly a matter to which the Society of Antiquaries or the Society for Medieval Archaeology could address itself; but so too could the CBA, which over the years has built up a fund of expertise in ecclesiastical politics and diplomacy. But perhaps the new Cathedrals Fabric Commission should take the lead? After all, its terms of reference provide for it.

One or several of these suggestions may take root. But there is a strong case for merging the lot into a concerted programme of research which is jointly sponsored by all the national bodies which have been mentioned. Nor should the international dimension be overlooked. As Christopher Wilson's recent book amply demonstrates, the English cathedral was but part of a much wider phenomenon (Wilson 1990), and it is not only British archaeology which needs and deserves an enterprise towards which it can rally. A European project on the archaeology of cathedral communities would be a timely enterprise.

Will it happen? Would that we now possessed the certainty expressed in the foreword to Winkles's *Architectural and picturesque illustrations of the cathedral churches*, published in 1838.

> An eminent and learned prelate has drawn a beautiful analogy betwixt a church, as displaying the admirable effect of the principles of architecture, and the Christian religion. The diverse order and economy of the one, seems to be emblematically set forth by the just, plain, and majestic architecture of the other: and as the one consists of a great variety of parts united in the same regular design according to the truest art, and most exact proportion, so the other contains a decent subordination of members, various sacred institutions, sublime doctrines, and solid precepts of morality digested into the same design, and with an admirable concurrence tending to one view – the happiness and exaltation of human nature.

This is a variant of the 19th century's theory of characteristic forms. Britton put it more pithily: "Every building of magnitude should be distinguished by decisive and positive marks of its purport". Britton saw a contrast between 18th- and 19th-century values in this respect. Thinking that his predecessors saw buildings as being merely pretty, he saw them as useful. If the Georgian could look at a cathedral to amuse, the Victorian would look to inform. What purpose may the 20th-century Elizabethan discern?

The torrent of study, writing, and illustration of the early 19th century was prompted not least by the fact that such systematic investigation had not been done before. When Britton published his volume on Canterbury he wrote:

> Many of its architectural features had never been published. The sections and elevations of its towers, nave, quire, transepts and crypts, have not been previously offered to the public; and these are indispensably necessary to display its construction, and exemplify its history. Without sections and strict geometrical elevations we can never attain correct information as to the curvature and proportions of arches – the true contour of columns, capitals, and bases – with the relative projections and recesses of various other members in our ancient buildings. With them we are furnished with satisfactory data, either for practical imitation or for antiquarian reference.

Antiquarian reference? There has perhaps been a tendency to downplay or even ridicule the efforts of architectural historians in the pre-Britton/Rickman era. The 19th-century mania for documenting the past was preceded by an age in which no reliable interpretative handbook could be interposed between an ancient building and the eye. In some cases the resulting commentaries were farcical, but even behind some exaggerated claims we might detect principles ancestral to those of structural criticism. It was, for instance, said of Thomas Gray that he "did not so much depend upon written accounts, as upon that *internal evidence which the buildings themselves give of their respective antiquity*". This looks encouraging, but Gray's credentials as an early structural critic are rather thrown into question when his biographer adds that Gray "arrived at so very extraordinary a pitch of sagacity as to be able to pronounce, at first sign, on the 'precise time' when every particular part of any of our cathedrals was erected" (Mason 1807, 239–40; cited in Clark 1962, 25).

The need for "antiquarian reference" remains with us. As explained above, our horizon has a circumference which is far larger than that perceived by our predecessors. The need for primary data remains as pressing now as it was in Britton's day not because the earlier data are inadequate, but because their range, and the issues upon which they can inform, has been massively extended. Nor should we forget that our capacity to destroy them, along with our environment, has been correspondingly enlarged.

Curiosity about ourselves and the products of human

aims and achievements is one of the characteristics which defines our species. When this is set against an ever-sharpening awareness of the extent and vulnerability of what there is *to be known*, our justification is complete. Often, the choice is to find out now, or never to know. Until very recently, there were a few deans and chapters who would take the "never" option; either because of a lingering complacent faith in the abilities of the likes of Thomas Gray, or out of defensiveness in seeking to assert pastoral over archaeological priorities, or simply on grounds of time and cost. But the deans, provosts, and chapters are themselves in some ideological turmoil. Not all, I think, are entirely convinced of the current, still less future, relevance of the buildings for which they strive to care. Recent tinkering with cathedrals and their contents – the visitor centres, treasuries, missions of tourism, the Mappa Mundis – could be seen as a symptom of deeper disquietude. Buildings are a focus for blame and complaint within the Church because they are conveniently mute and unprotesting objects upon which to project the consequences of inadequacy in mission.

Nowhere better than in and around a cathedral do we encounter the need to analyse the nature of our responses to the past. These responses are multiple, for a cathedral has many audiences – emotional, spiritual, academic, aesthetic – each of which is always changing. In such circumstances, no one audience can be "correct" in its reactions, or claim a monopoly on the management practices which its response at a given time may appear to require.

It is as well to realise that our archaeological culture in the 1990s is not so much conservationist as archival. Unable, at least for the time being, to develop our cathedrals with the ease and confidence enjoyed by earlier generations, we have turned inwards, paralysed by a kind of artist's block. Meanwhile, we steadily convert these buildings into archaeologically useless facsimiles of their former selves. In this process the archaeologist is depicted by some on the fundamentalist wing of followers of William Morris and John Ruskin as being compliant, neutral, an observer, documenting data which are themselves the by-products of a form of documentation. Indeed, there are those who regard the archaeologist almost as a kind of conservationist antichrist: someone who will, given half a chance, cause actual bodily harm to authentic fabric, and dissipate the mystery of a cathedral by forcing forth all its secrets.

The first criticism may contain some justice – but only to the extent that harm is being done to cathedral fabrics every day. Archaeological study and intervention are generally occasioned not by curiosity but by the responsibility to record fabric which is already doomed by rot, acid rain, decay, or the consequences of past mismanagement. Such fabric will be destroyed whether or not the archaeologist takes part in the exequies.

As to the second complaint – that the archaeologist may deprive a cathedral of its latent value (whatever that is), there ought not to be the slightest risk. All experience shows that investigation multiplies, not reduces, questions; and recent results are far more remarkable and unexpected than the antiquaries' fancies which preceded them. Nevertheless, the caricature of the archaeologist as a destroyer of dreams is something against which we need to guard. The drift of archaeology in the 1970s and 1980s has been towards the extraction of data by technicians, with no corresponding encouragement or support for the interpretation and synthesis of results, or the integration of those results with history. Such work might be thought appropriate for universities. But they too have their problems, and their critics.

In some sense, therefore, what is now to be looked for is an enlightened yoking together of the best of the last 200 years of study: an archaeology which catches something of the romance of the late 18th and early 19th century; the functionalism, enthusiasm, and continuing search for an informing theory of the mid-Victorian age; the range and precision of modern archaeological techniques; the best of Edwardian writing; and the discipline of co-operation. That is a tall order. But to shirk the challenge on grounds of helplessness, lack of imagination, or quarrelsome behaviour within the movement of conservation would be unforgivable.

Note

1 For a full bibliography of Willis's work see below (p.165–6).

References

Barley, M. W. 1986: *Houses and History.*
Bond, F. 1905: *Gothic architecture in England.*
Bond, F. 1912: *The Cathedrals of England and Wales.*
Clapham, A. W. 1934: *English Romanesque Architecture After the Conquest.*
Clark, K. 1962: *The Gothic Revival.* 3 edn.
Cross, C. 1976: *Church and People 1450–1660.*
Harvey, J. H. 1974: *Cathedrals of England and Wales.*
Harvey, J. H. 1978: *The Perpendicular Style.*
James, M. R. 1925: *Abbeys.*
Heyman, J. 1966: 'The stone skeleton', *International Jnl Solids Structures*, 2, 249–79.
Heyman, J. 1967: 'Spires and fan vaults', *International Jnl Solids Structures*, 3, 243–57.
Heyman, J. 1967–8: 'Beauvais Cathedral', *Trans Newcomen Soc*, 40, 15–32.
Heyman, J. 1968: 'On the rubber vaults of the Middle Ages, and other matters', *Gazette des Beaux-Arts*, 71, 177–???.
Mark, R. 1982: *Experiments in Gothic Structure.*
Mason, W. 1807: *Works of Thomas Gray, with a Memoir of his Life and Writing.* Vol. 2.
Morris, R. 1979: *Cathedrals and Abbeys of England and Wales.*
Morris, R. 1983: *The church in British archaeology.* CBA Research Report 47.
Peers, C. R. 1931: 'Recent discoveries in the Minsters of Ripon and York', *Antiqs Jnl*, 11, 113–22.
Phillips, D. 1985: *The Cathedral of Archbishop Thomas of Bayeux. Excavations at York Minster. Volume II.* RCHME.
Prior, E. S. 1905: *The Cathedral Builders in England.*
Rodwell, W. J. 1989: *Church Anthology.*

Sharpe, E. 1848: *Architectural parallels.*
Tatton-Brown, T. 1989: *Great Cathedrals of Britain.*
Taylor, H. M. 1978: *Anglo-Saxon Architecture.* Vol. 3.
Taylor, H. M. & Taylor, J. 1965: *Anglo-Saxon Architecture.* Vols. 1 & 2.
Thompson, A. H. 1925: *The Cathedral Churches of England.*
Wilson, C. 1990: *The Gothic Cathedral. The Architecture of the Great Church 1130–1530.*

Seventh-Century Work at Ripon and Hexham

Richard N. Bailey

INTRODUCTION

Drama attended the first appearance on the scholarly scene of the crypts at both Ripon and Hexham (Fig. 2.1). The Elizabethan antiquary William Camden provided the earliest notice of Ripon's structure in 1586, when his attention was understandably seized by its function as the setting for a local virginity test; unsullied maidens passed easily through a converted lamp-niche from the north passage into the main crypt chamber whilst others, with a more suspect history, were miraculously detained (Camden 1586, 406). Hexham's debut came somewhat later, with less folklore but a stronger element of farce. Here the very existence of a crypt had been forgotten in the post-medieval period until, in 1725, a workman engaged in constructing a buttress to shore up the thirteenth-century tower, inadvertently dropped into the north passage (Hodges 1888, 20). For over a century after this discovery the possible links between the two sites remained unnoticed until, in papers delivered in the 1840s, the Ripon historian John Walbran set out the connection and argued for the first time that both were the work of St Wilfrid (Walbran 1846; 1848).

To the visitor these crypts now offer a rare experience. Other English churches may contain seventh-century fabric but only at these two sites is it still possible to stand completely enclosed within walls and roofs built during the first century of English Christianity. For an historian this experience is further enriched by the knowledge that these crypts are firmly-dated structures – and thus rare phenomena in early medieval architecture – as well as

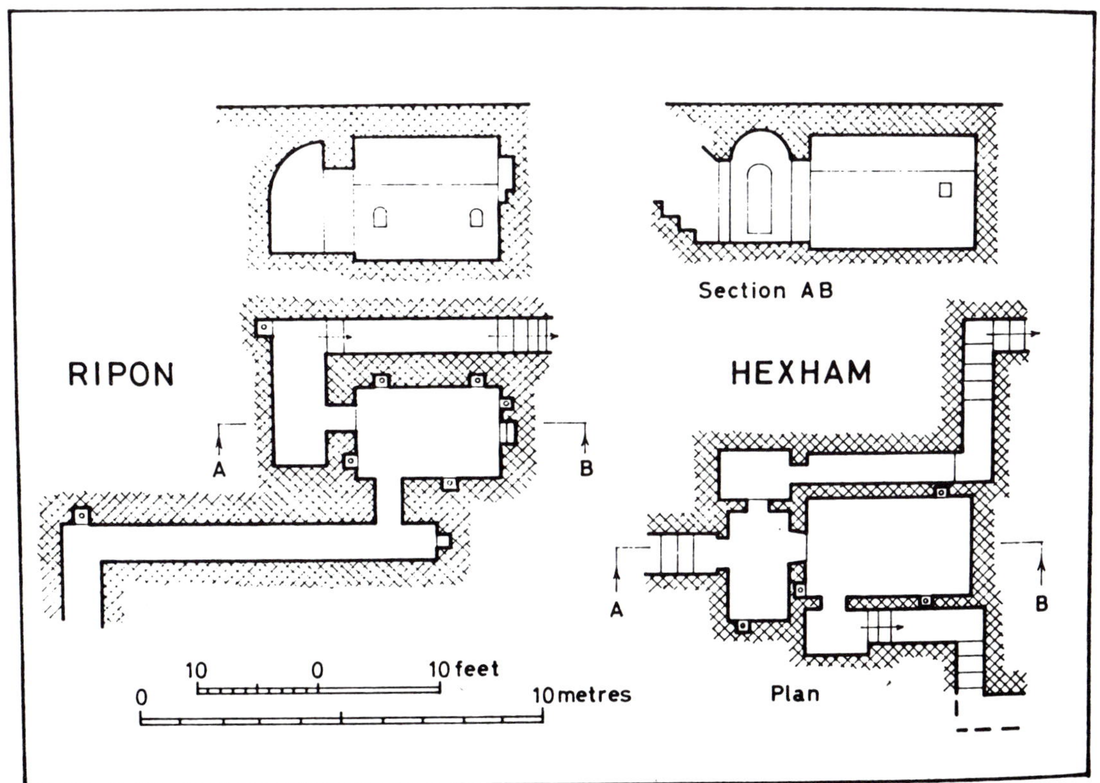

Fig. 2.1. Hexham and Ripon crypts (after Taylor and Taylor 1965–1978 by kind permission of the author and Cambridge University Press).

being the work of one of the most influential figures in the early church, St Wilfrid.

Since Walbran's day both crypts have, naturally, been the subject of scholarly study (Taylor and Taylor 1965–1978, 297–312, 516–18, 1014–17; Gilbert 1974; Bailey 1976; Hall forthcoming). But, despite excavations and documentary research at both sites, many problems remain unresolved. Some of the difficulties, and a few possible solutions, are outlined in what follows.

DATING

The date of the two crypts depends primarily on the identification of the existing structure at Hexham with the *domibus mire politis lapidibus* described by Wilfrid's contemporary biographer Stephen as forming part of the main monastic church built by the saint after he had received a land-grant in AD 671 x 673 (Colgrave 1927, 46; Roper 1974; Kirby 1983). I see no reason to question this identification. Not only has the whole area been so trenched and disturbed that any other crypt would have been discovered by now, but its plan and position only make sense as work of that period.

Ripon's crypt goes with Hexham's. Admittedly Stephen's description of the dedication of Wilfrid's church at this Yorkshire site (AD 669–678) makes no mention of a crypt but this was because it was not germane to his main purpose which was to record the impressive consecration ceremony and, vitally, the land-grants made at the time (Colgrave 1927, 34–6). Despite a lack of documentary support the two crypts are clearly the product of the same mind. Negatively, as we will see, they stand apart from all surviving early medieval crypts in Europe. More positively they share distinctive elements in their plans, their constructional techniques and their metrology. Both were built in large holes which were then backfilled against rising walls incorporating Roman stone; both were laid out in terms of 'northern rods' (Fig. 2.2) (see: Huggins, Rodwell and Rodwell 1983; Fernie 1985; Kjølbye-Biddle 1986); both show by a massive mortared buttressing against the east wall a similar solution to a stability problem (Bailey and O'Sullivan 1979, 153–4; Jones 1932,75). Both have western ante-chambers, with air vents to the surface, which preface vaulted main chambers of identical width. Both have northern passages of identical length flanking the main chamber. The two entrances to that main chamber stand in the same relationship to each other at both sites and are of the same height. Both have lamp-niches of a peculiar design in which a pyramidal head collected

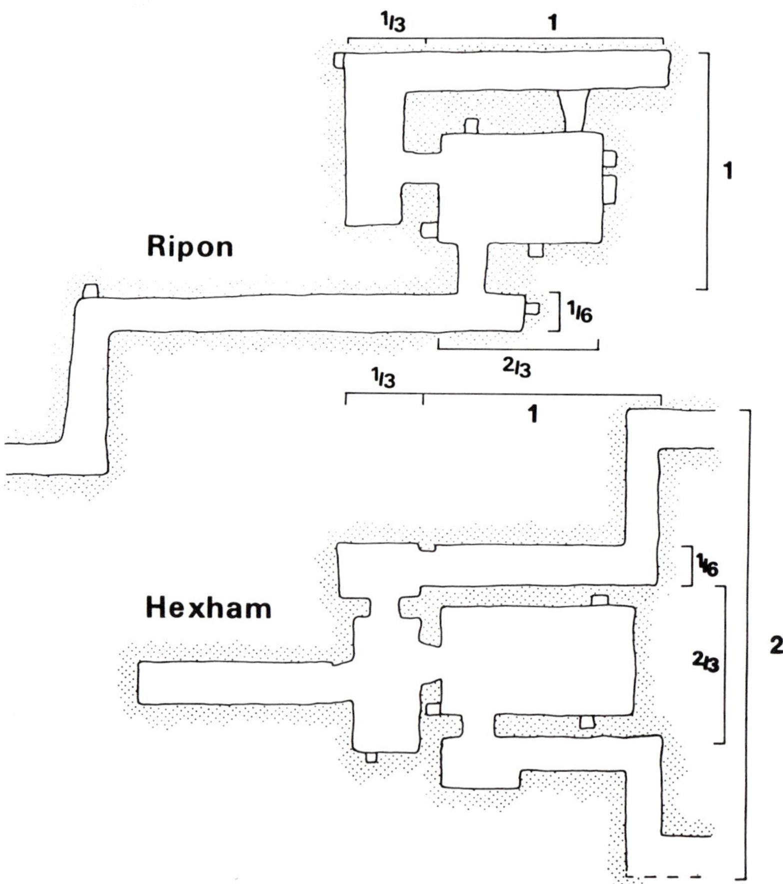

Fig. 2.2. Northern rod units and the crypts. The plan of Hexham is taken from Hodges and Gibson 1919; the plan of Ripon derives from Jones' plan prepared after excavations of 1930.

Fig. 2.3. Fish-eye lens view of Ripon crypt looking east (photo. courtesy S. Hill and York Archaeological Trust).

the soot (which was then perhaps re-cycled in the scriptorium). Finally both sites, according to Peers (1931, 116), used the same system of vaulting. There are, of course, differences but all are explicable in terms of the availability of materials and of the assimilation of lessons learned at one site (Ripon) in building at a second (Hexham). The landscape of Anglo-Saxon architectural history is littered with structures attributed by optimistic scholars to St Wilfrid. In the case of the crypts at Ripon and Hexham, however, the link seems unassailable.

Function

Some of the differences between Hexham and Ripon can be interpreted as a progressive sophistication of solutions to the dual function of crypts as identified by Taylor (1968); that of ensuring the security of the relics whilst giving access to those who wish to venerate them. Ripon's arrangement of passages suggests that the pilgrim passed *through* the main chamber; Hexham's addition of a third exit would obviate this necessity. It is usually assumed that, in the more developed system of Hexham, the pilgrim would approach the crypt *via* the western stairway but a stronger case can be made for an entrance at both sites through the northern passage. This would lead the visitor down a sharply-turning dark passage to a gloomy ante-chamber where he would suddenly be confronted by the revelation of the relics in the main chamber, their enshrining containers glittering in the light shed from the candles in the niches. It was precisely this combination of disorientation and sudden revelation which captured the imagination of William the Cantor in describing the tenth-century crypt at Winchester (Campbell 1950, 69). And the shuffling difficult approach down the north passage would also typify a characteristic of shrine architecture, identified by Brown, in providing a 'microcosm of pilgrimage' by 'playing out the long delays of pilgrimage in miniature' (Brown 1981, 87).

Relationship to the Above-ground Structures

Apart from fragments of architectural sculpture, which at Hexham betray an aggressively continental taste, little now survives above ground of the buildings of which the crypts once formed an integral part. Some indication of their extent and plan has, admittedly, been won by excavation over the last century and a half but the record is more one of opportunities lost than of advantages taken (Taylor and Taylor 1965–78, 297–311; Bailey 1976; Hall 1995).

Ripon was first attacked archaeologically in 1891 by Micklethwaite in a misguided attempt to locate the grave of St Wilfrid, which he believed to lie at the east end of the south passage (Micklethwaite 1892). This investigation incidentally revealed the existence of two relic deposits behind the lamp-niches on the south side of the main chamber and at the eastern end of the south passage. These deposits had been seen earlier by Carter in 1790 and by Walbran in 1858/9 and presumably represent assemblages of the Reformation period (Carter 1806;

HEXHAM 1978 **ROOF OF SAXON CRYPT**

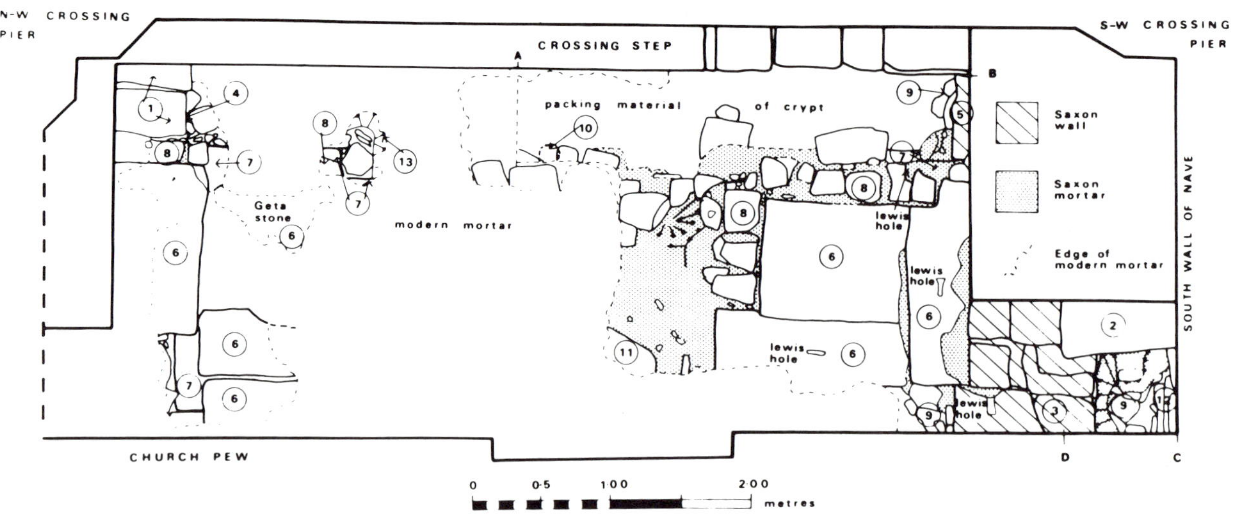

Fig. 2.4. Hexham: plan of 1978 excavation. Key 1. Roman decorated stones; 2. part of the medieval screen-platform; 3. Saxon wall; 4. foundations of crossing pier; 5. offset of Saxon wall; 6. roofing slabs of passages; 7. passage walls; 8. mortared packing of roofing slabs; 9. foundations of Saxon wall; 10. post-hole; 11. exposed top of vault; 12. footings of nave wall.

Walbran 1859,20). More important was Micklethwaite's observation that the outer face of the crypt walls was very rough, because this matches with earlier records, made when the organ was built in the 1870s that the outer face of the east wall of the main chamber was 'so irregular, some of the stones projecting far beyond others, that there can be no doubt whatever that it was never intended to be seen' (Micklethwaite 1882, 354; 1892, 192). The implication of all this is that the crypt was, from the first, entirely subterranean. This deduction is supported by Hall's 1974 excavations in the north passage which showed that the original steps lead up virtually to the level of the present floor (Hall 1977, fig. 3). Further evidence pointing to the same conclusion can be drawn from Peers' excavations over the crypt in 1930 for he discovered two substantial east-west foundations, flanking the crypt system, whose ashlar facing on the south side was only some 6 inches below the capstone of the adjacent passage (Jones 1932, 75). Though of pre-twelfth century date, these foundations cannot be assigned to the Wilfridian period with certainty and thus can only be used as supporting evidence for pre-Conquest floor levels. The same status must be accorded the flooring noted by Micklethwaite some 1 foot 7½ inches below the present paving (Micklethwaite 1892, 192).

Despite these reservations about the date of Peers' foundations and Micklethwaite's flooring, it is nevertheless clear that no part of the crypt was originally visible above ground level. It follows therefore that the large niche in the east wall of the crypt (Fig. 2.3) cannot be interpreted as a window. Nor can it have functioned as a *fenestella* offering a view of the relic chamber to the priest or congregation above, because there is no apparent break in the mortared rubble behind the backing of the niche. It is thus best seen as a setting for an important relic, analogous to the shallow, arched and stepped niches published by Magni from ninth-century Italy at churches like S. Felice de Pavie (Magni 1979).

At Hexham, excavations in 1978 clearly established that this crypt also was originally entirely underground and that the present nave-floor level equates with that of the Wilfridian church (Bailey and O'Sullivan 1979, 150–4). This conclusion emerged from the discovery of a wall, built at the same time as the crypt, which passes over the southern passage; at a later date it had been incorporated into the base of a thirteenth-century stone screen (Figs. 2.4, 2.5, 2.6, 2.7). Its plastered face and the level of its excavated foundations show that earlier attempts to propose a half-subterranean crypt with raised sanctuary above must now be abandoned.

No clear evidence for the above-ground Wilfridian church at Ripon has been traced archaeologically. It is possible that the foundations discovered by Peers, which incorporated two large cylindrical drums, date to the seventh century. But they could equally belong to re-building after Eadred's 948 sacking of the church (Peers 1931; Jones 1932; Hall 1995). Much more survived at Hexham but the story of its modern exploitation is one of continual frustration. The workman's precipitous descent into the crypt in 1725 occurred during building operations designed to stabilise the tower. The cause of its threatened collapse, apart from the void thus unexpectedly revealed, was the absence of a nave to the west of the crossing. By the eighteenth century this area had become a cemetery in

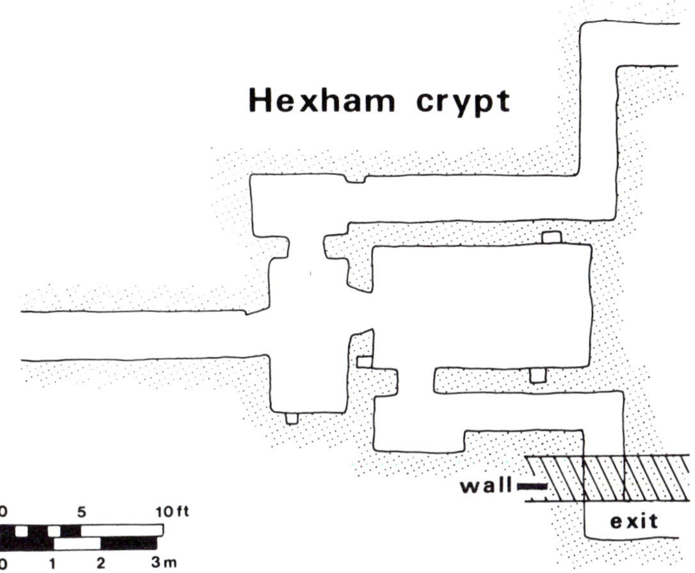

Fig. 2.5. Hexham: relationship of excavated wall and passage.

which a mass of inter-cutting graves were scattered among the foundations and partially standing walls of earlier structures on the site (Bailey 1976, 47). Nineteenth-century pamphleteers inveighed against the desecration and the insanitary conditions of this graveyard and these protests gradually forced its clearance in the course of the later part of the century. A local architect, Hodges (who produced a sumptuous study of the visible fabric in 1888), recorded the foundations and walls which were then revealed, both during this clearance and the subsequent operations connected to the controversial building of the new nave in 1907/1909.

Though he produced some indications of his observations and deductions in successive guidebooks (Hodges 1888; Savage and Hodges 1907; Hodges and Gibson 1919; Hodges 1921), Hodges could not be persuaded to produce a full study based upon his unrivalled knowledge of the site. This refusal was all the more frustrating for his correspondents because the evidence itself had now been sealed inaccessibly below the new nave. Eventually, in penury, he assembled a composite plan and section for Baldwin Brown who was then preparing the second edition of the architectural volume of *The Arts in Early England* (Brown 1925, 167). In the event Brown could make little of their information and the drawings languished unused until their re-discovery by Taylor who first published them in 1961 (Taylor and Taylor 1961). On the basis of Hodges' plan (Fig. 2.8) several reconstructions of the Wilfridian church have been attempted but all suffered from a series of fundamental flaws which were ruthlessly exposed by Cambridge in his re-assessment of Hodges' evidence (Cambridge 1979). He showed that the architect's drawings were selective in their record and that his method of identifying 'Saxon' foundations was ill-founded (Fig. 2.9). More seriously, he argued convincingly that all commentators had followed Hodges in two false assumptions. The first was that the documentary evidence of the *Chronicle of Lanercost* proved that Wilfrid's church was still standing to the west of the present crossing until the Scots' raid of 1296. The second was that there was no completed post-Conquest nave on the site. Cambridge exploded both of these myths and, in so doing, freed us from the need to identify *all* of the foundations recorded by Hodges as Anglo-Saxon in date.

A new reconstruction can therefore now be offered, with all due allowance made for its tentative nature (Fig. 2.10). This begins with Taylor's recognition that Hodges' drawing unwittingly recorded the existence of *two* Anglo-Saxon churches; a small apsed structure being set to the east of the main church, whose own east end ought logically to lie close to the crypt. This reconstruction also

Fig. 2.6. Hexham excavations 1978. The north side of the Saxon wall underlying the later screen platform. Note plaster adhering to the tooled face of the wall stone which bridges the passage and the lewis hole on the adjacent cover stone.

Fig. 2.7. Hexham excavations 1978 looking west. Saxon wall to left; passage capping stones with lewis holes in foreground.

draws upon the fact that the 1978 excavations revealed a wall (Figs. 2.4, 2.5, 2.6, 2.7), crossing over the crypt passage and contemporary with it, which must sit on the foundation, conventionally marked 'j', noted by Hodges and recorded on his plan (Fig. 2.8). Line 'j' must therefore be Anglo-Saxon and, indeed, Wilfridian.

This wall also has a bearing on the vexed question as to whether Wilfrid's church was a basilican building, its nave flanked by continuous aisles, or consisted of a large liturgical space surrounded by an envelope of porticus. The literary evidence of Stephen and Bede is ambiguous on this point (Colgrave 1927, 46; Colgrave and Mynors 1969, 530). Bede records that Bishop Acca created porticus within the walls of his predecessor's church but this need not imply that the building was not already compartmentalised. Colgrave's translation of Stephen's description of Wilfrid's church certainly conjures up a basilica: 'manifold building above ground, supported by many columns (*columnis*) and side aisles'. But Colgrave's 'many ... side aisles' renders *porticibus multis*, which could equally refer to the type of porticus-surround familiar from Reculver, Brixworth or Jarrow. Nor need *columnis* necessarily require an aisled structure for these might have taken a half-round attached form (Gilbert 1974, 103–4). The contemporary seventh and eighth century evidence does not therefore compel us to reconstruct Wilfrid's church as a basilica. And what evidence we have from the 1978 excavations about (what must have been) the main load-bearing wall on foundation 'j' was that it was solid and not arcaded. The attached reconstruction consequently follows the excavated evidence.

This drawing also, of course, depends on certain other assumptions. Two of them are crucial. The first is that Hodges accurately recorded the *full* length of foundation 'j' and thus established that the Wilfridian church extended no further west than the later medieval and present naves. The second assumption is that the same arrangement of passage and load-bearing wall obtained on the north side as was shown to exist by excavation on the south side; in other words, the wall passed over the south-north leg of the passage with the entrance/exit lying outside the main body of the church (Fig. 2.5).

The end result of all this argument and deduction is a building which is not far removed from the proportions of Benedict Biscop's near-contemporary Jarrow, as it can be established from excavated and other evidence (Cramp 1976, fig. 30). In view of the shared training and background of Wilfrid and Benedict Biscop this resemblance is not perhaps surprising; what is probably less expected is that the combined lengths of the two (admittedly often hypothetical) buildings at both sites are virtually identical.

Form and Meaning

The two crypts cannot easily be matched in form elsewhere in Europe (in general see: Thümmler 1958, 97–104; Taylor 1968; Grabar 1972, 436–52; Heitz 1977; Magni 1979). They certainly share elements of their planning with the so-called 'annular' types with which they have often been grouped. But there are significant differences from this set. There is for example the presence of ante-chambers, whilst the relative size of the main chambers at Ripon and Hexham suggests that they were not planned to function in quite the same way as most of the annular crypts spawned by St Peter's in Rome. Moreover

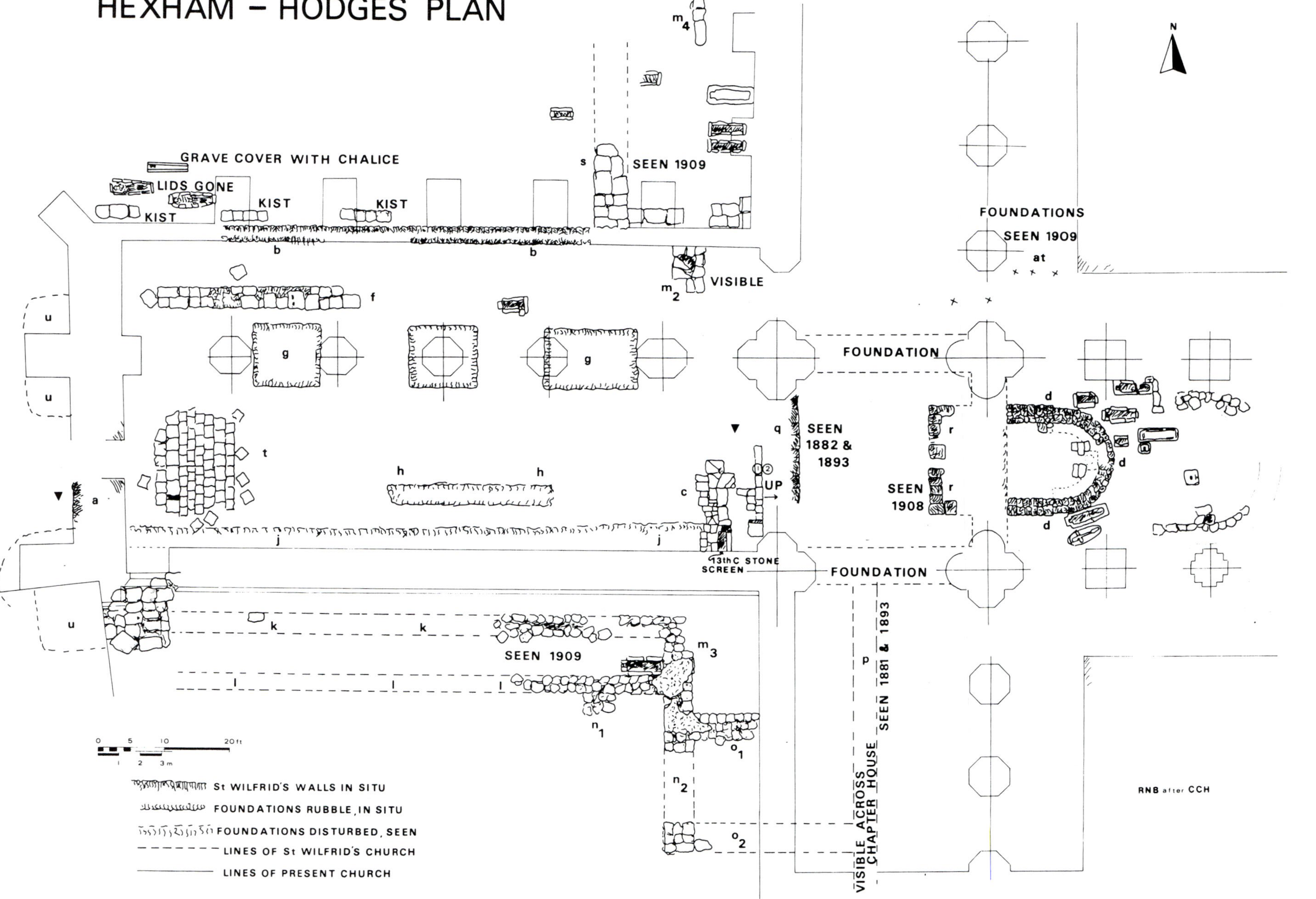

Fig. 2.8. Hexham: Hodges' plan. The key and all other descriptions are those shown handwritten on Hodges' plan. The letter identifications are those of Taylor and Taylor 1965–1978. The triangle at the west end marks the point where Hodges wrote "Piece of W. face W. wall in situ vide photographs and remarks by C.C.H.". The triangle west of line "q" marks a stuck-on label reading "E. wall of crypt about here".

Fig. 2.9. Hexham excavations 1978. Roman sculptured stone re-used in foundations of north-west pier of thirteenth-century crossing, contradicting Hodges' claim that re-use of Roman stone was diagnostic of Saxon foundations at the site.

eastern entrances to the entire crypt system and *western* entrances to the main relic chamber are very peculiar features to find in annular forms when placed under the *east* end of their respective churches; to his credit Micklethwaite (1882; 1896) realised this difficulty long ago though his own radical solution is no longer acceptable.

In view of these problems in fitting Wilfrid's crypts into an annular classification it is worth noting that there are non-annular forms surviving from Europe which may reflect other, now-lost, models available to the saint during his travels. At Grenoble, for instance, the eighth-century crypt of Saint-Laurent provides an example of a chamber flanked by passages which approach from the east whilst a church at Disentis in Switzerland preserves a crypt, inserted in the eighth century, which offers a parallel to Ripon in its combination of western and eastern passages (Sennhauser 1979, fig. 14).

Since, however, there are no close parallels available among surviving European crypts it is not unreasonable to suggest that Wilfrid may have had other forms of structure in mind when planning the subterranean chambers of Ripon and Hexham. Gem for example has recently drawn attention to possible inspiration in the catacombs of Rome from which many of the saint's carefully catalogued relics must have originated (Gem 1983, 3). Their combination of vaulted chambers and narrow passages might well have been one influence behind these Northumbrian crypts.

To any list of potential sources I venture to add another entry: the Holy Sepulchre in Jerusalem. As a whole series of studies has shown, the Anastasis church had an enormous influence on art and architecture across the medieval Christian world (Conant 1956; Krautheimer 1971a, 90–8; Krautheimer 1971b, 116–30; Heitz 1986). By the seventh century its impact can be traced in Merovingian Gaul, as Elbern's subtle study of the Hypogée des Dunes at Poitiers has convincingly demonstrated (Elbern 1961; Elbern 1962; Heitz 1987, 84; but see Grabar 1974, 12–14). That paper also (relevantly for our purposes) chronicles a tradition of Holy Sepulchre copies which use rectangular, rather than the expected circular, forms.

In suggesting that Ripon and Hexham, like their near contemporary in Poitiers, are in some sense a 'copy' of the Holy Sepulchre it is important to stress that the copying involved is of a distinctly medieval type. Krautheimer has well characterised this process as the 'disintegration of the prototype into its single elements, the selective transfer of those parts and their re-shuffling in the copy' (Krautheimer 1971b, 126). In this way copies of medieval buildings can emerge which, to modern eyes, bear little resemblance to each other and even less to their claimed original model.

What information about an Anastasis 'prototype' would be available to Wilfrid for 'disintegration', 'selective transfer' and 're-shuffling' in any copy? One source must have been travellers' descriptions brought to the West and one of the fullest surviving accounts from the early medieval period was supplied by the Gaulish bishop Arculf to Adomnan on seventh-century Iona; his narrative was later mined by Bede for his *De Locis Sanctis* (Meehan 1958). It is not claimed here, of course, that Wilfrid was familiar with Arculf's description but the bishop provides an accessible contemporary statement of what the saint *could* have discovered about the Holy Sepulchre when he was in Rome and Gaul.

From Arculf's text we can pluck some 'single elements' of the Anastasis church: a rectangular grave-chamber prefaced by an ante-chamber; a central area arched overhead and surrounded by walls and passages; an entrance from the east. Set out in this manner, the crypts at Hexham and Ripon *might* therefore be interpreted as containing iconographic references, in discrete form, to the Holy Sepulchre.

Two pieces of possible supplementary evidence can be marshalled in support of this suggestion. There is, first, some apparent stress on north-side activity at Ripon. Part of this may have developed at a relatively late date and be associated with the virginity-testing rituals noted by Camden. But it is possible that the foundation against the north wall (Fig. 2.3) is original and that the offerings placed by St Wilfrid's needle and recorded by Micklethwaite (1882, 350) reflect a long-lived emphasis on this part of the chamber. Foundation and tributes could, of course, be secondary and of no relevance to Wilfrid, but the arrangement of lamp-niches is certainly primary and they are so distributed as to throw most illumination onto the north and, specifically, the north-west side of the chamber. The relevance of this to copying of Anastasis is that Christ's tomb was known to lie on the north side of His burial chamber – and it is this well-publicised detail which explains the placing of Easter Sepulchres against the north walls of chancels and also accounts for the popularity of north-side burials in early contexts (Biddle 1986, 11; Morris 1989, 292). Are the organisation of the lamp-niches, the foundation and the tributes at Ripon all echoic of this feature of the Holy Sepulchre?

The second hint of Anastasis at Ripon and Hexham comes from metrology. The two main chambers differ in their length but are identical in width, varying between 7 feet 6 inches and 7 feet 9 inches at both sites. This measurement is of no significance in imperial or metric terms but in the so-called 'Drusian' system, which Kjølbye-Biddle has shown was employed in seventh-century Winchester, an imperial 7 feet 8 inches would yield exactly 7 Drusian feet (Kjølbye-Biddle 1986). And 7 feet was the frequently recorded length of Christ's tomb.

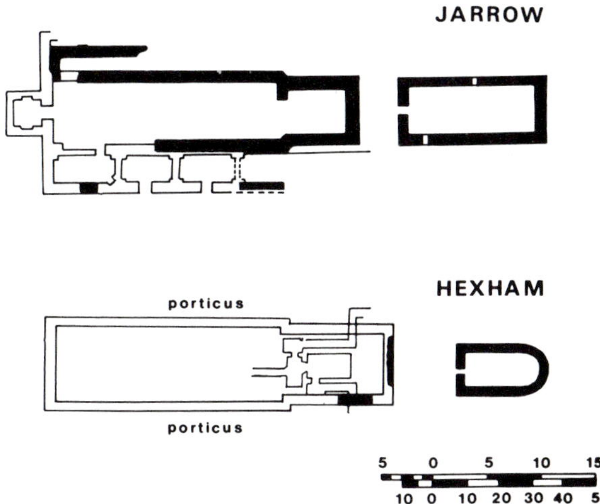

Fig. 2.10. Reconstructions of Hexham and Jarrow churches.

Envoi

This paper has finished with what will no doubt appear to be unwarranted speculation. My only defence can be that the solution to many of the problems posed by these remarkable crypts must now be sought as much on the continent and in the thought-processes of the seventh century as in further excavation and recording at the two sites.

Note

This paper is a shorter version of the lecture delivered at the Oxford conference. The complete paper has since been published: St Wilfred, Ripon and Hexham. In *Karkov and Farrell* (1991), 3-25; I am grateful to the editors' permission to include this abbreviated version here.

Since the submission of this paper the following important studies have appeared:

Cambridge, E. 1995: Hexham Abbey: a review of recent work and its implications. *Archaeol. Aeliana*, 5th Ser., 23, 51-138.

Hall, R. 1993: Observations in Ripon Cathedral crypt 1989. *Yorks. Archaeol. Jnl.* 65, 39-53.

Hall, R. 1995: Antiquaries and archaeology in and around Ripon Minster. In L.R. Hoey (ed.) *Yorkshire Monasticism. Archaeology, Art and Architecture from the 7th to the 16th Centuries (Brit. Archaeol. Assoc. Conf. Trans. 16)*, 12-30.

Bibliography

All books were published in London unless otherwise stated.

Bailey, R. N. 1976: The Anglo-Saxon Church at Hexham. *Archaeol. Aeliana*, 5th Ser., 4, 47–67.

Bailey, R. N. and O'Sullivan, D. 1979: Excavations over St Wilfrid's crypt at Hexham. *Archaeol. Aeliana*, 5th Ser., 7, 144–57.

Biddle, M. 1986: Archaeology, architecture, and the cult of saints in Anglo-Saxon England. In *Butler and Morris 1986*, 1–31.

Brown, G. B. 1925: *The Arts in Early England; II, Anglo-Saxon Architecture*, 2nd edn.

Brown, P. 1981: *The Cult of the Saints* (Chicago).

Butler, L. A. S. and Morris, R. K. (eds.) 1986: *The Anglo-Saxon Church* (*CBA Research Report*, 60)

Cambridge, E. 1979: C. C. Hodges and the nave of Hexham Abbey. *Archaeol. Aeliana*, 5th ser. 7, 158–68 (and *ibid.* 8, 1980, 172–3).

Camden, W. 1586: *Britannia.*

Campbell, A. (ed.) 1950: *Frithegodi Monachi Breviloquium Vitae Beati Wilfredi et Wulfstani Cantoris Narratio Metrica de Sancto Swithuno, (Thesaurus Mundi)* (Zurich).

Carter, J. 1806: Pursuits of Architectural Innovation. *No. XCIX. Gentleman's Mag.* 76 (2), 624–5.

Colgrave, B. (ed.) 1927: *The Life of Bishop Wilfrid by Eddius Stephanus* (Cambridge).

Colgrave, B. and Mynors, R. A. B. (eds.) 1969: *Bede's Ecclesiastical History of the English People* (Oxford).

Conant, J. 1956: The original buildings at the Holy Sepulchre in Jerusalem. *Speculum* 31, 1–48.

Cramp, R. J. 1976: 'Jarrow church' and 'Monkwearmouth

church'. *Archaeol. Jnl.* 133, 220–37.

Elbern, V. H. 1961: Das Relief der Gekreuzigten in der Mellebaudis-Memorie zu Poitiers. *Jahrbuch der Berliner Museen* 3, 148–89.

Elbern, V. H. 1962: Nouvelles recherches au sujet de la crypte de l'Abbé Mellébaude. *Bulletin de la Société des Antiquaires de l'Ouest* 4, 375–93.

Fernie, E. 1985: Anglo-Saxon lengths; the 'northern system', the perch and the foot. *Archaeol. Jnl.* 142, 246–54.

Gem, R. 1983: Towards an iconography of Anglo-Saxon architecture. *Jnl. Warburg and Courtauld Inst.* 46, 1–18.

Gilbert, E. 1974: St Wilfrid's church at Hexham. In *Kirby (1974)*, 81–113.

Girard, R. 1961: La crypte et l'église Saint-Laurent de Grenoble. *Cahiers d'Histoire* 6, 243–63.

Grabar, A. 1972: *Martyrium.*

Grabar, A. 1974: Recherches sur les sculptures de l'Hypogée des Dunes à Poitiers et de la crypte S. Paul de Jouarre. *Journal de Savants*, 3–43.

Hall, R. A. 1977: Rescue excavations in the crypt of Ripon Cathedral. *Yorks. Archaeol. Jnl.* 49, 59–63.

Heitz, C. 1963: *Recherches sur les rapports entre architecture et liturgie à l'époque carolingienne* (Paris).

Heitz, C. 1977: Cryptes préromanes du VIIIe au XIe siècle. *Université de Paris X – Nanterre, Centre de Recherches sur l'Antiquité tardive et le haut Moyen-age, Cahier* no. 11, 31–45.

Heitz, C. 1986: The iconography of architectural form. In *Butler and Morris (1986)*, 90–100.

Heitz, C. 1987: *La France pré-Romane* (Paris).

Hodges, C. C. 1888: *Ecclesia Hagustaldensis. The Abbey of St. Andrew, Hexham* (Edinburgh).

Hodges C. C. 1921: *Guide to the Priory Church of St. Andrew, Hexham* (2nd edn. rev. by J. Gibson, Hexham).

Hodges C. C. and Gibson, J. 1919: *Hexham and its Abbey* (Hexham).

Huggins, P., Rodwell, K. and W. 1983: Anglo-Saxon and Scandinavian building measurements. In P.J. Drury (ed.) *Structural Reconstruction* (BAR, Brit. Ser. 110, Oxford), 21–65.

Jones, W. T. 1932: Recent discoveries at Ripon Cathedral. *Yorks. Archaeol. Jnl.* 31, 74–6.

Karkov, C. and Farrell, R. (eds.): *Studies in Insular Art and Archaeology, American Early Medieval Studies* 1 (Miami, Ohio).

Kirby, D. P. (ed.) 1974: *St. Wilfrid at Hexham* (Newcastle upon Tyne).

Kirby, D. P. 1983: Bede, Eddius Stephanus, and the 'Life of Wilfrid'. *Eng. Hist. Rev.* 98, 101–14.

Kjølbye-Biddle, B. 1986: The 7th-century minster at Winchester interpreted. In *Butler and Morris (1986)*, 196–209.

Krautheimer, R. 1971a: Santo Stephano Rotundo in Rome and the rotunda of the Holy Sepulchre in Jerusalem. In *Studies in Early Christian, Medieval and Renaissance Art*, 69–114.

Krautheimer, R. 1971b: Introduction to an 'Iconography of Medieval Architecture. In *Studies in Early Christian, Medieval and Renaissance Art*, 115–50.

Magni, M. 1979: Cryptes du haut Moyen Age en Italie: problèmes de typologie du IXe jusqu'au début du XIe siècle. *Cahiers Archéologiques* 28, 41–85.

Meehan, D. (ed.) 1958: Adamnan's De Locis Sanctis (*Scriptores Latini Hiberniae*, 3, Dublin).

Micklethwaite, J. T. 1882: On the crypts at Hexham and Ripon, *Archaeol. Jnl.* 39, 347–54.

Micklethwaite, J. T. 1892: (Notes on the Saxon Crypt of Ripon Minster.) *Proc. Soc. Antiq.* 2nd. Ser. 14, 191–6.

Micklethwaite, J. T. 1896: Something about Saxon church building, *Archaeol. Jnl.* 53, 293–51.

Morris, R. 1989: *Churches in the Landscape.*

Peers, C. R. 1931: Recent discoveries in the minsters of Ripon and York. *Antiqs. Jnl.* 11, 113–22.

Roper, M. 1974: Wilfrid's landholdings in Northumbria. In *Kirby (1974)*, 61–79, 169–71.

Savage, E. S. and Hodges, C. C. 1907: *A Record of all Works Connected with Hexham Abbey since January 1899* (Hexham).

Sennhauser, H. R. 1979: Spätantike und frühmittelalterliche Kirchen Churrätiens. In J. Werner and E. Ewig (eds.) *Von der Spätantike zum frühen Mittelalter* (Sigmaringen), 193–218.

Taylor, H. M. 1968: Corridor crypts on the continent and in England. *North Staffs. Jnl. of Field Studies* 9, 17–52.

Taylor, H. M. and Taylor J. 1961: The seventh-century church at Hexham: a new appreciation. *Archaeol. Aeliana*, 4th ser. 39, 103–34.

Taylor, H. M. and J. 1965–1978: *Anglo-Saxon Architecture*, I-III (Cambridge).

Thümmler, H. 1958: Carolingian period. In M. Pallottina et al (eds.) *Encyclopedia of World Art* (New York) 3, 81–127.

Walbran, J. R. 1846: On a crypt in Ripon Cathedral, commonly called St. Wilfrid's Needle. *Trans. B.A.A. Winchester Congress 1845*, 339–54.

Walbran, J. R. 1848: Observations on the Saxon Crypt under the Cathedral church at Ripon, commonly called St. Wilfrid's Needle, *Royal Archaeol. Inst. York Meeting 1846*, 1–11.

Walbran, J.R. 1859: On St. Wilfred and the Saxon Church at Ripon. *Assoc. Archit. Socs. Reports and Papers* 5/1, 1-41.

The Cathedral Priory Church at Bath

Peter Davenport

There can be few of the great Norman cathedral foundations which followed the reorganisation of the English Church under William and his successors, which have so completely vanished from view, as that at Bath. Even those buildings such as York, which were entirely replaced in the Gothic centuries, retained their status as the *Sedes* of a Bishop. Bath lost that status in the changes that followed the Dissolution, and even came close to losing the late Perpendicular building that forms the core of what we see today, which serves merely as the Parish church for central Bath.

Historical Outline

The pre-Conquest see was at Wells, then a rural setting, and an establishment of no great intellectual or spiritual standing. The death of the last Saxon incumbent, Giso, in 1088 allowed William Rufus to appoint John of Tours or 'de Villula' to the bishopric. In accordance with the royal and papal policy of the urbanisation of the seats of Bishops, and no doubt by prior arrangement, John moved the see to Bath, to the site of the Benedictine Abbey of St Peter, which had a more lively reputation than Wells: Adelard, the great mathematician and geographer was probably in residence at this time or certainly during the latter part of John's episcopate. In addition, Bath clearly had an attraction for the physician in Bishop John, and he would have been familiar with the waters during his earlier stay in the town, if the traditional stories are true.

The house had been founded perhaps in 675 (see Sims-Williams 1975 for discussion), but was certainly in existence by 757, seemingly as a house of canons (Leland in Smith 1907, 143), when land was granted to the "brothers in the monastery of St Peter's" (Hunt 1893). It had a reputation as *monasterium celeberrimum* by 781, (Sims-Williams 1975, 9). In c.965–70 it was re-founded as a Benedictine monastery under the monastic reforms of Dunstan and Oswald.

After the failure of Odo's rebellion of 1088, the whole of the Saxon city passed into King William II's hands. It was granted to the Bishop in February 1090, "that with the greater honour, he may fix his pontifical seat there". (B.L Harleian MS 358, f.39; see Hunt 1893). Matthew Paris claims that John "anointed the King's hand with white [ie, silver] ointment", that is bribed him for this grant (Madden 1866–9). In fact, in modern terms, John simply bought the city from the King.

The move caused considerable disruption, both to the pride of the religious involved, and to the fabric of the city: approximately a quarter of the walled town was taken for the Cathedral precinct. Topographical analysis suggests that the main north-south street was truncated, and replaced by Stall Street, and the east gate moved north some 40 metres. It has been suggested that the northern suburbs may have owed their creation to the resettlement of a displaced population (Cunliffe 1986, 83). A much altered town emerged, with the independence of its abbey destroyed (Fig. 3.2).

The loss of cathedral status was always resented by the canons at Wells, and they fought long and hard to get it back. After several agreements, compromises and false starts, the see was finally declared a joint see of Bath and Wells in 1245. Thereafter, Wells was the more successful in asserting its supremacy, and the priory at Bath declined both physically and morally. It was not until Bishop King succeeded in 1496 that serious attempts were made to reinstate the Cathedral in Bath as a physical presence commensurate with its legal status. Total rebuilding followed, and continued until the dissolution in 1539.

The Norman Cathedral

"John pullid down the old Chirch of St Peter at Bath, and erectid a new, much fairer" (Leland in Smith 1907, 144). Of the "old chirch" we know nothing. Although its replacement has also vanished, we know considerably more about John's cathedral, with its "great and elaborate circuit of walls" (William of Malmesbury in Hamilton 1870) (Fig. 3.1).

It was certainly underway by 1106, when John refers to "the new work I have begun" (Hunt 1893, xliv). It seems probable that work had started soon after the move to Bath, and by 1122, at John's death, we are told that the lower vaults (*testudines inferiores*) were complete (Hunt 1893, 34).

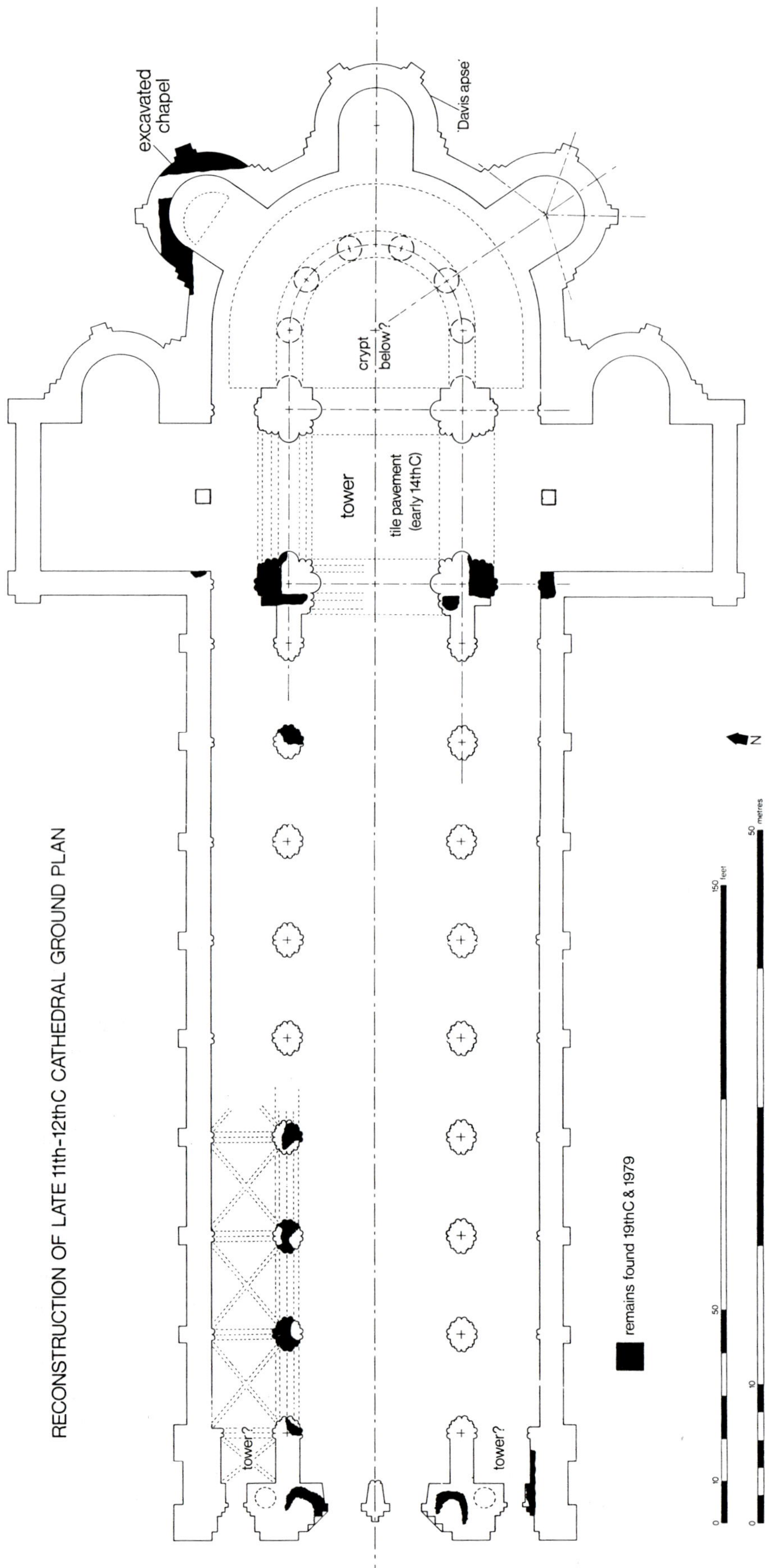

Fig. 3.1. After O'Leary 1980, modified after Bell in prep. *The north transept shows the minmum changes to the previous reconstructions cecessary. The south transept is reconstructed on the basis of ideas still being developed (Davenport* in prep.).

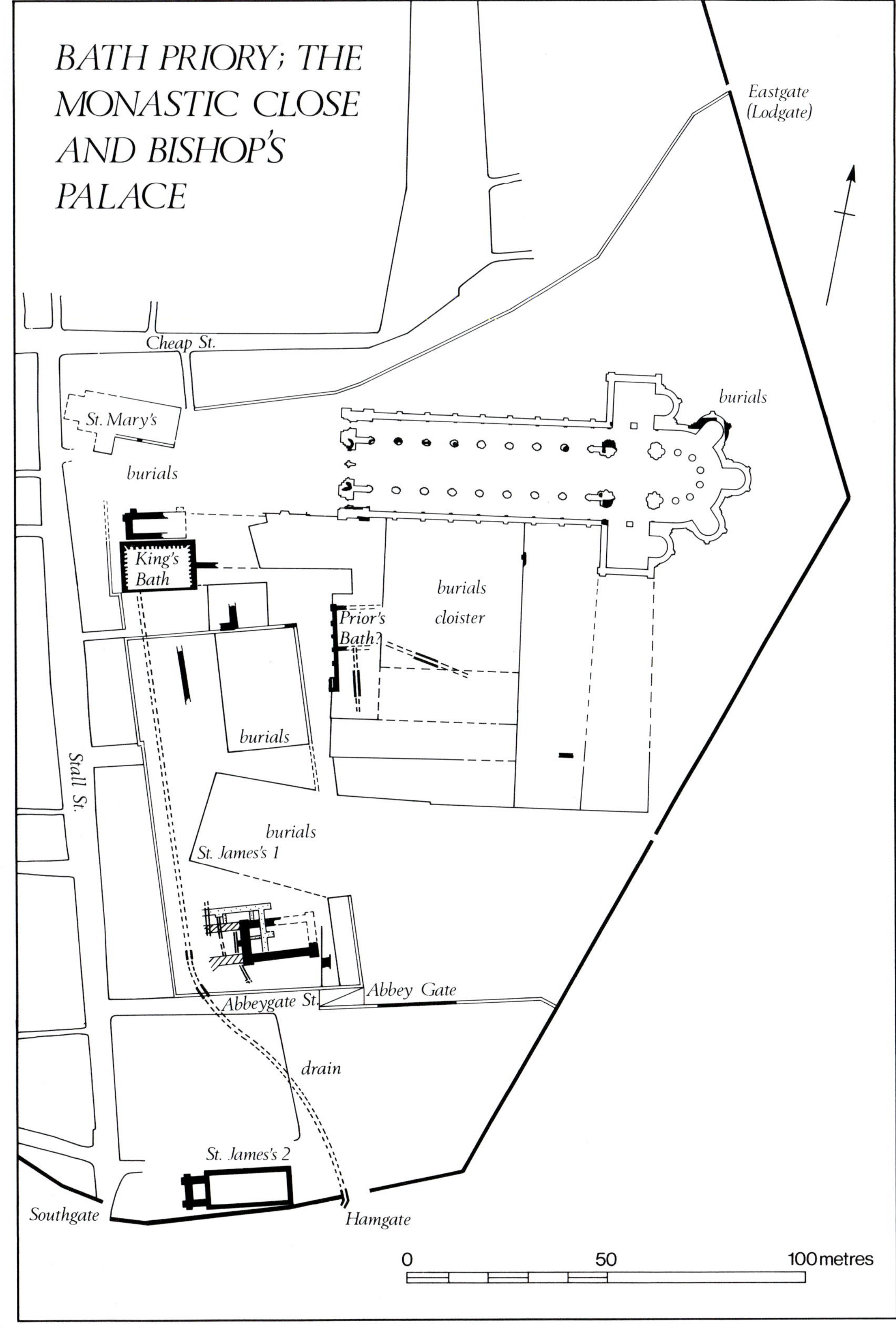

Fig. 3.2. The Cathedral and Bishop's Closes as established by John of Tours in the south east corner of the Saxon town after 1090. The city walls are marked in the thick black line; the cathedral close by the double line. The Bishop's Close is the double-outlined rectangle south of the King's Bath. Walls in solid black are archaeologically attested, single lines from post-mediaeval property boundaries.

The Physical Remains

The establishment of the ground plan is a continuing process (Fig. 3.1). Remains of the Norman work were first recorded in 1833, but interpreted as Roman (Mainwaring 1838, 425–9). The first attempt at properly recovering the extent of the Norman structure was made by James Irvine, during the restoration works of 1863–72, fully published in Irvine 1890. Excavation in 1979 by T. J. O'Leary for Bath Archaeological Trust (O'Leary 1980 and 1990) has fixed the general form of the east end (fig 3.1). Substantial new excavations carried out by the Trust in 1993 have, *inter alia*, revealed evidence for the south transept plan, and the Normancloister (Bell, in prep.).

Much yet remains to be revealed of the structure of the building, but it does appear to be possible to say that the Norman church was built entirely of the local Bath oolite. While there is no direct evidence, it seems likely that much use must have been made of Roman masonry. If so it was extensively reworked, from the large blocks we know were available nearby (Cunliffe and Davenport 1985, pl. XXIX). Irvine does claim that the "tufa" vault fragments (see below) came from the sides of Batheaston valley, about 5 miles north-east of Bath. (1890, 93).

Much of the stonework of the Norman church found its way into the present structure, in foundation work under the south transept and in the interior of the upper stages of the tower, where it has yet to be properly studied. Irvine was of the opinion that the sixteenth-century building simply reused the ashlar from its predecessor (Irvine 1890, 87), and in places the coursing visible today is rather shallow, which may support this view (Fig. 3.3). Little analytical work has been done on the present building, and much about the structural sequence and details awaits clarification.

While reporting on the recent archaeology, it has become essential to refer in some detail to the earlier work as follows. Irvine's efforts showed that the whole of the present building was built merely on the nave of its predecessor. The floor of the Norman church was nearly two metres below the sixteenth century floor, and this had ensured that the lower parts of the walls and piers of the Norman building survived remarkably well (Irvine 1890, fig. opp. 92). Irvine was able to demonstrate the nave arcade pier planforms, the position of the crossing piers, and the varying levels of the floors in the different parts of the building.

Most of the nave floor was 1.12 metres lower than the floor of the western bay, and the floor rose again just over half a metre into the crossing, which Irvine found still with its early fourteenth-century tile floor *in situ* (tile floors of similar date were also found in the nave aisles in 1833, Irvine 1890, 89). Steps at the junction of nave side aisles and presumed transepts showed a rise here of at least 0.75 metres (Irvine 1890, 88; 90–91 and Fig. 3.1). However, no floor was found here at 0.75 metres, and the relative heights of the shaft bases on the west and east sides of the crossing piers, suggest either a floor in the

Fig. 3.3. The springing of the transept arcade arch can be seen above the coping of the buttress, obscured by recent repair patches (lighter stone). The buttress was added in 1611.

transepts 1.5 metres higher than the nave, or a dwarf wall at this height (from which the crossing and choir arcade rose) separating the crossing and choir from the aisle and transepts (Irvine 1890 fig. opp. 92 and our Fig. 3.4). Irvine, indeed, refers to "the south wall of the crossing, which filled up the transept arch about 3'3" in height [1.5 metres above the nave floor]" (ibid, 92). The floor level around the transept pier found in 1993 was virtually the same as the nave. This supports the interpretation of the dwarf wall referred to above as a wallenclosing the choir, not supporting a raised transept floor to the south, unlike the raised north transept floor implied by the steps. The height of thesanctuary floor east of the crossing remains unknown. It is hard to disagree with Irvine that the purpose of these variations was to "' have added grandeur'.to the glory of the processions ' as they rose ' and advanced across the elevated platform toward the observers" (ibid, 93). However, practically, these variations may have been necessary to raise the sanctuary over a crypt. It would of

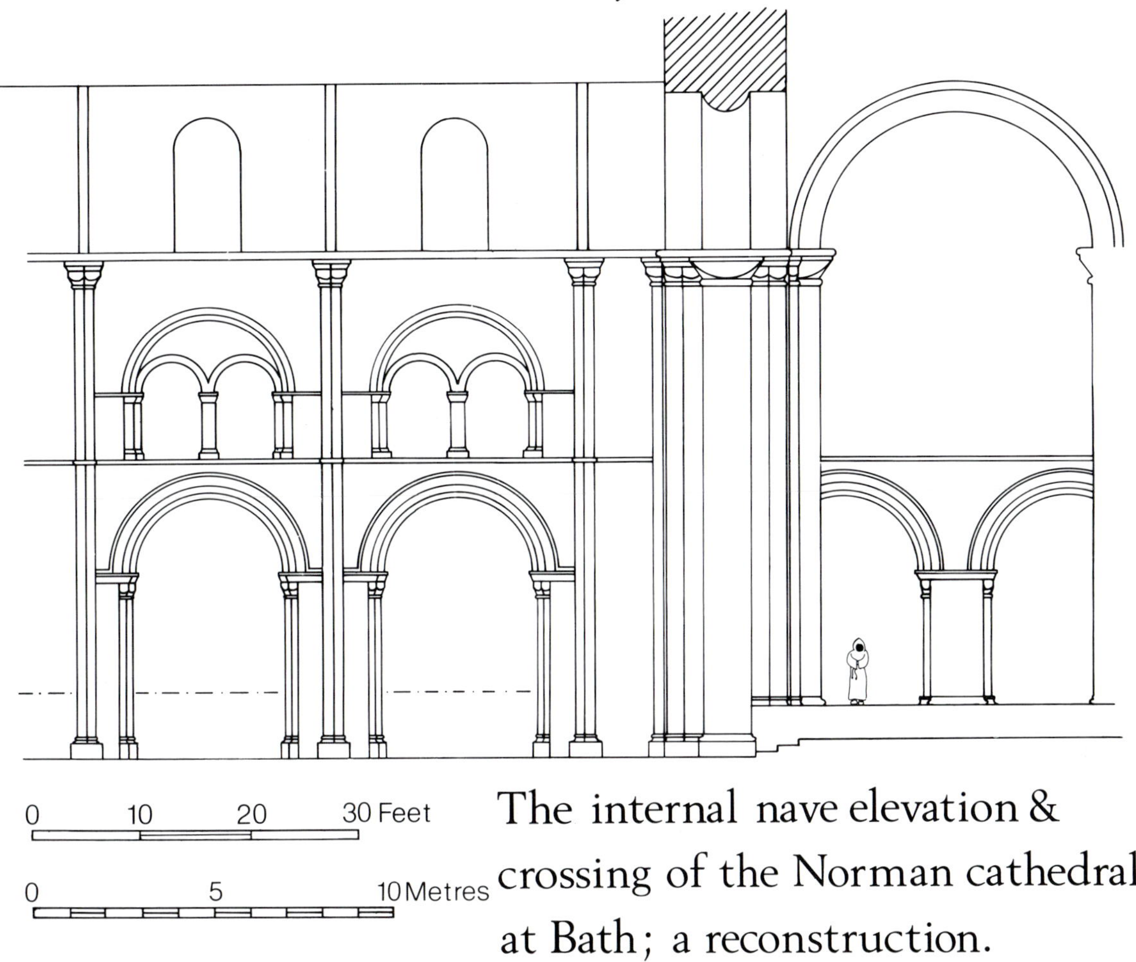
0 10 20 30 Feet
0 5 10 Metres
The internal nave elevation & crossing of the Norman cathedral at Bath; a reconstruction.

Fig. 3.4. The internal nave elevation & crossing of the Norman cathedral at Bath; a reconstruction. The chain-dot line shows the present floor level.

course be usual for a church of this status to have a crypt, and there is a record of the relics treasured by the cathedral, some of which may have been held there (Britton 1825, 24). A sub-surface radar survey was carried out in 1990, but the results were not of any practical use.

The position of the monk's choir is at present uncertain. Given the restricted space east of the crossing it might be expected that it occupied the crossing and continued into the nave, as at Norwich, for example. Irvine was of the opinion, based on the layout of the tile floor on the crossing, that the choir did not extend this far west, from what he was obviously imagining as a much longer east end. This is hardly tenable given what we now know of the east end layout, and in any case refers to the early fourteenth-century plan, and not the Norman. It is probably right to suggest that the choir projected even further west, leaving the crossing as the necessary space before the high altar.

The raised floor, and some slight evidence for the thickening of the walls, at the west end lends support to Warwick Rodwell's proposal that the west front had towers rising out of a species of *westwerk* (Rodwell and O'Leary 1990). Western towers are perhaps implied by reference to the "principal or central tower", probably soon after 1137 (Hunt 1893, 37 quoting the continuator of Florence of Worcester). Evidence for the plan of the transepts is extremely slight (but see below and Figs. 3.1 and 3.4). However, the east end has been bravely but convincingly reconstructed, from the fragments of structure recovered in excavation in 1979, as an apsed sanctuary surrounded by an ambulatory with three radiating chapels (O'Leary 1980 & 1990). This also takes into account the reported discovery of an apse by Davis, the City Architect, in 1895, which, if the earlier of two conflicting reports of its position is taken as correct, would fall neatly on the reconstructed position of the eastern apsidiole (Fig. 3.1 and Rodwell and O'Leary 1990).

Plan and Nave Elevation

The plan as presented in Fig. 3.1 is an interpretation, based on the most recent information (1994). Nonetheless, there is a pitiable amount of solid black on it at present. The plan reveals on what a large scale Bishop John was building. As befits a cathedral church, he planned a building comparable to all but the grandest of the other Norman cathedrals going up at the same time, with a length of 106.5 metres (330 feet).

While following the English fashion for a long nave, the church has a disproportionately short and cramped east end. There may have been site conditions of which we are ignorant, but it is noteworthy that the plan of the sanctuary is very close to that of some of the churches in the central Loire Valley region (Rodwell and O'Leary 1990) from which, of course, Bishop John hailed, and he may have called for masons from France. While apsidal east ends with radiating chapels were not uncommon in Norman abbey and cathedral building in England (Battle; St Augustine's, Canterbury; Gloucester, Norwich), Bishop John may well have been familiar with the French exemplars. The closest parallel for the sanctuary is probably St Etienne de Nevers, Niévre (AD 1097) (Evans 1938), but the general form is common there. Also shown on the plan (Fig. 3.1) are the positions of the probable arcades across the opening of the transepts into the crossing (see also Fig. 3.4). These are likely to have carried galleries at tribune level. They are most closely paralleled in Lanfranc's cathedral at Canterbury 1071–77 (Boase 1953 fig. 5). The piers have not been found, but are implied by the truncated arches seen springing from the east end of the present building in Speed's map of 1610 (Fig. 3.7). The stump of the northern arch can still be seen in the present fabric (Fig. 3.3).

We do have the wherewithal to go a little further into three dimensions. Irvine did recognise that one bay of the transept elevation survived, up to the top of the arcade, where the south nave aisle had entered the transept (now at the end of the south choir aisle). F. Bligh Bond later recognised that, in fact, enough survived, built into the later fabric, to reconstruct the elevation up to the springing of the triforium arcade (Bond 1918). This, the arches recorded by Speed, and the present survival of parts of them, enable yet more to be said of the probable appearance of the Norman church.

The elevation of the bay produced by Bond can be used, in the absence of any other evidence, to attempt a reconstruction of the nave arcade (Fig. 3.4). The arcade arches themselves were closely related to the surviving example, as shown by the following. The arch of the surviving bay is stilted, presumably to reach the same height at the crown as the nave arcade, being the transverse membrane of the nave aisle bay. Unstilted semicircular arches turned between the nave piers reconstructed with capitals at the same height do, in fact, crown at exactly this level. Stilting the cross arches of a rectangular bay is often done to ease the geometry of stone vaulting in Romanesque churches, and it seems likely that the aisles were vaulted, but the evidence is not conclusive for the nave. The reference to "lower vaults" in 1122 may certainly be thought to refer the aisles of the choir, and, perhaps 30 years after the start of building, we may imagine this to have also included the nave aisles. Irvine refers to "fragments" of the "tufa" vaulting of the aisles, but it is not clear if this is webbing, rubble or ribbing. Certainly vault ribbing of typically twelfth-century form is now displayed in the Choir vestry, of a scale that clearly belongs to the aisles, but whose find date and place is not known. It seems likely that these came from the investigations of Irvine, however. Further fragments were found in the excavations of 1979 on the site of the north-east absidiole (Rodwell 1990).

Above the vaulted aisles then, Bond's evidence suggests we should place a gallery giving on to the nave via double arched openings under relieving arches (Fig. 3.4). Without western aisles on the transepts the only connection between nave and transept tribunes would have to be through the thickness of the walls. However, the excavations of 1993 showed that the south side of the arch recorded by Bond, rather than being the junction of the west wall of the south transept and the nave aisle wall, was, in fact, a free-standing compound pier. This, and the paving around it, clearly imply a west aisle for the transept (Bell, in prep.). Indeed it can be argued that a west aisle strongly suggests sn eastern one (this and other details will be argued elsewhere). This has been shown on Fig.3.1 on the south transept, the north being based more directly on the earlier reconstruction (O'Leary 1980 and 1990).

The greater diameter of the inter-bay attached shafts on the arcade piers suggests that they rise through both lower storeys, which were probably separated by a moulded string course, to continue the bay division at gallery level. Above this we have not the slightest evidence to go on, and the drawing (Fig. 3.4) gives the minimum configuration (the clerestory could be completed with three-light windows perhaps, and the shafts continued upwards another storey) and assumes a wooden roof.

The east end is more problematical. There seems no reason to doubt the plan put together by Tim O'Leary and Warwick Rodwell, and the latter makes a plausible case for the ambulatory and absidioles having ribbed vaults prior to 1137 (Rodwell 1990,). It may be that the short sanctuary was roofed with a barrel vault and semi-dome. However, a timber roof or a rib vault are other alternatives.

There was a fire in 1137 (Hunt 1893, 36), which was particularly destructive of the claustral buildings, but it appears that the Norman church survived this catastrophe, as burnt mouldings of late eleventh/twelfth century date were found in the 1979 excavations with layers of whitewash over the burning, but only on the face of the stone, implying that the stones remained in situ to be re-whitewashed. We have it from Irvine that the Norman work he saw was whitewashed repeatedly (Irvine 1890, 88).

Bishop Robert of Lewes (1136–66) is credited with finishing the church, and most of the claustral buildings (Hunter 1840, 24). It is the latter that are likely to have suffered most in the fire of 1137, but clearly the church was damaged too. Consecration took place between 1148 and 1161, possibly in 1156 (Manco 1995, 85).

The building history of the Norman Cathedral is slight from the end of Robert's episcopacy. It should be borne in mind that the centre of affairs in the see gradually returned to Wells, (see above). It is also against the long drawn out battle for dominance between the two centres, that we should perhaps see the rebuilding of Wells; not yet with its cathedral status regained, yet planned on a cathedral scale, starting soon after the appointment of Robert's successor, Reginald fitzJoscelin, in 1174 (Rodwell, this volume). However, Bishop Reginald is recorded as having raised money for the repair of the Cathedral in 1180 (Hunt 1893, 154).

There are, nonetheless, some indications of work on the old fabric from time to time. In 1206, John, a monk at the Priory signs himself as *custos operum* (Hunt 1893, 42) but otherwise it is not until the 1260s under Bishop Bytton that substantial changes are heard of. In his time was rebuilt the Lady Chapel behind the high altar (Hunt 1893, 155). This was presumably a large replacement for the original eastern absidiolc, as occurred at several Norman cathedrals (e.g. Norwich, Gloucester). No trace of the structure of this is now known, but coloured and *grisaille* glass of this period was recovered in the excavations of 1979 near its presumed site (O'Leary 1990).

Bishop John of Drokensford (1301–31) bemoaned the ruined state of the building, in the context of the general decline of the Priory, and some work was set in hand in 1324. This may have included the fine tiled floor of the crossing recorded by Irvine (O'Leary 1990), but could not have amounted to a great deal as the work was consecrated by the following year (Rodwell 1990). More work was in hand by 1335 when Master Mason Richard Davy was in charge of the work. Unfinished early Perpendicular window tracery has recently been found discarded in contemporary deposits in the Priory precincts, and may be related to this phase of operations (Davenport 1990). Irvine has ingeniously suggested that this work may have included the provision of a spire to the Norman crossing tower, on the basis of a new Chapter seal of this date showing a church with such a spire. Even if true, this is hardly conclusive.

The last piece of work on the building seems to have taken place under Bishop Bubwith (1424–67). He gave 328 marks to the Priory for building works, which were to include a chantry chapel for him. The decorative appliqué revealed by Irvine (1890, 87 and fig. opp. 92) may represent his work, and was probably not very extensive.

The Present Building

The Priory seems to have nonetheless continued in physical and moral decay throughout the fifteenth century until the enthronement of Oliver King. This prelate had been worldly indeed, successfully bridging the reigns of Edward IV, Richard III and Henry VII, while remaining in high office under all. He came to the see of Bath and Wells in 1496, and in 1500 wrote to the Prior informing him of his resolve to rebuild the church anew (out of the monks' income) since it was "through the laxity of many priors that the church had not been repaired or rebuilt, and was ruined to the foundations" (Britton 1825 App IV). He calculated a yearly income of £480 for the monks, and directed the Prior to spend £300 of this on rebuilding the Cathedral church.

This decision was based on a dream that had come to King while, as Harington says, "lying at Bathe" (Harington, *Nugae Antiquae*, quoted in Britton 1825, 47–49). In it he saw a vision of the Trinity, and angels ascending and descending a ladder, at the bottom of which was an olive tree with a crown on it. He heard a voice saying "let an olive establish the crown, and a king restore the church." Thus moved to restore the church, and again according to Harington, King caused this to be recorded in high relief sculpture and in inscriptions on the west front of the church, including this, from Judges, 9: "Trees going to chuse their King/Said `be to us the Olive King'".

King died in 1503, yet, surprisingly as it may seem, the work went on consistently, and Leland implies that the work was completed by the 1530s (Smith 1907, 144). Indeed, under absentee Bishops including the Italian Cardinal Adriano de Castello, and Cardinal Wolsey, the prime impulse for the continuance of the building came from Prior Bird (1499–1525), who also added the fine chantry chapel on the south side of the chancel. His successor, Gibbs, alias Holleway, continued to spend money on the rebuilding of the church almost until the Dissolution (Leland in Smith 1907, 144) (Fig.3.5).

King gave the original commission to the brothers Robert and William Vertue, whom he may have known from his time at Windsor, although William was not given his major contract there until 1506. But in any case they were among the most eminent master masons of the period, William, by 1506 becoming joint King's Master Mason. They were practitioners of a particularly lavish and spacious late Perpendicular, specialising in complex vaulting effects. The pendant voussoir vaults at Henry VII's chapel at Westminster Abbey (1503–1519), are prime examples of their style, and pendants are introduced in the choir aisle vaulting at Bath, where they had promised Bishop King that there should be "none so goodely neither in England nor in France".

Irvine argued that they were replaced or their design altered in favour of local fashions, in particular, the abandonment of "eastern" four centred arches, for "western" two-centred ones. Such changes may reflect the influence of the local executive mason, Thomas Lynne (Wright 1973, 9.) or the master masons, Edward Leycester and John Multon (Irvine 1890, 89 n.1). Harvey, however, suggests that at least part of this change is due to a decision under the Vertues themselves (not implemented until 1860 in the nave) to vault the higher parts of the building, rather than fit a flat wooden ceiling (Harvey, 1984, 309). Evidence of such change could be traced in the masonry at the springing of the great west window, which was originally meant to be four-centred (Irvine 1890, 89 n.1); and in the awkward junction of the vaults with the flat-topped great east window, above which Irvine traced a large slot for a wall plate, which continued all around the choir walls just above the vaulting (ibid, 88). This in it-

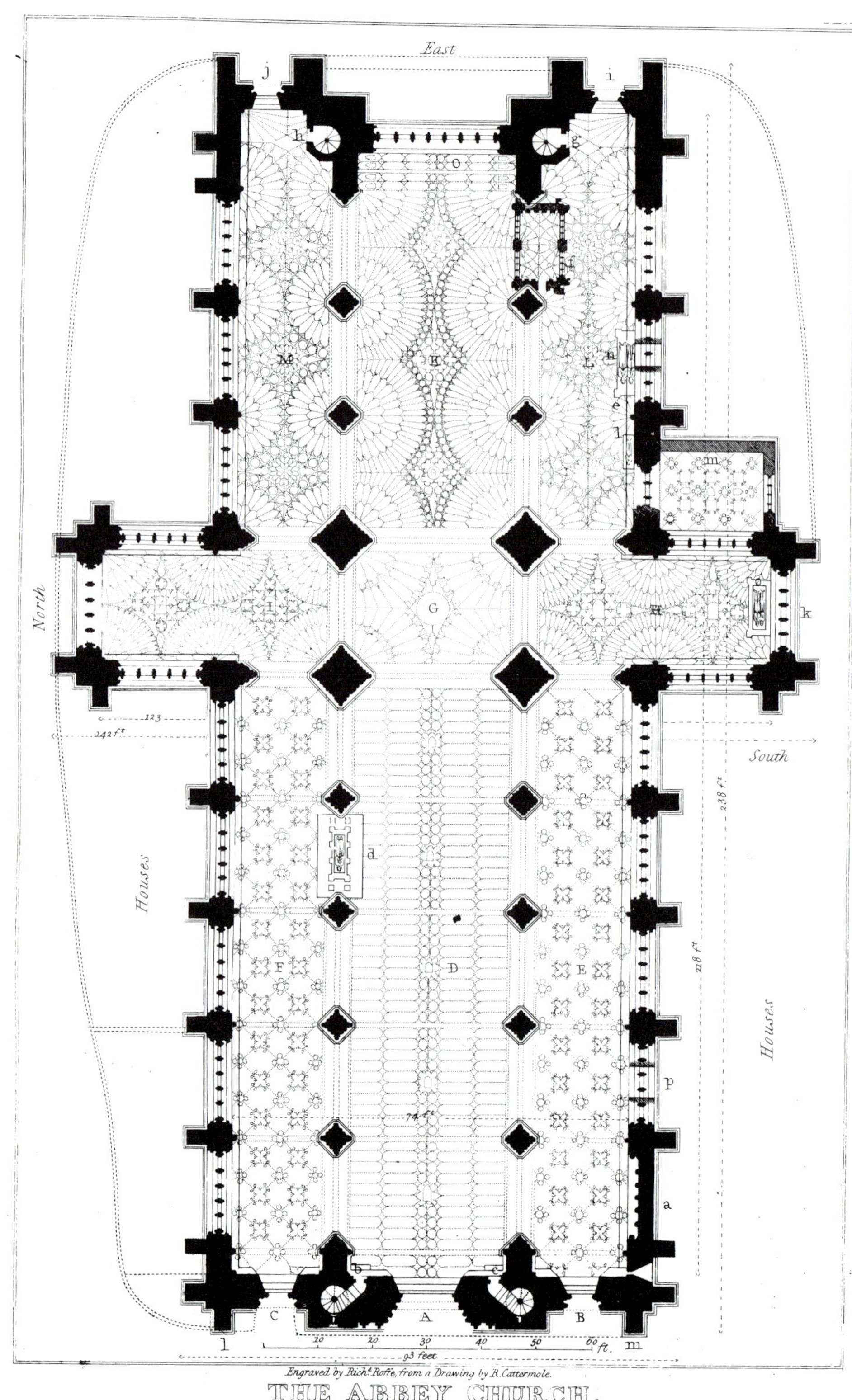

Fig. 3.5. Bath Abbey in 1816; from Britton 1825, pl.I

self implies that the walls were up to this height by the decision to vault in 1503.

Of the detailed progress of the work we know little. The old church must have been quickly demolished west of the crossing to allow the new to be erected, but Leland gives us to understand that the east end still stood around 1535, though unroofed (Smith 1907, 143–4). It has been argued (Manco 1995) that the East End of King's church was provided with a Lady Chapel. While the masonry discontinuities either side of the great east windoware *prima facie* evidence that such a chapel was intended, there are two reasons why it is likely never to have been started. The first is the continued existence of the old east end, with the tombs of the 12th century bishops still intact, until this late date. The second is the undamaged condition of the 14th century tile floor, and Norman wall in the south crossing arch (Irvine 1890) exactly where the massive footings of the south wall of the new chapel should be. It is likely that the old east end was kept in use until services could be held in the new church, which argues that the main energies of the builders were concentrated on the chancel. As we have seen, the chancel must have been up to roof level by 1503, and the roof and vaulting went up before 1518 as Cardinal Bishop Adriano de Costello's coat of arms (1504–18) appeared on the roof over the choir, according to Browne Willis (1746, 520, quoted in Britton 1825, 81), and are visible today, both in the main choir vault and the choir side-aisle vaults, along with Prior Bird's rebus. Similar evidence exists for the early completion of the west front (Britton 1825, 82). The arms here were indistinct, even by 1746, but the cardinal's hat indicates either Adriano or Wolsey. Recent cleaning has made it possible to see that two Cardinal's hats are still recognisable today high in the west gable. However, the faithful completion of the extremely elaborate sculptural scheme representing Bishop King's dream which dominates the west front argues that a substantial start was made here during King's lifetime. Harvey believes that the roofs were in progress in 1503 (Harvey, 1984, 309) suggesting incredibly rapid building of the main structure.

Both Cardinal Bishops were absentee prelates, Adriano not setting foot in England after his succession to the see. The setting of his arms on the work can only be the result of a commendable sense of rectitude on the part of Prior Bird, who, until his death in 1525, was the moving force behind the rebuilding.

The masonry shell of the building, and the eastern vaulting seem likely, then, to have been substantially complete by say 1518, if not much earlier. This is perhaps supported by the total homogeneity of the mouldings, pier forms, capitals etc throughout the building. Prior Gibbs great expenditure (Smith 1907, 144) is likely to have been for completing the fitting out of the church.

Without a great deal of detailed study of the fabric, it is difficult to be sure how much of the building as it stood before the restoration of 1833 is pre-1539. The pillage of the building after the Dissolution was considerable, resulting in the destruction of the roofing, leaving the nave totally uncovered, and the eastern vaults open to the sky; the removal of all window glass and frames, and the partial demolition of the south transept. Several pieaces of window tracery matching that of King's church have been found in the 1993 excavations, in post-medieval contexts. The degree of destruction can be gauged to some extent from the repair work indicated in the early seventeenth century list of benefactors of the rebuilding after 1572 (Britton 1825, app V).

When Edmund Colthurst gave the church to the city in 1572 (see below) "' though uncovered and much ruined ' yet the walls of the great tower and of most part of the church were then standing" (ibid 202). By 1581 the upper part was roofed and the north transept. The south transept was raised "neere from the ground" and roofed only in the first decade of the seventeenth century (ibid, 202) and the south aisle was "building uppe" between 1581 and 1604 (ibid, 203). Both choir aisles are recorded as having new walls, although the vaults are only repaired. However, as the east walls of both choir aisles are expressly said to have been rebuilt (ibid, 209), yet contain substantial Norman structure, the wording in these lists is clearly ambiguous. The nave was only roofed and given a stone and plaster barrel vault by Bishop Montague (1611–1616). Most of the windows were first re-glazed in the last decade of the sixteenth and first decade of the seventeenth century, also involving repair of the tracery "masonry work". The vaulting of the choir and choir aisles survived from the early sixteenth century work, as did the north transept, but the south part of the south transept vaulting was "made and beautified" by the Earl of Worcester in the early 1600s, very closely following the pattern of the existing work (ibid 208). Speed's map of 1610 (probably drawn in the 1590s) shows the very incomplete state of the south transept at that time (fig 3.7). The crossing vaulting was repaired at the expense of the city. The "ruines" of the other vaults were repaired (ibid, 209–210).

Nearly all this damage had been caused by demolition for scrap and salvage after the city had refused the King's Commissioners' offer of the Abbey for 500 marks, and it had been sold off to Humphrey Colles. The Colthurst family acquired it in 1548, and the church was given to the city by Edmund Colthurst in 1572. Almost the first thing the city did was to try to turn a profit by building houses on the narrow strip of land that had come with the gift. These houses, actually built on to the north side of the church, were not cleared away until the 1820s. However, the decline was halted and the process of repair began at this point. In 1574, Queen Elizabeth gave permission for a nationwide collection to be set in motion to repair the church, with results catalogued above. Fig. 3.6 shows the exterior of the church shortly after the completion of this work.

The church suffered few alterations to the basic fabric in the following two hundred years. Galleries were inserted in the choir aisles in the eighteenth century (the

Fig. 3.6 Bath Abbey in c.1650. Note the lack of flying buttresses on the nave.

east end of the church was the only part that functioned as a place of worship: the nave was little more than a covered cemetery) and the choir screen was replaced in the early part of that century and an organ built over it (Cobb 1980, 26). The north side of Prior Bird's chantry was defaced for a "Bishop's throne" (ibid), and of course, the whole of the lower part of the interior was plastered with memorials during this period. The openwork pinnacles at the east end were removed between 1790 and 1816, but little else changed until 1833.

Restoration

The clearance of the obscuring houses in the 1820s led to the realisation that the fabric so exposed was now in need of restoration and in 1833 the City Corporation engaged G.P. Manners, the City Architect, to begin a programme of repair and improvement. Apart from cosmetic patching where the old houses had been removed, this work involved replacing the roofs of the choir and transepts to a slightly lower position, following the line indicated by the weather slots of the early sixteenth century roof, and replacing the parapet balustrading. Similar work was carried out to the aisles (Mainwaring 1838, 423). New pinnacles were added to the east and west fronts (the eastern turrets being reduced from square to octagonal to match), the transepts and the tower (ibid, 424). The exterior ground surface was lowered to the sixteenth century level (and the Norman work now visible at the east end exposed). The major addition was that of the flying buttresses on the nave, whose position could be seen where the stubs of intended buttresses had been left by Prior Bird. As no vault was intended by Manners, these buttresses were hollow. The numerous monuments and inscriptions were moved to the periphery of the building, and Prior Bird's chantry chapel restored.

In the 1860s the church received the attention of Sir Gilbert Scott. The liturgical clutter so typical of eighteenth-century cathedral interiors had been only reduced a little by Manners, but was all cleared away under Scott (Cobb 1980, 27). The pinnacles on the west front were replaced yet again, in a style closer to the Vertues' work at Westminster (the tower and east end had to wait until 1908), and the parapet balustrades returned in large measure to their pre-Manners form (ibid, 26). The major change, however, was the replacement of the nave and nave-aisle plaster vaults with stone fan-vaulting copying that in the choir. The flying buttresses, now having a function, were rebuilt in solid stone (ibid, 26–7).

The west front was cleaned and restored in the 1890s, and in 1923 the covered cloister, now the choir vestry, was built. Notwithstanding, the building is still a splendid example of early sixteenth century Perpendicular Gothic; perversely perhaps, all the more so since its substantial remodelling under Gilbert Scott.

The Excavations of 1979

Research excavations were carried out in the traffic roundabout at Orange Grove in 1979, under the direction

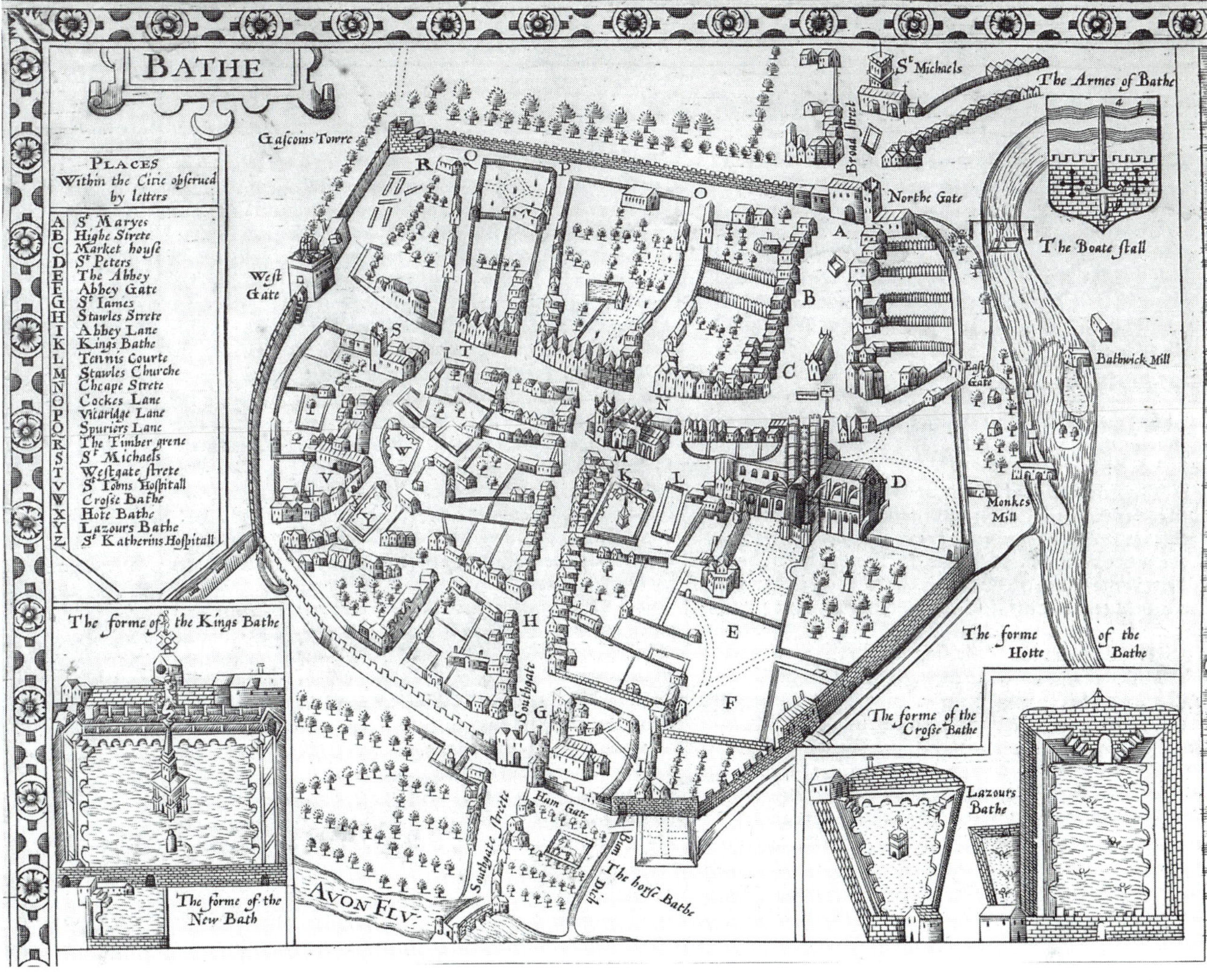

Fig. 3.7. Detail from the map of Bath published in 1610 by John Speed, in fact referring to the situation in c.1590.

of T. J. O'Leary for Bath Archaeological Trust, to try and ascertain the quality of archaeological remains and any clues as to the plan of the Norman Cathedral east end.

The walls recognised were heavily robbed, and no internal floors remained in the small area examined. However, it became clear that the trenches had come down on the north-eastern absidiole of an ambulatory-and-radiating-chapel east end. Only the foundation raft remained, but the robbing had been so gentle that impressions of ashlar jointing could be seen on the side of the robber trench, and the plan of multiple pilaster strips clearly recorded. Architectural mouldings were recovered from the robbing trench backfill, and stained glass fragments from the sixteenth century ground surface. A cemetery of fourteenth- to fifteenth-century date was partly investigated immediately to the north-east of the absidiole, containing burials of mixed sex and age, perhaps that of the abbey servants. A detailed picture was built up of the process of demolition and stone robbing of the post-dissolution years (O'Leary 1990).

Warwick Rodwell's study of the stone mouldings from the site shows that three building campaigns can be recognised (Rodwell 1990): early twelfth century; late thirteenth century and fourteenth century. This ties in well with the documentary evidence of John's church, the rebuild of the Lady Chapel c.1260 and the refurbishment initiated by John of Drokensford after 1324, and suggests that John's church remained essentially unaltered until 1500.

The Excavations of 1993

These were carried out under the direction of Robert Bell in advance of the creation of a new exhibition area for the Abbey: the Heritage Vaults. Excavation was possible along much of the south side of the present church, the nave of the Norman Cathedral. The north and east walks of the 12th century cloister were revealed, with paving intact on the north walk and the northern part of the east walk. The paving was c.70cm lower than the nave floor, suggesting that the cloister area was terraced level into the slight slope here. The east wall of the east walk survived up to 4.25 metres high where it had been incorporated into the early Stuart vestry. Unfortunately the Norman nave aisle wall at this point and in its junction with the cloister were obscured by 17th century work. However, evidence of steps rising up to nave level was found.

Evidence of the rebuilding of the north walk, occasioned by the new church, was also recovered. Medieval burials were found in echelon down the east walk, under the paving and respecting the east wall. Many were in 12th century head-niched cists. Others were found in the garth. Saxon burials were found cut by these and the cloister wall. Two large fragments of 10th century grave cover were also recovered. Two deep, narrow undercrofts were excavated running parallel to and east of the east walk. These were puzzling features, entirely robbed and backfilled in the mid 16th century, but seeming to be of 12th century origin.

East of these again, a small excavation showed that the south respond of the surviving Norman arch was a free-standing compound pier. This, and the position of the contemporary stone floor associated with it, implies the existence of a west aisle to the transept. The excavation was also able to show how the cloister garth and outer wall had been converted into the private garden of the Colthursts.

The cloister was continued to the west range which was level with the west end of the church. Its east end finished well short of the transept, even with its aisle. Therefore, the monks' night stair may have run into the south nave aisle. This rather strengthens the supposition that the monks' choir would have extended into the structural nave.

The Radar Survey

In late February 1990 a subsurface survey with ground-probing radar was carried out into the deep and complex stratified deposits underlying Orange Grove. It was hoped that this would provide data to assist the planning of a large scale research programme then being considered.

This relatively new technology seemed to hold out great promise for the non-destructive investigation of urban archaeological deposits, especially in areas where the disturbance of an excavation cannot be permitted other than for exceptional reasons; for example, in our cathedrals and great churches. The process is relatively quick and unobtrusive: the whole of the open space outside the east end of Bath abbey was covered in two nights, an area of 2500 square metres. However, results were disappointing: there seems to be no way to calibrate the readings or interpret them, and certainly no known features could be correlated with the print-outs, even massive things like cellars or the city wall.

For more details see Addyman and Stove 1989.

References

Addyman, P. & Stove, C. 1989: Ground probing impulse radar: an experiment in archaeological remote sensing at York. *Antiquity* 63 no.239, 337*ff*

Boase, T.S.R. 1953: *English Art 1100–1216* (Oxford)

Bond, F.B. 1918: Bath Abbey; discovery of part of the Norman triforium arcade in...the east wall of the south aisle of the choir. *Proc. Bath and Dist. Branch of the Somerset Archaeol. and Natur. Hist. Soc.* 1914–18, 48–49.

Britton, J. 1825: *The history and antiquity of Bath abbey church etc.* (London).

Cobb, G. 1980: *English Cathedrals: the forgotten centuries. Restoration and change from 1530 to the present day* (London).

Cunliffe, B.W. 1986: *The City of Bath* (Gloucester).

Cunliffe, B.W. & Davenport, P.A. 1985: *The Temple of Sulis Minerva at Bath* (Oxford Univ. committ. for archaeol. Monograph 7).

Davenport, P.A. 1990: *Archaeology in Bath 1976–1985* (Oxford Univ. Committ. for Archaeol. Monograph).

Evans, J. 1938: *Romanesque architecture of the Order of Cluny* (Cambridge).

Hamilton, N.E.S.A (ed) 1870: *Wilhelmi Malmesbiriensis monachi, de Gestis Pontificum Anglorum* (Rolls Ser. 52).

Harvey, J. 1984: *English mediaeval architects; a biographical dictionary down to 1550* (2nd edn) (Gloucester).

Holmes, T. 1906: Religious Houses, In *V.C.H. Somerset.* ii, 69ff.

Hunt, W (ed) 1893: *Two Chartularies of Bath Priory* (Somerset Rec. Soc. 7).

Hunter, J (ed) 1840: *Ecclesiastical Documents etc.* (Camden Soc. old ser. 8).

Irvine, J.T. 1890: Description of the remains of the Norman cathedral at Bath etc. *Jnl. of the B.A.A.* 1st ser. 46, 84–94.

Madden, F. (ed) 1866–9: *Historia Anglorum Matthiae Parisiensis etc.* (Rolls Ser. 44).

Mainwaring, R. 1838: *Annals of Bath from the year 1800 to the passing of the new municipal act* (Bath).

O'Leary, T.J. 1980: Excavations at Bath Orange Grove, the Norman cathedral and later development. *Popular Archaeol.* vol 1 no.11.

O'Leary, T.J. 1990: Excavations at Orange Grove and related studies. In Davenport (1990).

Rodwell, W. 1990: The stone mouldings. In O'Leary (1990).

Rodwell, W. and 1990: The ground plan of the Norman cathedral. In O'Leary, T.J. O'Leary (1990).

Sims-Williams, P. 1975: Continental influence at Bath monastery in the seventh century. *Anglo-Saxon England* 4, 1–10.

Smith, L.T. (ed) 1907: *The Itineraries of John Leland c1535–43* (London).

Wright, R.W.M. 1973: *Bath Abbey* (London).

The Origins and Development of the Twelfth-Century Cathedral Church at Carlisle[1]

M. R. McCarthy

The purpose of this paper is firstly, to outline what is known about the site of Carlisle Cathedral, and secondly to present an account of the visible remains of the church taking into consideration the restorations in the nineteenth century. No attempt has been made to assess the architectural affinities of the church with others elsewhere.[2]

The Setting

Carlisle has been a key focus of settlement in northern England for nearly 2000 years. It lies nine miles south of the border with Scotland and is traversed by Hadrian's Wall. The city is located on the south bank of the River Eden at the confluence with the River Caldew. On the north bank is the suburb of Stanwix on the site of the largest fort on Hadrian's Wall. The city is based upon boulder clay which overlies the grey Kirklinton and red St Bees sandstones of the Permo-Triassic Series. This has provided much of the building stone in both Roman and medieval Carlisle, and can be seen very clearly in two of Carlisle's major medieval buildings, the cathedral and the castle.

The early history of Carlisle

Carlisle was an important military and administrative centre in Roman times. Known as *Luguvalium* from at least as early as the mid 80s, the settlement can be shown to have extended over the whole of the later medieval walled area and almost certainly had the status of the civitas capital of the Carvetii. Recent excavations have located an important fort occupied from the early 70s to the 330s (Caruana forthcoming), many areas of housing, several major roads and a major public building tentatively identified as the forum (Fig. 4.1; McCarthy 1990).

By contrast the post-Roman period is much less well known. Although some Roman buildings can be shown to have continued in use into the fifth century, as at Blackfriars Street (McCarthy 1990) and at Scotch Street (Keevill, Shotter and McCarthy 1989), no archaeological evidence has yet come to light for occupation between the late fifth and late seventh centuries. It has been suggested, however, that Carlisle was the focal point of a sub-Roman diocese extending into south-west Scotland (Thomas 1981, 283) and that St Patrick was brought up close by in the late fourth or early fifth century (ibid. 311). Later, St Cuthbert, with the help of the Northumbrian King Ecgfrith and his Queen, founded a nunnery in AD 685 (Colgrave 1940). This has not been located but excavations have yielded many *stycas*, other artefacts and slight structural evidence including several instances of timber-lined pits and wells dated by dendrochronology to the late eighth or early ninth century. Three Anglian cross fragments were found, two in the garden of the second canonry (No.2) and one below the present garage of the third canonry (No.3), in the nineteenth century (Fig. 4.2) (Bailey and Cramp 1988). Although part of a tenth-century cross-head was recovered during building operations in the south transept wall in 1855 (ibid.), until 1988 the biggest remaining lacuna was the Anglo-Scandinavian period. This gap is now being filled.

Although much remains to be clarified about the chronology and shape of the pre-Norman settlement, the results obtained are consistent with historical analyses (Barrow 1975; Winchester 1987; Summerson 1993) which show that Carlisle was probably the centre of a shire. The estates centred on Carlisle may be represented by the churches, of which at least four, one being the Cathedral, may be tentatively identified.[3] Carlisle was not, however, an urban centre, a status which was not achieved in Cumbria until the twelfth century. In 1092 William Rufus occupied Carlisle, built a castle and imported settlers from the south. Henry I paid a visit in 1122 and it is from this point on that Carlisle may be considered urban. According to Symeon, King Henry gave money for the castle and town to be fortified with stone walls.[4] In addition he granted lands for the townsfolk and castle. It was about this time also that the silver at Alston began to be mined and placed under the control of the Sheriff of Carlisle (Summerson 1993). By 1135 Alston silver was being turned into coins at Carlisle. Henry's other decisive acts were to endow a house of Augustinian canons regular under Aethelwold of Nostell, and shortly after to create the Diocese of Carlisle. This began the process of removing Carlisle from the control of John, Bishop of

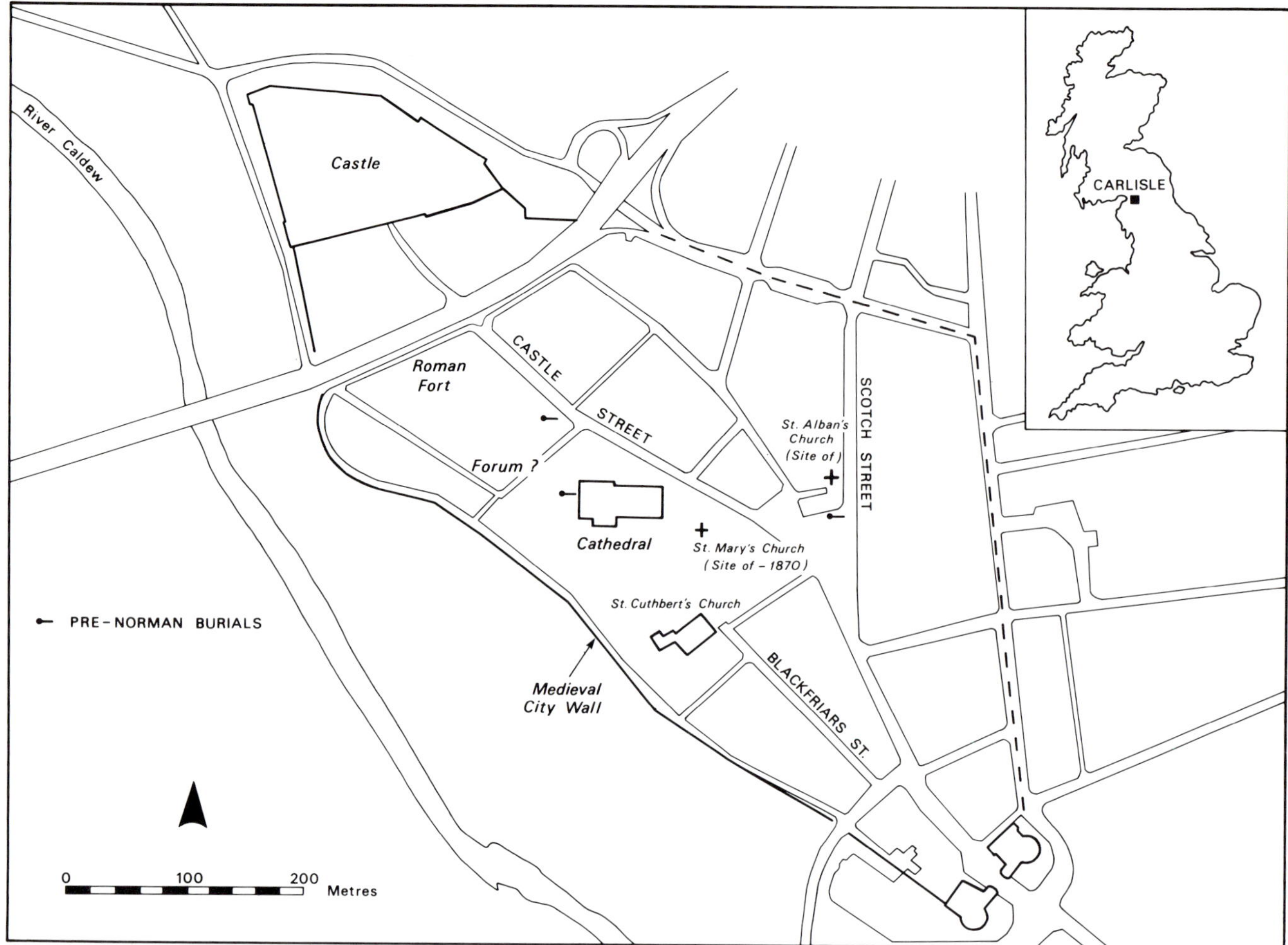

Fig. 4.1. Location of Carlisle Cathedral.

Glasgow. The Cathedral church of St Mary and the canons occupied the same building; St Mary's was located in the western five bays of the nave and was doubtless separated by a screen from the two eastern bays, the crossing and the eastern arm which was the domain of the Priory. The first prior of Carlisle was Aethelwold who held it plurally with Nostell, West Yorkshire. Aethelwold was consecrated Bishop of Carlisle in 1133.[5]

The traditional date for the foundation of the Priory is 1122, the year of Henry I's visit to Carlisle, but there has been some discussion over whether it might have been founded rather earlier in the reign (Dickinson 1945) by Walter the Priest. There is no doubt that a Walter the Priest was active in Carlisle at around this time, for a charter dated *c* 1127 endowed the canons with his lands, but it is not clear which church Walter was attached to. Although it is unlikely, as Dickinson has argued (ibid. 113), that there was a monastic community of any sort as early as Walter's traditional date of 1102, there is nothing improbable in the suggestion that Walter and the king cooperated rather earlier than 1122 in the foundation of a religious house as a means of stabilising the area (Summerson 1993).

Antiquarian interest in the Cathedral

Carlisle and its Cathedral have long attracted the attention of antiquaries. Whereas many of the earlier authorities, Dr Hugh Todd, or Bishops Smith and Nicolson, for example, were primarily concerned with the written record and the contents of the library in particular, those of a later date showed a particular interest in the fabric of the Cathedral. This was occasioned not only by the quickening pace of interest in medieval architecture in the early nineteenth century following Rickman's seminal analysis of medieval architecture first published in 1817, but by a succession of restorations. The sources for this paper include architects' drawings, those of Ewan Christian in the 1850s being especially fine and informative, architectural histories (eg Billings 1840), guides (eg Eley 1900) and articles in established journals. A most important additional source is the local press.[6] *The Cumberland Pacquet*, *The Carlisle Patriot* and *The Carlisle Journal* all contain references which have a bearing on the fabric. Much of this information, which includes opinions, eyewitness accounts and descriptions, may not appear anywhere else. An equally crucial source are paintings and engravings from the late eighteenth century on showing alterations which, whilst being referred to in the minutes of Chapter meetings, may not be apparent in the existing fabric.

One of the earliest and most radical changes was instituted by Bishop Lyttleton whose innovations, between 1762 and 1768, included the choir vault, a wall round the choir, a new position for the high altar and the removal of much medieval woodwork, to the chagrin of Storer (1816) and Billings (1840). In the early years of the nineteenth century a number of alterations were put in hand. The Dean and Chapter in 1799 resolved to repair the Cathedral[7] and in 1803 Prebendary Markham ordered that the plaster covering the capitals be removed.[8] It was also Markham who, according to Billings, discovered a door in the wall below the present east window (Billings 1840, 32). Between 1809 and 1811 the architect Robert Smirke worked on the Fratry and produced a design for a door into the south transept. Shortly afterwards a gallery was inserted into the aisles and the eastern bay of the nave. The drawing produced for Winkle's *Cathedrals* shows very cramped accommodation for a congregation facing towards the pulpit in the centre of the west wall. The pulpit was just below a three-light Romanesque-type window, which must have been a very recent addition as different windows appear on Carlyle's painting of *c* 1791.

The main restoration campaigns began in 1846 when a local builder who later became Mayor of Carlisle, Thomas Nelson, restored the north and south sides of the

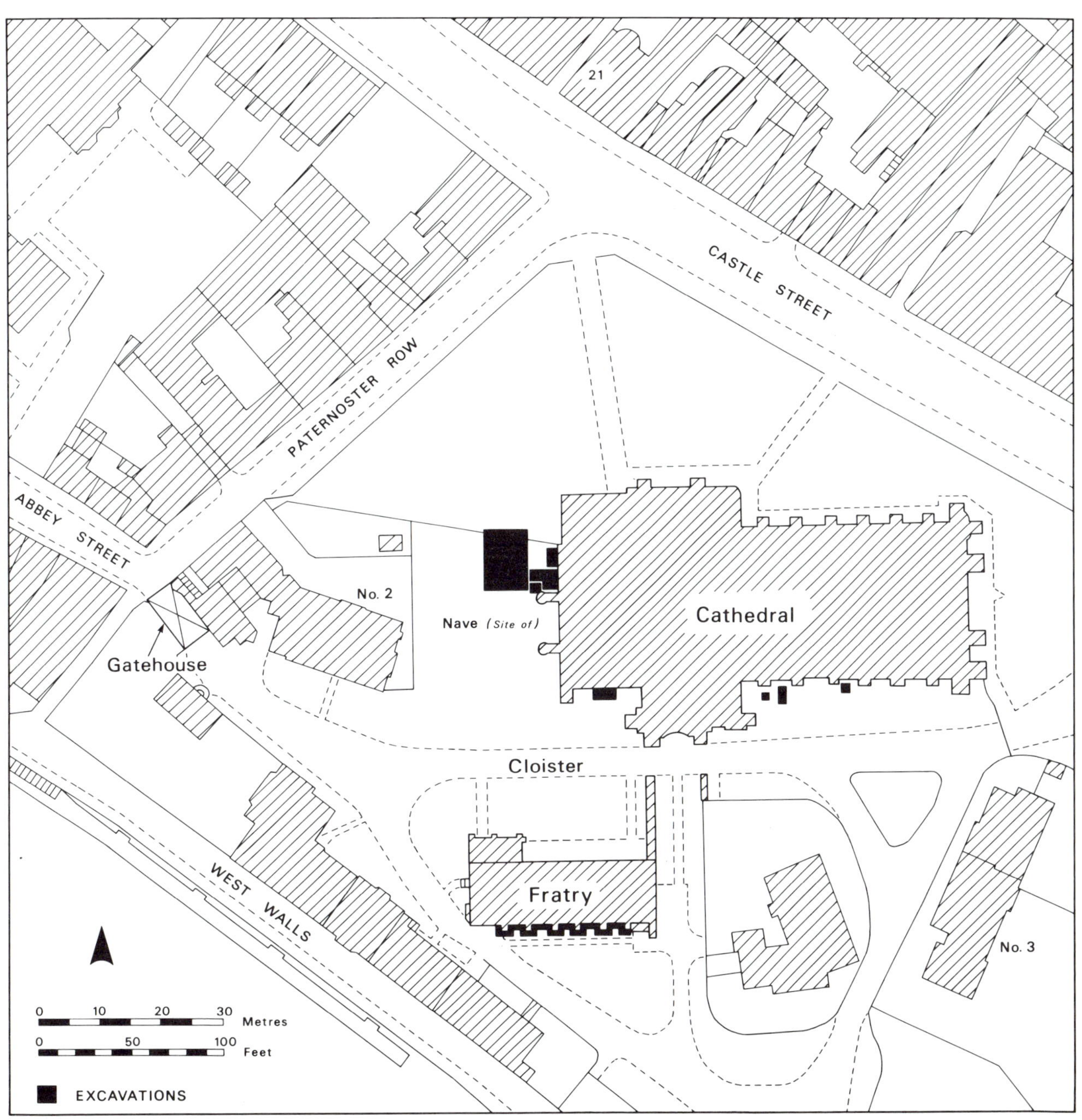

Fig. 4.2. Plan of the Cathedral precinct locating 1985 and 1988 excavations marked in black.

choir. Nelson was followed by Ewan Christian, the distinguished Victorian ecclesiastical architect, who between 1853–4 worked on the nave before dealing with the choir in 1855–6. When St Mary's church moved out of the nave into newly built premises elsewhere in the Cathedral precinct in 1870 (Fig. 4.1), Christian was once again employed, this time to remove the gallery and restore the nave. Shortly afterwards G. E. Street, another eminent ecclesiastical architect, was retained to remove and put right some of Lyttleton's excesses including the choir vault, the bishop's throne, the wall around the choir, and to restore the north transept. Street appears to have been appointed over the head of C. J. Ferguson, who was probably the Diocesan Architect.

The restorations were generally undertaken with a degree of care and sensitivity. Thomas Nelson, for example, regretted the "motley appearance" of the new red sandstone in contrast with the weathered stone of the tower, but continued "a few years seasoning will remove this eyesore"[9]. Nelson removed some of the original weathered stone to a folly he erected in the grounds of his house at Murrell Hill, Carlisle (Morton 1970, 125). There is also a tradition of an archway in a garden of Castle Street, Carlisle,[10] and the present writer has discovered window tracery, pinnacles and voussoirs identical to those in the fourteenth-century choir in the garden of 21, Castle Street. This stonework, together with two clerestory windows rebuilt in the garden of Bunkers Hill, near Morton some three miles to the south west, may all have been dispersed by Thomas Nelson, who was anxious to preserve the material. When the 1870 restoration was undertaken, Purday expressed concern about the style adopted in the restoration of some of the windows. He noted in particular the importance of the restored windows being

Fig. 4.3. View of the nave and south transept. From an engraving by Luke Clennel c 1811–17. Photo Cumbria County Library.

"sufficiently distinct in character to prevent their appearing to be a restoration of ancient work, where none existed".[11]

Sentiments such as these are of interest in the context of the varied fortunes of the nave and aisles in the nineteenth century. The south aisle of the nave, for instance, formerly abutted the cloister walk and would have been windowless. After the late seventeenth century, when St Mary's church was moved from its post-Restoration location in the choir into the two surviving bays of the nave, windows would almost certainly have been needed to light what would otherwise have been a very dark corner of the church. The plan reproduced by Browne-Willis in 1727 shows a single two-light window, and Hearne's pen and ink wash of *c* 1777 depicts two pointed, three-light windows with hood moulds. They may be original medieval windows inserted into the aisle in the late seventeenth century, or they may be eighteenth-century copies. The windows shown by Hearne were still there in *c* 1812 when Luke Clennel depicted the same view (Fig. 4.3), but they were replaced by very tall round-headed windows by 1838 and 1839 when Winkle and Billings (Fig. 4.4) prepared their views. Christian retained these windows in his 1853–5 restoration but they were later replaced by the present imitation fourteenth-century windows.

Despite the care and concern exercised over the fabric it was still possible for insensitive workmanship to destroy other features. Many traces of painting, for instance, appear to have survived up to the time of Christian's work in *c* 1854 when a painting, supposedly St Cuthbert dreaming, was washed off (Whyte and the Bishop of Barrow in Furness 1908; Purday 1859, 374). Similarly, the removal of white plastered voussoirs painted with red lines, discovered in the detritus of seventeenth- to nineteenth-cen-

Fig. 4.4. View of the nave and south transept. From Billings (1840). Photo Cumbria County Library.

tury demolition and restoration rubble in the 1985 excavations, must also be seen as part of a desire to clean up the fabric.

Whereas articles largely by prelates on aspects of the muniments, bells and seals continued to appear in the later nineteenth and twentieth centuries, the restorations prompted fresh enquiries into the history of the fabric itself (ibid.). Of particular importance to the story of Carlisle Cathedral were the Ferguson brothers. C. J. Ferguson was probably the Diocesan Architect and, although he published comparatively little about the Cathedral himself, he passed on much valuable information to his brother, Richard Ferguson, Chancellor of the Diocese and a most prolific and assiduous local antiquarian. He lamented (1875, 296), along with Billings thirty-five years earlier (1840), the fact that Carlisle Cathedral was so little known despite the "tractates" of various writers, including Archbishop Tait of Canterbury, formerly Dean of Carlisle. Billings had described the Cathedral as "this battered and comparatively unknown church of St. Mary's at Carlisle" (1840).

Following R. S. Ferguson's death in 1901 and that of his brother C. J. Ferguson in 1904, interest was maintained by J. H. Martindale, formerly Ferguson's assistant but now elevated to the position of Cathedral Architect. Martindale was himself assisted by C. G. Bulman who, with a faculty obtained from the Chancellor,[12] undertook excavations on the site of the original nave and revealed the pier foundations of the Norman church in 1934. Three years later he published the only major account of the Norman church (Bulman 1937) and followed it with an account of the church in the thirteenth and fourteenth centuries (Bulman 1949).

Archaeological interest went hand-in-hand with that of the restorers in the nineteenth century but then, with the exception of Bulman's work, it lapsed until the late F. G. Simpson excavated a shaft across the north wall of the nave in 1953 (Simpson 1988). No further work was undertaken until 1985, when Carlisle Archaeological Unit excavated six very small trenches for the Dean and Chapter (McCarthy 1987). In 1988 the Dean and Chapter appointed an archaeologist, Graham Keevill, to carry out the first major excavations in the precinct. Keevill's work, outlined below, was undertaken in advance of the building work for an underground Treasury; it was located immediately west of the present west wall in the former north aisle of the nave. These excavations are located and marked in black on Figure 4.2.

The pre-Norman Sequence at the Cathedral

In 1985 and 1988 archaeological excavations were carried out adjacent to the Cathedral church on behalf of the Dean and Chapter. The 1985 investigation, undertaken partly on behalf of English Heritage, and confined to very small-scale excavations against the south side of the choir and the nave and against the west wall, was intended to provide information about the foundations for the Surveyor to the Fabric. In addition to yielding valuable archaeological information, this work confirmed the stability of the foundations and suggested that movements observed in the walls were due to wind pressures.

The two principal results of this campaign included the discovery of a burial which provided a radiocarbon determination of Cal AD 680–820 (Har 7046) (McCarthy 1987, 271). Notwithstanding the danger of extrapolating from a single date, this discovery provided the first positive indication that a pre-Norman church may be located within the Cathedral precinct. The second important result concerns the foundations of the twelfth-century church. One of the nave piers was exposed and found to rest on a continuous sleeper wall which appears to be over 2m in width and at least 2.1m deep. The walls were of stone but the internal structure of the sleeper wall was not investigated. The north and south aisle walls, by contrast, were 2.2m wide but only 1.1m deep. Below the ashlar the foundation included pitched stone mixed up with a few large fragments of *opus signinum* (Fig. 4.5).

In 1988 Keevill's excavations comprised a trench 9.6m (NS) x 7.6m (EW) x 3m deep close to the west wall in the north aisle in advance of the construction of an under-

Fig. 4.5. View of the foundations of the south wall of the nave showing counterpitched stone in the 1985 excavations. Photo Carlisle Archaeological Unit.

ground Treasury. The report on these excavations is in preparation (Keevill forthcoming), but some of the salient results are outlined here.[13]

The excavations were terminated well above the natural subsoil in conformity with the depth of the building works. This left Roman deposits of the first and early second century uninvestigated and undisturbed. The main research objective was the establishment of a sequence of activities spanning the time between the later Roman period and the twelfth century; this was achieved.

The principal Roman features included a major metalled road, which may be identified with the main Roman road from the south also recognised in Blackfriars Street and Botchergate. Too little of the buildings on either side of the road were exposed to enable them to be identified, although one had plastered walls. The road was overlaid by a silt, which was in turn cut by the post-holes of a timber building tentatively attributed to the post-Roman period. At Blackfriars Street,excavated in 1977 (McCarthy 1990), the ultimate Roman timber buildings, which occur in a sequence not dissimilar to that at the Cathedral, are dated to the late fourth and fifth century. At the Cathedral, but not at Blackfriars Street, these buildings were overlaid by a "dark earth". No Anglian features were recognised, although fragments of metalwork and ninth-century *stycas* were recovered. Similarly no burials were attributed to this period, a point which may suggest that the radiocarbon date for the grave recovered in 1985, which in any case has only a 68% probability of being correct, may be misleading.

The "dark earth" was cut by a three-phase cemetery, of which 41 graves were excavated (Fig. 4.6). The graves in the first and final phases were oriented E-W but those in the middle phase were aligned ENE-WSW. Only three coffined burials were recognised, although other iron fittings which may be from coffins were recovered during building operations below the west wall of the nave. Some burials, however, were almost certainly placed in the graves without coffins, and one was lined with sandstone slabs, not dissimilar to the lintel graves at Peel Castle, Isle of Man (Freke 1988). The burials were associated with a fine collection of artefacts including strap ends of both Anglian and tenth-century date, Anglian pins, buckles of tenth-century type, as well as knives and a silver-capped whetstone of tenth- and possibly early eleventh-century date. Of special interest is part of a gold wirework

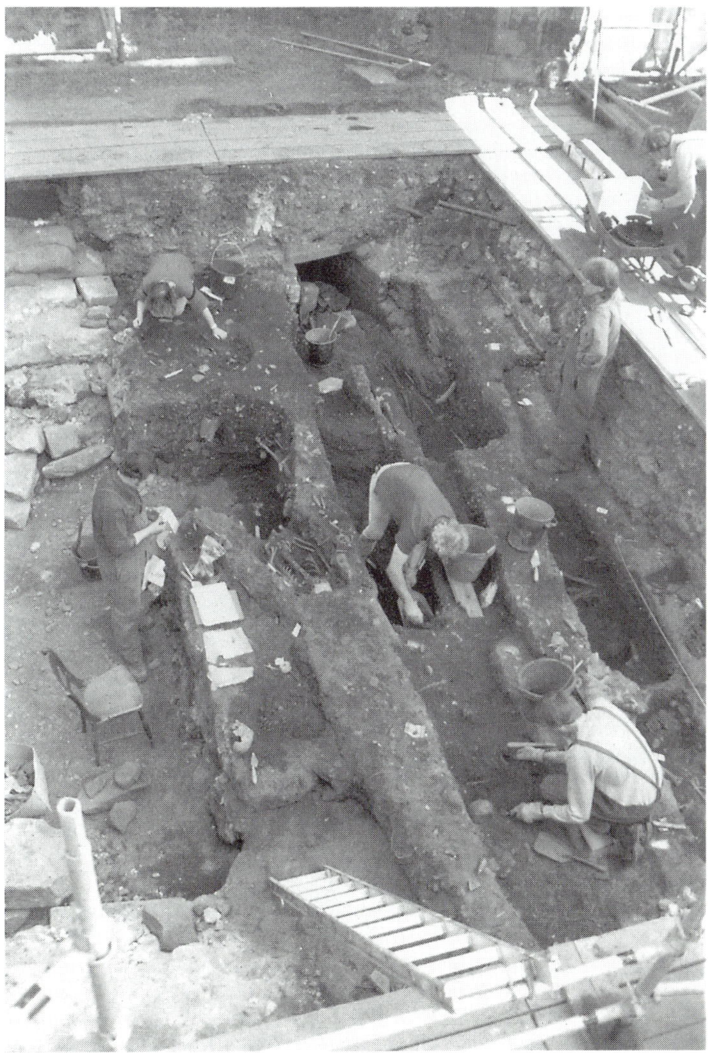

Fig. 4.6. View of the 1988 excavations of the tenth century cemetery in progress. Photo G Keevill.

braid from a cap, matched in this form by an example from a grave in Birka, Sweden (14). A penny of Aethelstan probably lost between 935 and 955 was found in the grave earth, and a halfpenny of Aethelred II lost between 979 and 999 was found in a later context. It seems very likely that some of these graves were those of Norse settlers arriving in the 920–30s.[14]

The Norman foundations were also uncovered and the results of the 1985 excavation confirmed. The building materials were largely re-used Roman stone, including part of a Roman altar dedicated to Concordia. Cutting through the grave deposits and overlaid by the floors were two possible post-pads and a post hole. Too little was exposed to allow a positive interpretation to be advanced, although they were seen as possible scaffolding positions for the Norman church. The floor levels were present as a hard mortar which may have been a base for a tiled or sandstone slab surface.

Description of the Fabric of the Twelfth-century Cathedral

The eastern arm, the tower and transepts (Fig. 4.7)

No trace of the original choir and east end survives above ground, but Bulman recorded (1937, 58–9) a two foot long, curved fragment of masonry which is present in the heating duct below the choir stalls on the south side.

Evidence for the position of the choir and the aisles can be seen in the lowest stage of the tower and the east walls of the transepts. The tower has piers with three orders of semi-circular attached shafts. The bases of the piers are relatively simple with a recurved lower roll, a scotia, a prominent upper roll and a steeply angled fillet next to the shaft. The square bases are partially below ground and barely visible, but the bases of the responds of the nave aisle arches, which project well above floor level, have spurs at the corners. The scalloped capitals of the tower are surmounted by a chamfered abacus which continues to east and west as a string course.

Immediately adjacent to the northern and southern piers are the arches into the aisles. The southern arch with its cushion capitals is bordered by a single band of chevron ornament above the outermost voussoirs (Fig. 4.8); the shafts and bases are identical to those of the tower piers. The abacus of the southern respond continues south as a string course which turns into the abaci of the arch into St Catherine's chapel (Fig. 4.7, c). The string then continues as far as the south wall of the transept.

The northern aisle arch, which also has a single band of chevron ornament above the voussoirs, is blocked up. The abacus and part of the capital are visible but the rest has been either concealed or removed. The voussoirs, abacus and blocking are also visible from the choir and the organ loft stairs.

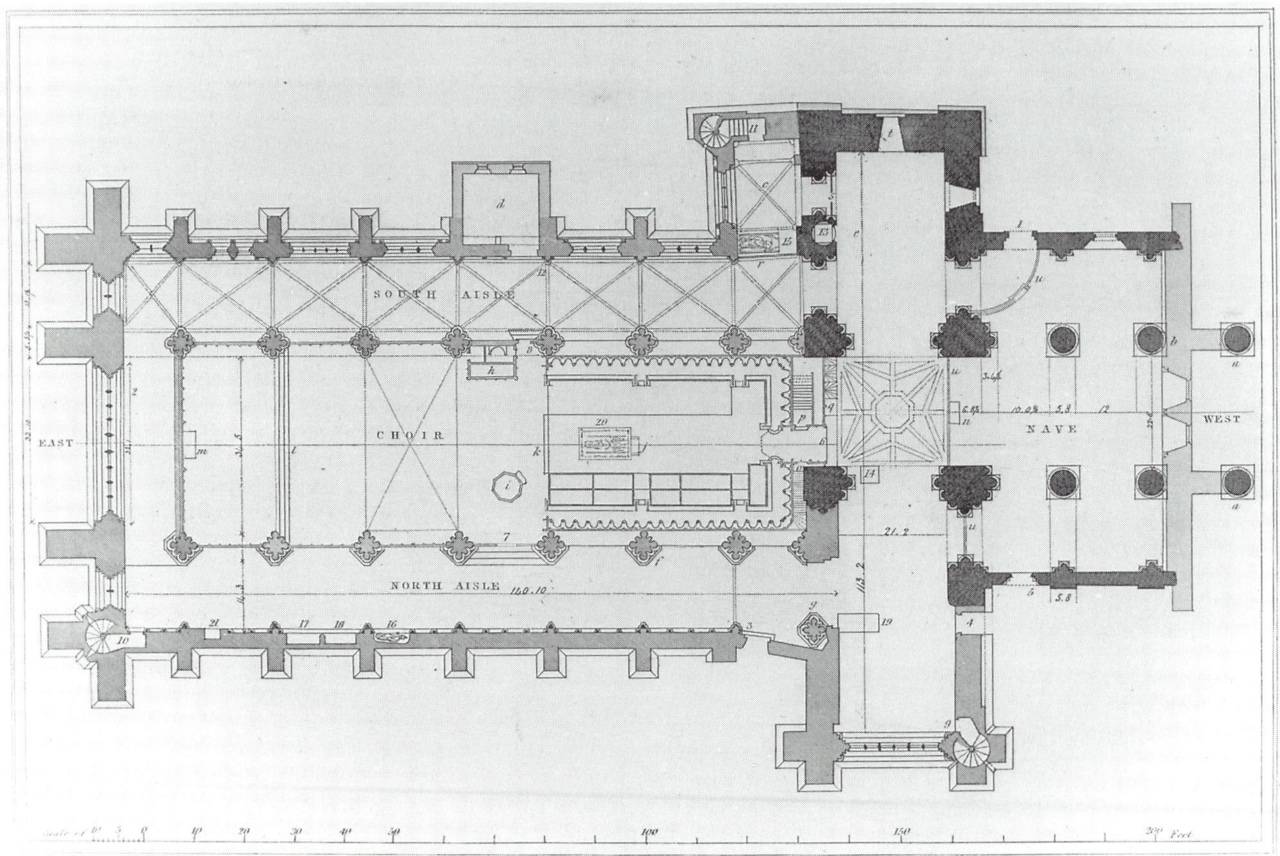

Fig. 4.7. Plan of the Cathedral, from Billings (1840). Photo Cumbria County Library.

Fig. 4.8. View across the transepts, from Billings (1840). Photo Cumbria County Library.

Seen from the transepts, the walling above both choir aisle arches is plain. On the opposite (eastern) face of this wall, however, there are blocked doors at triforium level. The southern door can be seen from the south aisle and the northern door can be seen from the choir. Above the latter door is the crease of a steeply pitched aisle roof, whilst below it can be seen the voussoirs for the blocked aisle arch.

Apart from the masonry immediately adjacent to the south east and the south west tower piers, the walling in the south transept is probably of one build with the aisle and chapel arches and those of the triforium as high as the clerestory string course. Above this string the wall is slightly offset on both east and west sides. In addition there is a vertical offset on the east wall between the tower pier and the north clerestory light. This offset is not matched on the west wall. A marked feature of the east and west walls of the transept is the subsidence affecting the aisle arches and the walls above (Fig. 4.8). The arches and the masonry slope down from south to north. The masonry immediately adjacent to the tower piers, is horizontal, however, suggesting the presence of a reconstruction.

A small side chapel dedicated to St Catherine leads off the south transept (Fig. 4.7, c). The arch has three orders with plain soffits and abaci linking it with a string course and the aisle arches. The east, north and south walls of the chapel are of thirteenth-century date. No trace of the chapel leading off the north transept survives above ground, although Charles Purday evidently saw the foundations in 1855–6 (1859, 373). The south transept is substantially intact and although restoration, especially that of Ewan Christian from 1855, involved a remodelling of the south wall and included some stone replacement, there is much original stonework including parts of two clerestory windows. This enables the transept to be reconstructed as a square. The three storeys are divided by a chamfered string course. There is a single, plain, narrow opening for an intramural passage at triforium level above the arch to St Catherine's chapel, but in the west wall there are two openings. The southern opening is a window with splayed reveals.

There are two windows at clerestory level in the east and west walls; these too lead to an intramural passage. The tall clerestory windows, bordered by a prominent roll, are supported on two shafts with capitals ornamented with a variety of geometrical motifs, some with volutes but with no anthropomorphic or floral motifs. The richness of the capitals matches the variety of mouldings seen on the external elevations of the clerestory. On either side of the shafts are plain, very narrow, subsidiary arches which also have a variety of decorated capitals The abaci on these subsidiary arches are linked by a chamfered string course but none continue along the south wall. The capitals in the south transept are all in red sandstone, compared with the grey used almost exclusively in the wall, the bases and shafts.

The most striking characteristic of the south transept is the distortion in the arches to the choir and nave aisles, the break in the string courses above and the crack in the masonry. The distortion can be seen on both north and south sides of the tower (Fig. 4.8). The north respond in the north aisle of the nave and the south responds of the south aisles have not been affected. It is interesting to note that the distortion apparent in the clerestory window shafts is not present in the window arches, a feature also present in the nave clerestory.

All that survives of the northern transept is the blocked aisle arch on the east wall and a short section of blank walling with a string course to the west. There is no evidence for the termination of the transept which was completely rebuilt and extended in the thirteenth century.

The nave

As a result of the demolition carried out in 1649–52 (Perriam 1987), the present nave is only two bays in length internally (Fig. 4.7). A third bay, in which the piers are linked to the present west wall by buttresses, can be seen outside. There is a triforium, a clerestory and two aisles.

The nave arcade consists of massive, plain, cylindrical piers rising from simple bases derived from the attic form. The capitals of the north arcade are moulded but quite plain, whilst those on the south side are scalloped with palmette leaves between each scallop. The soffits of the arches are plain but with hollow chamfers at the edges. The two eastern arches are distorted. There is a half-round attached shaft rising from the abacus on the two free-standing piers as high as, and integral with, the triforium string course. These shafts do not extend any higher and perform no useful function. Quarter-round shafts rise from the eastern abacus in the angle formed between the tower piers and the walling above the arches. These shafts also stop at the level of the triforium string course. Between the latter and the roof there is a flat pilaster which appears to be of one build with the tower pier at ground level.

The triforium arches are entirely plain and are slightly offset from the responds below. The walls are also plain as seen from the nave but the opposite face, especially that viewed from the south aisle, shows many signs of repair. The clerestory windows match those of the south transept in form and variety of capital, but the stonework is all grey Kirklinton masonry. The clerestory is not offset from the walling below, unlike that in the south transept. The arches of the windows are not distorted but there is evidence of subsidence in the string course and window shafts. This distortion can also be seen at the eastern end of the triforium and in the arcade below, but not in the triforium string course which is horizontal. The drawings of Ewan Christian, however, show that it was distorted in the mid-nineteenth century.

The arcade consists of a mixture of red and grey sandstone, but the overall effect is one of red. The stonework of the triforium and clerestory is, however, almost entirely in grey Kirklinton sandstone. At ground level the masonry is of one build and is integral with the tower piers. The triforium and clerestories may also be of one build, apart from the effects of the distortion and the nineteenth-century stone replacement. The north aisle divides into two bays corresponding to those of the nave arcade. The bays are divided by responds which are of three orders and which have scalloped capitals. The capitals are surmounted by abaci which stop with nothing above. The north wall is arched over in each bay and a centrally placed window lights the aisle. The window has a single round-headed arch, splayed reveals with a single shaft and scalloped capitals. The stonework of much of the windows has clearly been replaced. The eastern bay also contains the door to the clergy vestry built in 1955–6 but it originally formed the west door into St Mary's church. Once again much of the door masonry is replacement stone, and is decorated with two bands of chevron ornament and two orders of shafts with scalloped capitals and palmette leaves similar to those on the nave piers. The door in the western bay is of very recent date and is the entrance to the choir practice room.

The south aisle is similarly divided into bays by responds which stop at abacus level. There are no arches and the windows in each bay are Victorian additions. The eastern bay has a blocked-up door which formerly gave access into the cloister. On the inner face the door is almost wholly obscured by military memorials, but there is no evidence on either face of decoration. The string course above the door, together with some of the masonry, shows evidence of subsidence. Above the string most of the masonry is of one build with the windows and late in date.

The southern face of the spandrels of the south nave arcade is visible from the south aisle. An offset, corresponding to the string on the nave side of the arcade, marks the position of the triforium floor above. Above the offset can be seen the lower part of the triforium openings, now blocked. Between these blockings the masonry is grey Kirklinton sandstone in relatively small blocks typical of the twelfth century.

The external face of the twelfth-century church is readily distinguishable by its use of grey Kirklinton sandstone. Pilaster buttresses can be seen on the east and west walls of the south transept and on the north wall of the north aisle. The windows of the north aisle and the south transept are all decorated with a variety of motifs including chevron, billet and beakhead ornament as well as simple rolls. Above the windows there is a corbel table (Fig. 4.9).

Discussion

Bulman's main concern (1937) was to reconstruct the plan of the twelfth-century church. This he achieved partly by reference to the existing fabric and the plans of other Romanesque cathedrals in Britain, and partly by assumptions about the form of those parts of the church which can no longer be seen. Bulman's reconstruction consisted of a two-bay, apsidal-ended eastern arm with aisles which also had apses. The short, aisleless transepts had apsidal-ended chapels. Much of the crossing, together with two and a half bays of the nave and aisles, survive, but the rest of the western arm was demolished in 1649–52 (Perriam 1987), a decision taken by the church at a high level (Ferguson 1898, 27). Bulman reconstructed the nave as eight bays in length overall (1937), but Perriam (1989) has recently suggested that this may be an error and a seven-bay nave is more likely.

Bulman's approach was rather simplistic. He clearly regarded the church as being the product of a single building design and although some of the inconsistencies visible in the fabric, such as the functionless attached columns in the nave arcade and aisles, were noted, they were not seen as having any constructional importance. Furthermore, his reconstruction was partly based upon observations that nowadays would not be deemed sufficient.

In particular the evidence adduced by Bulman for the eastern arm must be questioned. His main concern was to establish whether the east end was of triapsidal plan, as at Durham, or whether there was an ambulatory, as at Norwich. Bulman satisfied himself that Carlisle had an apsidal-ended choir by crawling along the heating ducts

Fig. 4.9. View of the Cathedral from the north-west. Engraving by W H Nutter 1857. Photo Cumbria County Library.

below the south choir stalls. Some 14.6m (48 feet) east of the crossing he found "a fragment of masonry which begins a curve just before it is broken off, and is about two feet long. This I believe to be the foundation or footing of the original apse wall which terminated the early choir'' (Bulman 1937, 58–9). The present writer has also crawled along the same heating duct in order to clarify Bulman's assertion. The south side of this narrow duct forms the foundation for the fourteenth-century choir arcade, which must also be the line of the Norman choir arcade. At the end of the duct, which is also the end of the choir stalls above, there is a stone which appears to diverge from the line of the foundation. The eastern end of this stone is 0.3m north of the choir footings and it may be a remnant of the early church. The writer is not convinced, however, that this stone is capable of interpretation in isolation. Indeed, the point at which it occurs coincides with the third pier east of the fourteenth-century choir arcade and may be of that date.

As far as the aisle terminations are concerned Bulman had no evidence, relying instead on his assumption that "the simpler plan" consisting of the three apses was adopted. There is no evidence for the length or precise position of the east end of the Norman church at Carlisle, and the veracity of Bulman's claim can only be resolved by excavation. Indeed, a greater measure of doubt attaches to Bulman's reconstruction, as in 1949 he attributed the Norman church with three bays (1949, 116) in contrast with the two he advocated previously (1937, 57).

One factor overlooked by Bulman is the stonework on the eastern face of the crossing above the stairs to the organ loft. Not only does this contain the blocked arch for the north aisle, but it also contains a blocked round-headed door providing access into the triforium. Above the door is the crease of the steeply pitched aisle roof. A similar blocked door can also be seen over the south aisle arch.

Although the evidence for the eastern arm is meagre, nevertheless the position of the choir and aisles are established beyond doubt by the presence of much twelfth-century work at the crossing. The lowest stage of the tower is entirely twelfth century in date, and the three-storey aisleless transepts were square in plan as is clear on the south side.

The position of the nave and aisle is also clear beyond doubt and, although some confusion exists about the precise number of bays and the position of the west end, the position of the walls and the approximate position of the west end can be seen in Kip's engraving of *c* 1717 (Fig. 4.10). A seven-bay nave and the west end were established by Purday and Ferguson in the nineteenth century.

In 1878 C. J. Ferguson, following the 1853 observations of Purday, rediscovered the west end of the nave in

Fig. 4.10. Engraving of Carlisle Cathedral in c *1717 by Johannes Kip. Photo Cumbria County Library.*

the garden of the second canonry.[15] A fortnight after the letter containing this information was published, another appeared in which the west wall was said to be 2.1m (7 feet) thick with four flat pilaster buttresses 2m (6.5 feet) wide. The door in the centre of the wall was "of four recessed orders of arches, the outer arch having a span of 14 feet" (4.3m).[16] As a result of this Ferguson postulated a nave seven bays in length.[17]

Bulman, however, was unaware of this earlier discovery, and postulated an eight-bay nave and a west end in a different position to that of Ferguson on the basis of his own excavations. In 1934 Bulman carried out excavations to locate the nave piers and the west end. He thought that the nave was eight bays in length, believing that a "mass of rubble" in the garden of the second canonry was the west wall (1937, 61). It is possible, as Perriam has pointed out (1989, 19), that Bulman knew nothing of Ferguson's discoveries as they were not published in the local *Transactions*, but only reported in the press, notably *The Carlisle Journal* in 1878, *The Builder* in 1893 and *The Carlisle Patriot* in 1895.

The observations of Purday and C. J. Ferguson in identifying the west end[18] command respect if only because of their professional status in the building trade. Moreover, they were able to give precise details and measurements of the west elevation, thereby increasing confidence in the accuracy of their observations. Bulman, by contrast, relying on a statement by Eley (1900), could only point to "a mass of rubble" in the garden of the second canonry "from which", he admitted, "it seemed impossible to obtain any definite information". Bulman, in ignorance of the nineteenth-century discoveries, and no doubt partly following the views of his immediate superior J. H. Martindale, in whose office he worked, had misread the archaeological remains.

As a postscript to this aspect of the church plan, it is worth recording that neither the Ferguson brothers, nor Martindale, Bulman or Perriam has considered the possibility that the west end could have been adorned by twin western towers.[19] The documentary sources for the Cathedral before the Dissolution contain no information but they are very sparse, most having been lost or destroyed. A sixteenth-century map of Carlisle preserved in the British Library (BL *Cotton Ms Aug 1, i, 13*) depicts the Cathedral in *c* 1560, and shows a west end without towers, whilst seventeenth-century sources similarly make no allusion to the west end. Until such time as further excavation reveals the west wall, Perriam's analysis, based upon a detailed reading of the available sources, must stand. The one possible addition is contained in the 1988 excavations, which yielded weathered fragments of plain chevron-decorated voussoirs almost certainly from an external context. The nature of this context must remain uncertain, but given the apparent absence of any significant remains of twelfth-century work in the conventual buildings surviving into the nineteenth century, the voussoirs may well have originated in the church, perhaps the west door, although their radius is not inconsistent with a clerestory window.

The pre-Priory sequence

The 1988 excavations confirmed the presence of a major Roman road aligned at approximately 60 degrees to the church. The road is 4m wide, and consists of a solid deposit of cobble and gravel metalling probably as deep as the natural subsoil. The nature and solidity of the Roman structures on either side of the road is uncertain. By the late ninth or very early tenth century a considerable depth of soil had accumulated over the road. This is contemporary with the monastery of St Cuthbert which, from the evidence of artefacts and cross fragments in addition to the radiocarbon-dated grave excavated in 1985, probably lies close by. In the tenth century a densely packed cemetery cut through the soil deposits. This shows that the earliest Priory church (Period 1) was not an adaptation of an earlier building, which presumably lies to the south and may have been still standing in the 1120s.

The church, Period 1

The substructure of the Priory church (Period 1) revealed in the excavations of 1985 and 1988 consisted of the continuous sleeper wall which formed the base of the nave arcade. It is over 2m deep and probably rested on the Roman road in places. The aisle walls were much less substantial. This was a point noted by Ferguson (1898, 559), but Keevill has shown that on the north side they are stratigraphically contemporary[20] with the sleeper wall. The sleeper wall, together with the aisle foundations, is of one build with the nave arcade as high as the string course below the triforium arches. The nave arcade is also contemporary with the lowest stage of the tower and the transepts. The bases of the piers are all the same and are relatively simple, without being augmented with complex sequences of additional rolls, scotias and fillets. This strongly suggests contemporaneity. The capitals of the nave arcade, on the other hand, show some variation. Those on the north side of the nave are plain, whilst those on the south are scalloped, with a palmette leaf between each scallop. It is possible that this variation has a minor chronological significance, but it may equally have been the intention to vary the decoration. The bases, capitals and form of the piers are entirely characteristic of the first half of the twelfth century.

The church, Period 2

The masonry and other elements of the nave and aisles show that a break occurred in building after the nave arcade, the spandrels and string course above were completed. The break was followed by the completion of the church to roof level. The evidence for a break, and a change in building design, is threefold. Firstly, the responds in the aisles which stop in mid-air, as it were, perform no useful function. The builders clearly changed their minds as to the manner of the aisle roofs midway through the building programme. Secondly, the shafts rising from the abaci of the piers do not continue upwards into the triforium and again perform no useful function. A third factor, not in itself evidence of a change in design, but which may nonetheless be significant, is the widespread use of red St Bees sandstone in the nave arcade, contrasting with the use of grey Kirklinton stone in the upper levels.

A possible complication is the lack of distortion in the clerestory windows compared with the distortion visible lower down. This could be seen as another possible stage in the building sequence, but nineteenth-century illustrations show that this was not the case. The drawings of both Billings (1840) and Christian in 1853–4 show that the windows were formerly distorted and that it was Christian who restored them to their original shape.

The transepts are less easy to interpret because of the nineteenth-century repairs, but if the choice of stone colour is a true reflection of a change in building design, a break in building may also have occurred when the triforium string course was reached. The walling below the string is largely red sandstone and that above is almost wholly grey. There is little in the characteristics of the masonry, however, to determine the question either way.

Despite the fact that the arches to the nave and choir aisles and in the transept walls are badly out of true, there is no evidence in the fabric at Carlisle for a tower collapse in the twelfth century, as occurred in many other major churches. Settlement resulting in distortion probably took place over a prolonged period of time, beginning no doubt in the twelfth century, and disaster finally struck in 1380, when the tower collapsed.

Conclusions

Although analysis of the structural elements can only confirm two phases of building in the twelfth century, the apparent simplicity of the early building history could be deceptive. In the first place, too little survives to enable this straightforwardness to be pressed too far. It is not certain, for example, to what extent the break in the episcopate of nearly half a century, between the death of Aethelwold and the appointment of Bernard of Ragusa in 1204, had on the administration of the Priory and its fabric. There is clearly room for argument that the lack of a bishop had an impact in terms of prestige and revenues. Indeed the bishopric accounts for 1188 show that £16 15s 6d was spent on the cathedral, moneys diverted from the episcopal revenues to the canons by the king. Summerson has argued (1993) that the lack of a bishop may have had little impact, as the buildings were the responsibility of the Chapter who were probably presided over by the Archdeacon. Moreover, the canons, of whom there were as many as 26 in 1133 (ibid.), were sufficiently well endowed with land, churches and other property to enable them to complete the building programme.

Secondly, eighteenth- and nineteenth-century illustrations and accounts show just how chequered the fortunes of the surviving parts of the nave and aisles were. The fabric in some areas was affected to a significant extent, as Christian's fine series of ink and watercolour drawings testify. Much of the external stonework in the north and south aisle walls and the transepts, together with the windows and the entire corbel table, has been replaced. The clerestory, apart from the corbel table, has been affected much less although it was clearly blocked in 1717 (Fig. 4.10), but it had been re-opened by 1840 as shown in Billings (1840) and later by Nutter (Fig. 4.9). The internal elevations have escaped extensive restoration, especially the nave arcade, triforium and clerestory. Fortunately, Christian's drawings enable us to identify replacement stone which is not otherwise easy to recognise for what it is.[21]

Despite appearances, the north aisle wall contains little twelfth-century masonry *in situ*. The Romanesque-style door to the clergy vestry (Figs. 4.9–10) was built in 1813–14 as the entrance to St Mary's church. This must also have entailed considerable restoration to the window above (compare Figs. 4.9 and 10), for the entire arch in which the door and window are set has been renewed. The other Norman-style window is also a restoration and is shown in both Gilpin's view of 1765 and that of Robert Carlyle in *c* 1791, where it appears as a three-light arched window identical to those in the south aisle.

Although all is not what it may seem, nevertheless there is sufficient remaining to show that the Augustinian Priory church at Carlisle was not exceptional in its basic plan. Bulman's triapsidal reconstruction of the eastern arm is probably correct, although the evidence is lacking. The square transepts with apsidal chapels conform to the typical plan exemplified in many other priories.

To the citizens of Carlisle, a community remote from the centre of power and whose main claim on the attention of the crown throughout the Middle Ages occurred only when the borders were threatened or when the burgesses defaulted in their payment of the fee farm, the second quarter of the twelfth century witnessed a complete turn around in their fortunes. There was a massive building programme which included not only the Priory and its conventual buildings, of which we know nothing at this time, but also the city walls and the castle. Parts of Carlisle castle are exactly contemporary with the Priory (McCarthy, Summerson and Annis 1990), and the masons probably used the same quarries. The castle was conceived as one of the largest and strongest castles on the Anglo-Scottish border. It was one of the favourite residences of David I, and probably functioned as a royal palace. The acquisition of the castle and priory, together with all the craftsmen needed for building purposes, the city walls, the mint, the trade, and commercial activity, and the litigation which inevitably accompanied a community in which David 1, the sheriff, the prior and bishop were present, all confirmed Carlisle as a new but very important urban community in a hitherto remote rural setting. Carlisle Cathedral had a central role in the creation of this community in spiritual, economic and political terms.

Notes

1. I am extremely grateful to Tim Tatton-Brown, the Very Rev Henry Stapleton, Dean of Carlisle, Dr Henry Summerson, Denis Perriam, Graham Keevill and Catherine Brooks for reading and commenting on the text. Figures 4.1 and 2 were prepared by Philip Cracknell, Carlisle Archaeological Unit. Figures 4.3–4, 4.7–8 and 4.10 are taken from the Jackson Collection, Cumbria County Library. Figure 4.9 is in the Parsable Dawson Collection, Cumbria County Library.
2. The architectural affinities of the church is a complex issue which has not been pursued. There are possible links with Melbourne, Derbyshire, which was granted to Carlisle by Henry I at or about the time of Aethelwold's consecration to the new See in 1133. Of particular interest at Melbourne are the spurs on the bases of the nave arcade, the capitals of the nave on the south side and the capitals of the shafts at clerestory level, all of which resemble those at Carlisle.
3. In addition to the Cathedral church, other possible pre-Conquest foundations include St Cuthbert's church, which apart from its dedication, can be shown to be aligned on a former Roman road rather than the standard east-west Christian alignment. At 32–40 Castle Street, burials dated by radiocarbon to the pre-Norman period imply a church close by. Another post-Roman pre-medieval burial has been located south of St Alban's church. It is thought possible that St Alban's church is a pre-Conquest foundation although there is as yet no evidence. The location of these burials and churches is shown on Fig. 4.1.
4. T. Arnold, 1882, *Symeonis Monachi Opera Omnia, Rolls Ser* II, 267.
5. Paper by Richard Gem entitled 'Melbourne Church, Derbyshire' given at the B.A.A. Conference 1987. I am grateful to The Very Rev Henry Stapleton for this information. See also Summerson 1993, 35-36.
6. I am indebted to Denis Perriam for this information.
7. *Cumberland Pacquet*, 15/1/1799.
8. *Carlisle Journal*, 18/4/1803.
9. *Carlisle Journal*, 19/9/1846.
10. I am indebted to Denis Perriam for this information.
11. *Carlisle Patriot*, 10/6/1871.
12. I am indebted to Denis Perriam for this information.
13. I am grateful to Graham Keevill for information on the excavations.
14. Pers. comm. Dominic Tweddle, York Archaeological Trust.
15. I am indebted to Denis Perriam for this information.
16. *Carlisle Patriot*, 4/10/1895.
17. *Carlisle Patriot*, 18/10/1895.
18. The position of the west end is marked out in the footpath next to the south wall of the second canonry.
19. Melbourne Church, Derbyshire, has twin unfinished towers at the west end.
20. I am indebted to Graham Keevill for this information.
21. It is interesting to note that for the Cathedral church as a whole, at least 75% of the external stonework was replaced by Thomas Nelson and Ewan Christian: the whole of the east end, most of the tower, the entire choir clerestory and much of the north and south aisle walls. The external stonework represents an almost complete rebuild in the 1840s and 50s.

Bibliography

Bailey, R.N. and Cramp, R.J. 1988: *The British Academy Corpus of Anglo-Saxon Stone Sculpture Volume II: Cumberland, Westmorland and Lancashire North-of-the-Sands.*

Barrow, G. W. S. 1975: The pattern of lordship and feudal settlement in Cumbria, *J Medieval Hist*, 1, 117–38.

Billings, R.W. 1840: *History of Carlisle Cathedral.*

Bulman, G.C. 1937: The Norman Priory Church at Carlisle, *Trans CWAAS*, 2 ser. 37, 56–66.

Bulman, G.C. 1949: Carlisle Cathedral and its development in the thirteenth and fourteenth centuries, *Trans CWAAS*, 2 ser. 49, 87–117.

Caruana, I. forthcoming: *The Roman Forts at Annetwell Street, Carlisle: Excavations 1973–84.*

Colgrave, B, 1940: *Two Lives of St Cuthbert.*

CWAAS: Cumberland and Westmorland Antiquarian and Archaeological Society.

Dickinson, J. C. 1945: The origins of the Cathedral of Carlisle, *Trans CWAAS*, 2 ser., 45, 134–143.

Eley, C. King, 1900: *The Cathedral Church of Carlisle: a description of the fabric and a brief history of the episcopal See.*

Ferguson, C.J. 1893: article in *The Builder*, 6 May, 348.

Ferguson, R.S. 1875: The east window, Carlisle Cathedral: its ancient stained glass, *Trans CWAAS*, 1 ser., 2, 296–312.

Ferguson, R.S. 1898: *Carlisle Cathedral.*

Freke, D. 1988: Peel Castle, *Current Archaeol*, 110, 92–7.

Keevill, G. forthcoming: *Excavations at Carlisle Cathedral in 1985 and 1988.*

Keevill, G., Shotter, D.C.A. and McCarthy, M.R. 1989: A *solidus* of Valentinian II from Scotch Street, Carlisle, *Britannia* 20, 254–5.

McCarthy, M. R. 1987: Excavations at Carlisle Cathedral, *Trans CWAAS*, 2 ser. 7, 270–1.

McCarthy, M. R. 1990: *A Roman, Anglian and Medieval site at Blackfriars Street, Carlisle; Excavations 1977–9*, CWAAS Research Ser. 4.

McCarthy, M.R., Summerson, H. R .T. and Annis, R. G. 1990: *Carlisle Castle: A Survey and Documentary History*, English Heritage monograph 18.

Morton, J. 1970: *Three Generations of a Textile Family.*

Perriam, D. R. 1987: The demolition of the Priory of St Mary, Carlisle, *Trans CWAAS*, 2 ser. 87, 127–158.

Perriam, D. R. 1989: The search for the west end of Carlisle Cathedral, *Brit. Archaeol*, 11, 19.

Purday, C. 1859: The architecture of Carlisle Cathedral, *Archaeol Jnl*, 16.

Simpson, G. 1988: Further notes on Carlisle Cathedral excavations, 1953, *Trans CWAAS*, 2 ser. 88, 87–106.

Storer, 1816: *Graphic and Historical Description of the Cathedrals of Great Britain.*

Summerson, H.R.T. 1993: *Medieval Carlisle: The City and the Borders from the Late Eleventh to the Mid-Sixteenth Century*, CWAAS Extra Ser. XXV (2 vols.).

Thomas, C. 1981: *Christianity in Roman Britain to AD 500.*

Whyte, E.T. and the Bishop of Barrow in Furness, 1908: A wall painting formerly in Carlisle Cathedral, *Trans CWAAS*, 2 ser., 8, 234–5.

Winchester, A. J. L. 1987: *Landscape and Society in Medieval Cumbria.*

Archaeology and Chichester Cathedral

Tim Tatton-Brown

Compared to its huge neighbour at Winchester, Chichester Cathedral is a small structure; even with its five-bay Lady Chapel and western porch added, it is only just over 400 feet long externally. As originally built in the Romanesque period, it was only about 325 feet long externally. The aisled nave (without the later chapels) and presbytery is about 68 feet wide externally, and most noticeable of all, in comparison with Winchester, it has only small unaisled transepts.

Chichester Cathedral was also the smallest but one of the nine cathedrals of the 'Old Foundation' in the number of its canons. It had only 27 prebendaries and a dean, chancellor, precentor and treasurer and none of them had a particularly large income (Kitch 1978, 277). It is still today a comparatively little known and little visited cathedral, though one which is efficiently run and mostly in a good state of repair. It is also a building which in the last few decades has acquired many fine new works of art, thanks to the patronage of Dean Walter Hussey. A major campaign of restoration has been in progress for over thirty years.

Architecturally, Chichester Cathedral has no spectacular areas, but within the building there are many fine smaller details. To take but two examples, there are the exceptionally splendid early twelfth century 'Chichester reliefs' (perhaps part of a screen, see Zarnecki 1953), and the magnificent Purbeck marble capitals in the eastern ambulatory (Willis 1861, plate IV op.p. 21). To an archaeologist, however, the fabric of the building contains many very interesting details which make it possible to work out the numerous changes that have taken place. After its initial construction in the late eleventh and early twelfth century, the building never underwent any major campaign of rebuilding, no doubt because of its comparative poverty. Even after the devastating fire of 20 October 1187, the charred and calcined walls of the nave and presbytery were only refaced where necessary (ie, in the clerestory and main arcade, but not in the triforium). As a result, there still survives a remarkably large amount of the fabric of the early Norman church, although to view all of this it is necessary also to visit the galleries (triforia) and the cramped roof spaces above the vaults of the thirteenth century outer chapels. There are also many barely visible traces of the earliest building, like the indications of the position of the internal wall arcade in the south choir aisle (Andrew 1980, 305 and fig.5), the clues to the original apsidal ambulatory chapels, first spotted by Professor Robert Willis (1861, 8), or the evidence for the transverse gables on the thirteenth century nave aisle chapels (Willis 1861, 27).

As in so many cathedrals, it is Willis' architectural history that is the starting point for any modern work. His lecture at Chichester was given at the Archaeological Institute's summer meeting in July 1853. It was not, however, published immediately (due to the tardiness of others), but after the disastrous fall of the tower and spire on February 21st 1861, Willis wrote an important 'introductory essay' in which he analysed the reasons for the collapse, and then the whole was published in the same year. The documentary and architectural history was later expanded in W.H. Godfrey and J.W. Bloe's major contribution to the Victoria County History of Sussex in 1935, and this was accompanied by a good new measured plan of the building. Thirty years later Ian Nairn's and Sir Nikolaus Pevsner's fine description of the cathedral was written (considerably revised twenty years later in Pevsner and Metcalf 1985), but it has only been in the last decade or so that some important new archaeological work on around and on the fabric has taken place.

In 1958 the west end of the cathedral precincts was 'improved', followed by the east end in 1962–3. This has involved the almost complete removal of the old tombs and gravestones (they have also been cleared out of 'paradise' – the cloister garth). This was followed by the reduction of the ground level around most of the north side and eastern arm of the cathedral. Large areas of the eastern arm had also been underpinned and cross-ties and a ring-beam in a concrete bed had been inserted in the presbytery triforium by 1971. In 1968, for example, the buttresses on the north side of the presbytery north aisle were underpinned to a depth of 14 feet, A volunteer archaeological excavation carried out during the early part of this work was briefly able to record part of the foundations of the Romanesque semi-circular ambulatory chapel. Similar foundations were found on the south side in 1966 (Down and Rule 1971, 127–8).

In 1962 the Surveyor, Robert Potter, had produced a new survey of the cathedral with a suggested major programme of restoration work. A large appeal was launched, and a new Cathedral Works Organisation was set up in 1966 to carry out the work. This got underway on the underpinning as mentioned above. In 1966–71 the cathedral library, east of the north transept was totally rebuilt, and a new space for the library was created, under a new roof, above the earlier library. The work of lowering the ground level on the north side continued until 1971, and this was followed immediately by dropping the floor level inside the western porch and removing the steps at the west end of the nave. The Medieval west doors were removed (they are now stored in the bell-tower), and new glass doors were put in. A second pair of glass doors was erected at the entrance to the western porch. The lowering of the floor level in the porch exposed the original Romanesque bases outside the west doorway. This discovery halted the restoration of the thirteenth century Purbeck marble shafts and bases because they did not match the Romanesque ones. This dilemma was only resolved in 1989 when the Romanesque bases were boxed in and much new Purbeck marble was inserted (Tatton-Brown 1990, 8–11).

In 1974, the three central flying buttresses on the south side of the presbytery were taken down and rebuilt, and soon after that the hugely expensive job of restoring the external masonry of Scott's tower and spire commenced. In just over a century the Chilmark and Tisbury stone had in many places been greatly eroded by heavily saline winds from the south-west. This had not been helped by Scott's leaving the lantern stage of the tower open to the elements. Work on this stone replacement was finally curtailed in June 1986, and the following year, under the new Surveyor, Donald Buttress, various small-scale repairs were carried out in the presbytery area, The gable end of the St Mary Magdalen chapel as well as the top of the neighbouring pinnacle were rebuilt and two new small gables were added to the ends of the eastern presbytery flying buttresses. At the same time the underpinning and refacing of the large free-standing buttresss west of the north transept was started and plans were put in hand to carry out a major five year programme of restoration on the north side of the nave. Towards the end of 1987 I was invited to become the archaeological consultant to the Dean and Chapter, and in 1988 a new programme of recording of the fabric in advance of, and during, restoration work was started.

Studying the Fabric

As was said at the outset, it is Professor Robert Willis' study that has to be the starting point for any study of the fabric of the cathedral. This work, which as usual is well ahead of its time in studying the stratigraphic sequences, divides the architectural history of the cathedral into four main periods. Willis, however, only dealt in detail with the first two: the Norman cathedral and 'works consequent on the fire of 1186(sic)'. Though he studied the fabric carefully and made many excellent drawings and observations, his work can only really serve as a preface to a detailed study based on measured 'stone-by-stone' drawings.

Since Willis' time very little new work has been done, though a small number of important studies have added significant detail. First in time was E.S. Prior's brief paper of 1904 in the obscure Proceedings of the Harrow Architectural Club (quoted in Bond 1906, 23). In this, Prior proposed at least twelve 'different styles of masoncraft' between c. 1090 and c. 1450. By a careful examination of the masonry, he was able to demonstrate that early masonry, dressed diagonally with a pick and axe, gave way to vertical dressing with a claw chisel. He was also able to show the variations in the dressed work in different phases, and how different types of claw chisels were used. Early chisels (early thirteenth century) only had about six notches to the inch, but better tools were soon developed with 9, 12 and 14 notches to the inch. By the end of the thirteenth century, very fine dressed masonry using claw chisels with 16 or 20 notches to the inch is found.

More recently Martin Andrew (1980 and 1982) has studied aspects of the Romanesque fabric in more detail, though without making 'stone-by-stone' drawings, and Julian Munby (1981) has examined the high roof carpentry as well as aspects of the surviving masonry evidence for the early thirteenth century roof over the nave and presbytery.

As we have seen, a new programme of recording and studying the fabric of the cathedral was started in 1988. Over the next five years, this concentrated on the north nave area where the major restorations were taking place. Initially sketch drawings of the north elevation of the nave and of the west front (Fig. 5.1) were made, and a provisional analysis of the fabric was carried out. Then as cleaning and repair got underway, full-scale measured drawings at a 1:20 scale were made of each bay (working from east to west) on the north side of the nave (Fig.5.2). The sides of the flying buttresses and of the outer buttresses were also drawn, and it is hoped, at a later date, to add to these drawings more of the internal masonry (that is below the roof, and both above and below the vaults). Much of the upper part of the late eleventh century original outer wall is preserved at clerestory and gallery level, as well as buried late twelfth century buttresses, as Robert Willis first observed.

At Chichester one of the great advantages in analysing the masonry is that almost all phases of work use a different building stone. In the late eleventh and early twelfth century Quarr stone is used exclusively. Then by the mid-twelfth century Caen stone from Normandy was introduced, and it was the cutting of this fine stone, using better chisels, that evolved during the thirteenth century. A little later, large blocks of Binstead stone (similar to Quarr and harder than Caen) were used on the upper parts of the buttresses, flying buttresses and high corbel-tables and parapet. This was in the later thirteenth century, by

Fig. 5.1. Sketch elevation and provisional phasing of the masonry of the west front.: II –c.1100 Quarr stone masonry; V – rebuilding of SW tower after 1210 collapse; VII – rebuilt upper gable and added porch of the late 13th century; X – wooden mullions of great west window before mid-19th century restoration; also outline of the north turret before rebuilding of NW tower c. 1900.

which time it was recognised that a harder stone should be used in the more exposed areas. In the later Middle Ages a much softer upper greensand stone (almost certainly 'Green Ventor' or 'Bonchurch stone'from the southern part of the Isle of Wight) was used. This can be seen on the outer chapel parapet walls as well as in the detached bell-tower. A small amount of Fittleworth stone, characterised by its dark ironstone colour, is also used on the additions that were made to the tops of the flying buttresses in the more easterly bays of the nave. There are also Purbeck marble shafts on the outside of the later thirteenth century outer chapel windows (Fig. 5.2). The later repairs and restorations can also be distinguished by the different types of stone. In the seventeenth and eighteenth century some Portland stone was used, while Caenstone, but of a softer variety, was reintroduced in the early to mid-nineteenth century (R. C. Carpenter used this alone to restore the tracery in the windows in 1847). Some Bath stone was also used. Scott rebuilt the tower and spire (1861–6) with Portland and 'rag' from Purbeck in the tower piers, and then large amounts of Chilmark/ Tisbury stone in the outer walls. Pearson also used Chilmark for rebuilding the north-west tower. Early this century, Dean Hannah gave West Hoathly sandstone, from his own quarry, to the cathedral (Leeney 1947, 178), and this can be seen in the repaired bell-tower quoins as well as in the plinth to the rebuilt shrine platform behind the high altar. After the last war, a little Clipsham stone (from Rutland) was used for repairs (Leeney 1947, 179), but all major repair work in recent years has been with Lepine stone from near Poitiers, and other stones from France.

A provisional analysis of the west front of the cathedral (Fig. 5.1) shows that there are five main phases of masonry. Small block Quarr stone is used for the earliest (lowest) parts of the western towers. Then the south-west tower, after its collapse in 1210, was rebuilt with Caen stone. Massive buttresses to the south-west corner were added as well as a completely new top stage. It is also possible to see how a great crack up the middle of the

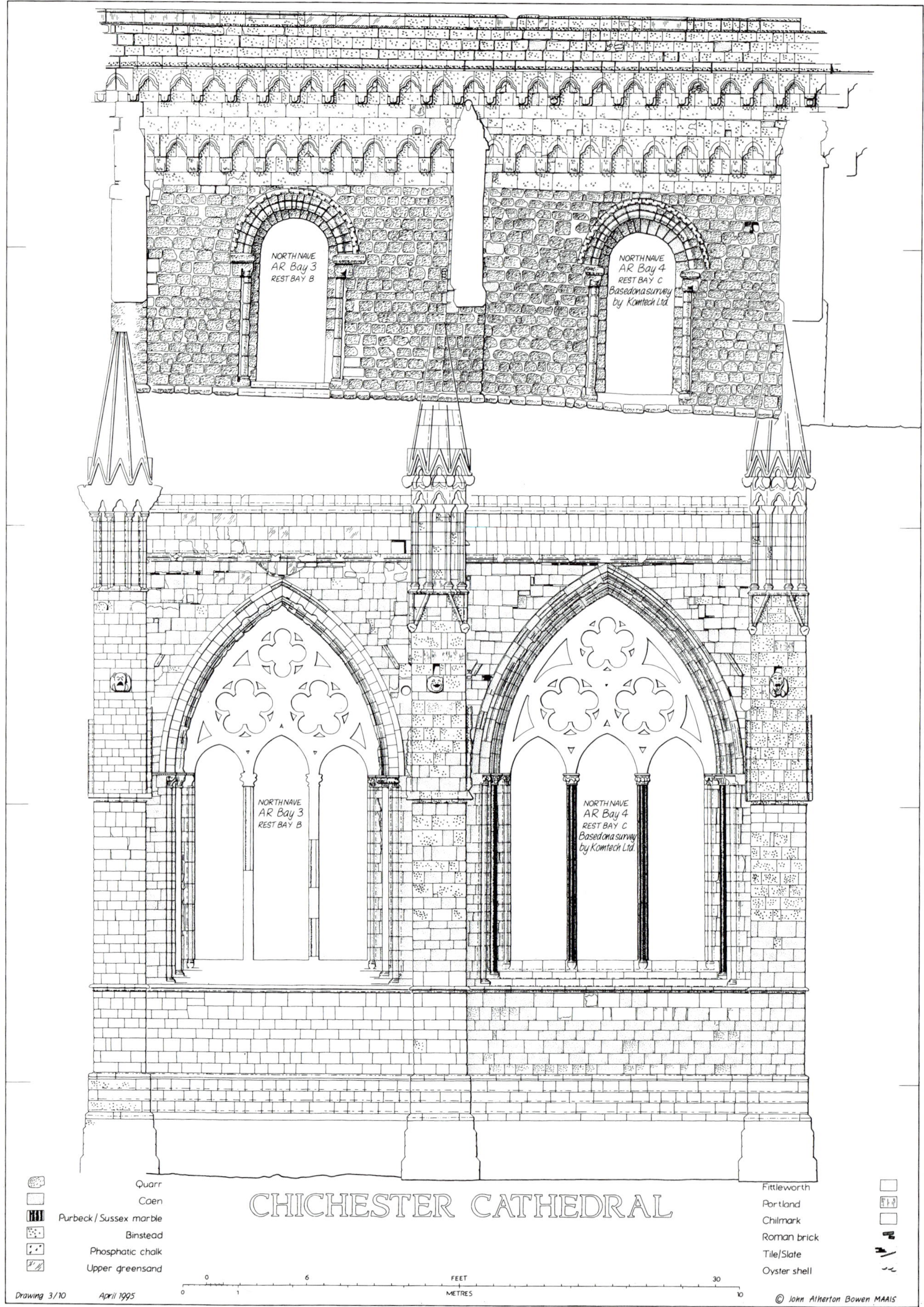

Fig. 5.2. Elevation of two bays in the north nave area (the Chapel of St Theobald) showing early Norman and thirteenth century phases of masonry (with some later work).

west face was repaired. Towards the end of the thirteenth century, the whole of the west wall of the nave was rebuilt in Caen stone with three lancets at the lower level, and over this is a 'great west window'. Above this again the gable end was raised and two more lancets were inserted. The heightened gable face was given a diapered decoration. Finally a porch was added which appears to be unfinished. The buttressing suggests that an upper chamber was planned but never executed.

In 1989 the main west doorway inside the porch was heavily restored and redesigned by the surveyor, Donald Buttress. At the beginning of the 1970s, as we have seen, the floor inside the porch was lowered by his predecessor, Robert Potter, and the steps at the west end of the nave were removed (the medieval west doors were also taken out at that time and replaced by doors of plate glass). The lowering of the floor revealed the original Norman bases, and, before these were boxed in, measured drawings of the west doorway and all the base mouldings and capitals were made (Fig. 5.3). Analysis of this (Tatton-Brown 1990) was able to demonstrate that, apart from the original bases, only the jambs showed any twelfth century work. The doorway itself and all the facework above it are all of finely tooled Caenstone of the later thirteenth century. When it was built a hood-mould was placed over the doorway, so no porch was planned at this stage. Soon afterwards, however, the porch was inserted, and large cracks (now filled) on either side of the doorway, clearly mark the break between the two periods of masonry.

The recording and analysis of all the masonry on the north side of the nave, which is not yet finished, has al-

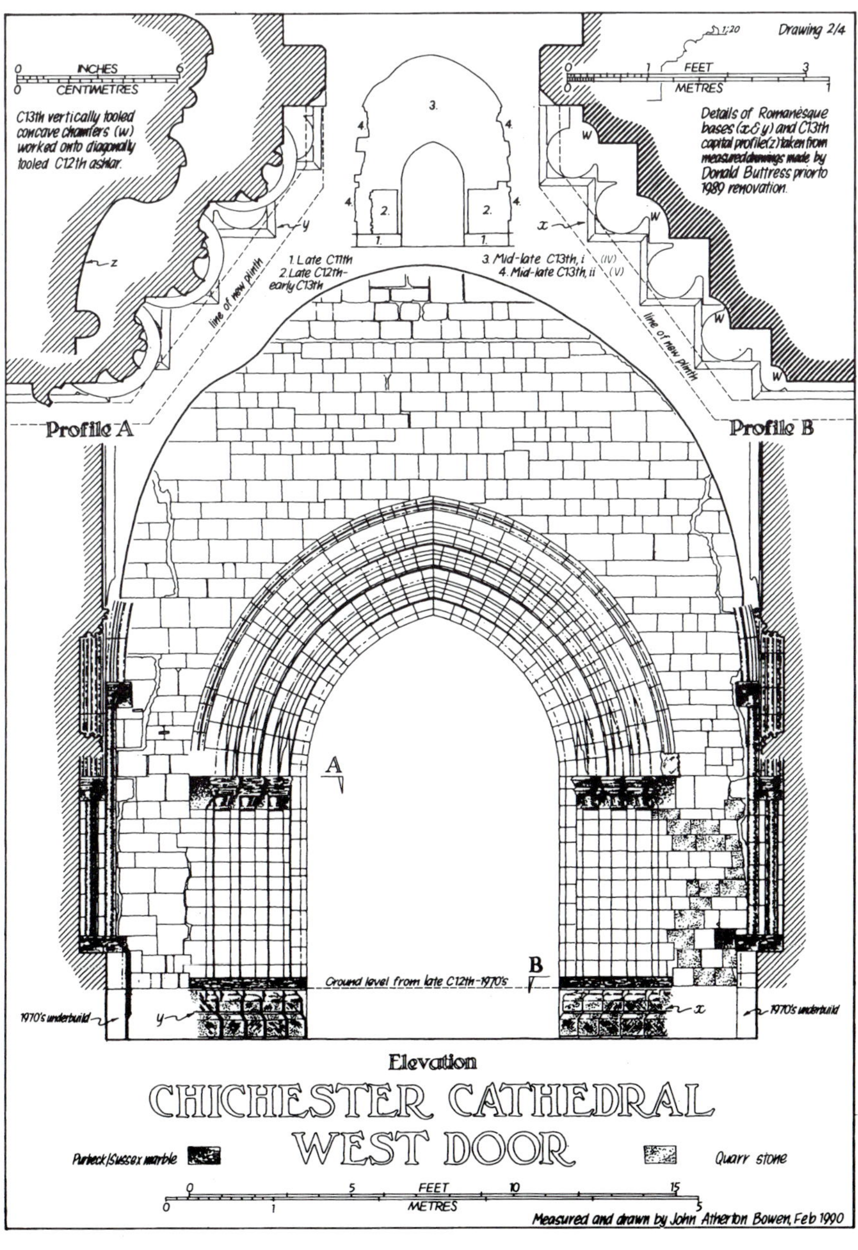

Fig. 5.3. Archaeological analysis of the west doorway area.

ready provided a great deal of new information about the various phases of work, but only certain aspects of this will be discused here. The earliest masonry can be seen in the eastern part of the clerestory where many of the blocks of Quarr stone with wide mortar joints survive. There can be little doubt that the Norman cathedral was started soon after the 1075 move from Selsey (Gem 1981). The clerestory windows have simple shafts on either side with cushion capitals and a roll moulding over the semi-circular head. In bay D (the fifth bay west of the crossing), the Norman masonry on either side of the clerestory is different, with the masonry to the west having much thinner joints as well as some very strange diagonal courses in the middle. There can be no doubt that this marks a major break in the work, perhaps between the 1080s and c. 1100, and this is confirmed inside the nave where there is also a clear break at this point in the triforium level. In the four eastern bays of the nave the triforium tympana has opus reticulatum, while the four western bays replace this with 'chip-carved' decoration on horizontal ashlar. The outside of the clerestory windows also show a stylistic change in the later, western windows. There are now carinations on the tops of the cushion capitals, as well as a hollow chamfer all the way round the outside edge of the window opening. The jointing in all the later masonry is also much thinner. The early Norman work also shows signs of a great deal of differential settlement having taken place at an early stage. On the gallery side of the fourth north triforium opening from the east, for example, an extra lower arch has been inserted, perhaps after a partial collapse which is reflected in the rebuilt head of the clerestory window above. This rebuilt head is easily distinguished by the use of some Caen stone and much close jointing.

The top of the clerestory walls on both sides of the nave are not only not level and much out of the vertical, but also bow-shaped in plan. This must have caused great problems after the fire of 1187 when a ribbed vault and flying buttresses were put in for the first time. It is perhaps for this reason that less than a century later the roofs were totally rebuilt at a higher level, once a completely new clerestory wall-top had been constructed. To make this new wall-top straight, much corbelling out was required on the north. Hence the use of a double corbel-table which partially dies out to the west. The new upper wall had to be built progressively higher from east to west (to give it a level top) because the old clerestory wall top slopes down to the west. The tops of the flying buttresses were also heightened at this time, and larger pinnacles were put on to the outer buttresses to counteract the increased danger of spreading. In the south triforium some extra flying buttresses at a lower level (below the roof) also had to be inserted (Willis 1861, plate 3). All of this is clearly shown in the phasing of the masonry.

At some time in the middle of the thirteenth century, the decision was made to build a series of chapels outside the aisles of the nave, starting with that on the north-east (probably the chapel of St Edmund of Abingdon). This first chapel was only a single bay long (all the rest were to be two bays long), but the masonry of its outside wall shows clearly that more chapels to the west were planned from the very beginning and the plinth and ashlar masonry up to the string-course below the windows were all built straightaway.The east jamb of the eastern window of the second chapel (perhaps that dedicated to St Theobald, Fig. 5.2) was built at this time and the jamb mouldings differ, in minor details, from the later jambs of the chapel windows. The chapels originally had transverse (ie. north-facing) gables with round windows in their heads (Fig. 5.2), and, though replaced in the late Middle Ages with a continuous parapet, the masonry still has plenty of surviving clues for the earlier gables. Most striking is the very small projecting gutter that ran down the edge of the gables before turning at right angles to run on diagonally down the sides of the buttresses.

Once the new higher nave roof and parapets had been built at the end of the thirteenth century, the rain water from the high leads was removed by allowing it to escape from spouts through the parapet onto the tops of the flying buttresses. These had carefully cut gutter blocks on their top side set into special 'kneeler' coping blocks (all made of hard Binstead stone) down which the water ran. It then passed through the buttress (below the pinnacle) and was shot clear of the wall from a large decorated spout. These spouts have now in part been replaced by Portland stone gargoyles. In the thickness of the buttress wall, below the water pipe, a lead damp-proof course was laid in the thirteenth century to stop water penetration. Much later, in the post-medieval period, lead sheets were laid onto the tops of the flying buttresses and the holes through the buttresses were blocked by more lead sheets. New gutters were then made which allowed the rain water to be piped under the chapel roofs and out into new lead boxes and down pipes beside the buttresses. The pinnacles were rebuilt by Scott in the 1860s (as is shown by the use of Chilmark stone) with completely new spirelet tops. Drawings and engravings of the north side of the nave before 1861 show the pinnacles with only flat tops, and a flat Portland stone capping survived on the westernmost pinnacle until replaced in the most recent restoration by Donald Buttress. This last pinnacle is unusual in that it is square in cross-section (the others are octagonal), and it seems to have been rebuilt at a later medieval date. The most recent masonry on the north side of the nave chapels is at the bottom of the outer wall. Here the plinth was extended downwards in Brauvilliers stone (from France) in the early 1970s, after the ground level had been lowered. Above this level are some earlier repairs to the original plinth in Portland stone.

Once all the masonry on the north side of the nave had been recorded, a complete stratigraphical sequence (of at least twelve main phases) was worked out and a detailed phasing proposed. Into this rough sequence, approximate dates (based on architectural styles) were inserted, as well as a few more exact dates from documentary and dendrochronological evidence. A series of new sections

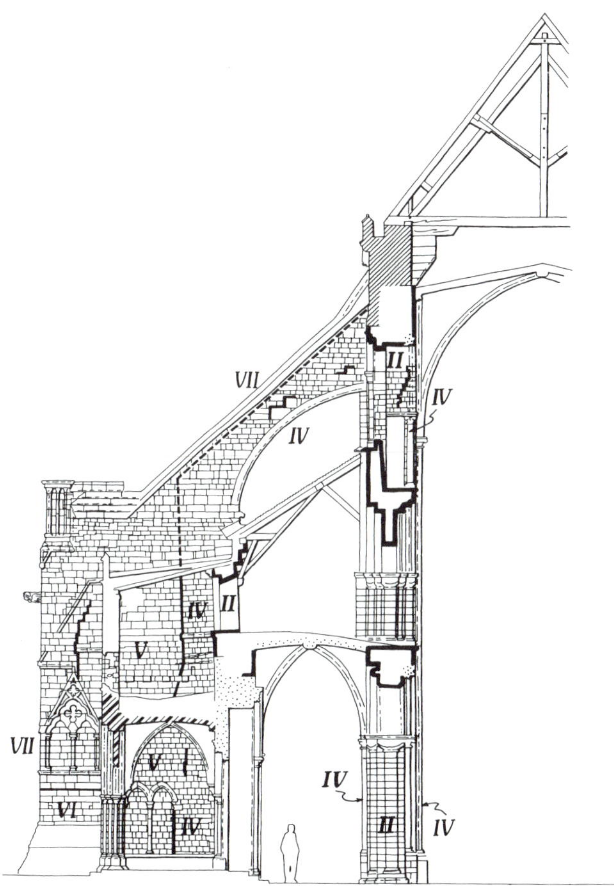

Fig. 5.4. Phased section through the north porch and north side of the nave showing late eleventh (II) to late thirteenth (VII) century phases.

(Fig. 5.4) through the bays of the north nave were then constructed to show each succeeding phase, as well as a new plan (Fig. 5.5). Many more years will be required to do this at all levels for the whole cathedral, but ultimately it should be possible to work out a complete sequence of all the building phases.

Apart from the cathedral itself, a small amount of new work has been carried out on the fabric of the cloisters (Tatton-Brown 1992) and in the associated buildings in the Close. Perhaps the most interesting of the new discoveries have been within the houses of the Vicars' Close. By examining the timber-framing of the roof and internal partitions, it is possible to show that there were originally twelve houses on either side of the main courtyard with probably four more in the return ranges at the south end (Fig. 5.6). A small covered walk (the 'Little Cloisters') ran around the inside of the courtyard, but this was destroyed in the eighteenth century. The remains of the octagonal base of an original chimney stack was also found, and it is likely that all the houses, which were built in the early fifteenth century, had chimneys from the beginning. The 28 houses in the Vicars' Close exactly match the known number of vicars at the time. Soon afterwards, however, the number of vicars began to drop and by the end of the sixteenth century there were only four. The west range of the Close was then converted into four large houses with enlarged gardens (Tatton-Brown 1991).

Most recently the topography of the bishop's palace has been carefully studied. Some magnificent elements of the medieval palace still survive (the chapel and the great kitchen) with their original roofs of *c.* 1300, but unfortunately, as at most English bishops' palaces, a huge amount

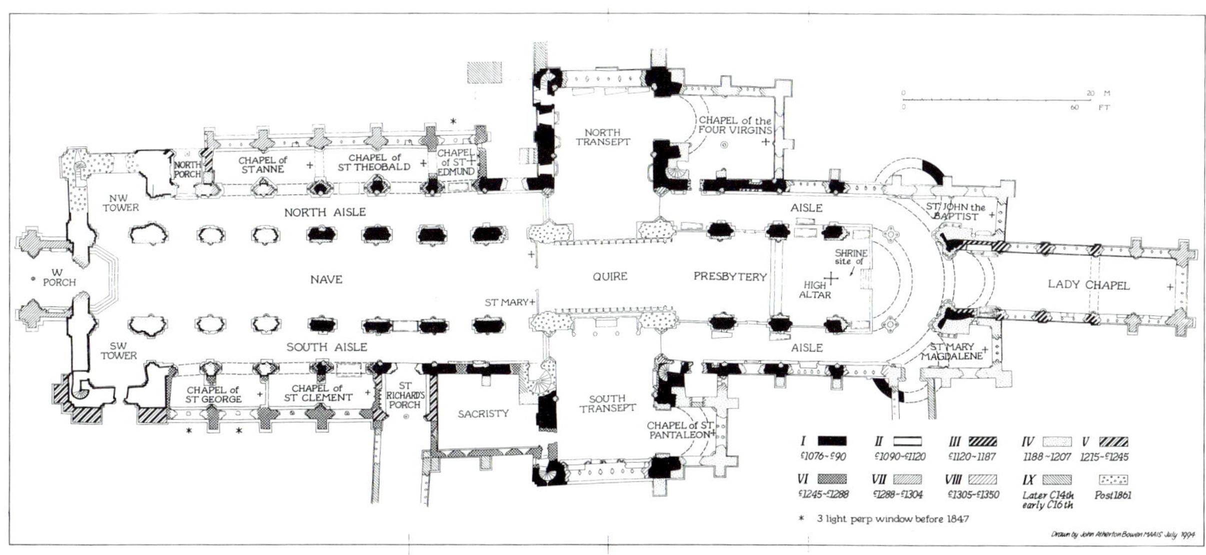

Fig. 5.5. New phased plan of the main constructional phases of Chichester Cathedral.

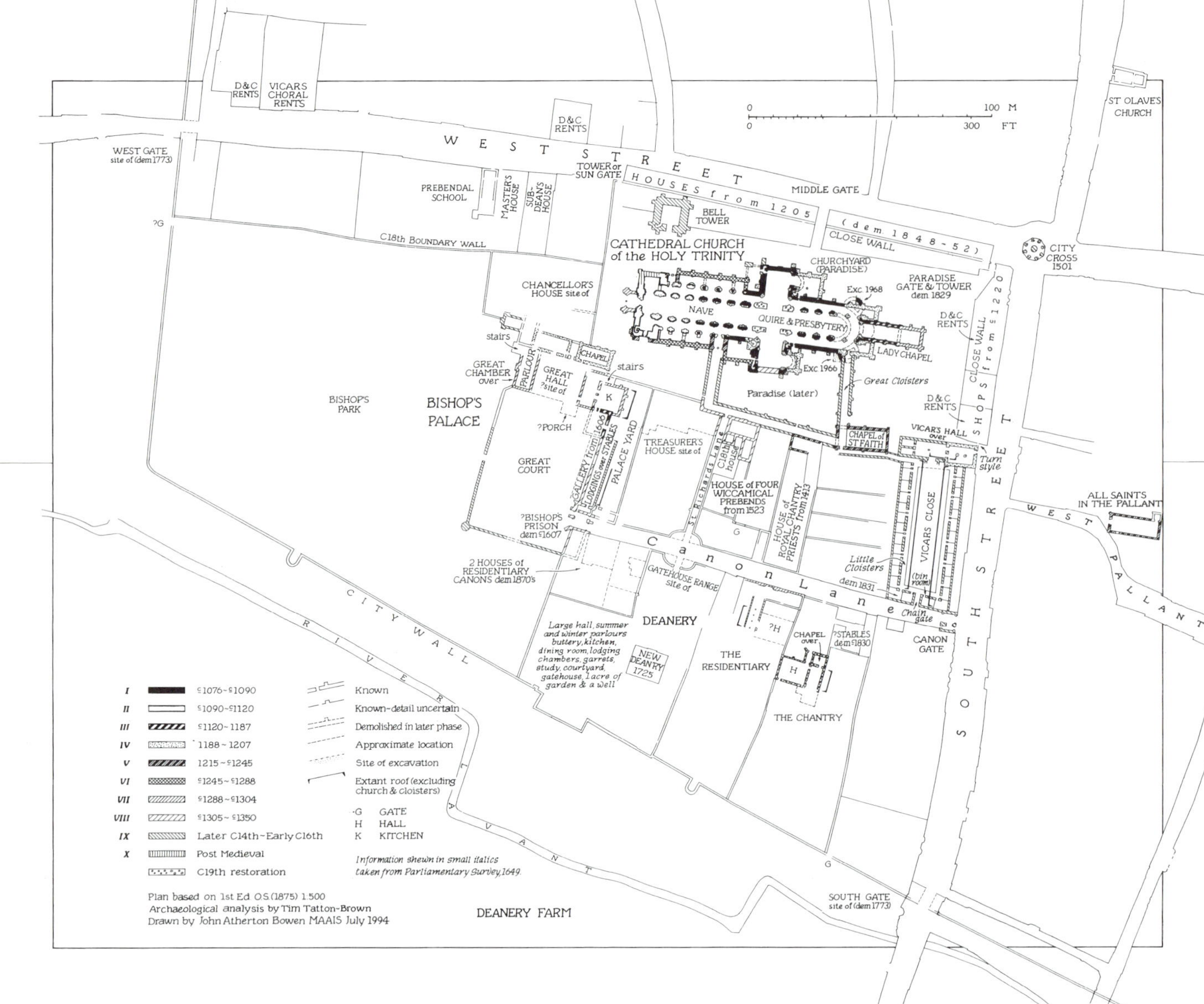

Fig. 5.6. New phased plan of the close of Chichester Cathedral.

of destruction work took place during the Commonwealth period. At Chichester the great hall has totally disappeared, but an examination of surviving medieval fragments suggests that it may be under what is now the front court of the late seventeenth century and later palace, with the great kitchen to the east and the parlour and chamber block to the west (Fig. 5.6).

References

Andrew M.R.G. 1980: 'Chichester Cathedral the original east end; a reappraisal' *Sussex Archaeol Coll.* 118, 299–308.

Andrew M.R.G. 1982: 'Chichester Cathedral: the problem of the Romanesque choir vault' *J.B.A.A.* 135, 11–22.

Bond F. 1906: *Gothic Architecture in England* (London).

Down A. and Rule M. (eds.) 1971: *Chichester Excavations* I (Chichester).

Gem R.D.H. 1981: 'Chichester Cathedral: when was the Romanesque church begun?' *Proc. Battle Conf. in 1980* (R.A. Brown ed.), 61–4.

Godfrey W.H. and Bloe J.W. 1935: 'Cathedral historical survey' in L.F.Salzman (ed.) *Victoria history of the County of Sussex* III (London), 105–146.

Hobbs M. (ed.) 1994: *Chichester Cathedral, an historical survey* (Chichester)

Kitch M.J. 1978: 'The Chichester Cathedral chapter at the time of the Reformation' *Sussex. Archaeol.Coll.* 116, 277–292.

Leeney O.H. 1947: 'References to Ancient Sussex churches in 'The Ecclesiologist' mainly as regards restoration and repair' *Sussex Arch. Coll.* 86, 155–186.

Munby J. 1981: 'Medieval carpentry in Chichester: 13th century roofs of the Cathedral and Bishop's Palace' in Down A.(ed.), *Chichester Excavations* V (Chichester), 229–253.

Pevsner N. and Metcalf P. 1985: 'Chichester' in *The Cathedrals of England* (Southern England) (Harmondsworth), 82–103.

Tatton-Brown T. 1990: 'The West Portal of Chichester Cathedral' *Chichester Cathedral Journal* 1990, 8–11.

Tatton-Brown T. 1991: 'The Vicars' Close and Canon Gate' *Chichester Cathedral Journal* 1991, 14–24.

Tatton-Brown T. 1992: 'The Cloisters at Chichester Cathedral'

Chichester Cathedral Journal 1992, 12–19.
Tummers H. 1988: 'The medieval effigial tombs in Chichester Cathedral' *Church Monuments* 3, 3–41.
Vallance W.H.A. 1947: *Great English Church Screens.*
Walcott M.E.C. 1877: 'The Early Statutes of the Cathedral Church of the Holy Trinity, Chichester ....' *Archaeologia* 45, 143–234.
Willis R. 1861: *The Architectural History of Chichester Cathedral with an introductory essay on the fall of the tower and spire*
Zarnecki G. 1954: 'The Chichester Reliefs' *Archaeol.J.* 110, 106–119.

Current Thinking on Glasgow Cathedral

Richard Fawcett

The state of Information on Scottish Cathedrals

The medieval cathedrals of Scotland are still not widely known, either within or beyond the border. This is partly because the country's limited resources in the middle ages meant that none of them was on the impressive scale of many European cathedrals; even the largest, at St Andrews,[1] was of little more than the middle English rank in size, while the smallest are essentially of parish church scale. Added to this were the losses suffered by the majority of them at the Reformation in 1560, as a result of which only Glasgow and Kirkwall survived into modern times in anything approaching a state of completeness. (Though Brechin, Dornoch and Dunblane have again been restored to – or in one case even beyond – something close to their original size).

The main cause of ignorance, however, must certainly be the paucity of adequate publication of their architecture. The study of Scottish architectural history was late in coming of age, and even now there are comprehensive accounts of the structural development of very few individual cathedrals. The first worthwhile survey of Scottish medieval ecclesiastical architecture as a whole was that published by David MacGibbon and Thomas Ross in the 1890s which, for a pioneering work, provided commendable accounts of nearly all major buildings (MacGibbon and Ross 1896–7). Most of the surviving cathedrals were covered more or less adequately so far as the scale of such a publication allowed although, inexplicably, there was only a passing reference to Dornoch Cathedral, of which there are substantial thirteenth century remains.

Great things might have been hoped for from the National Art Survey, which in the 1920s began to publish a splendid series of measured drawings of medieval buildings (NASS 1921–33). That venture ended with the publication of the fourth volume, however, by which time only one cathedral – that of Elgin – had been covered. (Iona was also covered, although the late medieval attempts to raise that abbey to the status of the cathedral of the Isles had been abortive, and so it cannot strictly be included amongst the medieval cathedrals.[2]

Mention must also be made of the efforts of local historians (many of whom were, of course, parish ministers) even if their strength tends to be on the historical rather than the architectural side. G. D. Bentinck' s account of Dornoch was exceptional for including a brief account of the structure of the cathedral by W. Douglas Simpson (Bentinck 1926). Dunblane has probably been the most fortunate of the cathedrals to be dealt with by local historians. Aspects of its story have been covered both in Alexander Barty's history of the town, which includes much useful information on the post-Reformation activities at the cathedral, and by James Hutchison Cockburn's account of the careers of its medieval bishops (Barty 1944; Cockburn 1959).

The inventories of the Royal Commission on the Ancient and Historical Monuments of Scotland have described a number of cathedrals. While the descriptions in the earlier volumes are too summary to be of great value, the accounts of St Andrews and Kirkwall are still worth reading (RCAHMS 1933, 230; RCAHMS 1946, 113). Lismore, the cathedral of the diocese of Argyll, was the first cathedral in an area covered by the Commission to receive full and scholarly coverage to modern standards, in the second volume of the Argyll inventory published in 1975, even if no amount of coverage of such a diminutive and largely featureless building is likely to attract great attention (RCAHMS 1975, 156). However, new ground was broken with the splendid account of lona, published in 1982, although it must be reiterated that Iona was only briefly advanced as a candidate for medieval cathedral status (RCAHMS 1982, 149).

Since, as a result of the vagaries of the arrangements made for church property after the Reformation and the Restoration, several Scottish cathedrals are partly or wholly in the care of the state, official guide books have also been published for a number of them by Historic Scotland. The accounts offered in those, however, since they have to be directed to a general readership, are inevitably not as full as might be wished by those with specialist interests.[3]

On a more hopeful note, the provision of adequate information has recently begun to improve at a number of cathedrals. Several papers on aspects of cathedral history have appeared in the *Innes Review*. Most notably for St

Fig. 6.1. View of the cathedral from the south-east, before the demolition of the western towers. (Collie)

Andrews David McRoberts edited a valuable volume of papers which had earlier appeared in two issues of that review (McRoberts 1976), and which in turn prompted a thought-provoking paper from Eric Cambridge (Cambridge 1977). For Kirkwall, Barbara Crawford has edited a volume of papers given at a conference in 1987, which attempts to place that cathedral in its wider cultural context (Crawford 1988). Beyond this, the Societies of Friends of some cathedrals have fostered the publication of a variety of useful short pieces either in their annual report or as occasional papers, most notably at Dunblane, Glasgow and Aberdeen. Also for Aberdeen, the recent publication of Leslie Macfarlane's fine volume on Bishop William Elphinstone has cast a fascinating side-light on the cathedral building operations (Macfarlane 1985). Apart from these, a valuable inititiative has been the founding of the Whithorn Trust, a leading purpose of which is to sponsor excavation around this most enigmatic of cathedral sites.

Publications on Glasgow Cathedral

However, it has been Glasgow which has been the most favoured of Scotland's thirteen Cathedrals of medieval foundation in receiving close attention over an extended period. As early as 1835 J. Collie published a handsome folio of measured drawings of the building which, since it predated the major campaigns of nineteenth century restoration, is an invaluable source of information (Collie 1835). Later that century George Eyre-Todd edited *The book of Glasgow Cathedral* (Eyre-Todd 1898), which included a perceptive architectural analysis by John Honeyman, as well as a number of other valuable contributions. Thomas Watson's *Double Choir of Glasgow Cathedral*, with its intriguing – if inordinately complex – theories on the development of the final design of the crypt below the eastern limb, appeared in 1901 (Watson 1901), and in 1914 the Bell's cathedral series published Peter Macgregor Chalmers' useful volume on Glasgow (Chalmers 1914). More recently several excellent papers have been published on aspects of its history, architecture and furnishing, most notably in the *Innes Review*, in the *Proceedings of the Society of Antiquaries of Scotland* and in the annual reports of the Society of Friends of the cathedral. In addition, the Friends have now instituted a series of occasional publications relating to the cathedral's history. An account of the cathedral has also been published in the *Buildings of Scotland* series (Fawcett 1990).

As a result of all this work the broad outline of the building chronology is well -if still not widely – known. Nevertheless, there has perhaps been a tendency to leave unquestioned a number of ideas which were initially advanced on the basis of inadequate consideration of the architectural evidence within its wider context. Although this paper will attempt to summarise the structural history as a whole, it will particularly concentrate on those aspects which have been the focus of recent re-evaluation.

Initially it has to be said that the most extraordinary feature of the various rebuilding operations at Glasgow from the twelfth century onwards is the number of changes of design which took place within a relatively short space of time, Consequently, at many points the architectural evidence is fragmentary and ambiguous, whilst such documentary evidence as there is frequently casts no more than an oblique light over the operations.

Bishop John's Cathedral

The first fixed point in the architectural history of Glasgow Cathedral is the dedication of a new building by David I's erstwhile tutor, Bishop John, in 1136. (*Chron. Holyrood*, 119).[4] This dedication possibly simply marked the completion of the first usable part of a new building rather than its finalization, with construction continuing after that date. One reason for thinking this is the painted decoration on a stone which was found during work below the choir floor in 1916, and which was probably the voussoir of a window or door rear-arch, with palmette decoration. Although a case has been made for this fragment being a part of the rebuilding by Bishop Jocelin in the late twelfth century, an operation which will be discussed below, its painting is now thought more likely to belong to a date nearer 1136 than 1197.[5]

Excavations in 1992-3, the results of which have not yet been fully assessed, located what may have been the west front of John's church, close to the third pier west of the north-west crossing pier (Driscoll 1992). A number of half drums from the cylindrical piers may also have come from John's church, suggesting it was a more ambitious building than had been thought.

Bishop Jocelin's Enlargement of the Eastern Limb

Bishop Jocelin set about 'gloriously enlarging' the cathe-

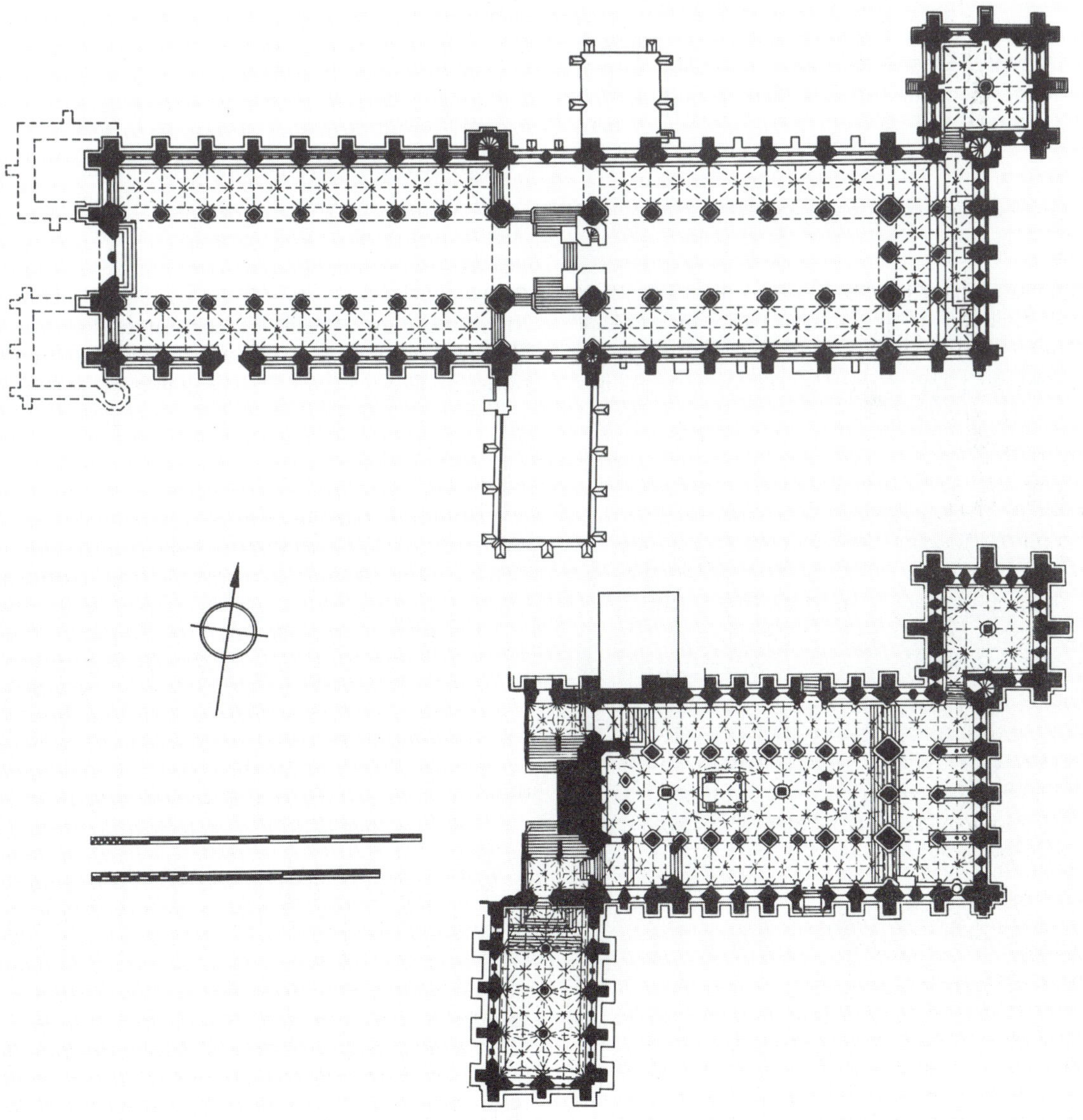

Fig. 6.2. Plans of the cathedral. (Historic Scotland)

dral in an operation referred to in the Melrose Chronicle for 1181. Jocelin was particularly zealous in promoting the cult of Kentigern (also known as Mungo) Glasgow's founder and patron saint, and commissioned a new and splendidly apocryphal *Life* from Jocelin of Furness (Jackson, 1958). He may also have been responsible for augmenting the chapter of canons. Because of this, and from the little we know of his building, it seems that his efforts were directed towards improving the setting of the tomb at crypt level and of the canons' choir at the main level. The one identifiable *in situ* fragment of this operation, a short keeled shaft facing westwards from a truncated spur of wall projecting into the south aisle of the crypt, was evidently originally part of a longer wall set out on a north-south axis. This suggests that it belonged to a lateral projection,[6] presumably intended to provide space for altars flanking both the tomb and the high altar above it. Assuming the provision of similar chapels on the north, as originally designed these chapels may have been somewhat similar in their relationship with the main body of the church as the lateral projections added to the east end of Hereford Cathedral at about the same time.[7]

Jocelin's campaign had been either prompted by or was interrupted by a fire, as a result of which King William the Lion was encouraged to further the work by exhorting benefactions, but enough was complete for a dedication to take place in 1197 (*Chron. Melrose* f.25). A significant feature of the surviving fragment is the way in which the cap is markedly out of proportion with the shaft, as if originally carved for a longer shaft. Its details also suggest it belongs to the later part of Jocelin's episcopate, and dates from not long before his death in 1199. The single sprigs of stiff-leaf foliage and the general form of cap and abacus may perhaps be compared with examples in the arcades of the choir at Cartmel, which is unlikely to have been started much before 1190. This points to the cap having been placed on the shaft as a make-shift expedient, either as part of post-fire repairs, or, perhaps more probably, in the course of later operations.

Fig. 6.3. The earliest surviving work in the cathedral, in the south-west compartment of the crypt. On the left is the spur of wall with a keeled shaft and water-leaf cap which belonged to Bishop Jocelin's building. On the right is the early thirteenth century wall which truncated Jocelin's work. (Historic Scotland)

The excavations of 1992-3 located many moulded and carved fragments from Jocelin's cathedral which had been either discarded or re-used in the foundations of the later stages of building. These excavations also revealed that very little of Jocelin's nave, which was apparently aisleless, was completed (Driscoll 1992).

The Early Thirteenth Century Enlargement

The limited surviving architectural evidence in fact shows that the extensions to the eastern limb as laid out by Jocelin were soon to undergo major modifications and, under the circumstances, it may be doubted if even they were ever completed. Perhaps this was partly because there could have been a hiatus of several years in building operations after Jocelin's death, as a result of lack of stability in tenure of the bishopric.[8] It is difficult to imagine that circumstances can have been propitious for work to resume in earnest before the long episcopate of Walter, between 1207 and 1232. Whatever the reason, a major replanning is evident from the relationship between the fragment of Jocelin's work and the adjacent south wall of the western bays of the crypt. The details of the keeled shafts along this south wall, which rise from water-holding bases of developed form, would certainly accord well with the episcopate of Walter.

It seems that in the course of this early thirteenth-century operation Jocelin's projecting chapel on the south must have been truncated by the south wall now seen in the south-western bays of the crypt, and presumably any corresponding chapel on the north was similarly treated. But this is not all. Comparison of the details of the south wall in the south-west corner of the crypt with those of the south and north walls of the nave indicates that they were together a part of a much larger campaign, encompassing a western limb on the scale of that eventually built.

Supporting the internal evidence, externally it can also be seen that the base course of the wall which truncated Jocelin's chapel continues back across the south transept (where it is now within the 'Blackadder Aisle') and along the south flank of the nave; the same base course runs along the north transept and north flank of the nave.

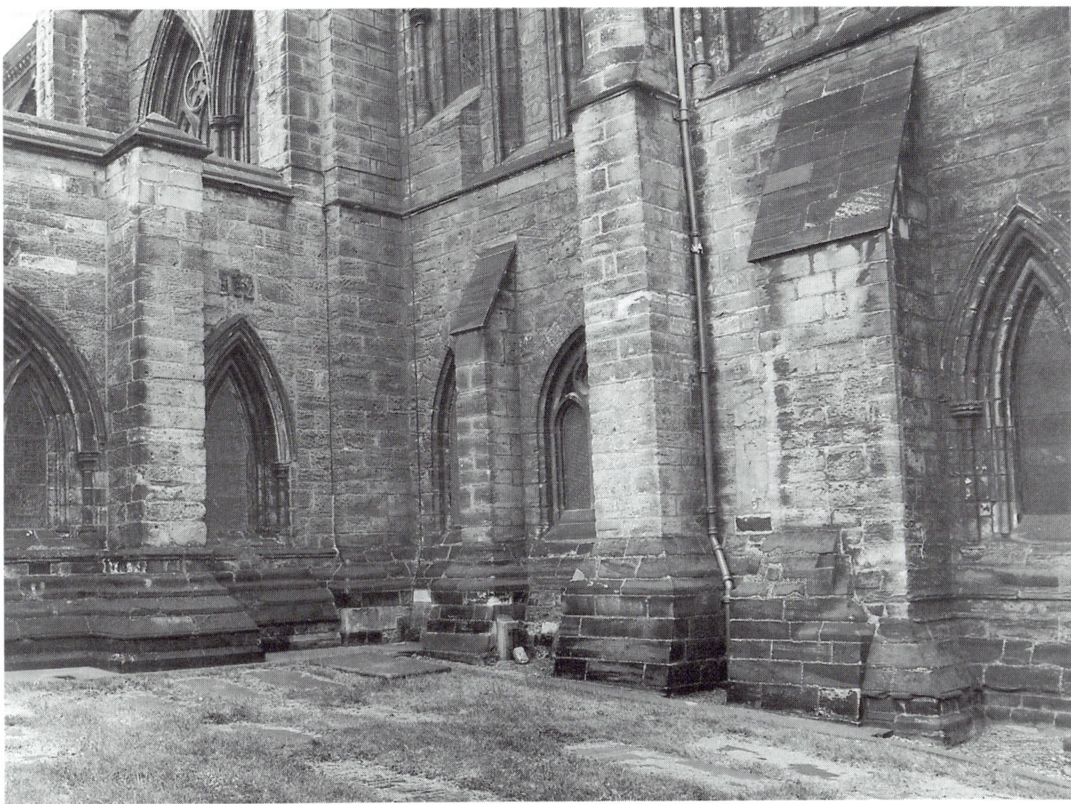

Fig. 6.4. The exterior of the south-east compartment of the crypt, showing the change of base courses between the work of Bishop Walter and the work of Bishop Bondington. On the left is part of the 'Blackadder Aisle', where it adjoins the south transept. (Historic Scotland)

Together with the evidence of the wall shafts, this points to an ambitious operation to rebuild the entire cathedral to an enlarged plan.

The evidence also shows that the curiously non-salient transepts of the cathedral as eventually completed were planned at this stage of the work, because the base course was given the extra projections necessary to carry the more massive buttresses required for a part of the structure rising to a greater height than the aisles. The attraction of placing the transepts in this position, rather than where the lateral chapels had been placed in Jocelin's plan, may have been that it allowed for a rather longer presbytery without disturbing the position of the tomb. So far as the nonsalient form of the transepts is concerned, a number of exotic parallels could be cited, though it is difficult to find convincing prototypes; it may simply have been that the steeply sloping ground made the designing mason nervous of high lateral projections.

Bishop Bondington's Extended Eastern Limb

How much of the eastern limb planned in the early thirteenth century was completed we have no means of knowing because – yet again – most of the evidence must have been obliterated by the next campaign of rebuilding. But within the nave the vaulting shafts along the aisle walls indicate that the walls must have been built up to about the height of the window sills, and the shaft are also of this date. By the time this stage had been reached, however, it was decided that completion of the nave should be postponed, and that instead the main thrust of energy should be diverted to rebuilding the choir to a yet more ambitious form. This decision is attributable Walter's successor, William Bondington, and in 1242 the faithful of all parishes were urged to contribute to the work throughout Lent (*Glasgow Registrum*, xxvii).

Up to the start of Bondington's campaign it seems unlikely that the successive designs for the eastern arm could have accommodated more than the high altar and presbytery at the upper level, with the canons' choir set in the crossing and eastern bays of the nave. It is perhaps also reasonable to assume that, in the early stages of the cathedral's architectural history, the high altar was more or less directly above the tomb in the crypt. But the rapid augmentation of the complement of canons at Glasgow, and the eventual adoption in 1258 of a constitution based on that of Sarum,[9] may have encouraged a view that the dignity of the establishment would be better expressed by the provision of an elongated eastern limb which could house both presbytery and choir, as was being provided at so many English cathedrals.

The new choir was set out with virtually the same length as the recently started nave, albeit with a more complex plan in order to accommodate a greater variety

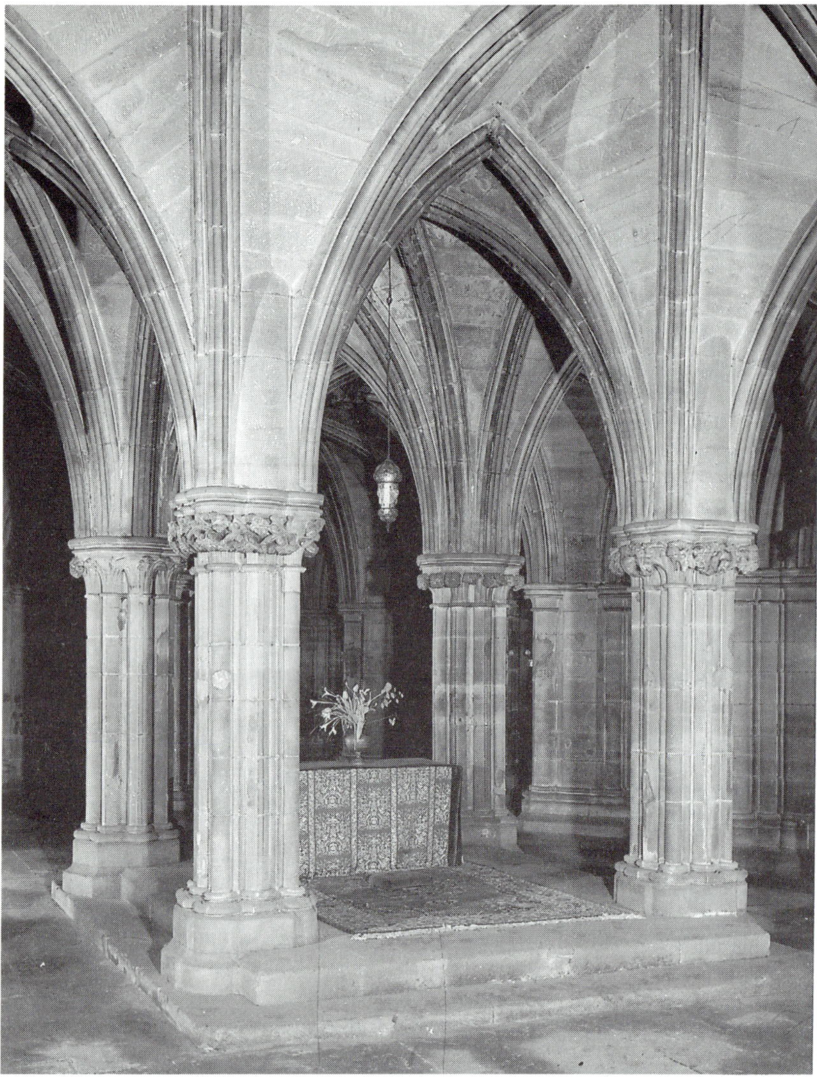

Fig. 6.5. The tomb area in the crypt. (Historic Scotland)

of functions. From records of the visit of Edward I to Glasgow in 1301 it appears there was a shrine of St Kentigern in the choir by then, as well as his tomb in the crypt (Stones 1967, 88), and the particular plan adopted for the choir may have been to allow for this from the start. The precise position of the shrine within the choir is not certain although, on analogy with earlier usage, it has been suggested that it continued to be set directly above the tomb (Radford 1970, 18). Yet this would place the shrine towards the western end of the extended choir, where it might be an encumbrance, and the choice of a plan which provided for a returned eastern aisle behind the presbytery, with a row of chapels beyond, might suggest instead that the shrine was in what was by this time the more usual place, behind the high altar. Such an ambulatory arrangement is well suited to allowing access to a shrine for pilgrims without disturbance to the services of the canons in the choir. (It should be said that fragments of a mid-thirteenth century miniature arcade thought to have formed part of the shrine base are now displayed in the crypt (Hay 1967), although there are no indications of its original position.)

Square ambulatory plans have a complex history in England (Hearn 1971) but, with the possible exception of Bishop Roger's York, they do not appear to have had a significant following in cathedral churches.[10] Undoubtedly their greatest popularity was within the Cistercian order,[11] for whom they had the merit of allowing a considerable number of altars within a relatively simple architectural framework. It has been suggested that the first Scottish variant of the plan may have been at Cistercian Newbattle (Wilson 1978, 36), founded in 1140 but probably only built some decades later, where the excavated plan could be interpreted as having been similar to that of Byland; if acceptable, this would certainly provide at useful link in the chain leading to Glasgow.

The crypt which continued to be necessitated by the fall of the land was, of course, of a similar overall plan to the choir itself. Within this matrix its layout was conditioned by the position of the tomb, by the retention of fragments of Jocelin's and Walter's work in the southwest corner, by the need to provide additional piers on the lines of the main arcades if its own arcades were not to be disproportionately wide and depressed, and by the eastward fall of land. These constraints did not prove to be a disadvantage to the master mason of this part of the cathedral; indeed, it is perhaps in the crypt that his genius is most finely in evidence and that the cathedral can best be seen as a building of more than Scottish significance.

The rectangular central area corresponding with the main body of the choir above was sub-divided into a series of spaces defined by the differing patterns of piers and by the complex rhythms of the vaulting they support, all of which was designed to concentrate attention on the site of Kentigern's burial. Despite the way in which the eastward elongation of the building created the potential difficulty of leaving the tomb arbitrarily towards the western end of the crypt, the master mason was able to model the space in a way which gave the impression of its being the focus of the building. An important element in this was the unusual placing of the Lady Chapel at the east end of the main body of the crypt,[12] and once this had been defined it was easier to give the tomb the appearance of a central position. The area of the tomb was further emphasised by four piers carrying a canopy-like bay of vaulting, to east and west of which were fascinating subsidiary spaces of three-by-three bays each with a central pier. Additional emphasis was given to the tomb by the more elaborate designs of its piers, with splendid stiff-leaf caps, and by its elevation upon a stepped podium.

Although changes of rib types suggest the design of the central area of the crypt was only finalised after several changes of plan,[13] the unity of the conception as a whole is confirmed by the relatively homogeneous character of the carving on the vault bosses. There is thus little reason to doubt that the design was fixed within a fairly short period.

Turning to the design of the main level of the eastern limb, the continuing influence of St Hugh's choir at Lincoln Cathedral on major Scottish architecture, which had earlier been apparent in the nave of Holyrood Abbey, is much in evidence in both the general elevations and in the lush growths of stiff-leaf on the arcade caps. But a more immediate inspiration for the elevations of Glasgow is likely to have been one of the later developments on the Lincoln theme, such as in the choir of Rievaulx Abbey, where work must have still been in progress when Glasgow's new choir was started. The debts to Rievaulx are most obvious in the inter-relationship of the arcade and triforium stages, and are particularly clear in the end bays of Glasgow where, as at Rievaulx, the sub-arches within each bay of the triforium are of the same arc as the containing arches.

At both Lincoln and Rievaulx, however, the main spaces had been designed for high vaults, with the associated implications for the design of the clearstorey, whereas at Glasgow the central vessel was to be covered by a wagon ceiling of slightly cusped profile. The inner skin of the clearstorey was thus designed as a continuous arcade interrupted only by the wall shafts defining the bay system. A relatively recent Scottish prototype for such a clearstorey had been designed for the nave of Jedburgh Abbey, a house in which Glasgow's bishops took a particularly close interest, as successors of one of the original co-founders.

A particular delight of Glasgow's eastern limb is the design of the windows, which provide a text book demonstration of the development of thirteenth century types, from the simple grouping of lancets, through plate tracery to the first forms of bar tracery. Among the most interesting are those of the choir aisles, which show some of the most inventive surviving variants of plate tracery. Again, it could have been Lincoln which provided some inspiration for these designs, in the triforium openings of its nave.

Fig. 6.6. South elevation of the choir and transept. (Collie)

Fig. 6.7. Longitudinal section through the choir, crypt and crossing. (Collie)

Fig. 6.8. East elevation of the choir; the two-storeyed chapter house is on the right. (Collie)

The Double Chapter House, Sacristy and Treasury

Glasgow is notable for the rectangular containment of the main core of its plan which results from the non-salient form of its transepts, and the square ambulatory and eastern chapels. Yet, outside this core, there were several projections, including the two western towers to which consideration will be given later. Apart from the towers there are two projections off the north side of the eastern limb, and a third projection off the south transept.

The block at the north-eastern corner of the eastern limb is of two-storeys, and rises to the same height as the choir aisles, with entrances from the north-east chapels of both the crypt and choir. Although many earlier writers had assumed that one level was used as a sacristy, it is now evident from a papal letter of 1406 that each level was used by then as a chapter house (Durkan 1975, 89), although it is difficult to understand why two were needed. Architectural and heraldic evidence makes it clear that there was much rebuilding of both levels of the chapter house after the fire to which the letter of 1406 refers, although there can be no doubt that the block as a whole is essentially an integral part of Bishop Bondington's building campaign.

The block which projects from the western bay on the north side of the choir is now of only one storey, and has suffered greatly since the Reformation, with subsequent harsh restoration by Edward Blore in the mid-nineteenth century. It has been shown that it was originally of two storeys, the upper of which served as a sacristy and the lower as a treasury (McRoberts 1966; Stones 1970), a reversal of the usual Scottish arrangement of treasury above sacristy, which was presumably occasioned in this case by the existence of a crypt. It had previously been conjectured that this block was the hall of the vicars choral (Eyre 1898a) and, although this idea has long been rejected, recent research on the cathedral precinct has shown that it was indeed connected to the vicars' hall by a bridge which crossed a thoroughfare on this side (Durkan 1986). From the base course which runs around the sacristy and treasury, it can be seen that, like the chapter house, it was a part of the mid-thirteenth century campaign; yet there is also a mutilated section of what seems to have been the same base course inside the building, which would suggest that it was only added as an afterthought in the course of the construction operations.

The 'Blackadder Aisle'

The third of these projecting structures is now known as the 'Blackadder Aisle'. This southward extending structure of two by four bays, which is attached to the lower walls of the south transept, was provided as the undercroft to an unbuilt structure at the level of the aisles of the main

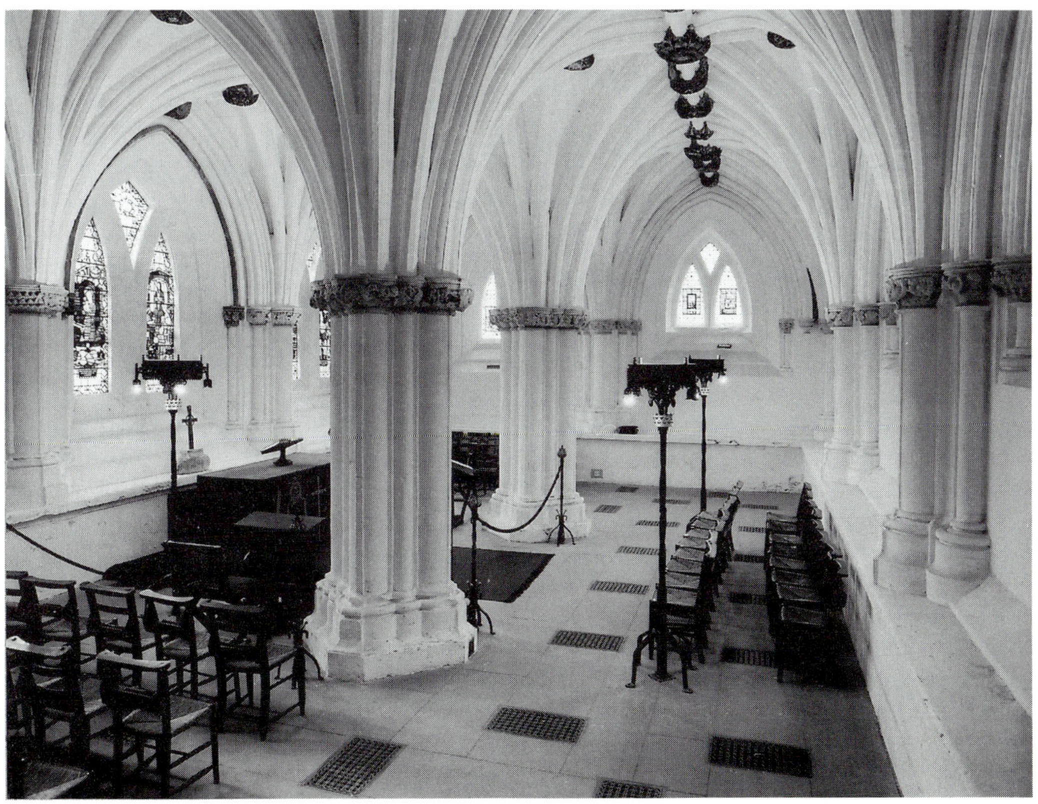

Fig. 6.9. The interior of the 'Blackadder Aisle'. (HistoricScotland)

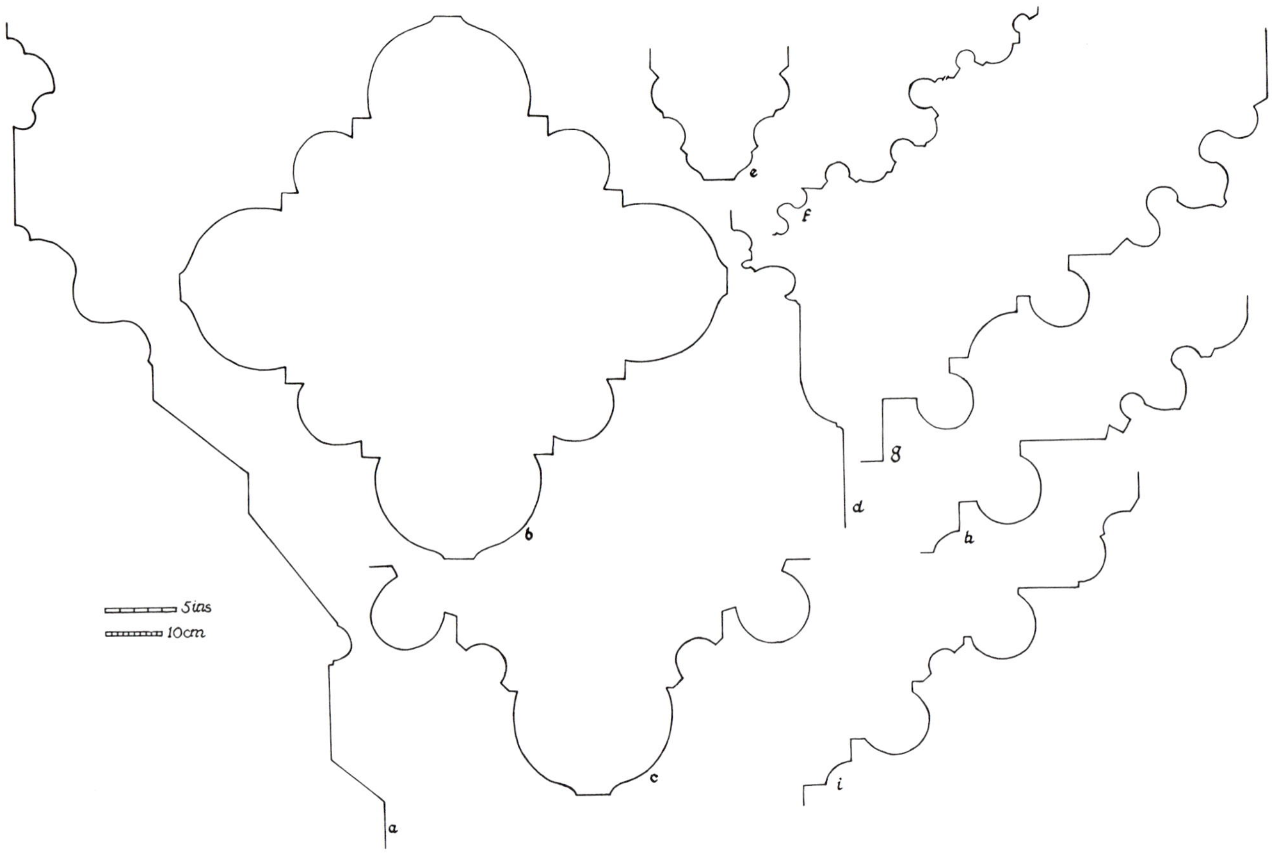

Fig. 6.10. Mouldings of the 'Blackadder Aisle': a) base course; b) piers; c) wall shafts; d) arcade bases; e) vault ribs; f) wall ribs and hood moulds; g) door from south transept; h) reveal of east windows; i) fragmentary reveal of upper window on west.

church, which may have been intended to be serve the cult of the holy man Fergus, whose hearse St Kentigern is said to have originally followed to Glasgow. The aisle has been generally accepted as being the work of Archbishop Blackadder at the turn of the fifteenth and sixteenth centuries. His arms are prominently displayed both on the external walls and on the vault which covers it, and a good case has been made for seeing its construction as part of a late medieval campaign to revive flagging interest in the cult of St Kentigern (McRoberts 1968). But, in the late nineteenth century, John Honeyman suggested that the walls should rather be seen as essentially of the thirteenth century (Honeyman 1898), and this idea has recently been argued afresh (Fawcett 1985).

Against the construction of the aisle by Blackadder, inspection of the placing of Blackadder's arms shows that there is no heraldic impediment to an earlier date for the walls of the aisle, since the arms are either set within work which is undeniably of his time, as in the vaulting, or it could be argued that they have been cut back into an existing masonry face. Nevertheless, it must be said that the architectural evidence is confusing, and it is only when the moulded details are closely examined that the early date appears more likely.

The prime difficulty in determining the chronological relationship of the aisle with the rest of the cathedral arises from the way it had to be constructed against a preexisting wall – the lower wall of the south transept as built in the early thirteenth century – and thus it has no organic relationship with any part with which it might be contemporary. It also seems that, if it is Bishop Bondington's work, he cannot have intended to build it when he first started his work, since the door cut through the base course of Walter's transept faces outwards, as if designed to provide a transeptal entrance to the church itself. Nevertheless, the mouldings of the plinth courses, piers, wall responds, bases and window reveals all point in the strongest way to the shell of the aisle being the work of the masons engaged on Bondington's eastern limb, even if its addition was an afterthought.

A first point of similarity to be noted between the choir and aisle mouldings is the design of the external base course, since in each case the top member is a strikingly similar string of beak-like section, and also in each case the main formation is terminated by a roll before a short vertical face and basal chamfer. Between these elements, however, there are differences which suggest that the plinth of the aisle could have been altered when the building was completed by Blackadder. In the external details of the windows there is a particularly close similarity

Fig. 6.11. Mouldings of the choir crypt: a) base course; b) lesser arcade piers; c) wall shafts; d) arcade bases; e) one of rib types in western compartment of central space; f) north door; g) reveal cof windows of outer eastern chapels; h) part of window reveal of central eastern chapels; i) reveal of windows along crypt flanks.

between the reveals on the eastern side of the aisle and those of the majority of windows along the choir crypt flanks. Apart from modifications to the glazing plane, the windows in the two parts are given almost precisely similar formations. If those of the aisle were indeed of the turn of the fifteenth and sixteenth centuries, it seems very strange that their designer should have followed those of the mid-thirteenth century crypt so very closely. On balance it would be far more convincing to see the Blackadder Aisle windows as being the work of the mason responsible for the choir crypt, albeit with later modifications to take the inserted Y-tracery.

Inside the aisle the mouldings are even better preserved, and the similarity of their formations with those in the crypt and choir can be yet more precisely noted.

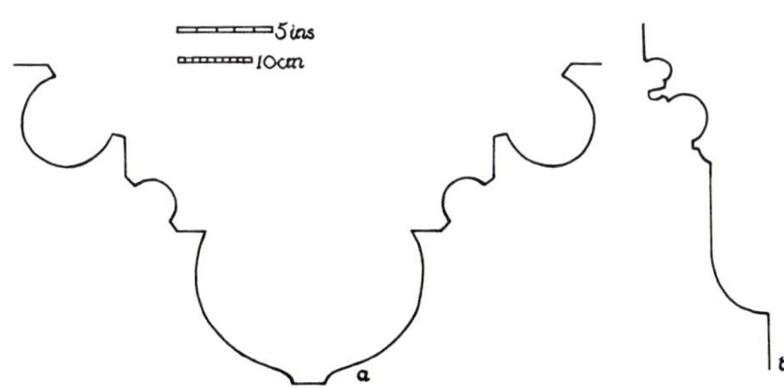

Fig. 6.12. Mouldings of wall shafts and bases in choir.

The wall shafts are virtually identical with those in the crypt aisles and the eastern chapels of the choir itself. The similarity of the wall ribs and internal window hood moulds to some of the ribs in the crypt also points to the presence of the same designing mason. The piers of the aisle tell the same story: although those of the aisle did not have to be so elongated as those of the eastern limb since they were not intended to support a major arcade on the upper storey, they show basically the same formation as the lesser piers of the crypt main arcade. In addition, the bases of these piers and their wall responds are closely paralleled by those in the choir.

The case for seeing all these details in the Blackadder Aisle as the work of the mason who designed the eastern limb would appear to be strengthened when it is seen that the mouldings of the vault ribs, which are undeniably Blackadder's work on the basis of the integral heraldic evidence, bear no relationship to anything in the eastern limb. Considered together, then, all of this evidence appears to be most consistent with the interpretation that, like the sacristy and treasury block, the aisle was started at some time after the instigation of work on Bondington's new eastern limb in about 1242, but as an extension of the same campaign.

The Transepts

Nevertheless, by the time the building campaign had

moved on from the choir and back to the transepts, started earlier in the century, plans for the completion of the Blackadder Aisle had apparently been abandoned. Instead of making provision for access to the upper stage of the aisle, the lower part of the south transept facade was pierced by a pair of windows containing fine examples of the newly fashionable bar traceried windows. Both on documentary and stylistic grounds work seems to have reached the transepts by the 1270s, at which time it is likely that Bishop Robert Wishart was the patron of the work. In 1277 there was a gift of timber for the bell tower (*Glasgow Registrum no.* 229), which points to construction in the crossing area, and this *terminus ante quem* for the work is supported by the known enthusiasm for the introduction of bar tracery into Scotland around the 1270s. It is at Elgin Cathedral, after the fire of 1270, and at Sweetheart, founded in about 1273, that the first datable Scottish examples are to be found, and the tracery at those churches relates closely to the designs in the Glasgow transepts (Fawcett 1984).

The Nave

Recent writers have tended to conclude that, once the transepts were complete, there was a considerable pause before work once again resumed on the nave (Radford 1970). But the architectural evidence would seem to suggest both that some work was in progress on the nave even while the transepts were being completed, and that the main thrust of operations moved directly onto the nave with unabated energy once the transepts were finished. The evidence also points to the structural shell being largely complete before the end of the thirteenth century, though the disturbances caused by the Wars of Independence almost certainly delayed the final stages of the operation.[14] In strong support of the continuity of work from transept to nave is the provision of responds of the same form as the nave arcade piers as an integral part of the crossing piers, whilst caps of the same multiple-moulded type as in the nave arcade are provided to some of the high shafts of the crossing piers. The heavy water-holding bases of the nave arcades are also closely related to the mid-century work further east, most notably in the use of concave flared sub-bases.

Nevertheless, there is a major problem in reaching a full understanding of the nave, which stems from the way in which certain aspects of the design were dictated by the early thirteenth century campaign. Certainly the biggest single conditioning factor was the bay width, imposed on the later master mason by the wall shafts built with the early thirteenth century aisle walls, which was considerably narrower than that in the choir.

Is it also a possibility that the design of the nave elevation was governed to some extent by the earlier designs? The most striking feature of the elevation as built is the vertical linkage of the triforium and clearstorey stages by pairs of embracing arches in each bay. Although this linkage was handled with great skill, and the reduction of the impact of the triforium stage was certainly an important theme in the architecture of the later thirteenth century, the particular form of the linkage at Glasgow might seem a little old fashioned by then. The closest analogy for it – albeit in an earlier architectural dress – is at St David's Cathedral, started in the last decades of the twelfth century. More sophisticated developments on the theme were, of course, to be developed later, as at Christchurch Cathedral in Dublin, although it is with St David's that Glasgow has the closest formal similarities.

Fig. 6.13. Longitudinal section through the nave; the roof is no longer as shown here. (Collie)

On the basis of these parallels could it be a possibility that the original design of the nave in the early thirteenth century was for something inspired by such a south-western prototype, and that the later mason - perhaps because of what had already been built – determined to adopt that earlier scheme as the starting point for his own design? Although this can be no more than speculation, it is worth remembering that the English West Country had earlier exerted its influence elsewhere in Scotland. In the first campaign on the choir of Jedburgh, for example, an elevation with linked arcade and gallery was chosen, a type now thought to have been first developed at Tewkesbury, although it was probably Romsey which was the direct inspiration for the idea at Jedburgh (Boase 1953, 152).

However, whether or not the elevation of Glasgow nave could point to the possibility of its having been prompted by an earlier design, as has been said, the architectural climate of the later thirteenth century was certainly sympathetic to the employment of a design in which a subordinated triforium was linked with the clearstorey. Among the various experiments to reduce the impact of the triforium stage, reference may be made to the choir of Southwell Collegiate Church, built around the central decades of the century. The linkage of the upper stages by a pair of arches in each bay there was certainly similar to Glasgow in elevation, although Southwell's triforium was more completely suppressed when seen obliquely because of the way in which the mural passage was set in front of the triforium openings rather than the clearstorey windows. In the last decade of the century the start of work on the nave of York Minster was to see a yet more sophisticated French-inspired means of achieving a similar end, in which the triforium was treated as an extension of the tracery of the clearstorey windows. Thus it could be argued that, whatever conditioning factors there may have been in the choice of design, Glasgow's nave must nevertheless be seen within a late thirteenth century architectural climate of thought in which a related idea was to be exploited in one of the most advanced buildings of northern England.

A late thirteenth-century date for the nave is further supported by many of its details. The mouldings of its two main doorways are of a type not far removed from those of the choir; whilst the general design of the west door, in its use of *trumeau* and arcaded tympanum, is characteristic of the later decades of the century. The design of the windows also argues for a similar date. The great west window, although augmented by Edward Blore in the 1840s[15] was clearly designed as a double permutation on the paired lancets and circlet theme, and is most unlikely to be far removed in date from the windows of the transept elevations of around the 1270s.

A slightly later type of tracery is employed in the windows of the south aisle. Since the main lay entrance to the cathedral was on this side, it was treated as a show front, and its windows were consequently made more elaborate than those on the north. They were designed with triplets of trefoils, which were uncontained by circlets and thus allowed to inter-act with each other, while the lunette over the doorway was filled with six individually uncontained trefoils, within a circle. The triforium openings have related tracery with a single uncontained trefoil above the trifoliate light heads.[16] Many analogies dating from the later decades of the century can be cited for tracery of this type in northern England, as in the nave of Howden which was completed by 1300 at the latest.

While the problems of reaching any firm conclusion on the date of the nave should not be minimised, the

Fig. 6.14. South elevation of the nave and south tower. (Collie)

weight of evidence is thus strongly in favour of the later thirteenth century. If this is the case, then the main body of the cathedral excluding the rebuilt central tower and the two demolished western towers, took roughly a century to build from the early thirteenth century remodelling of the crypt started earlier by Bishop Jocelin. Although a not inconsiderable amount of work was to be carried out on the building in the later centuries of the Middle Ages, most notably after the fire caused by a lightning strike in the time of Bishop Matthew Glendenning (Durkan 1975), and when settlement along the south side of the choir called for remedial action, these operations were not to involve any major modifications to the main body of the structure.

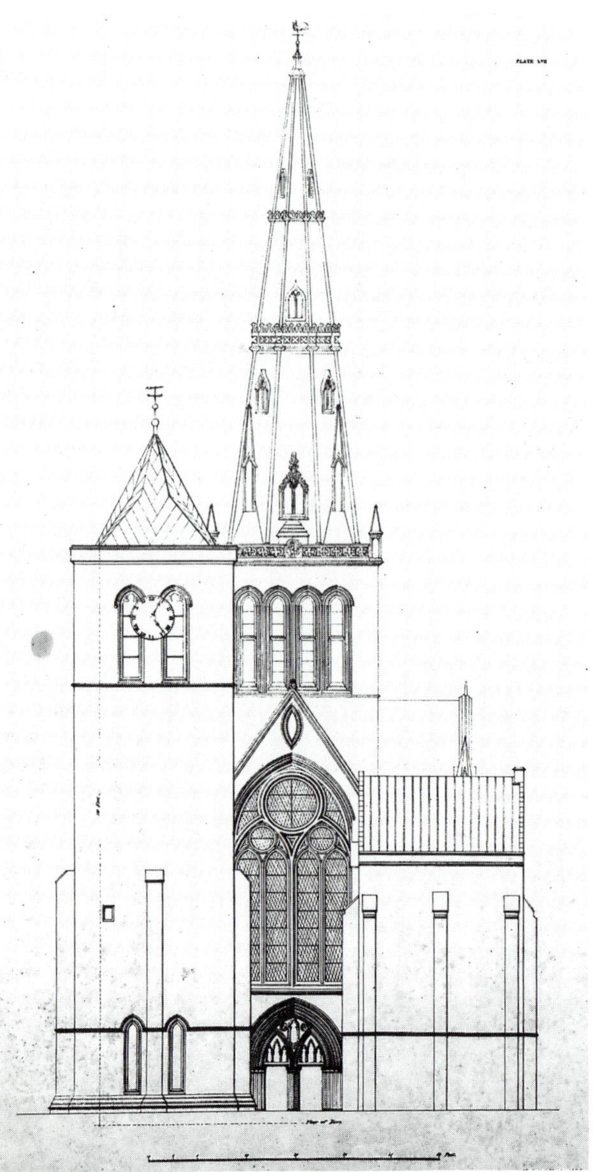

Fig. 6.15. Elevation of the west front before the demolition of the towers and the embellishment of the west window. (Collie)

The Three Towers

Of these later works, the main brunt of rebuilding the central tower and spire is firmly dated by heraldry to the episcopate of William Lauder (1408–c.1426), being finished by Bishop Cameron (1426–46). But the place of the two western towers in the cathedral's building history is rather more difficult to determine.

These two towers, which projected to their full depth from the aisle ends, were demolished in 1846 and 1848, and insufficient records were made of them before then to allow us to assess their dates with certainty simply from what we know of their architecture. Of the two, it seems likely the northern tower was probably started earlier. Collie's engravings suggest that its lower stages, with a deep base course and with lancets to either side of a central buttress, were of the thirteenth century. Beyond this, Archbishop Eyre's paper on the towers included an observation from the time of the demolition which suggested that the north tower had been added to the west wall of the aisle only after that wall had been built, but before its window was glazed (Eyre 1898b, 277), which, if correct, would confirm a thirteenth century date. The superstructure of this tower, and the whole of the southern tower appear to be of rather later date, however, and it is assumed that four finely carved corbels presently displayed within the cathedral, which appear to be of early-fifteenth century date, are from one of the towers (Fawcett 1994, 49).

In recent years there have been two opportunities to undertake archaeological investigation of the sites of the towers, although neither has produced conclusive information on dating. In 1973, a limited operation located part of the foundations of the north tower, and confirmed the basic accuracy of Collie's plan (Talbot 1975). More recently, in 1988 the Scottish Urban Archaeological Trust excavated the whole area occupied by the towers, in advance of landscaping operations. Their findings tended to confirm that the north tower had been started in the thirteenth century, and the south tower in the fifteenth (McBrien 1989). Thus it appears that, like others of the major Scottish churches, Glasgow was originally designed with no western towers, and that a single asymmetrical bell tower was added as an afterthought – as was also to happen at Dunkeld Cathedral and Inchmahome Priory, for example. At a later date a second tower was added at the west end of the south aisle, although it proved impossible to carry this up to the same height as that eventually reached by its northern couterpart if this had ever been the intention.

Conclusion

Thus, except for two of its three towers and a part of the third, the cathedral may be regarded as entirely the product of the thirteenth century and, as such, it is one of the most perfect and complete embodiments of the changing architectural tastes of a particularly momentous century of architectural development in Scotland. But the significance of the cathedral is not confined to Scotland. At a period when northern England and Lowland Scotland were still essentially a part of the same architectural province, Glasgow must be seen as occupying an important and highly creative place in the wider history of British medieval architecture.

Notes

1. St Andrews cathedral was probably planned to have a total length of about 125 m. but was eventually completed to a length of about 114 m. This hardly approaches the length of such as Winchester, of 161.5 m. Glasgow has a total length of around 91.5 m. excluding the western towers and the eastward projection of the chapter house.
2. For a summary of the situation see Cowan and Easson 1976, 59.
3. The guide books currently available to Scottish cathedrals wholly or partly in state care are: Richard Fawcett, *Dunblane Cathedral* (leaflet), 1980; C. A. Ralegh Radford and Gordon Donaldson, *Whithorn*, revised edn 1984; Richard Fawcett, *Glasgow Cathedral*, 1985; Stewart Cruden *St Andrews Cathedral*, revised edn 1986; Richard Fawcett, *Beauly Priory and Fortrose Cathedral*, 1987; Richard Fawcett, *Dunkeld Cathedral* (published by the Society of Friends), 1990; Richard Fawcett, *Elgin Cathedral*, 1991; William J. Morris, *A Walk through Glasgow Cathedral*, 2nd edn 1995 (published by the Society of Friends); James F. Miller and John C. Lusk, *Dunblane Cathredral* n.d. (published by the Society of Friends).
4. An abortive attempt to trace the east end of Bishop John's cathedral was carried out by Peter Macgregor Chalmers in 1899, with the permission of the First Commissioner of Works. See Chalmers 1904–5, p 184. Correspondence about the excavation is on file MW 169 in the Scottish Record Office. In 1978, in advance of changes to the heating system, further excavations were undertaken at the west end of the crypt, but failed to locate any evidence for the planning of the east end of the cathedral before Bishop Bondington's extension. See Gordon, 1980.
5. The later date for the voussoir was argued for in Radford and Stones 1964. Its association with Bishop John's cathedral was suggested in Fawcett 1985, and a detailed argument for this earlier date has been advanced in Cameron 1986.6. For a discussion of the possible planning of Jocelin's church see Radford and Stones 1964.
6. For a discussion of the possible planning of Jocelin's church see Radford and Stones 1964.
7. See the plan in Clapham 1934, fig 15.
8. For details of the bishops see Watt 1969, 143ff, and Dowden 1912, 294.
9. For the development of the chapter see Cowan 1967, 14.
10. In the course of his paper on Lichfield, Dr Warwick Rodwell made the important point that the early thirteenth century plan there also appears to have been similar to Bondington's plan for Glasgow, and pointed to significant parallels in their dimensions (this volume, pp 00–00). The differences between their architectural vocabulary, however, would seem to suggest that the same masons are unlikely to have been involved at both buildings.
11. See plans in Dimier 1949.
12. The documentary evidence for the placing of the Lady Chapel in the crypt was pointed out in McRoberts 1970.
13. The evidence for these changes was examined in Watson 1901, although his interpretation is rather over-elaborate.
14. The complaint was made of Bishop Wishart that timber given to him by the English for repairs to the bell tower was instead used for the making of siege engines: Palgrave 1837, 348.
15. His designs for doing this are preserved amongst the collections of his drawings in the Victoria and Albert Museum, 8724 1–38, and in the Mitchell Library, Glasgow, D 527941.
16. Diagrammatic sketches of all the Glasgow windows, set out in relation to comparable examples, are included in Fawcett 1984.

Bibliography

Barty, A.B. 1944: *The history of Dunblane* (Stirling).

Bentinck, C.D. 1926: *Dornoch Cathedral and parish* (Inverness).

Boase, T.S.R. 1953: *English art, 1100–1216* (Oxford).

Cambridge, E. 1977: The early building history of St Andrews Cathedral. *Antiqs Jnl* 57,50.

Cameron, N. 1986: The painted Romanesque voussoir in Glasgow Cathedral. *Jnl B.A.A.* 89, 40.

Chalmers, P.M. 1904–5: A thirteenth century tomb in Glasgow Cathedral. *Proc Royal Philosophical Soc of Glasgow* 36, 184.

Chalmers, P.M, 1914: *The cathedral church of Glasgow* (London).

Chron, Holyrood 1938, Anderson, M.O. (ed.): *A Scottish Chronicle known as the chronicle of Holyrood*, (Scottish History Society).

Chron. Melrose 1835, Stevenson, J. (ed.): *Chronica de Mailros*, (Bannatyne Club).

Clapham, A.W. 1934: *English Romanesque architecture after the Conquest* (Oxford).

Cockburn, J.H. 1959: *The medieval bishops of Dunblane and their cathedral* (Edinburgh).

Collie, J. 1835: *Plans, elevations, sections,. details and views of the cathedral of Glasgow* (London).

Cowan, I. 1967: Glasgow Cathedral and its clergy in the middle ages. *Annual Rep. of the Friends of Glasgow Cathedral.*

Cowan, I. and Easson, D. 1976: *Medieval religious houses, Scotland*, 2nd edn. (London).

Crawford, B. 1988: *St Magnus Cathedral and Orkney's twelfth-century renaissance* (Aberdeen).

Dimier, M.S.A. 1959: *Receuil de plans d'églises Cisterciennes*, Paris.

Dowden, J. 1912: *The bishops of Scotland* (Glasgow).

Driscoll, S.T. 1992: Excavations at Glasgow Cathedral: a preliminary report. *Glasgow Archaeol. Jnl.* 17, 63.

Durkan, J. 1975: The great fire at Glasgow Cathedral. *Innes Review* 26, 89.

Durkan, J. 1986: *The precinct of Glasgow cathedral* (Society of Friends of Glasgow Cathedral).

Eyre, Archbishop 1898a: The hall of the vicars choral. In Eyre-Todd 1898, 292,

Eyre, Archbishop 1898b: The western towers. In Eyre-Todd 1898, 277.

Eyre-Todd, G. 1898: *The book of Glasgow Cathedral, a history and description* (Glasgow)

Fawcett, R. 1984: Scottish medieval window tracery. In D.I. Breeze (ed.), *Studies in Scottish antiquity* (Edinburgh) 148.

Fawcett, R. 1985: The Blackadder Aisle at Glasgow Cathedral: a reconsideration of the architectural evidence for its date. *Proc. Soc. Antiqs Scotland* 115, 277.

Fawcett, R. 1985, *Glasgow Cathedral* (HMSO Official Guide, Edinburgh).

Fawcett, R. 1990: Glasgow Cathedral. In E. Williamson, A. Riches and M. Higgs, *The Buildings of Scotland, Glasgow* (London) 108.

Fawcett, R. 1994: *Scottish Architecture from the accession of the Stewarts to the Reformation* (Edinburgh)

Glasgow Registrum 1843: *Registrum Episcopatus Glasguensis* (Bannatyne Club).

Gordon, A. 1980: Excavation in the lower church of Glasgow Cathedral. *Glasgow Archaeol. Jnl* 7, 85.

Hay, G. 1967: Some architectural fragments in the lower church. *Innes Review* 18, 95.

Hearn, M.F. 1971: The rectangular ambulatory in English medieval architecture, *Jnl. Soc. Archit. Hist.* 30, 187.

Honeyman, J. 1898: In Eyre-Todd 1898, 234.

Jackson, K.H. 1958, The sources for the life of St Kentigern. In K.M. Chadwick (ed.), *Studies in the early British Church* (Cambridge) 273.

Macfarlane, L. J. 1985: *William Elphinstone and the kingdom of Scotland, 1431–1514* (Aberdeen).

MacGibbon, D. and Ross, T. 1896–7: *The ecclesiastical architecture of Scotland* (3 vols) (Edinburgh).

McBrien, H. 1989: *An interim report on excavations at the west front of Glasgow Cathedral* (Scottish Urban Archaeological Trust, Perth).

Mc Roberts, D. 1966: Notes on Glasgow Cathedral, the treasury of Glasgow Cathedral. *Innes Review* 17, 40.

McRoberts, D. 1968: The Scottish Church and nationalism in the fifteenth century. *Innes Review* 19, 3.

McRoberts, D. 1970: Notes on Glasgow Cathedral, the Lady Chapel of Glasgow Cathedral. *Innes Review* 21, 244.

McRoberts, D. 1976: *The medieval church of St Andrews* (Glasgow).

NASS 1921–33: National art survey of Scotland, *Examples of architecture from the twelfth to the seventeenth centuries* (4 vols) (Edinburgh).

Palgrave, F. (ed.) 1837: *Documents and records illustrating the history of Scotland* (London).

Radford, C.A.R. and Stones, E.L.G. 1964: The remains of the cathedral of Bishop Jocelin at Glasgow (c. 1197). *Antiqs Jnl* 44, 220.

Radford, C.A.R. 1970: *Glasgow Cathedral* (earlier version of HMSO Official Guide, Edinburgh).

RCAHMS, Royal commission on the ancient and historical monuments of Scotland, Edinburgh:
1933: *Inventory of Fife, Kinross and Clackmannan;*
1946: *Inventory of Orkney and Shetland;*
1975: *Inventory of Argyll*, 2;
1982: *Inventori of Argyll*, 4.

Stones, E.L.G. 1967: Notes on Glasgow Cathedral, the 'tomb' in the lower church. *Innes Review* 18, 18.

Stones, E.L.G. 1970: Notes on Glasgow Cathedral, the northern extension to the choir. *Innes Review* 21, 144.

Talbot, E.J. 1975: An excavation at the site of the N.W. tower of St Mungo's Cathedral, Glasgow. *Innes review* 26, 43.

Watson, T.L. 1901: *The double choir of Glasgow Cathedral, a study of rib vaulting* (Glasgow).

Watt, D.E.R. 1969: *Fasti Ecclesiae Scoticanae Medii Aevi*, 2nd draft, (Scottish Record Society, new ser. 1).

Wilson, C. 1978: In C. McWilliam, *The buildings of Scotland: Lothian* (Harmondsworth).

The Archaeology of Gloucester Cathedral

Carolyn Heighway

Gloucester is a Cathedral of the New Foundation, created in 1541, but it took over the church and conventual buildings of the abbey built in the late 11th century, which in turn had its origins in a minster of 679–81 (Finberg 1972b; building history, including unreferenced dates mentioned below, derive from the Abbey *Historia*, Hart 1863; see also Welander 1991, Hare 1993).

The Roman and medieval town of Gloucester occupies a peninsula of land overlooking the river Severn. The Abbey and precinct straddle the north-west corner of the Roman fortress and town. The Cathedral incorporates remnants of its Roman past; Roman bricks are built into walls in the Tribune Galley (Ashwell 1985b, 3/11), and there is a re-used Roman inscription built into the medieval fabric (*Britannia* vii, 1986, 429). There was a Roman building in the area of the south transept (Masse 1898, 22).

The topography of the Roman remains, allied with the natural hillock on which Gloucester stands, means that the site of the Cathedral is on a slope. This no doubt partly explains the many different levels which are found in the cathedral. Though the east end of a Benedictine house is usually raised above a crypt, at Gloucester there are many other changes of level from west to east. The presbytery and ambulatory are raised above the choir, this is in turn raised above the nave, which in turn is several feet higher than ground level outside the west end. The underlying Roman built environment has probably also affected the architecture: the subsidence of the south aisle (compensated for in the fourteenth century) may be due to the subsidence of the Norman foundations over the late Roman ditch (the Roman wall is further east than often shown on older plans: see Heighway 1974 for the updated Roman plan and cf. Morris 1985, 100 where the old plan is inadvertently used). However the subsoil under the Cathedral – sand over lias clay – is not ideal, and there may in addition be other causes of the subsidence deriving from the Roman topography of which we know nothing.

The original abbey was built 679-81; it was restored or rebuilt by Bishop Ealdred of Worcester in 1058 (Hare 1993, 17-20). The site of the Saxon churches is unknown, but Hare has argued for a site in the area of the present cloisters (Hare 1993,27-9).

The Building

Romanesque

The great Norman church was built by the first Norman Abbot, Serlo; its foundation stone was laid on 29 June 1089 and the church dedicated 15 July 1100. A remarkable amount of the Romanesque building survives; more can be reconstructed from surviving architectural evidence (Wilson 1985). There is a cut-away drawing by F. S. Waller showing the Romanesque building with thirteenth-century and later features taken away (Fig. 7.1) which has several times appeared in local guides (e.g. Massé, 15). Even the great Perpendicular choir is a casing of the Norman work. The form of the east end is known from piers under the reredos uncovered and recorded in 1873 (Massé, 51). The west end plan is uncertain, but there were certainly flanking towers. The south-west tower collapsed c. 1170; it must have been repaired, for it had to be rebuilt again in the 1240s. St John Hope (1897) thought that the west front was shortened when it was rebuilt by Abbot Morwent (1421–37), and that the adjacent west slype and chapel above were shortened at the same time. In fact it seems just as likely that the original west front was on the present line: alternative possible twelfth-century layouts are illustrated elsewhere (Welander 1991, 69-74).

Additional details about the Romanesque church come to light from time to time: for instance the polygonal ambulatory chapels had small single-splayed windows and were originally centrally planned with benches all round (Heighway 1993). Behind the south porch in the roof space can be seen the vestiges of one of the Romanesque strip-buttresses, and in the nave roof-space are remnants of two of the four corner towers which adorned the original Romanesque tower.

Thirteenth century

Little survives of the abbey's thirteenth century work. The nave vaulting is of this date, but the tower and spire and Lady Chapel have been superseded by later work. The screen in the north transept, which now forms an entrance to the Treasury, is thirteenth-century work, as are two doors in the north walk of the Cloister (Welander 1991, 109).

Fourteenth century

The south aisle, with its ball-flower ornament, was rebuilt c. 1319–29 (Morris 1985); the transepts were remodelled. The south face of the south transept was rebuilt reusing the Norman work (Ashwell 1985a). The choir was transformed (1337–51) by refacing the Norman work (see Fig. 7.1 and Massé, 52, 61); the great East window was built (1347–50). The north transept was modified 1368-74, and the superb Great Cloister was built 1364-1412 (Welander 1991, 215, 224-5).

Fifteenth century

Abbot Morwent (1421–27) rebuilt the west end and porch; the tower was built c. 1450; and the Lady Chapel completed shortly before 1500.

Cathedral Architects

Since the mid-nineteenth century there has been an unbroken sequence of Cathedral architects, all operating from the same office at 17 College Green, close to the Cathedral.

1862 Thomas Fulljames (of Waller and Fulljames)
1866 Gilbert Scott
1872 Frederick S Waller, appointed as Supervisor
1878 Frederick S Waller appointed Architect
1892 Frederick William Waller (with his father, who died 1905)
1933 Colonel Noel Nuxley Waller (with his father before 1933)
1960 Bernard John Ashwell
1985 Christopher Basil Comely

From the historical point of view, by far the most skilled and thorough of the architects was F. S. Waller. He was a scholar and draughtsman; many of his superb historical drawings are reproduced in 'Bells' (Masse 1898) and other guides. Although not appointed Cathedral architect until 1878, he had set up partnership with Fulljames in College Green in 1847 and had a long association with the Cathedral.

Record of Repairs

One disadvantage of the remarkable continuity of archiitects has been that more than a century of records accumulated in the architects office. The sorting of plans and drawings is now in progress and these are being transferred to the Cathedral Library. The files and written records are however still unavailable (it is unfortunate that English Heritage does not provide grants for written records as well as for drawings). Fortunately the principal records were summarised in Bernard Ashwell's Quinquennial Report (Ashwell 1985b); this includes extracts from the architects' log books of Fulljames and Walker which covered the periodc.1850-1885, and which are currently missing. There are however in the Cathedral Library a long run of Clerk of Works day books from 1878 to 1957 which detail wages payments and works being done; there are architects reports too in the *Chapter Act Books* although these were not included after about 1887. The Record Office holds a considerable collection of material from the eighteenth and nineteenth century, including accounts from which information about stone sources can be gleaned. Much also can be extracted from secondary sources and newspaper cuttings. A written/ photographic record outlines work done 1953-c.1976 (Ashwell n.d.).

Among the records are drawings and historical reconstructions by Waller, since often reproduced (e.g. by Massé 1898), although the reproductions do not convey the information, finely drawn and hand-coloured, on the original drawings. 1908 drawings by the Wallers of the tower were published early this century (Waller 1911). There are photographs (by the excellent Sydney Pitcher) of many of the early twentieth-century repairs; these are not in the Cathedral Library at present but there are copies in the National Monuments Record. Present day records are augmented by a thorough photographic record (on colour film) maintained and catalogued by the Clerk of Works.

Building Stone

The difficulties of obtaining building stone are described by Ashwell (1985b, 3/42). The medieval stone of Gloucester Cathedral was mostly taken from local limestone quarries in the Painswick and Minchinhampton area. Also used in the medieval building are special imported stones, although some of the 'Purbeck Marble' used for the shafts of the nave vaulting and elsewhere, may be lias stone from the Forest of Dean (inf. A. Price).

The Victorian architects experiimented with different stone. The south elevation of the south porch was restored in 1852-3 using in part a yellow dolomitic limestone from Anston, south Yorkshire. Bath stone was used here and elsewhere in the Cathedral form the mid nineteenth century onwards; the bath stone has not stood the test of time and much of it is now being replaced. Extensive research on quarries and stone use is being carried out by Arthur Price.

In the 1950s, stone still came from local quarries, but these are now worked out, and there are difficulties inherent in opening new quarries or extending old ones in areas of protected countryside. For a while Clipsham stone (Rutland) was used before it became unavailable (although the quarry is now re-opened). Attempts to use Box stone also failed (the source was restricted to work in Bath). In 1973–4 Lepine stone, from Chauvigny, east of Poitiers, France, was first used and is still used today.

Loose Worked Stone

The Victorian architects and masons were more ready to replace stonework than some modern masons. For instance in 1877 one buttress of the lavatory in the cloister was replaced solely 'in order to preserve it as a guide for the restoration of the others hereafter' (Ashwell 1985b, 5/23). I take this to mean it was their copy that was meant to last, not the fragment of stone they took out, which would show a touching faith in the power of human memory, for of course the stones could not be indelibly marked. For a long time odd pieces of stone removed in restoration or otherwise discovered were kept in the Tribune Gallery; when in the 1980s the gallery was used for the Cathedral Exhibition, the worked stone was removed to the crypt. A photographic inventory was made in 1989,

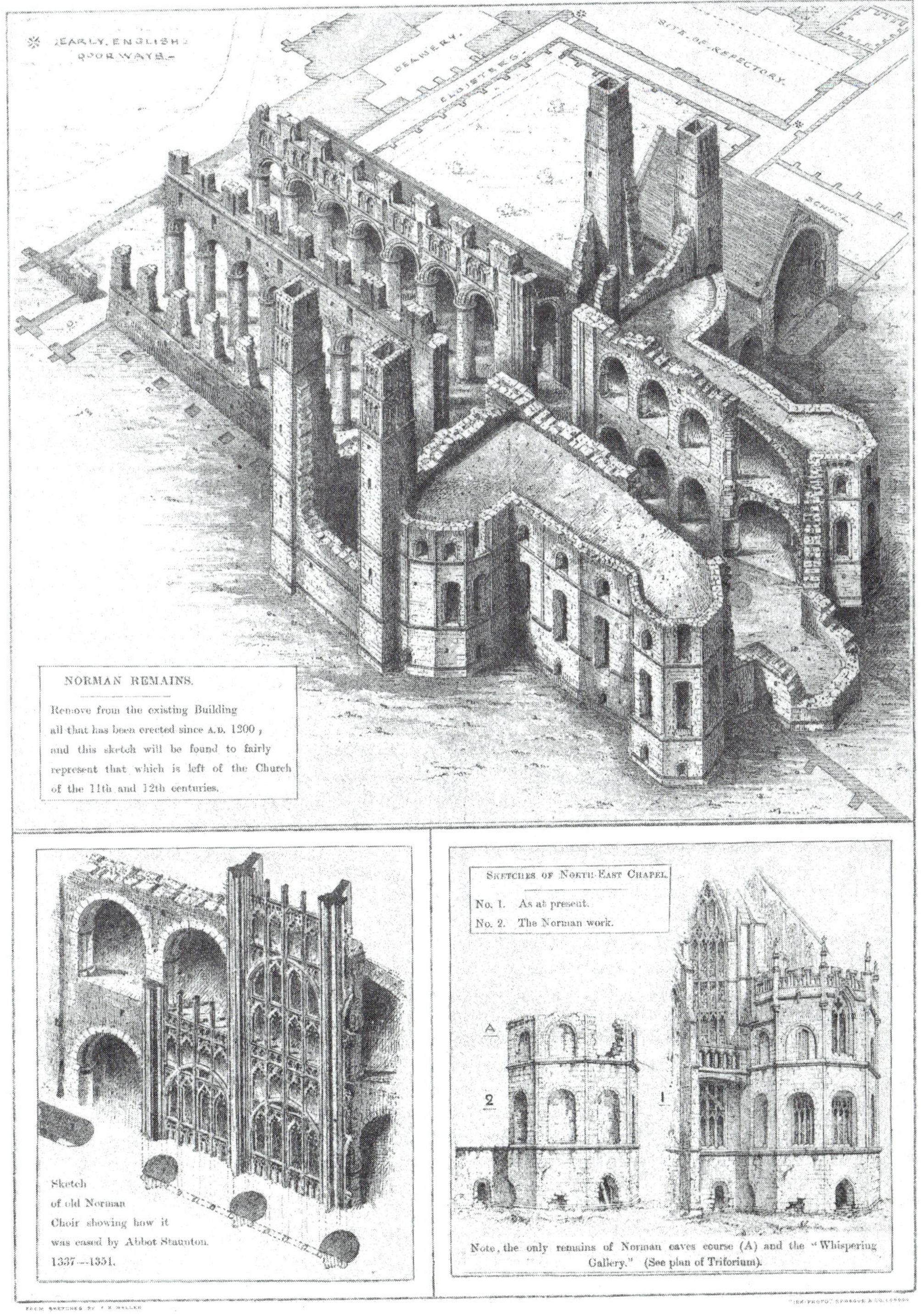

Fig. 7.1. Drawings by F. S. Waller showing the Romanesque parts of the Abbey Church, with later work omitted. and below details of how the Romanesque building was adapted. From Waller 1890, plate 4.

and the stone was marked; some of the stone was reburied, though most will be kept on racks in the crypt. The stone included fragments of ?medieval foliage possibly from the parapet of the west front which were discovered too late to be used as master examples for the new work which is now probably on its third copy. It should however be said that a medieval copy would not have matched the remaining Victorian work which was still in situ. The incident is a reminder, if one were needed, that much of the detail of the external Cathedral stonework bears only a superficial relationship to its medieval predecessor. This emphasises the importance of keeping the medieval

Fig. 7.2. Gloucester Cathedral: south elevation of the south transept, showing the suggested dating of the existing stonework and the new stone inserted in 1979–83. From Ashwell, 1985a.

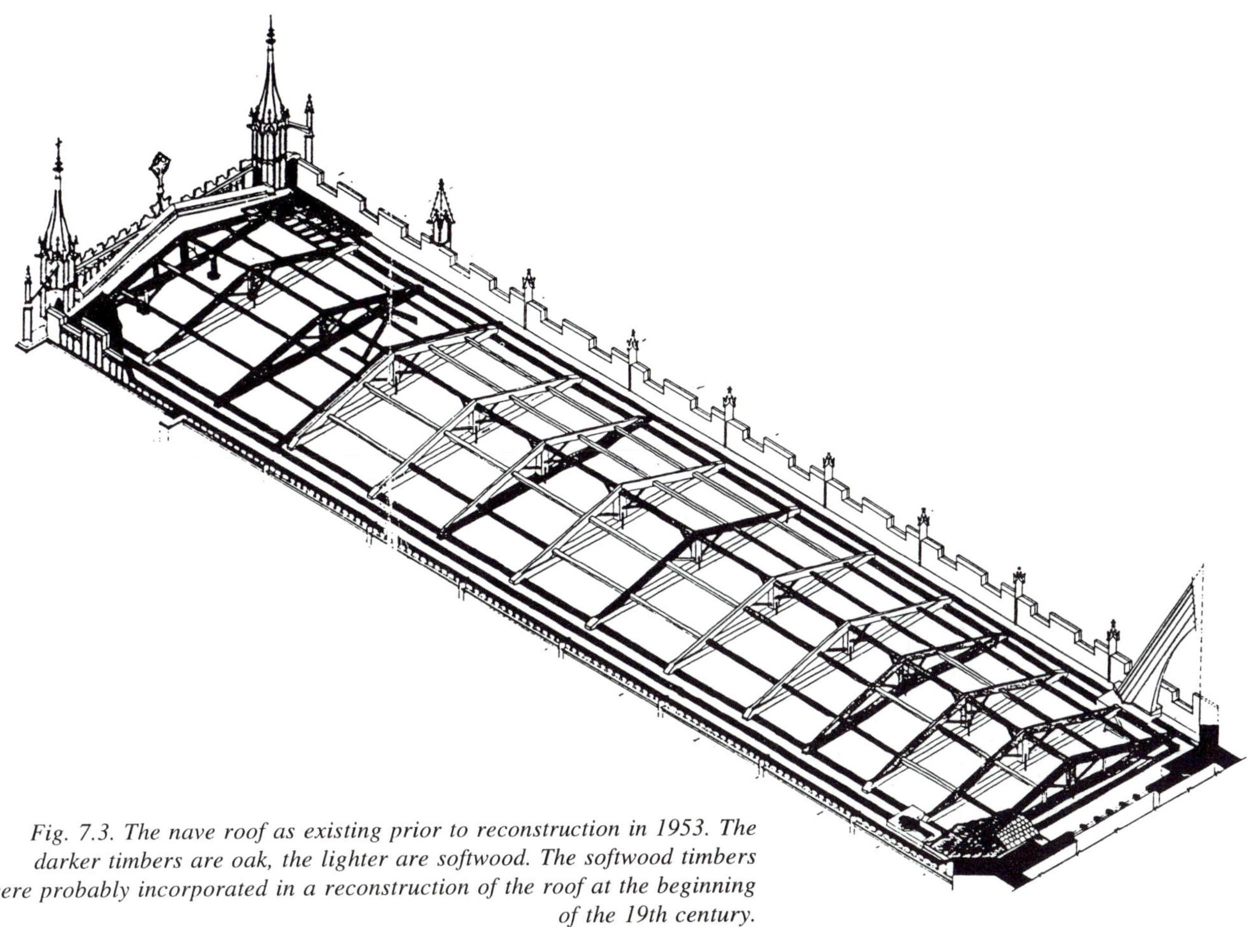

Fig. 7.3. The nave roof as existing prior to reconstruction in 1953. The darker timbers are oak, the lighter are softwood. The softwood timbers were probably incorporated in a reconstruction of the roof at the beginning of the 19th century.

worked stone, if any survives, to serve as working examples, but in any case to record the styles of the medieval masons.

Timber Roofs

Few of Gloucesters timber roofs survive, most having been replaced with steel trusses in the 1950s. The south transept has a softwood timber roof erected c. 1825 (Ashwell 1985b, 3/32); The roofs of the nave, presbytery, choir, and north transept all have galvanised steel roofs erected in 1953, 1953/4, 1957, and 1961 respectively (Ashwell 1985b, 3/32, 4/1, 4/2). The architect made a drawn and photographic record of the old roofs from which it is possible to deduce much information. The nave roof (Ashwell, n.d., Figs. 7–9, 26; see also Welander 1991, 516) show a low-pitched butt-purlin roof with fourteen king-strut principal trusses; the king-struts had raking struts to the principal rafters and the ridge-piece, and there were two purlins on each side. The design was similar to the pre-16th century nave roof at Tewkesbury (Hewett 1985, 68). The roof had been mostly renewed in softwood in the early 19th century and appears to be the roof shown on Ansted's cross sections (Britton 1829, Plate III, XVII, VIII, XVI). The end trusses of the roof had additional queen-struts between the ties and principals (Ashwell n.d. Fig. 9) which might represent an earlier arrangement. Ashwell thought the roof might be 15th century, and this is not unlikely, though the then Cathedrals Advisory Committee thought it contained no surviving medieval timbers.

The choir roof was different from the nave, having ten king-strut trusses but no ridge-piece, and the two purlins on each side supported by large queen-struts (Ashwell, n.d. Figs. 120, 131, 132). All but one of the ties had been scarfed, probably as post-medieval repairs; the roof was probably original 15th-century work.

The north transept had a four-bay roof with two tiers of clasped purlins held between collars and principal rafters, with two queen-struts supporting each collar, and curved wind-braces to the lower purlins, probably of late-medieval date (Ashwell n.d. Figs. 120, 131, 132). The north gable end of the transept shows the outline of a still earlier roof of steeper pitch; this steeper roof line is not visible on the north face of the tower, where it was overlain or rebuilt when the 15th century tower was built. The north aisle roof is still timber; the stone vaults of the north aisle are Romanesque , with two fifteenth century bays at the west end, and in spite of much alteration and repair the roofs above probably have surviving medieval timbers (some idea of the roof design and its variety is given by Britton 1829, plates III, XVI). The fifteenth-century porch also has a medieval roof, as does the Lady

Chapel. The medieval tower roof recorded by Waller (1911, Fig. 12; and also in Britton 1929, plate XVI) was repaired in 1948 but must still include some old timberwork; the two floors of the tower are fifteenth century (Hewett 1985, 150 and Fig. 144). In spite of the apparent paucity of medieval timber roofs at Gloucester, there is probably considerable scope for research and dendrochronological analysis.

Archaeology

The writer was appointed Cathedral Consultant Archaeologist in 1983, and has been a member of the Fabric Committee since its formation in 1988. The archaeologist receives Minutes of the monthly Architect's Meetings to check if any works are proposed which might need archaeological or architectural recording.

From about 1970 to 1983, Gloucester Museum and then the Gloucester Excavation Unit occasionally carried out watching briefs, but this was on an *ad hoc* basis and seldom included architectural recording. Prior to that architectural recording was occasionally done by the Cathedral Architect, who carried out a superb survey of the south transept south front (Ashwell 1985a; Fig. 7.2 above). The grant conditions imposed by English Heritage as well as the terms of the Cathedrals Measure have changed matters considerably. Photogrammetric survey has been carried out for most of the external elevations of the cathedral and these have proved, with very little augmentation, to be invaluable for marking-up stone-types and archaeological sequences.

Before the 1970s there had been no below-ground recording since the Wallers carefully recorded their findings in the major restorations of the late nineteenth century. As late as 1971 a one-metre deep trench was dug across the nave for a heating duct, without any archaeological observation. Many minor below-grounddisturbances mostly for services have been recorded in the past 20 years, showing among other things that a very patchy medieval tile pavement survives under the stone nave floor, at curiously diverse depths (a full publication of the medieval tiles of the cathedral is in preparation by Laurence Keen). Archaeological investigation of the south-east ambulatory chapel recorded several details about its original Romanesque design (Heighway 1993). Most small observations have only cumulative value; though unpublished for the time being, they are noted in local archaeological publications and copies of the annual reports of the Cathedral Archaeologist are kept in the Cathedral Library for reference.

Outstanding Problems and Research

♦ There is still disagreement about the Romanesque design, especially the choir elevations (Wilson1985; McAleer 1986, 165, 170-1).

♦ The plan of the Romanesque west ends is not certain. Indeed, it is clear that the whole of the west end is more complex than is indicated by summaries of the architectural sequence. Although the west end would indeed seem to have been built in the fifteenth century, presumably by Abbot Morwent (1421-37), the inside south wall of Morwent's west end has engaged shafts with roll-mouldings which now have no purpose and which clearly relate to a thirteenth-century weat end.

♦ The crypt is nearly all eleventh and early twelfth century (Waller 1876), but it would be interesting to know why the central area was lower (the present crypt floor level in the central area is mostly post-medieval infill).

♦ Some of the fourteenth-century work in the cathedral was carried out using Romanesque detail in architectural contexts, not just re-using stone. The south front of the south transept (Ashwell 1985a) is a conspicuous, but not the only example. Some of the choir roof-space windows (those which are of the least architectural importance, being functional rather than ornamental) were fitted with Romanesque engaged columns and bases. It is possible that the north transept also re-used Romanesque detail, as the south one did. There are also examples on buildings elsewhere in the Close and the extent of such architectural re-use needs further observation and research.

♦ More work needs to be done at Gloucester comparing architectural mouldings with those from elsewhere to establish architectural dates and styles. An obvious way to do this is to keep selectedmasons' templates; now that Gloucester has a full coverage of photogrammetry it should not be difficult to keep selected templates with their location for comparative work.

♦ The medieval floor tiles at Gloucester are an important collection and Laurence Keen's publication on these is eagerly awaited.

♦ Masons' marks are another subject of study. Many people take an interest in these but few publish them and, as with medieval tiles, each researcher has an individual collection of their own. A comprehensive list of sources of masons' marks at Gloucester is being attempted. Recent work on the tower produced a new crop of masons' marks in the form of weapons; a note should soon be published on these.

♦ There is no doubt that an overall assessment of all the archaeology of the cathedral Close would be of great value. This essay has been confined to the Cathedral Church itself, but the church is an inextricable part of its surroundings which incorporate two thousand years of a populous part of urban history. The buildings of the Close, often timber-framed,have present landscape value as well as extraordinary historical interest. An inventory of the whole resource is badly needed.

Acknowledgements
I am grateful to Canon David Welander and Basil Comely for commenting on earlier drafts of this paper; also to Julian Munby for contributing to the section on the roofs, and to Arthur Price and John Prentice for information about stone.

Bibliography

Ashwell, B. J. (n.d.) The Cathedral Church of St Peter and the Holy and Indivisible Trinity at Gloucester: Chronicle of the works of repair begun AD 1953 (Typescript).

Ashwell, B. J. 1985a: Gloucester Cathedral: the South Transept: a 14th century conservation project. *Antiq. Jn.* 65, 112–120.

Ashwell, B. J. 1985b: *The Cathedral Church ' of Gloucester. First Quinquennial Report to 31 July 1985.* (unpublished).

B.A.A. Conf. Trans. 1985: *Medieval Art and Architecture at Gloucester and Tewkesbury* (BAA Conf Trans 7).

B.G.A.S.: Bristol and Gloucestershire Archaeological Society.

Bazeley, W. 1885–7: Notes on the Early English Lady Chapel, AD 1224. *Records of Gloucester Cathedral* for 1885–97, 12–16.

Bazeley, W. 1891–2: Notes on the Early English Lady Chapel, Gloucester Cathedral. *Trans B.G.A.S.* 16, 1891–2, 196–200.

Bazeley, W. 1888–9: The early days of the Abbey of St Peter, Gloucester. *Trans B.G.A.S.* 13, 1888–9, 155–161.

Borg, A. 1985: 'The Gloucester Candlestick'. In B.A.A. Conf. Trans. 1985, 84–92.

Britton, J. 1829: *The History and antiquities of the Abbey and Cathedral Church of Gloucester* (London).

Carter, J. and Basire, J. 1807: *Plans, Elevations and Sections and specimens of the Architecture of the Cathedral Church of Gloucester* (London).

Cocke, T. H. 1985: 'Bishop Benson and his Restoration of Gloucester Cathedral 1735–1752'. In B.A.A. Conf. Trans 1985, 130–132.

Eward, S. 1985: *No Fine but a Glass of Wine -Cathedral Life at Gloucester in Stuart Times* (Salisbury).

Finberg, H. P. R. 1972a: Princes of the Hwicce. In *Early Charters of the W Midlands* (Leicester).

Finberg, H. P. R. 1972b: The Early History of Gloucester Abbey. In *Early Charters of the W Midlands* (Leicester).

Freeman, E. A, 1883–4: Gloucester and its Abbey. *Records of Gloucester Cathedral* 2, 79–155.

Garrod, A. P. and Heighway, C. M. 1984: *Garrod's Gloucester; Archaeological Observations 1974–81* (Bristol).

Garrod, A. P. and Heighway, C. M. 1981: Gloucester Cathedral 1980 *Glevensis* 15, 44–5.

Haines, Rev H. 1867: *A Guide to the Cathedral Church at Gloucester* (Gloucester).

Hart, W. H. (ed; 1863–7): *Historia et Cartularium Monasterii Scti Petri Gloucestriae,* Rolls Series 33, vol i (1863), vol ii (1865), vol iii (1867).

Heighway, C. M. 1974: *Archaeology in Gloucester: A policy for City and District* (Gloucester City Museum).

Heighway, C. M. 1984: Anglo-Saxon Gloucester. In J. Haslam, *Anglo Saxon Towns in Southern England* (Chichester).

Heighway, C. M. 1988: Archaeology in the Precinct of Gloucester Cathedral. *Glevensis* 22, 29–37.

Heighway, C. M. forthcoming: 'Topography' in C. Heighway and R. Bryant, *The Saxon Minster and medieval Priory of St Oswald at Gloucester* (Society of Antiquaries London).

Herbert, N. 1988: Gloucester Cathedral and the Close. In *VCH Gloucs* 4, 275–88.

Hewett, C. A. 1985: *English Cathedral and Monastic Carpentry* (Chichester).

Hope, W. H. St J. 1885–97: Notes on the Benedictine Abbey of St Peter at Gloucester, *Records of Gloucester Cathedral* for 1885–97, 90–131.

Kirby, I. M. 1967: *A Catalogue of the Records of the Dean and Chapter including the former St Peters Abbey* (Gloucester).

Masse, H. J. L. J. 1898: *The Cathedral Church of Gloucester* (Bell's Cathedrals, London).

McAleer, J. P. 1986: Some Re-used Romanesque material in the Choir Tribune at Gloucester Cathedral, *Trans B.G.A.S.* 104, 157–174.

Morris, R. K. 1985: Ballflower work in Gloucester and its vicinity. In B.A.A. Conf. Trans. 1985, 99–115.

Scott, G. 1867: The Cathedral Restoration. *Gloucester Chronicle*, 20 May 1867.

Thurlby, M. 1985: The elevations of the Romanesque Abbey Churches of St Mary at Tewkesbury and St Peter at Gloucester. In B.A.A. Conf. Trans. 1985, 36–51.

Waller, F. S. 1856: *General Architectural Description of Gloucester Cathedral* (London).

Waller, F. S. 1876: The Crypt of Gloucester Cathedral. *Trans B.G.A.S.* 1, 147–152.

Waller, F. S. 1880: *A Guide to the Cathedral Church of Gloucester*, 2nd edition (Gloucester).

Waller, F. S. 1884: The pinnacles of the cathedral tower, Gloucester. *Gloucestershire Notes and Queries*, 2, 245–8.

Waller, F. S. 1890: *Notes and Sketches of Gloucester Cathedral* (Gloucester).

Waller, E. W. 1911: Gloucester Cathedral Tower, *Trans B.G.A.S.* 34, 175–194.

Welander, D. 1991 *The History, Art and Architecture of Gloucester Cathedral* (Gloucester).

Willis, B. 1727: *A Survey of the Cathedrals of York, Durham, Carlisle, Chester, Man, Lichfield, Hereford, Worcester, Gloucester, and Bristol* (London).

Willis, R. 1860: [Architecture of Gloucester Cathedral. Report of his lecture] in *Archaeol. Jnl*, 17 (1860), 335–42.

Wilson C. 1985: Serlo's church at Gloucester 1089–1100. in B.A.A. Conf. Trans. 1985, 52–83.

Verey, D. and Welander, D. 1979. *Gloucester Cathedral* (Gloucester).

Archaeology and the Standing Fabric: Recent Investigations at Lichfield Cathedral

Warwick Rodwell

Although archaeological study of the fabric of cathedral churches has been carried out, in widely varying degrees of intensity, for more than a century, it is surprising how little systematic recording and analysis has actually taken place. Some cathedrals have fared better than others: Lichfield is one that falls into the latter category, despite an auspicious start in *c.* 1860. Indeed, the cathedral attracted the attentions of that notable antiquarian triumvirate of the era: Sir Gilbert Scott as architect for the restoration, James Thomas Irvine his Clerk of Works, and Professor Robert Willis. Irvine, who worked on many important buildings, was not a scholar of Willis's calibre, but was essentially an astute observer and methodical recorder of structural evidence. He published some of his work, but much has languished in manuscript. Unfortunately in the case of Lichfield, little has been preserved in either form.

Willis's own presence at the cathedral totalled a mere three days in August 1860. He coupled his own personal observations with those made previously by the clerk of works (not Irvine, at this stage), the master mason and a local doctor, and published a discourse which began as a conventional archaeological report and concluded as an architectural history (Willis 1861). For more than a century that paper has stood, augmented a little but effectively unchallenged, as the accepted structural history of the cathedral. Modern appraisals of the fabric (as opposed to the furnishings) have been very few in number, limited in scope, and art-historical in basis. However, considerable advances in analysis and synthesis have recently been made through the publication of a volume of studies based on the cathedral;the papers arose from a conference held by the British Archaeological Association in 1987 (Maddison 1993).

There has been a widespread assumption that Lichfield Cathedral holds little promise for the structural archaeologist: it was severely bombarded during the three Civil War sieges, it suffered lamentably at the hands of the Lichfield-born architect James Wyatt in the years around the turn of the nineteenth century, and was the object of a continuous programme of restoration by the Scotts between 1854 and 1908. However, despite these ravages – each of which is an important archaeological episode in its own right – a great volume of unappreciated structural evidence awaits recognition, recording and analysis (Fig. 8.1).

During the past thirteen years the Dean and Chapter have initiated several programmes of archaeological investigation, partly in response to opportunities presented during repair works, and partly in a conscious attempt to fill some of the more obvious lacunae in our understanding of the building's structural history. This enlightened approach, coupled with the enthusiastic support of the cathedral architect, Mr Martin Stancliffe, has resulted in a rapid expansion of knowledge in return for a relatively modest financial outlay. The yield of fresh information has perhaps been greater at Lichfield than might be expected at many other cathedrals, on account of the application of modern investigative procedures after a century of almost total archaeological neglect.

Even less attention has been paid by scholars, past and present, to the architectural history and archaeology of the Cathedral Close. Here, a rich inheritance of medieval, Stuart and Georgian houses survives, within the compass of an early fourteenth-century fortification. An appraisal of the documented history of the Close has recently been published by the Victoria County History (Tringham 1990), while that of the cathedral church appeared in 1970 (Kettle and Johnson 1970). A programme of archaeological investigation is currently in hand, in association with the restoration of buildings in the Close, as a complement to the documentary research. Also, series of basic survey drawings of many of the houses were prepared in 1986–87, by a team sponsored by the Manpower Services Commission and Staffordshire County Council, under the supervision of R.A. Meeson.

Lichfield has seen very little archaeological excavation, and none on a large scale. In 1976–77 Martin Carver cut a series of trenches on the site of the demolished Theological College, immediately south of the cathedral; this work demonstrated the considerable potential of the site, but was not on a large enough scale to reveal structural evidence *in extenso* (Carver 1981). In 1989–90 parts of the southern defences of the close, including the medieval gateway, were excavated.

Fig. 8.1. The central tower and the quire of Lichfield Cathedral from the south. This late eighteenth-century view shows the building in its restored state after the Civil War, but before the great era of restoration and alteration begun by James Wyatt. In the foreground is the south transept, and adjoining it to the right is the St Chad's Head Chapel complex.

The Norman and Early English Quires

Willis's most celebrated discovery at Lichfield was a Norman apse and other foundations beneath the floor of the Early English quire, but neither a satisfactory dating nor structural evolution for the sequence has been proposed. Moreover, a series of three round arches – evidently part of a low, vaulted building of late twelfth-century date – sandwiched between the south quire aisle and the consistory court and sacristy were wholly ignored not only by Willis, but even more recently by Pevsner (1971). Unpublished plans of nineteenth-century discoveries, including one showing a series of external buttress foundations alongside the quire, recorded by Irvine in 1882, compounded the confusion.

In 1986–7 fresh plans of the quire and aisles were made, and all archaeological evidence was replotted (Fig. 8.2). Stone-by-stone drawings were made of the internal aisle walls and of the enigmatic arches in the sacristy and consistory court. Examination of the cramped, unlit and evidently unexplored roof spaces above the aisles revealed not only the remains of a hitherto unsuspected Early English triforium and a rare system of early thirteenth-century aisle roofing, but also lengths of ashlar walling which were clearly older than the arcades of *c.* 1190 upon which they stood. Correlation and analysis of the evidence recorded on the different levels and planes yielded unexpected results, enabling a wholly new and more logical structural history for the eastern arm of the cathedral to be advanced (Rodwell 1987a; 1987b; 1993a).

In place of Willis's two principal periods of construction, an aisleless Norman apse of *c.* 1140 and a seven-bay square eastern termination of *c.* 1205, a revised sequence can now be offered, which includes (Figs. 8.3 and 8.4):

1. An ambulatory apse with radiating chapels (c.1085–1100).
2. An added Lady Chapel, *c.* 1150–60.
3. A reconstructed Transitional quire, feretory and four transverse eastern chapels, *c.* 1170–75.

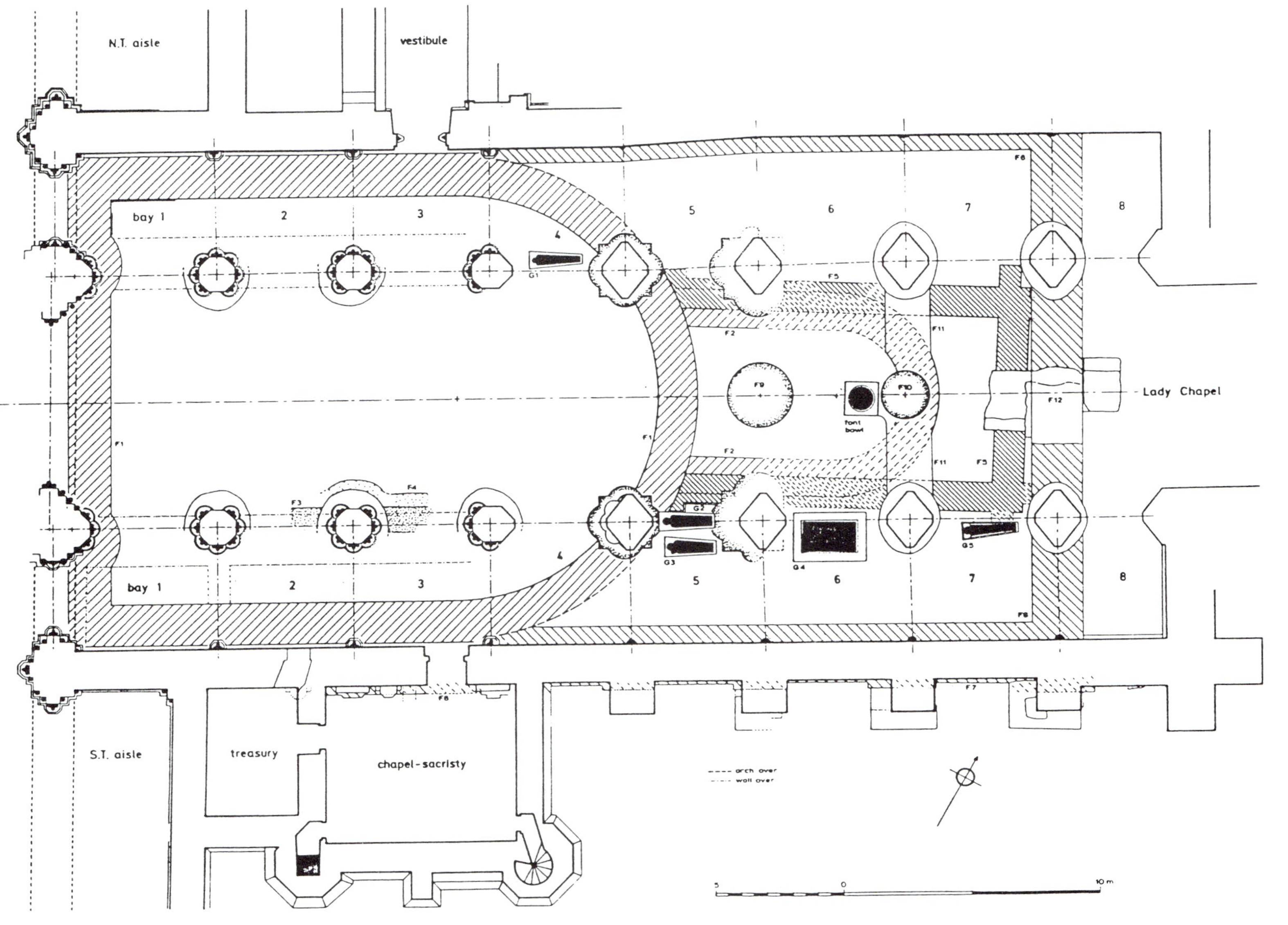

Fig. 8.2. Outline plan of the eight-bay quire and presbytery of Lichfield Cathedral, onto which has been plotted evidence for earlier foundations of all periods (shaded).

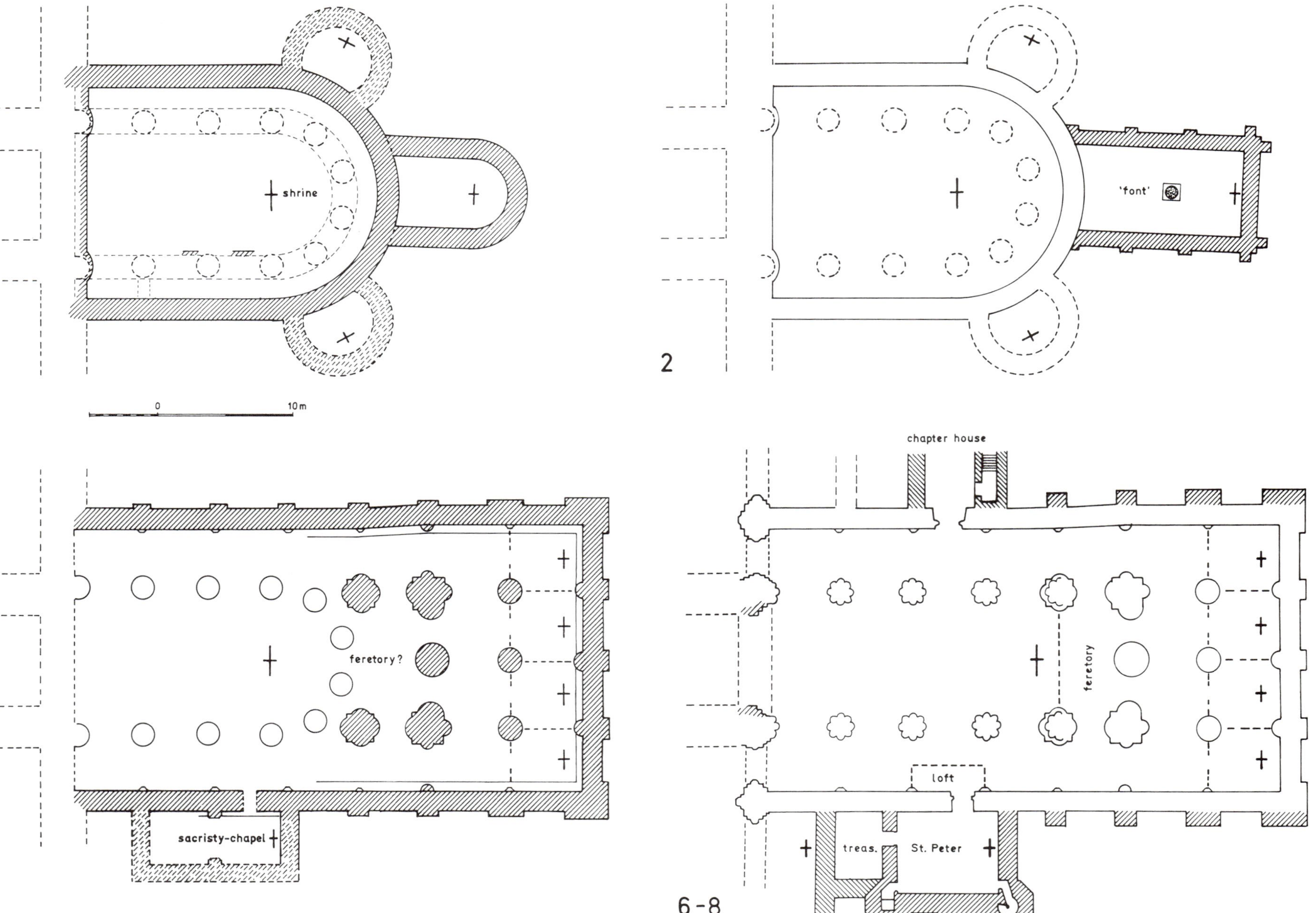

Fig. 8.3. Outline phase plans showing four of the principal stages in the development of the eastern arm of the cathedral, up to the mid-13th century. Shading represents new work of each period in turn. ***1.*** *Early Norman,* c. *1085–1100;* ***2.*** *Later Norman,* c. *1150–60;* ***3.*** *Transitional, phase I,* c. *1170–75;* ***6–8.*** *Early English, phases I–III,* c. *1200–40*

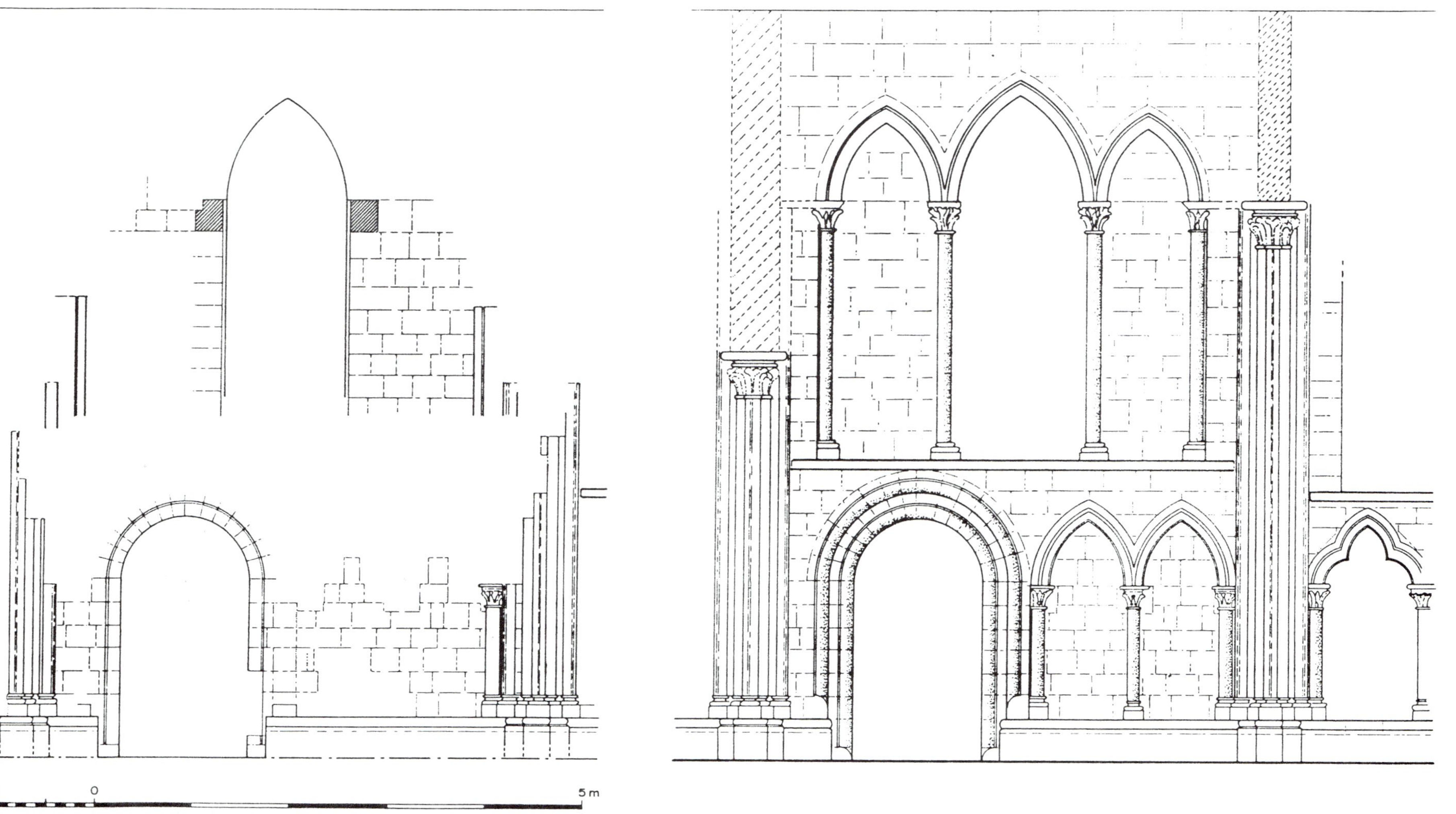

Fig. 8.4. Elevations of the third bay of the south quire aisle, showing the survival of late Norman masonry amongst subsequent work (left), and a reconstruction of the full elevation using fragmentary evidence from other bays (right).

4. Several modifications and embellishments, down to *c.* 1190.
5. Substantial reconstruction during the period *c.* 1200–40, with the addition of flanking chapels, a treasury and a possible proto-chapter house.

The St Chad's Head Chapel Complex

An enigmatic two-storey structure attached to the south side of the quire now houses a sacristy and consistory court on the ground floor and a chapel on the upper floor which, prior to the Reformation, was associated with the cult of St Chad's Head (Figs. 8.5 and 8.6). Although the common wall between this chapel and the quire embodies the three unexplained arches previously mentioned, the several elements here are clearly not contemporaneous. Furthermore, in 1981, when repairs were being carried out to the external masonry of the consistory court, a skeleton was discovered in an unmarked tomb in the south wall, at a height of 1.70 m above ground level (Rodwell 1983a; 1983b).

A detailed archaeological survey of the chapel complex was carried out in 1984–85, together with documentary research and an analysis of the many antiquarian illustrations in which this structure is depicted. It was shown that the present chapel complex – the third on the site – dates largely from *c.* 1230, and that the immured skeleton was William of Mancetter's (dean, 1222–54). The ground floor chamber, converted from lumber room to consistory court by Wyatt, is now identifiable as the medieval chapel of St Peter (Rodwell 1985a; 1985b). When William Stukeley visited Lichfield in *c.* 1715 the chapel was still adorned with the remains of its wallpaintings (Tringham 1987, 62).

Although the structure is of two storeys, with octagonal turrets at the south-east and south-west angles, no stairway linking the two levels was known; access to St Chad's Head Chapel is now via a fourteenth-century contrived wall-stair and relic-display gallery, leading off the south quire aisle. Early plans, however, show newel stairs within one turret or the other, or both; the archaeological survey demonstrated conclusively that, while there was a blocked stair in the base of the south-east turret, it could never have given access from ground to first-floor level. There was no

Fig. 8.5. The south side of the St Chad's Head Chapel complex. The thirteenth-century head-cult chapel is on the first floor, and below it is the consistory court room (formerly St Peter's Chapel). Dean Mancetter's burial (1254), in a stone coffin, is contained in the wall immediately below the sill of the lower right-hand window. Photo: Warwick Rodwell.

Fig. 8.6. East-west section through the St Chad's Chapel complex, showing the three levels of stone-vaulted chambers. The doorways in the two chapels communicate with the south quire aisle. The upper doorway is a thirteenth-century adaptation from a late twelfth-century quire window; and in the north wall of the lower chapel can be seen the remains of a Transitional Norman arcade belonging to an earlier phase of building.

stair in the other turret, the base of which contains a chamber housing a deep stone-lined shaft; although this is probably a medieval holy well, it has never been mentioned in any description of the cathedral. The well was excavated in 1992.

If the stair in the south-east turret did not ascend, it could only descend. It was hazily known that the Paget family had created a burial vault under the consistory court in 1797, and that there was an external access passage. A sketch published in the *Illustrated London News* in 1854 showed the lowering of the Marquis of Anglesey's coffin into the passage. Excavation duly located the entrance to the vault, via a nineteenth-century flight of steps and a fourteenth-century subterranean doorway. But internally the chamber proved to be yet earlier, an unrecorded barrel-vaulted crypt of the early thirteenth century, originally approached from St Peter's Chapel via the now-blocked newel stair. Thus the chapel complex is of three storeys, the lowest having been a subterranean treasury (Fig. 8.7). A second, barrel-vaulted, treasury was built at ground level in the mid-thirteenth century adjoining the chapels on the west, infilling the formerly open space between them and the south transept. This room is now the vergers' office.

Further study of a seemingly trivial series of scars and other features in the wall of the south quire aisle, adjacent to the chapel complex, demonstrated the likelihood that access to St Chad's Head Chapel in the thirteenth century was by timber stairs associated with a watching-loft, which overlooked the site of the principal shrine and feretory of St Chad in the centre of the quire. A structure akin to the surviving timber loft in the feretory at St Albans Abbey is envisaged.

Retrospectively, an allusion to the lower chapel and the crypt can be identified in the 1660 survey of squatters in the then-derelict parts of the cathedral: 'In the revestery part of God' s House' [ie St Peter's Chapel, now consistory court] lived Daniel Morgil, a labourer, with his wife and children; and 'In the lower vault of the same' [ie the crypt-treasury], were 'two women with children, both bastards, and one there lately brought to bed of a bastard' (Tringham 1984, 49). No-one apparently squatted in St Chad's Head Chapel, presumably on account of its being roofless.

The High Vaults of the Cathedral

The three-storey chapel complex was vaulted in stone at all levels., but the uppermost had been wholly destroyed, and a seventeenth-century timber roof substituted; the vault was renewed in 1897, when St Chad's Head Chapel was returned to use. The loss almost certainly occurred in 1646 when, after five days of bombardment by cannon-fire, the central spire of the cathedral was finally brought down onto the roofs below. Scant records survive of the damage wrought by the collapse, but archaeological mapping of repairs to the high vaults throughout the cathedral has recently provided a clearer picture of the physical effects of the cataclysm.

In 1985–88 a programme of cleaning and redecoration was carried out on the high vaults of the quire, transepts and crossing, and the opportunity was taken not only to study the structural history of the vaulting, but also of all the masonry and sculpture of the walls above triforium level, none of which had been accessible for study since *c.* 1870–94. The building sequences associated with the

Fig. 8.7. The thirteenth-century barrel-vaulted crypt beneath St Peter's Chapel. The doorway and steps leading up to the churchyard belong to a fourteenth-century modification. This chamber was originally constructed as a treasury, approached by a newel stair from the chapel above. In the eighteenth century the crypt was adopted by the Paget family for a mausoleum, and the tops of several tombs of the Marquises of Anglesey can be seen in the foreground. Photo: Warwick Rodwell.

central tower, transepts and quire were elucidated, and a short-lived system of early thirteenth-century wall-passages in the transepts (superseded by a second Early English triforium and clerestory arrangement) was fully recorded.

The dating and method of reinsertion of the vaults was also established: mid-thirteenth century in the nave, mid-fourteenth century in the quire, later fifteenth in the north and south transepts, and fifteenth or early sixteenth century in the crossing. As might be expected, Civil War damage was most severe in the bays abutting the central tower; here, it was found that some sections of medieval vaulting had been dismantled and re-erected, while others were entirely of seventeenth-century construction (Fig. 8.8). Some highly idiosyncratic carved bosses, with Gothic undertones, were introduced, to replace those damaged beyond redemption. One thirteenth-century boss has also strayed from the nave, to appear in a rebuilt section of the south transept vault. The study of the several series of masons' marks was vital to the elucidation of the sequence.

Likewise, masons' marks provided the crucial evidence to show that many stone mouldings of thirteenth-century origin were recycled in the fifteenth century, when the clerestories were rebuilt. As a result of the careful recording of large numbers of marks throughout the cathedral, and elsewhere in the Close, the recognition of datable workshop outputs is gradually emerging. One particularly unusual phenomenon is the dual marking of a group of mouldings by pairs of masons, in the period *c.* 1220–30; the paired marks occur in differing combinations, and are also known singly.

Fig. 8.8. A seventeenth-century vault boss decorated with a wreathed head, set into a network of fifteenth-century ribs, in the north transept. This is one of five new bosses introduced during the post-Civil War repair programme of the 1660s. Photo: Warwick Rodwell.

The South Transept

In 1988 a major programme of external stonework repair began which, over the course of a decade, will facilitate archaeological access to many high-level areas, including the entire west front, towers and spires. Commercial photogrammetry is being undertaken in advance of each phase of repair, providing a full set of elevation drawings at 1:50 scale for the use of both architect and archaeologist. Work has been completed on the great gable and facade of the south transept, where archaeological recording on a stone-by-stone basis has been undertaken. The entire central tower and spire have similarly been studied, from which much has been learned about the physical effects of the Civil War bombardment. Contrary to some accounts, the tower was not severely damaged, but the spire has been rebuilt.

The methodology employed at Lichfield is the same as that used during the conservation and recording programme on the west front of Wells Cathedral, 1976–87. The commercially-prepared drawings are rigorously checked and all detail that was invisible to the camera (behind pipes, parapets, etc) is added by hand measurement. Multiple copies of the corrected drawings are made and marked up to indicate stone-types, mortars, repairs, putlog-holes, masons' marks, and any other appropriate categories of information. One of the end-products is a set of colour-coded elevations, showing the phase of construction or repair to which each stone has been assigned, after analysis of the entire body of evidence. Another set of elevations is marked up with a full record of the present-day restoration.

The importance of distinguishing each phase of eighteenth, nineteenth and twentieth-century restoration, insofar as this is possible, cannot be stressed too strongly. A great deal can often be deduced about the form and chronology of lost medieval features through the careful study of the processes involved in their decay and removal, or renewal. It is instructive to note on the south transept that Scott, when undertaking the wholesale renewal of a moulding or repetitive band of decoration, attempted to retain just one original stone, which provides archaeological certification of the integrity of his restoration.

The Archaeology of Restoration

There has long been a tendency in cathedral studies for scholars and popular commentators to deprecate not only recent restorations and changes, but often also to condemn and dismiss out-of-hand the whole evolutionary process since the Reformation. Thus the post-medieval archaeology of British cathedrals is a virtually untouched field. Historians and art historians, although often strong in their lamentation of the physical losses which change has entailed, have nevertheless attempted to chronicle these works. Lichfield has received its share of attention (Frew 1978; Cobb 1980, 140–59; Lockett 1980a, 1980b; 1993).

These studies are primarily concerned with art-historical and liturgical changes, and with chapters in the biographies of the formidable succession of restoring architects at Lichfield. The first was James Wyatt (1787–93), followed by his assistant, Joseph Potter senior (1794–1842), who was eventually dismissed and replaced by Sydney Smirke (1842–56). He operated on his own at first, and then for a short while in tandem with Sir Gilbert Scott (1854–78). The latter was succeeded by his second son, John Oldrid Scott (1878–1908). The 120 years of almost continuous physical intervention with the cathedral and its site has yet to be chronicled and analysed in archaeological terms (Fig. 8.9).

Several episodes within this continuum have already been investigated, and some interesting insights into Victorian antiquarianism gained. One example of J. O. Scott's 'archaeological' approach to restoration has been cited, while another is superbly demonstrated in the great window of the north transept at Lichfield. Here, in 1892, he removed a huge Perpendicular window and reinstated the seven tall lancets which he claimed to have been the original arrangement of *c.* 1240. It is reported that when Scott dismantled the fifteenth-century window he discovered the masonry belonging to the original fenestration, and reinstated it. Since the later window involved a far larger expanse of glass, and much less masonry than its predecessor, it has always been difficult to accept Scott's claim, especially when all the accessible masonry in the lower parts of the reconstructed lancets is manifestly of the late

Fig. 8.9. Late twelfth-century walls and pier bases associated with a former chapel on the south side of the cathedral, seen here in Victorian heating ducts, after lifting the grills and clearing debris. These features were discovered by Scott in 1860 and left in situ, *but were unrecorded until 1985. Photo: Warwick Rodwell.*

nineteenth century.

However, when scaffold access to the heads of the lancets became available in 1987, it was immediately clear that about twenty medieval stones – voussoirs, springers, capitals and label-mouldings – were incorporated in Scott's work. The archaeological evidence is just sufficiently complete to vindicate the reconstruction in its entirety. These particular mid-thirteenth-century stones could not have been recycled in the Perpendicular window, but must have been employed to block a disused high-level intramural passage. Indeed, just such a section of clerestory passage remains alongside the transept window where Scott opened it up and left it as an archaeological feature. The passage is invisible from below, inaccessible without scaffolding, and appears not to have been previously recorded.

Unlike most other cathedrals, where post-medieval restoration was an advent of the late eighteenth century, at Lichfield it began in 1661. There is thus another full century of archaeology to explore (Cocke 1993). Indeed, Lichfield is perhaps the most important building for the study of later seventeenth and eighteenth-century ecclesiastical archaeology. Documentation is sparse and generally uninformative, and thus the study of the fabric has to begin from first principles.

In 1660 the only parts of the cathedral still adequately roofed were the vestry (later consistory court, discussed above) and the chapter house. Both were not only stone vaulted, but were also protected from cannon-fire and falling masonry by the vaulted chambers above them (St Chad's Head Chapel and the cathedral library, respectively). One might have supposed that the recognition of seventeenth-century work in the fabric would be no difficult task, and it is curious to relate that no attempt seems to have been made to identify it prior to 1986.

According to an unpublished sketch in the Bodleian Library, which is believed to have been drawn by William Dugdale, *c.* 1650, the central spire was almost entirely destroyed in the Civil War; the present spire should therefore be essentially a seventeenth-century artifact. Recent observations suggest that up to two metres of the base of the spire, on the west side only, may be medieval. Here again, the highly distinctive series of masons' marks of the seventeenth century is of critical importance for dating.

The archaeology of the high vaults has now been mapped, and that of the low (aisle) vaults will be undertaken to complete the picture. Recording on the south transept gable has provided the first opportunity since 1882 to study the great rose window. The original rose of *c.* 1220–30 would have been visible from the floor of the cathedral, but following the fifteenth-century vaulting of the transepts, it was marooned in the roof-space. Antiquarian illustrations differ markedly in their depiction of this window, showing it variously as spoked, rose-like, or catherine-wheel shaped.

The present rose window is basically wheel-shaped, with a central hub and eight radiating spokes, each being carved in baluster-form and ornamented with pronounced volutes. It is overtly classical and undoubtedly of the seventeenth century. The detailing, however, does not suggest a date after 1660, but somewhat earlier in the century: it must surely be pre-Civil War, adding greatly to its historical interest. The rose has been closely studied, showing that it has been at least partially dismantled on one occasion, and twice restored. The first restoration was in 1796, the second in 1892.

Spare Parts of the Cathedral

Using evidence remaining in the transept gable, and one surviving loose fragment of the medieval rose, it may now be possible to reconstruct the form of the window of *c.* 1220–30. This loose fragment highlights the archaeological importance of the collections of unlocated and usually, unlabelled stones which most cathedrals possess, but few cherish. Often regarded as tiresome heaps of curious rubble, many of these stones are artifacts of a very precious nature. They provide vital clues to the reconstruction of buildings, or parts, which have long since been destroyed, and are generally assumed to be lost beyond recall. In recent years, archaeologists and art historians have taken a fresh interest in these collections of 'spare parts', with some very interesting results.

Thus, at St Albans, further fragments of the great shrine have recently been located; and at Wells the lower part of a medieval statue that stood in one of the gable niches of the west front – and long since presumed lost – was found in a cupboard under some stairs in 1987, just after the conservation and study of the west front had been completed.

Lichfield also possesses a large collection of loose stones and figure sculptures, which have now been painstakingly catalogued by Dr Richard Morris. Amongst the collection are, for example, many pieces derived from the Norman cathedral; these, together with the results of recent surveys described above, will enable a much fuller reconstruction of the Norman cathedral to be attempted. Without the aid of excavation, structural archaeology has begun to recreate the eleventh and twelfth-century church in three-dimensional form. Hitherto it was known only as the plan of an undated apse.

A unique survival at Lichfield is a selection of late eighteenth-century Roman cement statues (some of which envelop the decayed remains of thirteenth-century sculptures). These were taken down from the west front during Scott's restoration and, for some unknown reason, were retained rather than discarded. Another sculpture that was brought down *c.* 1880 was the statue of Charles II, which had formed the crowning figure of tta central gable since the Restoration of the Monarchy. Charles stood on a bracket, and was protected by a crude shell-like hood. While the statue was retained as an antiquarian curiosity, the hood was discarded, along with much else from the west front.

In 1932 an object was dug up in the Close, hailed and published as an Anglo-Saxon stone chair, akin to those at Hexham and Beverley. It appears that nobody realised, at the time, that the so-called chair was actually the seventeenth-century stone canopy which, until *c.* 60 years previous, had protected the Carolean figure. The archaeological record was subsequently corrected by Jim Gould (1977).

Pavement Archaeology

The study of the quire and aisles at Lichfield brought to light a number of anomalies, concerning relationships between floors and adjacent pier-bases, wall-benches and doorways. The general belief that Scott had laid his new pavements at the medieval level had to be re-examined. One of the unexplained enigmas was the fact that the late twelfth-century wall-benches in the south aisle are too low to be used comfortably, while those in the north aisle are too high. Likewise, the plinths of the aisle-to-transept arches differ in height. These anomalies only occur in the western half of the quire, the fourteenth-century rebuilding and extension to the east being more finely balanced.

The difficulties were resolved by a variety of pieces of archaeological evidence which showed that the floor of the late Norman cathedral had sloped in sympathy with the local topography, the fall being about 30 cm from north to south. The initial levelling process had taken place, not in the eighteenth or nineteenth century for the laying of great pavements, as might have been supposed, but in the fourteenth century. This was probably found to be an aesthetic necessity at the time of introduction of ranks of ornate Gothic quire stalls.

Archaeological evidence surviving, but often unappreciated, around the bases of walls and piers in many cathedrals and parish churches, points to a complex history of sloping floors, steps, destroyed wall-benches, positions of former screens and other furnishings. Bristol Cathedral is another good example.

Ironically, it is the destruction of cathedral floors by the passage of innumerable visitors' feet that has focussed attention on their archaeology in recent years. Bristol is one of the few cathedrals to retain large areas of intact pre-Victorian flooring, in the Lady Chapel, quire aisles and transepts. A detailed archaeological survey of the south quire aisle floor in 1987 revealed that, what appears superficially to be a meaningless jumble of stone, marble and tile paving is in fact a composite artifact ranging in date from the Middle Ages to the early nineteenth century.

The few surviving medieval tile pavements in English cathedrals – as at Ely or Worcester – are generally well known and published, and it therefore came as a great surprise to discover that there is at Lichfield, in the chamber above the chapter house which is now the cathedral library, a large, almost intact, and wholly unrecorded pavement of *c.* 1300. The pavement was laid as a series of seven parallel 'carpets', each of a different design, with additional panels filling the two polygonal ends of the building (Figs. 8.10 and 8.11). Approximately half the floor is hidden by bookcases which were placed in

Fig. 8.10. Part of the polychrome tile pavement of c. *1300 in the cathedral library. This floor was laid as a series of seven 'carpets', each of a different design, with complementary arrangements in the polygonal apses at the east and west ends. Photo: Warwick Rodwell.*

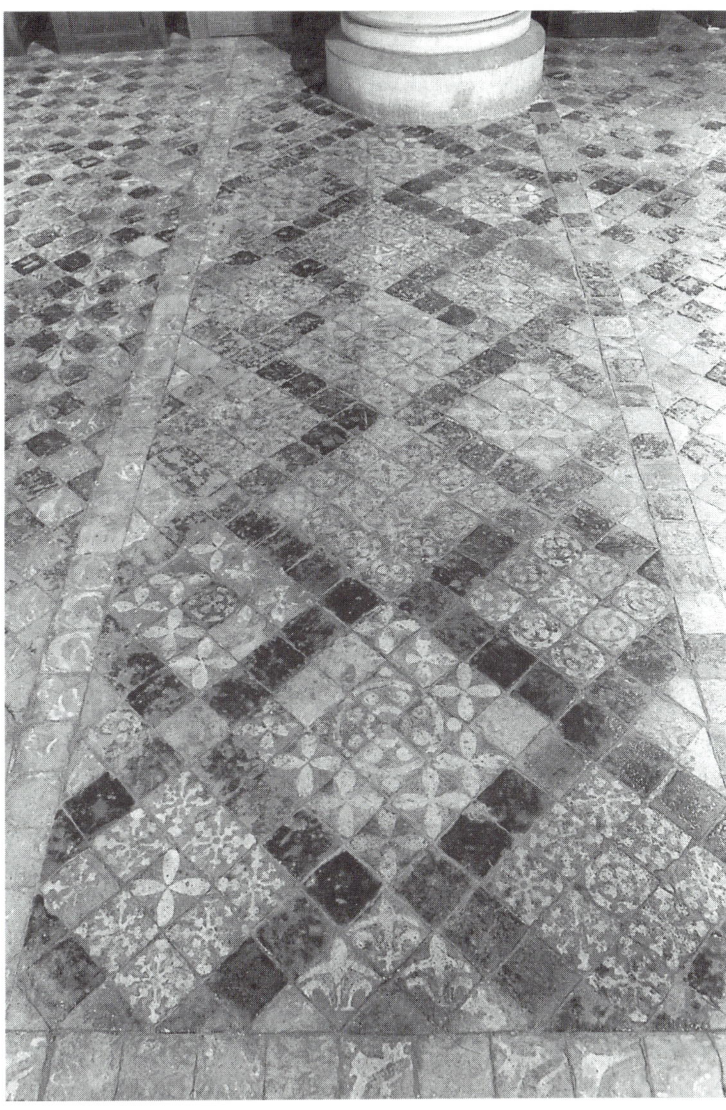

Fig. 8.11. Detail of the nine-tile and sixteen-tile patterns of the central 'carpet' of the library floor. Photo: Warwick Rodwell.

their present positions in 1910, and the visible tiling is mostly well worn. Possibly this accounts for the fact that Pevsner (1971), in company with all previous commentators, failed even to note its existence.

In 1988 it was determined that a full archaeological survey of the library pavement should be made, and the bookcases were accordingly removed. Rectified photography was employed to produce an accurate, coloured photo-mosaic at a scale of 1:10; plans, of both the complete pavement and individual panels, were drawn from a set of monochrome prints at a scale of 1:5. In this way, it was possible to detect and analyse minor misalignments of single tiles, or groups of tiles, which would have been virtually impossible to achieve by hand measurement. These misalignments, together with differential wear patterns, provided indications of ancient patching and repair.

Tiles in several parts of the floor had suffered from impact damage, the cause of which was apparently localised falls of masonry from the vaulted roof, another casualty of the Civil War bombardment. The principal damage to the pavement was, however, found to be of very recent date. The removal of the bookcases revealed that during the first 600 years of their life the tiles had suffered remarkably little wear, and some of the harder-fired examples are still in pristine condition; but in the last eighty years many of the exposed tiles – especially those in the principal gangways – have lost their glaze and much of their slipped pattern. The Lichfield pavement survey was conceived as a research project, but retrospectively it must be classed as a piece of rescue archaeology. The complete medieval design has been recovered, an achievement which would have been impossible had the project been deferred for another decade or so (Rodwell forthcoming).

Conclusion

Lichfield has often been dismissed as one of the least interesting of English cathedrals, on account of the thorough destruction and rebuilding that it is supposed to have suffered in the seventeenth century, and the successive waves of restoration in the eighteenth and nineteenth centuries. Certainly, its west front lacks anything to compare with the 297 medieval statues that Wells is able to boast, a contrast which is often emphasised. But the lack of this superficial glory has, albeit illogically, eclipsed archaeological interest in the great wealth of other fields of study which Lichfield has to offer. The Norman and Transitional quires were of unusual form; the St Chad's Head and St Peter's Chapel complex is a uniquely interesting survival, with pre-Reformation relic-cult associations; the library pavement is one of the half-dozen finest medieval floors in English churches; the archaeological potential for studying seventeenth-century fabric is without parallel in any cathedral (St Paul's, London, excepted); and few buildings can offer so much material for the structural archaeologist interested in the mechanics of cathedral restoration.

Acknowledgements

Serious archaeological investigations at Lichfield began in 1982 at the behest of the Dean and Chapter, who were anxious to discover the significance of many unrecorded features of the cathedral. The Dean and Chapter's continued interest in, and commitment to, archaeological investigation and recording during conservation and repair works is a model for emulation. The interest and support of the former Dean, Dr. J. Lang, has been a great encouragement; and the considerable assistance given by the former *Custos*, the Revd. Canon G. M. Smallwood, the present *Custos*, the Revd. Canon J. Howe and the Chancellor, the Revd. Canon A. N. Barnard is gratefully acknowledged. It is also a pleasure to record the excellent professional relationship that I have enjoyed with the Cathedral Architect, Martin Stancliffe, and the help continually given by Godfrey Hives, Head Verger. For assistance in other important matters I am grateful to, *inter alia*, Paul Drury, Jim Gould, Bob Meeson, Dr Richard K. Morris and Dr Nigel Tringham.

This paper is a modified and updated version of one which first appeared in 1989 (Rodwell 1989).

Postscript

Since writing this account, archaeological excavations have been undertaken in both the north and the south quire aisles, in conjunction with a reflooring programme. The excavations have not only substantially confirmed the structural sequence posited here, but have added much valuable detail. Parts of a hitherto unseen Anglo-Saxon cathedral church have also come to light (Rodwell 1993b; 1995).

Bibliography

Carver, M.O.H., 1981: Excavations South of Lichfield Cathedral, 1976–77. *Trans. SSAHS* 22, 35–69.

Cobb, G. (1980: *English Cathedrals: the Forgotten Centuries* (London).

Cocke, T. 1993: Ruin and Restoration: Lichfield Cathedral in the Seventeenth Century. In Maddison 1993, 109-14.

Frew, J.M. 1978: Cathedral Improvements: James Wyatt at Lichfield Cathedral. *Trans. SSAHS* 19, 33–40.

Gould, J. 1977: Saxon Cathedra or 17th-century Niche in Lichfield Cathedral. *Trans. SSAHS* 18, 69–72.

Kettle, A. and Johnson, D.A. 1970: The Cathedral of Lichfield. In *V.C.H. Staffs.* iii, 140–99. (London).

Lockett, R.B. 1980a: Sydney Smirke, Gilbert Scott and 'The Rearrangement of Lichfield Cathedral for Divine Worship': 1854–1861. *Research Bulletin of the Institute for the Study of Worship and Religious Architecture, 1980*, 3–38. (University of Birmingham).

Lockett, R.B. 1980b: Joseph Potter: Cathedral Architect at Lichfield, 1794–1842. *Trans. SSAHS* 21, 34–47.

Lockett, R.B. 1993: The Restoration of Lichfield Cathedral: James Wyatt to John Oldrid Scott. In Maddison 1993, 115-39.

Maddison, J. (ed.) 1993: *Medieval Archaeology and Architecture at Lichfield* B.A.A. Conf. Trans. 13.

Pevsner, N. 1971: The *Buildings of England: Staffordshire.* (Harmondsworth).

Rodwell, W.J. 1983a: Lichfield Cathedral, St Chad's Head Chapel: a Report upon the Investigation of a Burial found in the South Wall of the Chapel, 1982. (Lichfield Cathedral Library, manuscript report).

Rodwell, W.J. 1983b: The Skeleton in the Wall., *Forty-sixth Ann. Rep. Friends of Lichfield Cathedral.* (Lichfield).

Rodwell, W.J. 1985a: St Chad's Head Chapel and related structures at Lichfield Cathedral. (Lichfield Cathedral Library, manuscript report).

Rodwell, W.J. 1985b: Archaeology at the Cathedral: a new study of St Chad's Head Chapel, *Forty-eighth Ann. Rep. Friends of Lichfield Cathedral*, 10–14. (Lichfield).

Rodwell, W.J. 1987a: The Norman and Early Gothic Quires of Lichfield Cathedral. (Lichfield Cathedral Library, manuscript report).

Rodwell, W.J. 1987b: The Norman Quire of Lichfield Cathedral: its Plan and Liturgical Arrangement, *Fiftieth Ann. Rep. Friends of Lichfield Cathedral*, 10–14. (Lichfield).

Rodwell, W.J. 1989: Archaeology and the Standing Fabric: Recent Studies at Lichfield Cathedral, *Antiquity* 63, 281-94.

Rodwell, W.J. 1993a: The Development of the Quire of Lichfield Cathedral: Romanesque and Early English. In Maddison 1993, 17-35.

Rodwell, W.J. 1993b: Revealing the History of the Cathedral: Archaeology in the South Quire Aisle, *Fifty-sixth Ann. Rep. Friends of Lichfield Cathedral*, 23-33.

Rodwell, W.J. 1995: Revealing the History of the Cathedral 2: Archaeology in the North Quire Aisle, *Fifty-eighth Ann. Rep. Friends of Lichfield Cathedral*, 20-33.

Rodwell, W.J. forthcoming. the Archaeology of Church and Cathedral Floors. In J. Fawcett, ed., *Historic Floors at Risk: A Guide to Good Practice* (London) .

SSAHS: South Staffordshire Archaeological and Historical Society.

Tringham, N.J. 1984: Two Seventeenth-Century Surveys of Lichfield Cathedral Close. *Trans. SSAHS* 25, 35–49.

Tringham, N.J. 1987: An Early Eighteenth-Century Description of Lichfield Cathedral. *Trans. SSAHS* 28, 55–63.

Tringham, N.J. 1990: Topography: the Cathedral and the Close. In *V.C.H. Staffs.* xiv, 47-67.

Willis, R. 1861: On Foundations of Early Buildings recently discovered in Lichfield Cathedral. *Archaeol. Jnl.* 18, 1–24.

The Archaeology of Oxford Cathedral

John Blair

Although no older than 1542, the Henrician diocese of Oxford inherited the site and buildings of one of the oldest religious houses in the Upper Thames. St Frideswide's monastery, founded perhaps in the seventh and certainly by the late ninth century, stood above the broad, shallow crossing of the alluvial floodplain which gave Oxford its name. Medieval legend, probably not without some substance, made the first head of the minster a late seventh-century princess named Frideswide, daughter of the local sub-king who founded it (Blair 1987). Both the river-crossing and the minster had probably been long in existence when the planned *burh* was laid out around them *c*.900, and thereafter their presence powerfully influenced the development of the southern half of the town.

The early minster was by tradition a nunnery, but by 1004, the date of a charter of Æthelred II which provides the first solid evidence, the community had evolved like so many others into a college of secular canons. In about 1120 the minster was reconstituted as an Augustinian priory, and between the 1140s and the 1190s the reformed community carried out a total rebuilding of its church and premises, probably directed by the distinguished prior Robert of Cricklade (Blair 1990a). It was these basically Romanesque buildings that were appropriated by Cardinal Wolsey in 1524 and eventually, after many vicissitudes, incorporated into his great college of Christ Church. The twelfth-century and later arrangements are therefore known with some confidence; by contrast, the topography of the site before *c*.1140 can only be very partially reconstructed from indirect clues and from excavations of inadequate size.

The History of Archaeology at Oxford Cathedral

As the mother church of a great medieval town, St Frideswide's attracted antiquarian interest from an early date. In the 1120s the legend of the founder-saint was noted by William of Malmesbury, as well as being worked into a rather unstylish *Vita* which Prior Robert re-wrote more elegantly soon afterwards (Blair 1987). Robert quotes Æthelred II's charter which records the rebuilding of the minster after a fire in 1002, and adds his own deduction that Æthelred had enlarged the church around St Frideswide's grave because 'the grave, which had previously been on one side, came thenceforth to be the middle' (Blair 1987, 101). This seems to be based on the physical evidence of a church and grave-monument which Robert had himself seen (Blair 1990a, 247). The comment reflects the rather characteristic interest in the Anglo-Saxon past of a twelfth-century intellectual conscious of his house's venerable status.

Later in the twelfth century, a rumour that Frideswide's bones had been stolen led to more practical investigations (Blair 1987, 116–19). A group of canons entered the church at night and began to excavate the grave by torchlight. Finding an empty stone coffin they almost gave up, 'but urged by an astute man amongst them they set about digging deeper. For he said that it had once been a common practice to put empty coffins over the bodies of saints, so that if thieves came intent to steal the body they would go away deluded'. Thus encouraged, the excavators continued until they found a skeleton, whereupon all their torches were miraculously extinguished and rekindled. This story marks the early if rather dubious beginnings of archaeological excavation in Oxford: the canons are unlikely to have found Frideswide, but they may well have found part of the Anglo-Saxon cemetery now known to underlie the church.

The seventeenth-century antiquary Anthony Wood considered the development of the church with his usual thoroughness, reaching conclusions which are not so far from the current interpretation: ' 'twas wholy burnt in King Ethelred's dayes, and afterwards by him repaired; ruinated againe by time in William the Conqueror's dayes, and repaired in King Henry I time; and last of all burnt the second time anno 1190, and by the canons with severall others again re-aedified' (Wood 1890, 163). Later writers were more optimistic. In the 1830s James Ingram claimed a pre-Conquest date for the Romanesque tower (Sturdy 1990, 93), and later in the century the search for Anglo-Saxon fabric surviving above-ground was led by J.Park Harrison. Excavating with a team of workmen against the east wall of the north choir aisle, Harrison found what he interpreted as three apses entered through blocked openings still visible in the standing wall; all of this work he ascribed to the time of Frideswide herself (Harrison 1888). His conclusions were debated, with some acrimony, by the Oxfordshire Architectural and Historical Society in Michaelmas term 1887 (OA & HS 1886–93, 88–108). James Parker, who drew his own plan of the footings, commented that 'Mr. Harrison in his diagrams had drawn a good deal upon his imagination'; he accepted only one of the three apses, and for that 'there was no reason for putting the date earlier than Henry I'. Harrison responded with acid regrets 'that Mr. Parker did not wait until the stones which had been detached from the foundation-walls, some of them by the feet of visitors when examining the excavations, and so became trodden in, were removed, and the mounds of earth, which prevented accurate measurements being taken, had been levelled', and stuck to his guns. The problem was finally resolved by David Sturdy's excavation of 1963, which proved all three apses to be fictional and the standing wall to be late twelfth century (Sturdy 1990, 87–8).

Meanwhile other Victorian antiquaries were concerning themselves with the site. In 1863 the construction of Meadows Building, between the Priory cloister and Christ Church Meadow, involved a massive excavation, and the Oxfordshire Architectural and Historical Society commissioned a detailed report from the engineer, a Mr. Conradi, on the lost river-channel discovered there (OA & HS 1860–4, 217–22). In 1870 Gilbert Scott's heavy-handed restoration of the cathedral obliterated much archaeological information in the standing fabric, as well

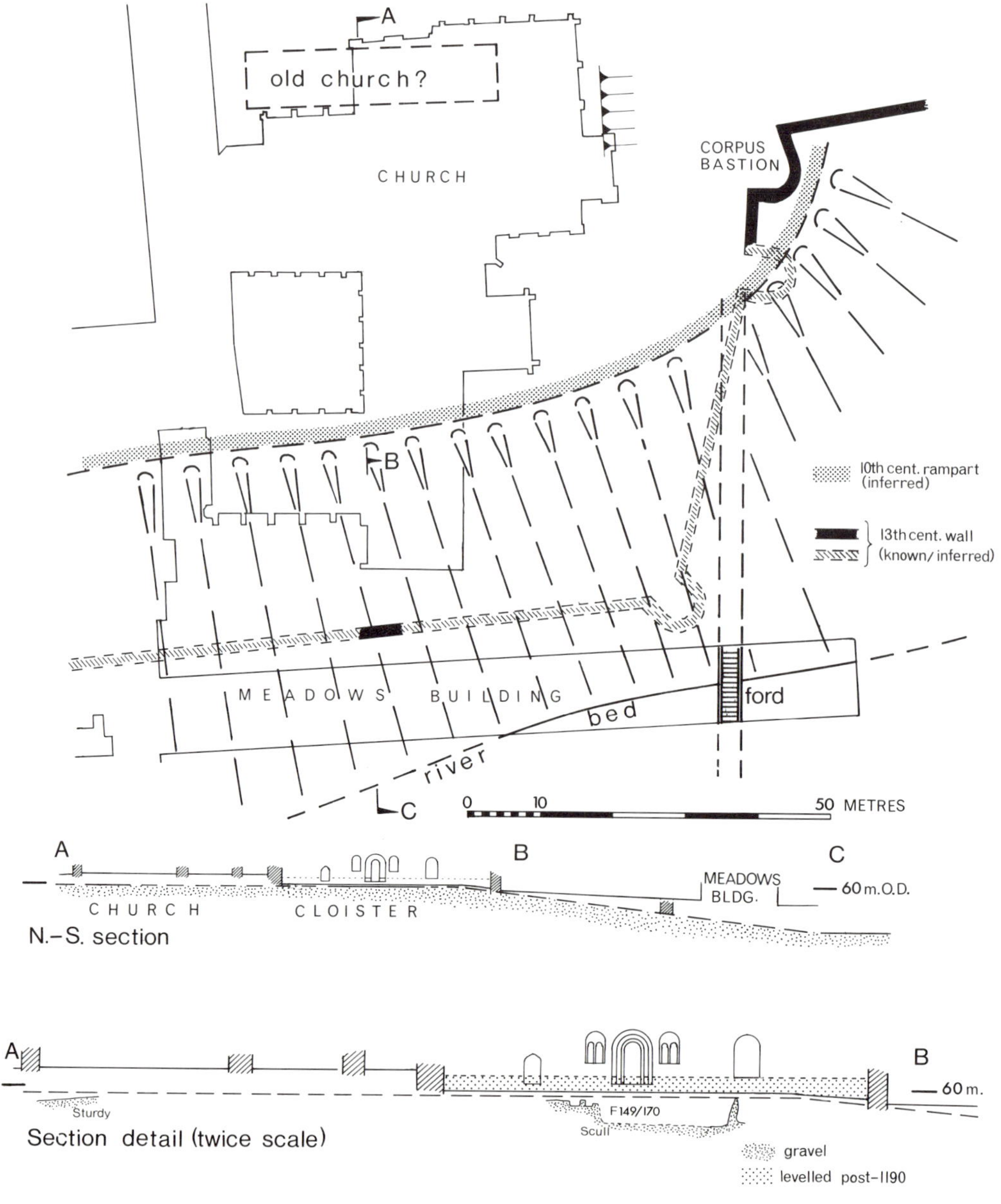

Fig. 9.1. The Priory buildings in relation to the City wall and the south edge of the gravel terrace, incorporating Conradi's observations. (After Blair 1990a, Fig. 92)

as revealing numerous re-used Romanesque fragments. Luckily the indefatigable J. C.Buckler was at hand, and made detailed sketches, plans and notes which compare favourably with much modern recording (Add.27765). Unfortunately Buckler's record, and the problems of interpretation which he raised, were ignored by the Royal Commission on Historical Monuments in its rather bland discussion of the building, and the recent analyses by Richard Halsey and Richard Morris are the first serious attempts to get to grips with its complexities (RCHM 1939; Halsey 1990; Morris 1990).

Modern excavations have been informative but small-scale. In 1962–3 David Sturdy dug a series of trenches in and around the north-eastern chapels, clarifying the Romanesque and subsequent phases of this part of the church without throwing any light on its Anglo-Saxon past (Sturdy 1990). In 1972, however, Tom Hassall observed two pre-Conquest charcoal burials in the south-east corner of Tom Quad, and Christopher Scull's larger excavation in 1985 revealed more graves from what was evidently a large cemetery established by the 9th century (Hassall 1973; Scull 1990). Only excavation on a large scale in Tom Quad or the Cathedral Garden, of which there is no immediate prospect, can hope to locate the Anglo-Saxon minster.

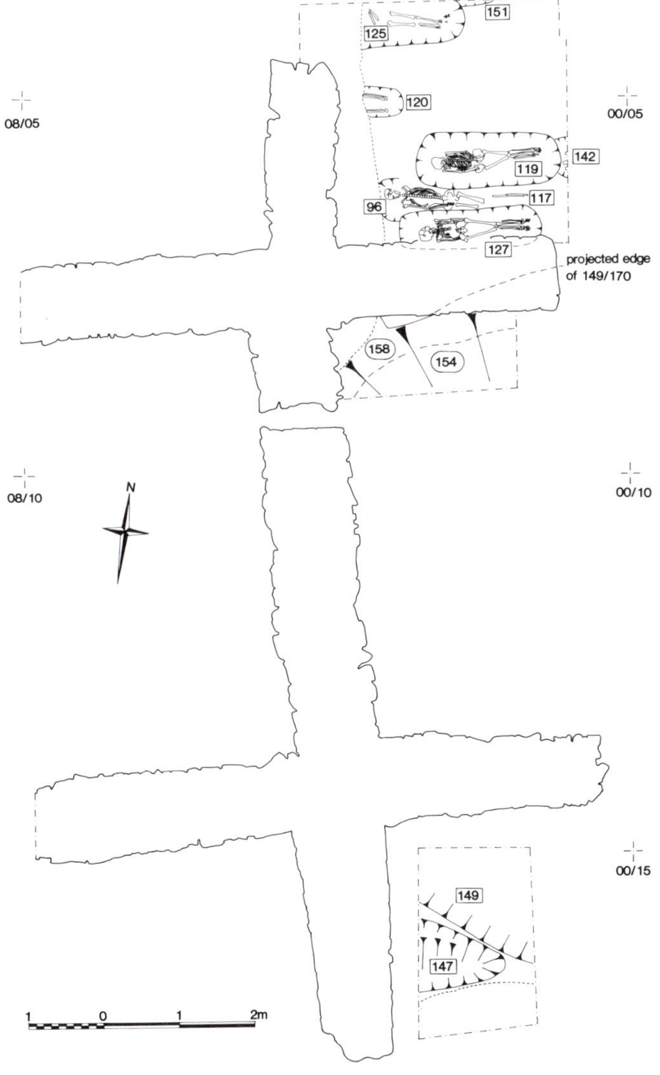

Fig. 9.2. Excavations in the Priory cloister, 1985: ninth- and tenth-century graves cut by the cross-shaped foundation of Wolsey's timber bell-frame. (After Scull 1990, Fig. 15)

The Site and the Monastic Buildings

The cathedral stands on the extreme southern tip of the Oxford gravel terrace, overlooking the Thames floodplain. Softened by centuries of dumping and levelling, the relief of the area is not conspicuous today, but in the early middle ages it would have appeared as a classic type of monastic site: a raised eminence overlooking water. Conradi's observations of 1863 showed that only a few metres south of the cloister the gravel terrace descends into a lost channel of the Thames, which probably served as a defensive ditch along the south side of the late Anglo-Saxon town (OA & HS 1860–4, 217–22; Blair 1990a, 228–32). The material found by Conradi includes the only archaeological trace of the Anglo-Saxon church that has yet come to light: a relief-impressed floor-tile of a kind now recognised as characteristic of rich early eleventh-century monastic sites (Biddle and Kjlbye-Biddle 1990).

Fig. 9.3. Reconstruction of mid eleventh-century pavement of relief-impressed tiles, based on the one extant example. (After Biddle and Kjlbye-Biddle 1990, Fig. 103)

The size of the early precinct is unknown: there are hints, both written and archaeological, that it may have extended westwards across the whole southern part of the early town, including two or three churches in line of which the most easterly is represented by the Romanesque priory church (Blair 1987, 88–9; Blair 1990a, 231–5). Another may be perpetuated as the parish church of St Aldate, the graveyard of which has produced a burial with a lavish eleventh-century gold ring (Graham-Campbell 1990).

At least four phases in the development of the Romanesque church and cloister can be identified (Halsey 1990; Blair 1990a; Munby 1990). The west range, including the dormitory and the chapter-house with its lavish entrance, was built in about the 1150s, probably by masons trained at, or influenced by, Reading Abbey who were also responsible for the local churches of St Peter-in-the-East and Iffley. The choir, probably built in the 1160s, introduced the 'giant order' elevation system which was later followed in the nave and aisles. Irregularities of plan suggest that the church was originally planned with two-bay, unaisled transepts, but as St Frideswide's cult pros-

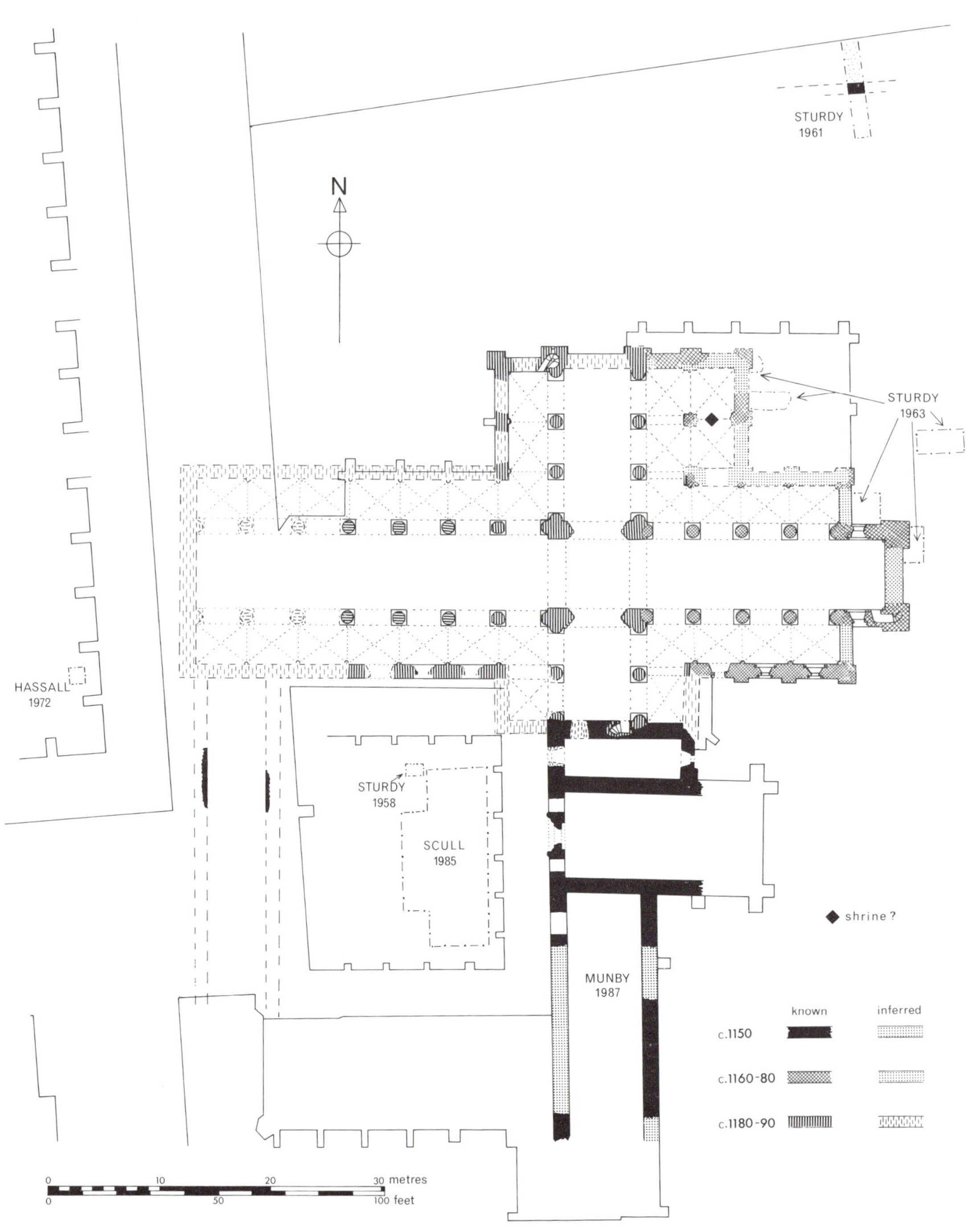

Fig. 9.4. Reconstructed plan of the Priory church and cloister as completed c.1200. (After Blair 1990a, Fig. 97)

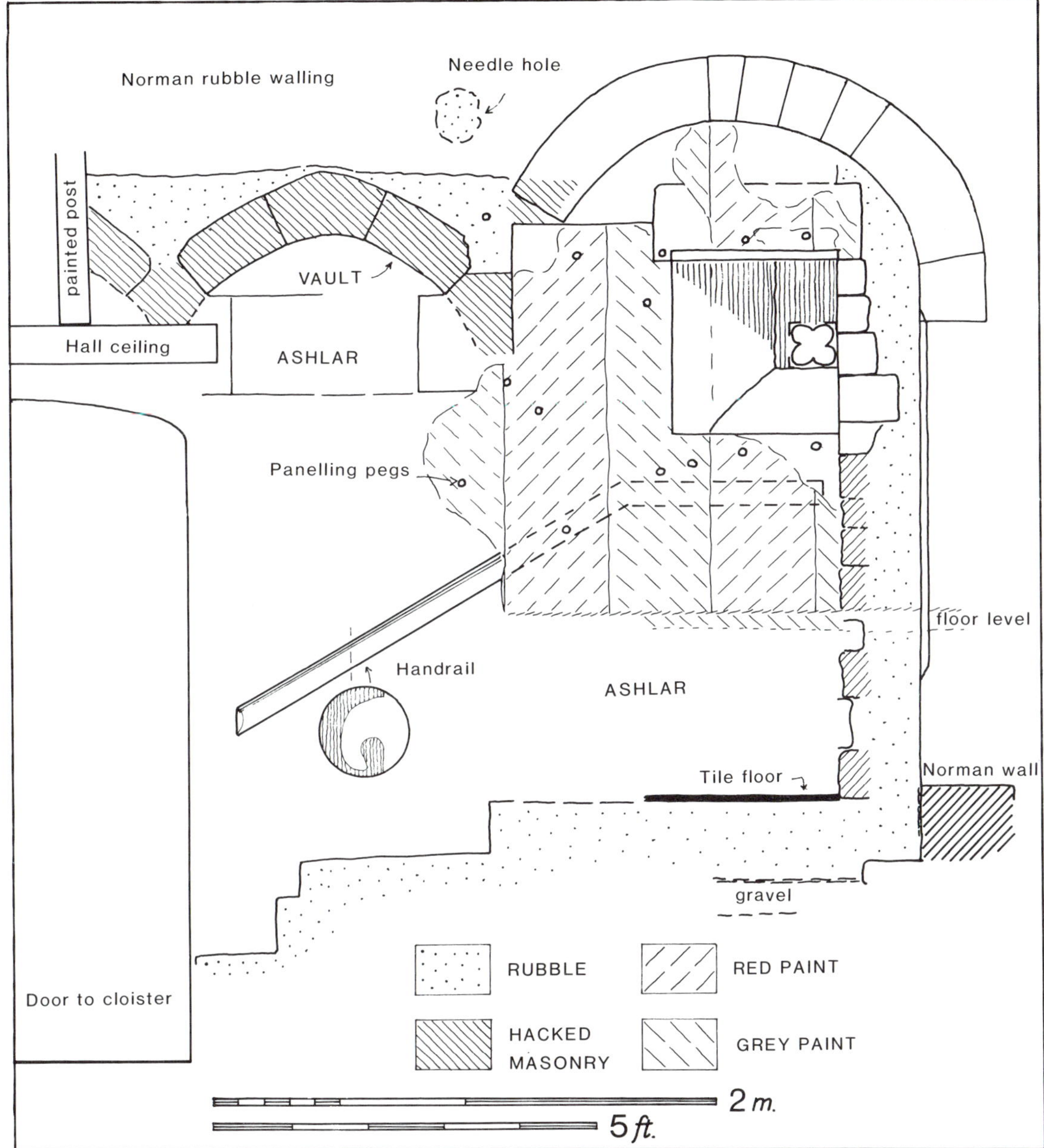

Fig. 9.5. West elevation of the twelfth-century doorway of the day-stair into the cloister, with features probably inserted during a refurbishment in 1489. (After Munby 1990, Fig. 79)

pered during the 1170s and 1180s the decision seems to have been taken to extend the transepts by one bay and provide them with western and eastern aisles. In the 1190s money seems to have run short, and the detail of the last bays of the nave is poorer than in earlier parts of the church. After a fire – almost certainly the one recorded in 1190 – the level of the garth was lowered and the chapter-house front remodelled, with new bases distinguishable from the earlier work on stylistic grounds and by absence of fire-staining.

Much remains obscure, but St Frideswide's illustrates how far knowledge of a building can be increased through correlation of successive below-ground observations combined with systematic study of the fabric. Although there is no substitute for large-scale excavation, the recording of minor observations as the opportunity arises is a cost-effective means of acquiring data with which to direct future work.

St Frideswide's Shrine and its Setting

The north-eastern chapels, in the angle between the choir and the north transept, must be one of the most complex areas of any English church, and rigorous three-dimensional analysis is required to unravel the successive phases between the mid twelfth and mid fourteenth centuries. Even with the help of Sturdy's excavation, uncertainties remain about the date and function of the chapels, but there is now a consensus that their main function was to house St Frideswide's shrine.

Footings and standing fragments represent a chapel built

in the 1160s or 1170s, almost certainly to receive the shrine made in 1180 when the relics were translated from their below-floor grave. Different reconstructions of the original plan are possible, but perhaps the most likely is a square of four bays with a central pier, the two western bays being absorbed shortly afterwards into the east aisle of the north transept (Blair 1990a, 242–4; Sturdy 1990, 94; Halsey 1990, 139–46). This arrangement, comprising vaults on a central pier, suggests an upper storey, and it seems possible that the chapel had a raised chamber or gallery for displaying the relics towards the north transept.

The relics were translated again in 1289, into the sumptuous Purbeck marble shrine of which portions still survive. The arcade between the two northernmost chapels may date from this occasion; more certainly, the shrine chapel itself (the present 'Latin Chapel') was lavishly rebuilt in about the 1330s, possibly by the St Albans master-mason Henry Wy (Morris 1990; Blair 1990a, 245–6). Fragments of a late medieval tile pavement recorded by Sturdy included an especially elaborate area, perhaps defining the liturgically important space in front of the shrine (Sturdy 1990, 80, 94–100).

The study of English saints' shrines has been hampered by an assumption that conventional arrangements applied universally: the guesswork of one generation becomes the 'tradition' of the next. At Oxford, careful analysis of the evidence shows that the shrine always occupied an unconventional position, which in turn makes it possible to interpret some once-puzzling features of the building. The case illustrates how much can still be recovered of the architectural settings of local cults, the systematic study of which has scarcely begun.

Dissolution and Rebirth

Work on Wolsey's vast quadrangle to the north-west of the old Priory buildings proceeded apace between January 1525 and October 1529 (Maclagan 1954, 228–31). The last three bays of the nave were demolished, and so near did the church come to destruction that scaffolding was bought in 1528–9 'for the takinge downe of the old stepull' (Biddle 1990, 206). A footing in the cloister has recently been interpreted as the foundation of a temporary timber belfry, built in 1529 to take the bells of St Frideswide's pending their transfer to Wolsey's new bell-tower (Scull 1990, 67–72; Biddle 1990). But Wolsey fell, his quadrangle and bell-tower stood uncompleted, and the truncated Priory church gained a temporary reprieve. Henry VIII originally planned to destroy the Cardinal's college completely, but grudgingly allowed it to continue on minimal endowments (Batey and Cole 1990, 212).

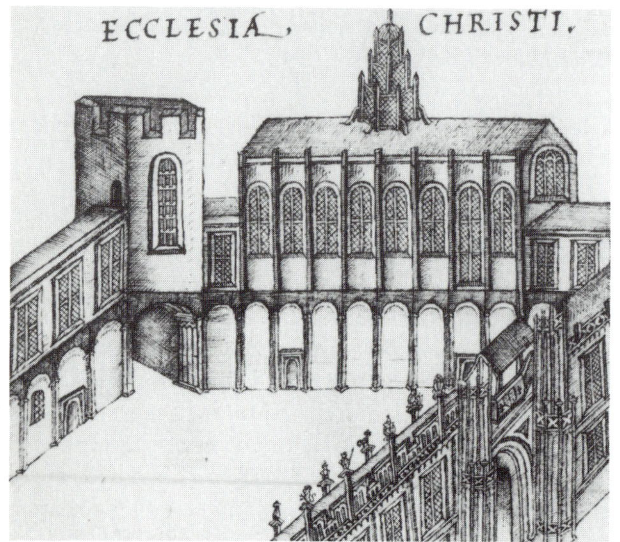

Fig. 9.6. Bearblock's drawing of Christ Church in 1566, looking S.E. (After Biddle 1990, Fig. 86. Reproduced by permission of the Curators of the Bodleian Library)

In 1542 the enormous diocese of Lincoln was divided,

Fig. 9.7. Reconstruction of the timber bell-frame built by Wolsey in the Priory cloister in 1529. (After Scull 1990, Fig. 33)

and a new see established at Oxford. Oseney Abbey was the first choice for the new cathedral, and the little that we know about it suggests that it had a much grander church and precinct than St Frideswide's (Sharpe 1985). But after a period of indecision the see was transferred, perhaps appropriately, to the mother church of Oxford; Wolsey's college (already refounded once in 1532 as 'King Henry VIII's College') was again surrendered and, in November 1546, united with the new cathedral as 'Ecclesia Christi Cathedralis Oxon' (Maclagan 1954, 231). Thus the old Priory church acquired its unique dual character as cathedral and college chapel, its canons forming part of the Christ Church governing body.

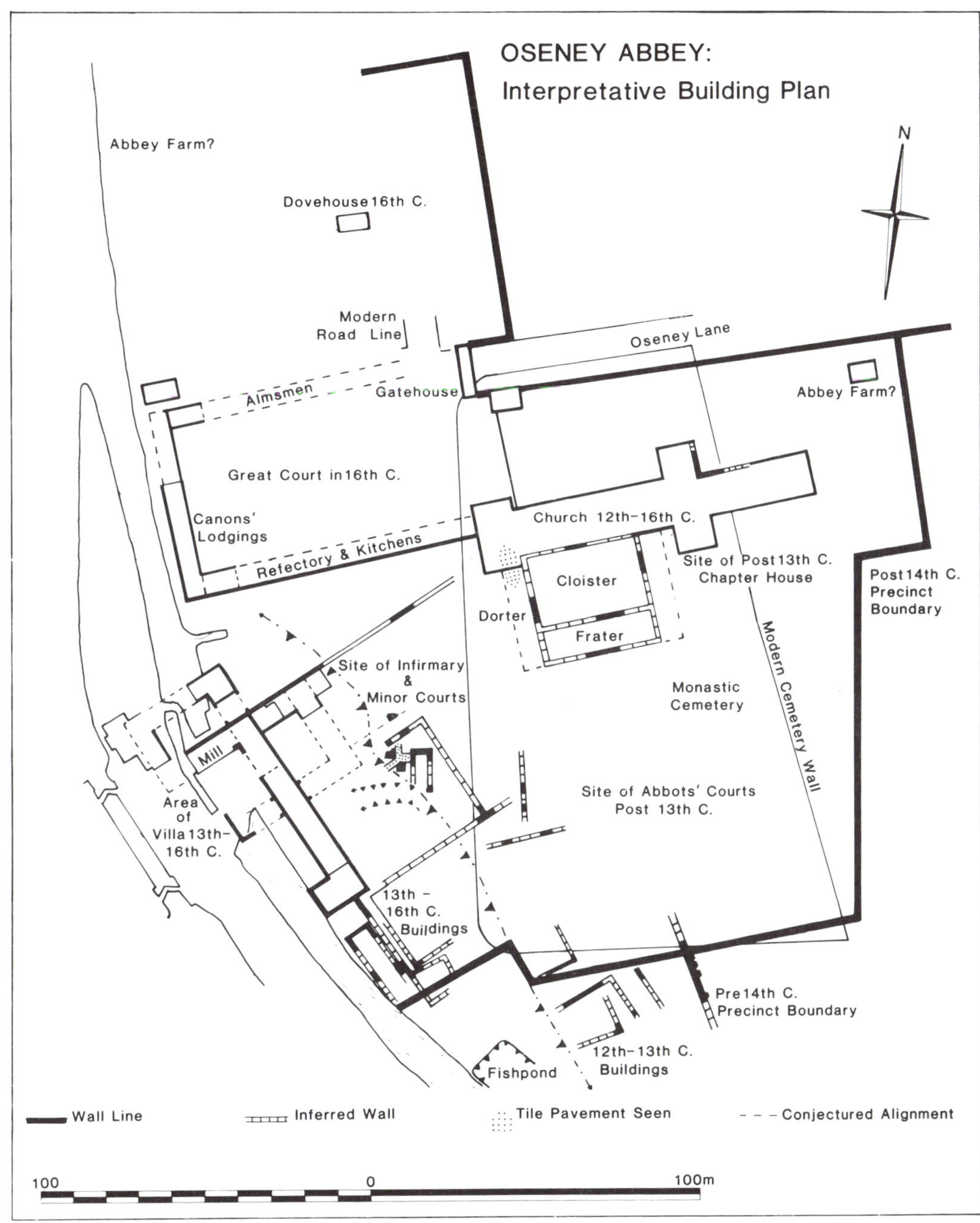

Fig. 9.8. Reconstructed plan of Oseney Abbey and its outbuildings. (After Sharpe 1985, Fig. 8)

Although Christ Church was generously endowed by the king, there was little surplus cash for new building. The gap left by Wolsey's demolitions in the nave was built up, and parts of the claustral ranges were converted into canons' lodgings; but the great quadrangle remained incomplete, a sad sight with its litter of masonry and rubble (Batey and Cole 1990, 213–14; Munby 1990, 191–2). The cathedral was maintained by the College, and indeed seems to have acquired the atmosphere and the liturgical routine of a college chapel; in 1847 the few public services held were said to be 'the most slovenly and irreverent' performed in any English cathedral (Cooper 1979, 369). Revived and restored by Dean Liddell in the later 19th century, the cathedral at last served its proper function. Yet it remains something of an anomaly: still attached to its cloister, closed off from the outside world by the vast open space of Tom Quad, too big for a college chapel and too small for a cathedral (and specifically exempted from the *Care of Cathedrals* Measure). Few informed visitors could long mistake it for anything other than a monastic church.

Bibliography

Add.27765: British Library MSS Add.27765 E, F and G: notes and drawings by J. C. Buckler.

Batey, M. and Cole, C. 1990: The Great Staircase Tower of Christ Church. *In* Blair 1990, 211–20.

Biddle, M. 1990: 'Wolsey's Bell-Tower'. *In* Blair 1990, 205–10.

Biddle, M. and Kjlbye-Biddle, B. 1990: An Early Medieval Floor-Tile from St Frideswide's Minster. *In* Blair 1990, 259–63.

Blair, J. 1987: St Frideswide Reconsidered. *Oxoniensia*, 52, 71–127.

Blair, J. 1990a: St Frideswide's Monastery: Problems and Possibilities. *In* Blair 1990, 221–58.

Blair, J. 1990: *Saint Frideswide's Monastery at Oxford: Archaeological and Architectural Studies* (published as part of *Oxoniensia*, 53 for 1988, and separately by Alan Sutton Ltd., Gloucester, 1990).

Cooper, J. 1979: Churches. In *V.C.H. Oxon.* iv, 369–412.

Graham-Campbell, J. A. 1990: The Gold Finger-Ring from a Burial in St Aldate's Street, Oxford. *In* Blair 1990, 263–6.

Halsey, R. 1990: The 12th-Century Church of S. Frideswide's Priory. *In* Blair 1990, 115–67.

Hassall, T. G. 1973: Excavations at Oxford, 1972. *Oxoniensia*, 38, 270–4.

Maclagan, M. 1954: Christ Church. In *V.C.H. Oxon.* iii, 228–38.

Morris, R. K. 1990: The Gothic Mouldings of the Latin and Lady Chapels. *In* Blair 1990, 169–183.

Munby, J. T. 1990: Christ Church, Priory House: Discoveries in St Frideswide's Dormitory. *In* Blair 1990, 185–93.

OA&HS 1860–4: *Proc. of the Oxfordshire Archit. and Hist. Soc.* new ser.1.

OA&HS 1886–93: *Proc. of the Oxfordshire Archit. and Hist. Soc.* new ser. 5.

RCHM 1939: *The City of Oxford* (Royal Commission on Historical Monuments).

Scull, C. 1990: Excavations in the Cloister of St Frideswide's Priory, 1985. *In* Blair 1990, 21–73.

Sharpe, J. 1985: Oseney Abbey, Oxford: Archaeological Investigations, 1975–83. *Oxoniensia*, 50, 95–130.

Sturdy, D. 1990: Excavations in the Latin Chapel and Outside the East End of Oxford Cathedral, Winter 1962/3. *In* Blair 1990, 75–102.

Wood, A. 1890: *Survey of the Antiquities of the City of Oxford by Anthony Wood*, ed. A.Clark, ii (Oxford Hist. Soc. 17).

Archaeology and Rochester Cathedral

Tim Tatton-Brown

The County of Kent is unique in having within it two dioceses, both of which originated in the years immediately after St. Augustine's arrival in England in AD 597. Because of this, the diocese of Rochester, which only occupies the western third of Kent, has always been in the shadow of Canterbury. In fact in the later Anglo-Saxon period, and for over a century and a half after the arrival in 1077 of Gundulf, its most famous bishop, it was totally controlled from Canterbury, with the bishop of Rochester being little more than a suffragen to the archbishop. Gundulf did, however, 'look after' the diocese of Canterbury during the long interregnunum between 1089 and 1093 and during Anselm's exile. Only in 1238 did the archbishop cease to hold the patronage of the bishopric (Thorpe 1769, 958).

During that century and a half, however, Rochester Cathedral gained much from the archbishop's patronage and Canterbury's great wealth, and as a result much of the medieval shell of the present cathedral was built during that period of 'subservience'. It is also important to remember that Gundulf's arrival as bishop saw the conversion of the cathedral from a secular to a major monastic one (there were over 60 monks by 1108) and the heyday of Rochester's Benedictine priory was from the end of the eleventh century until the early fourteenth century. By the end of the twelfth century, for example, it already had a library with over 300 books, and a fine collection of claustral buildings; the latter, most unusually, situated to the south-east of the cathedral (Hope 1900).

Since the late eleventh century Rochester Cathedral has always been overshadowed, literally, by a great royal castle which has undergone several major sieges (in 1088, 1215, and 1264). These periods of chaos naturally had an adverse affect on the cathedral and priory, which occupied a very constrained site between the castle, high street and city walls in the southern part of the city (Livett 1895). In 1215, for example, we know that king John desecrated the cathedral, and stole the silver retable from behind the High Altar (Hope 1898, 309).

Today the most noticeable thing about Rochester Cathedral is the evidence it exhibits, particularly the external evidence, for massive restoration and rebuilding campaigns in the last century and a half. These restorations, which affected almost all of the fabric of the cathedral, will be looked at further below, as they of course greatly influence any understanding of the earlier medieval fabric of the building. Despite this, Rochester still contains some exceptionally important remains (the mid-twelfth century west doorway, the remains of the uniquely early thirteenth century choir stalls and the early fourteenth century 'chapter room' doorway, to mention just three examples), and it is time for much more archaeological recording to take place in the cathedral.

As it happens, almost all previous archaeological work on the fabric of the cathedral, below and above ground, took place in the second half of the nineteenth century, and this too will be considered in more detail below. The culmination of this work was Sir William St. John Hope's monumental 'architectural history of the cathedral church and monastery of St. Andrew at Rochester' (Hope 1898 and 1900), and this is still unsurpassed as the standard work. It is, however, greatly in need of revision.

Restoring Rochester Cathedral

Before the major restoration campaigns of the nineteenth and early twentieth centuries, the cathedral was the subject of a number of repairs and minor restorations, the documentary evidence for which has been gathered by Hope (1898). The shrines of Saints Paulinus, Ythamar and William must have been smashed in 1538, followed ten years later by the altars, images, etc. In 1591, however, after a major fire in the chancel, a restoration (costing £5 5s. 6d.) was carried out. The Treasurer's accounts tell us that this included the making of a new pulpit with iron, wainscot, etc. Seven years later, Merton college, Oxford paid for a new monument for their founder, bishop Walter (1274–7). Archbishop Laud's Visitation of 1633 records that 'the cathedral suffered much for want of glass in the church windows', and the Dean and Chapter duly replied that 'there hath been of late years upon the fabric of the church, and making of the organs, expended by the church above one thousand pounds.'

Work on the west front is also recorded at about this time.

In September 1642 the cathedral was plundered and

damaged, though not as badly as Canterbury and many other cathedrals. After this,

> 'the body of the church (the nave) was used as a carpenter's shop and yard, several saw pits being dug, and frames for houses made by the city joiners in it' (Hasted IV 1798, 105).

Soon after the Restoration of Charles II, major repairs took place, and bishop John Warner (1637–66) left £2,000 towards this work in his will. We are also told that Dean Nathaniel Hardy (1660–70)

> 'took great pains to repair the whole of it, which was affected by means of the benefactions of the gentry of the county, and £7,000 added by the Dean and Chapter.'

Among particular areas of work mentioned are the south aisle wall restored and recased in 1664. This was no doubt required after the destruction in the 1650s of the neighbouring buildings of the bishop's palace. In 1670, 40 feet of the north aisle was 'rebuilt from the ground.' This was in the middle section, and evidence for this is still visible as it is here that the Romanesque pilasters and decorated string courses are missing. In 1680 repairs were also carried out to the tower and spire.

During the eighteenth century other repairs and refurbishings are also recorded in the Chapter Act Books, though the physical evidence for almost all of this was swept away in the 19th century. In 1707,for example, a new altar piece of 'Norway oak' was put up, while in 1742–3 the choir was repaired

> 'as to new wainscot stalls, pews, etc., at a large expense and very handsomely new paved in Bremen and Portland stone under the direction of Mr. Sloane, at which time the bishop's throne was rebuilt at the charge of bishop Joseph Willcocks' (Hasted IV 1798, 102).

Charles Sloane (1690–1764) was a typical eighteenth century man-of-many-parts. He lived at Gravesend and was a carpenter architect, surveyor and cartographer. In the 1730s he had been the rebuilder of St. George's church, Gravesend and the surveyor of various new Turnpike roads in West Kent. He also drew estate maps and in 1744 started to build the debtors' prison at Maidstone. Soon afterwards he became mayor of Gravesend. At Rochester cathedral in 1749 he also designed and 'started to erect a new steeple' (Erwood 1956,213). For this, we are told 'he made a wooden model, which was still preserved in St. William's Chapel in the late 18th century.' Sadly the model has subsequently disappeared. If it could be rediscovered, it might tell us much about the original 1343 spire which was destroyed in 1826. Whether Sloane built a brand-new timber and lead spire or just repaired the existing structure is unknown. The latter, however, is much more likely. Two years later, in 1751, two great brick buttresses were built to support the south-east transept 'on pursuance of the advice of the late Mr. Sloane' (Sloane did not in fact die until 1764, however). The following year, archbishop Herring, a former Dean of Rochester, gave £50 for furnishing the altar area. Twenty years later the south-east transept was still a great cause for concern with its considerable lean to the south. Its roof was then'lightened'(by removing the gable end), and the architect Robert Mylne was consulted.(He had also reported on the condition of the north-west tower at Canterbury Cathedral in 1768).

> 'By his direction piles of brick have been reared in the undercroft and within the aisle, and other methods used to discharge the weight of the upper works. The scheme has hitherto fully answered the purpose' (Thorpe 1788, 169).

Most of the brickwork put into the crypt at this time is still visible, though the outer wall was completely rebuilt half a century later by Cottingham. A little after this, the top of the bell-tower (Gundulf's tower, as it was now called) was removed and used 'for building material.' At least the rest of the bell-tower did not come down as it did at Salisbury Cathedral in 1790. In 1763 the pinnacles on the outer turrets of the west front were taken down, and the remainder of the north turret was rebuilt 'from the ground'. Shortly afterwards a crenellated top was added to this turret and to the west end of the nave aisle roofs (Thorpe 1788, 183). By the end of the eighteenth century the cathedral was in a sad state. It was described thus by the Kent historian, Edward Hasted (IV 1798, 106):

> 'Notwithstanding which [ie. the earlier restorations], time has so corroded and weakened every part of this building, that its future existence for any length of time has been much feared, but this church has lately had every endeavour used, and great repairs have been made which it is hoped will secure it from the fatal ruin which has threatened it, the inside has been beautified, and being kept exceeding clean, it makes at this time a very pleasing appearance.'

A decade or so later, however, there was to be more destruction, and the north and south transept gables were taken down and replaced by lower ones of 'debased classical character' (Hope 1898, 257 & 264).

In 1825 the first of a series of large-scale and very costly restorations (and rebuildings) got underway. This work culminated eighty years later with the rebuilding of the spire. and since that time (ie. about 85 years ago) no other major changes have taken place. The first of these campaigns, which cost nearly £10,000 was carried out by Lewis Cottingham from 1825–1830, and it is only possible here to summarize the main works:

a) The demolition of the spire and tower upper stage and the recasing of the lower stage and building of a large new tower upper stage with pinnacles.

b) The removal of the brick buttresses and recasing of the south-east transept with a new vertical face and gable above of Bath stone.

c) The taking down and removal of the great west window and the decorated spandrels over it, and the battlemented parapet above. The whole renewed in Bath stone. Hope (1898, 285) says that the remains of the old Norman diaper-pattern decoration was 'relegated to the crypt' (For this, now see Miele 1994).

d) Partial repair of two western corner turrets.

e) The arches into the eastern aisle unblocked, and the doorway and screen at the west end of the south choir aisle removed eastwards to the southernmost of the two arches at the top of the steps (Hope 1898, 285)

f) Complete refurbishment of the choir 'to the designs of Mr. Blore'. A new 'Gothic' organ case and west front to the pulpitum was also made after most of the 18th century woodwork was removed.

g) Provision of major new roofs over the choir and eastern arm.

h) Refurbishing of the presbytery, including the replacement of the high altar area.

During this work the painted effigy and tomb of bishop John of Sheppey (died 1360) was rediscovered. It had been walled up in 1681 behind the great monument to archdeacon Lee Warner. Unfortunately the effigy was subsequently heavily repainted, so little now survives to tell us anything about the medieval colours. An undated account of the tomb was published soon afterwards entitled *Some Account of an Ancient Tomb, etc., discovered at Rochester Cathedral by L.N. Cottingham,Arch.* There were also notes in the *Gentlemen's Magazine* (95 parts i and ii (1825), 76 and 225–6) and in *Archaeologia* (25, 122–6). This perhaps counts as the first 'archaeological' work at Rochester Cathedral. A little bit later on, while removing the choir pulpit, Cottingham uncovered the magnificent fragment of a 13th century 'wheel of fortune' wall-painting in the choir.

In 1853 Bishop Walter of Merton's tomb was once again totally rebuilt. All the 17th century work was swept away parts of this now lie in fragments in the cathedral lapidarium), and R.C. Hussey was comissioned to produce a new effigy. The earlier effigy was moved into the neighbouring north-east transept bay. It now seems to have disappeared (Blair 1994).

In 1871, George Gilbert Scott (knighted the following year) started work on an even larger campaign of restoration (the cost was over £30,000), and between 1872 and his death in 1878,the following major works were undertaken:

a) The underpinning of the south transept (1872) and the rebuilding of the gable wall above.

b) Rebuilding of the east end, including high gable restoration, and inserting three new '13th century windows' in the upper wall to replace 'an ugly late perpendicular window' (Hope 1898, 280 & 285). Also three lower lancets in east wall restored.

c) Much refacing of the eastern arm generallly (including north and north-east transepts) and replacing of decayed Reigate stone with Chilmark stone. Also new high-pitched gables and many pinnacles added to the tops of angle-turrets (the proposed new high-pitched roofs over the presbytery were never built).

d) Blocking of triforium passages and inserting of iron ties in the nave to counteract weaknesses in nave wall. Also underpinning of south nave aisle wall (1875–6).

e) Cutting of tunnel from crypt (west end) to under the pulpitum screen for the windtrunks for the organ bellows, also rebuilding of organ (1875).

f) Complete repaving and refurbishing of choir and presbytery with new high altar and reredos (1873–5). Rediscovery and repainting of 14th century wall-paintings behind the 18th century panelling behind the choir-stalls.

g) Start of west front restoration, but Scott died before much work was done (1878).

In a letter, to the Dean and Chapter, about this last stage of his work, Scott says:

> 'The Norman remains ....are almost too valuable to be interfered with. It is an open question whether a restoration, in part conjectural, should be attempted or whether it may not be best to adhere to the present form of the front, and to limit our operations to more necessary repairs.'

A very wise statement which should have been adhered to. The young William St.John Hope, who came to teach at Rochester just three years after Scott's death, said in summary (Hope 1898, 285):

> 'A good deal of necessary repair work was done to the stonework, and on the whole the 'restoration' was conservative and involved the destruction of very little old work.'

The restoration was certainly mild by Scott's standards, but several important features (like the perpendicular east window) were totally destroyed without drawn records. There is, however. a fine Buckler drawing of 1805 showing the east front before Scotts' 'restoration' (Fig.1) as well as several internal views. Scott's use of poor quality Chilmark stone, which he also introduced at Westminster Abbey, to replace Reigate stone, was very unwise. During the earlier part of the work, however, Scott used J.T. Irvine as his clerk-of-works (1872–6), and, as we shall see, the latter made many valuable notes and drawings.

Unfortunately the major campaign of restoration on the west front, which Scott had thought 'almost too valuable to be interfered with' was carried out by J.L. Pearson between 1888 and 1894. He had no qualms about destroying the 15th century inner north turret (Hope 1898, 279), and undertaking a totally conjectural reconstruction of the Norman work. At least no huge new 'Roman-

Fig. 10.1. East front of Rochester Cathedral in 1805 by J. Buckler (from a watercolour owned by the Dean and Chapter of Rochester Cathedral).

esque' crossing or western towers and spires were suggested here by J.L. Pearson, as he had proposed at Peterborough and was to propose at Chichester Cathedral. Pearson also wanted to remove the pulpitum screen and replace it with an new open stone screen. He was, however, prevented from doing this after many protests.

The final, and almost inevitable, restoration campaign after Cottingham's destruction in 1826 of the squat 14th century tower and large lead and timber spire, was its replacement. This was carried out in 1904 by C. Hodgson Fowler, and it now dominates the cathedral. Only very roughly does it reflect the medieval structure.

Thus, by the early years of this century almost the whole of the outside, and much of the eastern arm internal furnishings had been totally replaced at Rochester Cathedral with very few detailed records having been made. It is now time, therefore, to turn to archaeology – below and above ground- to see what contribution this has made to the architectural history of the cathedral.

Archaeology at Rochester Cathedral

As we have seen, archaeology can be said to have made an accidental and tentative start at the cathedral in 1825 when the tomb of bishop John of Sheppey was rediscovered. 'Archaeological recording' of sorts got underway 25 years later, when in June 1850 Sir George Scharf, 1820-95, (later director of the National Portrait Gallery) made eight fine drawings (now at the Society of Antiquaries of London) of the great west doorway (Kahn 1987). These supplement a few photographs and are invaluable for telling us what the doorway looked like before the start of J.L. Pearson's restoration in 1888.

The first actual archaeological investigation was that undertaken by Arthur Ashpitel (1807–1869) in the crypt in 1853. He made holes in the floor of the crypt 'by means of a boring rod' and discovered a massive wall foundation two bays east of the surviving early Norman two-bay groin vaulted crypt. He was therefore the first to suggest a square east end for the early Norman cathedral. St. John Hope, who was to investigate the same area some thirty years later felt that the 'borings were very unsatisfactory'. Asphitel tried to reconstruct the early Norman cathedral's plan and published his findings the following year (Asphitel 1854). He suggested that Gundulf's tower was the original north transept of this building, and that there had been a large arch in the south side of the lower level of the tower to connect with the church. No evidence, whatsoever, for this arch can be seen.

Next on the scene was the ubiquitous Robert Willis. During the summer meeting of the Archaeological Institute of Great Britain and Ireland in Rochester in 1863, he gave a lecture tour on the architectural history of the cathedral. Unfortunately this was not published at the time, but Hope did publish a transcript of part of the lecture in his own architectural history (Hope 1898, 233–242). As usual, Willis managed to work out the main structural history of the building and to find some documentary evidence which suggested the dates of completion(roofing and leading) of the new eastern arm. It was Willis who first suggested the actual order of the rebuilding of the cathedral in the late twelfth and thirteenth centuries(Hope 1898, 242):

(1) the crypt, presbytery, and eastern transept

(2) the choir and its aisles

(3) the north-west transept

(4) the south-west transept, with the eastern part of the nave.

Sadly none of his own notes and drawings appear to have survived. This is a particular loss because Willis was working in the cathedral before Scott's great restoration. It is also worth recording that during the Institute's summer meeting an area of plaster was stripped, for the members to inspect (Parker 1863, 263).

In 1872 Gilbert Scott's large restoration commenced and we are fortunate that his clerk-of-works from 1872–6 was J.T. Irvine, who was fresh from Scott's restoration work at Wells and Bath and was a keen observer of archaeological details. Irvine's Rochester notes were given to the Dean and Chapter after his death in 1900 (they are now in the Kent archives Office – Drc/Emf 77 – at Maidstone), but it was St. John Hope who first used them, and who corresponded with Irvine in later life. We should also be grateful to Irvine for saving some areas of the building which Scott wanted to rebuild totally. Hope (1898,268) tells us, for example, in relation to the south aisle/cloister wall that:

> 'The condition of this aisle wall became so threatening in recent years that Sir G. Gilbert Scott advised its rebuilding. But the entreaties of Mr. J. T. Irvine, who recognized its great historical value, led to the substitution of a flying buttress, which has successfully met the difficulty.'

Among the many discoveries that Irvine made during the restoration work, the following were the most important:

(a) He observed a Norman clasping pilaster buttress foundation exposed during underpinning work on the south wall of the south transept (1872).

(b) He drew the section (with layers marked on) of the tunnel (for the organ 'windtrunks') from the crypt to below the pulpitum (1874–5).

(c) He observed the foundations of the north wall of the nave during underpinning and noticed what may have been foundations for a tower at the western end (1875).

(d) He recorded pilaster buttresses and a constructional break on the south side of the nave during underpinning.

Fig. 10.2. Cutaway view of 'Gundulf's' tower and the neighbouring area of Rochester Cathedral, by J,A. Bowen, showing in outline the upper section of the tower which was demolished nearly two centuries ago.

He also observed an earlier transverse wall and apse (and opus signinum flooring), which were perhaps Roman (1875–6).

(e) He recorded the nave arcades during repairs and observed probable early Norman tufa voussoirs (concealed under plaster) on the outer sides (1876).

All of these discoveries were used by Hope who came on the scene a few years later.

W.H. St. John Hope graduated from Cambridge in 1880 (aged 26), and immediately afterwards was appointed a master at Rochester Grammar School. From 1881 until his appointment as assistant secretary at the Society of Antiquaries of London four years later, he spent many hours investigating both the fabric and the documentary history of the cathedral and its surrounding buildings. In October/November 1881 he tells us he 'sunk a number of holes in various places in the earthen floor of the undercroft (crypt), and had a trench cut down the centre line. My labours were fully repaid by the finding of the foundations of sundry walls. When carefully measured and plotted, the following facts became evident:

(1) That the church terminated, as Mr. Asphitel had surmised, in a square end, and not in an apse, built on a foundation eight feet wide.

(2) The eastern limb had aisles equal in length to the presbytery.

(3) Beyond the cross-wall was a small rectangular chapel about 6½ feet long by 9 feet wide, which it is to be noticed, projects from the middle alley of the central division of the undercroft, and not its whole width.

To make sure I followed the foundations of this chapel all round to their junctions with that of the great wall, with which it is contemporary' (Hope 1886, 329).

His workmen also found a 'box of bones' in this 'chapel'. Hope marked the outlines of these foundations on a new plan of the crypt, and was soon suggesting a superstructure for it with clasping buttresses at the outer angles. Since this time, Hope's suggested plan for the eastern termination of Gundulf's cathedral has been accepted almost without question. It might be worth adding that, in the view of the present writer, an eastern apse is still possible. Hope's central chapel could have been part of an eastern apse with its curved north and south sides cut away by the massive foundations for the large internal piers of the later crypt. Only a careful modern excavation would provide the answer.

In March 1884 Hope read a paper to the Society of Antiquaries on 'Gundulf's Tower at Rochester, and the first Norman Cathedral Church there' (Hope 1886). In this he communicated the results of his work and then went on to suggest his reconstruction of the 'peculiar' plan of Gundulf's church. This reconstructed plan remained almost unchanged in Hope's mind for the rest of his life, and it was fully published in the 'architectural history' (Hope 1898, plate I op.p. 202). The second part of Hope's 1884 paper was on Gundulf's tower, and here Hope went a stage further than earlier writers and suggested that it was built before the Norman cathedral, and that it was built 'primarily for defensive purposes'. He does, however, point out 'that at a very early period it was used as a bell-tower'. Hope's only apparent reason for making Gundulf the builder of the tower is that it is 'evident enough to anyone who is familiar with his peculiar mode of building' (ie. the use of tufa quoins, etc.). He also says that the tower was erected before Gundulf's cathedral because it blocks two of the four long narrow windows in the ground floor of the tower. In fact, only in the thirteenth century rebuilding were these windows blocked, and this 'peculiar mode of building' is found in the late eleventh and the first half of the twelfth century. Hope also failed to notice that there are a few reused Norman architectural fragments *in situ* in the south face of the tower.I would suggest, therefore, the 'Gundulf's tower' (the name does not seem to occur before the eighteenth century) was only a bell-tower that was perhaps built in about the second quarter of the twelfth century. As Hope himself pointed out, the mid-twelfth century Prior Reginald is documented as having 'made two bells and placed them in the greater tower (*in majori turri*)'. Other bells were also made and placed there in the later twelfth century (Thorpe 1769, 118). The tower, which contains no defensive features, though there may have been a spiral staircase in the north-east corner, is only peculiar because it is so close to the cathedral (Fig. 2.). This is certainly because space within the Roman walls was very tight at Rochester (Tatton-Brown 1991).

The problems of Gundulf's tower and the early plan of the Norman cathedral are two areas of Hope's work that need major reassessment. It should not, however, be forgotten that Hope investigated the whole of the cathedral and its surrounding buildings; in 1884, for example, he dug in the Deanery kitchen yard, and exposed and planned parts of the dorter undercroft. His account of the Benedictine priory buildings is still unsurpassed. He also drew together all the documentary evidence, and all earlier archaeological finds. His two major papers are still immensely valuable and only in recent years have a few new investigations been undertaken.

Hope left Rochester in 1885, and a few years later, in the autumn of 1888, work got underway on the underpinning of the west front. Luckily the precentor of the cathedral at that time (a minor canon) was a man called the Revd. Grevile M.Livett, who was probably the best 'church archaeologist' in Kent during the late nineteenth century and early twentieth century, (he died in 1951, aged 92), though he started his archaeological work with a major monograph on Southwell Minster in 1883.

Livett was able to record not only the remains of the early Norman west wall and doorway of the cathedral (probably Gundulf's work), which lay under the mid-twelfth century west front, but also the remains of an apse of what was almost certainly one of the buildings, if not the main building itself, of the seventh century Anglo-Saxon cathedral. This was on a more east-west alignment that the present building, and its apse lay immediately underneath the north-west corner of the Norman nave. A small fragment of north-south wall on the south side, which was also found, may have been part of a porticus. Livett very promptly wrote a full report of his discoveries, and made a fine plan and sections, and they were published the following year (Livett 1889). In the summer of 1894, more 'excavation and probing' was done outside the west front of the cathedral, and the west wall of the nave of the Anglo-Saxon church was discovered. The internal dimensions of the nave were found to be 42 feet long by 28 feet wide (Hope 1898, 212).

In January 1898, further excavations were carried out by the Rochester antiquary, George Payne, and St. John Hope in the garden immediately outside the south-west transept. These exposed part of a long wall, which may have been part of the twelfth century cellarer's range,or just possibly an outer court building of the bishop's palace, (McAleer 1993). The excavation was rapidly curtailed 'by a peremptory order of Dean Hole for the immediate stoppage of the work!' (Hope 1900,52).

With this work and the publication of Hope's magnum opus on Rochester Cathedral, all archaeological work on the fabric of the cathedral (both below and above ground) effectively came to an end. In this century all archaeological work has been on a very small scale indeed, and sadly quite a lot of it was never properly published. For example, in 1937 the area outside the south aisle of the nave was apparently re-excavated by Farley Cobb, the Cathedral Surveyor, and no trace was found of Irvine's apse of 1872 (Cobb 1938). In the same year the ugly yellow brick canon's house which covered the south-west corner of the cloister was demolished. It had been built in the early nineteenth century. The following year, 1938, saw the large-scale excavation of the area beneath and behind the house. The east side wall of the vaulted undercroft of the cellarer's range was uncovered , and at the south end the last compartment was stripped revealing fine twelfth century triple stone shafts in each corner. Only a very brief report (and no drawings) was produced (Forsyth 1939, but see now McAleer 1993)). Earlier, in February 1936, the chapter house doorway was re-opened and the area inside it was excavated. The only report on this work is in *The Times* of April 1936 where we read:

> 'The earth has been removed from the West end of the Chapter House and at a depth of 3ft. were found fragments of the encaustic tiling of the floor; a few pieces were still in situ, but most of the tiles were broken into fragments. Pottery and other small matters were also found, and a tiny object, apparently a coin, which has still to be identified. The bases of two piers in line with a fifteenth-century respond in the South wall have also been uncovered and provide evidence of a vaulted vestibule, possibly carrying a bridge, which communicated with the dormitory immediately to the South and with the choir. Some puzzling features, such as the foundations of a wall near the West end of the Chapter house, have appeared, and will perhaps be explained.
>
> It has always been believed that the Priors of the Monastery of St. Andrew had a right of burial within the Chapter House. At a depth of 2ft. 6in. to 3ft. below the paving a skeleton has been discovered, and there is reason to believe that another lies not far off. No vessels were found: the bones were not removed, and were covered up again within half an hour of their being disclosed. There was no sign of a coffin; probably the body was buried in a shroud.'

Ten years after Sir William St. John Hope's death (1919), Dr. F.H. Fairweather published a lengthy article about the plan of Gundulf's cathedral (Fairweather 1929). In this he criticised Hope's reconstruction of the early Norman plan and put forward his own. Unfortunately Fairweather's suggestions have almost no fabric evidence to support them, and his theory that the early part of the crypt is after Gundulf's time, and relates to a second phase of the Norman church cannot be correct. The situation is perhaps best summed up by Sir Alfred Clapham, who wrote a few years later (Clapham 1934):

> 'The plan of the early church is at present undetermined. the form suggested by Sir William Hope rests on little or no evidence and is neither reasonable nor probable. Dr. Fairweather has recently shown that a normal plan, similar to the of Lanfranc's church at Canterbury, is quite a possible layout for the site, but without excavation it is impossible to prove it.'

In the last half century or so only a handful of minor excavations and investigations have been carried out. Mr. Arthur Harrison and others have undertaken many small scale investigations in Rochester (including some within the cathedral precincts), which have thrown new light on the ancient topography of the city. Only once (in August 1968) has an investigation been carried out inside the cathedral. At this time leger and paving stones were removed from the north side of the crossing area during the installation of a nave altar platform. The cathedral surveyor, Mr. Emil Godfrey invited Dr. C.A. Ralegh Radford to investigate, and he published a brief note (but alas no plan) in the Cathedral Friends' Annual report (Radford 1969). Under the north crossing arch Dr. Radford apparently found parts of the walls of a building which predated the early Norman foundations in this part of the cathedral. However, no detailed investigations were undertaken.

In the last decade a few more small scale observations have been made. These include 'rescue' observations in the area outside the south choir aisle door (Bacchus 1985), the Sacrist's checker area (Tatton-Brown 1990) and, most recently, the chair store foundations on the north side of the nave in May 1990 (Ward 1991). Professor M.J. Swanton has also published an important paper on the twelfth century graffiti in the nave (largely on the piers) which, as he says, almost certainly 'represent the remaining evidence for an extensive programme of early medieval wall-paintings, although little of the original scheme can be reconstructed' (Swanton 1979, 129). In 1987 a reused fragment was removed from the inside of the south-west turret of the cathedral. This proved to be an important fragment of an early eleventh century gravestone, one side of which has decoration in the 'Ringerike' style. There are also remains of the original colour, and part of a Latin inscription on the edge. At the bottom of the spiral stair turret on the north-east corner of the north-east transept a very fine early door survives, decorated with ironwork. This has recently been studied by Dr. Jane Geddes (1990), who suggests that it dates from the late eleventh or twelfth century. Much later the door was given a new face and turned round, so that the original door is only visible on the inside.

Recent Work

In March 1987, a new fabric committee was set up by the Dean and Chapter, and with its support a new programme of archaeological investigation is getting under way. This has been encouraged by the current Surveyor to the Fabric, Mr. Martin Caroe, and the first major investigation to be undertaken was on the ruined west wall of the Chapter House. In 1989 measured drawings of both wall faces at a 1:20 scale were made by Mr. John Bowen after the surface had been cleaned. 1:4 drawings were also made of all the sculpture. The masonry was then examined and analysed by the present writer so that the different building materials could be identified, and the different phases of work (including restoration work) could be ascertained (Tatton-Brown 1989 and 1994). This has been most successful and it now seems likely that the ground floor arches of the chapter house west wall (and the neighbouring dormitory doorway) had been completely refaced in the mid-twelfth century. The core of the walls and the upper windows in the chapter house must date from c.1120, as it is documented that bishop Ernulf (1114–24) '*fecit dormitorium, capitulum, refectorium*' (Thorpe 1769, 120). Work was continued in 1990 and 1992 on the adjoining west wall of the dormitory undercroft, and the magnificent, but very worn, decorated doorway to the dormitory has also been cleaned and conserved. Between the lintel and the outer voussoirs, and holding the tympanum blocks together, is a unique system of original twelfth century ironwork set in lead. At its top end, and using a separate piece of iron, the whole structure is tied back to the original rubble core above the arch (Figs.3 and 4).

When this was completed, the cathedral's famous west front was cleaned and a similar exercise was undertaken

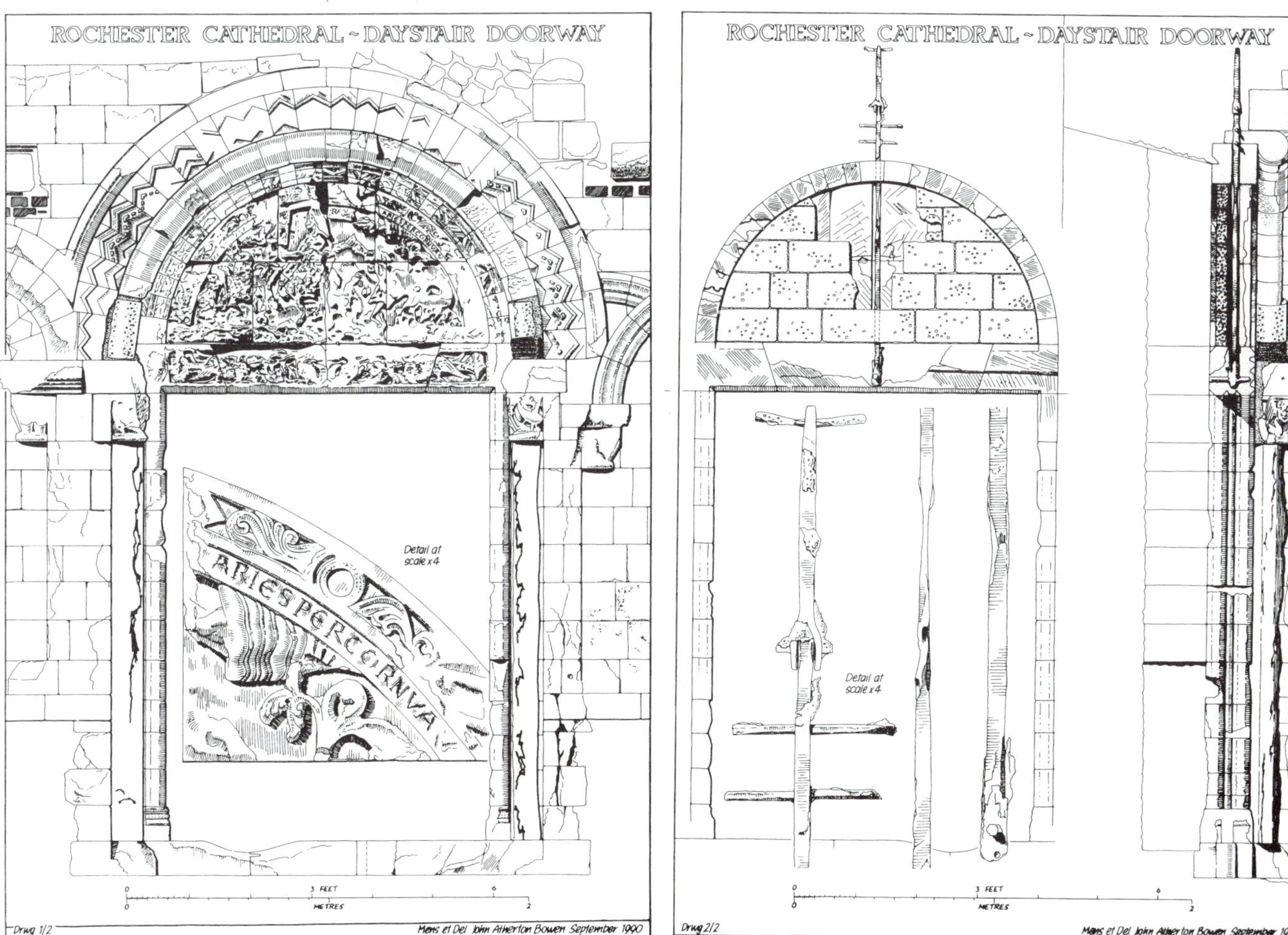

Fig. 10.3. Measured drawing, by J.A. Bowen, of the dorter doorway and its contemporary ironwork.

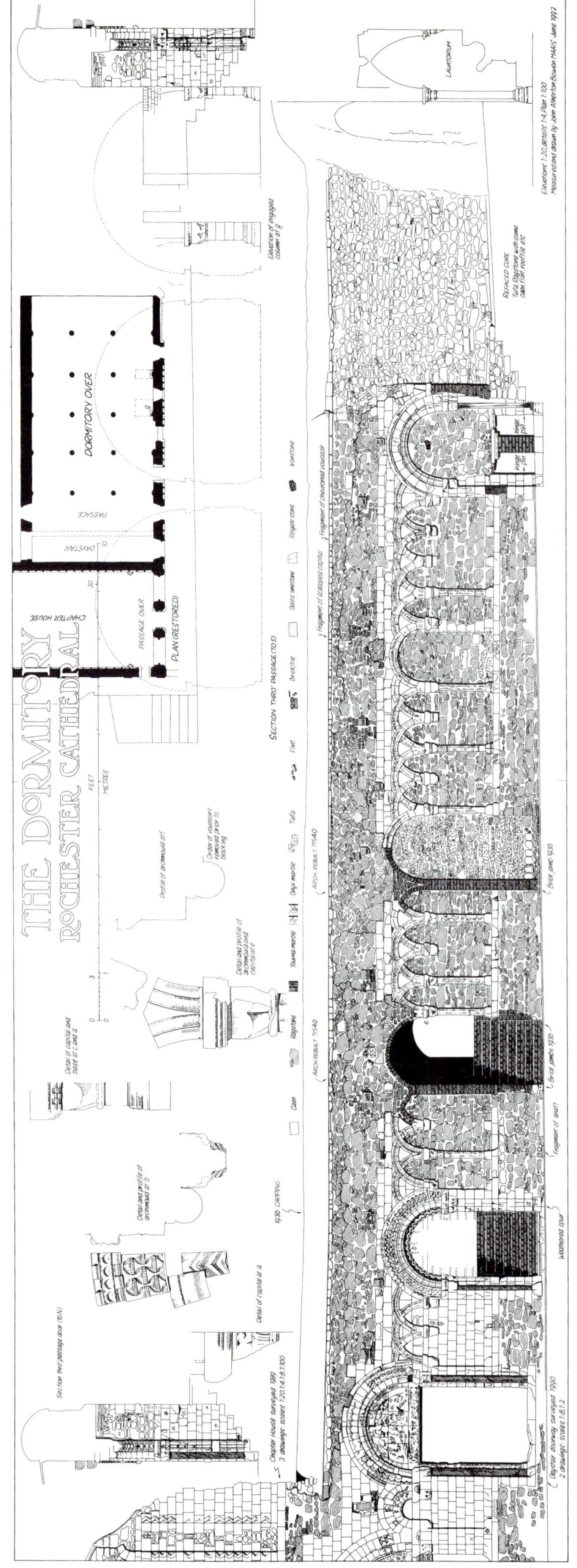

Fig.10.4. Measured drawing, by J.A. Bowen, of the northern part of the west wall of the dorter undercroft.

Fig. 10.5. Measured drawing, by J.A. Bowen, of the west front.

with measured drawings of the whole of the west front being made by John Bowen (Fig.5). This has allowed a more complete analysis of the west end of the building (McAleer 1983, 1985 and 1986), and should lead on to the detailed recording and analysis of other parts of the cathedral. Only then can a new architectural history of the cathedral be undertaken.

Bibliography

Asphitel, A. 1854: Rochester Cathedral. *Jnl. B.A.A.* 9, 271–285.

Bacchus, D. 1985: Rochester Cathedral, south door porch excavations. *Arch. Cant.* 102, 257–261.

Blair, J. 1994: The Limogesenamel tomb of Bishop Walter de Merton. *Friends of Rochester Cathedral: Report for 1993-4*, 28-33.

Clapham, A. 1934: *Early Romanesque Architecture after the Conquest* (Oxford).

Cobb, E.F. 1938: Explorations on the south side of the nave. *Friends of Rochester Cathedral: Third Annual Report*, 22–4.

Erwood, F.C.E. 1956: Miscellaneous notes on some Kent roads and allied matters. *Arch.Cant.* 70, 209–215.

Fairweather, F.H. 1929: Gundulf's cathedral and priory church of St. Andrew, Rochester: some critical remarks upon the hitherto accepted plan. *Archaeol. Jnl.* 86, 187–212.

Forsyth, W.A. 1939: Rochester Cathedral restoration of the Norman cloister. *Friends of Rochester Cathedral. Fourth Annual Report,* 20–2.

Geddes, J. 1990: Some doors in Rochester Cathedral. *Friends of Rochester Cathedral: report for 1989/90*, 19–22.

Hasted, E. 1797–1801: *The History and Topographical Survey of the County of Kent*, 12 volumes (2nd. edition, Canterbury).

Hope, W.H. St.J. 1886: Gundulf's Tower at Rochester, and the first Norman Cathedral there. *Archaeologia* 49, 323–334.

Hope, W.H. St.J. 1898: The architectural history of the cathedral church and monastery of St Andrew at Rochester I: The Cathedral. *Arch.Cant.* 23, 194–328.

Hope, W.H. St.J. 1900: The architectural history of the cathedral church and monastery of St Andrew at Rochester Church. II: The Monastery. *Arch.Cant.* 24, 1–85.

Kahn, D. 1987: The west doorway at Rochester Cathedral. In Stratford, N. et.al (editors), *Romanesque and Gothic: Essays for George Zarnecki* (Woodbridge), 129–134.

Livett, G.M. 1889: Foundations of the Saxon Cathedral church at Rochester. *Arch.Cant.* 21, 17–72.

Livett, G.M. 1895: Mediaeval Rochester. *Arch. Cant.* 21, 17-72

McAleer, J.P. 1983: The significance of the west front of Rochester Cathedral. *Arch.Cant.* 99, 139–158.

McAleer, J.P. 1985: Some observations on the building sequende of the nave of Rochester Cathedral. *Arch.Cant.* 102, 149–170.

McAleer, J.P. 1986: The west front of Rochester Cathedral: the interior design. *Arch.Cant.* 103, 27–43.

McAleer, J.P. 1993: Rochester Cathedral; The west range of the cloister, *Friends of Rochester Cathedral:report for 1992/3*,13–25.

Miele, C. 1994: The West Front of Rochester Cathedral in 1825: Antiquarianism, Historicism, and the Restoration of Medieval Buildings. *Archaeol. Jnl.* 151,400-19.

Parker, J.H. 1863: The buildings of bishop Gundulf. *Gentlemen's Magazine* 215, 255–268.

Radford, C.A.R. 1969: Rochester Cathedral; a new fragment of pre-conquest wall. *Friends of Rochester Cathedral: annual report for 1968*, 13–16.

Swanton, M.J. 1979: A mural palimpset from Rochester Cathedral. *Archaeol. Jnl.* 136, 125–135.

Tatton-Brown, T.W.T. 1989: The east range of the cloisters. *Friends of Rochester Cathedral: Report for 1988*, 4–8.

Tatton-Brown, T.W.T. 1990: Observations made in the sacrist's checker area beside 'Gundulf's' Tower at Rochester Cathedral – July 1989. *Arch.Cant.* 107, 390–394.

Tatton-Brown, T.W.T. 1991: 'Gundulf's' Tower. Friends of *Rochester Cathedral: Report for 1990/1*, 7–12.

Tatton-Brown, T.W.T. 1994: The Chapter House and Dormitory Facade at Rochester Cathedral Priory. *Friends of Rochester Cathedral: Report for 1993/4*, 20–8.

Thorpe, J. 1769: *Registrum Roffense* (London).

Thorpe, J. 1788: *Custumale Roffense* (London).

Ward, A. 1991: Rochester Cathedral. *Canterbury's Archaeology 1989–90* (14th Annual Report), 34–5 and *Friends of Rochester Cathedral: Report for 1990/1*, 13–15.

Above and Below Ground: Archaeology at Wells Cathedral

Warwick Rodwell

Wells has a relatively small cathedral, the focus of what is often claimed to be the smallest English cathedral city. The setting is overwhelmingly rural. It is perhaps not surprising, therefore, that neither the cathedral nor its environs was subjected to massive restoration campaigns in the 19th century; and in more recent times the closure of the railway lines in this part of Somerset has helped to relieve the city from the pressures of modern redevelopment. The more leisurely pace of life in Trollope's posited model for 'Barchester' was accompanied by an equally leisurely approach both to restoration and to scholarly research during the Victorian era.

The Dean and Chapter of Wells considered employing Sir Gilbert Scott to restore the west front of the cathedral, but were not impressed with him: no Scott – no big restoration. Without a major restoration, there could hardly be any great archaeological discoveries; and without these there was little call for Professor Robert Willis's attentions. Nevertheless, Willis found the excuse to contribute a brief paper on the subject (Willis 1868), while J. T. Irvine was availed of the opportunity to write a more lengthy discourse (Irvine 1873). But there was no real impetus for a major Victorian treatise on the development of Wells cathedral.

Nonetheless, neither liturgical change nor the urge for restoration bypassed Wells altogether. The 'great scrape', which began in 1842, purged the cathedral of its mantle of limewash and paint; and in 1848 Anthony Salvin reordered the quire. On this occasion archaeology passed unnoticed. Antiquarian attention was however drawn to the west front in August 1850, when one of the great statues of a king plummeted to the ground and was smashed to pieces. The architectural importance of the Wells west front was now firmly noticed, and C. R. Cockerell produced a monograph on it (1851). At the same time, a mild panic set in concerning public safety, and the need for a general restoration began to be felt. The shattered statue was duly stuck together and hoisted back into its niche; and after a twenty-year limbering-up period, the restoration of the west front finally began.

Although a major undertaking, the restoration of 1870–74 was a triumph of conservatism, and the catalyst for a long series of seminal papers by art and architectural historians. Meanwhile, antiquarian attention began to be turned towards another part of the cathedral, namely a walled garden known as The Camery, which adjoins the east cloister. Canon C. M. Church, Sub-Dean of Wells, was probably the first resident cathedral historian since the Reformation, and from his pen flowed a series of articles on many subjects: these included observations on the archaeological evidence for two successive medieval buildings that had formerly adjoined the cloister. Their site had been variously trenched in 1851 and 1875, apparently motivated by antiquarian curiosity, and Church's reconstructed plans showed a simple rectangular chapel and its predecessor, a buttressed octagonal building, akin in form and location to a chapter house (Church 1888).

Archaeology, Water and Cathedral Origins

Canon Church's researches constituted the first attempt at below-ground archaeology at Wells. Shortly afterwards, two pipe trenches were cut through The Camery, and walls were encountered which were not congruent with Church's plan. Hence, in January 1894 the cathedral architect, Edmund Buckle, was instructed to carry out archaeological excavations. Over the following four months labourers dug trenches and chased walls, an agreeable pursuit which Bishop Lord Hervey abruptly terminated by dying in June. The excavations had to be hastily infilled and preparations made for his lordship's burial in The Camery (Fig. 11.1).

Two successive medieval chapels, and sundry other features were revealed by Buckle's excavations: the supposed octagonal building was shown to be a myth. The earlier of the chapels, identifiable as the well documented Lady Chapel-by-the-Cloister (Church 1894), was seen to lie at an angle of 12 degrees to the axis of the present cathedral, but it was not until 1909 that an explanation for this overt anomaly was forthcoming. W. H. St. John Hope, in an address to the Somerset Archaeological and Natural History Society, observed that the diverent alignment of the early Lady Chapel corresponded to the topographical axis of the market place and city streets of Wells, and he advanced the theory that the medieval structures uncov-

Fig. 11.1. The only extant photograph showing the 1894 excavation in The Camery at Wells, immediately after the trenches had been backfilled. Here, the buttressed outlines of the south transept and eastern arm of Bishop Stillington's Chapel can be seen through the parched turf. The photograph was taken on the occasion of Bishop Lord Harvey's funeral on 14 June 1894. Photo: Phillips Collection, Wells Cathedral Library.

ered in 1894 reflected both the site and orientation of the Anglo-Saxon cathedral (Hope 1909). Hope's paper was received with incredulity.

A seventy-year lapse followed before it was possible, through large-scale excavation in 1978–80, to demonstrate that not only was Hope's topographical analysis correct, but that the core of the early Lady Chapel actually embodied the remains of a late Saxon building, which was itself the culmination of a developing sequence of religious structures, based on an axial line (Figs. 11.2 and 11.3; Rodwell 1981; 1982b). The discovery had almost been anticipated by Church (1888, 104). Fundamental to this planned layout are the natural springs of cold Mendip water which rise to the surface immediately east of The Camery. These gave Wells its name (L. *Fontinetum;* OE Wiella), and have appeared in numerous depictions of the cathedral from the eleventh century onward. Four of the springs, or wells, are now linked to form the lake in the grounds of the Bishop's Palace, while the fifth – the holy well of St Andrew – provides the eastern focus of a long line of liturgical features and spaces, extending as far as the market place. Although first mentioned in a charter of 766 as the 'great spring', these waters had attracted attention at a much earlier date, as evidenced by finds around the well mouth of Mesolithic and later flints, and Roman pottery.

The westward-extending sequence of structures erected alongside the spring derived its axis from the topography of the valley slope, a line which veered 18 degrees off true east-west. The market place and High Street adopted the same axis, being the essentials of a late Saxon planned town, laid out in front of the cathedral. The whole sequence has been described elsewhere (Rodwell 1980b; 1981; 1982a; 1982b; 1982c; 1984;

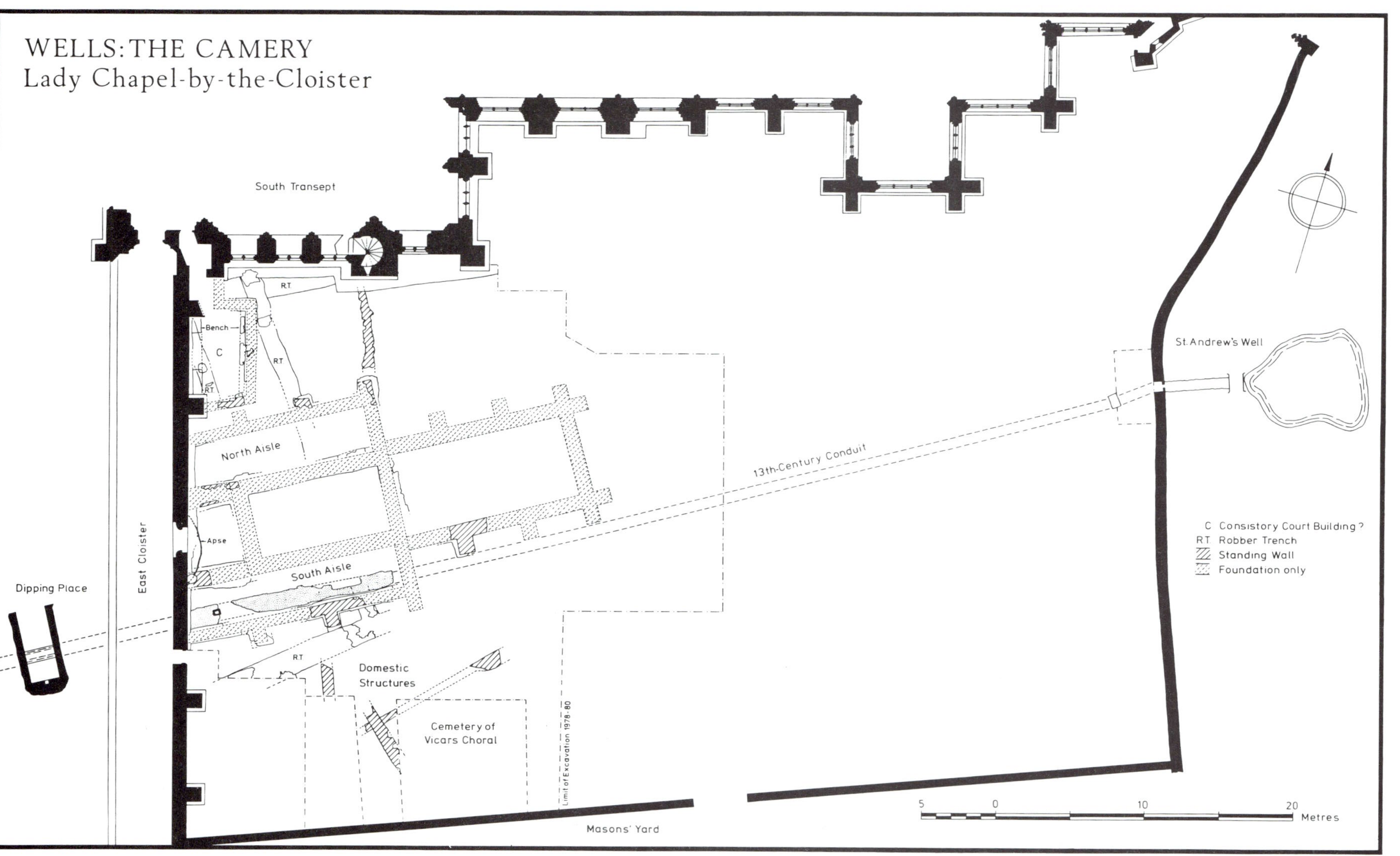

Fig. 11.2. Plan of the Camery, after the excavations of 1978–80, showing the divergent alignment of the thirteenth-century Lady Chapel-by-the-Cloister in relation to the Cathedral. The holy well of St Andrew and the original line of the great conduit running west are shown.

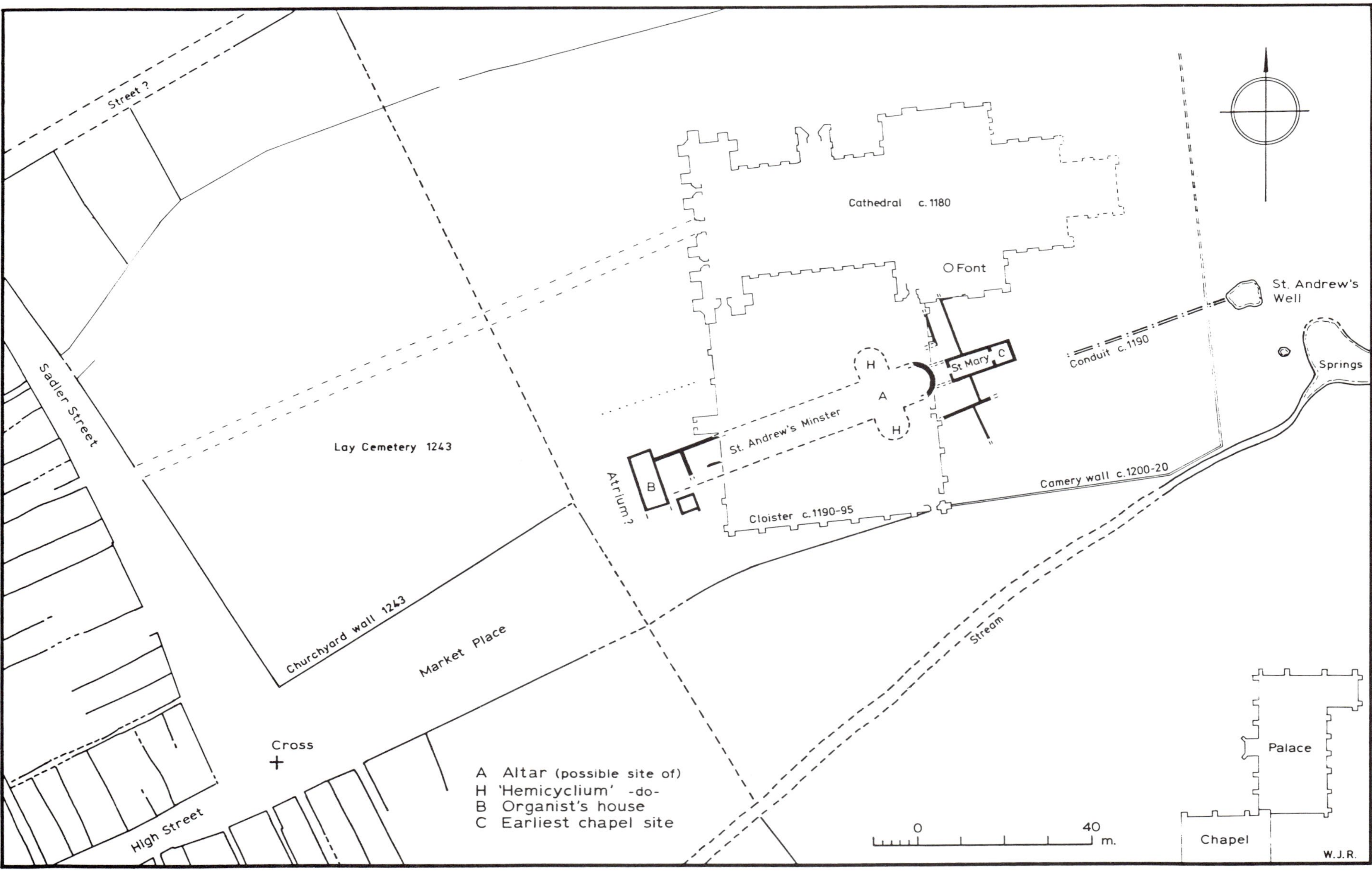

Fig. 11.3. Schematic plan to show the relationship between the Anglo-Saxon and Gothic cathedrals, and the local topography of the twelfth and thirteenth centuries.

1987; Scrase 1989). Here, it will suffice to recall that the earliest building was a small rectangular mausoleum of late Roman or sub-Roman date, robbed of its primary contents (for ritual translation?) and reused as an Anglo-Saxon ossuary.

Partly overlying the mausoleum was a middle Saxon mortuary chapel, containing, and surrounded by, contemporary burials. West of that chapel stood the minster church of St Andrew, the remains of which lie unexcavated and deeply buried beneath the Gothic cloister (Fig. 11.4A). The mortuary chapel in turn became enveloped by the sanctuary of a two-celled late Saxon church, for which a confident identification as the chapel of St Mary can be offered (Fig. 11.4B). Endowed by Giso, the last Saxon bishop of Wells (1061–88), this building stood initially as a detached chapel beyond the east end of St Andrew's Minster, and was later conjoined, becoming in effect an attached Lady Chapel. By this time, the minster church had a triple-apsed east end and was apparently crypted below the sanctuary (Fig. 11.4C).

Wells Minster was elevated to cathedral status in 909, when the diocese of Somerset was created out of Sherborne. Thus Wells became a cathedral of the Old Foundation, being served by a community of secular priests (who later had a dean as their capitular head). The canons lived amongst the local community, until bishop Giso of Lorraine (a former chaplain to Edward the Confessor) introduced the Lotharingian system of non-monastic communal residence. Excavations have revealed traces of ancillary buildings and domestic rubbish deposits of the period to either side of the Anglo-Saxon cathedral (Fig. 11.4D).

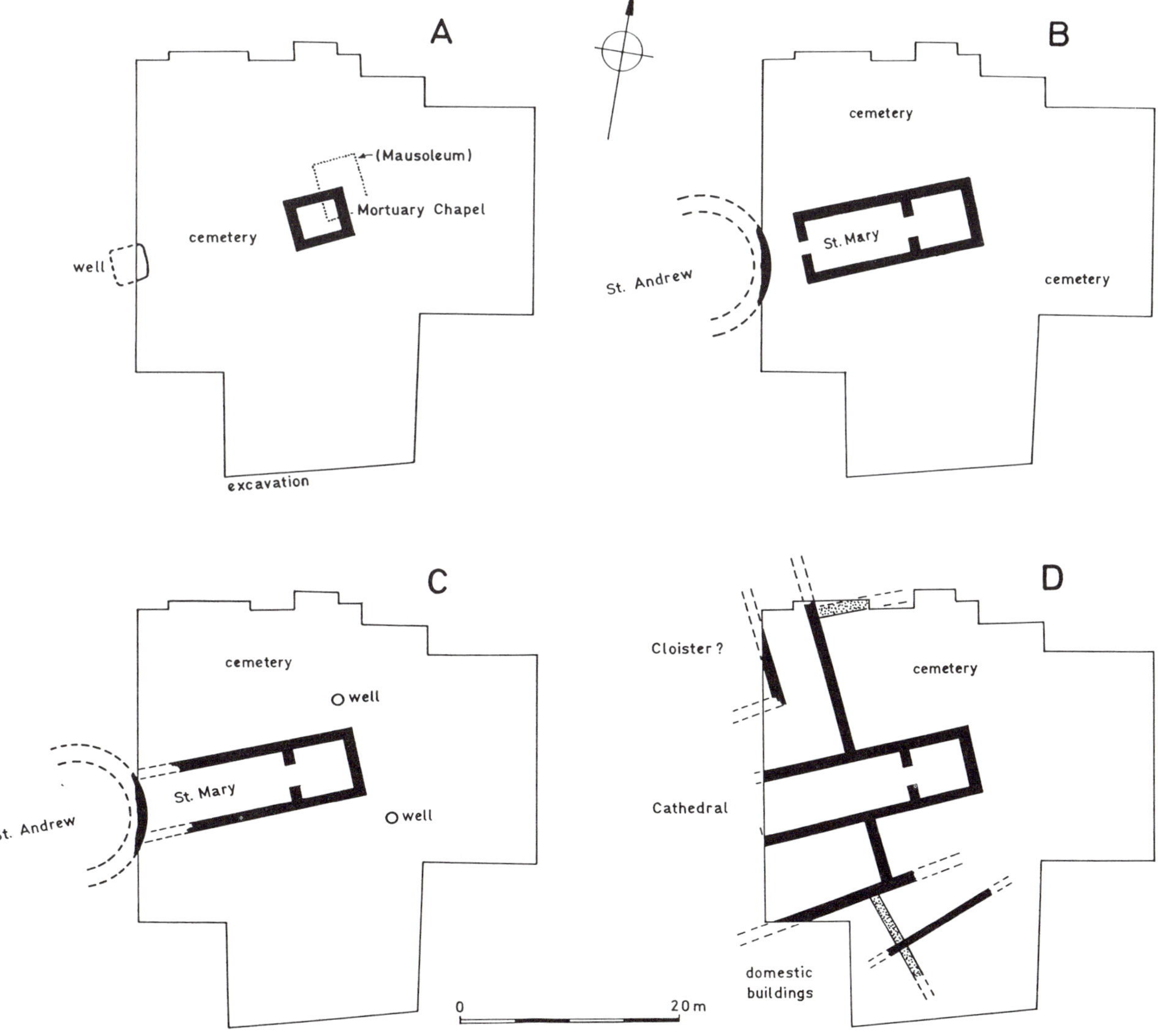

Fig. 11.4. Sequence of plans showing the pre-1170 phases of St Mary's Chapel (later, the Lady Chapel-by-the-Cloister). ***A.*** *Mortuary chapel of middle Saxon date, overlying a mausoleum of late Roman type.* ***B.*** *The sanctuary apse of the late Saxon minster church (St Andrew) and detached two-celled chapel of St Mary.* ***C.*** *The eastern termination of the cathedral in the mid-eleventh century. St Mary's Chapel was flanked by a pair of liturgical wells.* ***D.*** *In the later eleventh (and twelfth?) century the eastern arm of the cathedral was enveloped by ancillary structures, probably as a result of Bishop Giso's introduction of a communal life-style for the canons.*

A New Cathedral is Built

The effects of the Norman conquest on the community at Wells were curiously anomalous: to some extent, the Confessor's Norman influence must have arrived from Westminster with Giso in 1061. While there is no evidence that he set about rebuilding the cathedral in the same sense that his post-conquest contemporaries at Winchester, Worcester or Lichfield did in the 1070s and 1080s, the possibility awaits archaeological exploration. On present evidence it seems likely that when Giso died in 1088 the Anglo-Saxon cathedral was still standing. How extensive the modifications were that Bishop Robert dedicated in 1148 we cannot tell, but excavations have yielded some scalloped capitals and other architectural fragments of the period. The capitals appear to belong to free-standing arcading of a size appropriate to a cloister.

The Anglo-Saxon buildings, welded together and modified by Norman masons, almost certainly survived in a recognisable form until the very end of the twelfth century, long after other pre-conquest cathedrals had been razed and replaced by new structures, or else abandoned to ruin. The reason for this singular longevity is to be found in a complex ecclesio-political struggle of the late eleventh and twelfth centuries. Giso's successor, John of Tours, moved his bishopstool to Bath Abbey in or soon after 1088, demoting Wells to the status of college of secular canons. This was a mortally wounding blow to such a venerable foundation. The Anglo-Norman cathedral that should have been built at Wells arose instead at Bath (Davenport 1988; O'Leary and Rodwell 1991).

A series of appeals to the pope followed, under which the canons of Wells sought the return of the bishopstool, albeit without success for 156 years. Although the documentation of the struggle is sparse, the story can be fleshed out to a considerable extent through archaeological study. Sustaining the Wells claim to primacy over Bath demanded careful maintenance of the documentary and physical evidence relating to the cathedral's history and former status. First, an anonymous canon of Wells compiled a history of the foundation in *c.* 1175, known as the *Historiola*. Secondly, to have replaced the old church with a new one would have removed a large slice of the tangible evidence. Even if resources were available, there were good reasons for delaying the rebuild. But the time must eventually have come when the canons realised that their tenth-century church, with its eleventh and mid-twelfth century repairs and modifications was simply not a worthy building to serve as a cathedral in late Norman England. And their bishop may have told them so.

Sequence of Construction, c. 1175–1200

In the mid 1170s, during the episcopate of Reginald de Bohun (1174–91), a superlative effort was made – and who paid for it we do not know – to upgrade the fabric of Wells in a novel fashion. A wholly new church was built alongside the old cathedral and the Gothic style that was chosen had no precedent in England, and arguably, none in Europe. It bore no serious resemblance to the French Corinthianesque Gothic that was being introduced at Canterbury, following the fire of 1174 (Colchester and Harvey 1974; Harvey 1982, 52–5).

The date for the commencement of the present cathedral church at Wells has been much discussed. John Bilson (1928) argued that the Gothic of Wells must postdate the fine late Romanesque Lady Chapel at Glastonbury begun in 1184, after the abbey's disastrous fire. Dean Armitage Robinson, on the other hand, maintained that documentary evidence showed that Wells was under construction by the mid-1180s (Robinson 1928). A further review of the documents and of the fabric by L. S. Colchester and John Harvey (1974) pointed to a start on building work by *c.* 1180, at the latest.

The early dating of the present cathedral can now be further refined through a pincer movement involving two separate archaeological approaches. The first relates to the demolition sequence of the Anglo-Saxon cathedral, and the process of moving its treasures into the eastern arm of the new building (Rodwell 1982b). The second is based on a study by Jerry Sampson of the visible evidence for individual building campaigns in the masonry of the cathedral.

It had long ago been noticed that two sources of limestone ashlar were employed in the early Gothic fabric, the superior type being derived from the Doulting quarry, and the inferior from Chilcote (Colchester and Harvey 1974, 203). Doulting lay on the Glastonbury Abbey estate, and stone from its quarry was apparently only available for use at Wells when there was no prior call on resources from Glastonbury. Cross-linking between the recorded histories, and the extant fabrics, of the two churches has enabled a finely tuned chronology to be posited.

There is now little room for doubt that the design for Gothic Wells must have been conceived *c.* 1175, and that foundation trenches were being dug by 1176–77. The eastern arm was up by 1184. The eastern transept came next, and was complete by *c.* 1191; the crossing and south transept followed by *c.* 1196 (Fig. 11.5). The liturgical quire was then complete and ready for use, with access via a major processional door in the south transept.

Cathedral Removals

The move from the old church to the new probably took place in or around 1196. Of the innumerable furnishings and items of liturgical equipment that will have been transferred, archaeological evidence survives for two. One is the font, the other is the collection of corporeal remains of the Anglo-Saxon bishops.

The Anglo-Saxon Font

The font is an important but largely neglected furnishing of Wells Cathedral (Fig. 11.6). Until a study was carried

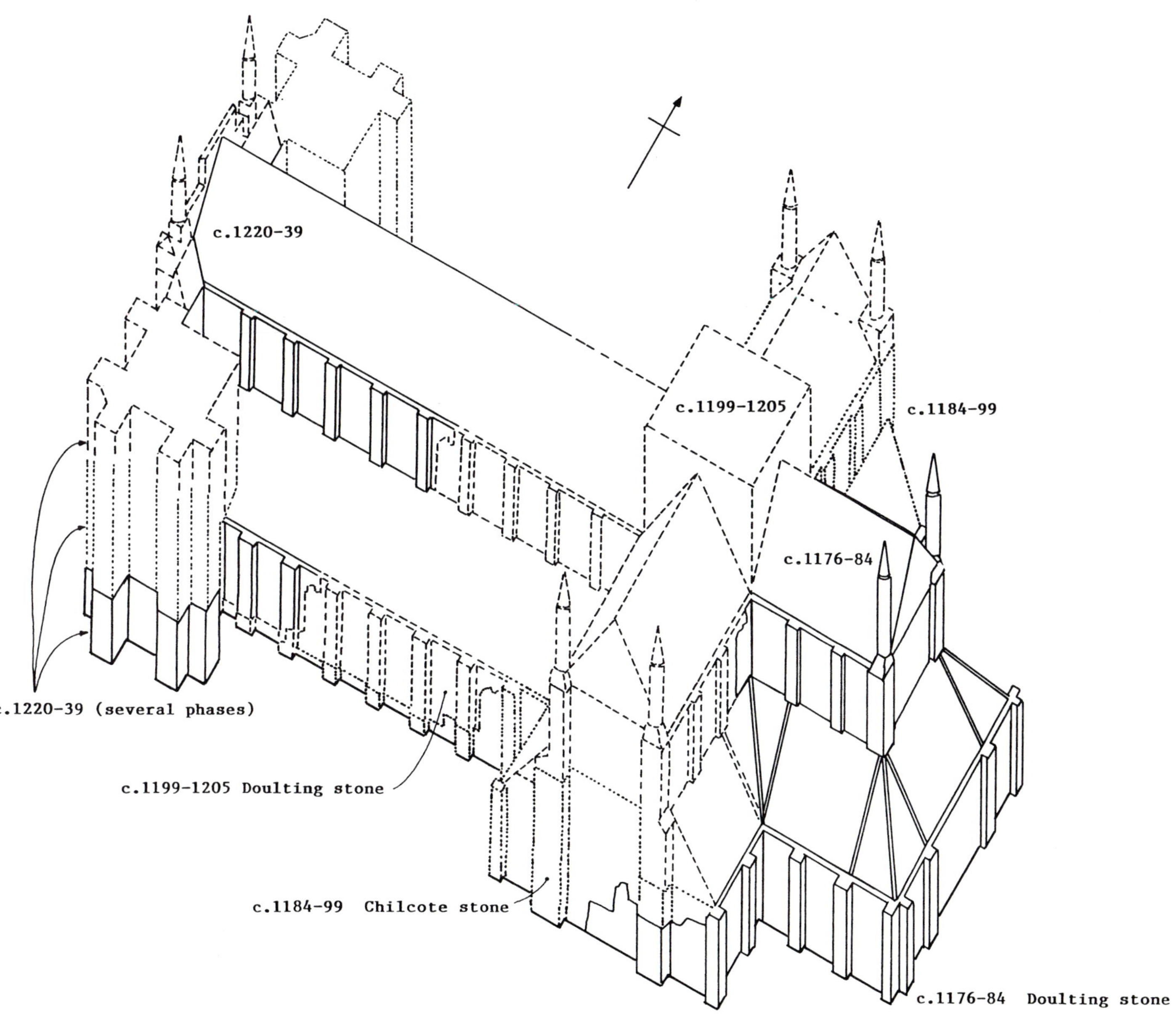

Fig. 11.5. Simplified axonometric reconstruction of Wells Cathedral in c. 1240, showing the form of the original eastern arm and the principal phases of construction based on visible building breaks and the separate uses of Doulting and Chilcote ashlar. Drawing after Jerry Sampson.

out in 1985, its antiquity was uncertain, but early Gothic features suggested that it was broadly coeval with the main period of the cathedral. The cylindrical bowl of the font is cut from a drum of Bath stone, set on a chamfered plinth and raised on a single step. The mildly pointed arcade of eight bays carved around the drum imparts an obvious Gothic flavour, but close inspection shows this to be a secondary arrangement. Not only was the original arcade round-arched and carried on square pilasters with chunky capitals and bases, but there were also eight haloed figures carved in bas-relief in the now-blank panels. The plain rim-band around the bowl has also been cut back, presumably to delete an inscription. A good deal of ground-coat for the original painting survives (Rodwell 1990).

While dating the Wells font remains a subject for debate, its pre-conquest origin is not in doubt: modernization of the bowl took place around 1200, when the present plinth and step were provided (Rodwell 1987, 19–20). No less interesting than the object itself is its location in the centre of the south transept. Liturgically the site is incorrect, since the prescribed place for a font is at the principal entrance to the church. In the case of Wells the central west door technically commanded that distinction, although in practice the north porch door fulfilled the function. But when the font was moved into

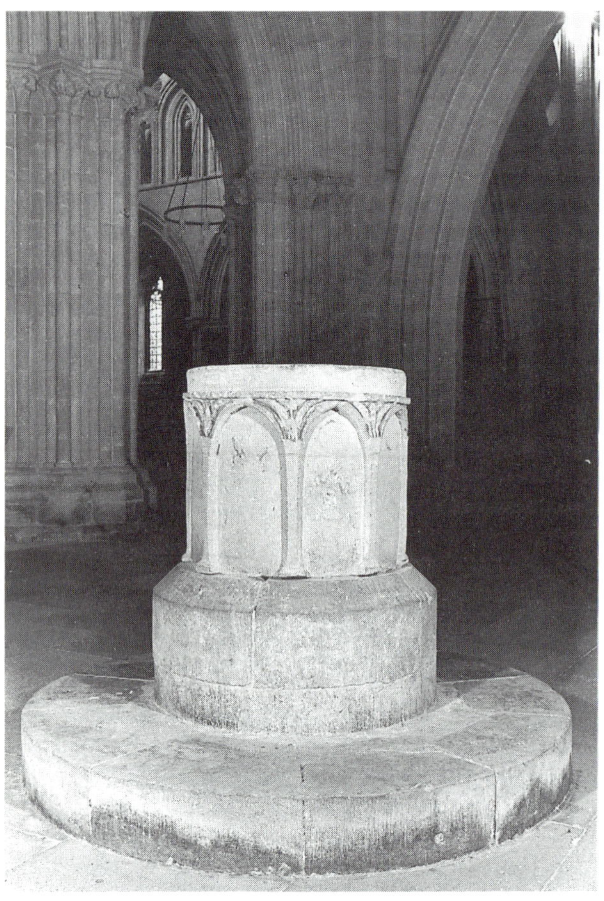

Fig. 11.6. The recut Anglo-Saxon font, mounted on a plinth and step of c. 1200. The blank arcading formerly contained relief figures of saints, and there was probably an inscription on the rim-band. Photo: Jerry Sampson.

the present building there was no west front or north porch, just the south transept door. Although only temporarily located in this area, after 800 years the font's position has acquired an aura of permanence.

Relics of the Anglo-Saxon Bishops

At least nine Anglo-Saxon bishops were interred in the old cathedral, and reverence would have demanded that their corporeal remains be solemnly translated into the new building when the quire was dedicated. This occurred *c.* 1196–1200. It would appear that the episcopal remains were placed in wooden chests, each beneath a life-sized effigy of the respective prelate (Fig. 11.7). Five imposing sculptures, dating from *c.* 1200, and two more of *c.* 1325, remain in the quire aisles today. They are of course retrospective effigies specially produced to adorn the Gothic church and to serve as powerful, ever-present reminders of Wells' ancient status as the seat of the *episcopus Somersetensis.*

The bishops' remains have been moved several times within recorded history – the last in 1914 – and although Dean Robinson had contributed two papers on the subject, many questions remained unanswered (Robinson 1914 and 1919). In particular, no osteological report had been attempted. Hence, in 1978 the Dean and Chapter determined that a fresh study of the effigies and the contents of the tomb-chests should be carried out. Many surprises were in store. The first concerned the number of individuals present. The skeletons were not only incomplete but also seriously jumbled, and the head-count revealed that the seven tomb-chests contained ten men – one more than the known total of bishops. Moreover, the

Fig. 11.7. The retrospective effigy of Eilwinus in the south quire aisle, lifted to one side of the tomb-chest upon which it rested, revealing the box containing the corporeal remains of the Anglo-Saxon bishop. Photo: Warwick Rodwell.

Fig. 11.8. A skull with a slice of bone removed by a sword cut: a presumed martyrial relic. Found amongst the bones of the Anglo-Saxon bishops, where it may have been concealed at the Reformation. Photo: Warwick Rodwell.

tenth skull exhibited a severe sword cut (Fig. 11.8), which was undoubtedly a death-blow (Rodwell 1982b, pl. 11). Since there is no record that any tenth or early eleventh-century bishop met a violent death, it may be permissible to suggest that we have here a martyrial relic that has somehow become muddled with the episcopal remains.

Another important discovery was a fragmentary inscription on a thin lead foil attached to the back of the mortuary cross that accompanied bishop Giso. The foil was evidently part of a triangular plaque that was probably attached to the bishop's coffin at the time of the original burial in 1088. It is inscribed with two excerpts from the Latin Mass for the Dead:

[AGNVS DEI QV]I TOLLIS[PECCATA MVNDI]

[DONA] EIS DO[MINE]
[REQV]IEM ET[ERNAM]
[LV]CEAT [EIS]*
[PERPETVA]
[ET LVX]

* (The fourth line is inverted, and the fifth and sixth are entirely missing. In order to make sense of this inscription, it must be presumed that the last three lines were all inverted and intended to be read upwards from the bottom).

In translation, the text reads, 'O, lamb of God that takest away the sins of the world: rest eternal grant unto them, O Lord, and let light perpetual shine upon them' (Rodwell 1982b, 21–2).

The most unexpected discovery – one which Dean Robinson assiduously avoided mentioning – was obvious veneration of the episcopal remains as saintly relics. Several of the skulls had been limewashed for the purpose of display, two had had discs of bone cut from the back of the cranium (presumably for use as amulets), and some were worn to a polished state in places where hands had been repeatedly laid upon them in acts of veneration (Fig. 11.9). Yet no bishop of Wells has ever been canonised, and thus the acts of veneration performed over these 'relics' were somewhat at variance with the prescriptions of Canon Law. This was not an uncommon happening.

Also accompanying six of the effigies are cast leaden plaques bearing the names of the bishops commemorated (Rodwell 1979). Moreover, it was found that at least some of the episcopal bones had been wrapped in red silk, a clear indication of their being treated with the reverence accorded to holy relics.

The Cloister: to be or not to be?

The cloister at Wells is a large, rectangular space enclosed by walks on only three sides. The inward-facing arcading and the upper stories over the east and west walks are all legacies of the fifteenth century, but the buttressed outer walls – and the five original doorways that pierce them – are of early thirteenth-century date (Rodwell 1980a). No work could have begun on the construction of the cloister until the demolition of the Anglo-Saxon cathedral had been substantially accomplished, a situation which did not obtain before the mid-1190s.

Fig. 11.9. Anterior and posterior views of four skulls from the tombs of the Anglo-Saxon bishops. The first and third have had roundels of bone cut from the cranium, post mortem, presumably for the manufacture of amulets; the other two skulls have been anciently limewashed to enhance their display as relics. Photos: Warwick Rodwell.

Recent research, prompted by discoveries made during the 1979 excavation, has suggested that the cloister was part of the original 1170s concept, and that the laying out of its foundations took place following the demolition of the central portions of the old cathedral. It appears that neither the extreme east end (Lady Chapel) nor the west end needed to be demolished for this operation, and they were left standing. Possibly the old Lady Chapel served as a temporary shrine for the remains of the Anglo-Saxon bishops, during the translation process. It is however clear from the arrangement of the foundations and plinths of the east cloister that the complete removal of the Anglo-Saxon chapel was envisaged, and that it was to be replaced by another structure, sited on the east-west axis of the cloister. There can be little doubt that the original intention was to build the chapter house here, as was done at Salisbury. But a decision was made in 1196 to retain and restore the old Lady Chapel, despite its anomalous siting and orientation. The rebuilt chapel was therefore physically bonded to the cloister.

Scrutiny of the cloister plan, and of ephemeral scars on the west wall of the south transept, reveals that a north walk was intended and perhaps begun, but certainly never completed. As conceived, the Wells cloister was thus a perfect square and was to have been integral with the construction of the transept and south-west tower. There would have been a narrow space between the north walk and the nave aisle, analagous to the Plumbery at Salisbury. The change of plan was precipitated by the evolution of the west front design, between the stages of conception and construction.

The ground plan of the west front, with its twin towers flanking the nave aisles, is original, but the exuberant superstruture was not conceived until after *c.* 1225. Its design is generally attributed to Thomas Norreys who succeeded to the position of master mason in 1229 (Harvey 1982, 62). The archaeological evidence synchronizes well with the art historical: the lower part of the west cloister is in bond with the south-west tower, while the upper part is an abutment to it. Hence, work on the cloister was halted while the west front progressed. The low-level niches and prominent angle-shafting to all the buttresses, which characterized the thirteenth-century design, effectively prohibited the completion of the cloister according to the original concept. Omitting the north walk overcame the difficulty of union to a considerable extent, but there was nevertheless an unavoidable conflict when the west walk was completed, towards the middle of the century.

A full study of the cloisters and all structures on the south side of the cathedral has been combined with a report on the archaeology of The Camery. The report was completed in 1993 and publication is awaited (Rodwell forthcoming a).

Archaeology on the West Front

The Dean and Chapter's decision in 1869 not to follow the example of Salisbury (1865) in commissioning Scott to embark upon a wholesale restoration of the Wells west front – with the attendant replacement of the figural sculpture – was responsible for bequeathing to posterity a staggering 297 medieval figures. In fact Scott's consultancy extended to no more than two days on site, which is somewhat puzzling since he nominated J. T. Irvine as clerk of works. The architect for the restoration was Benjamin Ferrey. At the time, Irvine was employed as Scott's own clerk of works at Bath Abbey, and he had henceforth to commute between Wells and Bath, spending three days per week at each. Irvine was thus availed of the opportunity to study the archaeology of Wells Cathedral, which he did in some depth, although his analysis of the main building sequence was later shown to be erroneous (Irvine 1873).

A remarkable record of the 1870–74 restoration was made by T. W. Phillips, a local photographer, and even more comprehensive recording took place when the west front was scaffolded again in 1906; a new study of the sculptures was prepared at the same time (Hope and Lethaby 1905). There is unfortunately little record of the work undertaken in the 1920s, but from the 1930s onward a remarkable series of diaries exists, having been compiled by the master mason, the late W. A. Wheeler. The diaries contain personal observations, as well as details of investigative and repair works throughout the cathedral and the liberty: they are invaluable as a source of archaeological information.

In 1975 the Dean and Chapter embarked upon a twelve-year conservation programme, providing a unique opportunity for a wide ranging study of the architecture, art history and archaeology of the Wells west front. The promotion of this aspect of the project owed much to the cathedral architect, the late A. D. R. Caroe (and subsequently to Mr Martin Caroe). In the first few years, recording was less than adequate and progress was hindered by some sculpture conservators who opposed the very concept of making systematic records of the work as it progressed. Nevertheless, an extensive recording project was carried out from 1980 to 1985.

The sculpture record comprises a dossier of photographic, drawn and written evidence for each figure. Condition before and after conservation is recorded, together with all evidence revealed as work proceeded. An unforeseen wealth of fresh information has been amassed concerning the schools of sculptors involved, the techniques of manufacture, fixing, decoration and former repair (medieval, as well as more recent) of the statues. In addition to the statuary there are some hundreds of specimens of foliage sculpture on capitals, spandrels, tympana, brackets, etc, which have been studied and recorded in the context of the complete architectural framework of the west front.

Wrapped around the twin towers and their buttresses, are no less than 49 separate faces to the west front, and the task of preparing accurate, hand-measured elevation drawings was considered impracticable. The entire composition was therefore recorded and plotted photogrammetrically at a scale of 1:50. Elevation drawings thus prepared have been used as the base-map for archaeological recording, including a stone-by-stone analysis of the fabric. Many fresh insights have been gained through prolonged study into the technical aspects of cathedral building and the mass production of medieval ornament. One interesting little detail is the striking lack of masons' marks on the thirteenth-century components of the west front. So complete is their absence that a matter of workshop policy must be reflected. Masons' marks abound on twelfth-century work at Wells, as they do on fourteenth and fifteenth-century constructions (including the upper parts of the twin west towers); but workshop practice in the early thirteenth century required no individual identification marks. Presumably Thomas Norreys, the master mason, ran his workshop on different lines from those of both his predecessor and his successors.

The Wells west front archive, housed in the cathedral library, has been compiled with two functions in view. First, it is an orderly and academically-based record of discoveries, observations, conservation treatment, practical experiments and research. Second, it is a working tool which will be available to inform and guide future architects and conservators. Repeatedly, it has been found that the most frustrating aspect to any piece of localised repair or conservation is the lack of an accurate and accessible record of previous interventions (Fig. 11.10). Hopefully, this deficiency has been permanently rectified as far as the west front of Wells is concerned. Publication of a substantial report, by Jerry Sampson, on the archaeology, architecture, sculpture and conservation of the west front is expected in due course.

William de Marchia: a failed saint

In common with the majority of English cathedrals, Wells lacks large scale, accurate survey drawings of most of its fabric. In the first place, there was until recently no ground plan to supersede that published in *The Builder* in 1891. The cathedral was therefore fortunate to obtain the services of two young architects for several months in 1978, during which time they prepared fresh survey plans, at two levels, at a scale of 1:100. Study of these plans, and of the less overt anomalies in the fabric that they reveal, has led to the reappraisal of several neglected areas.

One such area is the south wall of the transept. Here, in the centre of the wall, is an ornate tomb recess contain-

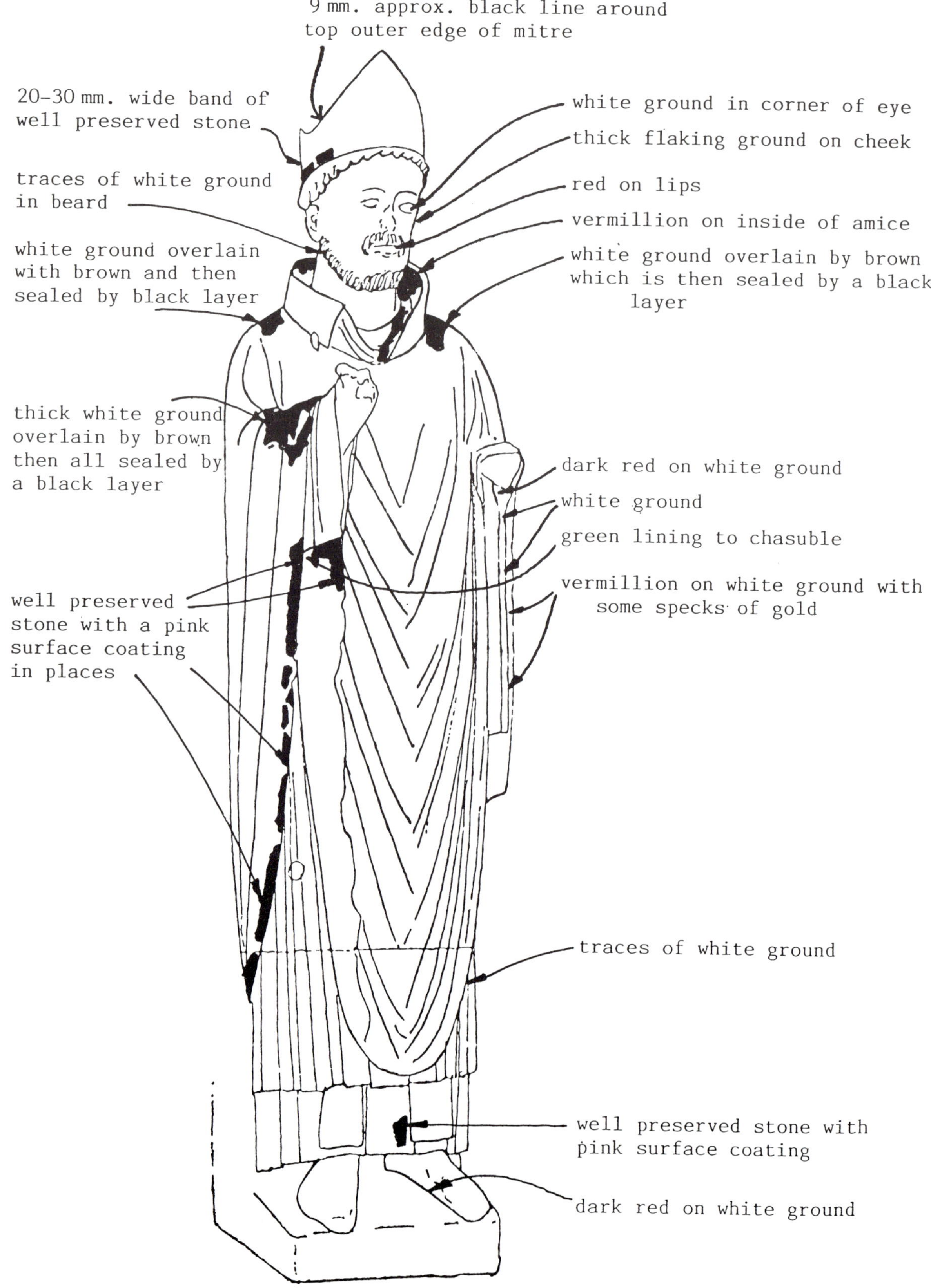

Fig. 11.10. Example of an annotated diagram from the sculpture conservation dossier for west from figure 227. Here the evidence for traces of medieval polychrome is recorded.

ing an effigy of William de Marchia, bishop of Bath and Wells 1293–1302. Twenty years after his death the Wells chapter made strenuous attempts to secure de Marchia's canonization, probably spurred on by Hereford's success, in 1320, in raising bishop Thomas Cantelupe to the status of saint. Since there is no obvious tomb-chest beneath de Marchia's effigy, the question arose: had the putative saint's remains been translated elsewhere? Eventually, with the aid of a small drilling and a cystoscope, the bishop's skeleton, accompanied by crozier and chalice, was located within the wall bench over which the tomb is built. But that was not the end of the enquiry.

Cut into the thickness of the transept wall above de Marchia's tomb is a short passage approached by a tiny intramural stair. In effect, this arrangement forms a gallery on top of the tomb, and must surely have been for the display of holy relics during the period of the attempted canonization. Moreover, it may be no coincidence that higher still – at triforium level – is a small and secure chamber contained within one of the buttresses of the transept wall. Plausibly, this is the chamber from which the cathedral's relics were 'brought down' in the Middle Ages, when required for procession.

Furthermore, set into the south transept wall, immediately east of de Marchia's tomb, is a second canopied recess, also of fourteenth-century date, for which no convincing explanation has yet been proposed (Fig. 11.11). The construction is certainly not a tomb recess, but is either a reredos or part of a shrine enclosure. In the back of the recess is a small chamber, evidently intended to house relics which could be seen through a traceried aperture. But there is a problem: the whole structure faces north, rather than west, and is therefore liturgically unusable in its present position. Suggestions that the construc-

Fig. 11.11. The fourteenth-century shrine-like structure set into the wall of the south transept beside the tomb of bishop William de Marchia. Photo: Jerry Sampson.

tion was the reredos of a chantry chapel that has been swung round on its axis through ninety degrees, since the Reformation, are archaeologically untenable. It is thoroughly built into a window embrasure in the south wall and has not been moved since the Middle Ages.

The possibility that the structure next to de Marchia's tomb might have been built from parts of a shrine enclosure deserves further consideration. Here it is necessary to turn to the east end of the cathedral, to consider yet another anomaly. The quire of the 1170s comprised three bays east of the crossing; this was extended by a further three bays, beginning *c.* 1320. East of the extended quire is the early fourteenth-century Lady Chapel, but between the two elements is an architecturally and spatially important link, the retroquire. This is an elegant space, graced with slender piers supporting a fine tierceron vault. The design bespeaks a feretory, and the arrangement bears a striking resemblance to contemporary Lichfield, where the retroquire was designed to be a worthy setting for the shrine of St Chad.

Most pre-reformation cathedrals housed the relics of at least one notable local saint, for whom a shrine and feretory were created. Wells was the major exception. Yet in the 1320s the architectural setting for a great shrine was being constructed. This can only have been with the presumptive canonization of William de Marchia in mind. But he had, by all accounts, been no saint in his lifetime, and the pope did not see fit to make him one in the hereafter. The Wells Chapter had evidently taken a gamble in building a feretory-retroquire, which has stood empty to the present day. Did they also commission the proposed shrine, or its reredos? If so, it is not inconceivable that some of its components were assembled to form the curious structure next to de Marchia's tomb in the south transept – a monument to a failed canonization.

The Cathedral in its Setting

Chapter House

Being a non-monastic cathedral, Wells was never encumbered by conventual buildings. It was, however, provided with a southern cloister which, apart from giving access to the old Lady Chapel, served only as an enclosed processional path. The chapter house was never built on its intended site adjacent to the cloister, but was contrived to fit into an awkward space alongside the north transept. Begun *c.* 1240, this two-storied octagonal building has given rise to a good deal of speculation; it has, for example, been suggested that the upper floor (containing the chapter house) is a substantially later build than the ground floor (treasury). It has also been observed that non-functional water-spouts appear to emerge from the buttresses at a level far below that of the present roof. This in turn has raised the possibility that the pierced arcade that surmounts the building above vault level – and which carries the roof structure – is an addition.

Study carried out during the restoration of the chapter house in 1988–89 indicated that the two main levels are a single, but perhaps protracted build, and that the contrast between the simplicity of the treasury-undercroft and the florid chapter house is related more to functional status than to chronology. While it has also been shown that the early fourteenth-century roof does not fit the building as snugly as might be expected, it would not appear to relate to a secondary raising of the walls. Moreover, the functionality of the enigmatic water spouts on the buttresses has been established. A curiously inept system of rainwater disposal had been contrived, whereby the parapet gutters discharged into vertical shutes (*c.* 4 m deep) contained within the angle buttresses. A concealed lead trough at the bottom of each shute directed the water to the externally projecting spouts. There was no means of access to clear blockages, and it is small wonder that the system was abandoned in favour of simple lead spouts at parapet level.

Vicars' Close

The same flight of stone stairs that gives access from the north transept to the chapter house also connects with a fifteenth-century bridge, known as the Chaingate, spanning the road which runs along the north side of the cathedral. The Chaingate was not only one of the entrance gates into the precinct but also carried a covered way connecting the cathedral with the common hall of the vicars choral. The hall and its undercroft form the southern termination of the Vicars' Close, a complex of buildings created by Bishop Ralph of Shrewsbury, and historically dated to 1348 (Rodwell 1982d). The unusually elongated plan of the Vicars' Close is less reminiscent of a college quad than, say, Hereford, but the basic principle of the layout was the same (Fig. 11.12).

The northern termination of the Vicars' Close at Wells comprises the chapel and library above, while the east and west flanks contain the forty-two houses occupied by the vicars (now numbered as 28 properties). In 1976–81 a major programme of repairs was carried out in the Vicars' Close, providing the opportunity to study every house and the viscissitudes of its history (many additions and alterations have taken place behind the largely intact fourteenth-century facades). At the same time, the first detailed plans of all floor levels were prepared. Although the basic plan and layout of the individual vicars' houses was originally similar, investigations have revealed that there was a good deal of variation in the positioning and detailing of the windows (Fig. 11.13).

More surprising was the revelation, through excavation, that the foundations for the houses are far from uniform or contiguous: they were not laid out *en bloc*. In fact, some of the units appear to have been built singly, while others were erected in groups of two or three. Squaring the structural evidence with the documentary is not easy, and it now appears that the erection of the houses

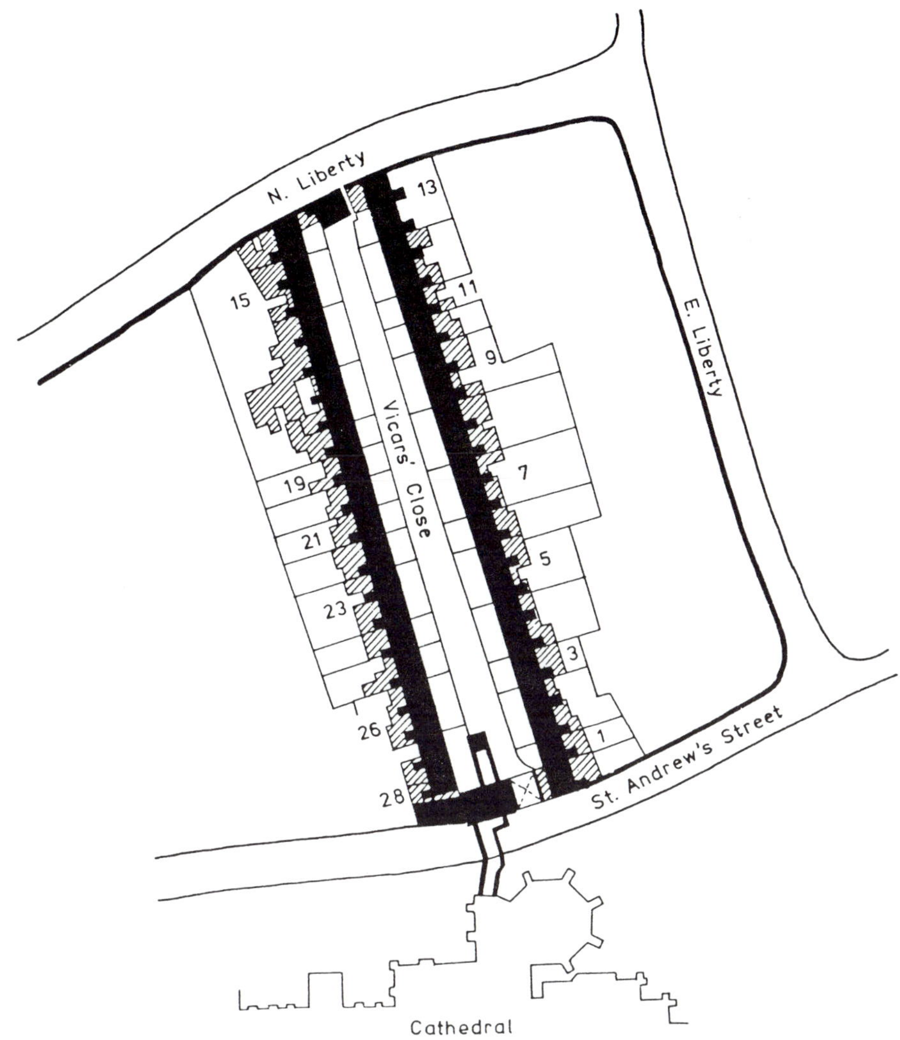

Fig. 11.12. Simplified plan of the Vicars' Close. The forty-two original houses, the chapel and the hall are shown in black, while the later medieval and post-medieval additions are shaded. The Chaingate provides a high-level link between the vicars' hall and the chapter house stair.

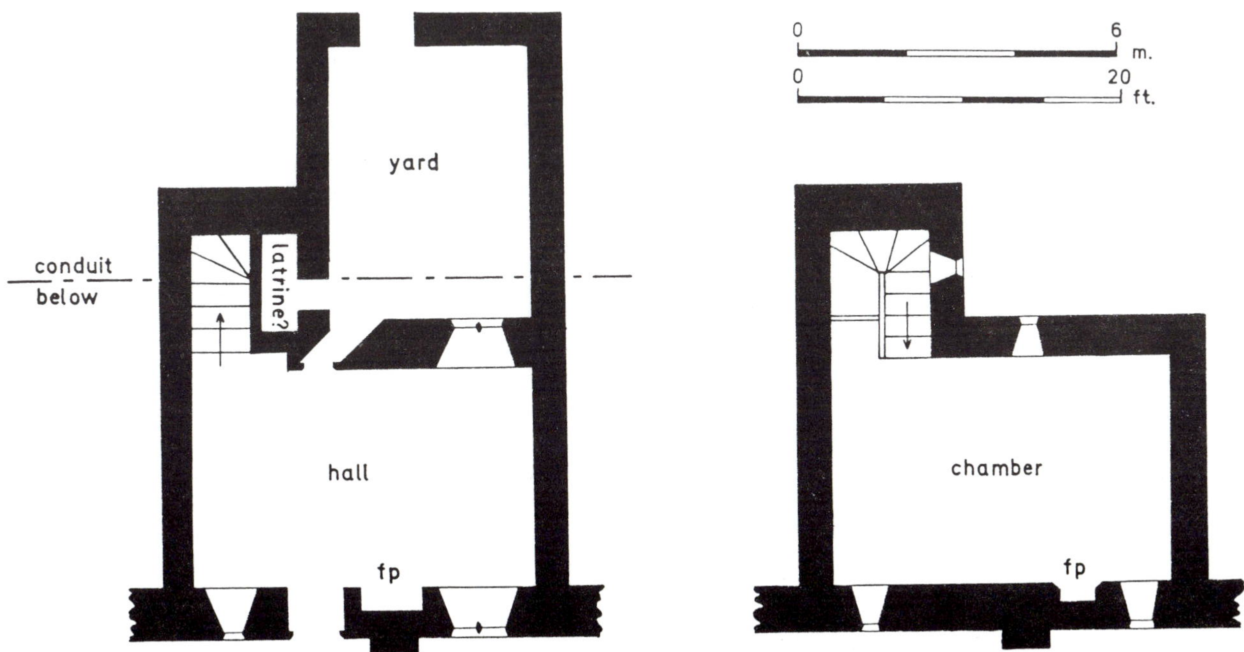

Fig. 11.13. Ground and first floor plans of a typical house for a vicar choral c. 1348.

was a piecemeal operation initiated before 1348, and not finished until some time after the Black Death. In that year the college was incorporated, and the bishop handed over 'a hall, kitchen and bakehouse, and all the other houses *built or to be built*' (my italics).

A further conundrum thrown up by archaeology concerns the chimneys. Every house has a stack projecting from the front wall, and since each stack carries an inset coat of arms of Bishop Bekynton or one of his executors, it has long been accepted that the chimneys (and hence the fireplaces) were mid fifteenth-century additions to formerly unheated houses. However, in each case where excavations or drainage works have exposed the foundations for the chimneys it has been demonstrated that they are integral to the construction of the houses themselves. It is now realised that the armorial plaques which ostensibly 'date' the chimneys are careful insertions, associated with a period of renovation.

A major refurbishment of No. 22 Vicars' Close was carried out in 1991, when much fresh information came to light, especially concerning the original staircase and latrine arrangements. A mid nineteenth-century decorative scheme by William Burgess was also recovered.

Also within the cathedral Liberty (at Wells the precinct has never been called a 'close') most of the medieval canonical houses remain, albeit as yet unstudied. The largest of these, the Old Deanery, is a major courtyard structure dating from the fourteenth and fifteenth centuries. No serious study of the building (now the diocesan office) had taken place until large scale restoration and alteration began in 1989, when a modest level of recording was put in hand and a fresh understanding of its development obtained.

Retrospect: Archaeology at Wells, 1860–75 and 1975–95

The foregoing account deals only with selected aspects of recent archaeology at Wells, above and below ground. Other observations and recording projects have been carried out on the high vaults of the cathedral, on the cloister vaulting, and the north porch, on parts of the precinct wall, in some of the canonical houses, in the grounds of the Bishop's Palace, and on the Cathedral Green. All have contributed to the global picture of the archaeology and architectural history of the cathedral.

A steadily increasing volume of tourists passing through the cathedral is rapidly bringing about the destruction of the historic floor surfaces and, particularly, the inscribed and decorated ledger slabs. This is a widespread phenomenon which has only recently begun to receive proper archaeological attention (Rodwell forthcoming b). In 1993 the Dean and Chapter of Wells initiated a full-scale surveyof the memorial slabs and plaques of the cathedral (Rodwell 1994).

For the most part, the cathedral, its ancillary and secular buildings, and their boundary walls had not been subjected to comprehensive works of repair or alteration since the 1870s. Now, however, the hundred-year cycle of renovation has come round again and the wheels of restoration have been churning incessantly. But now they are slowing down and the work is largely over. During those years we have witnessed the modernisation of the interiors of most of the domestic and office buildings; the conversion of unused spaces; adaptations to new uses; comprehensive re-roofing, repointing and reflooring; new drainage schemes and landscaping; alterations to boundary walls, gateways and access arrangements; the creation of car parks and service facilities.

During the course of these works a vast wealth of evidence has been revealed, bearing on the architectural, ecclesiastical and social histories of virtually all the buildings and structures in the Wells Liberty. A little of this new evidence remains visible, but much has been covered up again, and some has been unavoidably destroyed. Almost without exception, the works of restoration, conservation and adaptation have been specified and carried out to the highest levels of excellence currently attainable, with the result that losses have been minimised. Indeed, Wells has been a leader in several aspects of the conservation field, and work on the west front, in particular, has received interest and acclaim on a European scale.

The opportunities for study and recording have been legion, and the goodwill of all parties for so doing has been ever present. But one component has been lacking, namely the systematic provision for an adequate level of funding for the investigation and recording of archaeological evidence. Excavations in The Camery were supported by the Dean and Chapter, the Department of the Environment and the British Academy. The recording of the west front of the cathedral was sponsored entirely out of Dean and Chapter and Appeal funds. Despite the injection of large sums of public money into the major restoration programme at the Vicars' Close (funded by the Department of the Environment, Church Commissioners and Somerset County Council), it was impossible to extract a budget for recording. This was simply dismissed as 'unnecessary'. The limited archaeological work that was carried out was entirely due to the enthusiasm and good offices of Martin Caroe, the architect responsible for the project.

While small grants have recently been made by English Heritage for the limited recording of the east cloister, one canonical house and a length of precinct wall, other restorations of important buildings (including medieval gatehouses) have been supported by public funds, but the work has proceeded without adequate recording. The most disturbing aspect, however, of all the works carried out at Wells concerns the 'enhancement' schemes devised, funded and implemented by the county and district councils. The first project, carried out in 1981, was in the Vicars' Close. The entire central court was dug out by a mechanical excavator, in preparation for a new drainage and road-paving scheme. The budget for archaeological recording that had initially been earmarked was withdrawn as a 'necessary economy', leaving the County Archaeologist, with no resources at his disposal, merely to observe the archaeology of the Vicars' Close being carted away by a continuous stream of lorries. There was no technical need for this project to have been carried out: it was merely cosmetic.

The second 'enhancement' scheme related to the Cathedral Green. This had been landscaped in 1874, and once again there was no technical need for carrying out major uorks. Nevertheless, a hugely ambitious, but historically inappropriate, scheme was launched. Following several years of persistent pressure by the Cathedrals Advisory Commission, the Dean and Chapter and their Consultant Archaeologist, the projected undertaking was gradually whittled down in an attempt to reduce both the level of archaeological destruction, and the trivialising of the setting of the cathedral's west front. The minimal scheme implemented in 1988–89 has met with general approval. Once again, however, the budget for archaeology was excised as an economy measure, although it was possible on this occasion for the County Archaeologist, with very modest resources at his disposal, to carry out some small-scale investigations.

No English cathedral city can boast a more completely preserved ecclesiastical heritage than Wells. Apart from the cathedral, its cloister and immediate precincts, the wholly intact Vicars' Close, and the memorable Bishop's Palace with its great moat, there is the medieval deanery, a dozen canonical residences, the twelfth-century canon's barn, the fifteenth-century bishop's barn, Bubwith's fifteenth-century almshouses, the twelve houses of the *Nova Opera*, four great gatehouses, the Liberty walls, and much else besides. Post-medieval losses have been remarkably few: Bishop Stillington's Chapel (now excavated), two or three canonical houses, and a college of chantry priests.

For the most part, the historic buildings are statutorily Listed, and one gatehouse is a Scheduled Ancient Monument. Part of the Bishop's Palace is also Scheduled. But less than five percent of the area of prime and indisputable archaeological importance enjoys any form of protection. In 1979 the Department of the Environment intimated that it was proposing to schedule a substantial area around the cathedral. The matter was never pursued, and during the ensuing sixteen years several proposals were made for the revival of the scheduling, but to no avail.

In the 1860s and '70s, when there was no form of statutory protection for buildings and sites of historic importance, the Dean and Chapter of Wells, and their architects, carried out restoration programmes on their properties that were uncharacteristically conservative for the era. Likewise, although there was no machinery for implementing archaeological recording, or initiating programmes of research, these activities were somehow set in motion. We have already mentioned Phillips, the photographer, who recorded the west front, and Irvine, the clerk of works, who made drawings and wrote a substantial paper on the development of the cathedral. At the same time J. H. Parker was engaged in the restoration of buildings in the Vicars' Close and in antiquarian studies generally. His *Architectural Antiquities of the City of Wells* (1866) is a valuable record and assessment of all the major ecclesiastical buildings, the cathedral excepted.

Scholarly research, not specifically related to restoration works, was personally promoted by Canon Church, and he was responsible for the first archaeological excavation in 1894, voluntarily funded by the Dean and Chapter. It is sobering to reflect, as another hundred-year restoration cycle comes to a close, on the resources that were available for recording and investigation in a cathedral precinct in the 1970s and '80s. The similarities and the contrasts between the two centuries are striking. The current basic philosophy towards repair and conservation (not 'restoration') adopted by the Dean and Chapter, and their professional advisors, is almost identical to that of a century ago. While insisting that work of enduring quality must be carried out (no-one can afford to re-scaffold a major building every decade or two), the principle of minimal intervention with the historic fabric has been maintained for work on both the cathedral and the domestic buildings.

There has also been, in the two centuries, a similarly striking approach to antiquarian investigation, recording and research on the part of the Dean and Chapter and the several architects involved. Locally, the desire and goodwill for carrying out such studies has been continually present and, wherever possible, funds and assistance in kind have been made available.

The contrasts, however, between the two eras tell a sorry tale. Since the 1880s a panoply of machinery at both national and local government levels has been constructed not only to provide protection for historic buildings and buried archaeological sites, but also to fund preservation, repair *and* archaeological recording. The operation of this machinery has, however, left much to be desired. The majority of the archaeological recording of the last decade at Wells has been carried out *despite* the public provisions existing in the 1970s and '80s, rather than with their assistance. The problems encountered may be summed up in a single sentence: there has been a fundamental paucity of understanding of, and little interest in, the archaeology of cathedral complexes on the part of secular authorities, both national and local, and a reluctance to become 'involved'. That was certainly the position until 1990, when the passing of the Cathedrals Measure refocused national interest in these major buildings. At the same time, the advent of state aid for cathedral repairs began to release funding for the associated archaeological recording.At Wells, the major project to benfit from assistance given by English Heritage, so far, has been the recording of the east and south cloisters.

Another century will probably elapse before major opportunities once again arise for archaeological investigations in and around Wells Cathedral, and its associated building complexes. Posterity will surely find it hard to

Another century will probably elapse before major opportunities once again arise for archaeological investigations in and around Wells Cathedral, and its associated building complexes. Posterity will surely find it hard to excuse the saga of lost opportunities, inadequate records and destroyed evidence, when foreknowledge, goodwill and expertise were all present on the part of the ecclesiastical authorities, but the unwillingness of the secular bodies to collaborate, even after repeated requests, led to so much being sacrificed. Whereas in the 1970s and '80s the machinery existed to carry out an exemplary study of the archaeology and architectural history of our most completely preserved medieval cathedral complex, during some fifteen years of continuous restoration, the motivation to operate it was unattainable. Happily, in the 1990s a new era dawned.

ACKNOWLEDGEMENTS

This paper is dedicated to the late Linzee Colchester, Cathedral Archivist, whose tireless researches have so greatly advanced our understanding of Wells Cathedral and its history; so often, the dating and interpretation of archaeological evidence benefitted from his intimate knowledge of relevant documentation.

None of the results described here could have been achieved without the whole-hearted support of the Dean and Chapter of Wells; and the personal interest and involvement of the Very Revd. Patrick Mitchell, formerly Dean of Wells, has been of inestimable value. A great debt of gratitude is also owed to the three architects formerly engaged upon work at the cathedral, the late A. D. R. Caroe, Martin Caroe and Alan Rome, for their enthusiasm and cooperation; and similar thanks are due to Peter Cooley, the Superintendent of Works.

The sustained assistance of many colleagues in different aspects of the Wells project is gratefully acknowledged, and particular mention must be made of Dr Juliet Rogers, the late Norman Cook and Jerry Sampson.

Bibliography

Bilson, J. 1928: Notes on the Earlier Architectural History of Wells Cathedral. *Archaeol. Jnl.* 85, 23–68.

Buckle, E. 1894: On the Lady Chapel by the Cloister of Wells Cathedral and the adjacent buildings. *Proc. SANHS.* 40, 32–63.

Cather, S., Park, D. & Williamson, P. (eds.) 1990: *Early Medieval Wall Painting and Painted Sculpture in the British Isles.* (BAR, 216).

Church, C.M. 1888: Wells Cathedral. *Proc. SANHS.* 34, 98–113.

Church, C.M. 1894: Documents bearing upon the late Excavations on the South Side of the Cathedral Church of Wells. *Proc. SANHS.* 40, 20–31.

Cockerell, C.R. 1851: *Iconography of the West Front of Wells Cathedral* (Oxford).

Colchester, L.S. (ed.) 1982: *Wells Cathedral: A History* (Shepton Mallet).

Colchester, L.S. 1987: *Wells Cathedral.* (The New Bell's Cathedral Guides, London).

Colchester, L.S. and Harvey, J.H. 1974: Wells Cathedral, *Archaeol. Jnl.* 131, 200–14.

Davenport, P. 1988: Bath Abbey. *Bath History* 2, 1–26.

Faull, M.L. (ed.) 1984: *Studies in Late Anglo-Saxon Settlement* (Oxford).

Harvey, J.H. 1982: The Building of Wells Cathedral, I: 1175–1307. In Colchester 1982, 52–75.

Hope, W.H. St John 1909: On the first Cathedral Church of Wells and the site thereof. *Proc. SANHS.* 55, 85–96.

Hope, W.H. St John and Lethaby, W.R. 1905: The Imagery and Sculptures on the West Front of Wells Cathedral. *Archaeologia* 59, 143–206.

Irvine, J.T. 1873: The Fabric of the Cathedral Church of St Andrew at Wells, *Proc. SANHS* 19, 2–47.

O'Leary, T.J. and Rodwell, W.J. 1991: A Reconstruction of the Norman Cathedral Ground Plan. In P. Davenport, ed. *Archaeology in Bath, 1976-1985*, 32-8 Oxford Univ. Cttee for Archaeol., Mono. 28.

Parker, J.H. 1866: *The Architectural Antiquities of the City of Wells* (Oxford).

Pearce, S.M. (ed.) 1982: *The Early Church in Western Britain and Ireland* (BAR 102).

Robinson, J.A. 1914: Effigies of Saxon Bishops at Wells. *Archaeologia* 65, 95–112.

Robinson, J.A. 1919: *The Saxon Bishops of Wells.* (British Academy Supp. Papers 4, London).

Robinson, J.A. 1928: Documentary Evidence relating to the Building of the Cathedral Church of Wells. *Archaeol. Jnl.* 85, 1–17.

Rodwell, W.J. 1979: Lead Plaques from the Tombs of the Saxon Bishops of Wells. *Antiq. Jnl.* 59, 407–10.

Rodwell, W.J. 1980a: The Cloisters of Wells Reconsidered. *The Friends of Wells Cathedral.* Report for 1980, 15–19.

Rodwell, W.J. 1980b: Wells, the Cathedral and City. *Current Archaeol.* 7 (no. 73), 38–44.

Rodwell, W.J. 1981: The Lady Chapel by the Cloister at Wells and the site of the Anglo-Saxon Cathedral. *Medieval Art and Architecture at Wells and Glastonbury.* B.A.A. Conf. Trans. 4, 1–9.

Rodwell, W.J. 1982a: The Origins of Wells Cathedral. *Antiquity* 56, 215–18.

Rodwell, W.J. 1982b: The Anglo-Saxon and Norman Churches at Wells. In Colchester 1982, 1–23.

Rodwell, W.J. 1982c: From Mausoleum to Minster: the early Development of Wells Cathedral. In Pearce 1982, 49–59.

Rodwell, W.J. 1982d: The Buildings of Vicars' Close. In Colchester 1982, 212–26.

Rodwell, W.J. 1984: Churches in the Landscape: Aspects of Topography and Planning. In Faull 1984, 1–25.

Rodwell, W.J. 1987: *Wells Cathedral: Excavations and Discoveries.* Third edn. (The Friends of Wells Cathedral).

Rodwell, W.J. 1990: Anglo-Saxon Painted Sculpture at Wells, Breamore and Barton-upon-Humber. In Cather, Park and Williamson, 161–75.

Rodwell, W.J. 1994: Wells Cathedral: A Plan and Schedule of Tombs, Memorial Slabs, Commemorative Plaques and Inscriptions on the Fabric. (Wells Cathedral Library, unpublished report).

Rodwell, W.J. forthcoming a.: *The Archaeology of Wells Cathedral: Excavations and Structural Studies, 1979-93.* English Heritage Monograph.

Rodwell, W.J. forthcoming b.: The Archaeology of Church and Cathedral Floors. In J.Fawcett, ed., *Historic Floors at Risk:*

A Guide to Good Practice. (London).

Scrase, A.J. [1989]: *Wells: A Study of Town Origins and Early Development* (Bristol Polytechnic: Town and Country Planning Working Paper No. 12).

SANHS: Somerset Archaeological and Natural History Society.

Willis, R. 1864: Wells Cathedral. *Proc. SANHS.* 12, 14–24.

Recent Archaeology in Winchester Cathedral

John Crook

Introduction: brief summary of previous archaeological research

As in the case of so many major British cathedrals, Professor Robert Willis was the pioneer of the archaeological approach to the history of Winchester cathedral (Willis 1846). Although nearly a century and a half has elapsed since Willis's paper was published, no student of Winchester's architectural history can afford to ignore his findings, and subsequent investigations continue to confirm the penetrating accuracy of his analysis. Willis's work on Winchester does have some limitations. For example, he concentrated on features visible from the ground or at least from readily accessible parts of the cathedral, perhaps because his lecture was intended to introduce a tour of the building.[1] His assessment of documentary sources has largely been superseded by more recent work.[2] Nor did Willis concern himself overmuch with the place of Winchester cathedral in the wider perspective of European architecture; leaving to others the comparative approach, he treated the building as an isolated artefact, mentally taking it to pieces like a machine and examining the relationship of its various components – an analytical approach suited, perhaps, to the Professor of Engineering that he was.

As an architectural historian Willis was well ahead of his time, and for the next 60 years no further progress was made in the study of the fabric of Winchester cathedral, even though several building projects took place which might have shed useful light on the building's history. In 1886, for example, Dean Kitchin – a keen archaeologist and historian of the cathedral[3] – removed from the crypt a mass of fourteenth-century infill which had been brought in to raise the crypt floor above the winter water-table. This operation was inadequately recorded by today's standards, and Kitchin's published descriptions of the works seem limited to brief progress reports in local newspapers (Kitchin 1886), which were repeated in accounts submitted to learned societies by Canon Collier (1886) and T. F. Kirby (1887).

Likewise, the great underpinning operation of 1905–12, in which a deep-sea diver was involved (Henderson and Crook 1984), should have provided marvellous opportunities for archaeological investigation, for the foundations of the outer walls of the entire cathedral were excavated during the course of the underpinning process. Though the architect and his clerk of works kept copious notes (*Jackson Collection*), these were mainly concerned with technical procedures, and archaeological discoveries were noted only incidentally. Nevertheless, the surviving documentation has proved of some value in more recent investigations of the cathedral, providing evidence, for example, for the provenance of an important collection of sculptural fragments thought to have been associated with St Swithun's shrine (Tudor-Craig and Keen 1983; Crook 1985b).

At the time of the underpinning operation Charles Peers and Harold Brakspear were preparing a description of Winchester cathedral for the *Victoria County History (VCH Winchester*, 50-9). The scope of their analysis was wider than Willis's – they included, for example, many more of the cathedral's monuments and other artefacts in their detailed description of the visible fabric – but their survey added little to Willis's observation on the general architectural development of the church.

In the twentieth century successive architects to the Dean and Chapter of Winchester began to take a more informed interest in the structural history of the building in their care, and considered the historical implications of discoveries made during building work. T. D. Atkinson, Cathedral Architect from 1936, compiled notes on various aspects of the fabric;[4] perhaps in preparation for a book on the cathedral close like the one that he had already published for Ely (Atkinson 1933). He also submitted some useful, though regrettably brief, articles in the *Winchester Cathedral Record*. Published annually by the Friends of Winchester Cathedral, this journal has always had a strong historical and archaeological bias. Atkinson's successor as Architect, Wilfrid Carpenter Turner (who had previously held the post of Architectural Surveyor to the Dean and Chapter), was an equally enthusiastic architectural historian, and contributed to the understanding of particular areas of the building, complementing the work of his wife, Barbara Carpenter Turner, on the broader history of the cathedral and city.

The 1960s saw the largest archaeological investigation hitherto undertaken in a British city. Under the direction of Martin Biddle the site of Old Minster was discovered and its robber-trenches fully excavated - the results are only now being published in their definitive form after many years of painstaking analysis by Martin and Birthe Biddle (Biddle and Kjlbye-Biddle, forthcoming).[5] But the architectural development of the present cathedral lay outside the terms of reference of this excavation project.

The British Archaeological Association's conference at Winchester in 1980 provided new opportunities for coordinated research on various aspects of Winchester cathedral. Richard Gem (1983, 1–12) and Eric Fernie (1983, 13–19) contributed important articles on the place of the romanesque cathedral in the development of eleventh- and twelfth-century architecture, and the *Transactions* of that conference included valuable studies of wall-paintings, the tile pavements, certain sculptural fragments, and the roof timberwork of the cathedral and buildings in the cathedral close.[6]

More recently, a lively debate between Peter Draper and Francis Woodman (Draper 1978; Woodman 1983; Draper 1986) has clarified the question of the thirteenth-century remodelling of the east arm of Winchester cathedral.[7] Our own investigation of various aspects of the architectural history of Winchester cathedral owes much to this debate. In his 1986 paper, Peter Draper (1986, 73) emphasised that further progress in understanding the complexities of the thirteenth- and fourteenth-century building campaigns was likely to be limited by the lack of good measured drawings. The opportunity of providing such drawings arrived sooner than expected. Late in 1986 a hole for a temporary water supply was pierced through the crown of the crypt vault, and this allowed a precisely correlated datum to be established at main floor and crypt levels. During the following six months we undertook an accurate survey of the east arm of the cathedral. This was the basis for a two-fold research project. Firstly, we examined and re-assessed all evidence for the design of the romanesque east arm (Crook 1989). This part of the eleventh-century cathedral was completely replaced above pavement level between the thirteenth and sixteenth centuries, but enough evidence survives for both the plan and the elevations to be reconstructed with reasonable certainty. At the same time, a careful examination was made of the architectural development of the transepts (Crook and Kusaba 1991). Secondly, a more detailed investigation was undertaken of one of the most enigmatic areas of the cathedral: the so-called 'Feretory platform' behind the high altar screen, and the curious tunnel-like structure east of the platform, known an the 'Holy Hole'. This work turned out to form a logical sequence to the investigations of Martin Biddle and his collaborators on the cult of St Swithun in Old Minster - hence its eventual place of publication in the *Winchester Studies* series (Crook forthcoming 8).

Investigating the Romanesque crypt and eastern arm

The extant crypt of Winchester cathedral (Fig. 12.1) remains a supremely evocative example of eleventh-cen-

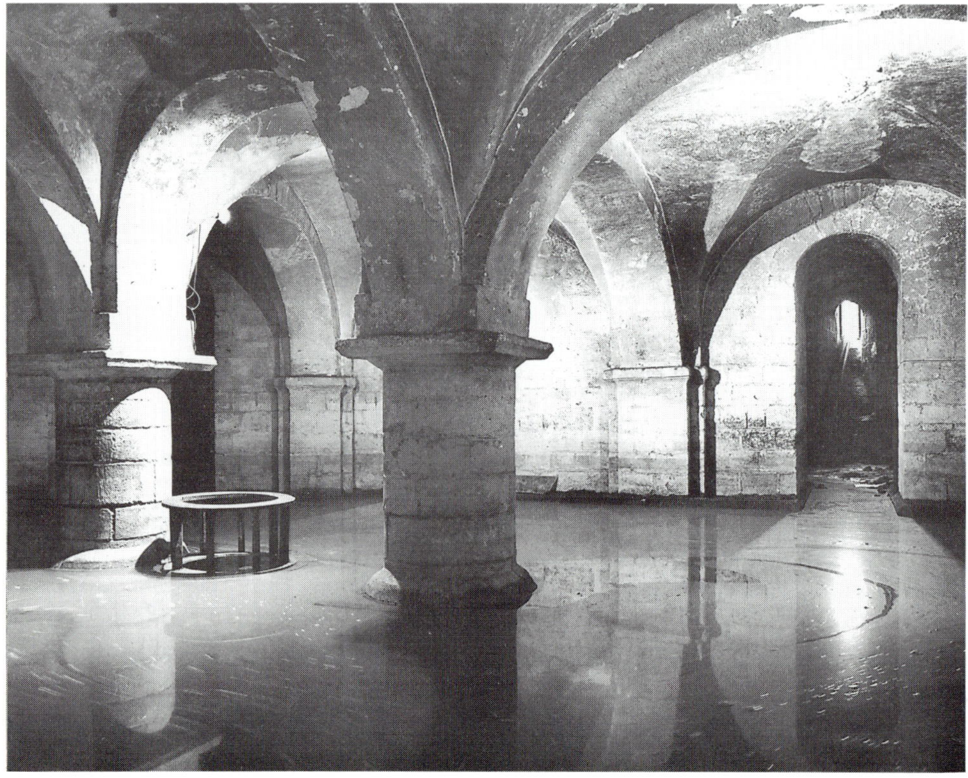

Fig. 12.1. The romanesque crypt, Winchester cathedral, during winter flooding. Photo: John Crook.

tury romanesque architecture. It underlay the entire original east arm, and provides the plan of this part of the eleventh-century church, which has been completely replaced above pavement level (Figs. 12.2, 12.3). One area that had never previously been satisfactorily investigated was the west end of the crypt, and especially its entrances (Fig. 12.4). Stone-by-stone examination and measurement of the masonry of the westernmost bay indicated that the crypt had been shortened by 1 m in the early twelfth century: a consequence of the rebuilding of the crossing tower on broader footings after its collapse in 1107. This had concealed any evidence for possible entrances in line with the nave aisles through the west wall of the crypt; the earliest surviving entrances were lateral ones from the transepts. These dated from the twelfth century, but in our view similar lateral entrances formed part of the pre-1107 scheme. Evidence for the twelfth-century crypt entrances had been excavated by Atkinson in 1934 during the installation of central heating pipes, but apart from a brief note in the *Winchester Cathedral Record* (Atkinson 1939) had never been adequately published. Enough features remained to indicate that twelve steps led down into the crypt from the transept (Fig. 12.5): the crypt door (whose rebated reveals and external jamb-shafts partially survive on the west side) was at the seventh step down, where there was a wider landing. The north-west crypt entrance was remodelled in the early fourteenth century (probably at the same time as the floor of the crypt was raised to cope with the water-table problem) and again in the nineteenth century. The equivalent entrance in the south-west corner of the crypt had also been remodelled *c.*1320, and again in the early sixteenth century.

One part of the crypt that still requires archaeological investigation is the west end of the central chamber, where three bays have been blocked off and (it is thought) filled in. The date of this infill is uncertain, but a date bracket of 1150–1320 seems most likely. The purpose of the infill was presumably to give greater stability to the crypt vaulting, though the groin-vaults of these three bays, where visible, appears intact. It might also be valuable to excavate the small area at the west end of the south aisle of the crypt, where the earth infill raising the floor was not removed by Kitchin; he had feared that its removal might jeopardise still further the stability of the cathedral walls in this area (Kitchin 1886b).

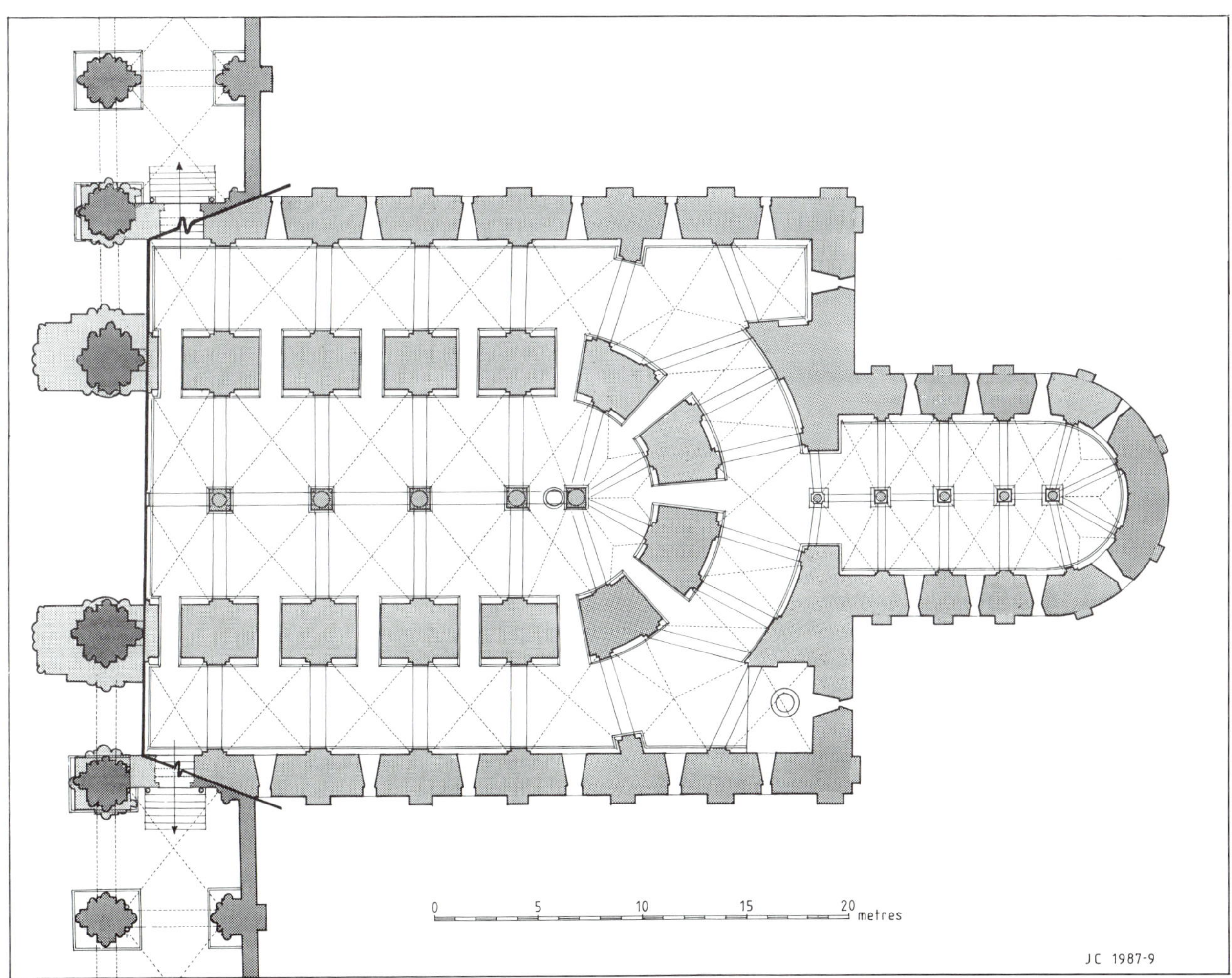

Fig. 12.2. Plan of the crypt, and of part of the crossing and transepts at main level, showing the eleventh- and twelfth-century tower pier profiles and twelfth-century lateral entrance to crypt.

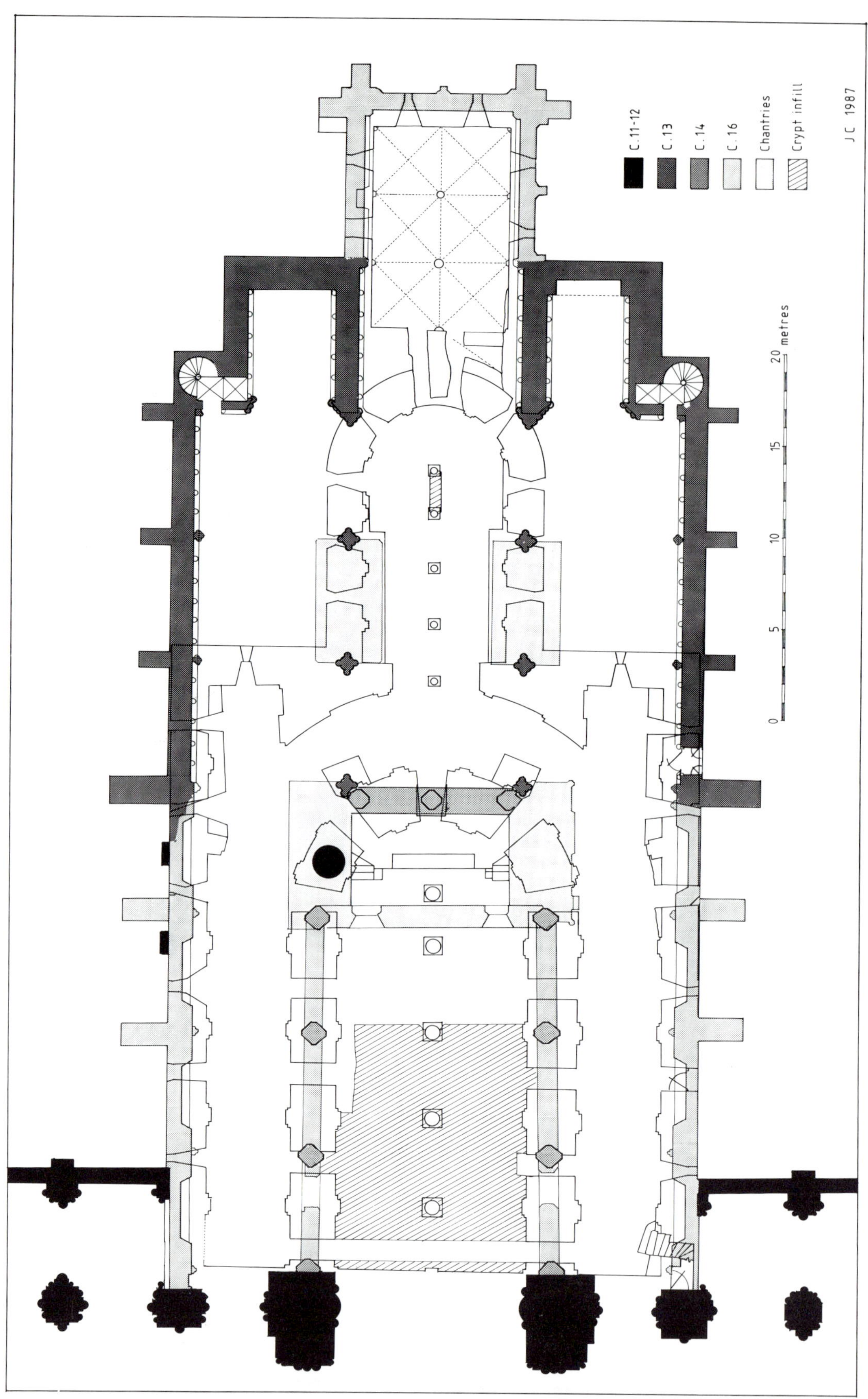

Fig. 12.3. Phased plan of the present eastern arm superimposed on the outline of the romanesque crypt.

Fig. 12.4. Three successive entrances to the crypt from the north transept: twelfth-century jamb and nook-shaft (visible within the central heating access pit, foreground); fourteenth-century arch (midway down stairs into crypt); present entrance arch of c. 1815. Photo: John Crook.

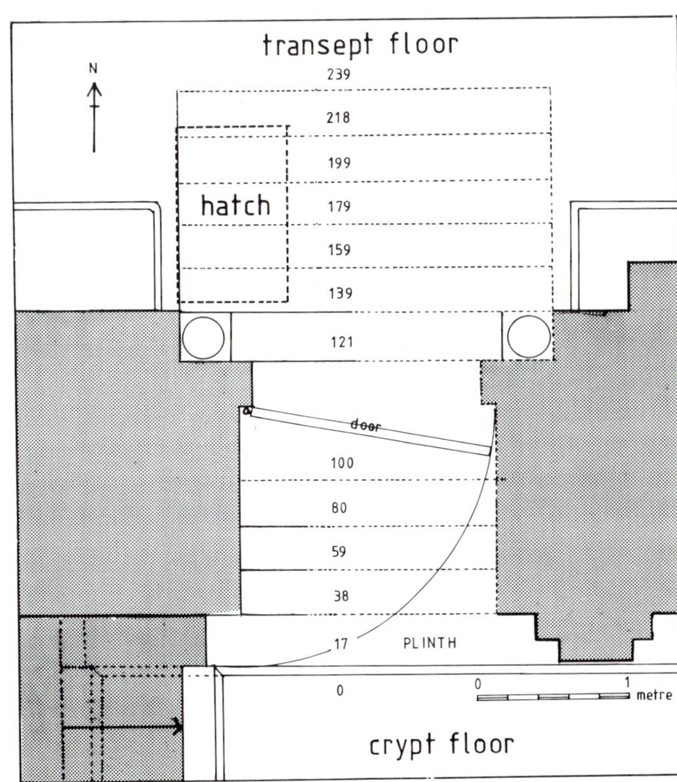

Fig. 12.5. Plan of the twelfth-century entrance to the crypt from the north transept. The pecked lines indicate conjectural elements, including the original position of the west wall of the crypt before the central tower was rebuilt after 1107. Figures indicate the height (in cm) of each step above the crypt floor.

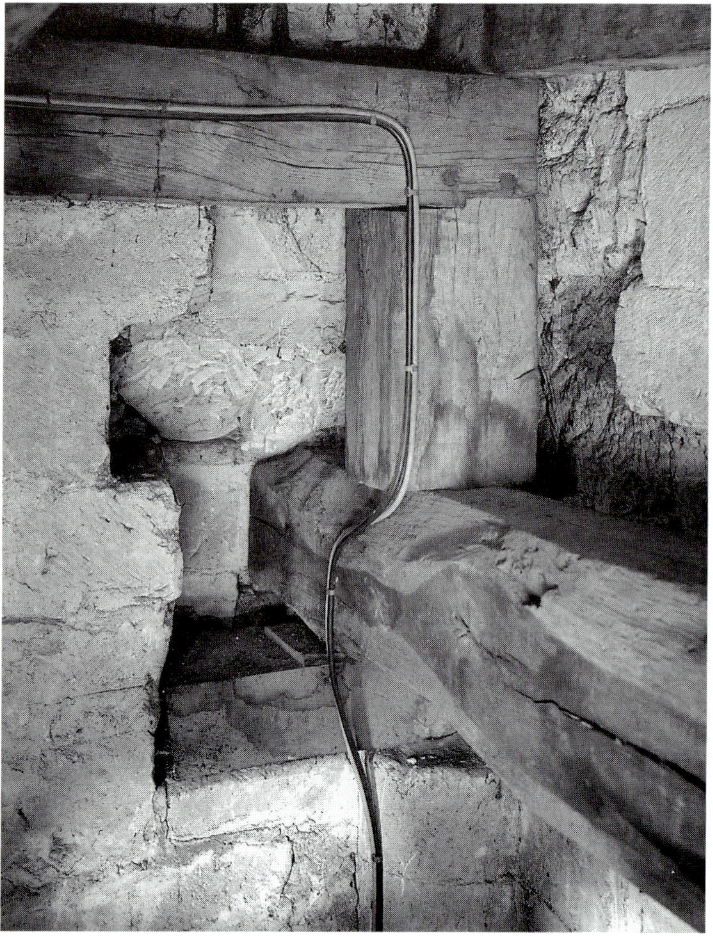

Fig. 12.6. Vestiges of the gallery respond shafts and capitals visible in the presbytery aisle roof space. They are embedded within the fourteenth-century presbytery wall at its junction with the east face of the north-east tower pier. Photo: John Crook.

The crypt preserves the plan of the original east end of the cathedral: an unusual hybrid of apse-and-ambulatory and apse-echelon formulae. In its plan, as in other aspects of its design, Winchester is unique. There is also some evidence for the elevations. The springing of arches survives at various levels against the east face of the crossing tower (Fig. 12.6), and these truncated elements provide the heights of the three storeys of the elevation of the eastern arm. The ground floor level of the romanesque choir and presbytery had been investigated by Wilfrid Carpenter Turner,[9] and we discovered independent evidence for the pavement level of the eleventh-century choir (55 cm below the present pavement) and for lateral entrances at the west end of the choir, aligned to the western aisle of the transepts. Until the west aisle of the south transept was infilled *c.* 1160 to form the Treasury attributed to Henry of Blois (Kusaba 1988) processions would have been feasible out of the choir, round the transept aisles, and down into the crypt.

It was also possible to examine the floor levels in the presbytery area. A *sondage* within an existing electricity conduit proved that the floor level of the high altar step was unchanged since the eleventh century, though the area in the apex of the apse, behind the high altar, had been elevated further still in the mid-twelfth century to form the Feretory platform.

The stylobate supporting the arcade of the romanesque presbytery had been excavated in 1969 during the replacement of the thirteenth-century tile pavement in the north aisle of the presbytery (Carpenter Turner 1969). Careful evaluation of oral accounts of the discoveries made at that time, together with comparison of alignments at crypt and main level, suggested that the outline of the stylobate preserved in the configuration of the modern pavement in the north aisle was correct, indicating an alternating system of piers in the straight bays.

One element of the arcade that survives above ground level had been discussed by Willis (1846, 43 and 77): the fragment of one of the five cylindrical piers in the romanesque apse, visible beneath an open flight of stairs leading to the higher level of Bishop Gardiner's Chantry chapel (Fig. 12.7). The tooling of the masonry of the chantry footings around the pier-base fragment suggested that it had been exposed in this way as an antiquarian curiosity *c.* 1820, when the floor between the Feretory platform and the Great Screen was lowered to its pre-Reformation level. Detailed measurements and drawing revealed that the romanesque pier-base had been incorporated in a thirteenth-century remodelling of the Feretory platform – a strong argument in favour of Willis's view (more recently challenged by Francis Woodman (1983, 95)) that the romanesque apse remained standing until the early fourteenth century.

Though the remains of the romanesque eastern arm are

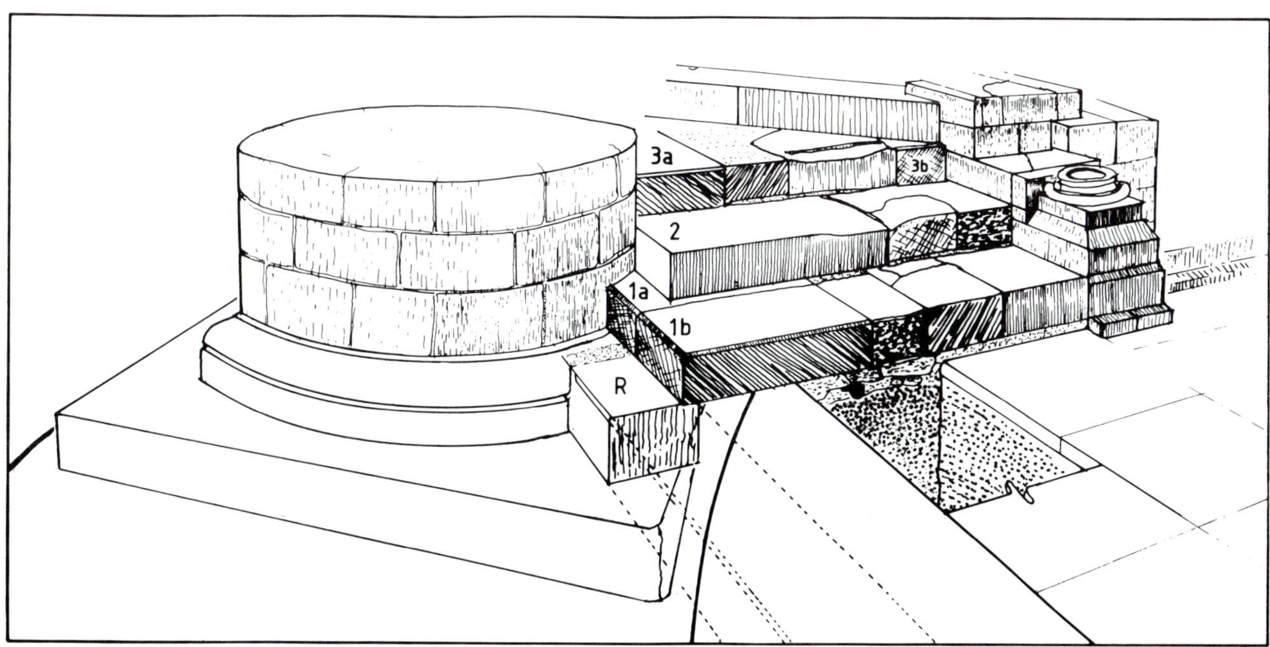

Fig. 12.7. Surviving eleventh-century pier base beneath stair to Bishop Gardiner's chantry chapel, and abutting thirteenth-century steps to Feretory platform.

fragmentary, enough survives for a reconstruction to be made of the elevations (Fig. 12.8) and, indeed, of the external appearance of this part of the eleventh-century cathedral (Fig. 12.9).

Investigation of the transepts

We found it somewhat surprising that the most extensive parts of the Norman cathedral to survive above ground level – the transepts – had scarcely been examined in detail since Willis worked out the general lines of their history in 1845. Some individual aspects had, however, been studied, notably in Charles Moore's paper on the aisle vaulting (Moore 1916), Kenneth Qualmann's report on the excavation of the 'Calefactory' (Qualmann 1986), and Yoshio Kusaba's investigation of the 'Treasury' of bishop Henry of Blois (Kusaba 1988). In the summer of 1988 Dr Kusaba and I undertook an intensive examination of the transepts with a view to checking and, if possible, refining, Willis's conclusions (Crook and Kusaba 1991).

Willis had noted (1846, 26–7) that the corner piers and responds had been strengthened in preparation for towers over the corner bays at the ends of the transepts; this reinforcement was secondary, so the towers did not form part of the original design. He did not, however, comment on the evidence for transverse arches over the east and west aisles at gallery level. These were required to support the corresponding wall of each tower, i.e. the north sides of the towers at the end of the south transept and the south side of their equivalents in the north transept. In fact, modified elements of these arches exist in all four cases, converted into pilasters after the tower scheme was abandoned. It is curious that Willis, normally so observant, should have missed them. Equally exciting was our discovery of the springing of a groined vault at clerestory level over the north-east corner bay of the north transept, and of a blocked access door into the chamber above the vaulting, leading from the newel stair in the corner of the transept. This evidence, together with the fragment of blind arcading in the north wall of the transept (which Willis *did* draw from ground level), suggested to us that the north-east corner tower was actually completed; a conclusion supported by the detail of subsequent modifications made when the tower was taken down.

The anomalous 'double-bay' system at clerestory level in the outer bays of the transept (Fig. 12.10) was also an afterthought introduced while preparations for the four corner towers were in progress, and retained despite the abandonment of the towers.[10] It appeared to have been adopted throughout the later bays of the nave. A stepped junction was identified in the surviving romanesque south aisle wall of the nave, showing that in the initial campaign (before the demolition of Old Minster in 1093–4) only three nave bays were completed. Once Old Minster, which partially occupied the site of the nave, had been taken down it was possible to complete the cathedral. The full-length shafts on dosserets, visible in the nave roof space (except where concealed behind fourteenth-century thickening of the walls associated with Wykeham's vaulting), occur only in every other bay, indicating that the alternating scheme at clerestory level was employed in these later nave bays.

We also noted the way in which the upper parts of the

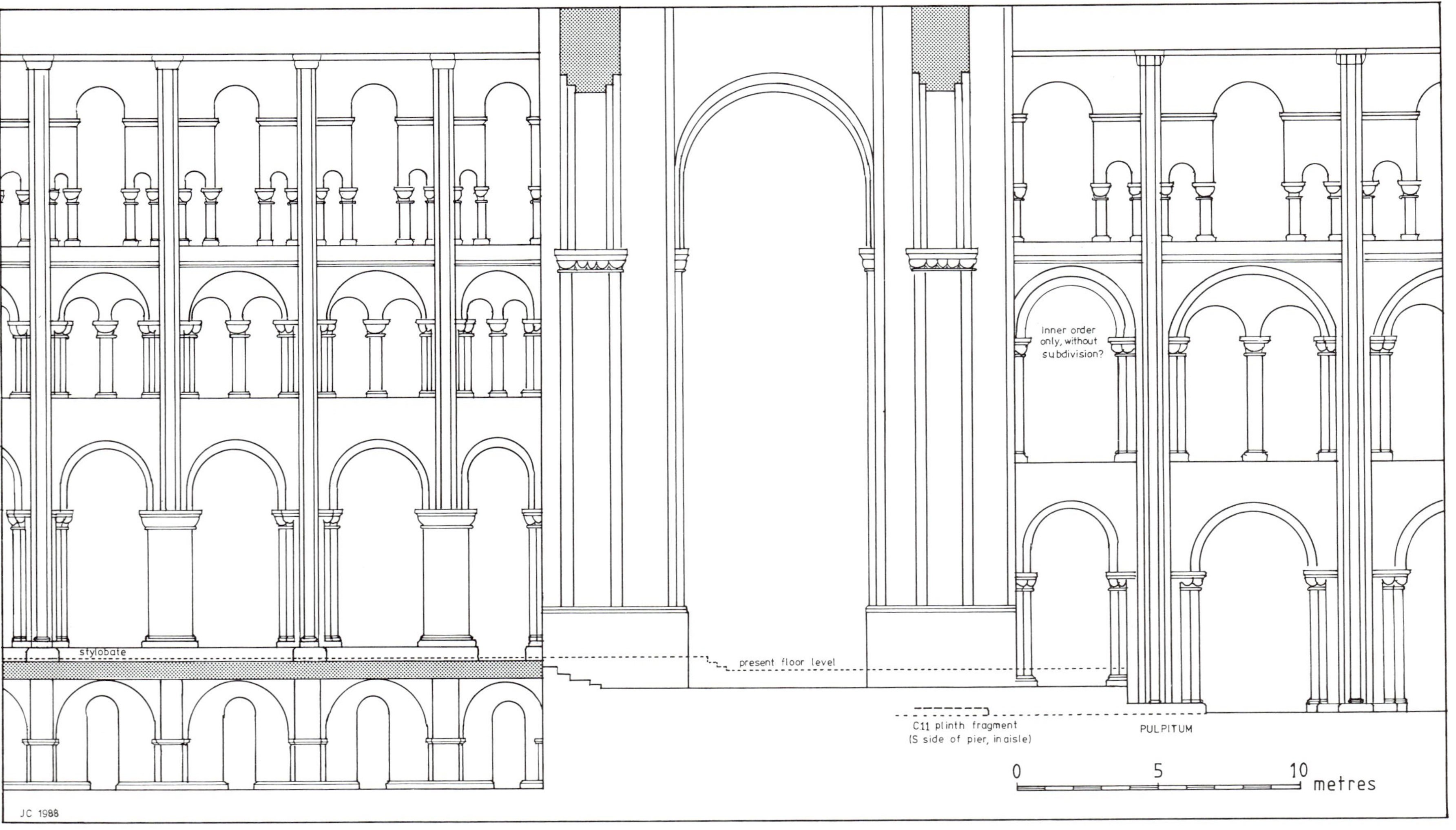

Fig. 12.8. Conjectural elevation of the romanesque eastern arm, crossing and part of the nave after the reconstruction of the central tower in the early twelfth century.

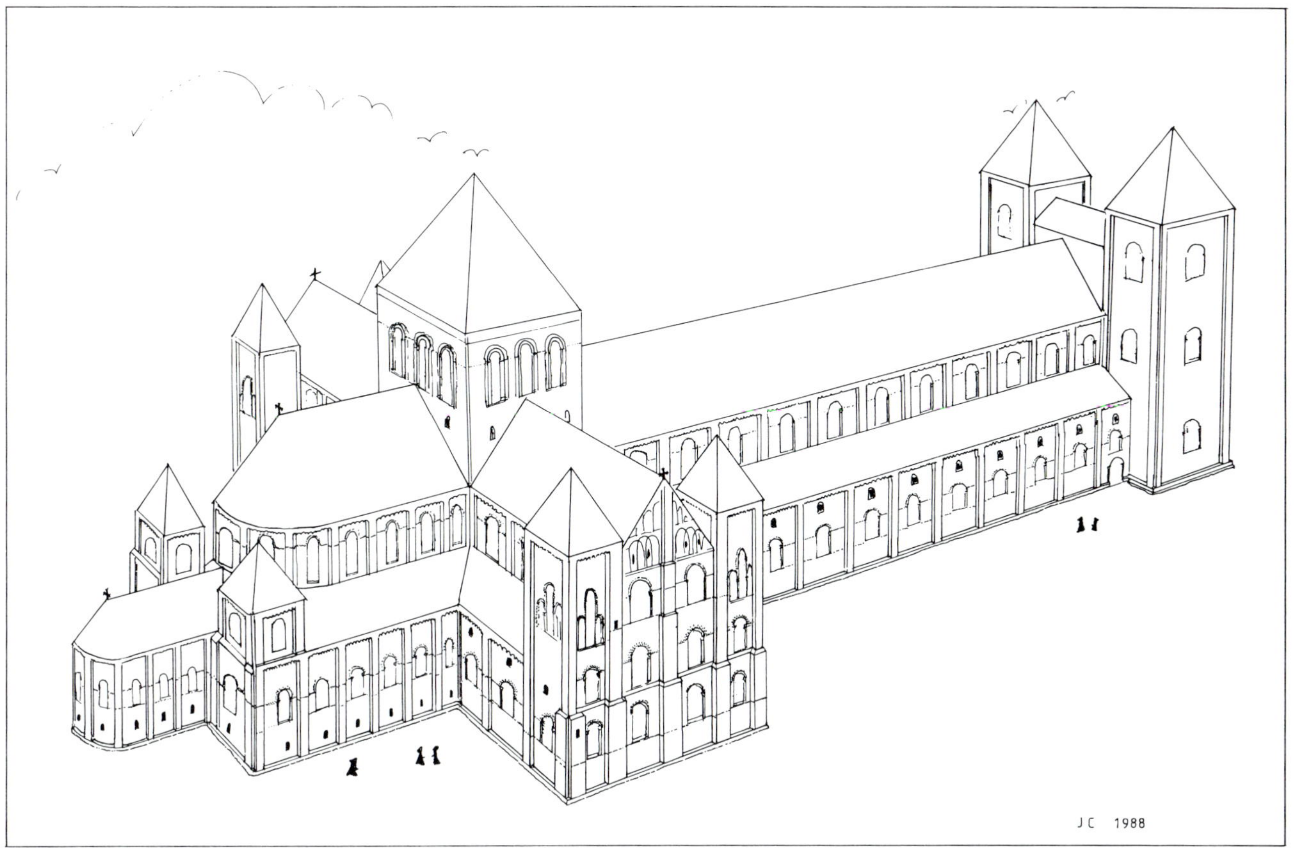

Fig. 12.9. Conjectural view of the romanesque cathedral at Winchester as it might have appeared in the early twelfth century had all intended features (including the transept towers) been adopted.

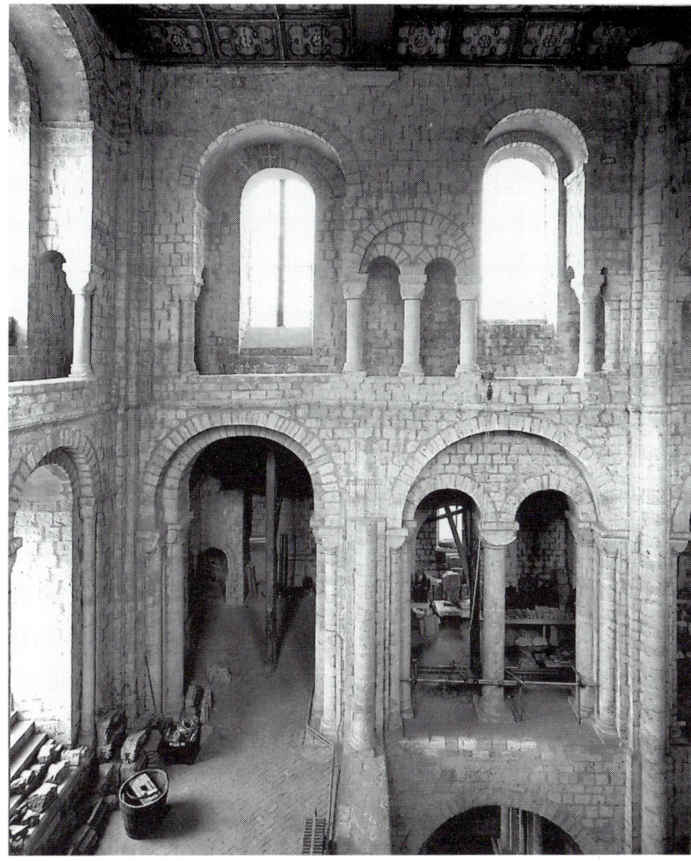

Fig. 12.10. East elevation of the north transept showing the secondary 'double-bay' system at clerestory level in Bays 3 and 4. Photo: John Crook.

transept elevations were modified during the course of construction, after the corner tower scheme had been abandoned. This confirmed that the towers at the end of the south transept (and possibly also the north-west tower in the north transept, where evidence was obliterated by fourteenth-century refenestration) were probably never completed.

Finally, the limited available documentary evidence allowed us to form some conclusions about the date of the various phases which we had described. It seemed probable that the transepts were completed by 1093, probably including the decisions first to build corner towers and then to abandon them (though the north-west tower may have survived for a few years longer). In April 1093 the monks of St Swithun's Priory moved from Old Minster into the new cathedral, and it is unlikely that they would have abandoned the old church until the essential parts of its replacement had been completed.

The Feretory platform and 'Holy Hole'

The most intensive recent archaeological investigation focused on the area behind the high altar screen, known as the 'Feretory' (Fig. 12.11). This area had been investigated by Willis (1846, 49–51) and more recently by St John Hope (1907, 414–5). The name seems to be of nineteenth-century origin, probably inspired by Willis's conjecture (1846, 49): previous researchers, such as John Milner (1798, ii, 57) referred to the area as the 'capitular chapel'. Here a raised platform occupies the site of the demolished romanesque apse (Fig. 12.12). To the east the platform is enclosed by the early fourteenth-century retrochoir screen, which replaced the apse. The central feature of the east face of this screen is a low gothic doorway, leading into a short tunnel-like structure known from as early as the mid-fifteenth century as the 'Holy Hole' (Fig. 12.13).[11] Behind the fourteenth-century work the masonry of the Holy Hole is of mid-twelfth century character, and we have associated this work with the documented movement of relics in 1158, when Bishop Henry of Blois is said to have exhumed the bones of pre-Conquest kings and bishops from a 'lowly place' and set them around the Holy Hole (Goodman 1927, 3).[12] In our view, the 'lowly place' was the 'memorial court' which, as Martin Biddle and Birthe Kjlbye-Biddle have shown, had been established at the west end of the present cathedral in the early twelfth century, around the presumed original site of Swithun's burial: the court was already failing into disrepair in the mid-twelfth century.[13]

The placing of the royal and episcopal remains around the Holy Hole seemed to indicate a focus of interest in this area; and we speculated that the remains were placed here in order to be close to Winchester's most potent relics, those of St Swithun, just as they had previously been placed near his first grave, an area which remained an object of veneration throughout the Middle Ages. It seemed probable that the Holy Hole allowed pilgrims limited access to the reliquary platform behind the high altar. To test our hypothesis that the Holy Hole originally

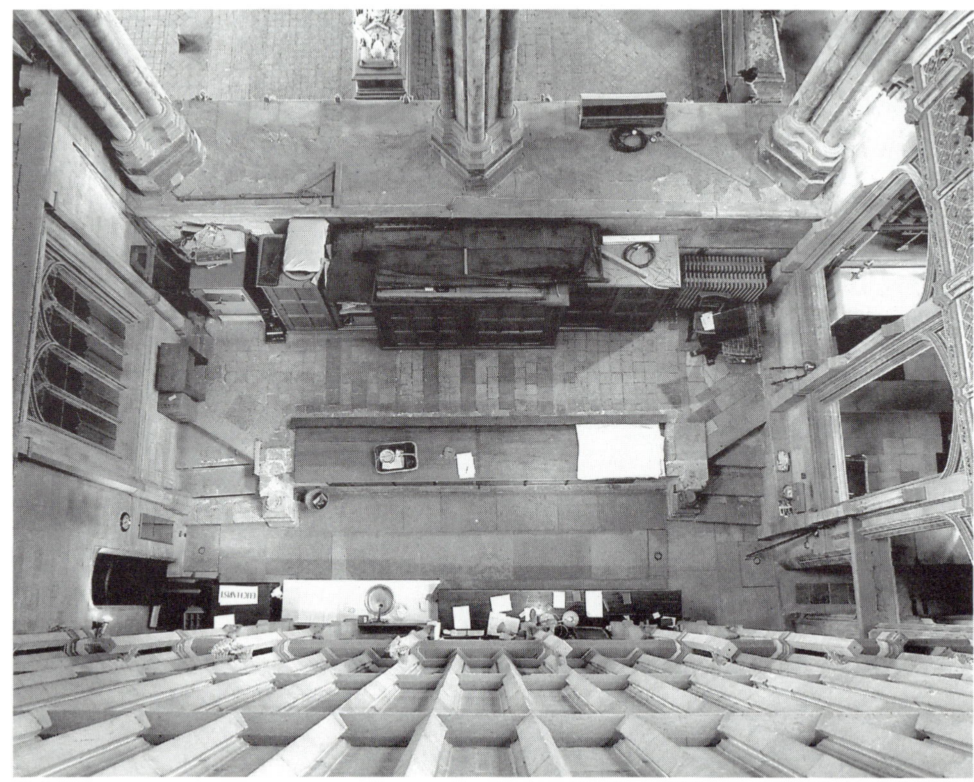

Fig. 12.11. The Feretory platform from the top of the high altar screen (east at top). Photo: John Crook.

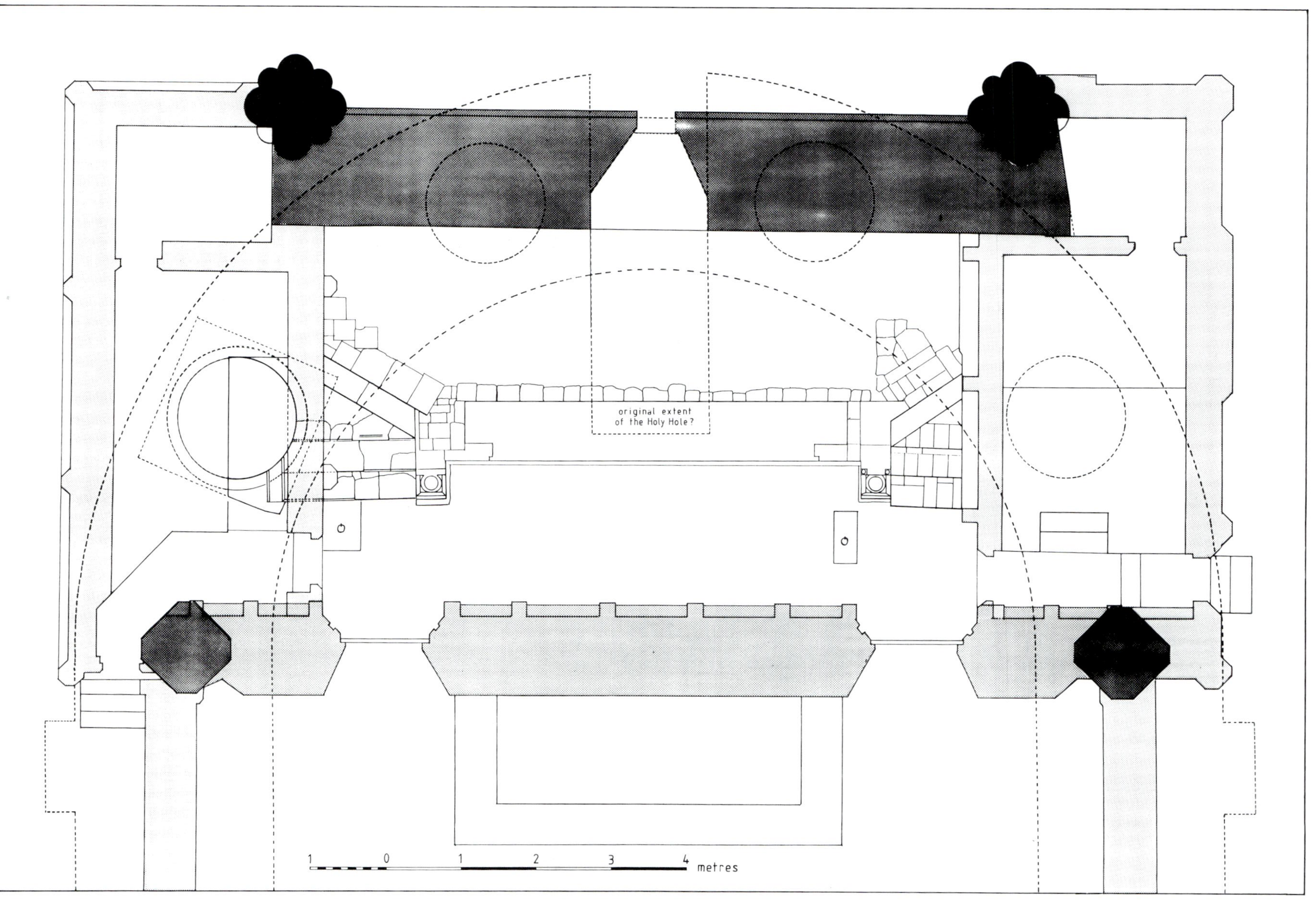

Fig. 12.12. Plan of the Feretory, showing original extent of the Holy Hole. The pecked lines indicate the position of the romanesque apse, demolished c. 1320.

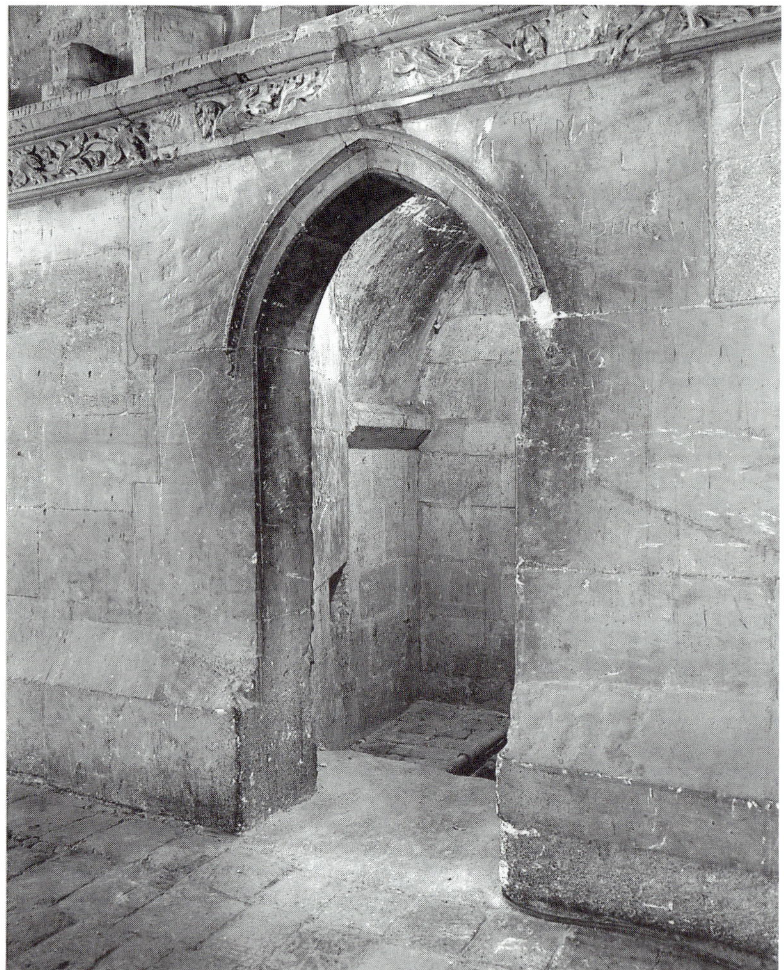

Fig. 12. 13. The 'Holy Hole', visible through the fourteenth-century arch in the east face of the retrochoir screen, showing the twelfth-century string course and masonry on the south side of the now truncated tunnel. Photo: John Crook.

extended further west than it does today, we removed a block from the sixteenth-century crosswall at the back of the Hole and excavated the floor and the infill behind. The side walls of the structure undoubtedly once continued further west. A larger excavation below the pavement of the actual Feretory platform provided evidence that the tunnel formerly extended across the full width of the platform (Fig. 12.14). The tunnel had been systematically destroyed at the Reformation, and dug over again and repaved in the early nineteenth century.

These findings contradicted the traditional suggestion that the thirteenth-century retrochoir was built to provide a suitably magnificent setting for the shrine of St Swithun.[14] In fact a mid-fifteenth century chronicle, as yet unpublished, specifically states that St Swithun's reliquary was still 'attached to the High Altar' as late as the fifteenth century (CCC 110, f. 336). But there was evidence for a thirteenth-century campaign in the Feretory area. Here a recess was inserted on the west side of the platform, presumably for the storage and display of secondary relics, which would obtain additional sanctity from the proximity of Swithun's relics. At this date, too, some sort of lateral arcading either side of the high altar was installed, evidenced by the bases which flank the Feretory platform.

Only in 1476 were the relics translated to their final location in the retrochoir, as part of a wide-ranging reorganisation of this part of the cathedral. This involved the construction of the Great Screen (Lindley 1989), which concealed the Feretory platform from the choir, making the Feretory redundant, and the erection of the chantry chapel of Cardinal Beaufort. The final translation was recorded in some detail in the Archiepiscopal register of Cardinal Morton (Wilkins 1737, iii, 610ff). The fifteenth-century shrine was a huge structure similar to the high shrine of St Thomas of Canterbury: it supported the new silver-gilt reliquary containing the saint's bones, over which a wooden cover could be lowered by means of a counterbalanced chain.

THE TOMB-SHRINE OF ST SWITHUN

The final part of our current research programme involved the examination of certain thirteenth-century Purbeck marble sculptural fragments that had previously been associated with the shrine of St Swithun, firstly by Le Couteur and Carter in the 1920s (Le Couteur and Carter 1924) and more recently by Pamela Tudor-Craig and Laurence Keen (Tudor-Craig and Keen 1983). Re-examination of the main fragment of the reconstruction showed

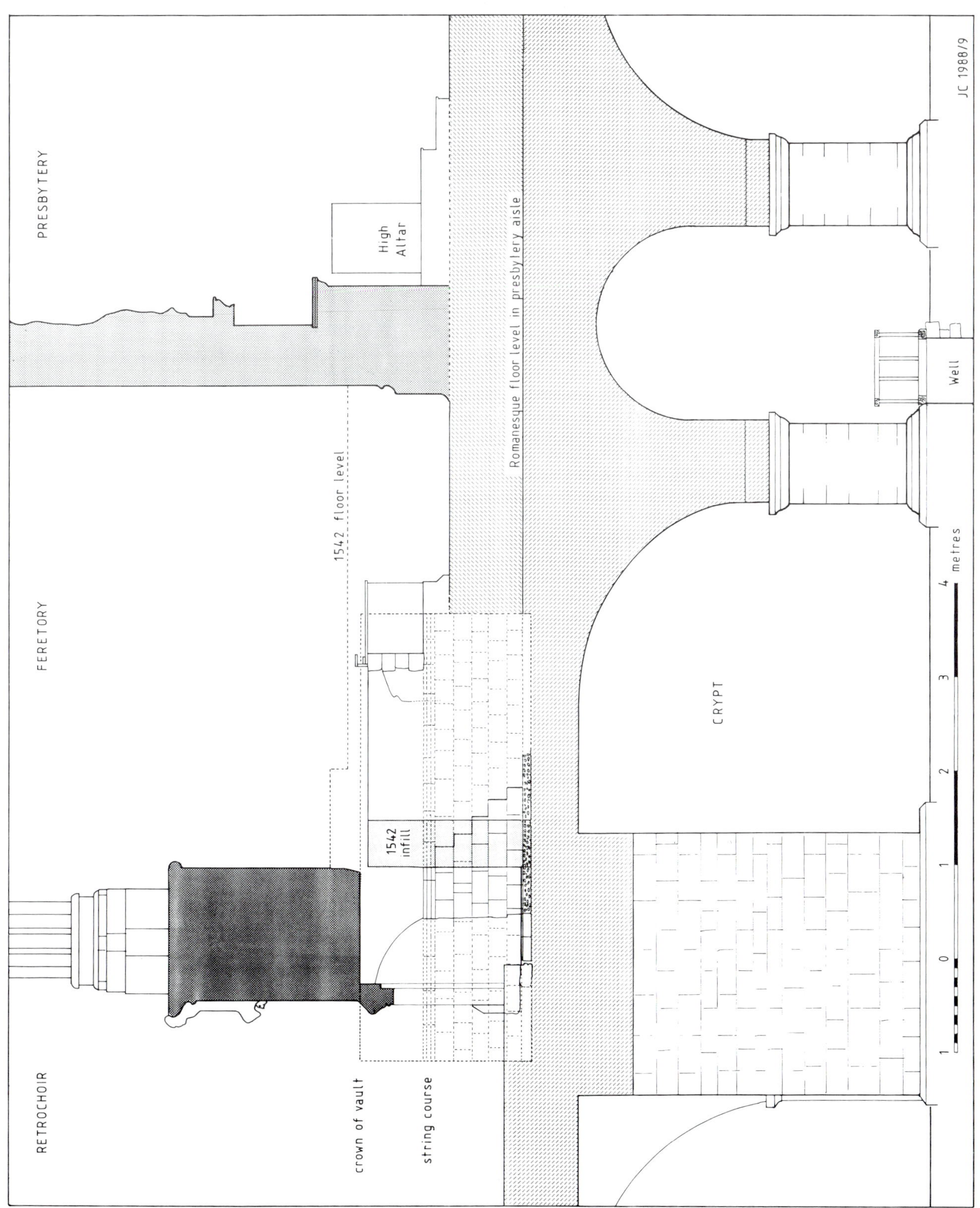

Fig. 12. 14. Cross-section of the Feretory area, showing the extent of the Holy Hole.

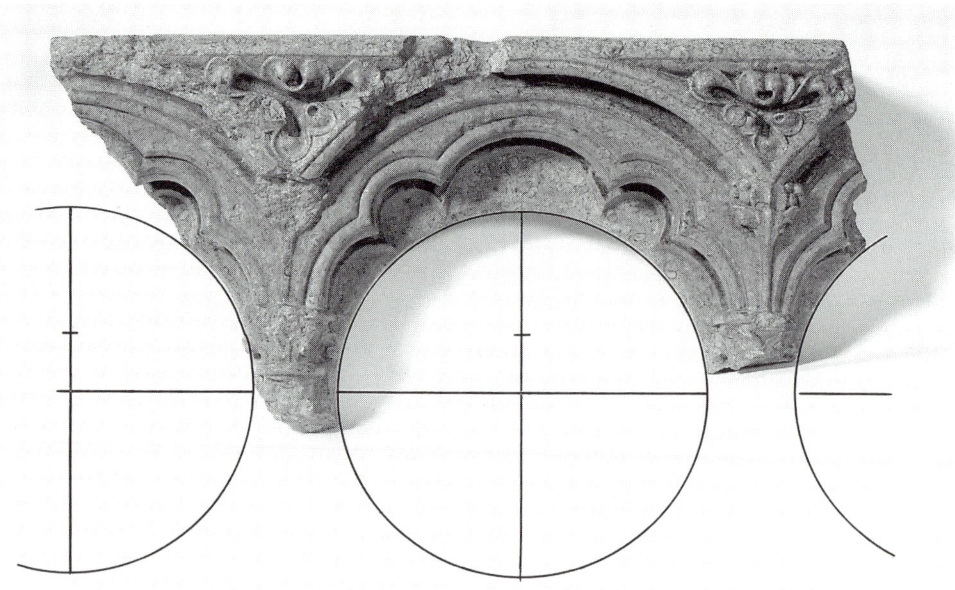

Fig. 12. 15. Fragment of the presumed Purbeck marble tomb-shrine panel, showing its geometry. Photo: John Crook.

that it derived from a panel pierced by at least three round holes arranged horizontally (Fig. 12.15) (Crook 1990). It was clear that it came from the type of structure to which we have given the name of 'tomb-shrine' (Fig. 12.16): a monument erected over the grave of a saint (whether occupied or empty), in contradistinction to the better-known 'high' shrines, which served to elevate a reliquary containing bones that had been exhumed. There are many examples of tomb-shrines erected over empty tombs – the prototype being the tomb of Christ in the church of the Holy Sepulchre, Jerusalem. At Winchester the site of the original burial of Swithun continued to be venerated long after the body had been removed from it. We associate the Purbeck fragments with the thirteenth-century structure which independent archaeological research shows to have been the last monument constructed in the Chapel of St Swithun outside the west end of the present cathedral (Biddle 1968, 278). This was a powerful alternative focus of veneration of Winchester's principal patron saint, and in the fifteenth century was recognised as a place where 'many miracles had taken place' (*AS 114*, f. 4).

Investigation of the Great Screen

Fig. 12. 16. Reconstruction of the tomb-shrine side panel, assumed here to have been in four bays.

AND OTHER SCULPTURE

The setting up of a permanent museum, the 'Triforium Gallery', involved above all a reassessment of the cathedral's collection of fifteenth-century statuary, much of which derived from the Great Screen behind the high altar.[15] Phillip Lindley's careful work on the provenance and date of these artefacts (Lindley 1989 and 1993) has important implications regarding the reorganisation of the Feretory and high altar area in the mid to late fifteenth century. As Pamela Tudor-Craig and Laurence Keen have rightly observed (Tudor-Craig and Keen 1983, 65), 'The archaeological approach to the movement of sculptural finds within our cathedral is a newly discovered historical weapon that might have been helpful had it been used in the past.'

MISCELLANEOUS RESCUE ARCHAEOLOGY

As well as the research projects described above, minor building works in Winchester cathedral have provided chance opportunities for archaeological study.

In 1984 a mezzanine floor supported on steel stanchions was inserted in the return aisle bays at the end of the south transept. The City Archaeologist was consulted, and the small areas of pavement involved were excavated before works began (Qualmann 1986). Some evidence was found in support of the traditional claim that this part of the cathedral served as a monastic 'Calefactory'. Perhaps the most interesting structure to be discovered was a chalk-lined water-course of uncertain function (Fig. 12.17), which presumably connected to the monastic drainage system as the 'Lockburn' (Crook 1984, 1985a). The excavations were too small to permit any firm conclusion to be drawn, but they gave a hint of the wealth of archaeology awaiting investigation beneath the pavement of the cathedral, and of the risk of damage to this archaeological record as a result of unsupervised work such as the cutting of electricity conduits.

Construction work for the creation of the 'Triforium Gallery' in the autumn of 1988 revealed that the floor of the romanesque gallery was originally 51 cm lower than its present level. It was raised in two phases: by 18 cm during the actual construction of the transepts, and by a further 33 cm in the early nineteenth century (Crook and Kusaba 1991).

In 1990-3 trial excavations in the cathedral close in preparation for the construction of a Visitors' Centre revealed the extent of the romanesque west end, and provided new information about the charnel chapel that stood within the cemetery, just south-west of the cathedral (Qualmann 1994).

With the passing of the Cathedrals Measure, archaeological recording has been undertaken on a more formal basis, with close co-operation between the cathedral architect, the works staff, and the cathedral archaeologist. In the past five years major repair work has taken place

Fig. 12.17. Excavation in the 'Calefactory' showing the water channel (foreground). The re-used shaft (background) appears to be secondary. It was drilled throughout its length and formed part of a piscina or basin draining into the channel. Photo: John Crook.

on two major parts of the cathedral: the crossing tower (Crook 1992) and the west front. Before work began, a photogrammetric survey was made of each area, and these surveys have facilitated a stone-by-stone survey of the fabric, providing informationabout the constructional phases. At the same time, the conservation of the thirteenth-century tile pavement of the retrochoir has provided an opportunity for a new study of the cathedral's floor tiles (Norton 1993). Forthcoming work on the south nave clerestory and the south transept will provide further opportunities for archaeological investigation; these areas will also be recorded photogrammetrically, and all these photogrammetric surveys will be linked by means of a control coordinate system now being established around and within the cathedral.

Notes

1. Willis's lecture was delivered in the morning of Wednesday, 10 September 1845, and in the afternoon, 'at four o'clock Professor Willis accompanied a large party to the Cathedral, and illustrated his lecture, delivered in the morning, by directing attention to various parts of that building, pointing out the grounds of his deductions, and showing the method of his researches, in a manner most gratifying to those who accompanied him.' (Willis 1846, xvii).
2. For the bibliography of early sources for Winchester cathedral (and an assessment of their reliability) see Crook (1989), footnotes 15, 51–2, 85, 87, 94. An edition of the fifteenth-century chronicles used by Willis is in preparation: J. Crook (editor), *Late medieval monastic chronicles of St Swithun's Priory, Winchester* (forthcoming).
3. Kitchin's damaging (but fortunately, limited) excavation of the Old and New Minster sites north of the present cathedral was virtually unrecorded. His main contribution to the history of Winchester cathedral was to edit several of its documents for the Hampshire Record Society in the 1890s.
4. MS. notes in Winchester Cathedral Library and, especially, at the Society of Antiquaries, London, MS. 783 (10 binders of notes).
5. Interim reports were published annually as the excavation programme continued. For a bibliography of these see M. Biddle, 'The Study of Winchester: Archaeology and History in a British Town', *Proc. of the British Academy* 69 (1983), 130.
6. Winchester's Cathedral Architects have always taken an interest in medieval carpentry, generally considered a recent area of study. A previous architect, J. B. Colson, had published illuminating accounts of the consolidation work on the roof of the nave at the end of the nineteenth century (Winchester Cathedral, a descriptive and illustrated record of the reparations of the Nave Roof, 1896–98,' in G. W. Kitchin and W. R. W. Stephens, *The Great Screen of Winchester Cathedral* (Winchester, 3rd edn. 1899), and *idem*, 'The Nave Roof, Winchester Cathedral,' *Proc. of the Hampshire Field Club and Archaeol. Soc.* 3 (1898), 283–93). Four years previously Norman Nisbett (Colson's eventual successor as Cathedral Architect) had written an account of the early fourteenth-century hammer-beamed roof of the Pilgrims' Hall (N. C. H. Nisbett, 'Notes on the roof of the Pilgrims' Hall, Winchester,' *Proc. Hants Field Club* 3 (1894), 71–4). The latter building is the subject of a new study: J. Crook, 'The Pilgrims' Hall, Winchester,' *Archaeologia* 109, 129-59.
7. The architectural development and sources for the retrochoir had previously been discussed by Nikolaus Pevsner, 'A note on the east arm of Winchester Cathedral,' *Archaeol. Jnl.* 116 (1959), 133–5, and *idem*, 'The east end of Winchester Cathedral,' *Winchester Cathedral Record* 29 (1960), 7–10). The late medieval evolution of this part of the cathedral has more recently been re-assessed by Peter Draper and Richard K. Morris in their joint paper, 'The development of the east end of Winchester cathedral from the 13th to the 16th century', in Crook (1993, 177-92).
8. A preliminary account of our discoveries has been published as J. Crook, 'St. Swithun of Winchester', in Crook (1993, 57-68).
9. Drawings deposited at the office of the architect to the Dean and Chapter of Winchester Cathedral.
10. This modifies our earlier suggestion (Crook 1989, 29) that the double-bay scheme was introduced *after* the tower scheme had been abandoned. See also J.Crook and Y. Kusaba, 'The perpendicular remodelling of the nave: problems and interpretation', in Crook (1993,215-30).
11. The earliest reference to the Holy Hole occurs in the early fifteenth-century chronicle attributed to Thomas Rudborne and published by Wharton (1691, i, 207): it is referred to as *locus nuncupatus The Hole Hole*'.
12. For the slightly earlier translation of saints' bones in 1150, see H. R. Luard, ed., *Annales Monastici*, ii (Rolls Series, 36), 1865, 54. The translation of 1158 is recorded in the *Chartulary*, MS, Winchester Cathedral Library, Item. 4, f. 1v, summarised in English by Goodman, (1927, 3).
13. Martin Biddle and Birthe Kjlbye-Biddle, pers. comm.
14. Cf. Sir Charles Peers, *VCH Winchester*, 54. Peter Draper (1978, 13) is guarded, correctly surmising that 'it is probable that at one time [the shrine of St Swithun] was placed in the centre of the retrochoir.
15. An earlier attempt at establishing a museum in the south transept gallery had not been successful. At that time the statuary was studied by T. D. Atkinson, Medieval figure sculpture in Winchester cathedral. *Archaeologia* 85 (1936), 159–67.

Bibliography

AS 114: All Souls' College, Oxford, MS. 114. The *Liber Historialis* of St Swithun's Priory, Winchester, transcribed in 1531 by the monk John of Exeter. For a note on other MSS of this text, see Crook 1989, 34 (note 85).

Atkinson, T.D. 1933: *An Architectural History of the Benedictine Monastery of St Etheldreda at Ely* Cambridge.

Atkinson, T.D. 1939: The Venerable Chapel. *Winchester Cathedral Record* 8, 6–9.

Biddle, M. 1968: Excavations at Winchester 1967, Sixth Interim Report. *Antiqs. Jnl.* 48.ii, 250–84.

Biddle, M. and Kjlbye-Biddle, B. forthcoming: *The Anglo-Saxon Minsters of Winchester* (Oxford, Winchester Studies, vol. 4.1).

Carpenter Turner, W. 1969: The Retrochoir. *Winchester Cathedral Record* 38, 57–66.

CCC 110: Corpus Christi College, Cambridge, MS. 110. Sixteenth-century copy of a MS. c. 1460: *Chronicon in quo continetur historia Angliae praesertim coenobii Wintoniensi a Lucio usque ad initium regni Henrici VI.*

Collier, Canon 1886: Report on the recent discoveries at Win-

chester Cathedral. *Jnl. B.A.A.* 42, 300–3.
Crook, J. 1984: Ethelwold and the conduits. *Winchester Cathedral Record* 53, 26–34.
Crook, J. 1985a: The Lockburn. *Winchester Cathedral Record* 54, 14–24.
Crook, J. 1985b: The thirteenth-century shrine and screen of St Swithun at Winchester. *Jnl. B.A.A.* 138, 125–31.
Crook, J. 1989: The Romanesque east arm and crypt of Winchester Cathedral. *Jnl. B.A.A.* 142, 1–36.
Crook, J. 1990: The typology of early medieval shrines: a previously misidentified 'tomb-shrine' panel from Winchester Cathedral. *Antiq. Jnl.,* 70.i, 49-64
Crook, J. 1992: .New findings on the tower of Winchester Cathedral. *Winchester Cathedral Record* 61, 15-17.
Crook J. (ed.) 1993: *Winchester Cathedral: Nine Hundred Years* (Chichester).
Crook, J. forthcoming : The architectural background for the cult of St Swithun in Winchester Cathedral, 1079–1538, in M. Biddle and B. Kjlbye-Biddle, *The Anglo-Saxon Minsters of Winchester* (Oxford, Winchester Studies, vol. 4.i).
Crook, J. and Kusaba, Y. 1991: The transepts of Winchester Cathedral. *Jnl. Soc. Archit. Hist. (USA)*, 50, 293-310.
Draper, P. 1978: A note on the east end of Winchester Cathedral. *Archit. History* 21, 1–17.
Draper, P. 1986: The retrochoir of Winchester Cathedral, evidence and interpretation. *Jnl. B.A.A.* 139, 68–74.
Fernie, E. 1983: The grid system and the design of the Norman Cathedral. *Medieval Art and Architecture at Winchester Cathedral* (B.A.A. Conf. Trans. 6), 13–19.
Gem, R. 1983: The Romanesque Cathedral of Winchester: Patron and design in the eleventh century. *Medieval Art and Architecture at Winchester Cathedral* (B.A.A. Conf. Trans. 6), 1–12.
Goodman, A.W. 1927: (ed.) *Winchester Cathedral Chartulary* (Winchester).
Henderson, I. and Crook, J. 1984: *The Winchester Diver* (Winchester).
Jackson Collection. MS. collection of notes relating to the preservation works of 1905–12, Winchester Cathedral Library.
Kirby, T.F. 1887: Excavations at Winchester Cathedral. *Proc. Soc. of Antiqs. Lond.* 2nd ser. 11, (1885–7), 99–102, 411–12.
Kitchin, G.W. 1886a: Letter to Editor [re. archaeological investigations at Winchester cathedral]. *The Hampshire Chronicle* 2 January 1886, 3.
Kitchin, G.W. 1886b: The crypts of Winchester Cathedral. *The Hampshire Chronicle* 17 April 1886, 3.
Kusaba, Y. 1988: The function, date and stylistic sources of the Treasury of Henry of Blois in the south transept of Winchester cathedral. *Winchester Cathedral Record* 57, 38–50.
Le Couteur, J.D. and Carter, D.H.M. 1924: Notes on the shrine of St Swithun formerly in Winchester Cathedral. *Antiqs. Jnl.* 4, 259–70.
Lindley, P.W. 1989: The Great Screen of Winchester Cathedral. *The Burlington Magazine* 131, No. 1038, 604–617.
Lindley, P.W. 1993: The medieval sculpture of Winchester Cathedral, in Crook (1993, 97-122).
Milner, J. 1798: *History and Survey of Winchester*, (London).
Moore, C. 1916: The aisle vaulting of Winchester transept. *R.I.B.A. Jnl.* 3rd ser., 23, Nos. 19–20, 314-20, 329–34.
Norton, C. 1993: The medieval tile pavements of Winchester Cathedral, iin Crook (1993, 167-76).
Qualmann, K.E. 1986: Archaeological investigation in the south transept of Winchester Cathedral – the "Calefactory". *Winchester Cathedral Record* 55, 11–14.
Qualmann, K.E. 1994: Archaeological investigation on the site of the cathedral visitors' centre. *Winchester Cathedral Record* 63, 21-6.
St John Hope, W. 1907: On the great Almery for relics of late in the abbey church of Selby, with notes on some other receptacles for relics. *Archaeologia* 60, 414–5.
Tudor-Craig, P. and Keen, L. 1983: A recently discovered Purbeck marble sculptured screen of the thirteenth century and the shrine of St Swithun. *Medieval Art and Architecture at Winchester Cathedral* (B.A.A. Conf. Trans. 6), 63–72.
VCH Winchester: W. Page (ed.), *The Victoria History of Hampshire and the Isle of Wight* V (London 1912), 50–9.
Wharton, H. 1691: (ed.) *Anglia Sacra sive Collectio Historiarum*, 2 vols, (London).
Wilkins, D. 1737: (ed.), *Concilia Magnae Britanniae et Hiberniae*, 3 vols. (London).
Willis, R. 1846: The Architectural History of Winchester Cathedral. *Proc. Archaeol. Inst. for 1845*, reprinted by Friends of Winchester Cathedral (Winchester 1980).
Woodman, F. 1983: The retrochoir of Winchester Cathedral: a new interpretation. *Jnl. B.A.A.*, 136, 87–97.

Robert Willis and the Study of Medieval Architecture

M.W. Thompson

I was invited to speak at the Oxford conference on the Archaeology of Cathedrals because I had been involved in writing the history of the Cambridge Antiquarian Society for its 150th anniversary.[1] Professor Robert Willis had joined the Society soon after its formation in 1840 following his resignation from the Cambridge Camden Society, the excesses of which had offended him. He was twice President in 1845–6 and 1850–1, the office being held for two years. He played an important role in the redrafting of the Society's rules in 1846, having the study of architecture written in as a specific objective, and he contributed two important papers to the Quarto Series, on the Sextry Barn at Ely and medieval nomenclature in architecture (Willis, 1843). Subsequently the newly-founded Archaeological Institute provided in its summer meetings the main platform for his studies of cathedrals, so he took very little part in the Cambridge Society's affairs in the last twenty years of his life.

Fig. 13.1 Professor Robert Willis, 1800-1875.

Early Years

To start from the beginning, Robert Willis (1800–75) and his sister were illegitimate children of Robert Darling Willis, a junior fellow of Gonville and Caius College, Cambridge. His father had philosophical interests, publishing a book that took a Burkean view of the French Revolution,[2] but he was primarily a medical doctor who had been called in to treat George III during his insanity. So there was a medical background to the home in which his son grew up.

Robert went into residence at Caius in 1821, was 9th Wrangler, took holy orders in 1827 (ordination was a condition of many fellowships), had fellowships at Caius and later Trinity College, and was Jacksonian Professor of Applied and Experimental Philosophy from 1837 to his death in 1875.[3] The title is confusing since he taught mechanical engineering. A list of manuscript sources and Willis' own publications is appended to this paper. A chronological perspective is the best way to understand his outlook and work.

The story begins with a youthful diary kept by Willis in 1819–20 which was acquired by Cambridge University Library in 1960.[4] Some of the entries are written in an as yet undeciphered shorthand, but most of what he wrote between 20/9/1829 and 21/1/1821 is legible. During this period he was struggling to make a harp (patented in 1819) but met with repeated setbacks, apparently only completing the work at the end of the entries. He took his first violin lesson on 17th October 1820; sound later became a professional interest. Although a tea-party with young ladies is referred to the abiding impression is of a very serious youth, intensely interested in practical things, particularly architecture: "Went to De Villes in the Strand to see the Holyhead Lantern and saw oil gas apparatus and manufactory" (1st December, 1819); "the convenience of the County Fire Office is sacrificed to the beauty as the offices on the ground floor are all darkened by the portico" (28th October, 1819); "...made a sketch of the greenhouse for the old man" (14th February, 1820). He was practical: "my tool box fell down" (6th November, 1820). There was a long blank in the summer of 1820 but we learn later that the summer holiday in Sussex took in Bognor, Chanctonbury Ring, Bramber and Arundel castle (p. 83).

The Society of Antiquaries of London has four volumes of drawings by Willis, mainly of buildings in Italy and on the Continent, but volume 3 has drawings from Norfolk in 1820, made when he was studying at King's Lynn, including plans and sections of Castle Rising castle. In volume 4 there are drawings of English ecclesiastical buildings including the Octagon at Ely. We have then a picture of a very serious-minded and practical young man who already in his youth was well acquainted with English medieval architecture; it was not long before this was extended to the continent. We have no precise chronology but he tells us in his *Remarks* (1835) that the book was based on a rapid tour through France, Italy and part of Germany in 1832–3. We know from his Introduction to Curzon's *Monasteries* (1849) that he had travelled in the Balkans, and was indeed regarded as an authority on Greek Orthodox monasteries.

Science and Architecture

Before Willis obtained the Jacksonian chair in 1837 his main teaching had been on sound. In the *Syllabus* of the Royal Institution for 1832 the four lecturers were: Willis on Sound, Faraday on Domestic Chemical Philosophy, Brande on Electricity, and Britton on Architectural Antiquities.[5] The association of Willis with Britton is of interest since he made much use of the latter's plans in later studies. Knowledge was less compartmentalised than today so architectural history could be studied with chemistry; the overtones of *Kunstgeschichte* had not isolated the former as is the case today. Of his first four published papers two deal with the physical aspects of speech, one with mechanics, and (the first) with his amusing exposure of a fraudulent chess player, allegedly automatic, but really operated by a man inside the machine.

Willis published his first work on architectural history in 1835, the *Remarks on the Architecture of the Middle Ages, especially of Italy* just mentioned, which relied on his drawings made in Italy that occupy fifteen plates at the end of the book (Figs. 13.2 & 13.3). While it is unwise to seek a long pedigree among Cambridge antiquaries for Willis there can be no doubt that William Whewell's *Architectural Notes on German Churches* (1830), to which he refers in his book, was uppermost in his mind. Whewell was a fellow scientist, a physicist and polymath, who became Master of Trinity College, and to whom Willis probably owed his later fellowship there. Whewell had concluded that the pointed arch had been adopted because it was necessary to reconcile the different radii of the vaulting ribs in a rectangular compartment to create a level line at the apex. Willis was quite categorical:

> "Among other objects I was naturally led to search for evidence that would throw light upon the origin of the pointed arch. There is a fascinating simplicity about that theory which would derive it from the requirements of vaulting that makes one wish to find it true; but I am sorry to say, that notwithstanding the favourable prepossessions with which I set out, I have been compelled to dissent from this ingenious hypothesis." (1835, 00)

It is not surprising that Whewell's study of Gothic architecture in the Rhineland led to very different conclusions from those of Willis in Italy, having regard to the great range of alternative forms of vaulting found in Italy from Classical times up to its very idiosyncratic 'Gothic'. While most students might admit an independent existence for the pointed arch, most surely would concede that the simple solution that it offered to rib vaulting gave a great fillip to its general adoption; reciprocity is usual in this kind of cause and effect.

The importance of the book however is that it states his theory of Gothic architecture, its merits and how it should be studied. Willis accepts the divisions of Rickman without demure, even with approval (p. 13) and goes on in the second chapter to a division "between mechanical and decorative construction":

> "The eye of an unpractised observer when viewing a magnificent building is never satisfied unless the weights appear to be duly supported, and it receives a corresponding pleasure when that is the case. Hence in all complete styles, part of the decoration is made to represent some kind of construction, and the more completely this is effected, the more satisfactory becomes the result." (1835, 00)

It is the structural element that interests him: this is the aestheticism of an engineer, which at once reveals the essential link between the two forms of his lifelong interests. It has something in common with the'honesty' of Ruskin or Morris, although it is perhaps a little more rational. He by no means dismisses 'decorative construction' although the closer it comes to merging with the mechanical (and in Greek and Egyptian architecture they do so) the better.

His drawings of detail in Italy, imposts, shafts, foliation, tracery, vaulting, mouldings, at the end of the book are used to work out his proposition (Figs. 13.2 & 13.3). Vaults, a transfer of the gravitational movement sideways to take a different course to the ground, occupy a major part of the book as we would expect with an engineer. The very marked regional variations of gothic style emerge, especially its Italian form.

Although we cannot speak of Willis as a revivalist yet the table comparing the 'Middle Age styles' with the 'Classical styles', comes down so heavily in favour of the former that there can be no doubt where his preference lay (1835, 158). For most revivalists (Pugin, the Cambridge Camden Society, Ruskin, Morris) it was the society, its Christian, non-industrialised aspect, symbolised by Gothic architecture, that attracted. Even for Gilbert Scott Gothic architecture was the native form of architecture as opposed to the alien, Classical form. For Willis the superiority rested on the correspondence of form with structure; the impedimenta of porticos and pediments, attached orders of columns and so on rendered the Classical inferior. Yet he was

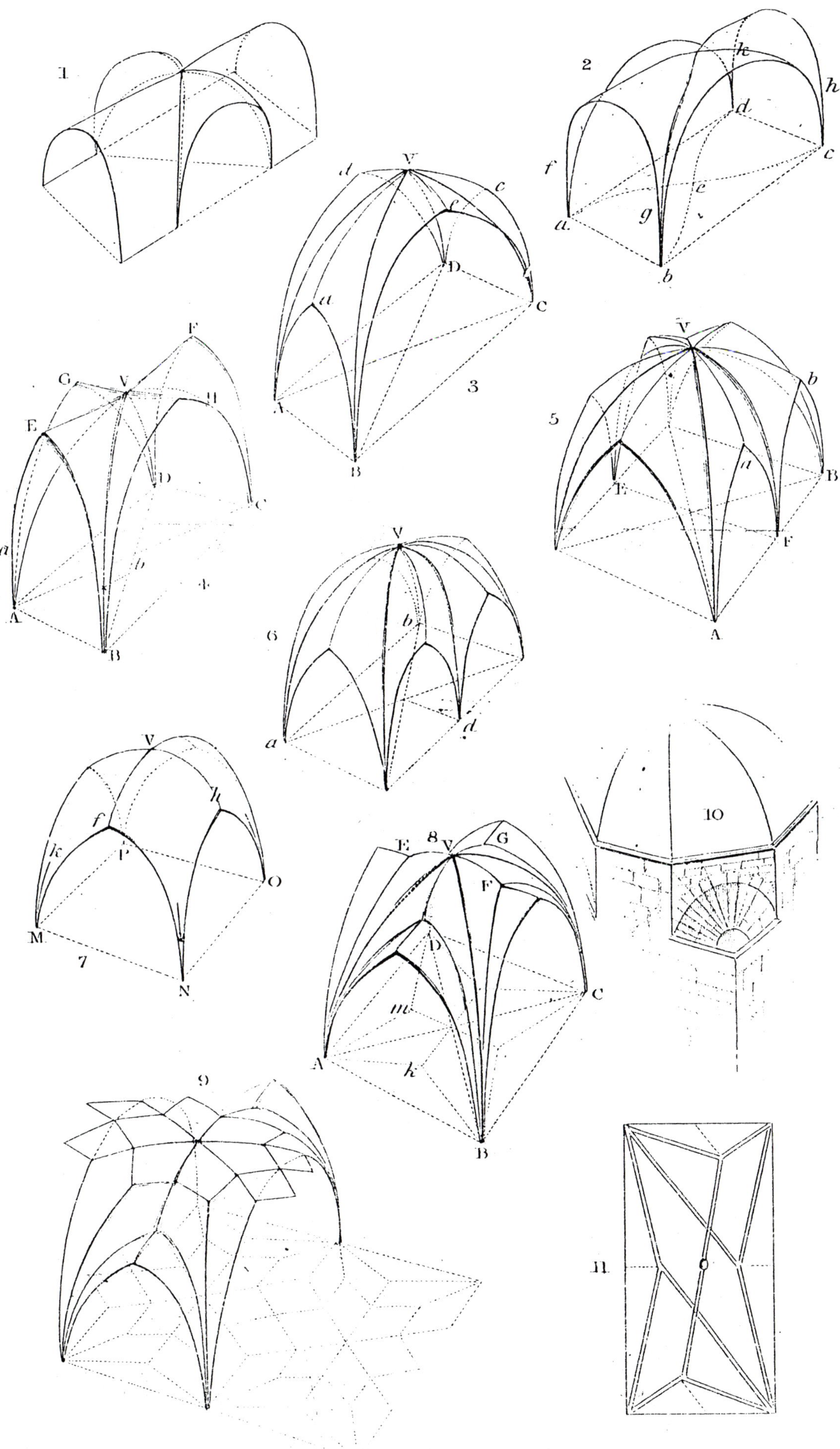

Fig. 13.2 Vaults, from Remarks on the Architecture of the Middle Ages, especially of Italy *(1835).*

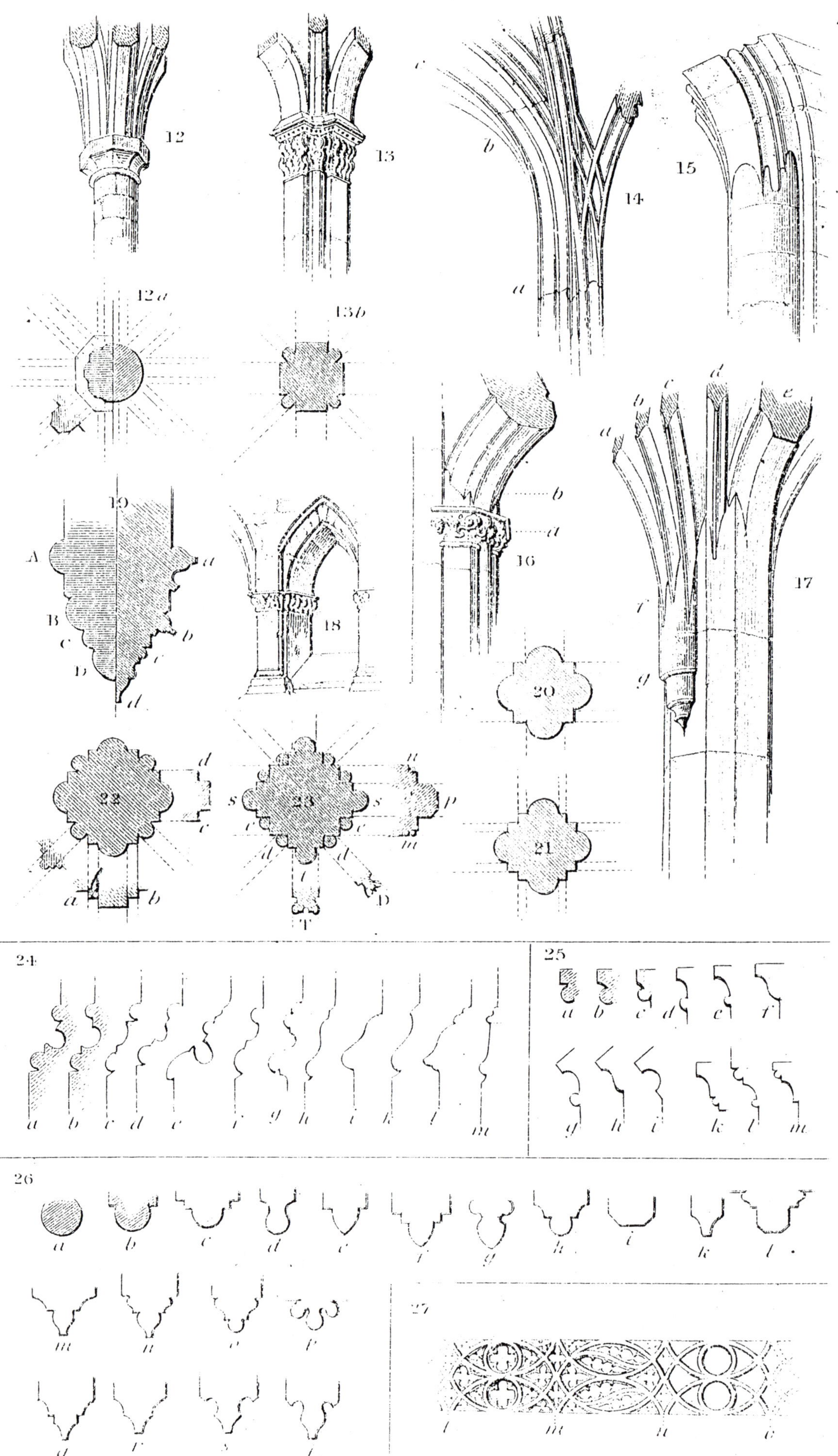

Fig. !3.3 Mouldings, from Remarks *(1835).*

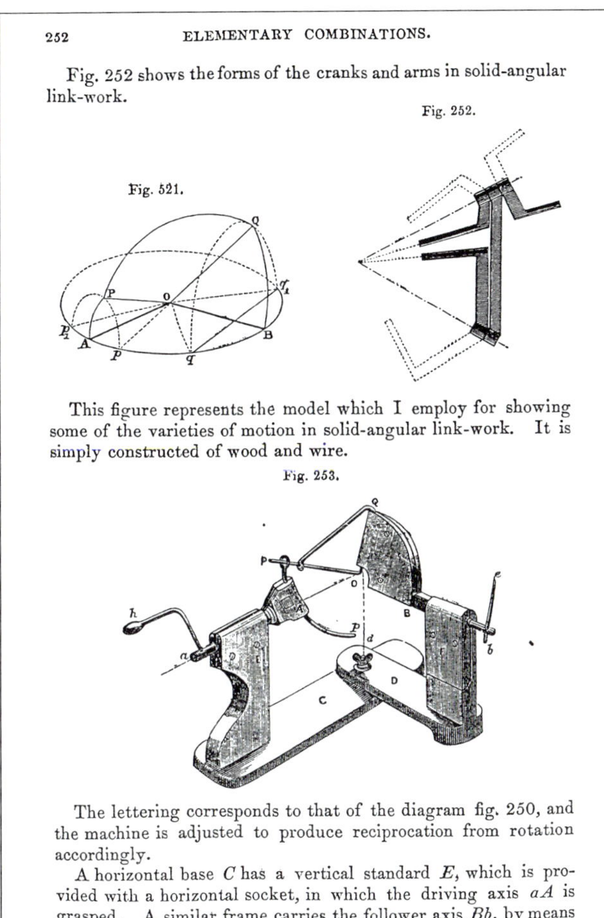

252 ELEMENTARY COMBINATIONS.

Fig. 252 shows the forms of the cranks and arms in solid-angular link-work.

Fig. 252.

Fig. 521.

This figure represents the model which I employ for showing some of the varieties of motion in solid-angular link-work. It is simply constructed of wood and wire.

Fig. 253.

The lettering corresponds to that of the diagram fig. 250, and the machine is adjusted to produce reciprocation from rotation accordingly.

A horizontal base *C* has a vertical standard *E*, which is provided with a horizontal socket, in which the driving axis *aA* is grasped. A similar frame carries the follower axis *Bb*, by means of a standard *F*. The two frames are connected by a bolt *d*, fixed to the lower or base board *C* and passed through a hole in

Fig. 13.4 Diagram from Principles of Mechanism *(1841).*

not a crude functionalist, like Frances Bond, as his dismissal of Whewell's origin for the pointed arch at once reveals.

His scientific papers had been published hitherto in the Cambridge Philosophical Society's *Transactions* but the paper 'On the Teeth of Wheels' of 1838 was published by the Institute of Civil Engineers. His election to the Jacksonian chair in 1837 meant that his main teaching commitment and the subject of his professional studies was now engineering; he straightaway wrote a textbook for his students, *Principles of Mechanism* (1841, 2nd edition 1870). The profuse illustrations, as in all his publications, were from his own hand and illustrated some of the machines that he constructed for demonstration to his students, a device that he had learnt from his predecessor in the chair. The resemblance between the drawings there (Fig. 13.4) and those in the articles on architectural history, particularly the flourishing application of upper and lower case letters for use in the text, will at once be remarked. In mechanics the object of the exercise was to reduce the problem to a mathematical formula, and although he did introduce numbers into his architectural drawings (for the good reason that the original builders had not done so) the mode of thinking in the two cases clearly had much in common, particularly with vaults where the problems are to a great extent engineering ones.

It was at this time that Willis wrote one of his most noteworthy papers, on vaults, ribbed vaults, how the curvatures were estimated and set out, and the best known section on fan vaults with axonometric drawings of their upper surfaces (Fig. 13.5; Willis, 1842). Vaults had been his main interest in Italy as we have seen. His short paper on 'The Interpenetration of the Flamboyant Style' won the admiration of Pevsner.[6] The invention of the 'cymagraph' (Fig. 13.6), a hook-shaped metal instrument for plotting moulding profiles was published in *The Civil Engineer*, a fair indication of the close association of the subjects in the mind of Willis. In the 'Architectural Nomenclature of the Middle Ages' he assembled a valuable body of material on medieval usage in the construction industry, amplifying earlier work and introducing matter from direct comparison between the sources and the surviving features. This may be regarded as the concluding part of what one might describe as the analytical background, the preparation for his studies of whole buildings for which he is best known.

At Hereford he had been invited by the Dean and Chapter to report on necessary repairs to the cathedral, especially the tower and crossing, but he inevitably became involved in considering the whole building. The report was published in two forms, in *The Civil Engineer* and by the Dean and Chapter. At about the same time he surveyed the thirteenth-century aisled Sextry Barn at Ely, before its demolition (Fig. 13.7; Willis, 1843). It was the only venture into the vernacular by Willis, but it meant that he had to consider an entire building, quite a large one. Willis' reputation rests mainly on his surveys and analyses of large buildings and building complexes, like Christchurch Priory and Cathedral, Canterbury or the Cambridge colleges, so a preliminary mastering of mouldings, vaults, tracery and so on was ideal training, a firm foundation for more comprehensive works.

Cathedral Archaeology

The initial summer meeting of the British Archaeological Association was held in 1844 at Canterbury, inspired and directly imitating, according to Roach Smith who was himself involved,[7] the Congrès archéologique at Caen in 1834 and held annually thereafter, a week in each summer being devoted to the study of the medieval architecture of different regions. Although the Association almost immediately split into two, the breakaway part that formed the Archaeological Institute continued the summer meetings. They were normally held in a cathedral town, which furnished Willis with an opportunity to study its fabric and history beforehand, and then to deliver a lecture to the Institute on the site. According to his nephew he lectured fluently without notes, holding his audience by the clarity of his exposition whether it were students or members of the Institute. The forthcoming lecture allowed intensive study of the cathedral by Willis, usually embodied in a monograph published independently or later in the Institute's *Journal*. Not the least achievement of Willis was to give an initial impulse to the Institute which caused it to become the main forum for medieval architectural history up to 1939, and to a great extent for all the periods since the war. Of his published accounts of cathedrals (Canterbury, Winchester, York, Chichester, Lichfield, Worcester) or other ecclesiastical (Sherborne, Glastonbury) or monastic buildings (Canterbury, Worcester), illustrated with his own drawings (Figs. 8–10), it is not possible to give a description here, even if the writer was competent to do so. That they are normally the starting point for fresh study goes without saying. The first and longest of the cathedral papers by Willis was that on Canterbury Cathedral (Willis, 1845) which has proved the most influential in later times.

Exceptionally rich documentary sources survive for Canterbury, Eadmer and Gervase being the best known names, so that Willis was able to achieve a dazzling symbiosis between written and material remains. His method, a strict separation of the initial history from written sources from the interpretation of the existing building, has been a model for later workers. The late Sir Charles Peers adopted this rigid division between 'History' and 'Description' in his guidebooks for the Office of Works and so it has continued even with English Heritage, although it tends to conflict with the fantasies of the marketeers. There is no doubt that any rational approach to the history of a building the separation is desirable, correlation being made during or after the description. At Canterbury Willis was able to make a conjectural reconstruction of the pre-Conquest church, and then analyse the existing remains: Lanfranc, Anselm, and the choir of William of Sens and William the Englishman (Fig. 13.8). His analytical powers are remarkable and the fact that a modern scholar working over the same ground seems to have revealed only one serious error testifies to this.[8]

His work in the cathedral was complemented by his equally famous account of the monastic buildings at Christchurch published almost at the end of his active life (Willis, 1868). After leaving Caius College, Willis seems to have been at Downing for a period before he secured a fellowship at Trinity, no doubt through the good offices of Whewell. The celebrated mid-twelfth century map of the monastery is in Trinity College library; it had already been published in the 18th century (*Vetusta Monumenta*, 1789) but Willis retraced his plan from the original. The plan showed both the inflow and outflow of water to the conventual buildings which Willis was able to distinguish by colours on a modern plan. The medieval plan is an almost miraculous survival from the time when the priory was at its height of power, forty years before Gervase, so the labels attached to the buildings identify their function beyond doubt when they were in active use. When the understanding of monastic ruins was still very rudimentary such information helped to explain many other remains. It is not unfair to say that these two studies of Willis gave a new sense of purpose and direction to the study of ecclesiastical architecture of the middle ages.

During the period he was studying cathedrals Willis wrote on other subjects. His engineering was not ne-

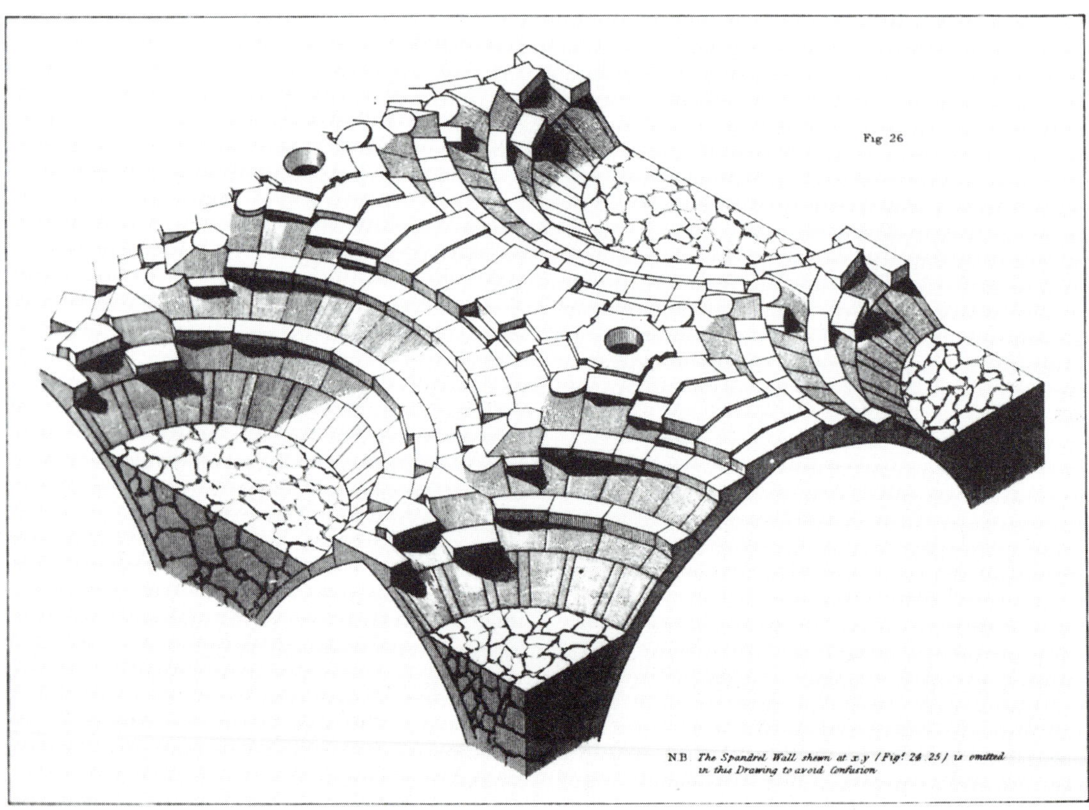

Fig. 13.5 Diagram of a fan vault, Trans. R.I.B.A. *(1842)*

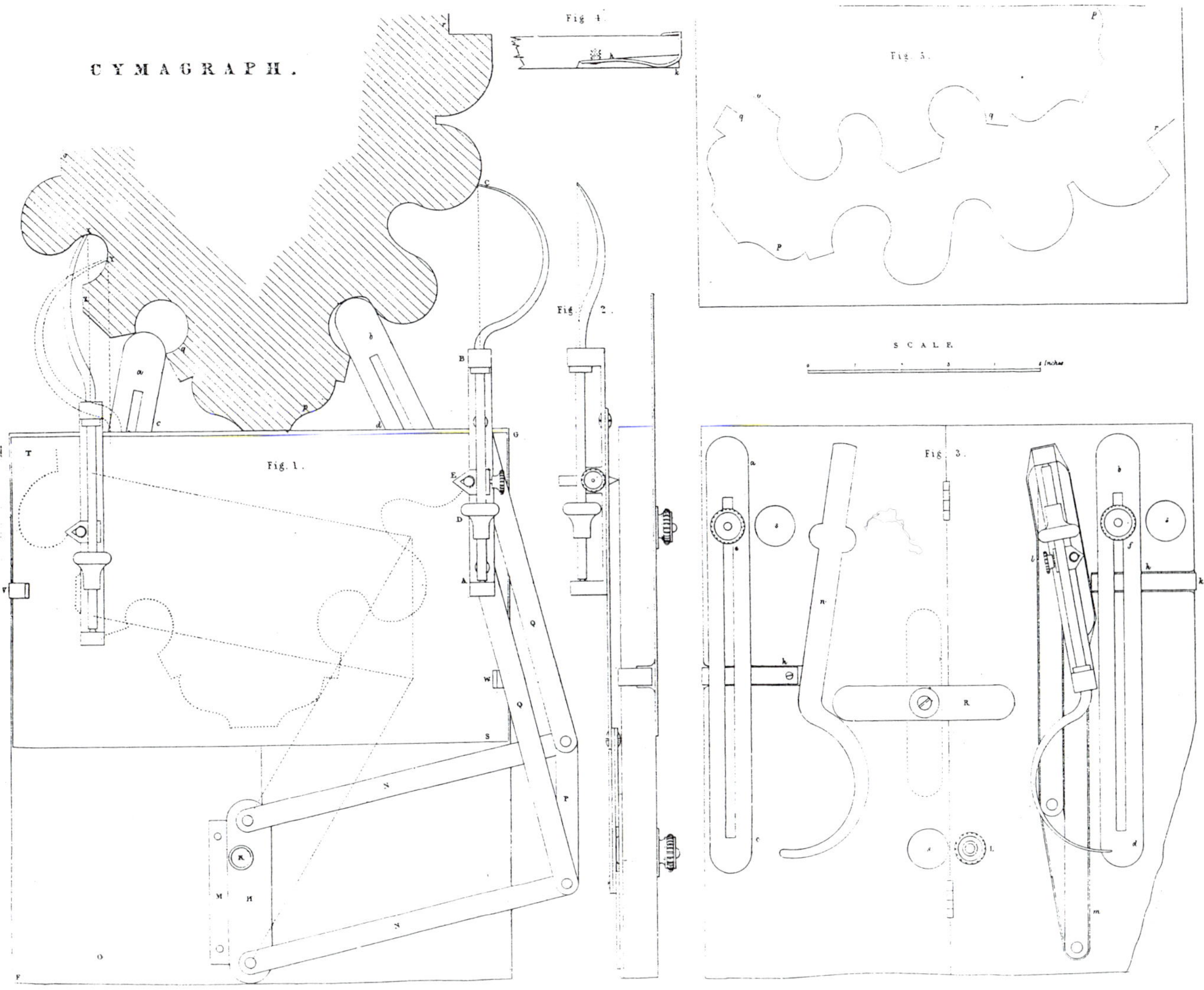

Fig. 13.6 The Cymagraph, The Civil Engineer *(1842).*

glected as shown by the list of publications given below. He was a juror in the machinery section of the Great Exhibition and lectured at the School of Mines. How can one apply the word antiquary to someone who was taking a significant part in the Industrial Revolution! He was President of the meeting of the British Association for the Advancement of Science held at Cambridge in 1862, which allowed him to give delegates a survey of the most recent advances of knowledge in each field of science. This aspect of his work does not however concern us here.

Willis' knowledge of Greek Orthodox churches has already been mentioned, but in 1849 he extended beyond this when he published his book on the Holy Sepulchre at Jerusalem (Willis, 1849). He had to rely on an ample literature, a model at the British Museum and oral advice. He distinguished five periods from Constantine and provided elaborate plans and sections. The predominantly Greek sources presented no problem for him. For contemporaries it was something of a *tour de force*, and although no doubt out of date (I am not conversant with modern work) still seems so today.

Following their publication on the Continent, Willis published a description of the 9th century St Gall monastic plan, so important for the study of the medieval cloister (Willis, 1848), as well as a translation and revised version of the French facsimile edition of the sketch-book of 'Wilars de Honecort', the 13th-century French master mason (Willis, 1859). Medieval courthand presented no problem for him as his publication of the Westminster fabric roll for 1253 shows (Willis, 1860). The point is an important one for it was his mastery of both sources of evidence that allowed him to move freely from one to another in his architectural histories. This took on a special importance when he was concerned with the Cambridge colleges.

Cambridge and Oxford Colleges

His final posthumous work, the four-volume (three of text and one of plans with overlays), *The Architectural History of the University of Cambridge and Colleges of Cambridge and Eton* (Willis and Clark, 1886), by which he is best known, has been re-issued by the Cambridge

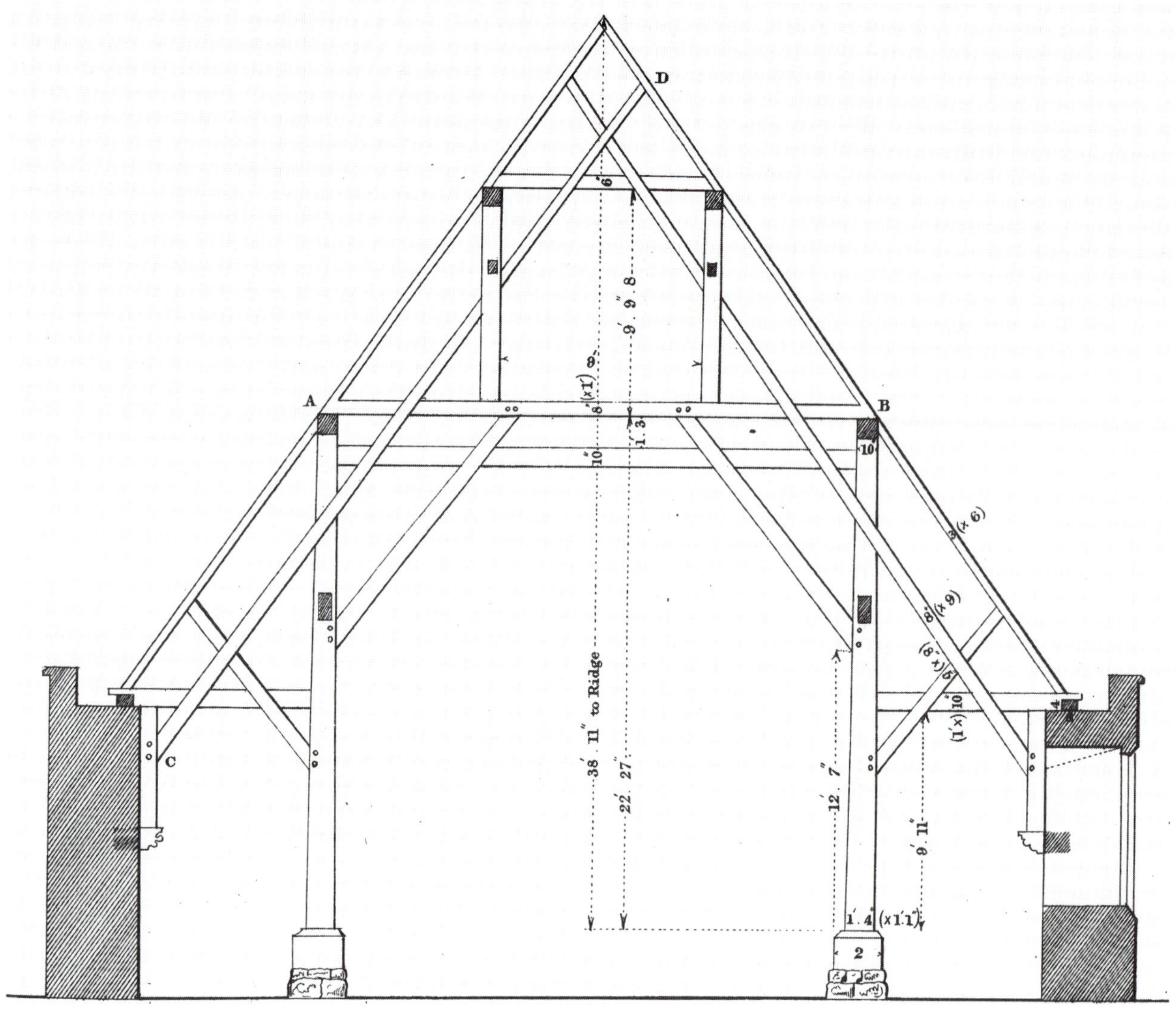

Fig. 13.7 The Ely Sextry Barn (now demolished).

University Press with a foreword by David Watkin, just after the centenery (1988). On 5th July, 1854, when the Archaeological Institute held its summer meeting at Cambridge, Willis speaking to the architecture section, presided over by Whewell, with the Prince Consort in the audience "delivered an admirable discourse on the Collegiate and other buildings in Cambridge".[9] The "vote of thanks was carried with more than ordinary enthusiasm". It is clear that Willis had already set out on the long road of collecting material for the architectural history that he followed until his powers failed him after the death of his wife. His papers passed to his nephew, J.W. Clark, after his own death in 1875, who pulled the whole project together and so created the volumes published ten years later.[10] There is no doubt that Clark was faced with a major undertaking, shuffling the papers around, repaginating, pasting in references and so on. Many of the sections are marked `Copied' by Clark, so much of the final text is unaltered Willis. The creation of the `Quad Style' and the comparison with Haddon Hall are clearly due to Willis.[11] The addition of Eton seems to have been Clark's idea, for, although Willis had lectured on Eton, Clark had been at school there. The real extent of the contribution of Clark could only be worked out from a detailed analysis of the bulky material in the University Library.

Willis constantly took Oxford into account and the history of college foundations ran from Merton at Oxford to Downing at Cambridge. On Cambridge he set out his intention:

> "The paper which I have proposed to myself in the present work is to trace the history of the colleges principally with reference to their topography and architecture, the acquirements and increase of their respective sites, the arrangements of their buildings and the additions they received from time to time. This is a very different investigation from that which has usually been proposed as the leading object – the necessary histories of the Universities or their colleges which have already appeared." (CUL MS Add. 5059)

The basis of the research was the documents in the bursars' offices of the colleges, which were predominantly concerned with property acquisition, leases, grants of

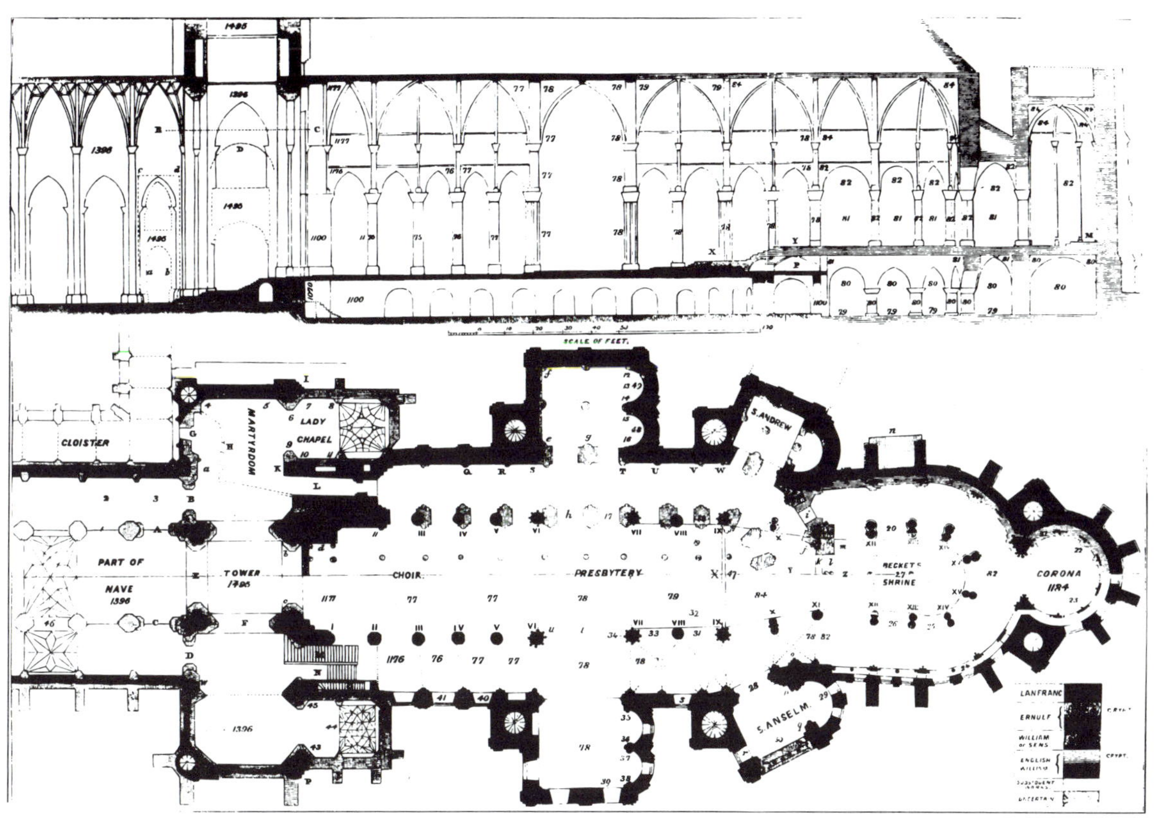

Fig.13.8 The choir of Canterbury Cathedral.

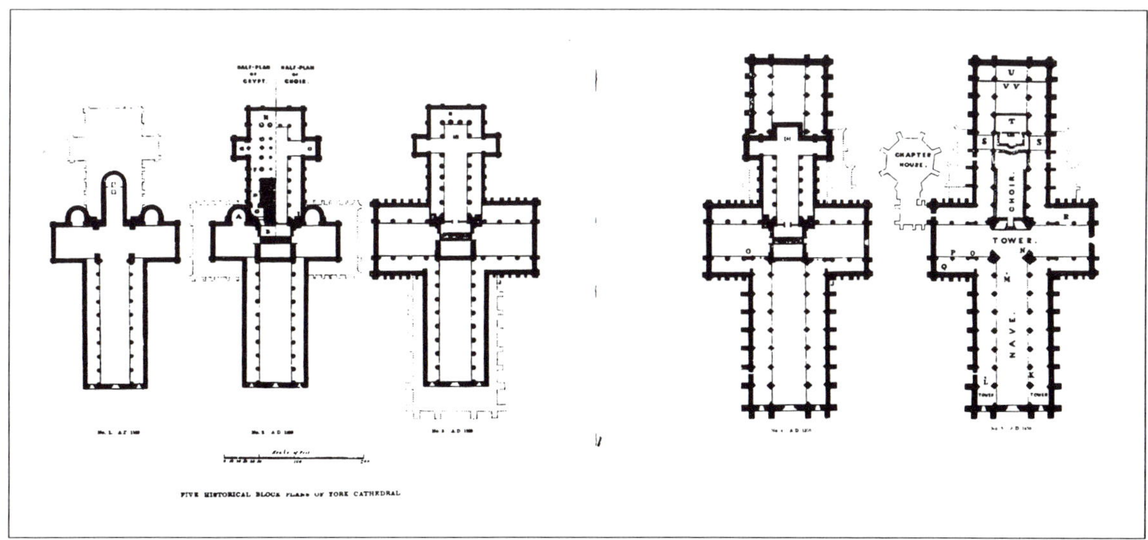

Fig. 13.9 The development of York Minster.

Fig. 13.10 Original and later bay in Winchester Cathedral.

rights, as well as with building works. At first sight it seems a fairly mundane objective; what prompted Willis to do this? The success of his marriage of documentary sources with the existing building at Canterbury no doubt suggested the idea that even with the documents unprinted in college offices something on a grander scale might be undertaken at Cambridge. His cathedral studies had made him familiar with the idea of organic growth, so characteristic of colleges, so the attraction of the project for Willis needs no long explanation. Study of the documents went hand in hand with the collection of much architectural detail: mouldings, doorways, windows, tracery, plans and so on.[12]

Although both the *Victoria County History* and *Royal Commission on Historic Monuments* have covered Cambridge, Willis and Clark have certainly not been superseded. Preoccupation with personalities and movements leads the normal historian into sentimental or sententious alleyways, and the 'art historian' is even more likely to lose himself in value judgements. The great strength of Willis and Clark is its single-minded devotion to an impersonal account of the ground plans and architecture, an engineer's account (except where Clark had overlain Willis) that adheres firmly to the brief. Socio-architectural history of the modern style would have been alien to Willis and very much out of place; single-mindedness was the key to the success of Willis and Clark.

Conclusion

Willis had exceptional gifts. His powers of analysis went hand in hand with his skills as an engineer. Whether he regarded a building as a machine to be taken to pieces as his nephew averred I am not sure but he did say: "The best instructor of all, perhaps, is a building which is being pulled down, but such opportunities are to be regretted" (Willis, 1842,3). His almost impassioned account of the collapse of the crossing tower at Chichester (Willis, 1861) revealed how closely entwined were his archaeological and engineering interests; they were like the obverse and reverse of the same coin.

His second gift was the mastery of original written sources; most architectural historians limit themselves to published sources or ignore them altogether; a rare example of someone who enjoyed a combination of both gifts was the late Alexander Hamilton-Thompson. Close marriage of analysis of the fabric with the written record played a major part in Willis' success.

The third gift that puts Willis into a class of his own was a practical one, skill with his hands of which there is so much evidence from his youth onwards. So far as we know he did not use a draughtsman and most of his drawings are signed by himself. No doubt this deepened his knowledge of the building, just as their revealing nature about the structure enhances the reader's understanding. The rib patterns of the Italian vaults (Fig. 13.2), the longitudinal section of Christchurch (Fig. 13.8) the axonometric views of the upper surfaces of fan vaults (Fig. 13.5), the alteration of the Norman bays at Winchester (Fig. 13.10) are examples that come to mind. Obviously a skill of this kind derived at least partly from an engineer's drawing.

> Changes in style may be best studied by following them throughout some great building that has occupied long periods in erecting and in which the inception of the parts will manifest itself even when no history remains (MS Add. 5029, 59).

Some of the influence of Willis on later generations has already been referred to, like the division between history and fabric analysis. His starting point, vaults, led to the well-known paper on vaults to which we may still turn (Willis, 1842). Without singling out special papers it is surely his general approach to a building that has most profoundly influenced later workers. He created a kind of developmental archaeology in which a structure is seen to be the end-result of a long process of accretion, demolition and replacement, in response to changes in need and fashion. He started by defining his periods by shading but had introduced colour by at least 1861 at Chichester. Subsequently the search for changes in construction at different dates became almost the main object of architectural history. For St John Hope, secretary of the Society of Antiquaries and an avowed disciple of Willis, the object of excavation on the site of a ruin was to extend the history underground in order to fill out the colour scheme on the dated plan. Even Romano-British archaeology was influenced by this producing a formidable series of 'periods' in its excavations. In this respect it perhaps owes more to Willis than to Pitt-Rivers.

Developmental archaeology was not confined to the building but in the case of the Cambridge colleges extended to the site; it was a way of looking at both buildings and the ground on which they stand. There is possibly an analogy with evolution in biology although certainly only a fortuitous one. To see an ancient structure as the final stage of a line of development is surely the only way to understand it, and in that respect Willis pointed us in the right direction.

Notes

1. Thompson, M.W. 1990: The Cambridge Antiquarian Society, 1840-1990 (Cambridge).
2. Willis, R.D. 1796: Philosophical Sketches of the Principles of Society and Government (London).
3. Clark, J.W. "Robert Willis' art", in the Dictionary of National Biography.
4. C[ambridge] U[university] L[ibrary] Add. MS. 7574.
5. Syllabus of Lectures, Royal Institution (1832).
6. Pevsner, N. 1970: Robert Willis (Northampton, Mass.); reprinted and expanded in Some Architectural Writers of the Nineteenth Century (Oxford 1972), 52-61.
7. Smith, C.R. 1883: Retrospections, Social and Archaeological, 3 vols. (London).
8. Woodman, F. [Canterbury] 1981, p.- for Willis error.
9. Proceedings of Cambridge Meeting of Archaeol. Institute. *Archaeol. Jnl.*, 11 (1854), 393.
10. Shipley, A.E. 1913: 'J': a Memoir of John Willis Clark (London)
11. C.U.L. Add. MS. 5059.
12. Ibid.

Bibliography for Robert Willis

A. *Manuscript materials*

The main body of papers of Willis are in the Cambridge University Library (C.U.L.):

Add. MSS 5022–45m 5058–82, 5103. A large quantity of notes, drawings etc in boxes or bound in volumes, sorted and arranged by J.W. Clark who bequeathed them to the Library in 1910

Add. MSS 5127–44. Partly arranged by individual buildings, bought by the Library in J.W. Clark sale at Bowes and Bowes.

There are also a number of letters in Add. MSS.

Add. MS 7574. Diary 1819–21 (partly in shorthand), gift in 1960 of S.M. Barry.

At the Society of Antiquaries of London are four volumes of drawings (some coloured) all from his early life, presented by J.W. Clark in 1900:

452 F. Vol. 1, France and Italy; 2, Italy and Germany; 3, Continent and Britain (Norfolk); 4, Cathedrals and Churches (Ely, Thetford, Gloucester etc.).

Patents: No. 4343 (1819) for a pedal harp, and No. 8384 (1840) for an apparatus for weighing; details in C.U.L., Cam.a.500.8(3-4).

B. *Publications*

Willis had been buying books from his youth and at the sale of his library in April 1872, it comprised 1,458 items (discussed by Pevsner op.cit. note 6, 24–5). His own publications were listed at the end of the second edition of *Principles of Mechanism* and this has been expanded below. Some of the publications appeared in more than one form and there is often a variation in the assumed date, especially if a printed version of a lecture appeared long after its delivery.

1821: An attempt to Analyse the Automaton Chess Player (London).

1830a: On the pressure produced on a flat plate when opposed to a stream of air issuing from an orifice in a plane surface. Trans. Cambridge Phil. Soc. 3, 129-40.

1830b: On the vowel sounds. Ibid. 3, 231-68.

1833: On the mechanism of the larynx. Ibid. 4, 323-52.

1835: Remarks on the Architecture of the Middle Ages, especially of Italy (Cambridge).

1838: On the Teeth of Wheels. Trans. Inst. Civil Engineers 2, 89-112.

1839: Syllabus of a Course of Experimental Lectures on the Principles of Mechanism (Cambridge).

1841: Principles of Mechanism (London).

1842a: On the construction of the vaults of the middle ages. Trans. R.I.B.A. 1 (pt. ii), 1-69 (repr. 1973).

1842b: On the characteristic interpenetrations of the Flamboyant style. Ibid., 81-7.

1842c: Report of a Survey of the Dilapidated Portions of Hereford Cathedral in the year 1841 (Hereford), repr. in *The Civil Engineer and Architects's Jnl.* 1, 374-80 (repr. 1973).

1842d: Description of the 'cymagraph' for copying mouldings. Ibid. 5, 219-20.

1843a: *A description of the Sextry Barn at Ely, lately demolished.* Cambridge Antiq. Soc. Quarto public. No. 7.

1843b: *Architectural nomenclature of the Middle Ages.* Cambridge Antiq. Soc. Quarto public. No. 9.

1845a: History of the Great Seals of England, especially those of Edward III." *Archaeol. Jnl.* 2, 14-45.

1845b: The Architectural History of Canterbury Cathedral (London) (repr. 1972).

1846a: The Architectural History of Winchester Cathedral, *Proc. Archaeol. Inst. Winchester* 1845, 1-80 (also repr. separately, and repr. 1972).

1846b: Principles of Tools for Turning and Planing Metals,

WHERE?

1848a: The Architectural History of York Cathedral, *Proc. Archaeol. Inst. York* 1848, 1-60 (also repr. separately, and repr. 1972).

1848b: Description of the ancient plan of the Monastery of St Gall, in the ninth century, *Archaeol. Jnl.* 5, 85-117.

1849a: The Architectural History of the Church of the Holy Sepulchre at Jerusalem (London).

1849b: Introduction to R. Curzon: Monasteries of the Levant (London).

1850: Edited, illustrated and added to J.H. Parker: A Glossary of Terms used in.... Gothic Architecture, 5th edn. (Oxford & London).

1851a: On the effects produced by causing weights to travel over elastic bars. In *Report of the Commissioners Appointed to Enquire into the Application of Iron Railway Stuctures* App. B.; repr. in Barlow: Treatise on the Strength of Timber.

1851b: A System of Apparatus for the Use of Lecturers and Experimenters in Mechanical Philosophy (London).

1852: On Machines and Tools for Working in Metal, Wood and other Materials, Great Exhibition Lecture, 7.

1853a: Manufacturing Machines and Tools, Great Exhibition. Reports of Juries: Class 6.

1853b: with Sir F.A.G. Ouseley and J. Donaldson: Crystal Palace Company: Grand Organ, Preliminary Report.

1857: Paris Universal Exhibition: Report on the Machinery for Woven Fabrics (London).

1859: Fac-Simile of the Sketch-Book of Wilars de Honecourt trans., ed. and with additions to the editions of Lassus and Quicherat (London).

1860a: A Westminster fabric roll of 1253, *Gentleman's Magazine* (July to December), 293-99.

1860b: [Architectural history of Gloucester Cathedral] Report in *Proc. of Archaeol. Inst. at Gloucester..... Archaeol. Jnl.* 17, 335-42.

1861a: The Architectural History of Chichester Cathedral, with an Introductory Essay on the Fall of the Tower and Spire (Chichester) (repr. 1972).

1861b: On foundations of early buildings, recently discovered in Lichfield Cathedral, *Archaeol. Jnl.* 18, 1-24 (repr. 1973).

1862: Presidential Address to the British Association for the Advancement of Science at its Cambridge meeting.

1863a: The architectural history of the cathedral and monastery at Worcester. *Archaeol. Jnl.* 20, 83-132, 254-72, 301-18 (repr. 1973).

1863b: The crypt and chapter house of Worcester cathedral, *Trans. R.I.B.A.* ['Papers read at'] 13, 213-30.

1865: The architectural history of Sherborne minster, *Archaeol. Jnl.* 22, 179-99.

1866: The Architectural History of Glastonbury Abbey (Cambridge).

1868a: The architectural history of the conventual buildings of the monastery of Christ Church in Canterbury, *Archaeol. Cantiana* 7, 1-206 (repr. separately London, 1869).

1868b: Speech on the Opening of the Conservatoire des Arts et Métiers. *The Builder* (4th July), 487.

1870: Principles of Mechanisms 2nd edition (London).

(Posthumous)

1886: with J. Willis Clark: The Architectural History of the University of Cambridge and the Colleges of Cambridge and Eton 3 vols. text and 4th vol. of plans with overlays (repr. with Preface by David Watkin, 1988).

1972-3: Architectural History of some English Cathedrals 2 vols. (Paul Minet, Chicheley) Reprints of Willis' papers on cathedrals and vaults, as noted above, and also prints from C.U.L. MS. 5036 a transcript of two lectures on the architecture of Salisbury Cathedral given to the Archaeol. Inst. at Salisbury in 1849.

Cathedral papers delivered by Willis to R.A.I. meetings:
[* denotes paper listed above]
1844 Canterbury*, 1845 Winchester*, 1846 York*, 1847 Norwich, 1849 Salisbury*, 1850 Oxford, 1851 Wells, 1852 Chichester*, [1854 Cambridge], 1860 Gloucester*, 1861 Peterborough, 1862 Worcester*, 1863 Rochester, 1864 Lichfield, 1865 Glastonbury.

Cathedral Carpentry

Julian Munby

Among my list of regrets I have set this memorandum:
'Did not ever draw a view of the Bell Tower at Salisbury.'
John Carter, *Gentleman's Magazine* 1803.[1]

The study of carpentry

John Carter, fulminating in his 'Pursuits of Architectural Innovation' at the destruction of medieval antiquities in cathedrals and elsewhere, was able to take some consolation in the fact that prior to the needless destruction of the Salisbury belfry, it had been surveyed by Price, in his remarkable work on that cathedral (Fig. 14.1; Price 1753, pl.10) But for the most part, carpentry work in cathedrals had been, and was to remain, a curiously neglected topic. Even though Professor Willis made his first major contribution in his exacting record of the threatened Sextry Barn at Ely (1843), and he lived in an age when the recording of threatened buildings was commonplace among architectural antiquaries, his notable series of papers on the archaeology of cathedrals did not prominently include carpentry in their subject matter. Amongst the broad stream of Gothic publications flowing from John Parker's publishing business, few dealt with carpentry except for framed buildings, and the Brandons' Open Roofs of the Middle Ages (1860) was the only work devoted to the topic. Practising architects could not afford to ignore the subject, however, and even Scott at Ely has been shown to be not insensitive to the needs of the renowned Octagon (Lindley 1987, 92ff), while Colson left a careful record of his repairs at Winchester (1899).

The French, who took the study of Gothic along with the steam engine from England, paid attention to carpentry from the beginning, as can be seen from the works of Violet le Duc and Caumont, and which culminated in the seminal studies by Henri Deneux.[2] The most wide-ranging study, covering much of western Europe, was Friedrich Ostendorf's history of roofs, *Die Geschichte des Dachwerks*, published in 1908. Ostendorf drew on an extensive knowledge of English publications, supplemented by his own surveys of a remarkable number of cathedral roofs (Fig. 14.2).

In England, amongst the last works of the great age of Gothic scholarship, Howard & Crossley's *English Church Woodwork* (1917), and Bond's various studies (1908 & 1910), largely related to visible works and fittings, and did not treat roof carpentry over vaults. The towering achievements of Nikolaus Pevsner, an avowed disciple of Willis, rarely extended to carpentry (though this is changing in the new editions of the *Buildings of England*). Little of relevance was published in the middle years of the present century beyond a paper on York (Hughes 1955), and Atkinson's work on Ely (1933). The major contribution of the RCHME in the field has been the rescue recording in the wake of the destruction wrought on the original roofs of Westminster Abbey (McDowall et al. 1966).

Given this background, the appearance in 1974 of Cecil Hewett's pioneering work on *English Cathedral Carpentry* (revised 1985), following on from his studies of Essex buildings and churches opened a new field of study which has been enthusiastically taken up by a large number of followers in his wake. The establishment of a vocabulary and framework of chronological development, aided by a virtuoso display of graphical communication (Fig. 14.7) by far outweighs any shortcomings of a relatively rapid and single-handed examination of so many major buildings.

The importance of cathedral carpentry

Hewett's contribution has been to reveal the skill of the medieval carpenter in coping with large-scale structural problems of covering wide (and high) spans between stone walls, and the solutions devised to deal with the special circumstances of polygonal roofing of spires and chapter houses. The problems had been examined before from the point of view of domestic buildings and barns, but not in the context of the designs and innovations of the great gothic masons (Smith 1958-1974).

The unique feature of the majority of cathedral roofs is their being obscured from everyday view, with their ingenuity being only apparent to the adventurous in dark and high places. To that extent, they represent pure engineering solutions to the design problems which they

Fig. 14.1 The lost belfry of Salisbury (Price 1753).

overcome, unaffected by aesthetic or stylistic considerations. Their relationship to stone walls sets them apart from framed buildings, whilst often providing valuable evidence for the chronology and sequence of their construction (Courtenay 1985, Munby 1981).

That such a major aspect of medieval engineering should have been ignored for so long may seem remarkable, but the amount of investigation currently being devoted to the subject is amply making up for lost time, and Hewett's account is continually being amplified and revised.

The carpenters and their work

Documentary sources for cathedral carpentry are surprisingly few, though much is known about medieval carpenters from better recorded buildings (Salzman 1967). Even

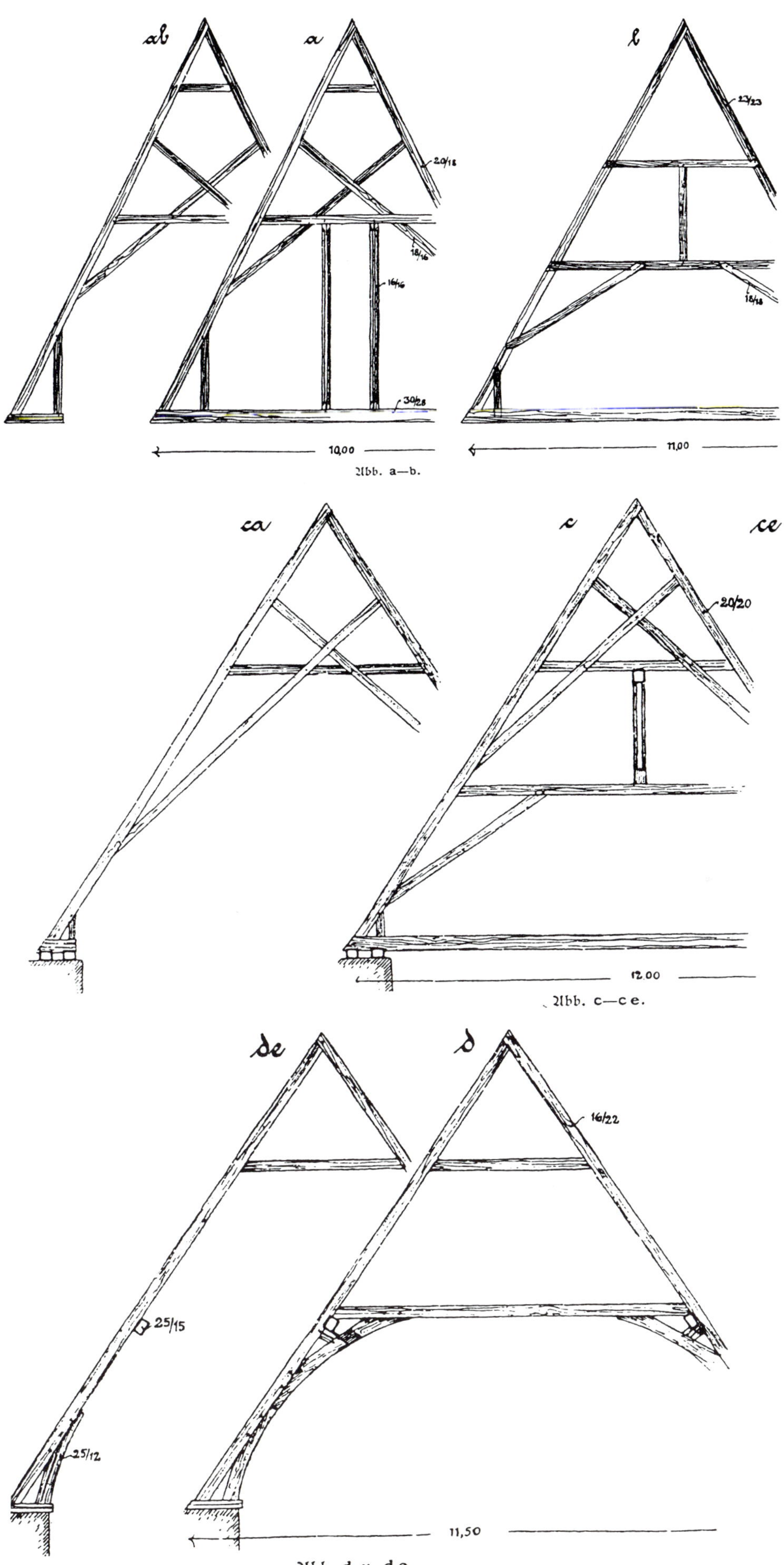

Fig. 14.2 Some roofs drawn by Ostendorf (1908):
A. Salisbury, north east transept; B. Winchester, nave; C. Exeter, nave; D. Wells, east choir.

where there are surviving sets of fabric accounts, as for Exeter, the accounting methods do not always serve to reveal what work is being done, or even consistently name the trades of the craftsmen (Erskine 1981 & 1983). The information gained from accounts is instructive on the general organisation of works, but tantalising in charting its progress. Indeed, the number of named carpenters who can definitely be associated with surviving works is remarkably small, and even then it is uncertain whether they were actually responsible for the design or just its execution (Harvey 1984, 383 ff.). The tendency to associate known masons with carpentry designs is perverse, and should surely be avoided, for even though they may well have discussed the design with the master carpenter, he is unlikely to have ceded such an important matter to one not trained in his craft. There is also little doubt (as at York in 1345) that there was generally both a master carpenter and a master mason in charge of the operations (Aylmer and Cant 1977, 157). One certain exception perhaps proves the rule: the mason Thomas Winton/ Witney's involvement in the Bishop's Throne at Exeter. Master Thomas 'de Winton' selected timber for it, though the carpenter Robert of Galmeton was much concerned with its construction; Master Thomas de Witney, likely to be the same man, was also much involved with new masonry work in the cathedral (Harvey 1984; Erskine 1981, 71; 1983, xx & xxx). The throne, an astonishing work of miniature architecture, might as easily have been built in stone as in timber, and the provision of a design would have well been within the capability of a master mason (Glasscoe and Swanton 1978). But the roof above it called for a different expertise, and there is no reason to suppose that Witney had a hand in that (Munby 1991a).

Unusually, in the case of Westminster Abbey we know the name of the major figure responsible for the carpentry for some twenty years, Master Alexander, who was the first to hold the office of King's Carpenter. He was involved in many projects for the king's works, especially castles, and built a detached belfry at Westminster in 1248/9; he is very likely to have designed the roofs of the east end of the church (Harvey 1984 for this and much of following). Another major figure was William Hurley, again a royal carpenter, paid £8 a year by the monks of Ely for his advice, which may have included the production or supervision of the design for the Octagon, and perhaps the stalls.

Gilbert of Corbridge was carpenter to the Archbishop of York in the second quarter of the thirteenth century, at the time the South Transept was built, and he may have been responsible for the timber vault and roof later destroyed by fire. Following an inquiry into the poor condition of the nave roof of York in 1345, when it was found that the old carpenter was no longer able to work at great heights, Philip of Lincoln was appointed master carpenter of the Minster for a weekly wage, together with the office of janitor of the Close, and received pay rises in 1350 and 1371. He erected and probably designed the timber vault of the Minster nave, for which timber was being collected as late as 1356 (Aylmer and Cant 1977, 158 & 190). At Canterbury, the carpenter John Wolward was excused jury service for eight years from 1390, and may have been master carpenter during the construction of the nave.

Most other references are to contracts for carving stalls, including such men as Geoffrey the carpenter, in charge of the St Albans Abbey choirstalls in 1314, and William Lyngwood, released by the Bishop of Norwich in 1308 to work at Winchester on 'a piece of work belonging to the craft of carpentry which he had already begun', presumably the existing choir stalls (Tracy 1987, 16) Finally, men such as Andrew Couper (repairs to Norwich campanile 1481-2), Hugh the carpenter (Worcester, 1359-96) and Lawrence Wright (Ripon, 1354-80) are to be seen more as jobbing carpenters, retained or hired for maintenance and minor works.

Apart from such rare instances, the authorship of the majority of cathedral carpentry must be considered anonymous, and the names of the master carpenters who made the designs are lost to us, though attributions on grounds of style may on occasions be possible. From better documented buildings the names of many carpenters are known, however, and much can be discovered about their work from written records, especially those of the king's works. We know that carpenters travelled across the country to aid the building of castles, and travelled abroad to construct engines of war (Taylor 1961; Harvey 1984 s.n. Houghton) The (unnamed) carpenter of Chichester Cathedral was excused from his job to go on crusade in *c.*1230 (Munby 1981, 243). It is mere coincidence that the roof applied to Chichester at the start of the next century (for which see below) was of such marked continental design, but it serves as a reminder that it may well be the design of an English carpenter who had crossed the channel, rather than being built by a French or Flemish carpenter.

Master carpenters were responsible for designing roofs, no doubt in consultation with the master mason. Drawings must have been prepared, and though none survive in England before the sixteenth century, the sketchbook of Villard de Honnecourt contains elevations of roof trusses.[3] The geometry of roof designs is as yet unexplored, but is a factor worth considering, given the known use of the compasses by carpenters as well as masons. Carpentry was often prepared in a framing yard at some distance from the site, and so could be laid out on the ground and to a certain extent be 'designed' at full scale.

As a preliminary, appropriate timber had to be selected, a process which involved the master carpenter riding to the woods to view the trees, as 'Winton' did for Exeter (see also Simpson, this volume, on selection and use of timber). It was felled, and after disposal of bark and branches (to wood and tanning trades), scappling (squaring) and any necessary sawing, it was carted to the framing yard (Rackham 1980). Usually, the timing of the process as revealed by building accounts indicates that timber was worked in the green; in the case of the timber selected for the Bishop's throne at Exeter, it was submerged in a millpond to let it season (Erskine 1981, 71). Boards for stalls, vaulting and doors was likely to be imported Baltic timber of oak or softwood, brought into the eastern ports of England in vast quantities for as long as records exist. Imported timber has been identified at Ely by means of dendrochronology, where the curves match exceptionally well with those for the Baltic; one of the doors in the York chapter house has been identified as being softwood.[4]

Roof frames were wholly assembled, marked and taken apart again, before being transported to site. Carpenters' marks made with a draw-knife are commonly found, identifying individual trusses and which way round they were to be reassembled (Fig. 14.9; Munby 1981, 234-5; Allan & Jupp 1981, 152-3). The final process of rearing need have involved no more than raising the timber to the top of the church by means of a crane, and fitting together the prefabricated pieces; it is unlikely that complete trusses were lifted whole.

It should be added that the entire business of building in stone necesitated much carpentry, as scaffolding had to be made, fitted with hurdles for walking on, and moved up and along as building progressed. Ladders, cranes, wheelbarrows, hods and tool handles all required a continuous input from the carpenter, and above all there was the construction of formwork for arches and vaulting (Fitchen 1961; Salzman 1967; Simpson, this volume Fig. 15.13, for surviving formwork). It is generally believed that vaulting was constructed after the roof was in place, which was certainly more convenient in roofs with tie-beams; the corollary of this is that temporary roofing may have been needed, if the roof and vaults were not built bay by bay. Some of the Wells roofs were actually built resting on the stonework of the vaults, and so must be secondary; at Chichester it would appear that the whole roof was built at one time (or in two parts for nave and chancel), and thus after the whole church had been vaulted. Exeter was continually building for almost a century, and by contrast the type of roof used there would allow for gradual building in short sections at a time, though it was perhaps made in only three or four sections (Munby 1991a).

Developments in roof design

Some attempt must be made to outline the progress of design of major roofs, in part to clarify Hewett's proposed sequence, and to suggest further lines of research. Given the lack of very early roofs, there is little that can be said of Saxon or Norman roof carpentry, though the examination of examples in France and Belgium has provided many examples that conform to a standard type.[5]

The earliest surviving roofs in England are fragmentary survivals of parts that were reused in later times. The most important recent discovery has been the orginal nave roof of Ely, whose profile has been reconstructed from reused rafters and the outline preserved on the west tower (see Fig. 15.4). The reconstructed truss has a tie and collar, king-strut, queen-struts and raking ashlars, all joined with open notch-lap joints. A dendrochronological date of 1105x40 is indicated, perhaps c.1120 (Simpson, this volume). This roof conforms with what is known of romanesque roofs on continental churches.

Towards the end of the century, the eastern part of the nave at Wells (possibly by Master Nicholas) has two collars and soulaces; the collars separated by a crown-strut, and the rafter feet supported with ashlars, the whole using notch-lap joints (Harvey 1984; Hewett 1985, 6). The western part, built after the interdict, is distinguished by the use of secret notch-lap joints (Hewett 1985, 11), though these had already been used at Canterbury in the south-east transept spirelet of *c.*1180 (Hewett and Tatton-Brown 1976). This type of truss seems to have been standard for the first phase of gothic roofing, as exemplified by the eastern roofs of Lincoln. Here an extensive programme of research on the form and dating of the roofs has examined the development of one basic design through the thirteenth century (Foot, Litton and Simpson 1986 and below, chapter 15). If the reused timbers in the roof of the Angel choir belong to the original presbytery, roofed about 1200, then it had scissor-braced trusses. The existing roofs over the choir and choir transepts of Bishop Hugh's church were built about the same time as the presbytery. They have two collars, with raking struts and soulaces trenched across secondary rafters (Hewett 1985, 7-10). The inner bay of the north-east transept has scissor braces across the lower collars. Tie-beams are present on every third truss, and the pitch of the roof requires such long rafters that some are made from two lengths, scarfed together. Dates for the timbers used at the east end suggest felling over a number of years but a single campaign of building. A variant of this design was used in the nave in the following decades, and in the roof over the Angel choir of the 1270s (Hewett 1985, 26 & 31). At the west end of Lincoln, the roof of the south-west chapel (Consistory Court), probably dating to the second quarter of the thirteenth century, employs a remarkable method to prevent the longitudinal movement of the rafters (racking). In addition to a standard Lincoln truss design of strutted collars, four outer rafters are bifurcated at their lower ends, with long struts passing through adjacent rafters to form a firm triangular base. The same roof has a raised tie-beam to prevent lateral spread and simultaneously clear the high vault apex (Hewett 1985, 18-21).

During the middle decades of the thirteenth century the use of collars with soulaces was common, especially in minor roofs, such as the chapter house of Oxford Cathedral (Fig. 14.3), but the use of scissor-braced truss became widespread, appearing at Peterborough in the roof of the nave and north-west portico (before 1238), the north-east transept of Salisbury (Fig. 14.2a), the presbytery and nave of Ely in the 1240s, and around the 1250s at Salisbury north porch, Gloucester Blackfriars,

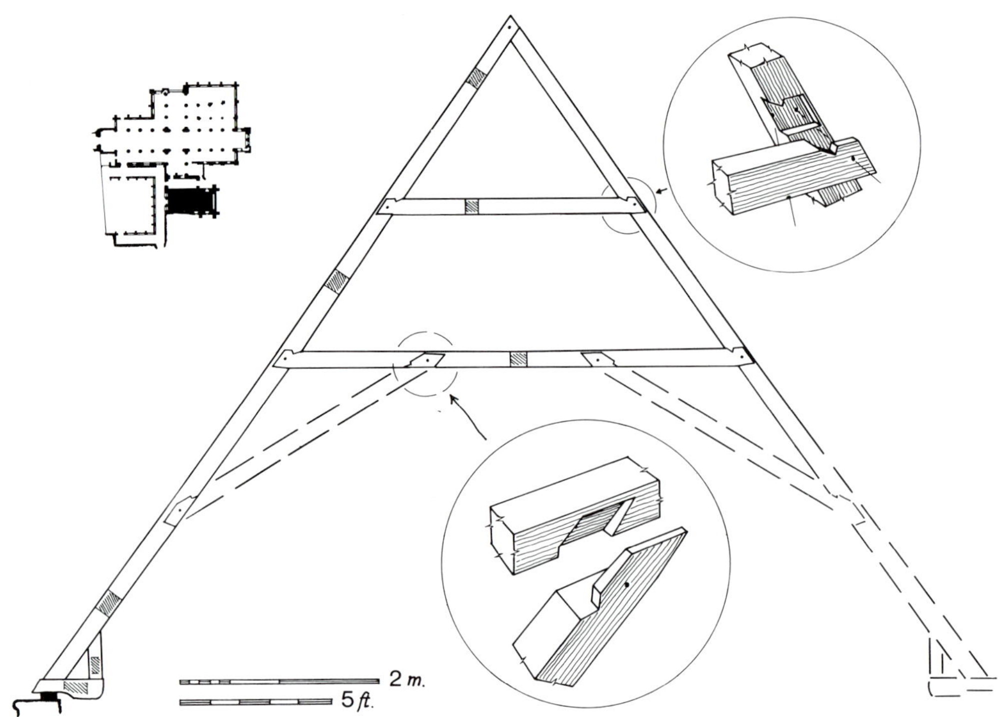

Fig. 14.3 Scissor-braced roof of chapter house, Oxford Cathedral, c.1250 (Ashdown et al., 1990).

and Westminster Abbey.[6] Attempts to provide longitudinal stability also appear in these roofs: the Salisbury porch has crown-struts on three trusses, connected to each other with cross-bracing; Gloucester and Westminster had diagonal braces applied respectively to the inner and outer faces of the rafters. The process had begun much earlier with the development of stabilising methods at the rafter foot, in the provision of wallplates and ashlar-bracing (Courtenay 1985), but it was the use of plates or purlins, longitudinal members resting on collars or supporting rafters, that became the standard method of providing stability against racking. Although purlins were first used in lean-to roofing merely to provide support for common rafters (e.g. Wells and Salisbury - Hewett 1985, 85-6), they were thought to have been first used in main-span roofing on the collars of the Angel choir at Lincoln, in the late 1270s, though these have now been shown to be secondary (Simpson 1987).

In the last decades of the thirteenth century the crown-post roof was developed, where a post standing on the tie-beam was strutted to a purlin running below the collars of the common rafters (Munby et al. 1983). An outstanding and unusual example is preserved over the whole length of Chichester Cathedral (Fig. 14.4), dating from the years around 1300, and which seems to have direct affinities with French examples in its elaborate vertical and lateral bracing (Munby 1981 & 1993; Hewett 1985, 14). At Exeter, which has one continuous roof space from east to west (Fig. 14.2c), the same basic design is used throughout, with only minor changes in detail: the collars of the principal trusses carry a crown-post and collar-purlin, with side-purlins trapped by struts; each truss has a scissor-brace, the common pairs with one collar, the principals with two. The chronology has not been fully elucidated, but roofing was probably in progress between the 1290s and 1330s.[7]

Surviving roofs of the fourteenth century are fewer in number. The eastward extension of the choir at Wells (Fig. 14.2d), probably during the 1330s, was roofed with two collars and trapped side-purlins (Hewett 1985, 35). The lower collars are supported by curved braces, which also occur in the undated and possibly earlier roofs of the western choir and south transept.[8] Curved, or bent timbers had been used in the late-thirteenth century Greyfriars' church in Lincoln, and waggon roofs had been built since the second quarter of the thirteenth century in Flanders; the choir of Carlisle is of waggon form, but its date is unknown, and is likely to be contemporary with the (restored) sixteenth-century ceiling.[9]

A major development is represented by the elaborate roof of the Guesten Hall of Worcester (Fig. 14.5), *c.*1340, now in the Avoncroft Museum of Building; this has principal trusses with arch-braces to the collar supporting side-purlins that have cusped windbraces (Wood 1965, 310-11; Morris 1978, 135). The inner structure is self-supporting and the outer covering of common rafters and laths can be added as a separate phase of construction. The double-framed roof with principal rafters and arch-braced trusses became a standard domestic type, though was less appropriate for cathedral roofs. A rather ver-

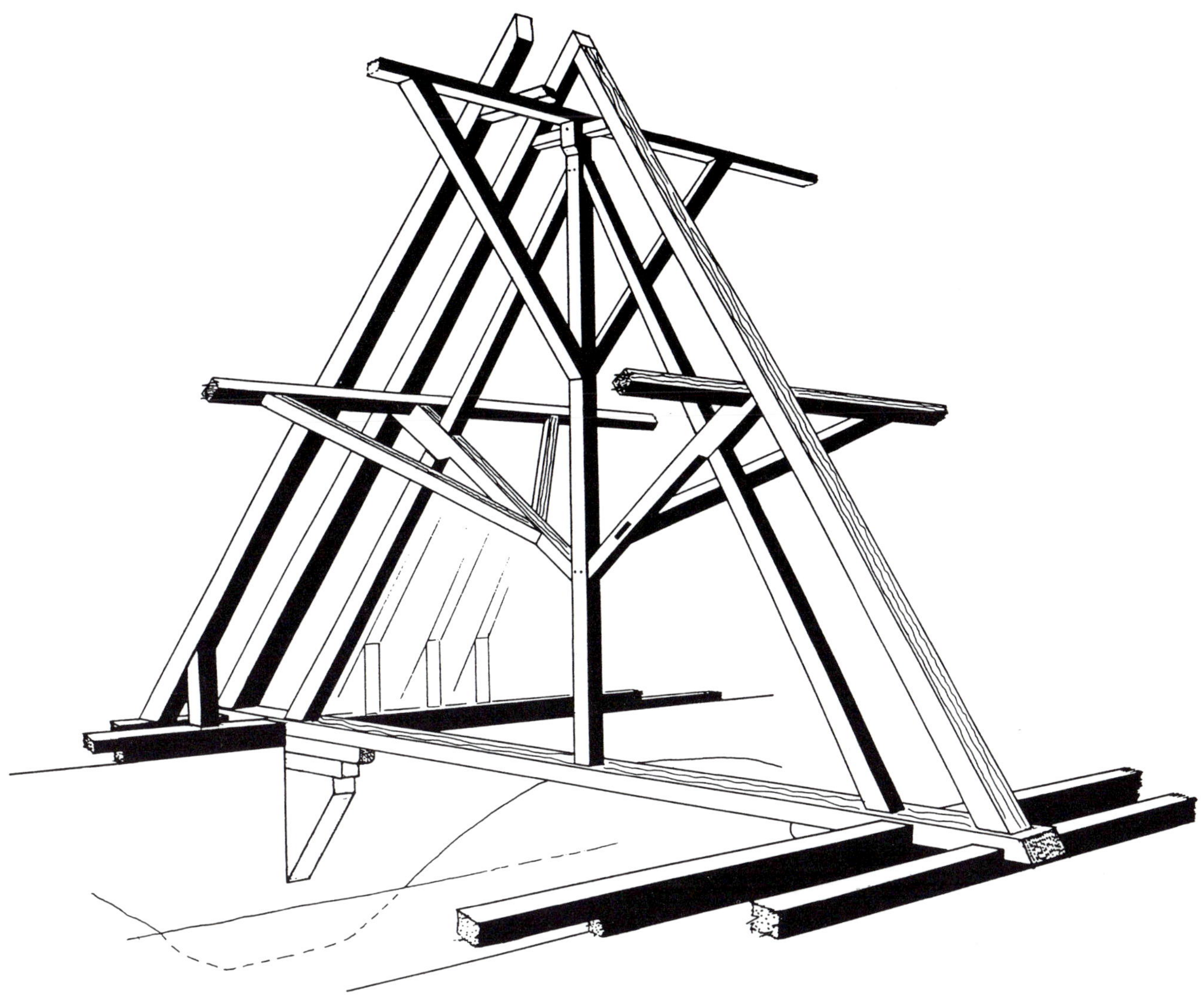

Fig. 14.4 Continental style roof of Chichester nave, c.1300 (Munby 1981)

nacular example of *c.*1340 is to be found over the Latin chapel of Oxford Cathedral, then only a minor Augustinian house (Ashdown et al. 1990, 200); the roof over the 'martyrdom' in the north-west transept at Canterbury, of *c.*1473, is rather more accomplished (Hewett 1985, 57; Woodman 1981, 185 & 262).

The earliest surviving roofs at Winchester over the nave and south transept (Fig. 14.2b), probably *c.*1400, are of conservative type, with plain collars and straight soulaces (Munby and Fletcher 1983, 102-3) They are steeply pitched, but elsewhere in the course of the fifteenth century the low-pitched lead covered roof became the norm. At Durham the dormitory was roofed in C.1404 by the carpenter Ellis Harpour, and has a ridge-piece supported on a low king-post and purlins supported on queen-struts, with tie-beams to each truss (Hewett 1985, 55; Snape 1980, 29). Where steeper-pitched roofs continued to be built, there was a continuing strain of inventiveness, as with the early sixteenth-century roofs of the choir and north transept at Winchester (Fig. 14.6). Here the tie-beams were raised to clear the tops of the vault, and the long braces to the collars were clasped and bolted between pairs of posts (Hewett 1985, 51-2; Munby and Fletcher 1983, 106). Of the same age were the roofs of Bath Abbey choir, combining hammer-beams and scissored inner rafters with strutted purlins, and King's College chapel, Cambridge with arch-braces and butted purlins.[10] The nave of Oxford Cathedral was given an open roof in place of intended vaulting at some date in the early sixteenth century (either in its monastic or collegiate phase); this is arch-braced with traceried spandrels, and was remodelled in 1816 (Ashdown et al. 1990).

Following the fire at Old St Paul's in 1561, extensive work was undertaken on the roofs,[11] but few roofs of the later sixteenth century were built or have been reported, and from the Reformation until the Restoration developments in roof carpentry have to be pursued elsewhere. When building and repair began again, as it did with some vigour in the 1660s, a revolution in the use of architectural source materials had taken place, and the influence

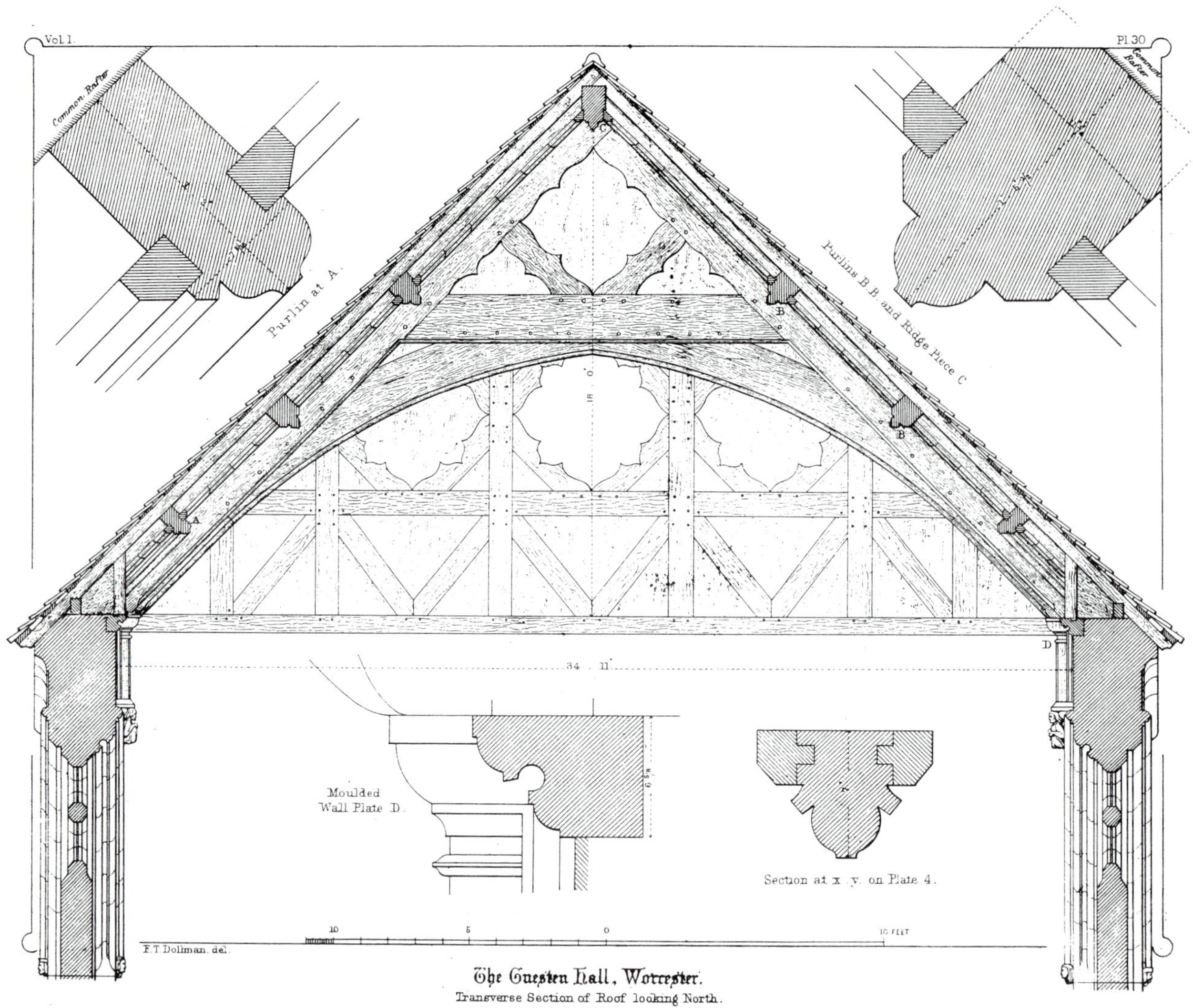

Fig. 14.5 Arch-braced roof of Guesten Hall, Worcester, c.1340 - (Dollman & Jobbins)

of classical pattern books was widely spread.[12] Essentially this meant the use of the principal trusses with a strutted king-post, rising from tie-beam to the apex of the roof (or held in tension by dovetails at the apex), the use of substantial squared timber (increasingly imported softwood) and ironwork supports. The north transept of Wells, of 1661, might use the old form of truss in softwood, all pinned with iron (and screw-threaded bolts), but at Litchfield the damaged church was re-roofed in the new manner from 1661-9 (Hewett 1985, 63-7). The strutted king-post is seen in its purest classical form, with a low-pitch, in Wren's St Paul's, after 1696, where a span in excess of 50 ft. necessitated a search for suitable timber (Hewett 1985, 68-9). At Winchester, repairs after a fire at the west end of the nave employed a less sophisticated roof, but still with a king-post (Hewett 1985, 71; Fletcher and Munby 1983, 105).

Throughout the eighteenth and nineteenth centuries increasingly complex and mechanical designs were devised, which cannot be described here (Yeomans 1984, 1992); perhaps the most remarkable were those by Cottingham at Rochester, where great lengths were taken to avoid failure of the trusses (Hewett 1985, 72-84). The twentieth-century experiments with steel, scarfed oak and laminated timber are another story that remains to be assessed.

Special roof structures

In addition to main-span roofing over the main body of the church, there were other types of roof which presented particular problems for carpenters and were treated with some of their most ingenious engineering solutions.

Aisle roofs are generally unremarkable in their relatively short span between stone walls, but some examples reflect specially adapted versions of main-span roofing, as with the original roofs of the triforium at Salisbury (Hewett 1985, 85-101).

Churches that had a polygonal termination at the east

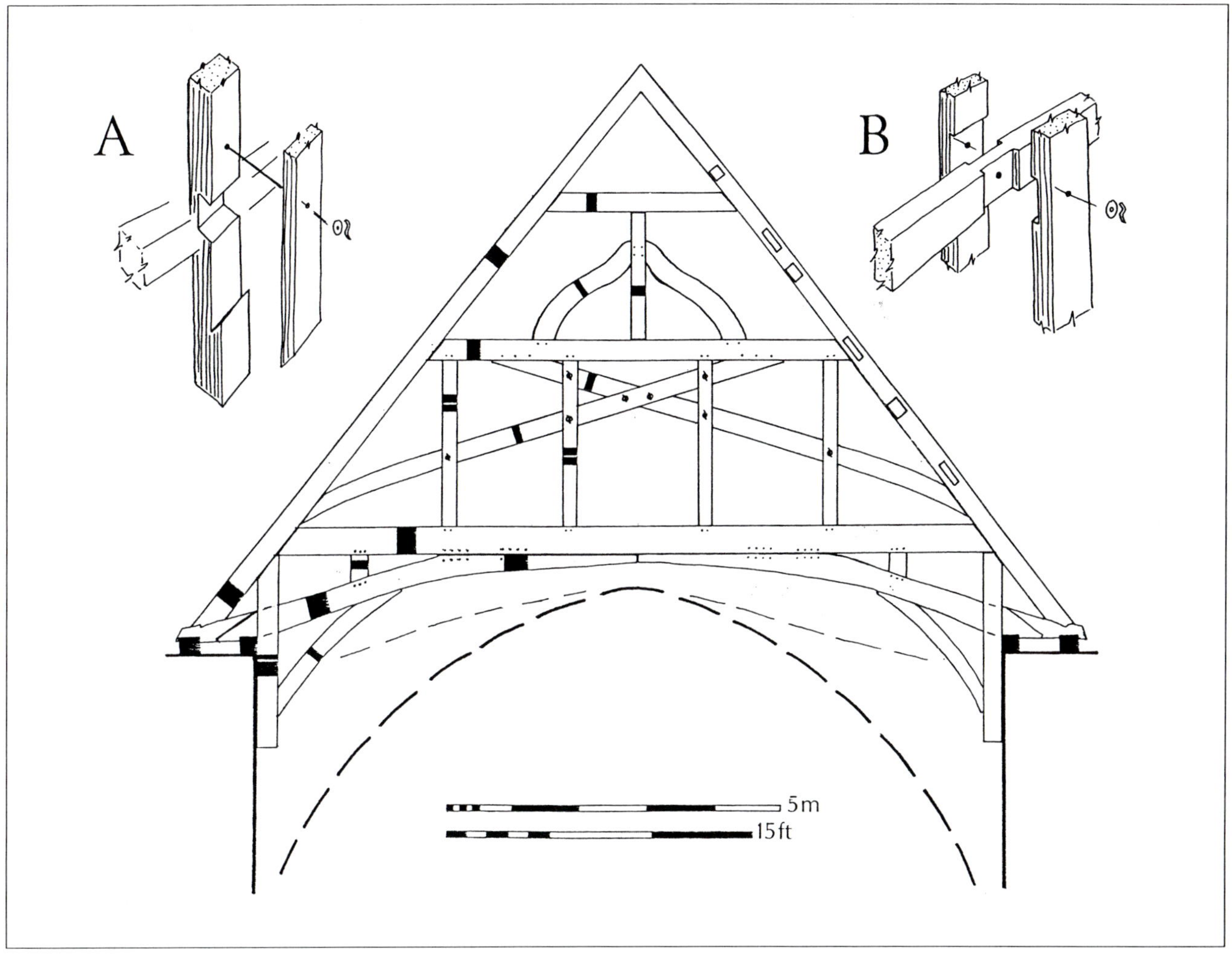

Fig. 14.6 Raised-tie truss, Winchester choir, c.1500 (Munby & Fletcher 1983).

end required special designs of some complexity. The eastern apse of Westminster Abbey, probably the work of Master Alexander and dating to before 1259, has a terminal king-post truss against which the radiating trusses rest (McDowall et al. 1966; Hewett 1985, 103).

Chapter houses required a yet more demanding type of polygonal roof. Some were flat, like the late thirteenth-century ones at Salisbury and Wells, the latter having an intermediate series of posts resting on the vaults, and both having rafters radiating from a central post (Hewett 1985, 106-11; Colchester 1988). But the most astonishing essay was attempted at York (Fig. 14.7), where the roof of *c.*1300 supports the timber vault over a clear span of some 64ft (19.5m). This is achieved by means of cantilevered supports to an inner ring-beam which is itself spanned by interlocking pairs of beams that clasp the central mast; similar pairs of beams are used at two higher stages, where they are also fixed to the principal rafters with double tenons. The roof uses an ingenious mixture of joint types from which the process of construction could be deduced. But despite the survey and modelling of this roof, its structure has yet to be fully analysed, let alone properly dated (Hughes 1955; Hewett 1985, 107-10).[13] Post-medieval solutions to the problem of polygonal roofing were no less ingenious, as is shown by the designs of James Essex for the Lincoln chapter house (Yeomans 1984).

Spires could be of timber, as the small twelfth-century one discovered at Canterbury (Hewett and Tatton-Brown 1976), but stone spires might also have a timber component. The renowned frame inside Salisbury spire (Fig. 14.8) is believed to have been used as part of the scaffolding during its construction, and now functions to dampen the force of the wind on the stone shell (Hewett 1985, 139-45). A reconsideration of the structure has shown that only the carpentry inside the spire itself (and not all of that) is medieval, and that the lower parts are much later additions; a proposed date of *c.*1300 for the tower and spire may possibly be refined by dendrochronology (Tatton-Brown 1991a).

Belfries were often accommodated inside towers and steeples, but were also built separately. As noted at the head of this chapter, the detached belfry at Salisbury was lost long ago. At Canterbury, the central tower has preserved the earlier roof of the tower as a floor from when the top was raised in the last decade of the 15th century

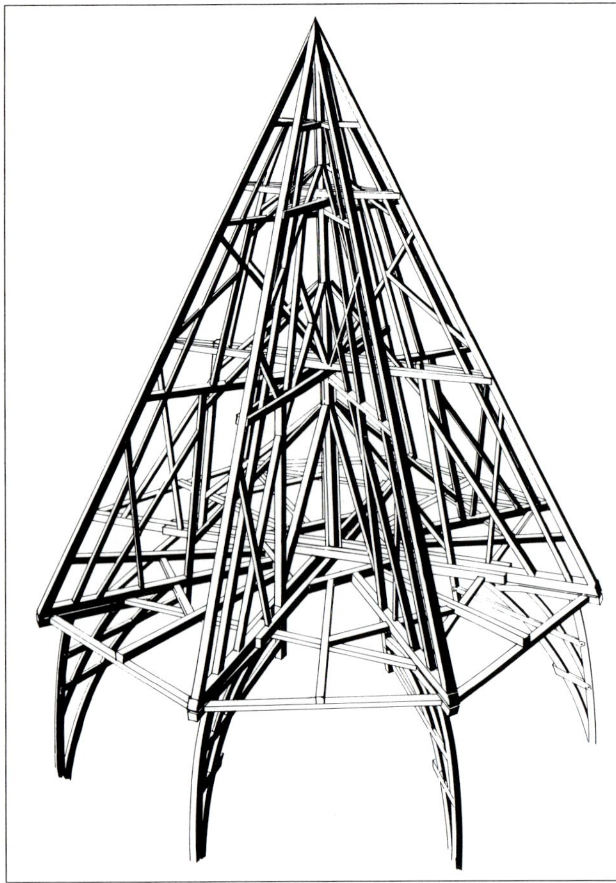

Fig. 14.7 York Chapter House, c.1300 (Hewett 1974).

(Hewett and Tatton-Brown 1976).

The Octagon at Ely, of the 1330s, is in a class of its own as one of the great technological feats of medieval carpentry. Although much altered over the centuries (Lindley 1987), enough of the original structure survives for its construction to be understood, and this has been analysed with great clarity by Hewett (1985, 114-22). As in the chapter house at York, the essential problem was to close the wide span (about 75 ft / 23m) to provide a firm base for the corner posts of the octagonal lantern; at Ely the curved supports for the floor and ring-beam also serve as the vaulted ceiling which creates much of the spatial and visual effect as seen from ground level.

Timber vaulting is found in some cathedrals where it has not perished by fire. The St. Albans presbytery may have the earliest example, from the mid-thirteenth century (Hewett 1985, 103-4; Pevsner and Metcalf 1985, 254), and the Lincoln cloisters were vaulted in timber at the end of the century (Howard and Crossley 1917, 130). The vaults of York have been burnt and replaced on several occasions, except that of the chapter house described above, while the underside of the Ely Octagon also takes the form of a vault. At Exeter (*c*.1320), the transepts have vaults that are partly suspended from the floor immediately above them (Fig. 14.9; Allan and Jupp 1981). The vaults at the east ends of Winchester and Carlisle have not been dated with certainty, and may both be sixteenth-century, like the roofs above them (see above).

The most outstanding piece of post-medieval carpentry in a special construction is the work supporting the outer lead roof in the dome of St Paul's Cathedral, which is based upon the middle cone of brickwork that supports the lantern (Hewett 1985, 154).

Furniture and fittings

Compared with structural carpentry, joinery has for long received scholarly attention, and much of it has been studied and photographed, or published in some form (e.g. Bond 1908, 1910; Howard and Crossley, 1917).

Seating for clergy has survived in many cathedrals, despite destruction and restoration. The misericords beneath lifting seats have long been the subject of attention for the variety of the subject matter of their carving (Anderson 1954; Remnant 1969). A general study of the development of stalls in some cathedrals down to 1400 has been published (Tracy 1987), with a further volume covering the period down to the Reformation (Tracy 1990). The remarkable feature of the changing fashions of stall design is inventiveness in canopy design, first breaking out from a flat two-dimensional gothic screen, and then extending upwards as fully developed 'tabernacle work'. Although the stylistic aspects of stalls have now received full attention, there is still scope for a structural study of their composition, and it is unfortunate that one masterpiece, the Bishop's Throne at Exeter Cathedral, of 1313-16, although having been dismantled in wartime and studied more recently from scaffolding, has not yet been fully surveyed as a piece of joinery (Howard and Crossley 1917, 191-5; Glasscoe and Swanton, 1978). The relationship of joinery techniques to those of large-scale structural carpentry would make an instructive comparison. The smaller Bishop's throne at St David's has been the subject of a recent study (Tracy 1988). The arm-chair at Hereford, sometimes thought to be of late twelfth/early thirteenth-century date, is a unique survival (Eames 1977, 210-11).

Doors from most cathedrals have been illustrated by Hewett, again opening up a new area of study (Hewett 1985, 155-87). Judging from medieval building accounts, doors were especially likely to be made from imported timber, and this is an area that could be investigated further. As previously mentioned, at least one of the York chapter house doors is made of softwood, but the use of fine imported oak boards can also be expected.

Cope chests now survive only in Cathedrals, though they must once have been more widespread, and they have been the subject of a recent study by Hewett (1988), who has demonstrated a sequence of changes in their construction which may have a relevance for other types of furniture. Other chests occasionally occur, of standard type, as that of the Hereford Vicars Choral, or the more elaborate 'Flemish' chest at York (Eames 1977, 145-8, 174-5).

Fig. 14.8 Carpentry in Salisbury Spire, c.1300 (Atherton Bowen).

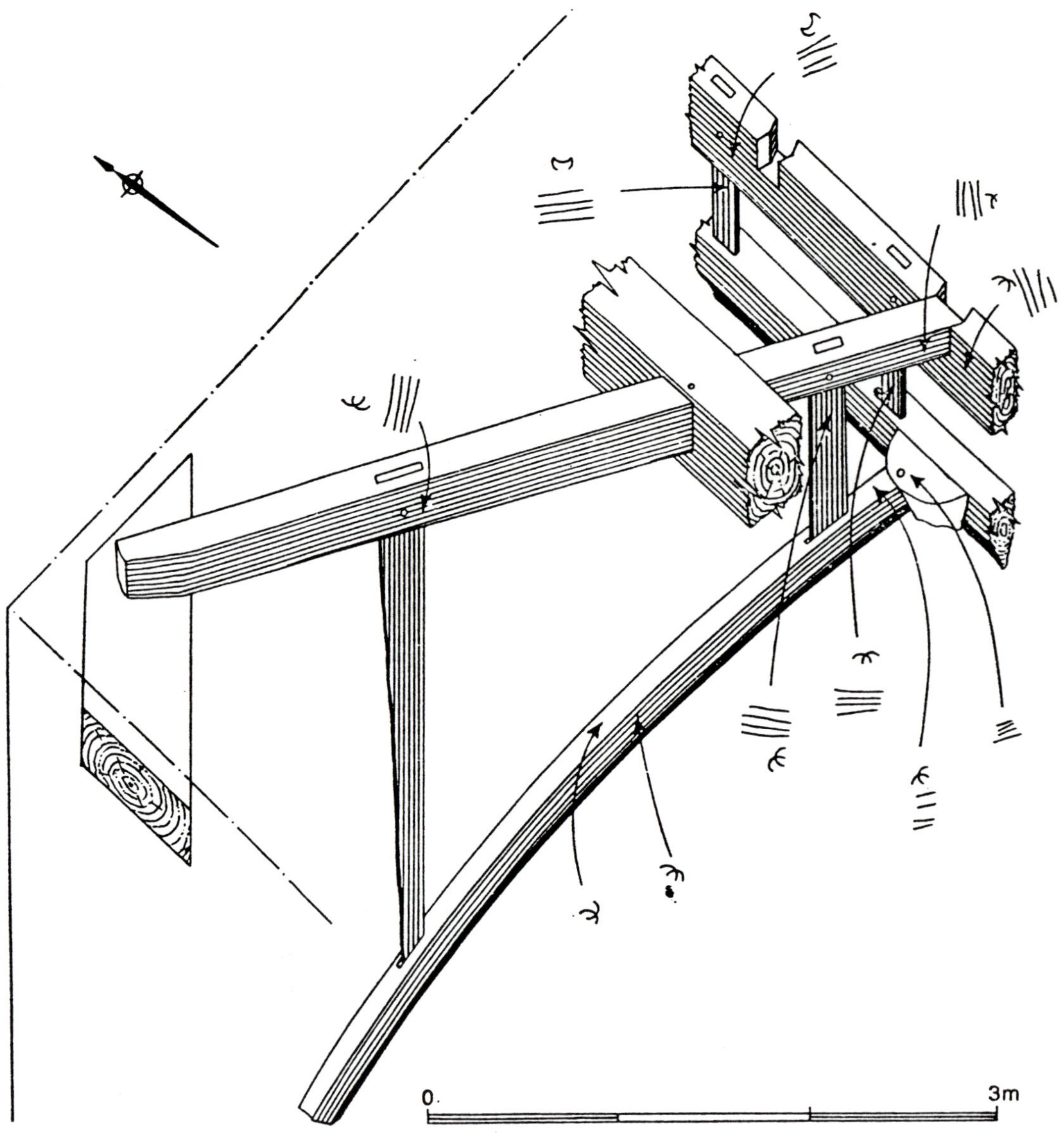

Fig. 14.9 Construction of the timber vault, south-west tower of Exeter, c.1320 (Allen and Jupp 1981).

Armoires or cupboards, of various forms, still exist in some cathedrals. Doors to stone lockers can be found at York in the de Zouche Chapel, dated by dendrochronology to the fifteenth century (Fletcher 1984, 123-4; cf. Eames 1977, 15-17). They are in a timber construction in the St Alban's 'Watching Loft', of the fifteenth century, and at Chester Cathedral of the late thirteenth century (Eames 1977, 17-20 and 44-6). The Muniment Room of the Vicars Choral at Wells is fitted with an armoire containing drawers for document storage, probably an original furnishing of the 1450s, and similar to those at Windsor and Winchester College (Eames 1977, 40-44). At Chichester is an enigmatic cupboard or 'machine', as Willis termed it (1861, 39), which may have held relics.

The vast bulk of ecclesiastical woodwork has fallen prey to the zeal of reformers and restorers, and the loss of statuary, roods and altarpieces in incalculable, though some has been brought back into cathedrals in modern times (e.g. the Carlisle reredos), while the rediscovery of the triptych for the Hereford Mappa Mundi is not the least benefit from that unhappy episode. The major screens in cathedrals are normally of stone, though smaller ones in side chapels may be of timber, and the presbytery screen at St David's Cathedral is of timber (Bond 1908, 18). A few wooden tomb effigies also survive, e.g. at Gloucester and Salisbury (Howard and Crossley 1917, 353-4; Fryer 1924). At Canterbury there is a late 13th-century effigy of archbishop Peckham, a fine canopy over archbishop Kemp's tomb as well as large wooden testers over the tombs of the Black Prince and Henry IV.

Lastly, there are some surviving examples of wooden lifting machinery, so important in the construction phase, though it cannot be certain that any of them have remained without alteration or replacement. Two types have been identified, the swinging arm or 'falcon', and the windlass or treadwheel turning a rope on an axle. Both a falcon and treadwheel exist at Canterbury, and windlasses may be seen at Peterborough and at Salisbury; the date of none

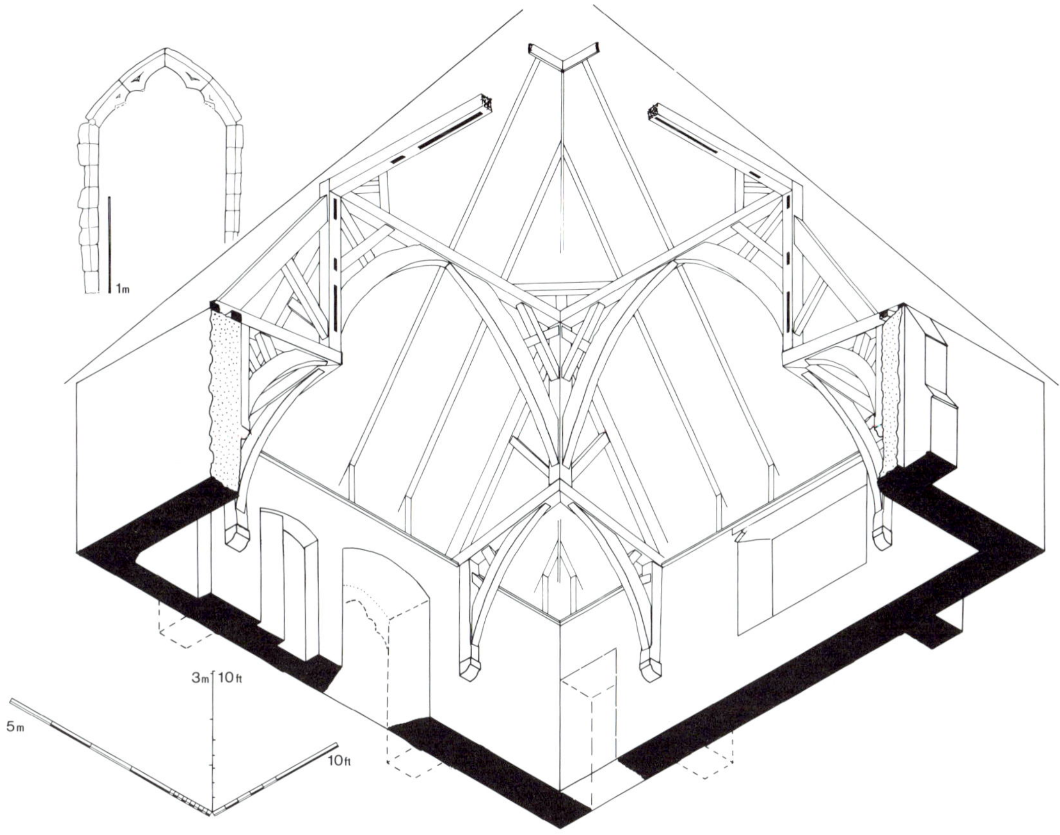

Fig. 14.10 The hammer-beam roof of the Bishop's Kitchen, Chichester, c.1300 (Munby 1985).

of these is certain, but they are of medieval type even if of post-medieval construction (Hewett 1985, 188-96).

The Cathedral Close

The architecture of the cathedral close is a large and distinct area of study, which cannot be treated in great detail here. It is important mainly for the survival of domestic and claustral architecture in multi-period buildings that are potentially well-documented. As with all such buildings there is a need for careful investigation before or during repairs and alterations, as ancient and unexpected features will always be found, and not necessarily recognised by those who uncover them.

Monastic cathedrals are in a class of their own, though the study of claustral buildings has mostly been developed in ruined structures (or below ground), and consequently there remains much of special interest to be found in those buildings which have continued in use. At Canterbury there is a unique pentice, once the most common feature of any medieval building complex (Willis 1868, 137) whilst the process of conversion from monastic to capitular use has preserved some fine medieval roofs there (Munby et al. 1983; Sparks 1990; Bowen 1990) At Winchester, the enigmatic 'Pilgrim's Hall' has yielded three different roof types in one contemporary build (Crook 1982 and 1991), and at Oxford an investigation of the Chapter House roof unexpectedly led to the elucidation of the changing means of access to the dormitory (Munby 1990).

In cathedrals of the Old Foundation, canonries often preserve extensive medieval houses hidden under later alterations, as has been shown by surveys at Ely and Lincoln (Atkinson 1933; Jones et al. 1984 & 1987) The roof carpentry of these (usually stone) buildings is of a different class from most cathedral carpentry, being designed for display, as with the fine surviving hall of the old Deanery at Salisbury (Drinkwater 1964). In contrast, houses for the Vicars Choral are often small-scale examples of collegiate planning, as at Wells and Chichester (Pantin 1959; Wood 1965, 180-1, 202; VCH Sussex iii, plan; Tatton-Brown 1991b).

Bishops' palaces are a grade higher than prebendal establishments, on a rank with their large rural manor-houses (of which they had many), and including large halls and chambers, with ancillary buildings such as chapels and kitchens. Hereford has preserved a remarkable timber aisled hall from the twelfth century (Blair 1987), and Chichester a unique kitchen of *c.*1300 (Fig. 14.10) with an early hammer-beam roof (Munby 1985). The study of surviving roofed examples is again of importance, since many palaces are only preserved as ruins, though those at Lincoln and Winchester have been excavated.

Methods of study

Arising from the initial stimulus provided by Hewett's pioneering survey of the whole field, several studies have been undertaken, as will be apparent from the references given above. But much remains to be done in the study of cathedral carpentry, and a few words may usefully be said about the appropriate methods of investigation.

An initial point is to stress the value of accurate measured surveys at an appropriate scale, which are not an end in themselves, but an important part of the discipline of careful observation that can reveal important aspects of the shape and configuration of timbers, differences between various parts of the building, and also have practical uses for others concerned with the fabric (see below). Written descriptions are vital, as are photographic records, whilst attractive three-dimensional drawings are very instructive for purposes of interpretation and communication, but cannot be considered as a prime method of recording.

Surveys of timberwork are not in themselves sufficient without due consideration of the structural context, i.e. the same process of investigation applied to archaeology below ground. Although the principals of structural analysis were developed some 150 years ago by Professor Willis, and have been given due prominence in the writings of Nikolaus Pevsner and by more recent practitioners, they are still not generally understood by all who are concerned with the fabric of cathedrals. The elucidation of the constructional sequence of timberwork is little different from that of stonework, and it is essential to consider the context of carpentry in the development of the building. For instance, the stonework at the east end of Chichester Cathedral provides a key to the phasing of the roof, where it can be shown that the present roof is not the first one to be built over the new east end in the early thirteenth century, and that it was probably added when the eastern gable was modified with the insertion of a rose window and the parapets were added (Fig. 14.11; Munby 1981). It is instructive to note that a small part of the earlier gable line has survived on the outside for nearly 700 years, but would perhaps be unlikely to survive a radical replacement of stonework here. At Wells, the addition of parapets is also a key to the phasing of the roofs, though the date of this is not yet known with certainty (above at note 8).

Apart from the relationship of stone to timber, the sequence of elements within a roof that has been repaired and modified requires study, as has been attempted for the nave of Winchester (Munby and Fletcher 1983). The re-use of timbers can allow the reconstruction of an earlier form of a roof, as has been possible to do in the Bishop's Chapel at Chichester, and the nave roof of Ely (Munby 1981, Simpson, this volume). Careful analysis of a single-period construction, taking into account the jointing and carpenters' marks, enhances the understanding of a structure (e.g. the south tower at Exeter), and the collection of such data may later be of use in deciding whether other works are contemporary (Allan and Jupp 1981). Where a roof is taken down for repair, analysis of the conversion and use of timber is possible, as has been done at the Gloucester Blackfriars and at Lincoln (Rackham et al. 1978). The study of dendrochronoly is separately dealt with in this volume, and it is clear from the programmes of work at Lincoln and Exeter that much information can be gained from a detailed study of a large number of timbers from one building, giving results that go beyond the simple matter of dating.

Following on the application of scale modelling of stone structures towards an understanding of the design of masonry, work has begun on the modelling of timber roofs, so far only completed for the roof of Westminster Hall, but this is a promising area that will repay further application (Mark 1982; Courtenay and Mark 1987).

There remains the historical side of the study of timberwork, and this has been insufficiently exploited. The linking of written sources to existing buildings is often fraught with difficulty, even where there are apparently good source materials. It must always be remembered that the purpose for which building accounts were drawn up does not necessarily mean that they readily answer the questions put to them by the architectural historian. But even where medieval documentation is thin, there is nearly always a large amount of later material, including architect's drawings (cf. Lindley 1987) and even models, and this has rarely been made full use of by investigators, though it has great potential for informing the more recent phases of repair and restoration.

Future work

Having discussed some of the methods of studying cathedral carpentry, this can be put in the context of what is now required. For if a claim has succesfully been made for the importance of considering this previously neglected topic, it follows that there remains much to be done. Even at the most basic level, there is a need for surveys of what carpentry remains in cathedrals, to amplify Hewett's findings, and assess the importance of what remains. Such surveys, which should include accurate measured drawings, will need a chronological dimension, which can best be provided by detailed programmes of dendrochronology. Until a larger number of roofs have been firmly dated, much of the existing chronology can only be based on stylistic considerations.

Apart from these purely academic desiderata, there are very practical reasons for paying due attention to carpentry. The incomparable loss of thirteenth-century roofs at Westminster Abbey, wholesale replacement by steel at Gloucester, and the minor losses at e.g. Canterbury, Norwich and York have been at the hands of responsible architects in the course of restoration; the tragic fire at York is just a more recent reminder of what has always been the greatest threat to cathedral roofs.[14]

Investigation and survey prior to such events would

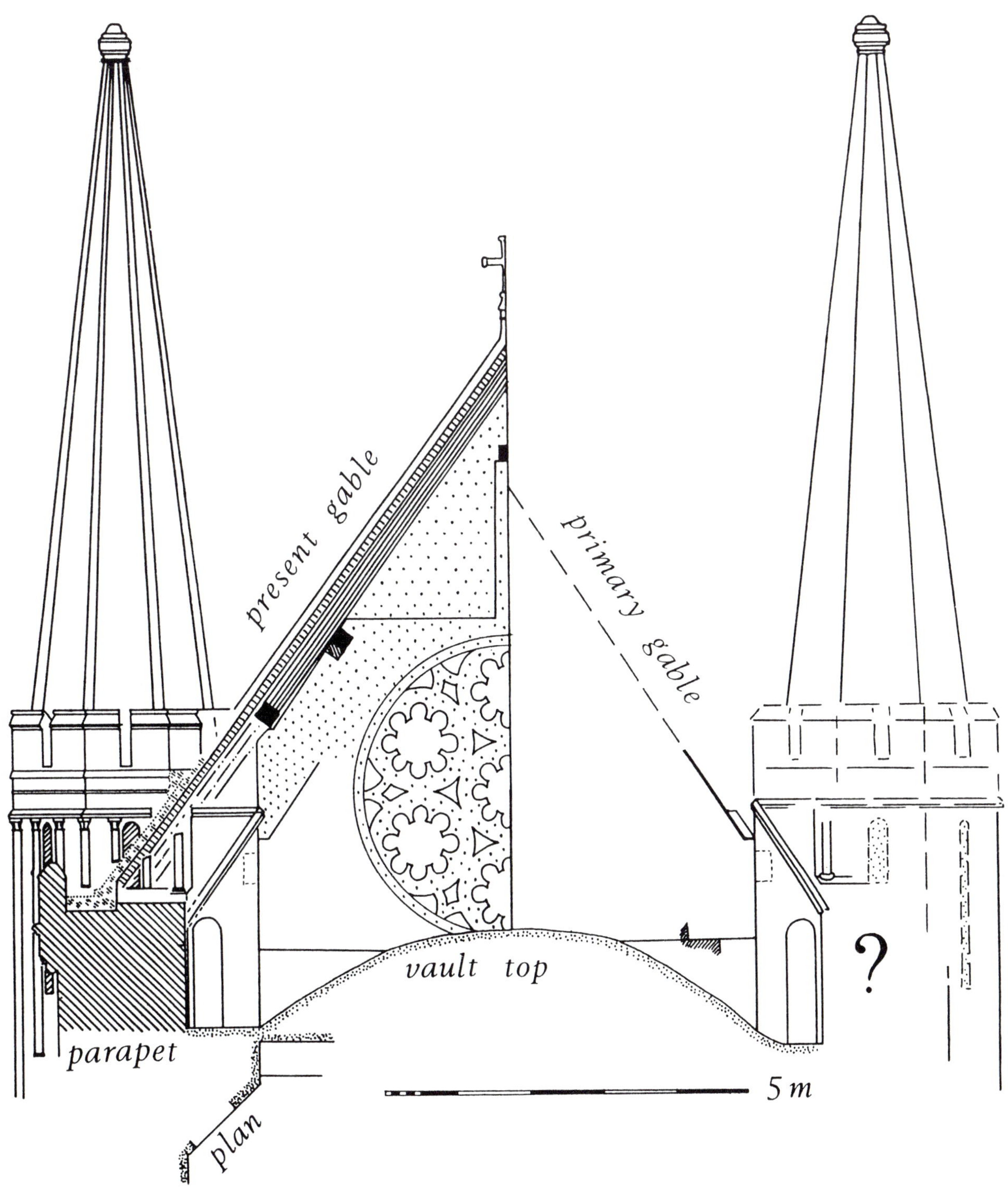

Fig. 14.11 The archaeology of the choir roof: east gable of Chichester (Munby 1981).

minimize the danger of loss, especially where expert investigation and assessment is undertaken before decisions are made (even the post-fire archaeological work at York was a vital part of the process of restoration). Repairs planned with full knowledge of the historical importance of the fabric are likely to be less destructive, and appropriate conserving measures may be taken to minimize the loss of original features. But however carefully prior investigation may be undertaken, further information is likely to come to light during repairs, and it is necessary to maintain a watch during work, especially with a view to observing the use of timber in roofs and collecting samples for dendrochronology.

Cathedrals preserve a unique body of material for the study of medieval and later carpentry, which has until recently been a neglected aspect of their history and has much to contribute to the history of technology. The realisation of what still exists can both further academic needs, and play a part in conservation for the future.

References

1. Carter's *Pursuits* are conveniently gathered together in Gomme 1890.
2. 'Notre archaéologie nous est venue de l'Angleterre, comme la diligence, les chemins de fer et les bâteaux à vapeur' (Stendhal), quoted in Pevsner 1972, 22; see also Watkin 1980; Viollet-le-Duc *Dictionnaire* 1854-68 s.n. Charpentes; and Deneux 1927.
3. Paris, Bibliothèque Nationale MS. Français 19093, f.17v; facsimile repr. in *Album de Villard de Honnecourt* (Bibliothèque Nationale, n.d.)., and most recently by Erlande-Brandenburg et al., 1986.
4. Simpson, this volume; pers. comm. Jane Geddes; for timber imports, see Salzman 1967, 245-9; Rackham 1980, 151; and Munby 1991, 382 n.8.
5. For Romanesque roof carpentry, see Currie 1983 and refs. there cited, especially Deneux 1927, Janse and Devliegher 1962, and *Charpentes* (Paris, Centre de Recherches sur les Monuments Historiques, n.d., c.1960).
6. Oxford: Ashdown et al. 1990; Peterborough: Hewett 1974, 17-18, and idem 1985, 5; Fletcher and Spokes 1964, 182-3; for its date Pevsner and Metcalf 1985 (North), 273; work in progress by Simpson, pers. comm.; Salisbury transept: Hewett 1985, 22 (but N.B. the side-purlins are a later addition); Ely: Simpson, this volume; Salisbury porch: Hewett 1985, 30; Gloucester Blackfriars: Rackham et al. 1978, 107; Hewett 1985, 38; Westminster: McDowall et al. 1966, 164-5; Hewett 1985, 29.
7. Hewett 1985, 46-7; inspection of the Exeter choir roof (Munby 1991a) reveals no conclusive evidence for a distinct design as proposed by Hewett 1985, 41; for dating from the fabric rolls see Erskine 1983, xxv-xxxvi; for dendrochronology see Simpson, this volume.
8. On the date of eastern choir of Wells, see Pevsner and Metcalf 1985 (South), Colchester and Harvey 1974, Draper 1981 and Colchester 1987, who agree generally on the date, but dispute the date of inception; the parapets truncating the rafter feet must here be later still. The roof of the western part of the choir could be of any date, and is also cut by parapets, but these may be prior to the extension of the new choir, and copied from the Lady Chapel and so of about 1320, Colchester 1987, 55; cf Pevsner and Metcalf 1985, 303.
9. Lincoln: Hewett 1985, 28; Pevsner et al. 1989, 508-9; Flanders: Janse and Devliegher 1962; Carlisle: Hewett 1985, 53; for dating see Pevsner and Metcalf 1985 (North), 47.
10. Hewett 1985 60-62; but note that the diminished haunch joint used after 1510 at King's College was not an innovation, but had previously been used, e.g. All Souls College, Oxford, in the 1440s.
11. Colvin et al. 1975, 63-5; *Wren Society* I (1924), pls. vii-viii.
12. See discussion of classical and renaissance sources in Yeomans 1986, his full study in Yeomans 1992 and Munby 1981, and refs there cited.
13. York Chapter House provides an excellent example of the difficulties of dating, proposed completion dates ranging between 1285 and 1367. Gee thought it was completed by 1285, which concurs with the evidence of the glazing, Aylmer and Cant 1977, 136-41, 337-9. Coldstream 1972 believes that the stonework was completed before the nave was begun in 1291, but appears to accept a date for the parapet in the 1330s, and the plumbing contract of 1367 as the date of the roof. Pevsner agrees with a completion date of 1291, Pevsner and Metcalf 1985 (North), 341-2. Discussion of the building has studiously avoided analysis of the roof carpentry, and its relationship to the stonework.
14. Professor Buckland, speaking at the Canterbury congress of the British Archaeological Association, characteristically suggested that spontaneous combustion of accumulated pigeon guano in thunderstorms was a potential fire hazard, B.A.A. *Proceedings at Canterbury*, 1844 (1845).

Bibliography

Allan, J.P. & Jupp, B. 1981: Recent Observations on the Central Tower of Exeter Cathedral. *Devon Archaeol. Soc. Proc.* 39, 141-54.

Anderson, M.D. 1954: *Misericords* (Harmondsworth).

Ashdown, J., Fisher, I. & Munby, J. 1990: The Roof Carpentry of Oxford Cathedral. *Oxoniensia* 53 (for 1988), 195-204; repr. as J. Blair (ed.) *St Frideswide's Monastery at Oxford: Archaeological and Architectural Studies* (Gloucester).

Atkinson, T.D. 1933: *An Architectural History of the Benedictine Monastery of St Etheldreda in Ely* (Cambridge).

Aylmer, G.E. & Cant, R. 1977: *A History of York Minster* (Oxford)

Blair, W.J. 1987: The 12th-century Bishop's Palace at Hereford. *Medieval Archaeol.* 31, 59-72.

Bond, F. 1908: *Screens and Galleries in English Churches* (Oxford).

Bond, F. 1910: *Wood carvings in English Churches I - Misericords, and II Stalls and Tabernacle Work* (Oxford)

Bowen, J., 1990: Architectural History of 'Meister Omers' and the Buildings to the North. In J.C. Driver, J. Rady and M. Sparks *Excavations in the Cathedral Precincts* (The Archaeology of Canterbury IV), 67-78.

Brandon, R. & J.A. 1860: *The Open Timber Roofs of the Middle Ages* (London).

Colchester, L.S. 1987: *Wells Cathedral* (London, New Bells Cathedral Guides).

Colchester, L.S. 1988: note in *The Friends of Wells Cathedral, Report for 1988.*

Colchester, L. and Harvey, J. 1974: Wells Cathedral. *Archaeol. Jnl.* 131, 200-14

Coldstream, N. 1972: York Chapter House. *Jnl. B.A.A.* 3rd ser. 35, 15-23.

Colson, J.B. [1899]: *Winchester Cathedral. A Descriptive and Illustrated Record of the Reparations of the Nave Roof 1896-8.* Bound in Kitchen, G.W. & Stephens, W.R.W. 1899: *The Great Screen of Winchester Cathedral*, 3rd edn. (Winchester).

Colvin, H.M. et al. 1975: *History of the King's Works III 1485-1660* (Part I) (London).

Courtenay, L.T. 1985: Where Roof Meets Wall: Structural Innovations and Hammer-Beam Antecedents, 1150-1250. In P.O. Long, *Science and Technology in Medieval Society* (Annals of the New York Academy of Sciences 441), 89-124.

Courtenay, L.T. and Mark, R. 1987: The Westminster Hall Roof: A Historiographic and Structural Study. *Jnl. Soc. Archit. Hist.* (USA) 46, 374-93.

Crook, J. 1982: The Pilgrim's Hall, Winchester. *Proc. Hants Field Club* 38, 85–101.

Crook, J. 1991: The Pilgrim's Hall, Winchester. *Archaeologia* 109, 129–59.

Currie, C.R.J. 1983: A Romanesque roof at Odda's Chapel, Deerhurst, Gloucestershire, *Antiqs. Jnl.* 63, 58-63.

Deneux, H. 1927: L'Evolution des Charpentes du XIe au XVIIIe Siècle. *L'Architecte* nouv. ser. 4, 49-53 etc.

Draper, P. 1981: The Sequence and Dating of the Decorated Work at Wells. In *Medieval Art and Architecture at Wells and Glastonbury* (B.A.A. Conf. Trans. 4).

Drinkwater N. 1964: The Old Deanery, Salisbury. *Antiquaries Jnl.* 44, 41-59.

Eames, P. 1977: Furniture in England, France and the Netherlands from the Twelfth to the Fifteenth Century (*Furniture History* 13).

Erlande-Brandenburg, A., Pernoud, R., Gimpel, J. and Bechmann, R. 1986: *Carnet de Villard de Honnecourt XIIIe siècle* (Paris, Stock).

Erskine, A.M. 1981, 1983: The Accounts of the Fabric of Exeter Cathedral, 1279-1353 (*Devon & Cornwall Record Society*, new ser. 24 & 26).

Fitchen, J. 1961: *The Construction of Gothic Cathedrals* (Oxford).

Fletcher, J.M. and Spokes, P.S. 1964: The Origin and Development of Crown-Post Roofs. *Medieval Archaeol.* 6, 152-83.

Fletcher, J.M. and Tapper, M.C. 1984: Medieval Artefacts and Structures Dated by Dendrochronology. *Medieval Archaeol.* 28, 112-32.

Foot, N.D.J, Litton, C.D. and Simpson, W.G. 1986: The High Roofs of the East End of Lincoln Cathedral. In *Medieval Art and Architecture at Lincoln Cathedral* (B.A.A. Conf. Trans. 8), 47-74.

Fryer, A.C. 1924: *Wooden Monumental Effigies in England and Wales* (London, 2nd edn.)

Glasscoe M., and Swanton, M. 1978: *Medieval Woodwork in Exeter Cathedral* (Exeter)

Gomme G.L. (1890): Gentleman's Magazine Library, *Architectural Antiquities* (London).

Harvey, J.H. 1984: *English Mediaeval Architects, A Biographical Dictionary down to 1550* Revised edn. (Gloucester)

Hewett, C.A., 1974: *English Cathedral Carpentry* (London).

Hewett C.A. 1980: *English Historic Carpentry* (Chichester).

Hewett, C.A. 1982: *Church Carpentry* (Chichester).

Hewett, C.A., 1985: *Cathedral and Monastic Carpentry* (Chichester).

Hewett, C.A. 1988: English Medieval Cope Chests. *Jnl. B.A.A.* 141, 105-23.

Hewett, C.A. and Tatton-Brown, T.W.T., 1976: New Structural Evidence regarding Bell Harry and the South-east spire at Canterbury. *Archaeol. Cantiana* 92, 129-36.

Howard, F.E. and Crossley, F.H. 1917: *English Church Woodwork* (London, 2nd edn. 1927).

Hughes, J.Q. 1955: The Timber Roofs of York Minster. *Yorkshire Archaeol. Jnl.* 38, 474-95.

Janse, H. and Devliegher, L. 1962: Middeleeuwse Bekappingen in het Vroegere Graafschap Vlaanderen. *Bulletin de la Commission Royale des Monuments et des Sites* (K.C.M.L.) 13, 308 ff.

Jones, S., Major, K., Varley, J., and Johnson, C. 1984: *The Survey of Ancient Houses in Lincoln I: Priorygate to Pottergate* (Lincoln Civic Trust).

Jones, S., Major, K., and Varley, J., 1987: *The Survey of Ancient Houses in Lincoln II: Houses to the South and West of the Minster* (Lincoln Civic Trust).

Lindley, P. 1987: 'Carpenter's Gothic' and gothic carpentry: Contrasting attitudes to the restoration of the Octagon and removals of the Choir at Ely Cathedral. *Archit. Hist.* 30, 83-112.

McDowall, R.W., Smith J.T. and Stell C.F., 1966: Westminster Abbey The Timber Roofs of the Collegiate Church of St Peter at Westminster. *Archaeologia* 100, 155-174.

Mark, R. 1985: *Experiments in Gothic Structure* (Cambridge Mass. & London).

Morris, R.K. 1978: Worcester Nave: From Decorated to Perpendicular. In *Medieval Art and Architecture at Worcester Cathedral* (B.A.A. Conf. Trans. 1), 116–43.

Munby, J.T. 1981: Medieval Carpentry in Chichester: 13th-Century Roofs of the Cathedral and Bishop's Palace. In A. Down, *Chichester Excavations 5* (Chichester), 229-53.

Munby, J.T. 1985: Thirteenth-century Carpentry in Chichester. In Proceedings of... Royal Archaeol. Inst. at Chichester, *Archaeol. Jnl.* 142, 13-17.

Munby, J.T. 1990: Christ Church Priory House: Discoveries in St. Frideswide's Dormitory. *Oxoniensia* 53 (for 1988), 185-93; repr. as J. Blair (ed.) *St Frideswide's Monastery at Oxford: Archaeological and Architectural Studies* (Gloucester).

Munby, J.T. 1991: Wood. in J. Blair and N. Ramsay (eds.) *English Medieval Industries.*, 379–405.

Munby, J.T. 1991a: Roof Carpentry. *Exeter Cathedral A Celebration.* (Exeter), 61–3.

Munby, J.T. 1993: Chichester Cathedral Roofs. *The Chichester Cathedral Journal 1993.*

Munby, J.T. and Fletcher, J.M. 1983: Carpentry in the Cathedral and Close at Winchester. In *Medieval Art and Architecture at Winchester Cathedral* (B.A.A. Conf. Trans. 6), 101-11.

Munby, J.T., Sparks, M. and Tatton-Brown, T. 1983: Crown-post and King-strut Roofs in South-East England. *Medieval Archaeol.* 27, 123-35.

Ostendorf, F. 1908: *Die Geschichte des Dachwerks* (Leipsig and Berlin; repr. Hannover 1982).

Pantin, W.A. 1959: Chantry Priests' Houses and other Medieval Lodgings. *Medieval Archaeol.* 3, 216-58.

Pevsner, N. 1972: *Some Architectural Writers of the Nineteenth Century* (Oxford).

Pevsner, N. & Metcalf, P. 1985: *The Cathedrals of England: Southern England, and Midland, Eastern and Northern England* (Harmondsworth).

Pevsner, N., Harris, J. and Antram, N. 1989: *The Buildings of England Lincolnshire* (2nd edn.) (Harmondsworth).

Price, F. 1753: *A Series of particular and useful Observations, Made with great Diligence and Care, upon that Admirable Structure, the Cathedral-Church of Salisbury* (London).

Rackham, O. 1980: *Ancient Woodland* (London).

Rackham, O., Blair, J. and Munby J. 1978: The Thirteenth-century Roofs and Floor of the Blackfriars Priory at Gloucester. *Medieval Archaeol.* 22, 105-22.

Remnant, G.L. 1969: *A Catalogue of Misericords in Great Britain* (Oxford).

Salzman, L.F. 1967: *Building in England down to 1540* 2nd edn. (Oxford).

Simpson, W.G., 1987: Work on Lincoln Cathedral Roofs.

Archaeol. Jnl. 144, 443-4.

Smith, J.T. 1958: Medieval Roofs: a Classification. *Archaeol. Jnl.* 115, 111-49.

Smith, J.T. 1965: Timber-Framed Building in England, its Development and Regional Differences. *Archaeol. Jnl.* 122, 133-58.

Smith, J.T. 1970: The Reliability of Typological Dating of Medieval English Roofs. In R. Berger (ed.), *Scientific Methods in Medieval Archaeology* (Berkeley, Calif.).

Smith, J.T. 1974: The Early Development of Timber Buildings: the Passing-Brace andReversed Assembly. *Archaeol. Jnl.* 131, 238-63.

Snape, M.G. 1980: Documentary Evidence for the Building of Durham Cathedral and its Monastic Buildings. In *Medieval Art and Architecture at Durham* (B.A.A. Conf. Trans. 3), 29.

Sparks, M. 1990: The 'New Foundation' and its Domestic Buildings. In J.C. Driver, J. Rady and M. Sparks *Excavations in the Cathedral Precincts* (The Archaeology of Canterbury IV), 21-36.

Tatton-Brown, T.W.T 1991a: Building the tower and spire of Salisbury Cathedral. *Antiquity* 65 (246), 74–96.

Tatton-Brown, T.W.T 1991b: The Vicars' Close and Canon Gate. *The Chichester Cathedral Journal 1991*, 14–24.

Taylor, A.J. 1961: Castle Building in Wales in the later thirteenth century: the prelude to construction. In E.M. Jope (ed.), *Studies in Building History, Essays....B.H.St J. O'Neil* (London), 104-33.

Tracy, C. 1987: *English Gothic Choir Stalls 1200-1400* (Woodbridge).

Tracy C., 1988: St David's Cathedral Bishop's Throne... *Archaeol. Cambrensis* 137, 113-18.

Tracy, C. 1990: *English Gothic Choir Stalls 1400-1540* (Woodbridge).

Viollet-le-Duc, E-E. 1854-68: *Dictionnaire raisonné de l'architecture française du XIe au XVIe siècle* (Paris).

Watkin, D. 1980: *The Rise of Architectural History* (London).

Willis, R. 1843: *A Description of the Sextry Barn at Ely, Lately Demolished* (Cambridge Antiq. Soc. Quarto publ. 7).

Willis, R. 1861: *The Architectural History of Chichester Cathedral* (Chichester).

Willis, R. 1868: The Architectural History of the Conventual Buildings of the Monastery of Christ Church in Canterbury. *Archaeol. Cantiana* 7, 1-206.

Wood, M.E. 1965: *The English Mediaeval House* (London).

Woodman, F. 1981: *The Architectural History of Canterbury Cathedral* (London).

Yeomans, D. 1986: Inigo Jones's Roof Structures. *Archit. Hist.* 29, 85-101.

Yeomans, D. 1984: Structural design in the eighteenth century: James Essex and the roof of Lincoln Cathedral Chapter House. *Design Studies* 5.1, 41-8.

Yeomans, D. 1992: *The Trussed Roof: its history and development* (London).

Dendrochronology in Cathedrals

W. G. Simpson and C. D. Litton

Introduction

In the second half of this century archaeology has been revolutionised by the application of scientific techniques and new technology to the analysis of artefacts and archaeological and environmental data. In general, these advances have occurred in response to the demands of archaeologists involved in excavation or the study of artefacts in museums and those applying archaeological techniques to the study of proto-historic or historic aspects of human culture not involving excavation have been rather slower to embrace it. It is ironic that dendrochronology was developed by a physicist using tree-ring data obtained from the timbers of prehistoric and historic buildings in south-western USA, not for the study of those buildings *per se* but to collect information about the intensity and periodicity of sunspot activity and its effect on climate (Baillie, 1982, 28). In Europe interest in the potential of the technique developed as master chronologies became available and art historians were among the first to apply it for the dating of paintings on oak panels.

The tree-ring dating of vernacular buildings in Britain has increased dramatically over the last decade as the lists in recent volumes of *Vernacular Architecture* bear witness. During this period dendrochronological investigations have also been undertaken in cathedrals such as Canterbury, Ely, Exeter, Lincoln and Winchester. In broad terms, the dendrochronological techniques used to date vernacular buildings are the same as for more prestigious buildings. Cathedrals, however, pose considerable problems. Typically they have extensive roofs that may be over seven hundred years old and have been subjected to many repairs and alterations. Even within a single roof many phases of work may be present (Fig. 15.1). Given a particular problem, which timber or group of timbers should be sampled to solve it?

In this article we intend to describe very briefly the principles underlying dendrochronology, as applied to the analysis of timber from cathedrals. We will demonstrate how tree-ring dating in conjunction with detailed survey work and the analysis of documentary evidence may be used to illuminate aspects of the development of a cathe-

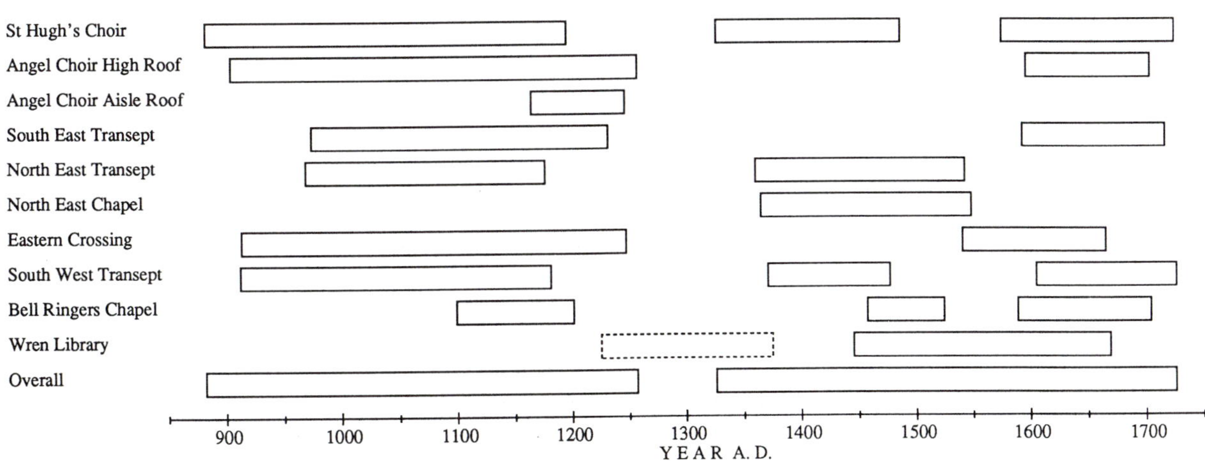

Fig. 15.1. Lincoln Cathedral Roofs. Bar chart showing the time span of timbers from different locations. (Compiled by C.D. Litton)

dral and its carpentry. This will be illustrated in a series of case studies based upon work by the Nottingham Tree-Ring Dating Laboratory at Ely and Lincoln Cathedrals.

The principles of dendrochronology

The following brief introduction to tree-ring dating should be sufficient to allow the reader to follow the main points of this article. Baillie (1982) and Eckstein *et al.* (1984) give more extensive discussions of tree-ring dating and Laxton and Litton (1988) describe in detail the construction of a regional master tree-ring chronology for the East Midlands of England.

The growth of oak trees, as seen in the widths of their annual rings, varies from year to year. The amount of variation is dictated by conditions, principally the weather, during the growing season. Over time these variations give rise to a sequence of consecutive annual rings whose pattern of ring widths is, more or less, unique for each particular span of years. Consequently samples of timber from the same phase of a building may be cross-matched if they show a similar pattern in their rings. An average or site chronology is formed from these samples.

From several buildings in a locality, or phases of a building, an extended sequence of ring widths can be constructed. This represents the average growth of oak in that region in each year and forms a master, or reference, chronology. It is anchored in the present by including ring measurements from recently felled trees each of whose felling date and, thus, last ring date is known. Once a master chronology for a region has been established and tested, it can be used as a reference against which other samples can be cross-matched and dated. At Nottingham all cross-matching and comparison is carried out by statistical analysis using a computer (see Litton and Zainodin 1987). The Student's t-value is used as a statistical measure of the quality of a match between two tree-ring sequences. A t-value of 5.0 or above against a master chronology is interpreted as a very good match. (See Laxton and Litton 1988 for further discussion of the interpretation of t-values.)

Samples are usually taken using an annular corer attached to a power drill. After the samples have been extracted, the holes, which are just over one centimetre in diameter, are plugged and disguised. Several cores, usually six or more, from a single phase of a building are usually required to provide enough data for statistically acceptable dates to be achievable. The sequences of ring widths from these samples are measured and then cross-matched. Usually a group of contemporary samples will show a pattern of similar ring widths and a sequence of consecutive average ring widths can be formed into a site, or average, sequence. If this has sufficient rings, (about 80+), then the dating indicated by cross-matching it with master chronologies can usually be accepted with confidence.

It must, however, be stressed that tree-ring dating for various reasons does not always work. The most frequent difficulty encountered is that the timbers have too few rings, (about 50 minimum). Also phenomena such as insect attack or flooding may have caused the tree, from which the timber was cut, to grow in a uncharacteristic manner in certain years.

If the samples do, however, match with the master chronologies then there are other considerations. If complete sapwood is present the felling date will be the year following the date of the last ring and even if it is not present it is often still possible to make a reasonably accurate estimate of it. This is because the outer or sapwood rings of an oak tree form its lymphatic system. There are between about 15 and 50 of them on a mature oak, but on average about 30 (Hughes, *et al.*, 1981; Hillam *et al.*, 1986). They contain the vessels which carry the sap and are usually lighter in colour than the core of the tree, or heartwood. If say 12, sapwood rings survive on a sample then by adding extra rings to the total of 30, the felling date can be estimated. The range of possible dates is given in this case by adding $15 - 12 = 3$ and $50 - 12 = 38$ to the date of the last ring measured. Usually some timbers can be found in a medieval building with sapwood surviving. Since medieval carpenters usually used green (unseasoned) timber in constructing a building, its use would have followed soon after the trees were felled. To take samples which will give the actual felling year(s) means identifying those timbers where a waney edge marks not the heartwood/sapwood transition (HST) but the complete sapwood, preferably with the bark intact.[1] However, unfortunately the sapwood is the softest part of the tree and most vulnerable to insect attack and to decay so generally, unless special conditions of preservation prevail, the older the timber the less chance there is of finding complete sapwood which will bear the stresses of core-drilling. A complete cross-section of a timber cut with a chain-saw is much kinder to fragile sapwood than a core-bit. Of course, this method of sampling is often not possible. The invention of a satisfactory conservation method to toughen-up fragile sapwood and maintain its adherence to the heartwood in the coring process would be an invaluable contribution to dendrochronology.

Master chronologies and cathedrals

Because cathedrals are often of ancient foundation and liable to contain timber of many different periods, dendrochronologists have looked to them for samples which would help them to construct or extend their master chronologies. Lincoln (Laxton and Litton, 1988), Glasgow (Baillie, 1977), Winchester (Barefoot, 1974) and Exeter (Bridges, 1983; Mills, 1988) cathedrals have all contributed significant data to master chronologies of their respective regions of England and Scotland. Boards making up doors, chests and other cathedral furnishings rather than actual structural timbers were preferred for chronology development by Fletcher (1977) who observed that they were usually radially split from the log and often contained very long ring-sequences. Unfortunately the often exceptional length of the samples was off-set by less favourable factors, some of which have only become apparent in recent years (Eckstein *et al.*, 1986). Very often the boards were imported from the Baltic and anyway timber used for quality furnishings is generally less likely to have sapwood surviving than construction timber. These factors made comparison with West European master chronologies and the determination of felling dates for the timber, very difficult. Continental cathedrals have also been important in providing samples for chronology building. Hollstein's (1980) West German master chronology for example contains tree-ring data derived from timber sampled in Aachen (imperial throne and roof shingles), Cologne (Merovingian coffin boards; choir stalls), Minden (Romanesque window frames), Speyer (fifteenth century window frames), Trier (coffin, chest, staircase, door, construction timber) and Xanten (choir stalls) cathedrals. While in Southern Europe and Asia Minor Kuniholm and Striker (1983) include tree-ring data from 33 churches and mosques to construct a master chronology for oak from the present back to the early twelfth century.

A distinction must be made, however, between the sampling of timber to make master chronologies and the use of dendrochronology as part of a concerted archaeological or architectural study of a cathedral or its furnishings, supplemented by the information that historical and documentary records can provide. Dendrochronology in this triple-disciplined approach to cathedral research may often provide a link between the other two kinds of evidence which was not otherwise apparent so that the three sets of data together are interdependent and each supportive of the other allowing new hypotheses to be built upon their firm triangular foundation. A number of continental workers have recognised the value of this approach as for example D. Eckstein with colleagues Wrobel and Neugebauer (1982) working on the roofs of St Jacob's and St Katherine's churches, the Hospital of the Holy Ghost (with Brauner, 1985) and other buildings in the Hansa town of Lübeck; also, in Belgium P. Hoffsummer working with the University of Louvain has dated the roofs of a number of medieval churches in Liege and elsewhere; and Kuniholm and Striker (1977) have published on the structural analysis of a Greek Byzantine church in relation to the dendrochronology of the tie-beam system in the nave arcade (cf. Wilcox, 1981). The work of Hollstein at a number of German cathedrals has already been mentioned. His work with Kempf (1968; 1975) at Trier, where he was able to tree-ring date beech and pine as well as oak timber, is also notable for the number (over 400 samples) and variety of the artefacts sampled. Most impressive is their use of timber from scaffold holes, floor beams and boards used for centering arches and vaults in the walls of the westwork to document the progress of construction of the walls, including the north-west tower, between c.1040 and 1060. The south-west tower however was not started until the following decade and not completed before the twelfth century (Hollstein, 1980, 162; Baillie, 1982, 173).

The Survey of Cathedral Roofs and their Dating

No such dendrochronologically related investigations of the lifts of a masonry structure have been undertaken in this country in a cathedral or any other type of building. Indeed apart from the work of Fletcher, referred to above, most of the tree-ring dating of cathedral timber relates to the roof structures. A detailed survey is an essential preliminary to the sampling of any structure or furnishing for dendrochronology. Cathedral roofs are not only often of large dimensions but also of great age and frequently repaired. A tree-ring date is only as good as the sample it comes from – which is equally true of other scientific dating methods. The quality of the sample and its context are therefore all important. It should be established that the samples are taken from timbers which are original to the structure or event being dated. Experience has shown that within a single large cathedral roof it is possible to find timber of varying periods and qualities, as the example of the Angel Choir roof of Lincoln Cathedral will serve to illustrate (Table 1).

The roof survey methods used by the Nottingham workers are primarily designed to give a visual record and interpretation of what is there. It is the timber equivalent of, for example, the work of Sutherland and Parsons (1984) on the masonry of Brixworth Church. It is their misfortune that they rarely have materials which are closely datable in association to assist with their interpretation of the structure. As with such surveys of masonry structures, detailed surveys of roofs are however often of value in their own right, irrespective of the dendrochronology for the information they give about their construction, the history of the building, the number of trees used (Rackham, 1972; Rackham *et al.*, 1978) and carpentry practice in general. The conclusion to be drawn from a recent discussion about the value of such detailed surveys is that one should know what is worth the effort and learn when to stop. (Ferris; Meeson; Smith. 1989.)

Preliminary work in the survey of a large cathedral roof involves the making of a scale drawing of the structural unit(s) typical of it. In the case of the nave roof of Ely Cathedral it is a medieval scissor-braced frame (no 37 was the one selected, but cf. Figs. 15.2 and 15.3) without later repairs or additions, while for the roof of St Hugh's Choir, Lincoln Cathedral they are a medieval frame with sole pieces, another with tie beam and queen posts, a truncated frame inserted c.1500, an eighteenth century frame and another rebuilt in pine in the nineteenth century (Foot *et al.*, 1986 figs. 3,5a and b and 11–13). These drawings are reduced to approximately 1:50 scale so that they fit onto A3 paper. This is the optimum size: although only the minimum practical for the recording of such large timber roof units, it is about the maximum practical considering the safety and mobility factors involved in working at up to 40ft above the vaults or ceilings of cathedrals. These drawings of 'typical' frames are copied onto both sides of A3 xerox paper

TABLE 1

Angel Choir Roof: Timber qualities and their recognition

CATEGORY		TIMBER QUALITY	FELLING DATE RELATIVE TO ROOF CONSTRUCTION (X)	IDENTIFYING FEATURES
A		**Old timber** (oak)		
	1.	First used seasoned – re-used twice	X – c.200 years	Two sets of redundant joint beds
	2.	First used seasoned – re-used once	X – c.130 years	One set of redundant joint beds; No use of saw
	3.	First used green in previous roof	X – 80 years	One set of redundant joint beds; or carpenter's marks
	4.	First used seasoned – not previously used	X – 40 years	
B		**Green timber** (oak)		
	1.	Felled within a year or two of construction	X = 1275–79 AD	No redundant joint beds, mortises intact and carpenter's marks, carpentry, scantling consistent throughout roof.
C		**Repair timber** (oak)(Phase 1 – c.1704)		
	1.	Of categories A and B (above) re-used	X – c.200 years up to 1275–79 (X)	Use of nails; redundant joint beds, evidence of reduction in size.
	2.	Re-used from another building	X + 275	Atypical joint beds and carpenter's marks.
	3.*	From the timberyard – seasoned	X + c.400 years	Use of nails, later types of joints used, no redundant joint beds.
	4.	Green – felled within a year or two of repairs	X + 430 years	Different scantling and carpentry. No carpenter's marks.
D		**Repair timber** (mixed, oak and pine)(Phase 2 – c.1763)		
	1.	Of categories A, B and C (above) re-used	X – c.200 years to X + 430 years	As C1, above.
	2.*	Re-used from another building	X + n years	As C2, above.
	3.*	From the timberyard – seasoned	X + c.470 years	As C3/4, above.
	4.*	Green – felled within a year or two of repair	X + 487 years	
	5.	Imported Baltic pine (P. Sylvestris)	X + c.480 years	Power sawn. Bracking marks.
E		**Repair timber** (mixed, oak and pine)(Phase 3 – c.1842)		
	1.	Of categories A,B,C and D (above) re-used	X – c.200 years to X + 430 (490*) years	As above.
	2.*	Re-used from another building	X + n. years	As above.
	3.*	From the timberyard – seasoned	X + c.540 years	As above.
	4.*	Green – felled within a year or two of repair	X + c.570 years	As above.
	5.	Imported Baltic pine (P. Sylvestris)	X + c.660 years	As above.

* Presence of timber of this quality is theoretically possible but has not actually been recognised.

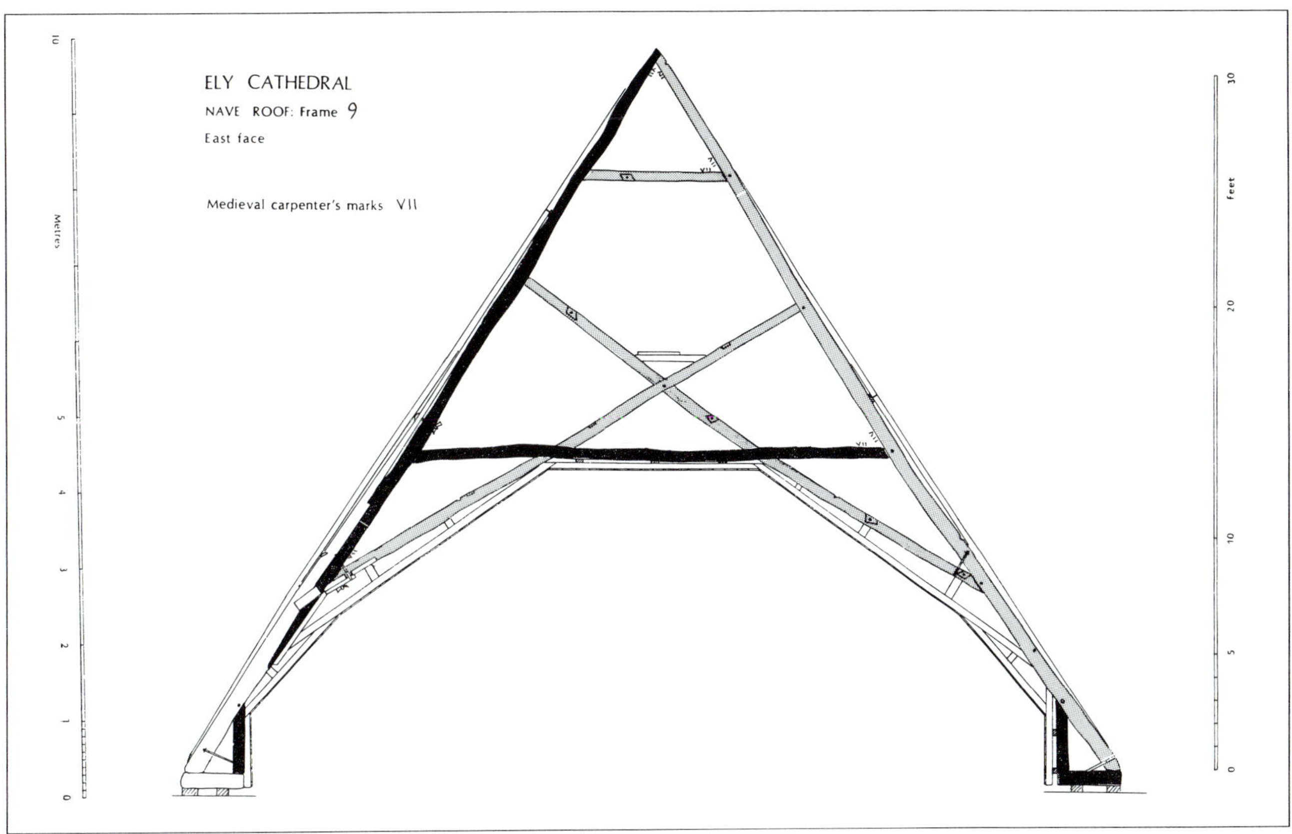

Fig. 15.2. Ely Cathedral, nave roof, frame 9, oak timbers. Dark shading – c.1240. Light shading – reused Norman timbers from roof built c.1120. (Drawn by Elaine Guilding)

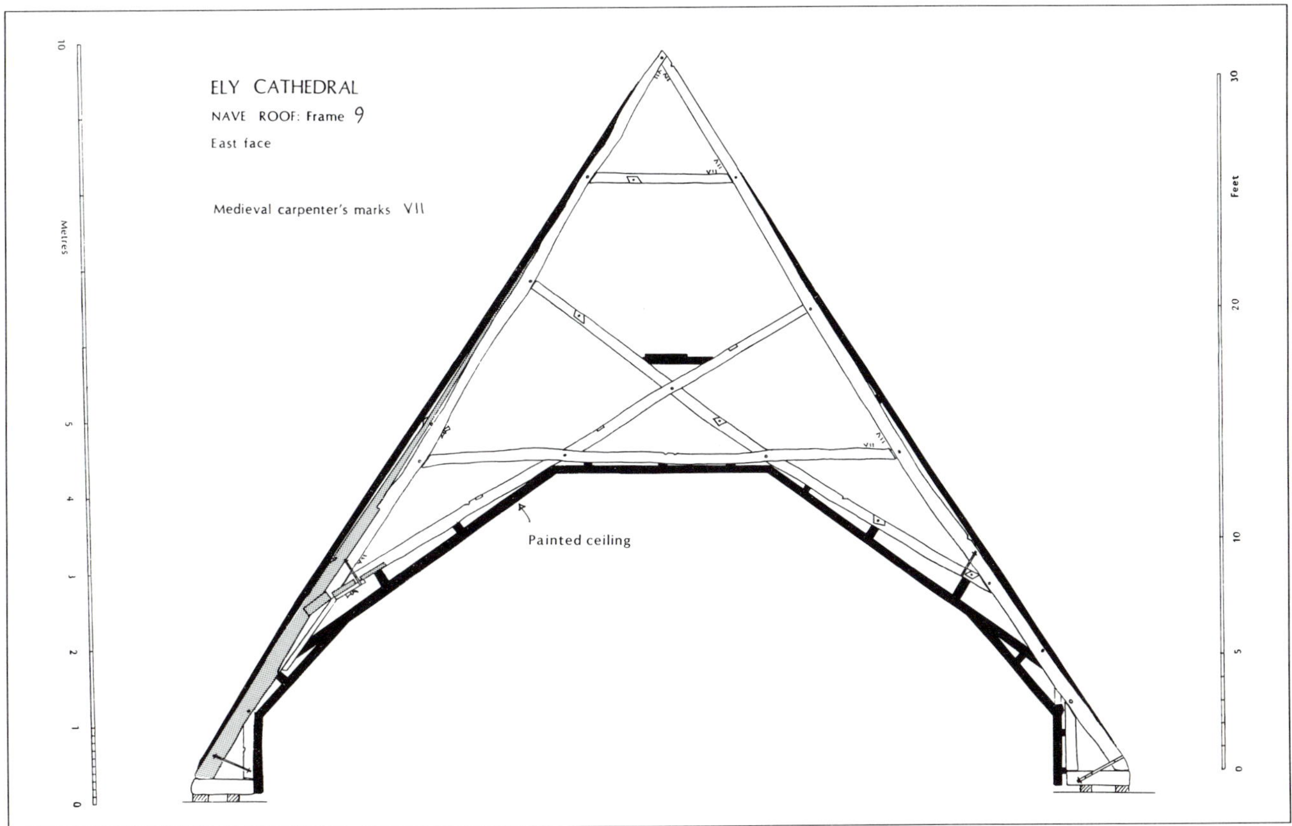

Fig. 15.3. Ely Cathedral, nave roof, frame 9, pine timbers. Dark shading – Victorian. Light shading – 17th–18th century. (Drawn by Elaine Guilding)

to the number of those units in the roof and are used as basic record sheets which can be altered by using correction fluid and/or indian ink. Features on both faces of the frames are recorded and methods have been devised for recording (often in profile) features observed on the other two faces of the individual timbers. When a roof has a lot of longitudinal members – e.g. purlins, ridge piece, wind braces – the clearest presentation of its form and the best means of emphasising significant features is often by means of a perspective isometric drawing.[2] Colours are used to differentiate between timbers of different species or qualities and between wood and metal (pegs and nails for example). The sample number and origin of all samples taken for dendrochronology are marked. Any explanatory notes do not normally need to be extensive and are made on the relevant sheet. A sheet is completed for each frame in the roof and photographs are taken and drawings made of particular features which require illustration in greater detail. These records are sufficiently detailed to provide the data for an isometric or axonometric projection of the complete roof, or for a variety of analyses such as the percentage of original timber to repair timber, changes or inconsistencies in the carpentry, the situations in which particular types of nail are used, features associated with the construction techniques employed (e.g. lifting points for crane ropes) and most importantly waney edges, particularly those associated with partial or complete sapwood.

It will be seen from Table I, which summarises and interprets the qualities of timber used in the Angel Choir roof, Lincoln Cathedral, that the only timber of any value in dating its actual construction is that of Category B, or timber of that quality which can be identified reused in later repair contexts (C1, D1 etc). The B1 timbers, on the basis of dendrochronology and documentary evidence, discussed in greater detail below, are thought to have felling dates between 1275 and 1279. This period is represented as X in column 3 and timbers dated by dendrochronology earlier or later than that are assigned their respective number of years (usually approximate) plus or minus X. Unfortunately it is usually impossible to differentiate between green timber (B1) and seasoned timber not previously used (A4), except by dendrochronology.

Synopses of the principal results and conclusions of dendrochronological work in British cathedrals

1. Lincoln Cathedral

(Foot et al., *1986; Laxton and Litton 1988)*

The sampling of timber being taken out of the roof of St Hugh's Choir in the course of repair work was begun by the Nottingham University Tree-Ring Dating Laboratory in 1980. By 1982 this work for the building of an East Midlands master chronology was being supplemented by a keener interest in the roofs themselves and particularly in their structural survey. All the medieval roofs have been studied except those of the western chapels, the chapter house vestibule and the old library. The pine roofs of the north-west transept (1842) and of the nave triforia also require more detailed survey.

The earliest roofs are the high roofs to the east of the central tower and timber for their construction was felled in 1195/96. However a certain amount of timber was reused from the old Romanesque cathedral (cf. Angel Choir roof, Categories A1/2 – Table 1) both from the original building and from repairs made after the fire c.1140 (Pevsner and Metcalf 1985, 200; Esling *et al.*, 1990). Seasoned timber not previously used (category A4) is also found. There are no documentary records for the source of any of this early timber but undisturbed natural woodland, probably a royal forest, (cf. Rackham, Blair and Munby, 1978, 121; Rackham, 1980, 153) seems likely for much of it is from very large trees, long past maturity, which contrast with the smaller mature trees used in the later thirteenth century roofs. Tree-ring dating and documentary sources together suggest that construction of the roof of St Hugh's Choir was in progress in 1208/9. If the Interdict affected this work, as at Wells (Colchester, 1987, 95), then it seems unlikely that it was completed much before the last years of King John's reign and likewise the famous 'crazy' vaults beneath. The carpentry to the east of the tower, and probably originally in the western transepts too, has many differences in detail from the roofs built over extensions to the ends of the east transept c.1250 (Esling *et al.*, 1990) and those of the nave (where more sampling for dendrochronology has yet to be done) and the Angel Choir built between 1276 and 1280. There are close parallels with churches in northern France and it is suggested that characteristics of the earliest carpentry indicate the French origin of Geoffrey de Noiers and their extent in the building the limits of his work.

The earliest repairs to the roofs are tree-ring dated to the very end of the fifteenth or early years of the sixteenth century when curious truncated frames little higher than the lowest collars of the medieval frames were inserted into the roofs of St Hugh's Choir and the nave (Esling *et al.*, 1990). Their purpose is enigmatic but they may have been designed in some way to prevent those roofs from racking. Certainly by this time the cathedral roofs were in a serious condition as demonstrated by the loss of the spire from the central tower in a storm in 1548. It crashed across the centre bay of the north-east transept and its northern chapel which, together with the tower were given new roofs c.1550 (Esling *et al.* 1989; Esling *et al.*, 1990). The ring sequences of the timber from these roofs almost fill the gap in the Lincoln master chronology between the later thirteenth century and c.1330 (Fig. 15.1). There was little building in progress during this period but it is to be hoped that in due course samples taken from the old library, from choir stalls and screens, and from re-used timbers in the roof of the central tower will provide more data than they have as yet.

The biggest repair programme on the cathedral roofs immediately followed the Restoration, though for various reasons dendrochronology has not confirmed its full extent (see p. 29). The Honywood Library was built in 1674–5. The contract between the builder William Evison and Sir Christopher Wren stipulated 'no firre ' but for the floor and stairs and boards under the lead ' all the rest of the wood and timber shall be Oak and that of the better sort and well seasoned'.[3] The quality was indeed fine but the felling date of at least some of the roof timbers was 1674. Evidence of repairs has been found in the high roofs of the east end in the later seventeenth century but it seems that the major repairs that were required there did not really get underway until the early years of the eighteenth century. The Fabric Accounts detail the annual purchases of lead and timber and also record the craftmen's wages (Fig. 15.8).[4] This information together with dendrochronology and tree-ring analysis is giving a detailed picture of the extent and location of roof repair programmes in the first half of eighteenth century. Appeals were made for funds for cathedral restoration in the 1720's. From the mid-eighteenth century the cathedral had a consultant architect on a more or less regular basis. James Essex, the son of a Cambridge carpenter was appointed c.1760 and he seems to have been responsible for introducing the regular use of pine baulks for roof construction, as in his Chapter House roof of 1762 (Yeomans, 1984; Simpson, 1987) though deal for roof boards had been in use since the late-seventeenth century. The Fabric Accounts indicate that this timber was imported from the southern shores of the Baltic. This evidence is complemented by possible bracking marks on the timber itself (Fig. 15.17). These graffiti informed the merchants buying at the Baltic ports about its quality (Albion, 1926, 148). The last major repairs when complete roofs (e.g. that of the north-west transept) were rebuilt or extensively repaired (e.g. the Angel Choir) seem to have been in the 1840's using mostly pine. Thereafter repairs have been made by piecing new timber onto the old, and in this century oak, and even chestnut, have been used in preference to pine.

2. *Ely Cathedral*

A survey and tree-ring dating of timbers of the nave roof were undertaken in association with Phase 1 of the Cathedral Restoration in 1987–8. Timbers of the present scissor-truss roof were tree-ring dated to the years 1237–40 (Esling *et al.*, 1989). There was no evidence of extensive repairs except towards the east end. Tie beams from the previous Romanesque roof were re-used in the thirteenth century roof as rafters, after reduction in length and scantling. Two original rafters were re-used as scissor-arms in Frame 9 (Fig. 15.2). From these timbers it was possible to reconstruct the form of an original roof frame, 21ft high, with a pitch of 45° and tie beams 46ft long which extended to the outer edges of the walls. In the use of lap joints and simple bracing of struts and collars it is very similar to, though larger than, continental roofs of the twelfth century such as those of Soignes Abbey, Belgium (Fletcher & Spokes, 1964, 156) or St Pierre, Montmartre, Paris.[5] Its tree-ring dating, on the evidence of only one sample with HST, was c.1120 (Fig. 15.4; Esling *et al.*, 1989).

The survey revealed much incidental information about the process of dismantling the original roof and the construction of its thirteenth century replacement. This was something of a technical achievement since the roof spans 35ft without any tie beams and mortice-and-tenon joints were used to fasten both ends of the scissor-arms into the rafters, where lap joints would have been a much easier, though structurally weaker, option (Rackham *et al.*, 1978, fig. 2). The reason for the new roof when the original one was probably still serviceable, may have been a desire to give the building a roof with a high pitch and gutters along the eaves to provide access for maintenance and repair of the lead (Colchester, 1987, 55–7). There may also have been an original intention to suspend a painted ceiling beneath it as at Peterborough (Ruprich–Robert, 1881, ii, Pl. 86).

The eastern quarter of the roof (Frames 1–22) had been extensively repaired and in places rebuilt using pine (Fig. 15.3). The form of the associated series of secondary carpenters' marks and the observation of James Essex in 1757 that pine was used in the nave roofs suggests that this work was perhaps done in the seventeenth century.[6] That further repairs were made using oak and Baltic pine in the eighteenth and nineteenth centuries is indicated by further tree-ring dates of oak timbers (Esling *et al.*, 1989) and possible bracking marks on the pine. The last repairs were made in 1861 following the insertion of the ceiling of 'one and one-quarter inch Petersburg battens' (pine boards) which carries the painting of Le Strange and Gambier Parry.[7]

Riven oak boards imported from Baltic ports, no doubt through Kings Lynn, at an earlier period were also identified re-used as roof battens beneath the lead, mostly on the north side (Owen 1984, 352–3). Tree-ring dating showed that the timber was felled c.1295. There was no indication of where the boards were used in the first instance (see p.21).

During recent repairs to the fine hammer-beam roof of the south transept seven core-samples were taken for tree-ring dating. Complete sapwood remained on two and their final rings grew in 1427 or early 1428 which would allow completion of the roof c.1430.

3. *Exeter Cathedral* by Dr Coralie Mills

A large number of timbers from the Cathedral Church of St Peter in Exeter have been successfully cross-matched and dated through the use of standard dendrochronological procedures (Mills 1988). A total of 79 timbers from the Cathedral roof have been dated, through inclusion in the new chronologies XMEAN52 (AD 1137–1332), XMEAN60 (AD 1662–1783) and

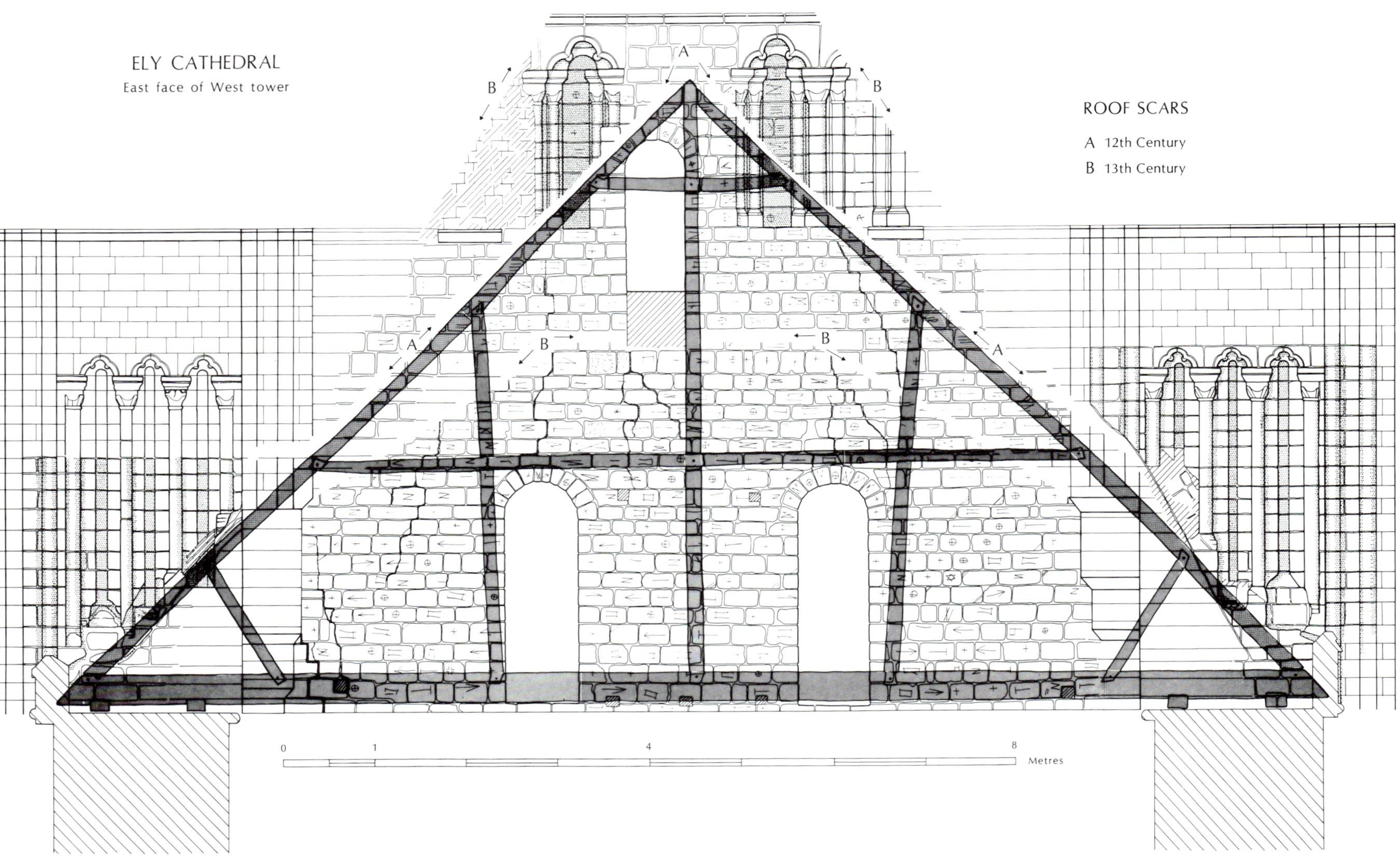

Fig. 15.4. Ely Cathedral. Drawing of the masonry (including masons' marks) of the east face of the West Tower from the tops of the nave walls to the apex of its roof with a reconstruction of one of the original Norman roof frames superimposed. (Drawn by W.G. Simpson and David Taylor)

EXMED11 (AD 1367–1616). Of these timbers, it is only sole-plate sequences which date to anything other than the medieval period. Prior to this research, it was thought that all oak timbers in the roof were medieval. However, the dendrochronological results revealed a major phase of repairs in or after the late eighteenth century, when many sole-plates were replaced. In addition, a small group of dated sole-plates may represent repairs in the early sixteenth century. However, these timbers could be part of a later repair phase which employed some re-used or stored timber.

There is a great difference in the dating quality of the medieval and post-medieval timbers. Most of the medieval timbers do not retain any sapwood, while many of the replacement sole-plates retain complete sapwood and bark. The lack of definite felling dates limited the extent to which the dendrochronological results could be used to re-evaluate the architectural history of the Cathedral for the medieval period. However, the evidence for an east to west direction of construction allowed earliest possible construction dates to be identified for different portions of the roof. These showed that the eastern arm was roofed in or after 1298 and that some of the timber used in the nave roof was felled in or after 1334, although the completion date remains unknown.

4. Glasgow Cathedral

Between 1909 and 1912 the high roof of the choir and of the nave and its triforia were restored and repaired under the direction of W. T. Oldrieve for H. M. Office of Works. His subsequent report on the work (Oldrieve, 1916) is difficult to follow due to lack of any drawings or detailed information and analysis of the structures. However, records of this kind were made and are now housed in the Historic Buildings and Monuments (Scotland) Office at Edinburgh. The drawings together with the report make it clear that Oldrieve undertook a very scholarly analysis of the roofs and restored them so that their present state is what he considered to be their original appearance.

The drawings show that both roofs were of scissor-truss design but of very different character. The roof of the nave was an open roof with a span and height of 25ft. Oldrieve inserted tie-beams at every sixth frame, but whether they were there originally is dubious. It required repairs because it had no internal longitudinal bracing, not even wall-plates, and its 48 trusses were racking badly towards the central tower (Fawcett, 1985, 23). Apart from the tie-beams and its smaller size it would seem to be very similar in both its form and its carpentry to the nave roof of Ely Cathedral.

The roof of the choir is about the same size as the nave roof but much more sophisticated in its carpentry and ambitious in its design. It may be compared in a general way to the former roof of the nave at Peterborough, (probably built c.1220) in that a timber ceiling or vault is suspended beneath the scissor trusses. The soffits of the ashlar pieces and lower scissor arms of the principal trusses were of slightly curved profile and were, together with the soffits of the collars and of the arch-braces between them and the scissor arms, moulded and their sides slotted to take oak boards. Thus the lower members of the principal trusses projected a little below the ceiling boards and defined a space of slightly ogival form. These transverse arches occurred every fourth frame of the roof and subdivided the ceiling into a series of half-bays relative to a complete bay of the masonry structure. The ceiling was further subdivided by three longitudinal, and a series of diagonal, ribs pinned to the soffits of the roof members. All these components of the ceiling would, like the battens covering the rafters beneath the lead, have helped to prevent the roof trusses from racking. The builders also took another precaution to prevent it by putting plates mortised and tenoned at either end between the mid-points of the collars of the principal trusses. In the original work the rib-intersections would have been covered by carved and illuminated bosses and the whole ceiling painted.

By the early years of this century when Oldrieve came to restore the roofs all this timber vaulting had been removed and replaced by a lath and plaster ceiling. The nave roof had been similarly excluded. It seems that these changes were made in the early eighteenth century (MacUre, 1736; Oldrieve, 1916, 157). Engravings in Brown (1822) seem to show the nave roof ceiled but the choir still in its original form. However this is probably deceptive for Oldrieve remarks (1916, 163) that he found 'the original division of the ceiling into panels had been followed when the plaster ceiling was substituted, although the character and spirit of the original work had been entirely lost'. This information together with his analysis of the roof structure above enabled him to restore the vaulting to what he considered to be its original form.

Rotted and decayed timber cut out of the roofs during the restoration was fortunately not thrown away but put into store at Newark Castle, Greenock. There it was sampled in 1976 by Dr M. Baillie of the Palaeoecology Laboratory, the Queen's University, Belfast to provide data for the construction of a master chronology for southern Scotland (Baillie, 1977). Of the 20 samples he took 14 cross-matched to give a 415 year chronology covering the period 946–1360AD. The dendrochronology defined timbers of two distinct phases and as there were indications of sapwood in both instances Dr Baillie was able to estimate that the timbers were felled c.1258 and c.1385.

Paradoxically evidence can be adduced to show that either of these dates could apply to the choir roof but neither of them correlate well with what is known from documentary sources about the history of the nave. The 1258 date would accord well with Bondington's work on the choir[8] or, alternatively, the choir roof may not be original but a replacement built by Bishop Wardlaw (1367–87) for MacUre (Gordon, 1872 i, 60; Oldrieve, 1916, 163) observed that over the high altar 'on the roof of the area is his coat-of-arms finely illuminate'. The roof of the nave on typological criteria should be earlier than that of the choir. However the building itself was largely constructed in the last decades of the thirteenth century. Although its completion was certainly delayed by Bishop Wishart's (1271–1316) close involvement in the Wars of Independence, and his conversion into siege engines of timbers originally supplied for the building operation,[8] a delay of nearly a century between completion of the masonry building and its roofing seems excessive. Fortunately all these uncertainties could be resolved by a thorough archaeological investigation of the timbers at Newark Castle to determine which roofs they come from and how the tree-ring dates relate to them.

5. Hereford Cathedral

The results of tree-ring dating of the timber aisled-hall of the Bishop's Palace at Hereford have recently been published (Haddon-Reece *et al.* 1989, for details and bibliography). One sample retained complete sapwood which gave the felling year 1179.

6. Christ Church Cathedral, Oxford

A timber from the roof of the chapter house of St Frideswide's Priory (Oxford Cathedral) has given a tree-ring date of 'after 1250' and another from the stair-frame of the Priory House dated 'after 1450' (Ashdown *et al.*, 1988).

Case Studies

1. The construction of the roof of the Angel Choir, Lincoln Cathedral

Survey and tree-ring dating of the roof of the Angel Choir has shown that it is contemporary with the building it covers, or very largely so, for it includes later timber, oak, pine and very recently chestnut, introduced in repairs (Table I and Foot *et al.*, 1986). There are three significant changes in the original carpentry and they coincide with the division between the second and third bays of the building from the east and also with the eastern edge of the wall foundation of St Hugh's presbytery in so far as this can now be ascertained (Fig. 15.5; Kidson, 1986, fig. 1). The joints at the lower ends of the queen posts to the tie beams were simple lap-joints in the eastern bays and lap-dovetail joints with square housed shoulders in the western bays (Foot *et al.*, 1986, fig. 7, c and d). The last frame of the eastern bays (no. 25) has inferior carpentry and is the only frame in the roof without carpenter's marks. Thirdly the western bays contain a substantial amount of timber re-used from the roof of the presbytery built by St Hugh which was demolished to make way for the Angel Choir (for tree-ring dates of samples from such timbers see Foot *et al.*, 1986, 60). The start of work must have been sometime after Henry III gave the Dean and Chapter a licence to demolish the city wall to make space for the new building in 1256.[9] It was complete (presumably) and consecrated in November, 1280.

In April 1276 Edward I gave the Dean and Chapter fifty oaks from Sherwood Forest of which six were for *transversaria* or tie beams.[10] Did this grant come before work had started on the roof or when it had progressed some way and more timber was required in order to complete it? The solution was to be found, it seemed, in tree-ring dating all the tie-beams which still survived out of the original total of nineteen in order to identify the six given in 1276. Unfortunately, however, there were problems which made it difficult to carry out this apparently simple project. In the last big repair programme in the roof in the 1840s the consultant architect Charles Hollis had advocated:

> As most of the tie-beams require to be replaced it would be injudicious to trust so extensive a building to so many pieced and repaired tie-beams. It would be proper to introduce some new beams and truss framing and connect the rafters by purlins.[11]

The repairs were evidently carried out according to these proposals except that the rafters have no purlins, only a series of planks of this date nailed across their inner faces to brace them; some of the collar plates also seem to have been introduced at this time. The good lengths of two tie-beams were pieced together to make one and big baulks of Baltic pine were introduced to make up the resulting deficiencies. Thus, although a part of nearly every original tie-beam still survives only one (no. 52) was still complete, and many were not in their original positions (Fig. 15.5). The identification of the original locations of the 1276 tie-beams in the roof was essential in order to reach a solution to the question. Fortunately nearly all the tie-beams had carpenters' marks not only at their ends (which had, of course been mostly cut off in the repair works) but also beside the joint beds holding the bases of the queen posts. It was therefore possible by reference to these carpenters' marks, in nearly every instance, to match up each length of tie-beam to its proper frame and so determine its original position in the roof.

Having solved this archaeological problem a dendrochronological one remained. Although waney edges could be found on most tie-beams they nearly always marked the HST and little or no actual sapwood survived. Thus the very best that could be hoped for from the tree-ring dating was an *estimate* of the felling date of each timber rather than an actual felling year. However, if it is assumed that the 1276 timbers of the king's gift are those with the latest HST dates, then it would seem that the grant was made before work on the roof construction had begun (Fig. 15.5). The tree-ring dates do not show any trend from east to west and a random distribution of felling dates is indicated. There was no evidence either that any tie-beam was re-used in its original context (Table I, Category A, 1–3), but some timbers (e.g. nos 19 and

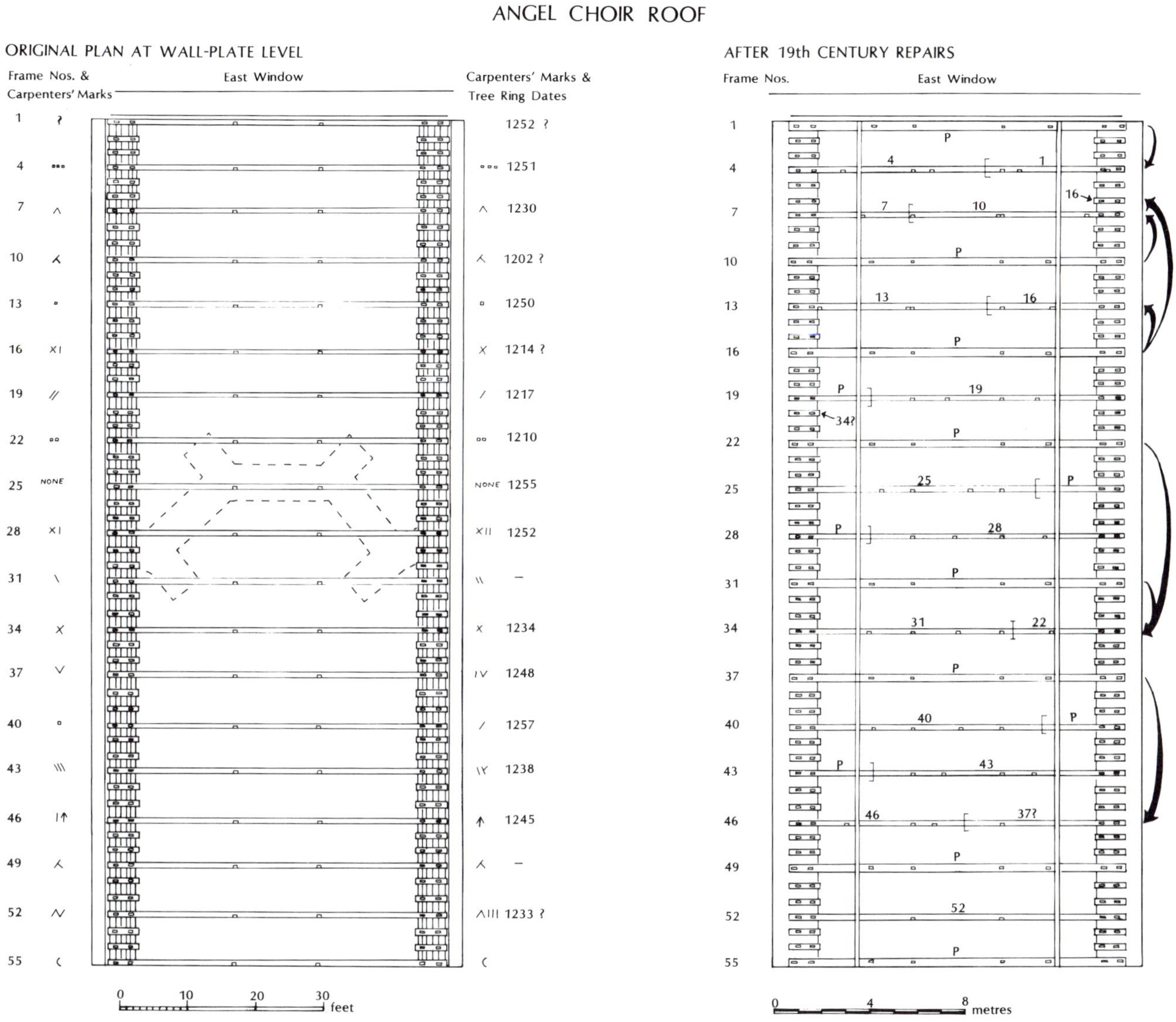

Fig. 15.5. Lincoln Cathedral, Angel Choir roof, plans at wall-plate level. ***Left*** *Tie beams and sole pieces as originally laid down with outline of the east end of St Hugh's presbytery shown, centre. The tree-ring dates are for HST except possibly in the cases indicated by ?* ***Right*** *Tie beams and sole pieces following 18th and 19th century repairs. The arrows and numbers on the plan indicate how parts of tie beams have been combined. P = inserted pine timbers. (Drawn by Elaine Guilding)*

22) had HST dates so early as to suggest that they were seasoned, having lain in the cathedral timberyard for a number of decades (Category A4) awaiting the day when the master carpenter had need of them.

The archaeological, documentary and dendrochronological evidence together therefore suggest that the Angel Choir roof was built in not more than four and a half years between April 1276 and November 1280. Still unexplained is the reason for the break in the roof carpentry. It could indicate an actual halt in construction. The total construction time need not have been much more than a year. For example, the high roofs of the nave and choir of the medieval St Paul's Cathedral were entirely rebuilt, with the high pitch of the Gothic originals (Dugdale, 1673) in just two years after a disastrous fire in 1561 (Kitching, 1986, 128). Building technology had not advanced greatly over the three centuries separating the two projects to justify any suggestion of a faster rate of work in sixteenth century, although there may of course have been differences in the size of the labour forces. Indeed a slower rate of work might be assumed for the later project. Because the fire was extensive and unexpected there was insufficient timber to hand and the master of the works had to search throughout the country for supplies.

The restricted distribution of the old timbers re-used from the roof of St Hugh's presbytery to the three western bays overlying its foundations might be coincidental. Perhaps only at this point did a scarcity of new timber for construction of the upper parts of the roof become apparent to be supplemented by the only other source readily to hand. An alternative explanation, however, is that the old timbers were not available for the roofing of the first two bays because the old work had not yet been demolished. This explanation would require that there was actually a halt in the roof construction at the point marked by this change in the queen post joints while the old presbytery was demolished, followed by the setting up of the piers, triforium arcades and clerestories of the three western bays of the new work before the western part of the roof could be completed. It is not intended to adduce further evidence for or against this hypothesis here but it is one which should be seriously considered.

2. Dendrochronology and documents: Bishop Northwold's new works at Ely

The tree-ring dating of the nave roof (see p. 9) firmly puts its construction in the second phase of the building programme initiated by Bishop Northwold in 1234 (Draper, 1979, 26), five years after his accession. The first phase included the start of work on the presbytery which extended the Romanesque church beyond its apsidal east end. It is possible, however, that the first years of Northwold's incumbency were occupied with the completion of works initiated by his predecessor, Bishop de Burgh. He received royal grants of 200 oaks from Inglewood Forest for building the 'turris' of his church in April 1226 and 40 oaks for unspecified work from Mansfield Wood in Sherwood Forest in February 1228 – the year of his death.[12] This 'turris', considering the quantity of timber involved – about the same amount as in the nave roof – can only have been for a lead-covered timber spire. It may have been for the 'stepil' or campanile to the north of the west end of the church which is first mentioned in 1325–6 (Chapman, 1907:ii, 57) and which was demolished in 1354 (Chapman, 1907:ii, 165) or for the central tower of the church. It is unlikely that it was the western one completed c.1200 for the first major project initiated by Bishop Northwold in 1234 was the construction of a 'turris' on the western tower (Wharton, i, 636). For this the king granted 100 oaks to Northwold which were to be selected by his carpenter in the royal forests of Weybridge (Hunts), Brigstock Park (Northants) and Kingswood (Essex) in 1234–35.[13] Another grant of 16 oaks was given by the king from Weybridge for unspecified work in the church later in 1235.[14] A list describing roof timbers and giving their lengths, but not their quantities, survives among the annual accounts for the bishop's new works. It must date between 1235 and 1246 and, since it includes timbers supported on corbels (*corbiliones* – cf. the medieval belfry at Salisbury. Price, 1753, Pl.10) and the lengths do not fit the nave roof, may be the master carpenter's requirements for the western 'turris' (Stewart, 1868, 75).[15] Timber for the nave roof probably came either from the bishop's estates or by purchase at local fairs, as certainly happen in the fourteenth century (Fig. 15.6; Chapman, 1907: i, 29, 51; ii, 47–8, 83). Either way, the cost of the timber and of the labour must have been borne by the bishop and is probably included in the sum of £156.18s.9d. expended in 1239–40 and of £184.7s.6d. expended in 1240–2 (Draper, 1979, 27).

At the east end the completion of the aisle walls, the arcades and the clerestories must have been near in 1247–8 when the king granted another 34 oaks from Kingswood.[16] These, however, would have been less than half the number required to roof the new presbytery. Although the roof has gone, a sketch of a typical frame giving its dimensions was sent to James Essex at his request in 1760 by William Wiles, who was probably the carpenter who built the present pine scissor-truss roof.[17] The original roof was clearly of the same design as that of the nave and must have been built in 1247–49 when expenditure was averaging £350 *per annum*, the greater part being borne by the bishop (Draper, 1979, 27). Expenditure falls abruptly in the latter part of 1250 and the work must have been largely completed by the following year, with the dedication of the new building taking place on seventeenth September, 1252 (Wharton, 1691 i, 636).

3. The fall of the spire at Lincoln Cathedral and the ensuing repairs

The archaeological evidence of this event, which is recorded with few details in a brief note appended to the Chapter Acts (Cole, 1920, 171) has become apparent gradually over the last few years (Simpson, 1988). Survey of the high roof of the north arm of the east transept revealed an unexpected diversity in its character (Foot *et al.*, 1986, 48–51, 54). The scissor-truss roof over the inner (aisle) bay seems superficially much the same as that over the centre bay and that over the outer bay is unlike either but matches that over the outer bay of the south arm of the transept which has been tree-ring dated to c.1250. The differences in the carpentry of the roof over the inner bay and that of the centre bay were revealed after a detailed survey and they are set out in Table 2. Clearly the two bays were not roofed by the same carpenters, even if they were more or less contemporary. Dendrochronology in fact demonstrated that their dates were very different. The roof in the inner bay is original, built of trees felled c.1195/6 and probably completed by 1200. It is the earliest surviving scissor-truss roof in the country and also the highest and most steeply pitched of its type. The roof over the centre bay turned out to be much later. One of the four samples (no. 358) taken from the roof had complete sapwood (16 rings) indicating that the timber had been felled in 1542/3 and the other three all had HST surviving so that it could be estimated that all were felled sometime between 1522 and 1584. One (no. 360) had its HST at 1534. If it had the same sapwood complement as sample 358 then the felling date of the timber would have been

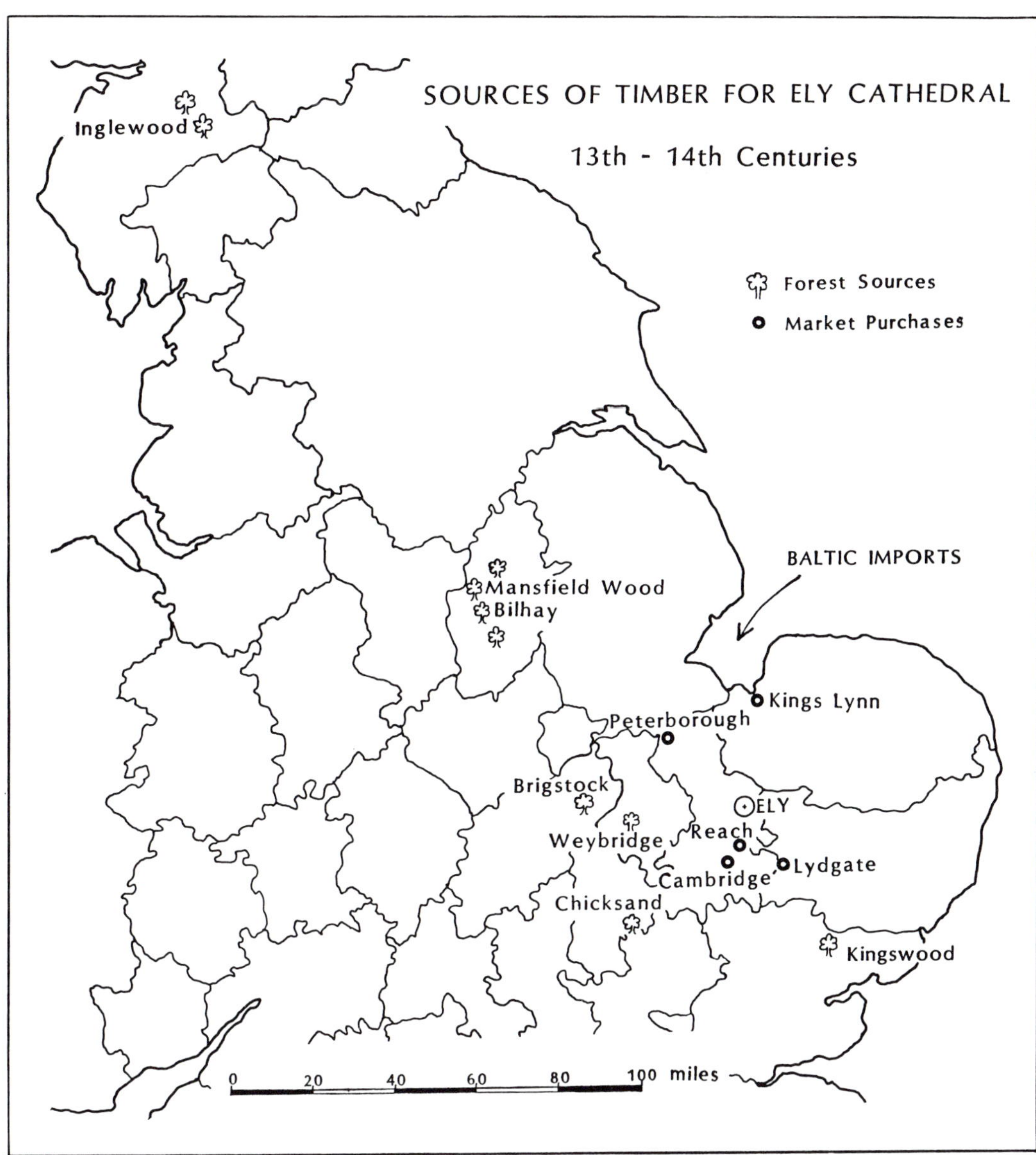

Fig. 15.6. Ely Cathedral Priory. Sources of timber for building in 13th and 14th centuries. Cambridge had two markets or fairs which sold timber, at Stourbridge and Barnwell Priory. (Compiled from data in Sacrist and Close Rolls by W.G. Simpson, drawn by Elaine Guilding)

TABLE 2

Roof of the north arm of the east transept
Differences in details of the carpentry

Inner Bay	Centre Bay
Rafters of a single timber	Rafters with scarf joints
Trees mostly over 120 years old	Trees mostly less than 120 years old
Large scantlings	Lesser scantlings
Timbers riven and axe squared	Squared by notch and chop technique
No evidence of sawing lengthwise	Timbers sawn lengthwise
No carpenters' marks	Carpenters' marks
Half-lapped joints single-pegged	Half-lapped joints double-pegged
No use of nails	Occasional use of nails

1549/50. Evidently the centre bay is not covered by an original roof but by a mid sixteenth century reproduction (Fig. 15.7; Esling *et al.*, 1989).

As our work of surveying and tree-ring dating the Cathedral roofs progressed it became apparent that the north chapel of the east transept which was demolished by James Essex in 1772 (Venables, 1883, 187) still had the western bay of its king-post roof surviving above the reconstructed apsidal chapel. Wenceslas Hollar's view of the east end of the Cathedral shows the earlier chapel with its low pitched roof before its demolition (Dugdale, 1673). Three samples taken from its timbers had complete sapwood and the felling dates were 1544, 1546/7 and 1548/9.

By now it seemed clear that these two restricted areas of the north transept roofs in line with the central tower had had to be rebuilt because they had been damaged by the fall of its 250ft high timber and lead spire in 1548.

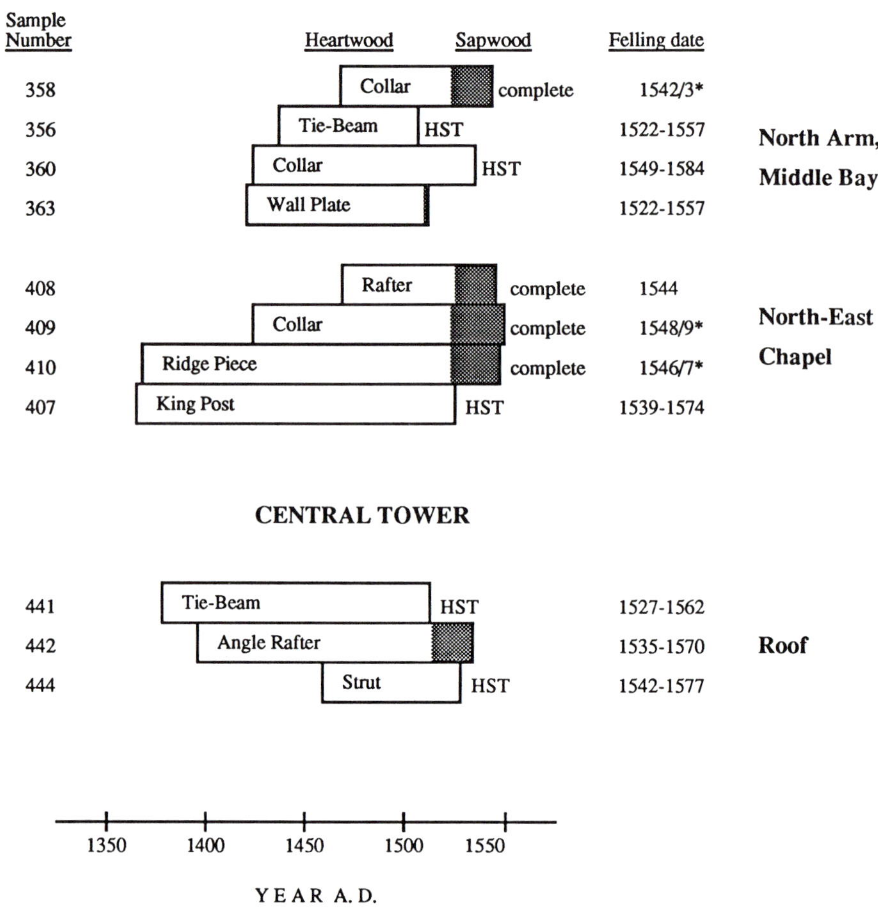

Fig. 15.7. Lincoln Cathedral. Bar chart to show the relationship of samples taken from the north arm of the east transept and from the central tower roofs – areas damaged by the fall of the spire in 1548. (Compiled by C.D. Litton)

The dating of samples taken from the roof of the tower, including one of its great 46ft long tie-beams, demonstrated that it was also of the mid-sixteenth century (Fig. 15.7; Esling *et al.*, 1990) and not, as Hewett (1985, 145) thought, the surviving base of the original spire. What may have influenced Hewett's judgement is the large post supporting the roof which looks much like the stump of the great mast around which the frame of the spire must have been built. Perhaps it was, indeed, intended to use it as the foundation of a new spire one day.

4. Lincoln Cathedral: timber supply and roof repairs, 1650–1750

The dendrochronology of the tie-beams in the Angel Choir roof indicates that they were of both green and seasoned timber but, for lack of complete sapwood, it was difficult to be precise about felling dates (Case Study 1). In those areas of the east transept roofs which have been identified as being rebuilt c.1550, however, complete sapwood is present and it is clear that while some of the timber was felled in 1548/9 and therefore probably used green, other timber was felled some six or seven years earlier and must have been well-seasoned (Case Study 3). These two pieces of evidence imply the existence of a stock of timber or a timberyard both when the building of the cathedral was in progress as well as when increasing age and decay made maintenance and repair work a constant necessity. The first documentary evidence of the Dean and Chapter's stocks of timber is an inventory made shortly after the Restoration. It is quite short and so may be quoted in full.

'An inventory (made in 1665/6) of the timber and lead which these Accountants have to the use of the Fabric and thereunto belonging viz:

In timber

Item Seven pieces of timber, ten yards a piece in length and about 16 inches over, lying in the Minster.
Item Two small pieces of timber, lying in the woodyard.
Item One short piece of timber, lying in the Minster, 5ft and a half long and 29 inches over.
Item Three small pieces of timber for piecing of Sparrs lying in a Chapel.
Item Three shores bought for the Great roof (i.e. the nave).
Item One piece of timber lying in the steep south (i.e. east transept) roof which was cut off the old great tree which lay in the Minster.

These pieces of timber are all that remains of those several pieces which were belonging to the Fabric when the Accountants were chosen Masters of the Fabric in September 1664.'[18]

The Fabric Accounts give a detailed picture of the annual costs of carpenters' and plumbers' work and the purchase of oak timber and deal boards from this time onwards (Fig. 15.8). The figures must reflect the amount of roof repair work in progress and they can to some extent be correlated with other documentary sources and with tree-ring data. The twelve year gap in the purchase of timber between 1695 and 1707 implies a period when stocks were running down after the big purchase in 1690. The continuing purchase of deals and amounts of the plumbers' bills show that roof repairs, if only largely external, were still continuing. Thus the two purchases of timber in 1707 costing £28.10s.0d. and £4.14s.0d. from William Hobman and John Earland respectively, came when stocks were almost exhausted. Tree-ring analysis suggests that the larger of these purchases was of oaks felled in 1703 and 1704 and that they were used to repair the roof of the Angel Choir. The timber comes from trees which all seem to be about a hundred years old and are remarkable for their very low numbers of sapwood rings (14–19). The uniformity of the quality of the timber suggests that it all came from a single tract of woodland, probably a plantation (Fig. 15.9). Repair of the roof over the south end of the east transept seems to have started within about ten years of the completion of work in the Angel Choir roof. The quality of the timber used here is much more variable and its felling years extend from 1705 to 1717 (Fig. 15.10). Since the area of roofing involved is so small there can be no doubt that the timber with the earlier felling dates was used seasoned and that the actual repairs were made either in 1718 following the big purchase of timber in that year, or in the following year. In the next decade it is interesting to note that the high tradesmen's bills and timber costs of the mid 1720's coincide with, rather than follow, the appeals for funds made in 1723 and 1726 (Foot *et al.*, 1986, 63). Although little timber was purchased in the decades 1730–1750 there was probably timber in stock. Repairs were made to the roof of St Hugh's Choir, probably in the 1730's and, as deals were being purchased and plumbers' bills were high relative to carpenters' bills reboarding and releading were probably the main activities.

The seventeenth century inventory already quoted indicates that what little timber was then in stock was in various parts of the Cathedral rather than in any central store, much as today. The woodyard referred to may have been a fuel store for the lead-casting house to which the 'two small pieces of timber' had been consigned as having no other value. If there was an outdoor timberyard there is little evidence for it except that in March 1778 the Dean and Chapter made an agreement with the Cathedral mason, John Hayward and the carpenter Thomas Lumby that they should tidy up and level the old stone [masons'] yard (the area to north and west of the cloisters) and fill in the old saw-pit there.[19] The blacksmiths shop and the plumbery were on the opposite side of the Cathedral in the Galillee Porch (Venables 1883, 395n).[20] The redundancy of the saw-pit may have had something to do with the changes in the supply of timber initiated by James Essex on becoming surveyor to the Cathedral in 1761. His new roof on the Chapter House is the first to be built entirely of Baltic pine, which continued to be used for well over a century. It was shipped up the Trent and landed at Gainsborough where there was probably a sawmill where it could be sawn to the dimensions required by the Clerk of Works at Lincoln.[21] Deals (sawn planks of fir) were also of Baltic origin and purchased from merchants at Boston and less often Hull and Gainsborough. They also sold fir poles for scaffolding.[22]

5. The use of imported Baltic oak at Ely and York

In the course of the repair of the nave roof at Ely Cathedral in 1988 areas of riven oak boards or battens were revealed, mostly on the north side, covering the rafters immediately beneath the lead. Redundant nails, groups of nail holes and their relative spacings showed that they had been used for a similar purpose once or twice previously. Six boards were selected from a total of 47 collected, for tree-ring dating and one, with an ogee-headed arch cut out, was also taken from among the pieces of dismantled fourteenth century choir stalls now stored in the choir gallery (Bond, 1910, ii, 37; Tracy, 1987; Alexander and Binski, 1987, no 532, 431).

Dendrochronology separated the boards into three groups of one, two and four boards which all matched well against the master chronology for Poland (Wazny, 1986; Eckstein *et al.*, 1986) with *t*-values of 7.0, 8.0 and 5.2 and last measured ring dates of 1288, 1303 and 1289 respectively. These *t*-values must be compared with those obtained by cross-matching with chronologies compiled from native British oak, in particular those for the British Isles[23] and the East Midlands of England (Laxton and Litton 1988) which both span the period 1000AD to the present. When the Ely chronologies are cross-matched against them no *t*-values above 4.5 are recorded and certainly none as high as those against the Polish chronology (see Table 3). Thus, in the light of the extremely good

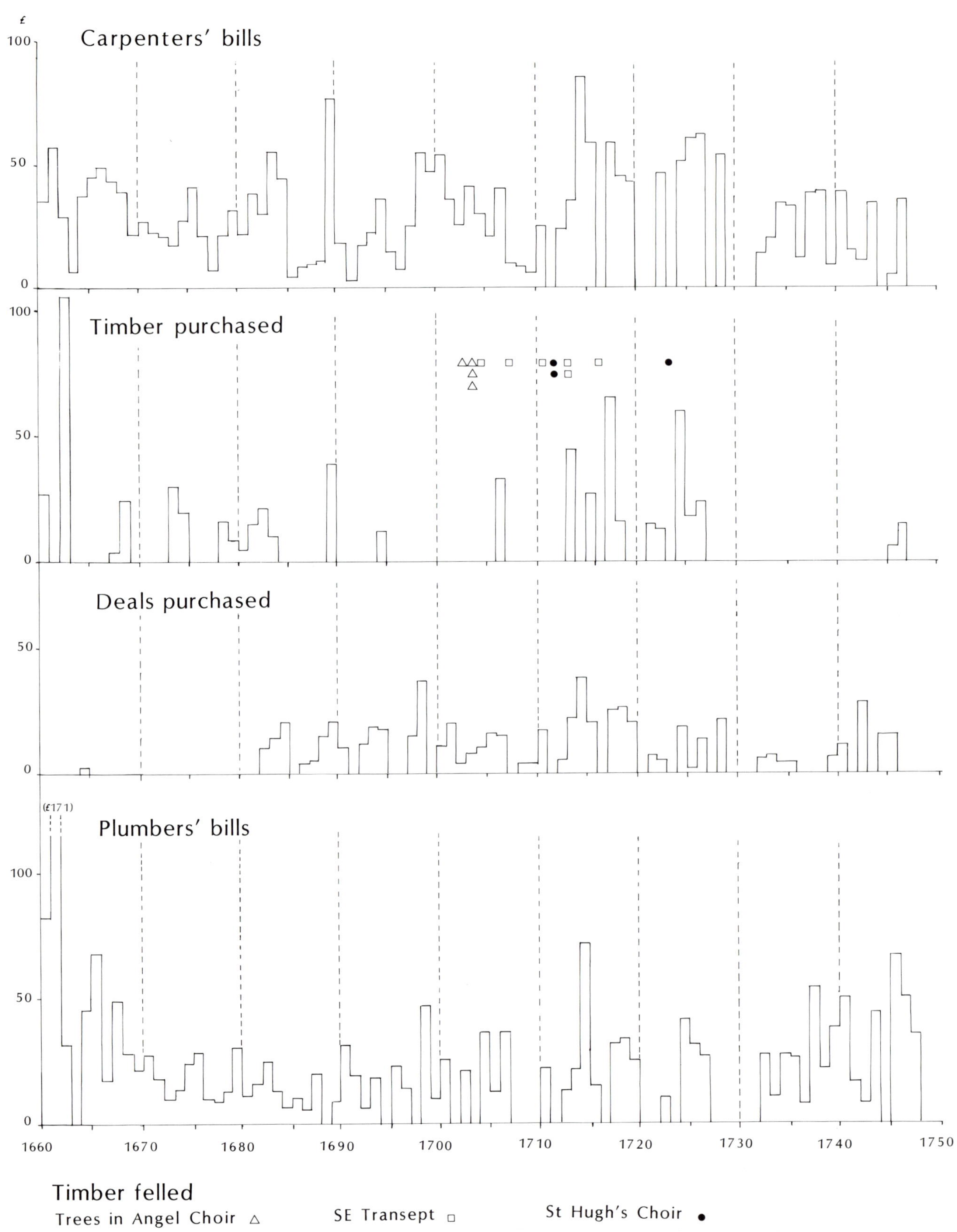

Fig. 15.8. Lincoln Cathedral. Analysis of Fabric Account entries indicating the extent and intensity of roof repairs in the period 1660–1750. Tree-ring evidence for the felling dates of individual timbers is shown in relation to the purchases of timber for the period 1700–1725 only. (Compiled by W.G. Simpson, drawn by Elaine Guilding)

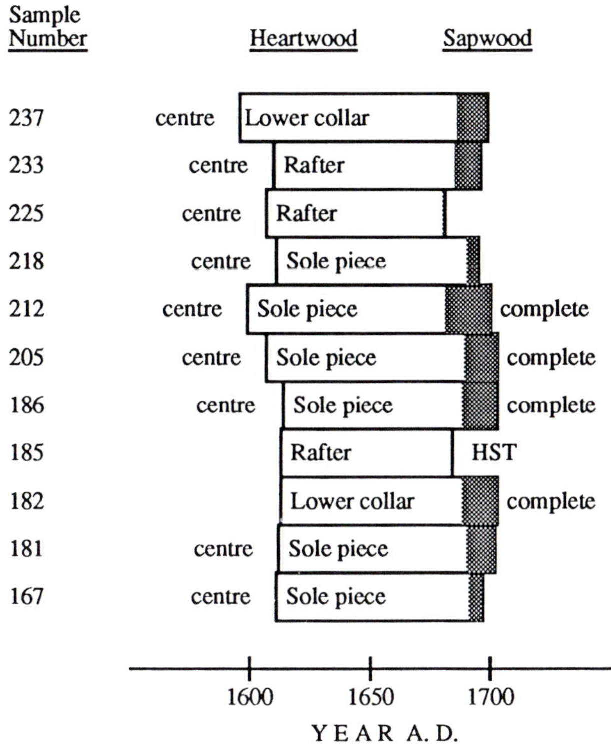

Fig. 15.9. Lincoln Cathedral, Angel Choir high roof. Bar chart of timbers felled in 1703–5 and used for repairs. The uniform character of the timbers suggests they came from a plantation. (Compiled by C. D. Litton)

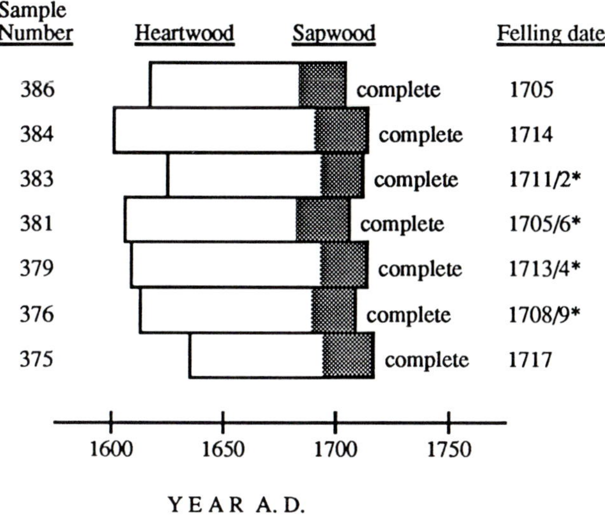

Fig. 15.10. Lincoln Cathedral, roof over the south end-bay of the east transept. Bar chart of timbers felled between 1705 and 1717 and used for repairs. About half of them seem to have been felled during the winter months when the sap was down. (Compiled by C. D. Litton)

matches against the Polish master, it is inferred that the Ely boards were almost certainly imported from the Baltic.

As the boards from the roof had indications of sapwood, the felling dates of the trees from which they were split could be estimated at c.1295. However, the board from the choir stalls had a final ring grown in 1303 and no indication of sapwood. There was therefore no basis for estimating the felling date of the timber since an unknown number of heartwood rings may have been removed in addition to the sapwood. All that can be said with certainty is that the felling cannot have occurred much before 1320, since East European oak has on average no more than 15 sapwood rings (Eckstein *et al.*, 1986). The construction of the stalls in fact seems to have been in progress in the decade from 1335 (Chapman, 1907, i, 44, 57–60). This would allow that the board under discussion might have been part of a batch of 500 'estrich' boards bought for the 'New Work' at Kings Lynn in 1334–35, the purchase of which is recorded in the surviving Sacrist Roll for that year (Chapman, 1907, ii, 72), though it would seem more likely that they were intended for roofing the Octagon since the entry is closely followed by others recording the purchase of 500 'bordnayl' and more than four fothers (about four tons) of lead.

The chronologies for the Ely boards also showed significant matches against three of Fletcher's master chronologies, denoted by Ref 1, Ref 4 and Ref 7, (Fletcher, 1977) composed of data taken from boards making up chests and cupboards at Westminster Abbey and from panel paintings which, it is now recognised were often laid on boards of Baltic origin, though usually painted in West European countries (Fletcher, 1986). Furthermore, Laxton *et al.* (1990) describe the dating of further timber in the East Midlands against the Polish chronology. Included are oak boards from a bench at Croxton Kerrial church, Leicestershire, 1299–1449 (t = 5,7); oak panels from a screen at Eaton church, Leicestershire, 1174–1438 (t = 4.7); boards from a chest at Ewerby church, Sleaford, Lincolnshire, 1074–1315 (t = 7.5) and planks from a granary from Tadlow, Cambridgeshire, 1145–1386 (Black *et al.*, 1984) (t = 6.0). A bar chart showing the relative dates of these imported timbers is given in Fig. 15.11. There were also significant matches (see Table 3) between the above chronologies and one compiled from data obtained from boards making up doors and cupboards in the de Zouche Chapel at York Minster (Fletcher and Morgan, 1981).

TABLE 3

Chart of the t-values between the Polish chronology and boards of Baltic origin found in Britain

CHRONOLOGIES	Poland	Ref7	Ref4	Ref1	York	Ely Cathedral 39	40	41
POLAND		5.9	9.6	6.3	4.4	5.2	8.0	7.0
REF7			4.5	N/O*	4.9	4.8	1.4	3.3
REF4				5.9	9.5	4.8	7.8	5.2
REF1					4.9	N/O	3.3	N/O
YORK						4.8	3.0	1.9
ELY (39)							4.0	3.4
ELY (40)								3.3
ELY (41)								

*N/O = No overlap.

Poland	996–1985	York	1118–1386
Ref7	993–1267	Ely 39	1109–1289
Ref4	1136–1355	Ely 40	1097–1303
Ref1	1254–1553	Ely 41	1133–1288

The building of the Chapel started in the mid-fourteenth century but was not completed until much later, although it must have been roofed by 1394. The Polish chronology is the first from eastern Europe to give a complete sequence of ring-width data beginning with modern trees of known felling years and extending back a millennium. It makes all these York timbers, previously matched against West European chronologies, five years later. However, this affects their actual felling date hardly at all for Fletcher and Morgan were allowing a complement of c.20 sapwood rings, or five more than the recent research results would allow. Thus the timber used in the de Zouche Chapel was felled sometime between 1390 and 1417 with a date c.1396 being most likely. Allowing time for transport and seasoning the doors and cupboards were probably made in the earliest years of the fifteenth century.

Other Lines of Research and some Problems

The doors of the cupboards of the de Zouche Chapel at York Minster were made up of short, vertical boards fastened to horizontal battens. But for this simple construction it would probably not have been possible to measure the ring-widths. Although imported Baltic boards in our experience almost invariably have long sequences of narrow rings which make them most suitable for dendrochronology they are often not easy to sample because their ends cannot be seen when they are used as panels framed within a screen, a door, a pew or stall or

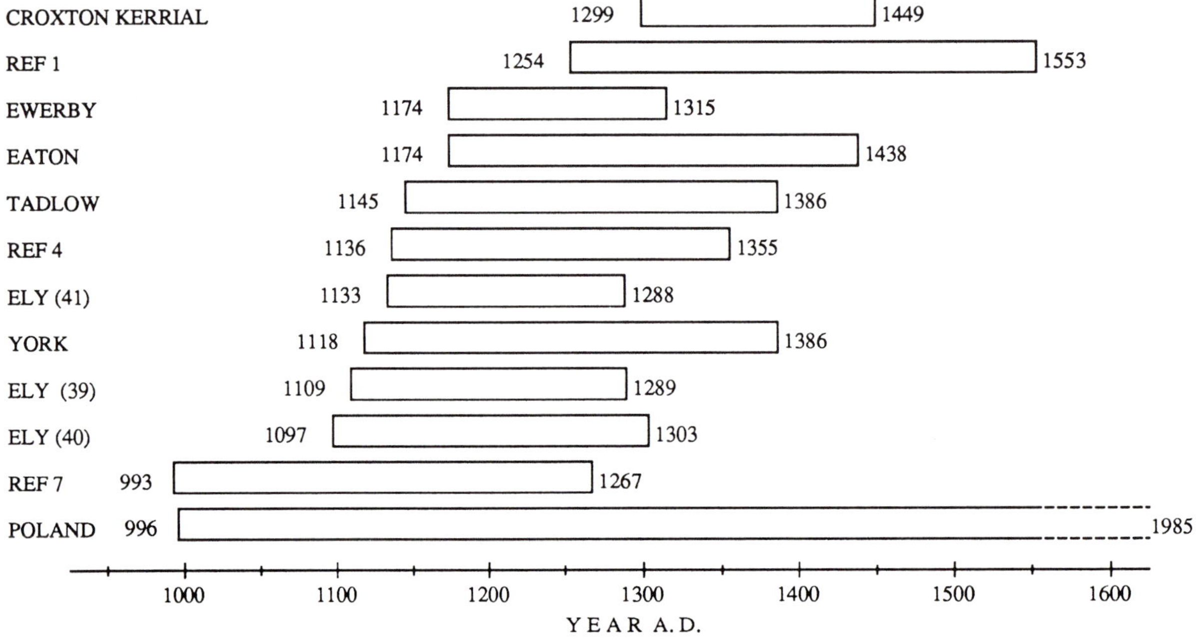

Fig. 15.11. Bar chart showing the chronological relationship between samples from Baltic boards from various locations in UK and the master chronology for Poland. Compiled by C.D. Litton

some other furnishing. Moreover, when they are used for cabinet work rather than structural carpentry care has usually been taken to remove all sapwood which is usually the starting point of any insect infestation. Thus the best samples for dating cathedral furnishings may often be obtained by taking out samples by coring – which it is not possible to take from boards because of their thinness – from, for example, the frames and jambs of doors or stalls, or the ground sills or top-plates of screens. These are likely to be of English oak and probably have fewer rings compared with the boards, but are more likely to exhibit a waney edge, indicating the presence of sapwood, somewhere along their lengths (Black *et al.*, 1984). As with roofs, furnishings are liable to have been repaired on more than one occasion in the past and sometimes elements of a number of different antique pieces may have been combined to make a single, or even a series, of complete furnishings as, for example the screens of the transept chapels at Lincoln Cathedral.

It can often be seen from impressions left in the mortar on the soffits of vaults that boards have been used for their centering. Although this has usually been completely dismantled sometimes some of the boards have become partly incorporated into the mortar and may not have been entirely removed, or their ends may survive around the edges of the vault or where it meets some feature in ashlar masonry. Such instances are usually in parts of the cathedral far from the public gaze, as for example, in the wall-passages and stairways of the west tower at Ely or in the tower and transept at St Albans Cathedral[24] or the crypt of Winchester Cathedral (Crook, 1989, 11). Perhaps, the most complete example of centering remaining *in situ* in any cathedral is in a small, high, vaulted room off the stair on the west side of the north arm of the east transept at Lincoln (Fig. 15.13). The boards centering the web of the vault are laid with one end on the extrados of the ribs and the other on top of the walls. However no sampling for dendrochronology has been done here not only because it is felt that such a complete example should be preserved but also because it is clearly made up almost entirely of re-used material. Some of the planks are lime-washed and so do not show up very clearly in the picture. The re-use of many of the others is demonstrated by the nails in them and at one point a piece of hurdlework made of willow rods (identification by Dr C. R. Salisbury) fills the space between two boards (Fig. 15.14). Such constructional timber which is actually partly incorporated within the masonry is excellent for dating the construction of the work if it can be shown that it is neither old nor re-used. Staves from old barrels, for example, would be very suitable material for centering on account of their size and curving profiles which would approximate to that of a vault (Colvin, 1971, 140, 152). Obviously there is a high probability that old timber would be used for construction work when available. Probably much the same applies to timber found in put-log holes.

Another problem with the extensive use of old timber has been encountered at Lincoln Cathedral. All the original roofs here seem to have been built without internal, longitudinal bracing to prevent racking. At some time, or at different times, this omission has been made good by inserting one or more plates over all the collars (Alcock *et al.*, 1989, fig.4c, 23; Foot *et al.*, 1986). Unfortunately no accurate tree-ring dates for these additions have been obtained because invariably the plates are of re-used timber. The only alternative strategy would seem to be either to tree-ring date samples from a large number of plates and so hope to arrive at a *terminus post quem* close to the event or to get radiocarbon dates for a few of the pegs which secure them to the collars, trusting that they are made from green timber.

All that has been written in this paper so far has been relevant only to oak. When other species are encountered, as for example at the east end of the nave roof at Ely, radiocarbon assay may be the only means of obtaining a date. Master chronologies have been established on the continent however for some of them (e.g. Hollstein, 1973; Becker *et al.*, 1970; Becker, 1978). There has also been some success both there and in this country in dating floating chronologies (i.e. those not starting with data obtained from modern timber of known felling years or not otherwise dated in calendar years) composed of tree-ring data from other species against established oak master chronologies (e.g. Hollstein, 1980, 160ff. for fir; Morgan, 1988, i, 149ff. for lime). However, in our experience, occasions when this would be of value in Cathedral studies are rare.

The Quality of Timber and its Influence on the Carpentry

It has been the aim of this paper to demonstrate how dendrochronology can be used with documentary evidence and archaeological survey of the roofs to learn more about the history and development of cathedrals. In conclusion we return to a subject touched upon earlier. From the examination of the surfaces of timber as well as by analysis of the tree-rings much can be learnt about its quality which is an important consideration in the development of carpentry. From the ring-widths, and their consistency or variability, as the case may be, it is possible to determine the rate of growth, which in turn may indicate the conditions under which trees were growing. It is possible to determine the age-range of the trees, to estimate their sizes and even to suggest the type of woodland from whence they came (Rackham, 1972; Rackham, 1980, 153; Rackham *et al.*, 1978). The size of many cathedrals, their antiquity and their various extensions and restorations affords a range of timber covering nearly a millennium, from which it is possible to learn much about the traditions and variations in carpentry standards and techniques throughout the Middle Ages up to the present time. Dendrochronology provides the chronological framework for these studies.

In a previous article (Foot *et al.*, 1986, 62) contrast

was drawn between the quality of the timber used in the earliest roofs of Lincoln cathedral and that used in the latest of the medieval roofs. Before about the middle of the thirteenth century our work at Ely and Lincoln suggests that the cathedral carpenter had available to him timber from natural woodland growing in conditions which had not been subjected to human interference. The trees were tall, often long past maturity (i.e. over a century), straight-grained and of narrow average ring-width. Their trunks were relatively knot-free and branched extensively only towards the crown. Where it has been possible to relate timber of this quality to documentary evidence it appears that royal forests were places where such trees grew. They were established as hunting preserves at a time when the great programme of Norman church building was only just beginning. Ironically there was human interference involved here but it was interference which, on account of the game, tended to conserve or even on occasions extend, the forest. It was particularly from the beginning of the thirteenth century that by sale and by gift of timber and by assarting and disafforestation the natural resources became depleted (Young, 1979). In their prime it is probable that the royal forests yielded timber comparable in quality to that available to the prehistoric and Roman carpenter (Hillam and Morgan, 1986). Examination of such timber in archaeological contexts and experimentation has shown that the earliest agricultural communities in this country were capable of converting the largest oaks for construction purposes using only a mallet and wedges (Morgan, 1988, 25). It is probable that these simple tools remained the principal ones used for converting timber of the best quality well into the thirteenth century although, of course, the axe, adze and two-man saw were also available, at least from Roman times (Adam, 1984; Gaitzsch, 1983; Darrah, 1982). Timbers of eleventh and twelfth centuries date identified at Ely and Lincoln cathedrals are often so finely finished that one has difficulty in seeing any toolmarks whatsoever. A fine example visible to the visitor is the re-used SE-NW, lower intermediate cross-tie between the valley rafters of the eastern crossing at Lincoln Cathedral. It has HST at 1115, was felled c.1145 and was probably used about that time in repairs or extensions by Bishop Alexander (Pevsner and Metcalf 1985, 200). No doubt the fact that both Romanesque cathedrals had open timber roofs is part of the explanation of the quality of the carpentry. In St Hugh's work at Lincoln the quality of the timber is still high but the finish is not so careful as to eliminate all waney edges or evidence of working methods. It is in the roof of St Hugh's Choir that rafters of two pieces scarfed together make their first, infrequent appearance. Otherwise they are of a single 44 foot length, as in the earlier work.

By the late 1270s when the roof of the Angel Choir at Lincoln was under construction the only timbers of comparable size and quality are the tie beams. All the rafters are of two pieces scarfed just below the middle collar. The poorer quality of the timber is demonstrated by complete trunks which are used in many cases for the rafters. In general the trees used approximated in their dimensions to the requirements of the carpenters. They are often waney and sometimes round in cross-section, less than a century old, knotty, wide-ringed and showing some evidence of sawing in converting the timber (Foot *et al.*, 1986, 61–2). The earliest evidence of the use of the saw in timber conversion at Lincoln is in the roofs of the western chapel, which have been tree-ring dated to c.1230. The extensive re-use of old timber in the west end of the Angel Choir roof is evidence either that funds were running out or that suitable timber was difficult to obtain. A rather better situation may be seen in the roof of the nave at Ely (c.1240) which is, however, not as high as the Lincoln roofs. The rafters are mostly single trunks thirty-five feet long and the saw is used only for converting the original Norman tie-beams to the appropriate dimensions for re-use as rafters.

Undoubtedly the poorer quality of the timber required the carpenter to invent new joints and construction techniques so that the roof structure remained as effective as ever. At Ely Cathedral where the rafters in the nave roof sometimes run out of length towards the top collar, a unique type of scarf joint about five feet long, covered by a flap or flange, was used to secure the extension (Fig. 15.12). At Lincoln, in the Angel Choir roof the need to have all the

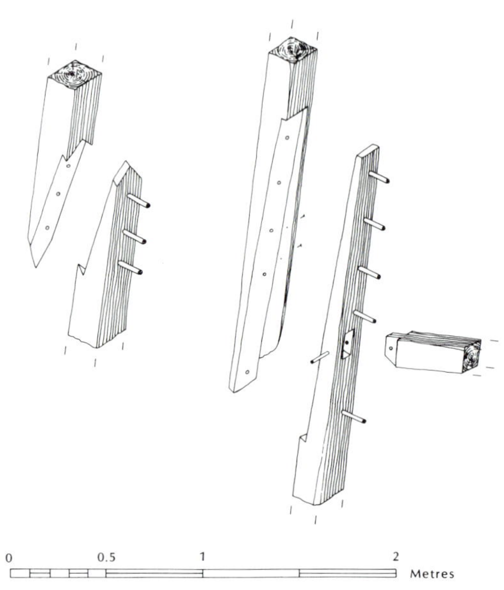

Fig. 15.12. Scarf joints in rafters. ***Left*** *Stop-splayed scarf with undersquinted and sallied abutments with three face pegs, used just below the middle collars throughout the roof of the Angel Choir, Lincoln Cathedral, 1276–80.* ***Right*** *A splayed scarf with square, undersquinted abutments with five face pegs. It is transfixed by the tenon of the top collar and has a single edge flange secured by two nails. Used occasionally in the roof of the nave at Ely Cathedral to make up the top length of a rafter c.1240. (Drawn by David Taylor)*

Fig. 15.13, Lincoln Cathedral. View of the vault of a small room off the staircase on the west side of the north arm of the east transept showing many of its centering boards still in place. (Photo C. R. Salisbury)

Fig. 15.14. LincolnCathedral. Detail of Fig. 13 showing the nail holes indicating the re-use of boards and also a piece of willow mat or hurdle forming part of the centering. (Photo C. R. Salisbury)

rafters in two sections was turned to advantage, it seems, by scarfing them all at the same height. This would have allowed the roof to be assembled in two stages. The lower two-thirds of the framing could have been constructed piece by piece at wall-top level and once this work had progressed some way a crane could have been set up on the lower collars and the apex rafters, tied at the base by the middle collars, raised fully assembled. The upper soulaces with notched-lap joints at either end served to lock the two parts of each frame together (Foot *et al.*, 1986, fig.5c).[25] Temporary boards, some still *in situ*, nailed across between collars and between struts served to stabilize the unleaded or partly completed roof skeleton during these difficult operations (Fig. 15.15; Simpson, 1987).

The advantage in forming the roof members by cleaving and hewing the timber is that where the line of cleavage is in a radial direction it will tend to follow the medullary rays of the timber which are its source of strength. Likewise when worked in other directions (e.g. tangentially) it will tend to follow the natural course of the grain. Sawing, on the other hand, will cut across natural weaknesses in the timber rather than eliminate them. It is generally the more laborious and expensive means of converting timber (Albion, 1926, 102). Many long saw-cuts would be necessary to convert a large trunk into planks (slabbing).[26] Splitting boards radially from a trunk using a mallet and wedges was a better option but could only be done easily where timber of the quality of that obtainable from natural woodland was available (Rackham, 1980, 145, 151). The boards collected from the nave roof of Ely Cathedral seem to be of such a quality. Areas of open or recently regenerated woodland tended to yield timber which was twisted and subject to knots and shakes in the trunk. It would not cleave straight or easily. It is timber of this quality that is beginning to appear in the roof of the Angel Choir, Lincoln. One means of slabbing poorer quality timber at an economic rate was by mechanization of the sawing and it is probably no coincidence that the French architect Villard de Honnecourt had this in mind around the middle of the thirteenth century (Adam and Varèene, 1985). The first records of the importation of Irish and Baltic boards into England also occur about this time (Salzman, 1952, 245–7; Colvin, 1971, 366). The development of this trade in oak, as well as pine, is well documented not only for the building industry but also for shipping (ibid; Albion, 1926). It was not so much the Baltic shores that were being exploited but the great forests bordering the rivers which flow into the Baltic. Here natural forest with timber of the required quality could still be found and its importation probably increasingly became the cheapest and most practical alternative to poorer quality or sawn English planks. As they came from the log the radially split boards had an isoceles cross-section. Simply by cutting a V-shaped groove along the thick edge of one board a form of groove and tongue joint could be made with the feather-edge of another (Innocent, 1916, fig. 44 nos 2 and 5). Boards (not necessarily of Baltic origin) fitted together in this way were nailed to the soffits of the joists and tie-beams of the floor at the base of the tower at Salisbury Cathedral to form a temporary vault (Spring, 1987,49). With a little trimming of their feather-edges they could be squared up to make rough battens to cover a roof, as at Ely Cathedral and with more adzing and planing they became fine timber for cabinet work or panel paintings (Fletcher and Tapper, 1984, 122–6).

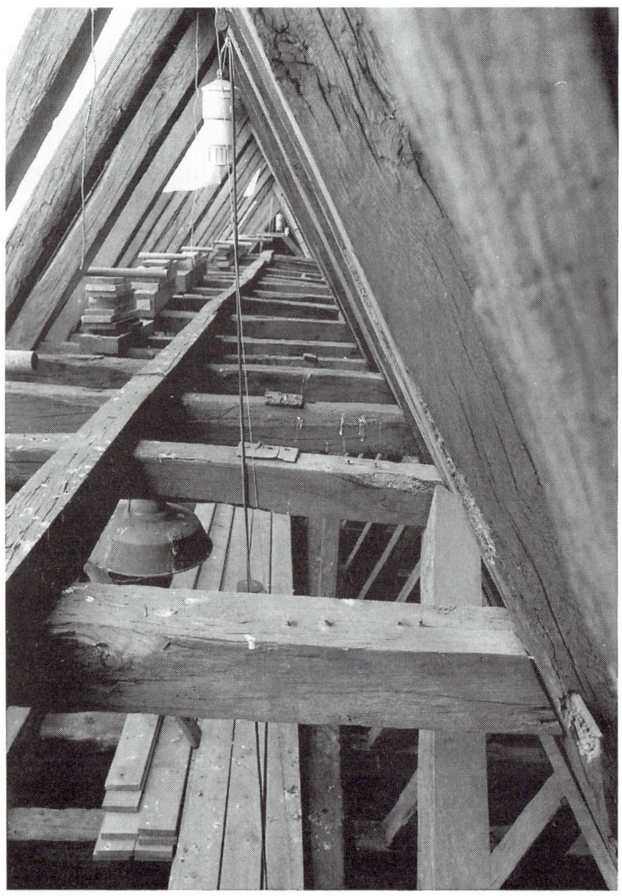

Fig. 15.15. Lincoln Cathedral, apex of the Angel Choir high roof showing the stub-ends of boards nailed across the top collars to steady the structure during construction. Nails for lost boards can also be seen on the two collars nearest to the camera. The central collar-plate is a 19th century addition. (Photo C.R. Salisbury)

One reason for the steady decline in the quality of native timber available in the thirteenth century is chronicled in the Close Rolls by the numerous gifts of timber from royal forests for all kinds of building projects by Henry III and Edward I. Relaxation of the forest laws, land clearances by the Cistercians and other orders as well as commercial exploitation also contributed to the depletion of the timber sources (Young, 1979; Holdsworth ii, 1974, 342–4).[27] A decline in the quality of timber is also apparent on archaeological sites, particularly in towns (Morgan, 1982, 35) and dendrochronologists have encountered a problem attributable to the same cause. When building regional master chronologies difficulty has been experienced in finding timber with sufficient rings to span the fourteenth century (Baillie, 1982, 213–15; Laxton *et al.*, 1982). But the quality of the timber is dependent not only on its availability but also on the status of the building concerned and the use to which it was put therein. In the early fourteenth century the sacrist of Ely was able to buy 'seventy great oak logs' at a local market for 3s.10d. each or 20 trees of extraordinary size for 9s. each from the estate of a Gilbertine priory (Chapman, 1907, ii, 33 and 83) for his building programme at the cathedral priory (Fig. 15.6). Likewise in the late fifteenth century to mid-sixteenth century the Clerk of the Fabric at Lincoln could still find over 20 tie-beams of dimensions equivalent to or, in the case of the eight across the top of the tower, in excess of the medieval originals. However, now, to convert the timber the saw was used in preference to mallet and wedges. The axe and the adze, however, was used initially to baulk the trunks using the 'notch and chop' technique. This is well illustrated in a German engraving of 1531 which shows both the axe used to chop out the notches and the broad axe used to dress the intervals between them (Salzman, 1952, 196). At Lincoln on the mid-sixteenth century scissor-truss frames there are tool-marks of both types of axe but in the example illustrated (Fig. 15.16) the timber has been dressed with an adze.

The timber was probably of very local origin, from estates administered by the Dean and Chapter on behalf of the bishop. There is no specific reference to the supply of timber to the Cathedral but in drawing up contracts for leases of their properties they 'always reserve to the bishop and his successors the great trees and wood growing there'. Thus in the lease of the manor and rectory of Greetwell, just to the east of Lincoln, in 1548 the Dean and Chapter promised 'to allow and assign within their woods at Kynthorpe, co. Linc. or nigh thereunto, or in any other place within seven miles of Lincoln ' great timbers, as post, panne and balke' which might be required for the repair of the said property (Cole, 1920, 51–2). This contract is unique in stipulating an annual planting of ash, oak, elm and willow trees on the estate though this may only be as a result of an act of parliament four years earlier which was intended to look after the long-term needs of the navy (Albion, 1926, 122). Be that as it may, it seems that from about this time the supply of timber for building construction is increasingly influenced by affairs of state and the requirements of the navy. When the sapwood is complete it can be seen that the Lincoln carpenters were getting a fair amount of winter felled oak. This was always preferred by the navy on account of its better resistance to insect attack and decay, although it was usually more expensive as the bark could not be peeled for sale to the tanners when the sap was down (Albion, 1926, 7–14; Tyson, 1987). During the Interregnum the Dean and Chapter, like many other owners of large estates, seem to have lost most of their woodlands (Albion, 1926, 127–30). In 1664 charges were brought against Henry Mansford, the Clerk of the Fabric at Lincoln. He was accused, among other things, of choosing rotten timber from Lord Castleton's plantations,[28] 'not one tree of the Minster wood

Fig. 15.16. Lincoln Cathedral, high roof of the north arm of the east transept, middle bay. Evidence of the use of the notch and chop technique in squaring timber can be seen on the right hand scissor-piece in this roof which was rebuilt c.1550. (Photo C.R. Salisbury)

at Harby – just west of Lincoln – being left after the late Civil Wars' (Williamson, 1956, 32).

About the time of the Restoration the demand for indigenous timber far outstripped supply. This was due not only to the depletion of stocks but also to increased demands of the building industry following the Great Fire in London and the need for the navy to repair and build many new ships after the Dutch Wars. There was a particular shortage of oak plank and it seems that the regular purchases of imported deal boards from c.1680 by the Clerk of the Fabric at Lincoln must be ultimately attributable to these causes (Fig. 15.8; Albion, 1926, 217, 225–8). His purchases of oak timber at this time all seem to be very local (e.g. from Ingleby, Saxilby and Reepham) though it is not always clear if the seller is a merchant, an estate owner or a bailiff. The £33 of timber purchased in 1707 (see p.20, above) was felled at its maturity and certainly gives the impression of having come from a well-managed plantation. Though such uniformity of quality is not maintained over the next half century the overall quality is good and it seems likely that the abandonment of the use of oak for cathedral building and repairs by James Essex c.1760 was due as much to his need for timber of exceptional scantling for the new roof of the Chapter House as to the cheaper price of imported Baltic timber (Fig. 15.17). After this time oak has been seldom used in the cathedral until recent years and then it is usually imported.

Acknowledgements

The funding of work at Lincoln Cathedral has been by the SERC, Lincoln Cathedral Preservation Council, the Royal Archaeological Institute and the Robert Kiln Charitable Trust. We are also grateful for the help and support of the Dean and Chapter; Mark Dicken and Roger Parsons, successive co-ordinators of the Preservation Council; Keith Murray and Dr J Baily, successive Surveyors to the Fabric; Peter Hill and John Baily, successive Clerks of the Works and Mick O'Connor, Norman Bonner and other members of the Works staff.

The funding of work at Ely Cathedral has been by the Dean and Chapter, Gonville and Caius College, Cambridge and the Society of Antiquaries of London. We are also grateful for the help and support of the Dean and Chapter; Peter Miller, the Surveyor to the Fabric and David Aldridge and Jane Kennedy of Purcell, Miller, Tritton and Partners, Norwich; Roy Blunt (site agent) and Geoff Carter and staff

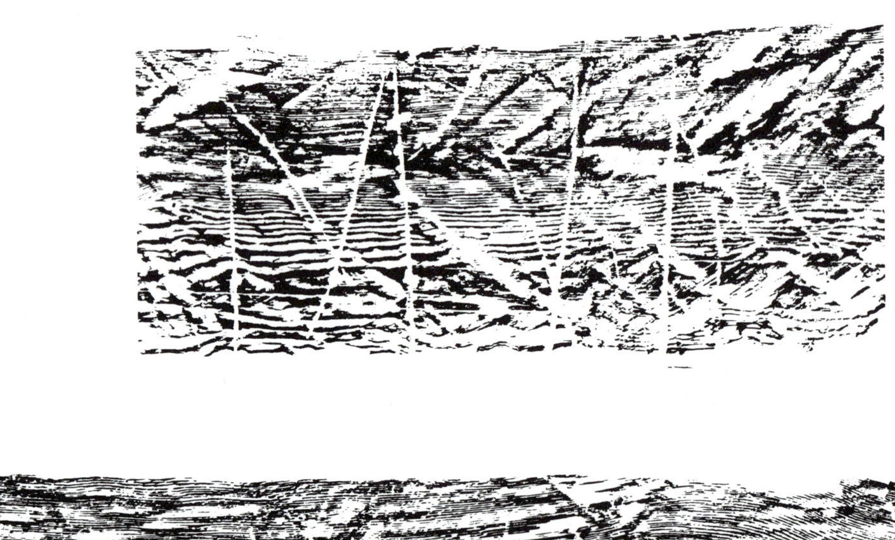

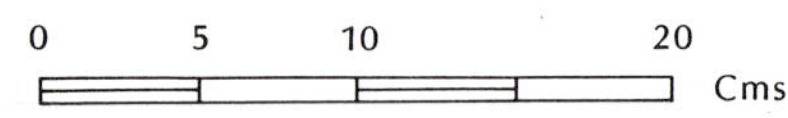

*Fig. 15.17. Rubbings of possible bracking marks (?) on imported Baltic pine in Lincoln Cathedral roofs. **1.** From the Chapter House, c.1760, exported through Riga. **2.** From the Angel Choir, c.1840, probably exported through Memel. C.R. Salisbury and W.G. Simpson.*

of Rattee and Kett of Cambridge, principal contractors for the Cathedral restoration.

The research at Exeter Cathedral was funded by a SERC/CASE award, sponsored by the Royal Albert Museum in Exeter and was undertaken at the Department of Archaeology and Prehistory, University of Sheffield.

We are grateful to Robert Howard and John Esling who have taken and processed all the samples for tree-ring dating; to Professor D Eckstein, Ordinariat für Holzbiologie, Universität Hamburg for the master chronology for Poland; to Chris Salisbury who has taken all the photographs; to David Taylor and Elaine Guilding for the line illustrations and to Maureen Mahany, Elaine Guilding and Chris Salisbury who have assisted with the roof surveys. Our thanks also to friends and colleagues for help, discussion or advice particularly Jenny Alexander, Mike Baillie, Thomas Cocke, Richard Fawcett, Nicola Foot, Richard Gem, Bob Laxton, Norman Pounds, Dorothy Owen and Oliver Rackham.

Finally we are deeply indebted to Mrs Jo Frampton for patiently typing the manuscript.

Notes

1 A worked timber usually has four plane surfaces meeting at four corners. If one or more corners are rounded through meeting the curved outside of the log, the timber is said to be *waney*.

2 Standard terms are used to describe individual timbers. For those who are unfamiliar with them reference should be made to Alcock *et al.*, 1989; Hewett, 1985, or to the glossary at the back of any volume of N. Pevsner's 'Buildings of England' series (Penguin).

3 *Wren Society* 17, 76–7.

4 Lincoln Archives Office. Fabric Accounts Bj/1/8–16.

5 Centre de Recherches sur les Monuments Historiques, *Charpentes*. (Paris, Ministère de la Culture, 1982) i, D6938.

6 British Library, Add. MS. 5842, f. 345; Cambridge University Library. EDC. 4/5/17a.

7 Bacon, J. 1871. *A Record of the Restoration, Repairs ...done in and about Ely Cathedral since 1818*, (unpublished ms. by a former Clerk of the Works. Original in the Chapter Office, Ely. Copy in Cambridge University Library – EDC MS. 37).

8 Richard Fawcett, pers. comm., 1990.

9 *Cal. Patent Rolls*, 1247–58, 506.

10 *Cal. Close Rolls*, 1272–79, 277.

11 Lincoln Archives Office. *D & C*. The Ark, no. 22.

12 *Cal. Close Rolls*, 1224–1227, 106 and 1227–1231, 17.

13 *Cal. Close Rolls*, 1231–1234, 468 and 1234–1237, 45.

14 *Cal.Close Rolls*, 1234–1237, 129.

15 British Library, Cotton MS. Tiberius B. ii, f.248.

16 *Cal. Close Rolls*, 1242–1247, 508 and 1247–1251, 34.

17 British Library. Add. MS. 6772, ff. 222–3.

18 Lincoln Archives Office, Fabric Accounts, 1660–1668. Bj/1/8, f 49. The spelling of the piece here quoted has been modernised.

19 Lincoln Archives Office, *D & C* A/4/13.

20 British Library, 'Some account of Lincoln Cathedral' unpublished ms. by J. Kerrick, 1774. Add. MS. 6763, f. 4.

21 Lincoln Archives Office, Fabric Accounts. Bj/1/15 (e.g. Jan-May, 1763).

22 Lincoln Archives Office, Fabric Accounts. Bj/1/9 (e.g. in 1685).

23 J. R. Pilcher and M. G. L. Baillie, pers. comm., 1981.

24 R. D. Gem, pers. comm., 1988.

25 We owe this suggestion to Nicola Foot. In Foot *et al.*, 1986, p.53 it is incorrectly stated that the rafters are scarfed between the middle and the top collars rather than just below the middle collars as shown in the figure on the opposite page.

26 Riven Baltic timber imported into Britain is always referred to as 'estrich', 'Eastland' (etc.) *boards* never *planks*. In this article board refers to riven, and plank to sawn, timber of similar dimensions.

27 V. C. H., *Nottinghamshire* ii, 113–14, 126–8.

28 See Fig. 15.8 'Timber purchased' *sub anno* 1663.

Addendum

Since this article was completed tree-ring dates for a number of English and Welsh cathedrals, and short notes on the results, have been published in *Vernacular Architecture* as follows:

VA 21 (1990), 37-9: Ely, Lincoln
VA 22 (1991), 40-3: Ely, Lincoln & Salisbury
VA 23 (1992), 51-6 & 59-60: Ely, Lincoln, Chichester, Salisbury & Durham
VA 24 (1993), 40-1 & 52-3: Ely & Chichester
VA 25 (1994), 38 & 40: Brecon
VA 26 (1995), 47-9: Ely, St Albans, Lincoln & Worcester

The following publications have mostly appeared since 1990 and are not otherwise referred to in this paper:

Bonde, N. 1992: Timber Trade in Northern Europe from the 15th to the 17thCentury. *Medieval Europe*, 1992 (5) Exchange and Trade (Medieval Europe, York), 191-6.

de Vries, D.J. 1987: Monumenta dendrochronologisch gedateerd, (2). *Bulletin van de Koninklijke Nederlandsche Oudheidkundige Bond*, 86. no.2, 85-9 (and reports in successive annual volumes).

Hoffsummer, P. 1989: *L'évolution des Toits à deux versants dans le Bassin Mosan: l'apport de la dendrochronologie.* (Université de Liège, Faculté de Philosophie et Lettres, unpublished doctoral thesis).

Hoffsummer, P. 1995: *Les Charpentes de Toitures en Wallonie: typologie et dendrochronologie, 11e - 19e siècle.* 3 vols.(Liège).

Janse, H. 1989: *Houten kappen in Nederland, 1000-1940.* (Delft UP).

Orcel, A., Orcel, C., & Tercier, J. 1991: La dendrochronologie appliquée aux stalles gothique. *Stalles de la Savoie médiévale: catalogue de l'éxposition.* (Musée d'art et histoire, Génève), 75-9.

Simpson, W.G. 1992: Notes on Innovations in Structural Engineering and Carpentry Practice in North-West Europe, 1150-1400. *Medieval Europe, 1992* (3) Technology and Innovation (Medieval Europe, York).

Thun, T. 1992: Norwegian Pine Chronologies. In O. Eggerston (ed.) Tree-rings and Environment: proceedings of the international dendrochronological symposium, Ystad, S. Sweden, 3-9 September, 1990. *Lundqua Report*, 34 (University of Lund), 324-6.

Wazny, T. 1992: Historical Timber Trade and its Implications on Dendrochronological dating. In Eggerston *op cit.*, 331-3.

Bibliography

Adam, J.-P. 1984: *La Construction Romaine* (Paris).

Adam, J.-P. and Varène, P. 1985: La scie hydraulique de Villard de Honnecourt et sa place dans l'histoire des techniques. *Bulletin Monumental*, 143, no. 4, 317–32.

Albion, R.G. 1926: *Forests and Sea Power*. (Cambridge, Mass.).

Alcock, N.W., Barley, M.W., Dixon, P.W. and Meeson, R.A. 1989: *Recording Timber-Framed Buildings: an illustrated glossary*. (London, Council for British Archaeology).

Alexander, J. and Binski, P. (editors), 1987: *Age of Chivalry: Art in Plantagenet England, 1200–1400* (London).

Ashdown, J., Fisher, I. and Munby, J.T. 1988: The Roof Carpentry of Oxford Cathedral. *Oxoniensia*, 53, 195–204.

Baillie, M.G.L. 1977: An Oak Chronology for South-Central Scotland. *Tree-Ring Bulletin*, 37, 33–44.

Baillie, M.G.L. 1982: *Tree-Ring Dating and Archaeology*. (London).

Barefoot, A.C., Hafley, W.L. and Hughes, J.F., 1978: Dendrochronology and the Winchester Excavations. In J.M. Fletcher, (ed.), *Dendrochronology in Europe* (Oxford, BAR, 51, Int. Ser.) 161–70.

Becker, B. 1978: Dendroecological Zones of Central European Forest Communities. In J.M. Fletcher, (ed.), *Dendrochronology in Europe* (Oxford, BAR 51, Int. Ser.), 101–114.

Becker, B. and Giertz–Siebenlist, V. 1970: Eine über 1100 jährige mitteleuropäische Tannenchronologie. *Flora* Abt. B, 159, 310–346.

Black, G., Laxton, R.R. and Simpson, W.G. 1983: The Repair and Dendrochronological Dating of a Medieval Granary from Tadlow, Cambridgeshire. *Proc. of the Cambridge Antiq. Soc.*, 72, 79–87.

Bond, F. 1910: *Woodcarving in English Churches*. 2: Stalls and Tabernacle Work. (London).

Brown, W. 1822: *Three Views of Glasgow Cathedral*. (Glasgow).

Chapman, F.R. 1907: *The Sacrist Rolls of Ely*. (Cambridge).

Colchester, L.S. 1987: *Wells Cathedral*. (London, New Bell's Cathedral Guide).

Cole, R.E.G. (ed.) 1920: Chapter Acts of the Cathedral Church of St Mary of Lincoln, 1547–1559. *Lincoln Rec. Soc.*, 15.

Colvin, H.M. 1971: *Building Accounts of King Henry III*. (Oxford).

Crook, J. 1989: The Romanesque arm and crypt of Winchester Cathedral. *Jnl. B.A.A.* 142, 1–36.

Darrah, R. 1982: Working unseasoned oak. In S. McGrail, (ed.) *Woodworking Techniques before AD 1500*. (Oxford, BAR 129, Int. Ser.), 219–30.

Draper, P. 1979: Bishop Northwold and the cult of St Etheldreda. In *Medieval Art and Architecture at Ely Cathedral* (B.A.A. Conf. Trans., 2), 8–27.

Dugdale, W. 1673: *Monasticon Anglicanum*, (London).

Eckstein, D., Wrobel, S. and Neuebauer, M. 1982: In *Lübecker Schriften zur Archäologie und Kulturgeschichte*, 6.

Eckstein, D., Brauner, G. and Neugebauer, M. 1985: In *Lübecker Schriften zur Archäologie und Kulturgeschichte*, 11.

Eckstein, D., Baillie, M.G.L., and Egger, H. 1984: Dendrochronological Dating. *Handbooks for Archaeologists*, 2 (Strasbourg).

Eckstein, D., Wazny, T. Bauch, J. and Klein, P. 1986: New evidence for the dendrochronological dating of Netherlandish paintings. *Nature*, 320 (3 April) 465–6.

Esling, J., Howard, R.E., Laxton, R.R., Litton, C.D. and Simpson, W.G. 1989: Nottingham University tree-ring dating results. *Vernacular Archit.*, 20, 39–41.

Esling, J., Howard, R.E., Laxton, R.R., Litton, C.D. and Simpson, W.G. 1990: Nottingham University tree-ring dating results. *Vernacular Archit.*, 21 (forthcoming).

Fawcett, R. 1985: *Glasgow Cathedral*. (Edinburgh).

Ferris, I.M. 1989: The archaeological investigation of standing buildings. *Vernacular Archit.*, 20, 12–18.

Fletcher, J.M. and Spokes, P.S. 1964: The origin and development of crown-post roofs. *Medieval Archaeol.*, 8, 152–83.

Fletcher, J.M. 1977: Tree-ring chronologies for the 6th to 16th centuries for oaks of southern and eastern England. *Jnl. Archaeol. Science*, 4, 335–52.

Fletcher, J.M. and Morgan, R. 1981: The dating of doors in the Zouche Chapel, York Minster. *Yorkshire Archaeol. Jnl.*, 53, 45–9.

Fletcher, J.M. and Tapper, M.C. 1984: Medieval artefacts and structures dated by dendrochronology. *Medieval Archaeol.*, 28, 112–132.

Fletcher, J.M. 1986: Dating of art-historical artefacts. *Nature*, 320 (3 April), 466.

Foot, N.D.J., Litton, C.D. and Simpson, W.G. 1986: The high roofs of the east end of Lincoln Cathedral. In *Medieval Art and Architecture at Lincoln Cathedral* (B.A.A. Conf. Trans., 8), 47–74.

Gaitzsch, W. 1983: Arbeitsspuren antiker Handwerker. *Das Rheinische Landesmuseum Bonn Berichte* 3, 38–41.

Gordon, J.F.S. (ed.), 1872: *Glasghu Facies: a view of the city of Glasgow*. by J.M. MacUre (Glasgow).

Haddon-Reece, D., Miles, D.H. and Munby, J.T. 1989: Tree-ring dates from the Ancient Monuments Laboratory, Historic Buildings and Monuments Commission for England. *Vernacular Archit.*, 20, 46.

Hewitt, C.A. 1985: *English cathedral and monastic carpentry*. (Chichester).

Hillam, J. and Morgan, R. 1986: Tree-ring analysis of the Roman timbers. In T. Dyson, (ed.) *The Roman Quay at St Magnus House, London* (London & Middlesex Archaeol. Soc., Special Paper 8), 75–85.

Hillam, J., Morgan, R. and Tyers, I.G. 1986: Sapwood estimates and the dating of short ring sequences. In R.G.W. Ward, (ed.) *Applications of tree-ring studies: current research in dendrochronology and related areas* (Oxford, BAR 333, Int. Ser.).

Holdsworth, C.J. (ed.) 1974: *Rufford Charters*, 2 (Thoroton Soc. Rec. Ser., 30).

Hollstein, E. 1968: Dendrochronologische Untersuchungen an den Domen von Trier und Speyer. *Kunstchronik*, 21, 168–181.

Hollstein, E. 1973: Jahrringchronologie mosel- und saarländischer Rotbuchen. *Mitteilungen des Deutschen Dendrologischen Gesellschaft*, 66, 165–172.

Hollstein, E. 1975: Dendrochronologische untersuchungen an Hölzern des 10. Jh. aus dem Trierer Dom. *Das Munster*, heft 1/2, 20–21.

Hollstein, E. 1980: *Mitteleuropäische Eichenchronologie*. (Mainz am Rhein).

Hughes, M.K., Milsom, S.J. and Leggett, P.A. 1981: Sapwood estimates in the interpretation of tree-ring dates. *Jnl. Archaeol. Science*, 8, no. 4, 381–90.

Innocent, C.F. 1916: *The Development of English Building Construction*. (Cambridge; repr. Newton Abbot, 1971).

Kempf, T.K. 1968: Zur Baugeschichte des Trierer Domes nach Ergebnissen dendrochronologischer Untersuchungen. *Kunstchronik*, 21, 164–8.

Kempf, T.K. 1975: Die ottonische Bauperiode der Trierer

Bischofskirche. *Das Munster*, heft 1/2, 8–20.

Kidson, P. 1986: St Hugh's Choir. In *Medieval Art and Architecture at Lincoln Cathedral.* (B.A.A. Conf. Trans., 8) 27–42.

Kitching, C.J. 1986: Re-roofing old St Paul's Cathedral, 1561–66. *The London Journal*, 12, no. 2, 123–133.

Kuniholm, P.I. and Striker, C.L. 1977: The tie-beam system in the nave arcade of St Eirene: structure and dendrochronology. *Istanbuler Mitteilungen Beiheft*, 18, 229–240.

Kuniholm, P.I. and Striker, C.L. 1983: Dendrochronological investigations in the Aegean and neighbouring regions, 1977–1982. *Jnl. of Field Archaeol.*, 10, 411–420.

Laxton, R.R., Litton, C.D., Simpson, W.G. and Whitley, P.J. 1982: Tree-ring dates for some East Midland buildings. *Trans. Thoroton Soc. of Nottinghamshire*, 86, 73–78.

Laxton, R.R. and Litton, C.D. 1988: *An East Midlands Master Tree-Ring Chronology and its use for Dating Vernacular Buildings*, (Monograph Series III, Dept. of Classical and Archaeol. Stud. University of Nottingham).

Laxton, R.R., Litton, C.D. and Simpson, W.G. 1990: Dating some oak boards from the East Midlands. *East Midlands Archaeol.* (submitted).

Litton, C.D. and Zainodin, H.J. 1987: Grouping methods for dendrochronology. *Science and Archaeology*, 29, 14–24.

Mac Ure, J.C. 1736: *A view of the City of Glasgow.* (Glasgow).

Meeson, R.A. 1989: In defence of selective recording. *Vernacular Archit.*, 20, 18–19.

Mills, C.M. 1988: *Dendrochronology in Exeter and its Application.* (Sheffield, unpublished Ph.D. thesis).

Morgan, R.A. 1982: Tree-ring studies on urban waterlogged wood: problems and possibilities. In A.R. Hall and H.K. Kenward, (eds) *Environmental Archaeology in the Urban Context.* (CBA Research Rep. 3), 31–39.

Morgan, R.A. 1988: *Tree-Ring Studies of Wood used in Neolithic and Bronze Age Trackways from the Somerset Levels*, (Oxford, BAR 184, Brit. Ser.).

Oldrieve, W.T. 1916: The ancient roof of Glasgow Cathedral. *Proc. of the Soc. of Antiq. of Scotland*, 50, 155–73.

Owen, D.M. 1984: *The Making of King's Lynn: a documentary survey.* (Brit. Acad. Rec. Soc. & Econ. Hist. new ser. 9).

Pevsner, N. and Metcalf, P. 1985: *The Cathedrals of England.* (Harmondsworth).

Price, F. 1753: *A Series of ' Observations ' upon ' the Cathedral – Church of Salisbury.* (London).

Rackham, O. 1972: Grundle House: on the quantities of timber in certain East Anglian buildings in relation to local supplies. *Vernacular Archit.*, 3, 3–8.

Rackham, O., Blair, W.J. and Munby, J.T. 1978: The thirteenth-century roofs and floor of the Blackfriars priory at Gloucester. *Medieval Archaeol.,* 22, 105–122.

Rackham, O. 1980: *Ancient Woodland.* (London).

Ruprich-Robert, V. 1881: *L'Architecture Normande.*

Salzman, L.F. 1952: *Building in England before 1540.* (Oxford, 2nd edn., 1967).

Simpson, W.G. 1987: Work on Lincoln Cathedral Roofs. *Archaeol. Jnl.* 144, 443–4.

Simpson, W.G. 1988: A summary report on the survey and dating of the roofs of Lincoln Cathedral during 1987. *Archaeol. Jnl.* 145, 395.

Smith, J.T. 1989: The archaeological investigation of standing buildings: a comment. *Vernacular Archit.*, 20, 20.

Spring, R. 1987: *Salisbury Cathedral.* (London, New Bell's Cathedral Guides).

Stewart, D.J. 1868: *On the Architectural History of Ely Cathedral.* (London).

Sutherland, D.S. and Parsons, D. 1984: The petrological contribution to the survey of All Saints Church, Brixworth, Northamptonshire . *Jnl. B.A.A.*, 137, 45–64.

Tracy, C. 1987: *English Gothic Choir Stalls, 1200–1400.* (Woodbridge).

Tyson, B. 1987: Oak for the navy: a case study, 1700–1703. *Trans. Cumberland and Westmorland Antiq. and Archaeol. Soc.,* 87, 117–126.

Venables, E. 1883: Architectural History of Lincoln Cathedral. *Archaeol. Jnl.* 40, 159–92 and 377–418.

Wazny, T. 1986: Dendrochronologie in Nordpolen. *Acta Interdisciplinaria Archaeologica*, 4, 123–8.

Wharton, H. 1691: *Anglia Sacra.* (London).

Wilcox, R.P. 1981: *Timber and Iron Reinforcement in early Buildings.* (Society of Antiquaries Occasional Paper, n.s. 2).

Williamson, D.M. 1956: *Lincoln Muniments.* (Lincoln, Friends of the Cathedral).

Yeomans, D. 1984: Structural understanding in the eighteenth century: James Essex and the roof of Lincoln cathedral chapter house. *Design Studies*, 5, no. 1, 41–8.

Young, C.R. 1979: *The Royal Forests of Medieval England.* (Leicester).

Mouldings in Medieval Cathedrals

Richard K. Morris

In no other country in Europe is the study of moulding profiles as rewarding as in England, and many of the most significant examples are found in our cathedral churches and their associated buildings. The rewards include documentation for dating, evidence for the sequence of design and construction, and attribution to particular masons; as well as an appreciation of the beauty and inventivity of craftsmanship which many profiles display.

Mouldings of sufficient variety to be useful for some of these purposes appear during the second half of the twelfth century, with the inception of Gothic style and the introduction of new mouldings of northern French origin (Morris 1992). In the north, Archbishop Roger of Pont l'Eveque's choir at York Minster (known only from surviving fragments) and the choir of Ripon Minster, both probably begun in the 1160s, were amongst the pioneers of the new movement with their use of keel and grooved roll mouldings (Wilson 1986, fig. 5). Within a decade, the same spirit of invention is evident in southern cathedrals in the linear bundles of roll mouldings in the arcades of Wells, *c.* 1175 sqq. (Bilson, fig. 4), and in William the Englishman's use of the roll-and-fillet moulding in his contribution to the new east end at Canterbury, 1179–84. Indeed, it is an apt commentary on the growing sophistication of mouldings in the late twelfth century that they permit us to distinguish between William the Englishman's work, as in his capitals and bases of circular plan in the east transept, and that of his French predecessor, William of Sens. The pioneer phase was completed with the emergence of Lincoln Cathedral after 1192 as another major centre of moulding design, to be especially influential in the midlands and the north. The profiles of St Hugh's choir are characterized both by curvilinear and angular mouldings (e.g. the scroll, free-standing fillet, and chamfered mitre),[1] lending a new subtlety to the appearance of the arches.

Workshops like Lincoln and Wells ushered in what one may justifiably describe as 'the golden age' of mouldings in the thirteenth and fourteenth centuries, both for variety and quantity. Complicated mouldings like the three-quarter hollow, wave and double ogee came into regular use in England (Morris 1978a, 1979), though virtually unknown on the continent, and the changing fashions in mouldings during this period provided the nineteenth-century antiquaries with evidence to differentiate between the so-called Early English, Decorated and early Perpendicular styles (e.g. Paley 1847). All English cathedrals possess fabric exhibiting important examples of mouldings from at least one of these periods. Many encompass two of the periods, e.g. Bristol,[2] Ely, Hereford, Lichfield, Lincoln, Oxford, Peterborough, St Albans, St Davids, Salisbury, Southwell: and some all three, e.g. Beverley, Wells, Winchester, Worcester, York.

However, during the later fourteenth century, the range of mouldings in use diminished and the character of the Perpendicular style was established. Throughout the fifteenth and early sixteenth centuries, mouldings therefore appear rather standardized and are generally less helpful, in our current state of knowledge, for the purposes of dating and attribution. More research into their regional variations is required, following the studies already made in Hertfordshire and Norfolk (Roberts 1972a, 1972b, 1973; Fawcett 1975, 1982), though these have concentrated mainly on parish churches. For cathedrals, the foundations for future study have been laid by John Harvey in his published selection of Perpendicular profile drawings from Beverley, Chichester, Durham, Exeter, Gloucester, Hereford, Norwich, Wells, Worcester and York (Harvey 1978, 246–62). With the demise of an overtly Gothic style at the Reformation, there has been a tendency traditionally amongst archaeologists and architectural historians to neglect the continuing potential for the evidence provided by early Renaissance mouldings in this country. In fact, the increased uniformity imposed by printed architectural treatises such as Serlio did not really take effect until well into Queen Elizabeth's reign. In the meantime individual and historically meaningful designs continued to be created (Morris 1989), amongst which must be numbered profiles on some post-Reformation monuments and furnishings in cathedrals, e.g. Bishop Knight's pulpit at Wells, *c.* 1545.

The cathedral is particularly important for the study of mouldings because frequently it offered the most consistent employment for skilled masons in its area and thus became the centre for an influential local workshop or lodge. This may be inferred from case studies such as my own for Hereford, which showed that the tracery, mouldings and ballflower decoration employed in the remodelling of the cathedral's aisles and towers, *c.* 1290–1320, were quoted immediately in numerous churches within a twenty-mile radius (Morris 1973, 1974b). Some of these works appear to have been detailed by the cathedral master mason (e.g. Leominster priory), and others by local masons familiar with the workshop (e.g. Madley parish church). In some instances, cathedral workshops could provide almost continuous employment over several generations, as at Wells between *c.* 1175–1250 and again between *c.* 1280–1350.

'Cathedral' as a term should be interpreted in the widest sense to include all the related ancillary buildings, such as bishops' palaces, conventual buildings and gatehouses, many of which contain fine mouldings. For example, the profiles of Bishop Burnell's hall and chapel in the palace at Wells (*c.* 1280–90) usefully complement the sequence of early Decorated mouldings in the cathedral church (Morris 1974a, 32–6). At Worcester, profiles from the monastic refectory and the prior's guest hall correlate with the rebuilding of the cathedral nave during the fourteenth century (Morris 1978b). And at Norwich, the great gatehouse into the Close, St Ethelbert's Gate, is a well dated structure (*c.* 1316) incorporating one of the very first examples of the double ogee moulding. With regard to recording and conservation of moulded stonework, it should be noted that many of these buildings are owned or administered separately (e.g. Worcester refectory – the cathedral school; St David's bishop's palace – Welsh Heritage; Coventry, remains of the west end of St Mary's cathedral priory – Coventry Corporation).

Creating a database to provide a sound framework for the analysis of mouldings requires a series of independently dateable examples, and in this respect the cathedrals are unrivalled as an architectural group. As a result of the dissolution of the monasteries, the fabric of cathedrals has come down to us in a more complete state than that of most of other great churches, and cathedral records are second only to those of the royal works, for which virtually no buildings survive except castle ruins. The relatively complete fabric accounts for Exeter Cathedral in the first half of the fourteenth century allow us to pinpoint the execution of various parts of the architecture and fittings (Erskine 1981, 1983); and thus to date the moulding profiles with exceptional accuracy (Morris 1991). It was Master Thomas of Witney who introduced the wave moulding to the cathedral workshop shortly after 1317, and the sunk chamfer in 1318; and Master William Joy introduced the double ogee about 1346. No other cathedrals can rival Exeter for this quantity and quality of information, but an adequate chronological framework can be produced for many of them through a cumulation of chronicle evidence, chapter act books, dated monuments and the like. Canterbury, Ely, Gloucester, Wells and York are good examples amongst the major cathedrals. At Gloucester, the *Historia et Cartularium* not only provides useful information to chart the development of the incipient Perpendicular style there after 1329, with its distinctive vocabulary of mouldings new to the region (see Harvey 1961, 134–7); but also one of the few dateable examples of ballflower work and associated mouldings in the area, in the nave south aisle, 1318–29 (Morris 1985, 100–103).

Few documentary dates should be taken at their face value, however, without interpreting their application to the standing structure, a process in which mouldings play their part. The date of 1372 traditionally associated with the monastic refectory at Worcester, on the strength of a brief entry in the seventeenth-century notebook of Prebendary Hopkins, looks too late by about forty years for the style of the existing building. However, the refectory pulpit can be demonstrated to belong to the 1370s, from the detail of its capitals, and is probably the work implied in Hopkins' note; thus indicating that his information is likely to have been extracted from a medieval roll or record which has since disappeared (Morris 1978b, 126–7).

Some cathedrals are almost devoid of documentary records for their fabric, such as Lichfield and Chester, and it is common to find major parts of many others completely lacking in dates, e.g. the smart thirteenth-century north transept of Hereford. The analysis of mouldings and worked stonework comes into its own in such situations, as one of the tools of the archaeologist and architectural historian. In the nineteenth century, Robert Willis, the master of this art, noted the paucity of recorded dates for the long drawn-out rebuilding of the nave of Worcester Cathedral between *c.* 1320 and 1377, and proceeded to diagnose the main stages of reconstruction from the evidence of the fabric (Willis 1863, 108–117 and figs 4, 5). My own research at Worcester, based specifically on the mouldings (Morris 1978b), has confirmed his conclusion that, unusually, one side of the nave (north) was rebuilt before the other (south); and has also discounted Brakspear's assertion that the change from Decorated to Perpendicular between the two sides resulted from the advent of the Black Death. In fact, the new style appears to have been an aesthetic preference introduced by a fresh master mason about 1340. Another cathedral where this type of investigation has produced fruitful results is Chester, as interpreted in the researches of Virginia Jansen (1979) and John Maddison (1983). As Maddison (1983, 31) aptly remarks about the choir of the cathedral:

> There can be few buildings in England that manage to compress quite so many evident hesitations and changes of design into so small a compass, and it is this phenomenon which makes it such an interesting structure to the student of medieval masonry.

From a close examination of the details of the monastic choir (*c.* 1260–1340), he has been able to disentangle an intricate archaeological sequence of development in the fabric and relate the stages to at least six master masons with their own preferences for mouldings. His article is a modern model of its kind, and essential reading for everyone interested in proof of the value of studying mouldings.

Perhaps this methodology is most beneficially applied when parts of a cathedral survive only as fragmentary ruins or as loose stones, and identification and dating come to rely very substantially on specialist knowledge of medieval masonry. Frequently they provide the only detailed information about episodes in a cathedral's history no longer represented in the standing fabric, and it is therefore vital that such remains are properly appreciated. The only visible remnants of Old St Paul's in London are the partial foundations of the chapter house and several hundred loose stones on shelving in the south triforium of Wren's cathedral (Fig. 16.1). It may seem surprising, given the outstanding architectural importance of Old St Paul's, that a definitive catalogue of these stones has never been made. In addition, the south-east corner respond of the fire-damaged medieval crypt still exists below ground in St Paul's churchyard, and its detail substantiates the general accuracy of Hollar's famous pre-fire engraving of the crypt's interior (Morris 1990, 77–79). Unfortunately its surviving features in Purbeck marble are decaying through damp, and conservation of this important vestige of London's medieval cathedral is urgently required.

In the case of another lost church, the cathedral priory of St Mary at Coventry, a considerable amount of thirteenth-century moulded stonework exists *in situ* in the exposed west bay of the nave, and a comparative analysis of this material with contemporary midland sites such as Lichfield could produce more precise information with regard to date and design affiliations (Morris 1994). Lichfield is also a cathedral like St Paul's with a significant collection of loose stones, and these were catalogued between 1983 and 1985 at the request of the dean and chapter. Amongst them are the only surviving stones from the Ronanesque predecessor of the present church, and numerous high quality pieces from lost Gothic furnishings. These include the late medieval reredos of the high altar, obviously imported from a workshop in the limestone belt (Morris 1993). Such collections also frequently contain high quality pieces of sculpture, as at Winchester, where the displaced statuary from the high altar reredos has been recently identified and reconstructed by Phillip Lindley (1989).

Modern archaeological excavations within cathedral precincts are likely to add to the number of worked stones requiring storage, recording and analysis. When the site of the monastic chapter house at St Albans was excavated in 1978, an unexpectedly large quantity of fragmentary worked stones was recovered. Specialist examination has allowed most of these to be identified with the documented remodelling of the chapter house in the 15th-century (*c.* 1452–60 and *c.* 1480–92); and provided enough

Fig. 16.1. London, St Paul's Cathedral. Moulded stones from Old St Paul's, mainly from the chapter house and cloister, stored on shelving in the south triforium of the present cathedral. (Photo: R.K. Morris)

information for the main features of its elaborate lierne vault and window tracery to be reconstructed (Morris forthcoming/b).

Where cathedrals contain examples of documented works by master masons, they provide evidence for the attribution of a set of profiles and associated architectural details to a named designer. Close study of the mouldings of the chapter house foundations from Old St Paul's, and of relevant pieces from the collection of loose stones (Fig. 16.1), has allowed the architectural vocabulary of Master William Ramsey (fl. 1323–49) to be defined (Harvey 1961; Wilson 1980). Ramsey was exempted from jury service in 1332 on account of his engagement on the cathedral chapter house and cloister (Harvey 1984, 242) and, as king's master mason, pioneered many features of the Perpendicular style, including the use of the double ogee moulding and bell bases (Morris 1978a, 35–9; 1979, 28–9). The architectural details of his documented intervention at Lichfield Cathedral in 1337 corroborate his style. At the same time the fabric there indicates that some moulded stones cut before his arrival were used up in the east bay of the retrochoir clerestory before his own profiles were introduced. Practical considerations of this kind often fudge the break in mouldings between the builds of two consecutive masters. It is evident that in some cathedrals the profiles of standard components like capitals and vault ribs might be carried on from one master to another with only minor modifications, e.g. the rib profiles of Exeter, 1280s–1340s, under Masters Roger, William Luve and Thomas of Witney (Morris 1991, 62).

Numerous instances could be listed where the name of a master is unrecorded, but where the mouldings and other minutiae testify to the arrival of a new designer whose style can be identified in other buildings. Even at a smaller cathedral like St Asaph's, the use of wave and sunk chamfer mouldings for the rebuilding after the burning of 1282 permits a convincing association to be made with contemporary work at Caernarfon Castle, and thus a tentative attribution to Henry of Ellerton, master of works at the castle after 1309 (Maddison 1978, figs. 27, 28). To take another case, under discussion by architectural historians and archaeologists at the time of writing, the famous tower and spire of Salisbury Cathedral has been disassociated (correctly) from a document of 1334 signed between the dean and chapter and Master Richard of Farleigh (Harvey 1984, 106; Spring 1987, 15–17); and Roy Spring has suggested a new date as early as 1280. However, any dating for the tower needs to take account of the striking similarities of the mouldings laden with ballflower ornament to those of Wells chapter house (1290s–1306) and especially to the crossing tower at Hereford (*c.* 1310–19). the profiles of mullions and window jambs at both towers, not to mention other details, are so similar that there must be a direct link between the two works (Morris forthcoming/a).

Another very recent case illustrates how useful discoveries can still be made from a close study of the standing fabric, especially in areas 'behind the scenes'. The Decorated architecture of Wells Cathedral is generally regarded as well researched, and yet the details of the crossing tower (documented in building, 1315–22) have been neglected,[3] because it has been assumed that the Perpendicular remodelling of the tower after 1439 was more extensive than is actually the case. On a recent visit into the upper stage of the tower, the author was surprised to discover not only that the Decorated mouldings were still complete, but that their profiles and associated details were instantly recognizable as by the same master who detailed the main features of the choir of Bristol Cathedral. The arrangement of large ogee mouldings in the piers and arches is especially characteristic (Fig. 16.2). This discovery is particularly helpful because the Wells tower supplies a closely dated comparison for the extremely important but more loosely dated work at Bristol (1298–*c.* 1340), and implies that the most memorable features of the latter were designed no earlier than the second or third decade of the fourteenth century.

The mouldings of furnishings in cathedrals can be studied to equal effect. The author's survey of mouldings in major churches in the Decorated period (Morris 1978, 1979) revealed, for example, that the elaborately moulded piers and bases of the reredos (shrine platform) at Beverley Minster (1330s) were cut from the same templates as those of the pulpitum at Exeter Cathedral (1317–25). All the pieces are in Purbeck marble, thus adding testimony to the geographical extent of the trade in highly detailed prefabricated components in this material, emanating from Corfe (the Exeter fabric accounts make it clear that Corfe was the source of supply). But what is particularly interesting is that the combined evidence of mouldings and documents suggests that the designs were originally supplied by the Exeter Cathedral master, Thomas of Witney, to the Canon family of Corfe, who in turn re-employed them a decade later for a suitable job at Beverley (Morris 1991, 79, note 14).

For those charged with the care of medieval fabric of our cathedrals, I hope that this selection of case studies has demonstrated that worked stones are historical documents, and as important as more conventional records in cathedral libraries. When plans are laid to erect a scaffold for essential works (e.g. roofing, glazing, etc.), the cathedral archaeologist should make arrangements for the drawing of any profiles not yet recorded and not otherwise easily accessible. Whenever moulded stonework actually needs to be repaired or replaced, accurate full-size drawings should be made of the repertoire of profiles found on the existing stones, as part of a complete archaeological record. For example, for a window of uniform design, a sample of profiles would typically consist of sections through a jamb, the arch, one or more mullions, a representative point in the tracery (if different in profile to the mullion), the sill, and capitals and bases if present. Most important of all, the resultant drawings must be deposited in a publicly accessible place connected with the cathedral (e.g. the cathedral library), and their existence notified to the National Monuments

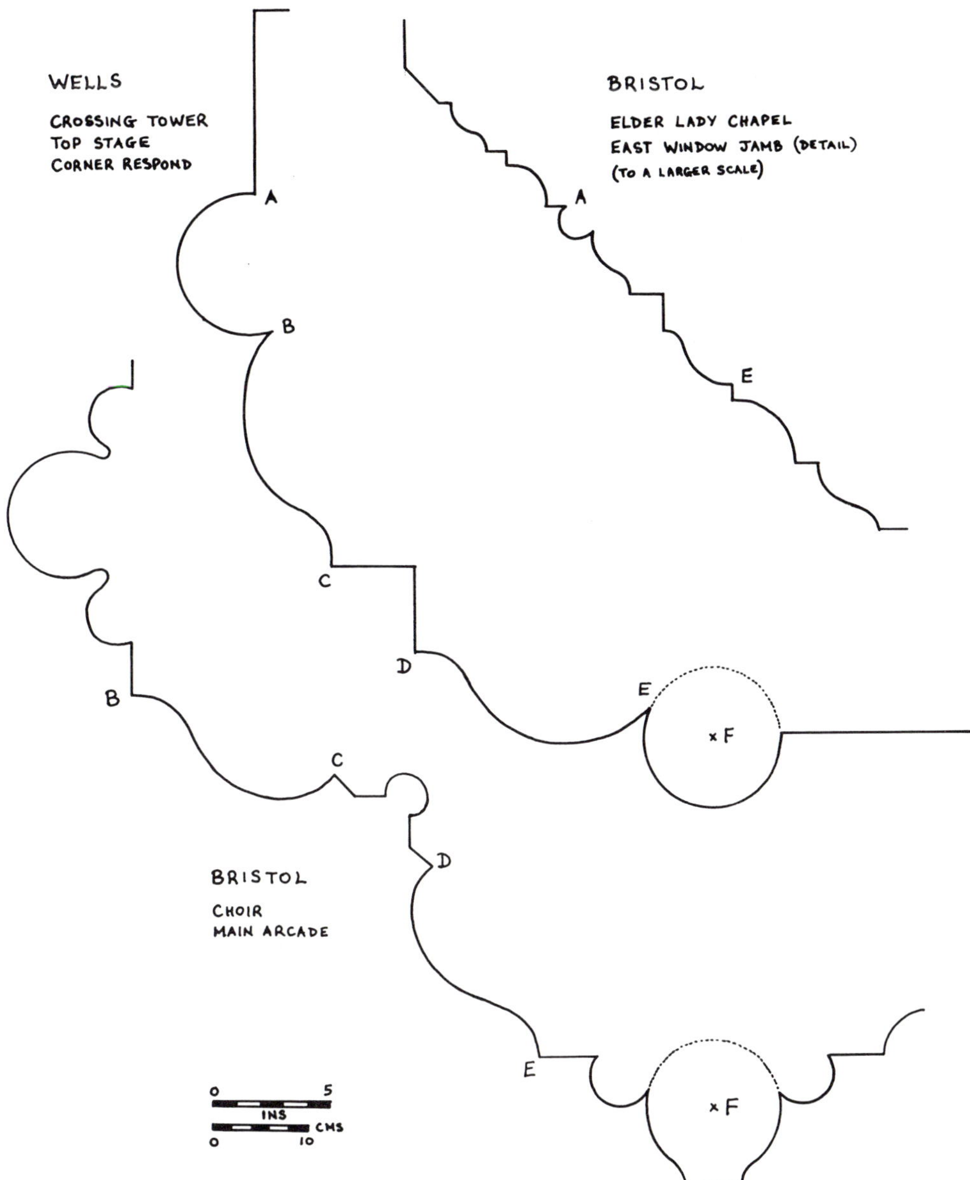

Fig. 16.2. Wells Cathedral crossing tower and Bristol Cathedral, profiles compared. Note the use at Wells and in the Bristol main arcade of large ogee mouldings (EC, DE) and shafts of similar radius (F). Also the same design of a roll moulding followed by a pair of affronted ogee mouldings at Wells and in the east window of the Elder Lady Chapel at Bristol (A-E). (Drawing: R.K. Morris)

Record. All too often, potentially useful records made during restoration work (e.g. photographs, working drawings) are dispersed – typically by the architect or contractor – without the client receiving copies for a permanent record.

Collections of measured drawings made by antiquaries or architects during the Gothic Revival period are a useful resource, as they can be used to check existing mouldings against any changes made in more recent restorations or loss of detail through weathering. Neale (1978) for St Albans is an excellent example, published just before Lord Grimthorpe's severe restorations. Many splendid profile drawings are also to be found in various nineteenth-century 'sketchbook' publications (e.g. the *Architectural Association Sketchbook*, 1867 sqq.), for which a comprehensive topographical index was published earlier this century (Victoria and Albert Museum 1908). Where profiles need to be drawn today, the template former (or 'moulding comb') is an invaluable tool. In addition to a small commercially available template former, the author uses one specially made, 12 inches square, incorporating slats of reinforced plastic sliding in a metal frame, with bolts at one end for adjusting the compression (Fig. 16.3). The basis of this design was the brain-child of Peter Lasko, when he was chairman of the Fine Arts Department at the University of East Anglia, inspired by nineteenth-century devices such as Willis' 'cymagraph'. Modern template formers provide a quicker method for producing full-size profiles than the traditional architectural measured drawing, provided care is

Fig. 16.3. The large Warwick template former. The width between the metal clamps at each end is 12 inches (30.5 cms); the pair of knurled adjusting bolts is visible on the right. (Photo: Robert Kilgour)

taken to ensure the accuracy of the copy (see further the author's contribution in Council for British Archaeology 1987, 36–9). The Warwick Mouldings Archive can provide further advice on this, as well as on all matters related to the recording and analysis of moulding profiles.[4]

Notes

1 For the freestanding fillet, see Morris 1978a, 46–9. The chamfered mitre is an angle-fillet with a flat termination, resembling in section three sides of an octagon, undercut by hollow mouldings (Morris 1979, 12, 'polygonal termination'; Morris 1992, 11-15).

2. In this paper the term 'cathedral' denotes all churches of cathedral status, whether bestowed in the middle ages, at the Reformation (as in the case of Bristol), or more recently.

3. Except by Dr John Harvey; it was his interest in the tower as a possible work by Master Thomas of Witney which prompted me to take another look at it.

4 . Dr R.K. Morris, Warwick Mouldings Archive, History of Art Department, Warwick University, Coventry CV4 7AL.

Bibliography

Bilson, J. 1928: Notes on the earlier architectural history of Wells Cathedral. *Archaeol, Jnl.* 85, 23–68,

Council for British Archaeology 1987: *Recording worked stones* (London).

Erskine, A. 1981: *The Accounts of the fabric of Exeter Cathedral, 1279–1353: part 1 1279–1326* (Devon and Cornwall Record Society, new ser, 24).

Erskine, A. 1983: *The Accounts of the fabric of Exeter Cathedral, 1279–1353: part 2 1328–1353* (Devon and Cornwall Record Society, new ser. 26).

Fawcett, R. 1975: Later Gothic architecture in Norfolk, an examination of the work of some individual architects in the 14th and 15th centuries (unpublished Ph.D. thesis, University of East Anglia).

Fawcett, R. 1982: St Mary at Wiveton in Norfolk, and a group of churches attributed to its mason. *Antiq, Jnl. 62*, part 1, 35–56,

Harvey, J.H. 1961: Origin of the Perpendicular style. In M.E. Jope, (ed.), *Studies in building history, essays in recognition of the work of B.H.St.J. O'Neil* (London).

Harvey, J.H. 1978: *The Perpendicular style 1330–1485* (London).

Harvey, J.H. 1984: *English mediaeval architects, a biographical dictionary down to 1550* (Gloucester); and *Supplement* to the same (Pinhorns, Isle of Wight, 1987).

Jansen, V. 1979: Superposed wall passages and the triforium elevation of St Werburg's, Chester. *Jnl. Soc. Archit. Hist. (U.S.A.)* 38/3, 223–43.

Lindley, P. 1989: The Great screen of Winchester Cathedral I. *Burlington Magazine* 131, 604–15.

Maddison, J. 1978: Decorated architecture in the north-west midlands, an investigation of the work of provincial masons and their sources (unpublished Ph.D. thesis, Manchester University),

Maddison, J, 1983: The Choir of Chester Cathedral. *Chester Archaeol. Soc. Jnl.* 66, 31–46.

Morris, R.K. 1973: The Local influence of Hereford Cathedral in the Decorated period. *Woolhope Naturalists Field Club Trans* 41/1, 48–67.

Morris, R.K. 1974a: The Remodelling of the Hereford aisles. *Jnl. B.A.A.* 38, 21–39.

Morris, R.K, 1974b: The Mason of Madley, Allensmore and Eaton Bishop. *Woolhope Naturalists Field Club Trans* 41/2, 180–97.

Morris, R.K. 1978a: The Development of later Gothic mouldings in England 1250–1400, part I. *Archit. Hist.* 21, 18–57.

Morris, R.K. 1978b: Worcester nave: from Decorated to Perpendicular. *Medieval Art and Architecture at Worcester Cathedral*, (B.A.A. Conf. Trans 1), 116–43.

Morris, R.K. 1979: The Development of later Gothic mouldings in England c. 1250–1400, part II. *Archit. Hist.* 22, 1–48.

Morris, R.K. 1985: Ballflower work in Gloucester and its vicinity. *Medieval Art and Architecture at Gloucester and Tewkesbury*, (B.A.A. Conf. Trans 7), 99–115.

Morris, R.K. 1989: Windows in early Tudor country houses. In D. Williams, (ed.), *Early Tudor English* (Woodbridge, Harlaxton symposium proceedings for 1987), 125–38.

Morris, R.K. 1990: The New Work at Old St Paul's and its place in English 13th-century architecture. *Medieval Art, Architecture and Archaeology in London*, (B.A.A. Conf. Trans for 1984).

Morris, R.K. 1991: Thomas of Witney at Exeter, Winchester

and Wells. *Medieval Art and Architecture at Exeter Cathedral*, (B.A.A. Conf. Trans 11), 57-84.

Morris, R.K. 1992: An English Glossary of medieval mouldings: with an introduction to mouldings *c*. 1040-1240. *Archit. Hist.* 35, 1-17.

Morris, R.K. 1993: The Lapidary collections of Lichfield Cathedral. *Medieval Archaeology and Architecture at Lichfield Cathedral*, (B.A.A. Conf. Trans 13), 101-108.

Morris, R.K. 1994: The lost cathedral priory church of St. Mary, Coventry. In G. Demidowicz (ed.), *Coventry's First Cathedral* (Stamford), 16-66.

Morris, R.K. forthcoming/a: The Style and buttressing of Salisbury Cathedral tower, *Medieval Art and Architecture at Salisbury Cathedral*, (B.A.A. Conf. Trans 17, in press).

Morris, R.K. forthcoming/b: The 15th-century chapter house of St Albans Abbey. In M. Biddle and B. Kjolbye-Biddle (eds), *Report on the 1978 excavations of the chapter house site at St Albans Cathedral*, (St Albans and Herts. Archit. and Archaeol. Soc., forthcoming).

Neale, J. 1878: *The Abbey church of St Albans, Hertfordshire* (London).

Paley, F.A. 1847: *A Manual of Gothic mouldings* 2nd edn. (London).

Roberts, E. 1972a: Robert Stowell. *Jnl. B.A.A.* 35, 24–38.

Roberts, E. 1972b: Thomas Wolvey, mason. *Archaeol. Jnl.* 129, 119–44.

Roberts, E. 1973: Perpendicular architecture in Herefordshire, a search for medieval architects through mouldings (unpublished Ph.D. thesis, London University).

Spring, R. 1987: *Salisbury Cathedral* (London, New Bell's Cathedral Guides).

Victoria and Albert Museum 1908: *Topographical index to measured drawings of architecture in principal British architectural publications* (London).

Willis, R. 1863: The Architectural history of the cathedral and monastery at Worcester. *Archaeol. Jnl.* 20, 83–132.

Wilson, C. 1980: The Origins of the Perpendicular style and its development to c. 1360 (unpublished Ph.D. thesis, London University).

Wilson, C. 1986: The Cistercians as 'missionaries of Gothic' in northern England. In C. Norton and D. Park, (eds), *Cistercian art and architecture in Britain* (Cambridge), 86–116.

Masons' Marks and Stone Bonding

Jennifer S. Alexander

Introduction

In the search to understand the way that cathedrals were designed, laid out and built the masonry of the buildings themselves is now being scientifically examined. The advent of photogrammetry has made accurate recording of whole sections of major buildings feasible and has greatly facilitated the planning of restoration projects (Dallas 1980). Petrological studies, that combine geological and archaeological methodologies, can provide detailed pictures of the sources of building stone (Sutherland and Parsons 1984).

Recent research has been focussed on the surface details of the masonry; on the marks made by stonemasons during the construction of the building. These marks, which served a number of different purposes, are to be found on dressed and squared walling stone and on mouldings, but rarely on rubble, or less well finished stonework. The marks were made as part of the construction process and acted as a means of communication that was understood by the workforce using it. First recorded during nineteenth-century antiquarian studies of major buildings, the distribution patterns of masons' marks are now being analysed by computer to reveal valuable insights into the working practices of the medieval cathedral builders.

Marks were made on stonework by the masons involved in constructing the building for a number of reasons. Preliminary design drawings were worked out on the materials available to hand, either before these were used in the building, or afterwards, with the walls themselves used as a form of drawing board. Most marks however were a form of autograph, to identify an individual mason's work, and consist of a series of intersecting lines in a geometric pattern. Other marks, of similar form, were used to ensure correct assembly of critical sections of stonework. A further type of mark identified the quarry source.

Banker Marks

The majority of marks found on masonry are those made by banker masons working in the lodge who prepared the stone ready for use by the walling masons. Marks were needed when a piece-work system was operated, to identify an individual mason's work for the paymaster. Evidence for this system can be found in some of the surviving building accounts. The contract between Richard of Stow, mason, and the dean and chapter of Lincoln for work on the cathedral in 1306 specifies different types of payment for work on plain walling and carved stone. The carved work was to be paid for by the day whereas the plain walling was to be paid for by measure (Pownall 1789). One would therefore expect to find marks on the blocks of the walling built under this contract, the upper levels of the crossing tower, and that is indeed the case.

When masons were paid regular wages they had no need to mark their work. Exeter cathedral has few masons' marks on the walling of the eastern parts of the structure, for which the fabric rolls survive in part. The rolls reveal that the masons and other craftsmen were paid weekly wages on a regular basis, with occasional payments 'at task' for specific pieces of work such as carved bosses. The masons would not therefore have needed to mark the walling stone (Erskine 1981).

The banker or masons' marks have been cut freehand using a punch or a narrow edged chisel struck decisively (Fig. 17.1). Marks are primarily based on intersecting straight lines with considerable variety in both the numbers of lines used and the complexity of the forms. Most are made up of two, three or four strokes, fewer have five or six strokes and a very few have more (Fig. 17.2). Marks may resemble masons' tools, such as axes, and one mark found in Lincoln cathedral is clearly based on a mason's square, with particular care taken to reproduce the irregular lengths of the arms of the square and the angles of the ends (Fig. 17.3). Another mark may have been used by a capital sculptor since it is shaped like a lobe of stiff-leaf foliage, although curves are not often found and circles, where they appear are obviously drawn with dividers.

Some marks are clearly based on the same design, but have been given extra strokes to differentiate between them. For example, a series of marks from Lincoln cathedral that resemble the letter W seem to form a 'family group'. 4wl is the basic form of a spread capital W, 5wl

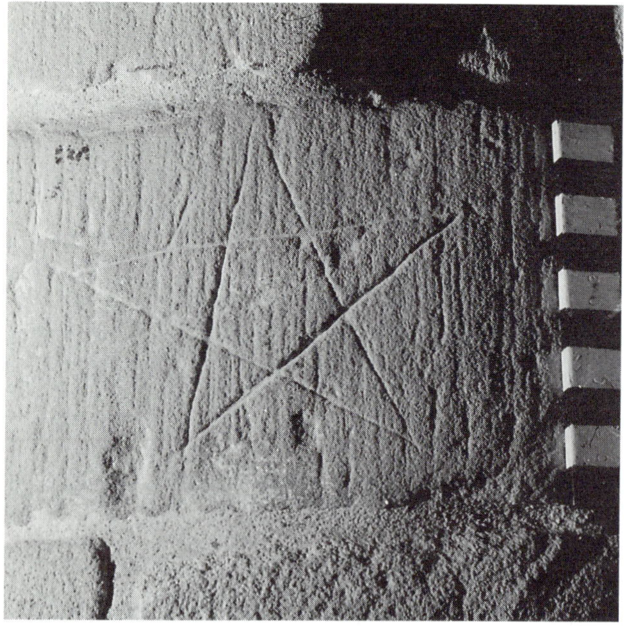

Fig. 17.1. Banker mason's mark. Buildwas abbey chapter house pier. c. 1135–1200.

Fig. 17.2a⇑ and b⇐. Banker masons' marks. Lincoln cathedral Angel Choir east wall. c. 1255–80.

Fig. 17.3. Banker mason's mark in the shape of a mason's square on ashlar block dressed with a claw chisel. Lincoln cathedral Angel Choir walling above high vault c. 1255–80.

is a W with a bar joining up the top and 7wl and 8wl have extra short strokes at the ends of the arms (for this nomenclature see below). It seems likely that there may be a formal relationship within these 'family groups' of marks, with perhaps the simpler forms used by the foremen and the more complex ones by the men working under him. Alternatively the more complex marks could be those of the men trained by a particular mason who have adapted his mark for their own. This is a practice that is still current; one of the masons employed in 1987 at Wollaton Hall, Nottingham, derived his mark from that of the mason to whom he was apprenticed.

Banker marks are easily identified since they were made before the blocks of stone were installed. The chisel strokes of the marks do not extend over neighbouring stones even when the tool has been dragged across the surface of the block and the mark has not been finished cleanly. The same mark can often be seen in different orientations on regularly shaped blocks of plain walling. Marks are also frequently found sealed behind free-standing shafts or sections of blind arcading, and set in positions where they could not have been cut after installation.

Moulded stone, for vault ribs as well as for doorways and windows, was also marked, examples can be seen on door mouldings at Lincoln (Fig. 17.4) and on window tracery at Beverley Minster (Morris 1979, 64). More elaborate work, which may have been the work of a single mason, may only have a single mark.

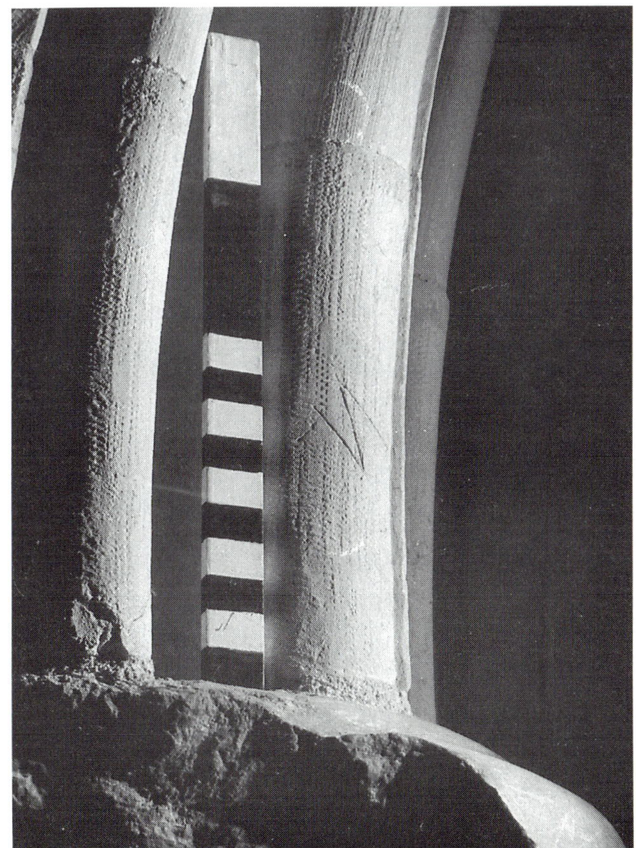

Fig. 17.4. Banker mason's mark on archmoulding. Lincoln cathedral north-east transept north chapel c. 1192–1200.

Assembly marks

Marks of similar appearance but different purpose can sometimes be found. Those based on a numbering system acted as assembly marks to ensure correct installation of critical sections of stonework. They closely resemble the carpenters' marks found on roof trusses and have been made for the same reason. An example of their use can be seen on the window jambs of the chancel windows of North Luffenham church in Rutland where each stone is marked with a loose version of a Roman numeral to ensure correct assembly of the window. The sequence is I, II, III, IIII, IV, IIV, V, IIIIV, IX. A very similar system has been recorded in St Laurence's church Ludlow, for the construction of the west door (Jackson and Northway 1976).

Assembly marks were also used on the ribs of bosses that had to be inserted in a particular orientation and they can often be seen on the mating faces of dismantled bosses. At Reims cathedral Coulton (1953, 158) has described the use of this system to ensure correct positioning of the column figures of the west front portals.

A type of assembly mark may be found cut at the edge of one stone and continued across the joint to a second stone. These marks, usually consisting of numbers of straight lines, were made before the stone was used in the structure and ensure precise alignment of critical blocks within courses. At Lincoln cathedral the courses of curved stonework of the tops of the parapet stair turrets show both types of assembly marks, each course has its own numeral and stones within each course have marks across their joints (Fig. 17.5). Assembly marks can also be found in the pre-medieval period, their use has been recorded for example on column drums and capitals of classical Roman buildings (Adam 1984, 54).

Quarry marks

Stone buildings or more correctly, stone faced buildings under construction today have stone delivered to site ready for assembly in the structure. The stones are marked with several different marks, to identify where in the building the stone is to be placed, its orientation and also the mark of the quarry where it has been cut. These marks are more usually stencilled on to the surface and like all marks today, placed on the bedding plane of the stone.

Quarry marks have been used since the period of ancient Greece and we have evidence of their use from medieval accounts. Sometimes these marks were to identify a particular grade of stone as the accounts from the 1440s for Gloucester castle show. They refer to a mason and his servant sorting stone at the quarry for the works and marking the stones of sufficient quality for the building (Salzman 1952, 126). Selecting stone at the quarry in this way was part of the master mason's job, as the Louth building accounts from the sixteenth-century demon-

Fig. 17.5. Assembly marks. Left, to identify the course and centre, to line up the blocks within the course. Lincoln cathedral Angel Choir inner face of turret of south parapet stair c. 1255–80.

strate. Initially the master, with a lay overseer, travelled to the quarry which was about thirty miles away, to inspect the stone. During the busiest building period however, a masons' lodge was actually set up in the quarry and stone was prepared there before transport (LAO Louth Par 7/1). The practice continued beyond the medieval period and the selection mark used by Sir Christopher Wren has been recorded at the Portland stone quarries in Dorset (Beaumont-Slegge 1950, 73).

Pre-medieval masons' marks

Marks resembling masons' marks have been recorded on stone structures from as far back as the Bronze Age. Sir Arthur Evans recorded several sequences of marks in the buildings at Knossos which he used as part of the dating evidence, as well as marks that were clearly assembly marks on terracotta well linings (Evans 1930). Detailed recording and analysis of these marks has suggested that the marks may have had a less direct role in the construction process, their relationship to early writing perhaps giving them a more mystical significance (Hood 1987). Inscribed marks from the later Greek and Roman periods have been identified more simply as constructional masons' marks with different types used by quarrymen, stone transporters and walling masons; these large and easily visible marks have been noted at sites throughout the Mediterranean region (Adam 1984, 42).

Marks found on classical buildings are also based on intersecting lines and have similar shapes to those on medieval and later buildings. This similarity of form was noted by writers in the nineteenth-century and it has added a level of complexity to their interpretation. Godwin, whose paper was one of the first to draw attention to masons' marks in medieval buildings, remarked on the similarity between the marks he had recorded and the characters of a Punic inscription found at Carthage, which he described as 'a curious coincidence' (Godwin 1844, 120). More recently the apparent close resemblance between medieval marks from Salisbury and certain Minoan marks in eastern Crete has been used as evidence that these Minoan marks did function as constructional masons' marks, although without explanation of why this should be so (Hood 1987, 210).

To understand why the marks should be similar, the cultural context of masons' marks needs to be examined, Gaur (1984, 23–5) has noted the importance of geometric signs and symbols for all societies in which writing was restricted to a particular group, where they were used as a simpler means of identification accessible to others. They represent a utilitarian form of writing and are closely related to the primary elements from which script developed. The geometric form of these signs, abstract designs based on triangles, zigzag lines, combs, loops, spirals etc. found first in prehistoric and later rock drawings, reappears at all periods in connection with property marking, as marks of identification and to indicate authorship. Masons' marks should be seen as part of this group of 'property' marks. The use of masons' marks as personal identification marks on chisels at the Ham Hill quarries in the 1940s perhaps completes the sequence (Beaumont-Slegge 1950, 78).

Masons' marks had ceased to be displayed on the face of the stone by the seventeenth-century (Morris 1979, 64). By this time stones were more usually marked on the bed rather than on a dressed face, although marks continue to be seen on the face of stone used for bridges and aqueducts from the eighteenth century (Cunnington 1946, 379). There seems to have been a revival in the nineteenth-century when masons' marks were first studied. A good example of a late nineteenth-century banker mark can be seen on stone used in Pearson's rebuilding of the arcading next to the chapter house at Lincoln cathedral

Fig. 17.6. Banker mason's mark. Lincoln cathedral east cloister rear wall arcading c. 1890

cloister, which has erroneously been identified as a medieval mark (Coulton 1953, 147 n.2) (Fig. 17.6).

Documentation of masons' marks

There are few documentary records of marks and their use, with one notable exception. The sketchbook of Villard de Honnecourt has drawings of marks on the templates for certain mullions, jambs and bases for use at Reims cathedral. The same marks also appear on two of the elevation drawings, f.30v and f.31v, at the sites where the templates were to be used (Erlande-Brandenburg *et al.* 1986, pls. 60, 62, and 63). The presence of these marks on elevation drawings from Reims but not on other similar drawings in the sketchbook has led Bucher (1979, 23) to suggest that they show Villard's direct involvement at Reims. He regards the masons' marks as a record of the work assigned by Villard, in his role of sub-contractor from *c.*1228–33, to the masons that he supervised. The mark of the mason responsible for each section was entered on the relevant part of the elevation drawing and logged on the template drawing. It is possible however that they simply demonstrate Villard's method of recording the site use of certain templates (See Addendum).

There was no form of registration for masons' marks in England and a strictly *ad hoc* method of assigning marks existed (Davis 1954, 44). A registration system would have needed to be like that used for heraldry in which individuals demonstrated their right to a particular device by reference to a central register. Not only does no such register survive but more importantly, no reference is made to it in any of the regulations governing the conduct of stonemasons' operations, The only reference to any documentation of masons' marks is contained in the Schaw Statutes of 1598 published by Knoop and Jones (1949, 260). The Statutes lay down the conditions of employment for masons in Scotland and differ in several respects from English ordinances. The section that covers admission to the lodge requires that a new mason must enter his name and masons' mark in the lodge book. It should therefore be possible to compile a list of named Scottish masons and their marks from lodge books where they survive.

The shortage of documentary evidence has led some writers, Coulton for example, to make suggestions based on the well documented practices of masons in Germany (1953, 157). There, named masons are found depicted in sculpture or wall painting, holding a square or level and compasses and with their masons' mark clearly displayed in a heraldic form. At Bamberg, Erasmus Braun is represented on a corbel as a full length figure, holding his mallet in one hand, with a shield bearing his mason's mark beside him from *c.*1570. The head of Hans Augstaindreyer, a mason of *c.*1470, is depicted in the chapel of Tubingen castle on one shield held by an angel while his mark occupies a second (Gerstenberg 1966, 161, 185).

There is no tradition of this display in England and France and depictions of actual masons are harder to identify. Masons are shown at work in manuscript illustrations and in sculpture, but no examples survive that show a mason with his mark. The nearest parallel is the illustration on the tomb slabs of masons where the figure is usually accompanied by his instruments. The tomb of Hugh Libergier for example, now in Reims cathedral, shows the figure holding a model of a church in one hand and his staff of office in the other. His square and compasses are at his feet and an inscription runs around the edge of the slab but there is no depiction of any mark.

The German use of the masons' mark may well have been a more public expression and indeed the word for a masons' mark used in the Torgau statutes of 1462 'Ehrenzeichen' means 'a distinction or honour'. The Torgau statutes of 1462 and 1563 are explicit about the allocation and use of marks, with regulations about the assigning of marks, marks for temporary workers in the lodge and procedures for changing marks (Coulton 1953, 157–8). There is nothing comparable in any of the English ordinances, even in the case of the London Masons'

Ordinances of the fifteenth and sixteenth-centuries which are very detailed.

Marks resembling masons' marks occasionally appear in documents, used as ciphers, and these may provide some form of identification of individual masons. Salzman (1952 pl. 11) illustrates a stone contract from 1536 that is 'signed' with three masons' marks, presumably those of the three masons named in the deed. From the same century the Louth spire building accounts have what appears to be the mark of the master mason Christopher Scune. It occurs in the top margin of the entry for 1508–9 in which the churchwarden lists the financial transactions with the master.(LAO Louth Par 7/1 166).

In some cases marks have been associated with named masons, by linking marks found in buildings with the documentary evidence. The name 'Malton' with a masons' mark beside it has been found on the nave wall of Beverley Minster and identified as that of William de Malton, appointed master mason of the Minster in 1335 (Petch 1981, 38).

Publication of masons's marks

Medieval masons' marks were first described in publications in the mid-nineteenth-century by both French and English writers (Godwin 1844, Didron 1845), although an earlier publication had noted the Roman masons' marks at Pompeii (Mozois 1824). Further papers in England and France rapidly followed as nineteenth-century writers sought to draw attention to the existence of masons' marks on major buildings. From an early date the marks were recognised as personal marks to identify the work of individual masons and authors stressed the need for comprehensive listing of marks to enable comparisons to be made between structures. Masons' marks were recorded in cathedrals and major buildings in England, France and Germany and published as reduced scale drawings. G. E. Street's volume on the major Spanish churches (Street 1865) includes drawings of masons' marks with the groundplans, but since he was unable to find similarities between the marks he felt they were of little interest.

At this early period distinctions had not been drawn between the various types of marks and all were considered simply as banker marks. The illustrations of the marks usually only referrred to whether they were found on the interior or exterior of the building and no reference was made to the number of times each mark occurred. An exception is the listing of the Westminster Hall marks (Freshfield 1887) which used diagrams of bays and stone courses to site the marks, but this approach has not been widely followed.

Publications in the first part of the twentieth-century concentrated on listing marks from parish churches (for example Bloe 1923, Davis 1938, Cunnington 1946 and Beaumont-Slegge 1950). Davis dealt with a specific group of churches from the Perpendicular period and related the evidence of the masons' marks to the documented history of the buildings. By using the same approach at Edington church it was possible to establish a connection between the constructdon of the parish church in the mid-fourteenth century and the rebuilding of the west end of Winchester cathedral (Cunnington 1946).

The first attempt to analyse masons' marks scientifically was made in the 1950s (Davis 1954). Davis presented a catalogue of marks classified by shape, listed with the building in which they occur. The declared aim was to use the marks as evidence for dating, since by finding marks of similar type he hoped to link undated buildings with those whose dates are known. Davis noted that the simpler marks can be found on buildings of all periods and that only the more elaborate ones are certain to be specific to one man. The catalogue is therefore primarily useful for the later medieval period when these marks occur.

Amongst the more elaborate marks that appear in buildings of the Perpendicular period are some that are clearly based on contemporary script, and whilst marks based on intersecting lines can be found at all periods, script based marks have only been found in buildings of the later period. Lettering underwent a change in the later Middle Ages, with the rounded shapes of 'Miniscule' script replaced by a more angular form with letters made narrower and more vertical. By the end of the period this had culminated in the development of the familiar 'black letter' script (Tschichold 1946). Later masons' marks seem to reflect this development and share the characteristic shape of lettering of the 'Textura' type that was used from the fourteenth century onwards, with marked lozenge shapes to heads and feet of letters and suppression of curves. Marks of this type have been recorded at a large number of late fourteenth and fifteenth-century buildings such as All Souls College Oxford from *c.*1438–43 and Peterborough cathedral from *c.*1496–1509 (Davis 1954, 71,51). Similar marks can also be seen in King's College Chapel (Fig. 17.7). Although their similarity to script does not enable the marks to be dated precisely the resemblance does provide a *terminus post quem* for their use.

More recent research has made use of the evidence of masons' marks in the analysis of individual structures. At Saint Denis, Crosby (1966) identified the original masonry from Abbot Suger's period by the presence there of masons' marks not found in later parts of the building. The evidence of the marks corresponded with the stylistic evidence and strengthened the connection between the chevet chapels and the work on the west block. In two other French buildings, Bourges cathedral and Toulouse Saint Sernin, the masons' marks were found to be specific to particular types of stone used only for certain parts of the buildings (Blanc *et al.* 1982, Lyman 1978). A considerable corpus of work on masons' marks now exists for buildings in Europe and Scandinavia, largely organised by the Centre de Recherche Glyptographique of Braine-le-Château but unfortunately not easily acces-

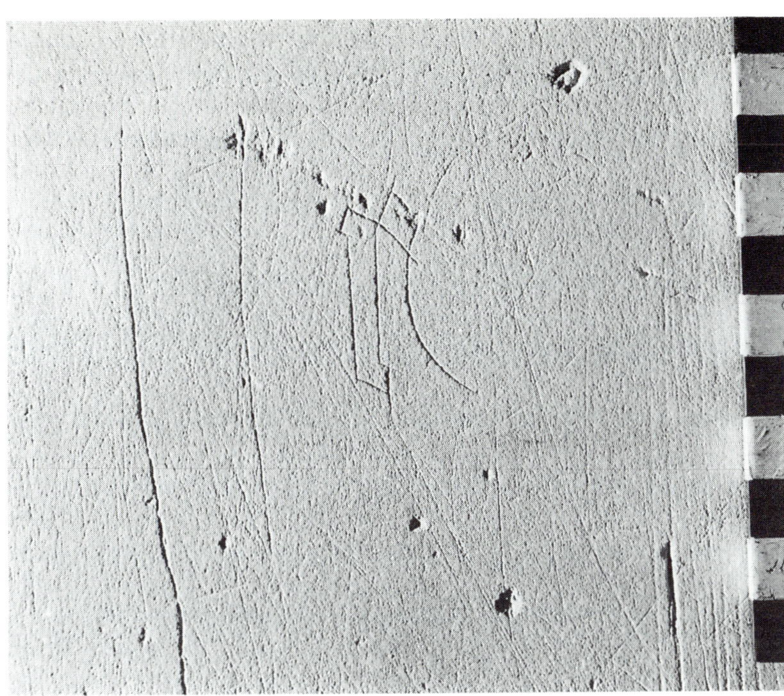

Fig. 17.7. Banker mason's mark based on late medieval script. Cambridge King's College Chapel choir north wall c. 1448.

sible outside France (for example Sansen 1975).

In Ireland Stalley has recorded masons' marks in the Cistercian abbeys and used them to support his argument that the buildings were the work of professional masons from outside the Cistercian order. At Mellifont the size of the thirteenth-century workforce has been estimated from the evidence of the masons' marks (Stalley 1987, 42–3).

Marked stones have been noted in a number of excavations, for example at Lismore Achanduin Castle in Scotland where comparisons between the marks in the castle and those of both Lismore cathedral and Inverlochy castle have been made to establish the date of the castle courtyard buildings (Webster and Cherry 1974, 197). Similarly the church at Wharram Percy has been related to the manor house, discovered by excavation, on the basis of the masons' marks (Wilson and Hurst 1965, 187).

There is no central register of masons' marks found in buildings in this country or any systematic programme of recording although the Royal Commission for Historic Monuments (England) does now include lists of masons' marks in its record of specific monuments (for example Phillips 1985).

Recording marked stonework

Marks inscribed on stonework are revealed under a raking light. This method can also be used with binoculars to examine inaccessible areas if a powerful torch is used and the light can be positioned at the correct angle. It is even possible to find marks on high vault ribs this way, from a position in the clerestory passages. A thorough inspection of a building to record all its masons' marks, or equally importantly to discover the sections of the building that do not have any, will require considerable work. A sampling technique is best adopted as a first stage, with one bay at several levels examined. Less public parts of the building, such as newel stairs are useful sites to sample.

Recording of marks is a twofold task. The mark itself needs to be recorded and its site precisely plotted. Rubbings are recommended for most surface details on stonework, but there can be problems with the background 'noise' of stone tooling and extraneous markings in some cases. The possible damage that rubbing can cause to friable stonework has also to be considered. If the stonework is in good condition and the mark is clearly defined then rubbings taken with pencil on various grades of paper can produce excellent results. Wax or heelball is usually too coarse to make a good rubbing.

For publication marks should be photographed with a scale under controlled lighting. The camera must be set up square to the surface to be photographed and not at an angle. For marks on the interior of buildings a flashgun held off the camera and angled across the surface of the stonework is the simplest method to use. Different tooling will need different angles of lighting to isolate masons' marks and a very shallow angle is not always the best. The angle can be tested by using a torch. The flashgun can either be held at arms length or be mounted on a second tripod in the required site and it should be set on a manual setting.

The main value of masons' marks is within the building in which they occur and they therefore need to be precisely coded to identify their site. A coding scheme was devised for Lincoln cathedral, based on the plan at four levels with allowance made for exterior surfaces and for wall passages. The building was divided into its major sections, nave, Bishop Hugh's Choir, Angel Choir etc. and then into bays within each section. Piers and responds were numbered within section and the coursing of all plain walling coded from a declared base line. At ground level this was the top of the plinth, above the high vaults the courses were counted down from the wall plate. Individual stones were then numbered within each course or other unit. The site coding system is made much simpler on the exterior of buildings where photogrammetric drawings are available.

The marks themselves also need to be coded if there are sufficient numbers to warrant analysis. A simple numbering system is adequate but dull and has little mnemonic value. A more complex system, which is easier to consult for comparison of marks, is one based on the marks themselves and for Lincoln a scheme based on the number of lines needed to draw the mark was used. This was combined with a letter of the alphabet, based on a loose resemblance, with a final number to make each one unique. Thus an alpha shaped mark made up of three lines is coded as 3a4, that is three lines arranged as a greek letter A, and is the fourth such mark in the group.

A certain amount of comparative analysis is possible by hand but the task of sorting several hundred marks is best left to a computer, and the time spent entering all the marks is well justified if a whole building or section of a building is involved. For most sample sizes a modern personal computer, preferably with a hard disc is ideal. The complete record for input into the will consist of a six column entry, made up of one code for the mark and five codes to locate it within the building, with an additional data number that is generated by the programme. Using a purpose-written programme the database can be interrogated for such things as all occurrences of a particular mark, or of all marks within one section of a building. Relationships between groups of marks can also be established by examining where they occur together. The significance of building breaks and changes in the building can also be assessed by comparison of the marks in those areas. The following buildings have been examined in part at least for masons' marks and the results made accessible. Computer analysis has been demonstrated at Lincoln.

Ely

No systematic recording of the cathedral has been undertaken but advantage was taken of the presence of scaffolding inside the west end of the nave during the cleaning of the ceiling in the late 1980s to record the marks on the east face of the late twelfth-century west tower wall. The marks have been plotted out on a measured drawing of the wall to give the precise location of each occurence (Fig. 15.4). A few marks were recorded on the exterior of the wall above the roof level but most of the exterior surface had become too weathered for these very lightly inscribed marks to survive. Unfortunately the archive does not contain rubbings or photos of the marks and they have been recorded diagrammatically rather than to scale. No analysis has yet taken place or comparative study in other parts of the structure undertaken but the existence of this archive should facilitate further study and provide encouragement for further recording in similar circumstances. The archive has been deposited at the cathedral. More recently the south-west transept has been surveyed archaeologically and analysis of the sequence of the masons' marks used to demonstrate the progress of construction (Fearn *et al.* 1995).

Exeter

Restoration work at Exeter cathedral has been monitored by the Exeter Museums Archaeological Field Unit as part of a long term project, with recording carried out in advance of conservation and replacement of weathered stonework. The south transept tower and the west front have been under observation. The transept tower dates from the twelfth-century and is built entirely of Salcombe stone. The west front dates from the mid-fourteenth and fifteenth centuries. Masons' marks have been noted on the exterior masonry, with some sited on the bedding plane of the stone rather than on the prepared face. This study is still in progress (Gaimster *et al.* 1989, 174). Masons' marks had previously been recorded in the high vault (Allan 1983, 5).

Lichfield

Analysis of the masons' marks has been carried out at Lichfield cathedral as part of the elucidation of the sequence of vault erection and repairs after the Civil War damage (Rodwell 1989). A series of masons' marks was identified and used to demonstrate that mouldings from the thirteenth century had been recut in the fifteenth century when the clerestory was rebuilt. At Lichfield it has been suggested that individual workshops can be identified and their output dated by analysis of masons' marks from the cathedral and nearby buildings. The methodology used to analyse the marks has not been published.

Lincoln

The Angel Choir of Lincoln cathedral has been systematically examined and all instances of masons' marks recorded. The marks and their precise site locations were coded and analysed by computer (see above) to discover the relationships between different parts of the choir. Using the evidence of the marks it was possible to demonstrate the construction sequence of the Angel Choir built over a short period in the second half of the thirteenth century. Further analysis related the screen walls around the high altar and the choir stalls to the later work in the choir, and demonstrated that the elaborately decorated work had been done 'in house'. Analysis of the masons' marks in the cloister has shown the extent of the controversial restoration programme at Pearson in the late nineteenth century (Alexander 1994, 141).

Wells

A comprehensive record of the masons' marks in Wells cathedral was undertaken in the 1940s and augmented by further researches in the 1960s (Wright and Wheeler 1971). The marks are presented in tabular form and referenced to bays within sections of the building. An introduction by Linzee Colchester relates the results to the surviving fabric accounts and shows the relationship between the marks and sections of the building.

Drawings

The plain walling of buildings may often reveal part of the design process of the overall structure since the materials readily to hand were used for small scale preliminary drawings. Drawing on parchment only seems to have occured after the mid-thirteenth century (Branner 1963, 131) and the high cost of the material must have restricted its use in the workshop. Examples of trial drawings can be found on stone and even on timber intended for roof beams that have survived when the materials were used in the building.

Both small and full scale drawings were clearly necessary but each served a different purpose. The tracing floors on which full scale drawings were made of tracery and other moulded stone, known from several major buildings in England and further afield, were only needed when the designs were fully worked out, to cut the templates. Earlier stages in the design need not have been made at full scale. An example of such a drawing at St Albans, for a rose window, is less than 3 metres in diameter. It also serves to demonstrate the continuity of the process since it is for the nineteenth-century rose built by Lord Grimthorpe (Branner 1963, 133).

Many examples of preliminary drawings and full scale layout drawings are known from European buildings and it has often been possible to relate these drawings to features in the buildings themselves. At Trogir cathedral in the former Yugoslavia for example, the drawings on the flat flagstoned roof above the aisles of the thirteenth-century cathedral have been identified as the design drawings for the additions made to the building in the fifteenth and sixteenth centuries. The drawings demonstrate three stages in the design process, early projects, the working out of decorative details and full scale layouts for template cutting. They were originally on the outside of the aisle roof and were preserved when a low parapet and tiled roof was raised over them (Gibson and Ward-Perkins 1977).

In this country all major buildings will have had a laying out shop for the full scale drawings, but only those of York and Wells have been published in detail (Harvey 1968, Colchester and Harvey 1974). The site of Ely's shop has been tentatively identified above the west porch although the small scale of the drawings recorded there may cast doubts upon its specific use as such (Pritchard 1967, 37–8). Not all shops may have been as well appointed as the tracing house at York, indeed the Wells site, over the north porch, has very little headroom, and it is possible that temporary floors, such as that used to plan the wooden vault ribs at York after the 1984 transept fire may have been common.

A number of drawings have been recovered in the recording and archaeological excavation of monastic sites. Some, inscribed in the plaster, must have disappeared when the buildings were unroofed, others such as the tracery design at Castle Acre priory survived into the late nineteenth century (Coulton 1915, 61). At Byland abbey evidence of the design drawing and the layout for its west rose have been recorded. A preliminary drawing of the rose window can be seen inscribed on the interior face of the west wall and a full scale layout drawing of the rose on a plaster floor was revealed in the 1930s (Harrison and Barker 1987, 141–2).

Lincoln cathedral Angel Choir has two sets of small scale drawings which show different stages in the design process. A single stone in the walling of the Longland chapel, but originally on the exterior, was used for working out the configuration of cusps in a circle for a tracery motif. It is incomplete because the drawing was done before the stone was cut to size for use, that is, the design was worked out while the stone was in the masons' lodge (Fig. 17.8). The second example was cut *in situ*. It consists of a series of drawings made with dividers on the rear of the screen wall of the south triforium and shows part of the evolution of the design of the Bishop's Eye, the circular window in the south west transept (Fig. 17.9). From the position of the drawings on the wall it is obvious that they were done when the stone was in place and their presence may suggest that a workshop, perhaps for training apprentices was sited there. There is insufficient room for a full-size tracing floor in the gallery.

Small scale design drawings on the walling stone probably survive in most cathedrals where the plain walling has not been damaged. As with masons' marks they are most visible in a raking light and should be recorded under the same conditions.

The numerous other drawings that can also be found, gaming boards, scraps of music and script, depictions of fanciful beasts and monsters as well as religious illustrations showing varying degrees of skill, belong perhaps with the graffiti of generations of visitors to the study of social rather than architectural history (Pritchard 1967).

Stone tooling

The mason working at a bench is responsible for preparing the individual blocks of stone that the walling masons will build with. After bringing the stone to its required shape each surface of the stone, with the exception of the back, will be brought to a degree of finish suitable for its purpose. That is the jointing faces will be keyed for mortar or shaped for metal clamping and the visible faces will be dressed. The act of dressing the stone is carried

Fig. 17.8. Design drawing for a cusped circle on ashlar block later used in exterior wall of Lincoln cathedral. Now in Longland chapel of the Angel Choir south aisle c. 1255–80.

Fig. 17.9a. Preliminary drawing for Bishop's Eye window. Lincoln cathedral Angel Choir south triforium.

Fig. 17.9b. Bishop's Eye window. Lincoln cathedral south west transept c. 1235–50.

out by driving a metal implement across the surface of the stone in a series of vertical or diagonal strokes or drafts. The resulting series of regular marks is refered to as tooling. Although different chisels and axes produce different marks, in practice these can be hard to distinguish on the finished stone due to the nature of the work.

Accounts differ as to the usefulness of tooling as an aid to research. The CBA handbook on stone (1987) suggests that tooling can probably contribute to the dating debate, whilst acknowledging that differences will occur with geology and with regional tradition. However as Hill has noted, stonemasons' tools have changed little over time and differences between tooling marks may not indicate differences in date (1981, 7). Not all dressed stone will have tooling marks visible, sometimes these will have been removed by rubbing with a piece of sandstone to leave a perfectly smooth surface and there is always the possiblity of refaced stonework. Even within these constraints however, the evidence afforded by tooling can be valuable. A catalogue of tooling marks categorised by date as well as by the tools involved facilitates analysis (for example, Bessac 1986).

Squared and dressed stone was only widely used as a mass walling material for buildings in England after the Norman Conquest, and evidence for Saxon tooling has to be sought from carved slabs and grave markers. Buildings from late eleventh-century England and Normandy demonstrate the use of the same sort of tooling, bold diagonal marks deeply incised, with vertical marks of the same type used for shafts. Tooling of this type is almost universal in Anglo-Norman buildings and it is the only type that can be assigned to a particular building period with any confidence (Fig. 17.10).

It is not possible to determine what sort of implement was used for this tooling since experiments have shown that both the axe and the broad chisel can produce these marks (Phillips 1985, 191). It had been suggested that a change from diagonal to vertical tooling occured *c.*1200 (Clapham 1934, 116), but this is clearly an over-simplification. Vertical tooling was already in use by the first quarter of the twelfth century for the massive drum piers of Gloucester and Tewkesbury, and both types of tooling can be seen in the eastern transepts at Lincoln from *c.*1192–1200.

The axe, the adze and the pick have all been identified as tools used for the rough dressing of stonework, and the axe can be used to dress ashlar. The chisel is thought to have been first used for dressing stone in the twelfth century, although as Salzman (1952, 333) has noted, its use for sculpture must predate that. Chisels must still have been novel in the 1170s since their use is one of the new methods commented on by Gervase in the rebuilding at Canterbury (Salzman 1952, 374).

There are a variety of different types of chisel, classified according to width. Those over 50mm are known as boasters or bolsters, and are used for the final dressing of stone surfaces. The most commonly used chisels for architectural as opposed to sculptural work are the 12mm, 25mm and 50mm widths (these are the modern equivalents of the half-inch, one inch and two inch chisels). Gouges or bull nosed chisels have rounded ends and are used for creating concave surfaces. The claw chisel has a series of straight or pointed teeth and is used either to bring the surface to a state where a straight chisel may be

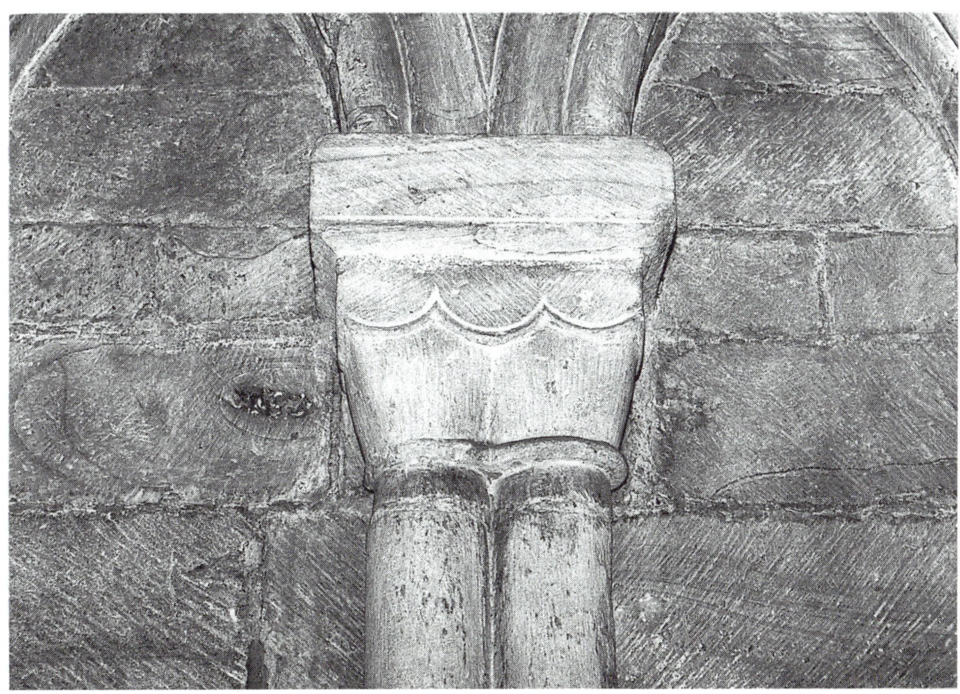

Fig. 17.10. Anglo-Norman tooling. Durham cathedral north nave aisle. First quarter of the twelfth century. Photo: J. F. King.

used or as a finishing tool itself (Hill 1981, 11). A form of toothed axe, known as a drag, was used for dressing stone in the thirteenth century in France, but it does not seem to have been popular in England.

The marks made by the different chisels and axes are often very similar, particularly when successive drafts have overlapped, disguising the width of the grooves left by the tool. Stones of different types and degrees of hardness will also produce different effects (Fig. 17.11). The claw chisel is the main exception, leaving a distinctive combed pattern on the dressed surface (Hill 1981, 12) (Fig. 17.3). Tooting created by a claw chisel is widely found in buildings of the thirteenth century but the date of its introduction is uncertain. In the north it can be seen in buildings of the third quarter of the twelfth century, introduced between the building of the choir at Ripon *c.*1160–70, which has diagonal tooling exclusively, and the church of Byland abbey from the next decade which has a small amount of claw tooling used (Wilson 1986, 115n). At Salisbury the claw chisel was introduced between 1220 when the building was started and 1225 when the Trinity altar in the eastern chapel was consecrated. It was not used on the stonework at ground level in the east end but is present in the upper levels of the chapel. The claw chisel was used by the Romans and its reintroduction and widespread use in the medieval period may have been due to personal choice by the masons. Further examination of stonework is needed, particularly of buildings in the south of England, to complete the picture.

When used within single structures, the evidence of the tooling can make a valuable contribution to the analysis, as has been demonstrated at York (Phillips 1985). Stone used in Archbishop Thomas of Bayeux's cathedral has tooling characteristic of the late eleventh century, and comparable to that of the near contemporary stonework at Richmond castle. Tooling marks were revealed on stone found in the excavation of the area under the central tower and formed part of the dating evidence. The tooling was made by either an axe or a boaster and comparison was made with the claw chisel tooling used by masons at York after *c.*1200. It was also noted at York that the differences between the finishing of the stonework in different parts of the building could be attributed to a number of factors outside the control of the banker masons, such as the amount of time allotted to the work and the demands of the patron (Phillips 1985, 189–91).

Earlier writers such as John Bilson, in his analysis of the building sequence at Wells, had used the evidence of the change in tooling from diagonal to vertical at the point where the stone course sizes change, to support his argument for a break in construction during the building of the nave (Bilson, 1928). The similarities between the architectural sculpture on either side of it suggested that the break was not a long one. As Harvey (1982, 61) has subsequently noted, the changes in the stonework, in the accuracy of cutting as well as in the block size and tooling, suggest a more radical change of method. This, coupled with the evidence of the roof timber jointing, which is more sophisticated after the break, seems to point to a 'technical revolution' by the time that work was resumed. Harvey also cites the evidence of the masons' marks, which show that over half the workforce employed on the eastern part of the nave continued to work after the break, as further evidence for the break being of short duration.

Fig. 17.11. Fifteenth-century tooling and banker mason's mark. Mount Grace Priory church tower east wall.

Stone Jointing

There are a number of different materials used for jointing stone of which mortar, although most often encountered, represents only one. There are some circumstances in which a method is necessary that will provide protection against lateral movement that mortar cannot supply. Metals are to be found here, either introduced in a molten state or as premade clamps linking sections of stone. Short lengths of other materials have also been used in the past to act as ties across stone joints. These have included wood, pieces of stone and even the leg bones of small animals. An example of this last use can be seen on the reused Caen stone blocks of the tomb chest to Sir Thomas Moyle from Eastwell church, Kent now in the Victoria and Albert Museum (Physick 1973, 10).

Mortar is used in stone buildings to provide stability, not to act as an adhesive (mortar has a very low tensile strength), to join stone in a way that keeps separate the individual stone blocks (Hill 1981, 5). It is intended to provide a measure of flexibility in the structure, as was discovered at York Minster (Phillips 1985, 173). There the mortar joints in the eleventh-century work absorbed the settlement caused by the extra weight of the tower added in the thirteenth century which caused distortion, but not damage, to the eleventh-century walling beneath.

The setting times of the medieval lime mortars, which behave differently to modern Portland cements, have been the subject of much speculation in the literature with figures of months and even years quoted but recent analysis has demonstrated that this is not the case (Mark 1982, 18). Lime mortars undergo a two stage process. In the first stage, the actual setting time is determined by chemical reaction to form calcium hydroxide plus evaporation of the moisture content and hence is subject to atmospheric conditions; this need not be a long process. The second stage, in which a chemical reaction occurs between the calcium hydroxide and atmospheric carbon dioxide (to form calcium carbonate) takes considerably longer due to the formation of a protective skin of calcium carbonate on the surface of the calcium hydroxide and this second process may never be completed. However, the mortar can be regarded as dry after the first stage.

Scientific analysis of lime mortars has been undertaken using the Carbon-14 method with varying success. Early attempts in the 1960s and early 1970s produced conflicting results (Delibrias and Labeyrie 1965; Baxter and Walton 1970), but a refining of the technique in the mid 1970s in which extracted elements of the mortar were studied has demonstrated its potential for dating structures (Folk and Valastro 1976). By separating the quicklime from any aggregate that has been used to make up the bulk of the mortar, it is possible to analyse its C14 content. The technique was first used successfully on the Roman site at Stobi and has since been repeated on the medieval church of Saint-Benigne at Dijon (Malone *et al.* 1980).

Mortar was little used by Greek and Roman builders before the first century AD for monumental stone buildings. Precise block cutting ensured stability in the structures with jointing achieved by the use of shaped metal clamps set in the bedding faces of the stones. Sections of column were linked by metal dowels run in with molten lead (Coulton 1982). Later builders used clamps shaped like modern staples, a method described by Vitruvius (book 2, 8) for attaching facing materials to rubble walls. Dowels and clamps have also been reported on the voussoirs of bridges and aqueducts as well as in barrel vault construction (Blake 1947, 217).

Medieval builders used similar techniques to resist lateral movement. Metal clamps, shaped like a double ended dovetail measuring *c.*25cm long by 8–10cm wide, were set into recesses cut into the bedding planes of the stones, on the tops of medieval screen walls for example Fig. 17.12) and in spires (e.g. Salisbury). The use of dowels and clamps continues to the present day to joint sections of stone in particular situations such as pinnacles or more prosaically gatepiers, where the stonework is built up as a stack rather than as part of a coursed wall.

Fig. 17.12. Beds cut for metal clamps on top of fourteenth-century screen wall. Lincoln cathedral south-east transept.

Lead used on its own is also sometimes found as a jointing compound in medieval structures. It can be employed in a number of different ways but the reason for using it will be the same in all cases, that is to make a joint that is strong and sets instantly. Lead acts as a key between two pieces of stone, it works in the same way that a clamp does but with additional advantages. It can be used for joining vertical faces as mortar can; unlike a mortar joint the joint using lead can be assembled fully before the jointing compound is used (Fig. 17.13). The mating faces are carefully prepared by having a series of channels arranged in a connected sequence, often like the veins of a leaf, with one end left open for the lead to be poured in.

An advantage of using the poured method is that as the lead sets almost instantly the joint is immediately fully made and requires no further support. For this reason lead joints are often found in high vaults, linking vault bosses and lengths of rib. Their use has been reported at Exeter cathedral in joints in the ridge rib (Allan 1983), and the intended site of this sort of joint can be seen at Lincoln cathedral. Here in the nave the ridge rib of the high vault is unable to connect with the ridge rib of the west block vault due to their different alignments and there is a space between the bosses at the ends of each vault. The channels in which the lead was to run are clearly visible on the last nave vault boss (Fig. 17.14). The Lincoln boss illustrates as well the additional protection against lateral movement that is provided by the key formed by the lead running into the holes drilled in the boss.

Poured lead joints, whether used between sections of rib in high vaults or between pieces of moulded stone, are often invisible in use, sometimes disguised by the use of mortar pointing. They can only be observed when the joint has been dismantled. Many cases of vault bosses or sections of moulded stone or window mullions may be cited, that are *ex situ*, where the lead channels are clearly visible. In most instances their use has not been identified (for example Daniels 1986, 268–9) probably because the lead has not remained. Lead has always been an expensive material and it seems unlikely that it would have been left either in abandoned structures, or in those being dismantled. In some cases lead jointed stones with the lead still attached are recovered archaeologically and these demonstrate conclusively how the method was used, an example is the fourteenth-century vault boss from the cloister at St Albans (Fig. 17.15).

A further use for lead jointing is in wall arcades where monolithic shafts, particularly those of Purbeck marble, have been used. In numerous examples, from the late twelfth century until the phasing out of these shafts in the early fourteenth century, lead can be seen between the neck of the capital and the top of the shaft, with a hole bored through the bell of the capital for the lead to be

Fig. 17.13. Poured lead joint in place.Rievaulx abbey novices room.

Fig. 17.14. Roof boss prepared for poured lead joint. Lincoln cathedral nave ridge rib from west c. 1235.

Fig. 17.15. Roof boss with poured lead joint in place. From St Albans abbey cloister. Fourteenth century. Photo: R. K. Morris (University of Warwick).

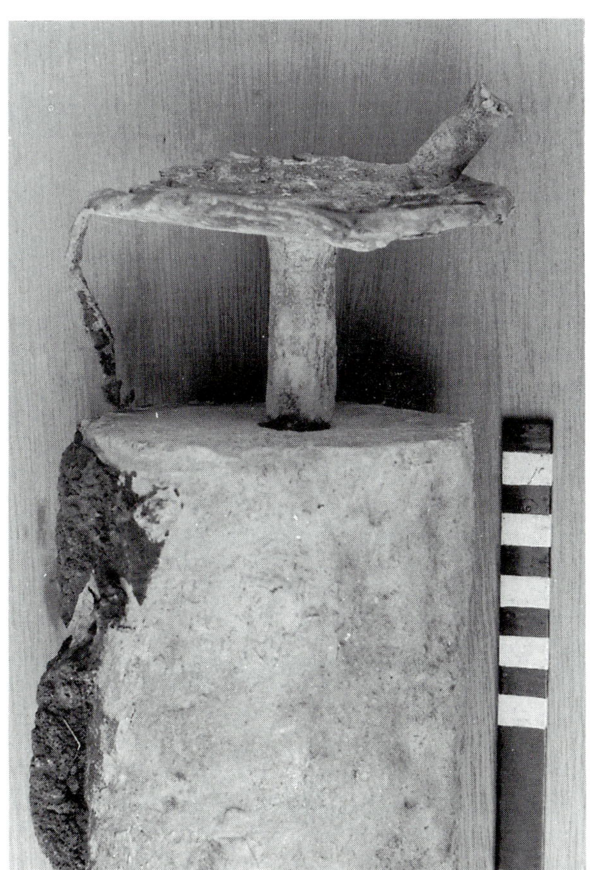

Fig. 17.16. Dismantled shaft from Lincoln cathedral west front with poured lead joint between capital and shaft partly removed. Pouring spout from neck of capital visible on right.

poured (Fig. 17.16). When it has been done skillfully it is often difficult to see, and arcades at ground level seem to have been done with greater care than those higher up in buildings. The reason for using lead in this situation can be explained by the action of the walling at this point. In building a wall arcade the capitals and bases will have been built in with the coursed masonry of the wall and will have undergone the slight settlements inevitable as the building rises higher. Any monolithic shaft already in place would crack or burst in that situation and to avoid this problem the shafts would have been added later. In order to make a firm joint in a situation where the shaft has had to be offered up under the neck ring of the capital and space would be limited, the ideal jointing material is molten lead. This method can also be used to replace damaged shafts.

To prevent seepage of the molten lead poured either vertically or on to a flat joint a clay collar is fitted round the joint. The consistency of the clay is important as it must be malleable enough to take up the shape of the stone but not too damp or spitting will occur. The remains of clay collars often survive around the tops of monolithic shafts where they join the capital. At Exeter cathedral wax, pitch and rosin were bought for this purpose, where the technique is described in the building accounts as 'soldering' the stones (Erskine 1983, 292).

Lead may sometimes be observed between sections of monolithic shafts, particularly Purbeck ones, where it has been used as a means of joining shafts to get the required length. The joints have been made very neatly and trimmed back to remove any trace of a pouring spout and must have been done before the shafts were put into place.

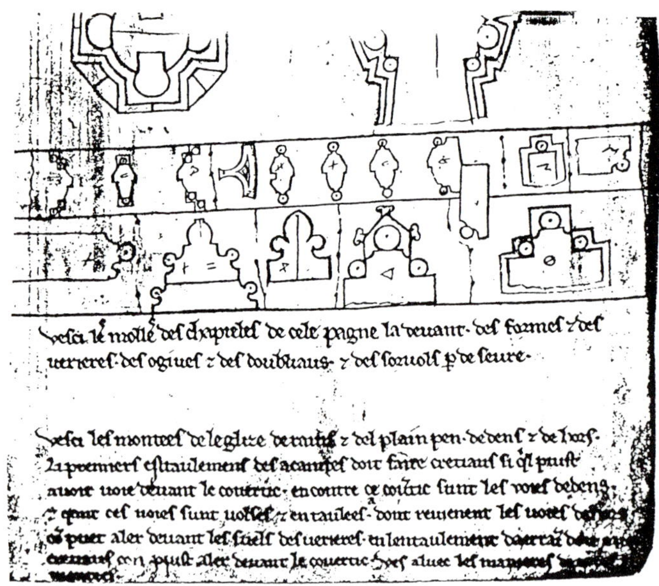

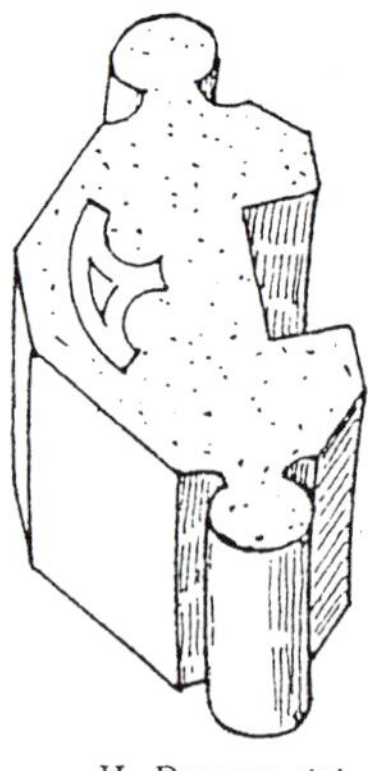

Fig. 17.17 Reims Cathedral dismantled window tracery with mark on bedding plane, and Villard de Honnecourt Sketchbook, f.32 detail.

In thirteenth-century buildings these joints often occur at an annulet although at Salisbury the massive Purbeck shafts surrounding the main crossing piers have brass rings in place of the annulets to tie the shafts into the central core. On dismantling these leaded joints one would expect to find that the shafts would have holes sunk into their mating faces for the lead to make an immovable joint. Although grouting inserted under pressure is often used today to make repair joints and is a less difficult material to work with, molten lead is still used in certain conditions.

Close study of the masonry of a cathedral or major church can reveal the methods employed in its construction, the organisation of its workforce and in some cases, the workings of the design process itself. Building sequences can be demonstrated by the plotting of changes in method, such as the use of different tooling and by the distribution pattern of the masons' marks, and restorations identified. The medieval mason developed techniques still in use today and the marks cut into the stonework represent a part of that process. Archaeological examination of these buildings with systematic recording and analysis of the marks is part of the process of elucidation.

Addendum

Villard's method of using marks at Reims can be demonstrated by an examination of the building to see whether marks from the sketchbook can be found on the stonework. A unique opportunity was presented during repairs to the damage caused in the first world war and the report was published in the 1920's (Deneux 1925). Deneux did not examine Villard's involvement in the construction of Reims and he published the masons' marks that were discovered as part of the archaeological evidence revealed in the restoration. A considerable number of marks was recorded by Deneux, the majority being assembly marks such as those used to install the west portal sculpture, but he also recorded several marks that occur in the sketchbook. One mark, a triangle that is shown on the drawing of the chevet chapel (f.30v), was recorded by Deneux in one site of the south side of the chevet. Asecond mark, shown on the transversearch of the 'lateral' high vault by Villard (f.31v.), was found by Deneux on the springing of the high vault of the nave between bays five and six.

The most interesting correlation between the sketchbook and the building occurs on a window mullion from the south window of the axial chevet chapel. The bedding plane of one of the oculus stones was found by Deneux to be marked with a drawing of a pierced soffit cusp. It is of identical form to that drawn on f.32 of the sketchbookbeside a window mullion of the same profile (Fig. 17.17). In each case the use must be the same, to identify the stone as part of the inner order of the oculusto which the soffit cusp was to be fitted. Since cusped oculi were a new developmentat this date it would have been necessary to provide a reminder for the construction masons who were working with an unfamiliar idea. Both the soffit cusp mark and the template marks are a form of assembly mark, possibly specific tothis one building, and serve to demonstrate the flexibility of this communication system.

Acknowledgements

I should like- to acknowledge the assistance of the masons at several buildings, in particular Mick O'Connor, foreman mason at Lincoln cathedral and of colleagues in the department of archaeology and of Dr R. G. Jones of the department of chemistry, University of Nottingham in the preparation of this study.

Bibliography

Adam, J-P. 1984: *La Construction Romaine*, (Paris).

Alexander, J. S. 1994: Early Decorated Architecture in the East Midlands c.1250-1300: an analysis of the major building campaigns. Unpublished P.H.D. thesis, Department of Archaeology, University of Nottingham.

Allan, J. 1983: Restoration and Archaeology in Exeter Cathedral. *Devon Archaeol.* 1, 1–5.

Baxter, M, & and Walton, A, 1970: Radiocarbon Dating of Mortars. 225. 937–938.

Beaumont-Slegge, W. 1950: Masons' marks in Dorset Churches, *Dorset Nat. Hist. and Archaeol, Soc*, 71, 73–83.

Bessac, J-C. 1986: l'Outillage Traditional du Tailleur de Pierre de l'Antiquité à nos Jours. Revue Archéologique de Narbonnaise Supplement 14. *Editions de Centre National de la Recherche Scientifique.*

Bilson, J. 1928: Notes on the earlier architectural history of Wells Cathedral, *Archaeol. Jnl.* 85, 23–68.

Blake, M. E. 1947: *Ancient Roman Construction in Italy from the Prehistoric period to Augustus*, (Washington).

Blanc, A. Lebouteux, P. Lorenz, J. and Debrand-Passard, S. 1982: Les Pierres de la Cathédrale de Bourges. *Archeologia* (Dijon) 171, 22–35.

Bloe, J. W. 1923: Masons' marks in Essex. In RCHM , 4, 181–2.

Branner, R. 1963: Villard de Honnecourt Reims and the Origin of Gothic Architectural Drawing. *Gazette des Beaux Arts* 6th ser. 61, 129–146.

Bucher, F. 1979: *Architector* vol 1, (New York).

Clapham, A. W. 1934: *English Romanesque Architecture after the Conquest*, (Oxford).

Colchester, L, S. and Harvey, J. H. 1974: Wells Cathedral. *Archaeol. Jnl.* 131, 200–214.

Coulton, G. G. 1915: Medieval Graffiti. *Proc. Camb. Antiq. Soc*, new ser, 13, 53–62.

Coulton, G. G. 1953: *Art and the Reformation*, (Cambridge).

Coulton, J. J. 1982: *Greek Architects at Work*, (London).

Council for British Archaeology 1987: *Recording Worked Stones: a practical guide.* (Handbooks in Archaeology no.1), (London).

Crosby, S. McK. 1966: Masons' marks at Saint-Denis. In P. Gallais and Y-J. Riou (eds.) *Mélanges offerts A René Crozet*, (Poitiers), 711–717.

Cunnington, B, H. 1946: Mason's marks on Edington Church. *Wilts. Archaeol. and Nat. Hist. Mag.* 51, 378–80, 470.

Dallas, R. W. A, 1980: Surveying with a Camera: Photogrammetry, *Architects Jnl.* 171, 249–255.

Daniels, R. 1986: The Excavation of the Church of the Franciscans, Hartlepool, Cleveland, *Archaeol. Jnl.* 143, 260–304.

Davis, R. H. C. 1938: Masons' Marks in Oxfordshire and the Cotswolds. *Archaeol. Soc. Rep.* 84, 69–83.

Davis, R. H. C. 1954: A Catalogue of Masons' Marks as an Aid to Architectural History. *Jnl. B.A.A.*, 3rd ser. 17, 43–76.

Delibrias, G. and Labeyrie, J, 1965: The Dating of Mortars by the Carbon-14 Method. *Proc. 6th Internat. Conf. on Radiocarbon and Tritium Dating*, 344–347.

Deneux, H. 1925: Signes Lapidaires et Epures du XIIIe Siècle à la Cathédrale de Reims. *Bulletin Monumentale* 84, 99-130.

Didron, A. 1845: Documents sur les artistes du Moyen Age, *Annales Archeol*, 223–236.

Erlande-Brandenburg, A. Pernoud, R. Gimpel, E and Bechmann, R. 1986: *Carnet de Villard de Honnecourt XIIIe siècle*, (Paris).

Erskine, A. 1981: The Accounts of the Fabric of Exeter Cathedral part 1, 1279–1326, *Devon and Cornwall Record Soc*, new ser. 24.

Erskine, A, 1983: The Accounts of the Fabric of Exeter Cathedral part 2, 1328–1353. *Devon and Cornwall Record Soc*, new ser. 26.

Evans, Sir A. 1930: *The Palace of Minos at Knossos*, vol 3. (London).

Fearn, K., Marshal, P., and Simpson, W.G. 1995: The South-West Transept of Ely Cathedral: Archaeological Interpretation. Unpublished report for Dean and Chapter of Ely Cathedral.

Folk, R. L. and Valastro, S, 1976: Successful Technique for Dating of Lime Mortar by Carbon-14. *Jnl. Field Archaeol*, 3, 203–208.

Freshfield, E, 1887: Masons' Marks at Westminster Hall. *Archaeologia* 50, 1–4.

Gaimster, D. R. M. Margeson, S. and Barry, T. 1989: Medieval Britain and Ireland in 1988. *Medieval Archaeol*, 33.

Gaur, A, 1984: *A History of Writing*, (London).

Gerstenberg, K. 1966: *Die Deutschen Bauneisterbildnisse des Mittelalters*, (Berlin).

Gibson, S. and Ward-Perkins, B. 1977: The Incised Architectural Drawings of Trogir Cathedral, *Antiq. Jnl.* 57, 289–311.

Godwin, G, 1844: Masons' Marks observable on Buildings of the Middle Ages. *Archaeologia* 30, 113–120.

Harrison, S. and Barker, P. 1987: Byland Abbey, North Yorkshire: the West Front and Rose Window Reconstructed. *Jnl, B.A.A.* 140. 134–151.

Harvey, J. H. 1968: The Tracing floor in York Minster, *40th Annual Rep. Friends of York Minster.*

Harvey, J. H, 1982: The Building of Wells Cathedral, I 1175–1307, In L. S. Colchester (ed.) *Wells Cathedral a History*, (Shepton Mallet) 52–75.

Hill, P. R. 1981: Stonework and the Archaeologist, *Archaeol. Aeliana* 5th ser. 9, 1–22.

Hood, S. 1987: Masons Marks in the Palaces. The Function of the Minoan Palaces. *Proc. Fourth Internat. Symposium the Swedish Inst. in Athens*, 205–212.

Jackson, J. W. and Northway, E. F. 1976: *St Laurence's Church, Ludlow.* Typescript.

Knoop, D. and Jones, G. P. 1949: *The Medieval Mason*, (Manchester).

L.A.0. Lincolnshire Archives Office.

Lyman, T. W. 1978: Raymond Gairard and Romanesque Building Campaigns at Saint-Sernin in Toulouse. *Jnl. Soc. Archit. Hist. (USA)* 37, 71–91.

Malone, C. M. Valastro, S. and Varela, A. G, 1980: Carbon-14 Chronology of Mortar from Excavations in the Medieval Church of Saint-Benigne, Dijon, France. *Jnl. Field Archaeol*, 7, 329–343.

Mark, R. 1982: *Experiments in Gothic Structure*, (Cambridge, Mass,).

Morris, R. K. 1979: *The Cathedrals and Abbeys of England and Wales*, (London).

Mozois, C. F. 1824: *Les ruines de Pompeii*, (Paris).

Petch, M. R. 1981: William de Malton Master Mason. *Yorkshire Archaeol. Jnl.*, 53, 37–44.

Phillips, D. 1985: *The Cathedral of Archbishop Thomas of Bayeux, Excavations at York Minster vol 2.* (London).

Physick, J, 1973: *Five Monuments from Eastwell,* (London).

Pownall, T, 1789: The Origins of Gothic Architecture. *Archaeologia* 9, 125.

Pritchard, V. 1967: *English Medieval Graffiti*, (Cambridge).

Rodwell, W, 1989: Archaeology and the Standing Fabric: Recent Studies at Lichfield Cathedral. *Antiquity* 63, 281–294.

Salzman, L. F. 1952: *Building in England down to 1540*, (Oxford) (2nd, edn. 1967).

Sansen, R. 1975: Lointains Messages de la Pierre. *Annales du Cercle Royal d'Histoire et d'Archéologie d'Ath et de la Région et Musée Athois*, 42, 1–144.

Stalley, R. J. 1987: *The Cistercian Monasteries of Ireland*, (London). Street, G. E. 1865: *Some Account of Gothic Architecture in Spain*, (London).

Sutherland, D. S. and Parsons, D. 1984: The Petrological Contribution to the Survey of All Saints church Brixworth, Northamptonshire: an Interim Account. *Jnl, B.A.A.*, 137, 45–64.

Tschichold, J. 1946: *An Illustrated History of Writing and Lettering*, (London).

Webster, L. E. and Cherry, J, 1974: Medieval Britain in 1973, *Medieval Archaeol*, 18.

Wilson, C. 1986: The Cistercians as "missionaries of Gothic" in Northern England. In C. Norton and D. Park (eds.) *Cistercian art and architecture in the British Isles,* (Cambridge) 86–116.

Wilson, D, M. and Hurst, D. G. 1965: Medieval Britain in 1964. *Medieval Archaeol*, 9.

Wright, G. A. A. and Wheeler, W. A. 1971: *Masons' Marks on Wells Cathedral Church*, 2nd edn. (Wells).

The Care of Cathedrals Measure 1990

Richard Gem

When the Ancient Monuments Bill was being discussed in Parliament in 1913 there was a view that this should allow the inclusion of cathedrals and churches in the Schedule, since these buildings formed a preeminent part of the nation's heritage. However, the political influence of the Church of England was sufficient to exclude 'ecclesiastical buildings in ecclesiastical use' from the scope of the Act (as the influence of houseowners was sufficient to exclude also domestic buildings). In return for this acknowledgement of its special position, Archbishop Davidson undertook to review the operation of the Church of England's own system of control, the Faculty Jurisdiction, the origins of which went back to the thirteenth century. From the period following the passing of the 1913 Act, with several subsequent commissions and pieces of legislation, dates the emergence of the Faculty Jurisdiction as it exists today. The Faculty Jurisdiction, however, applies solely to parish churches which come under the authority of the bishop of a diocese: it does not extend to cathedral churches, which have been subject only to their own statutes granted by the Privy Council.

However responsibly cathedral chapters might discharge their duties in maintaining the historic fabric of their churches (and the majority have consistently during this century set a high standard which did not fall behind contemporary standards applied to buildings in the secular field), there has always been the possibility that things might go wrong because of inadequate consultation or inadvised action -and in some cases things have occasionally happened that should not have done (it would be invidious to name names!). With the increasingly high standards set by succesive pieces of Parliamentary legislation, therefore, there has been corresponding pressure to bring cathedrals within a framework of statutory control. The turning point came when the Church of England, in response to a Government request related to the provision of state aid from the Historic Buildings budget towards the repair of churches, established a Commission to review the workings of the Faculty Jurisdiction. The Commission, under the chairmanship of the Bishop of Chichester, Dr Eric Kemp submitted its report in 1984: this was entitled *The Continuing Care of Churches and Cathedrals*. The report had in fact examined not only the workings of the Faculty Jurisdiction, but had looked also at the care of cathedrals and made a series of recommendations for bringing them under mandatory control: these recommendations the Government then pressed the Church of England to implement.

The Church of England as by law established posseses the right to initiate legislation on Church matters. Such legislation begins its course in the General Synod, where it is subject to three stages of debate and to two committee stages; it then passes to Parliament where it is scrutinised by the Ecclesiastical Committee to see whether it is 'expedient' before being read once in each of the two houses. Subject to Parliamentary approval the legislation then passes to the Royal Assent, whereupon it becomes part of the statute law of the land – though termed a 'Measure' rather than an 'Act'. The new Care *of Cathedrals Measure 1990* began its passage throught the General Synod in 1987 and was finally approved by Parliament in 1990: it is to come into operation on 1st March 1991. The Measure itself will be supplemented by a number of Rules, which will also have statutory effect. The matter of sanctions to enforce the provisions of the Measure is under continuing review.

The provisions of the Measure have not sprung from nowhere, but represent a codification of the best practices in the care of cathedrals that have developed over recent years, modified and extended in the light of the recommendations made by the Kemp Commission, and in the course of debate in the General Synod, as well as in discussion with the Government. They represent, therefore, a position that in principle is acceptable alike to the Government, to the General Synod and to the majority of cathedral chapters. The theory of the Measure, however, remains to be translated into practice in many of its details, and this is an important task ahead for the next few years.

The central provision of the Measure is that in future the administrative body of a cathedral has to obtain *approval* before implementing any proposal that would materially affect the architectural, archaeological, artistic or historic character of the cathedral church or of any ecclesiastical building in its precinct, as well as proposals that would affect any archaeological remains within the precinct or affect the setting of the cathedral. Additionally approval is required for the sale, loan or disposal of any object of architectural, archaeological, artistic or historic interest; or for the adddition of new objects to the cathedral. This necessary approval is to be obtained from one of two bodies: in the case of certain specified matters, from the national Cathedrals Fabric Commission for England (CFCE, successor to the present Cathedrals Advisory Commission, CAC); or from a local Fabric Advisory Committee (FAC) at each cathedral, nominated jointly by the administrative body and by the CFCE. When an application for approval is made the proposals must also be advertised and notified to the Local Planning Authority; additionally when the application is made to the CFCE notification must also be made to English Heritage and the national Amenity Societies. Such bodies then have a specified period within which to comment before the application is determined. The administrative body may appeal against an FAC decision to the CFCE, or against a CFCE decision to a specially constituted tribunal called a Commission of Review, whose judgement is final.

Archaeological Provisions of the Measure

At one level archaeological considerations are not singled out for exceptional treatment in the Measure precisely because they form one of the principles undergirding the whole structure. As early as 1914 the Dibdin Commission had recognised that there were four main principles that were fundamental to any systern of caring for church buildings, these were: architecture, archaeology, art and history; and precisely these four are central to the Care of Cathedrals Measure. That being recognised, there are additionally some specific provisions relating to archaeological matters.

In general the Measure establishes statutory control by the FAC or the CFCE over any proposal that a Dean and Chapter may wish to implement which potentially affects the archaeological character of the cathedral church or of any building in ecclesiastical use in the precinct (that is, any building excluded ipso facto from Listed Building Control or Ancient Monument Control). Furthermore it establishes control over any proposal that may affect archaeological remains anywhere within the precinct (the 'precinct' to be designated on a map by the CFCE), whether or not those proposals are also subject to Scheduled Monument Control: 'archaeological remains' are defined as 'the remains of any building, work or artefact, including any trace or sign of the previous existence of the building work or artefact in question' (cf. the Ancient Monuments Act 1979). As a supplementary provision, the Dean and Chapter must notify the CFCE of any application they make for Scheduled Monument Consent so that the CFCE may comment thereon.

The sale, loan or disposal of any object of archaeological interest is also brought under control. The Dean and Chapter have to compile and maintain an inventory of all objects in their possession which the FAC considers to be of (inter alia) archaeological interest, and the FAC must consult the CFCE on the designation of any objects that are to be considered of outstanding interest. The CFCE is required to issue guidance on the format of such inventories.

A Dean and Chapter are already under a statutory obligation to appoint a Cathedral Architect, and now they are under a similar obligation to appoint a Cathedral Archaeological Consultant. The Consultant must be a person who possesses such qualifications and expertise in archaeological matters as the CFCE may recognise as appropriate; and the CFCE has a discretionary power to dispense the Dean and Chapter from appointing a Consultant if it considers that the archaeological interest of the cathedral does not justify this (one might think of a twentieth-century cathedral on a new site). The statutory responsibilities of the Consultant are: first, to attend meetings of the Fabric Advisory Committee; and, secondly, to consult with the Cathedral Architect on the preparation of a written report every five years, setting out those works which the Architect considers should be carried out in the next quinquennium and advising on their priority. There is also an obligation for the Dean and Chapter to keep a record of all works actually carried out.

Role and Duties of Cathedral Archaeological Consultants

The appointment of an Archaeological Consultant is not a provision incorporated in the Measure without a previous background in actual practice. For a number of years there has already been a network of such Consultants serving the majority of cathedrals and appointed with the advice of the Cathedrals Advisory Commission and the Council for British Archaeology. The CAC in 1987 produced guidance notes on the role and duties of such consultants, and has in preparation a draft for a specimen Memorandum of Agreement that can serve as a model contract for the appointment of a Consultant. A basic job description for a Cathedral Archaeological Consultant therefore exists, and it is in relation to this that the new statutory functions will need to find their context.

The Consultant is above all the professional adviser to the Dean and Chapter on all matters in which the latter have archaeological responsibilities. He or she, therefore, must have not only experience and understanding of the archaeology of standing buildings and of sites, but also a familiarity with the statutory framework for archaeology and planning proceedures. His primary responsibility is to ensure, insofar as lies within his power, that the archaeological aspect of all Dean and Chapter proposals has been properly evaluated at an early stage, and that steps have been taken to incorporate a suitable archaeological component into those proposals, with due resources assigned for the realisation of that component at the fieldwork and post-fieldwork stages. This function extends as much to the standing fabric as to archaeological deposits below ground level, and ranges from making provision for the recording of ancient masonry that is being renewed, to arranging for the possible excavation of archaeological deposits in advance of works (where preservation in situ is not possible).

The Consultant is not as such expected to be an executant archaeologist and may usually be in the position of making arrangements for work to be carried out by other archaeological bodies. On the other hand, in some cases the Consultant may have the resources of an archaeological team or unit behind him and will be able to offer to carry out a major piece of work, where such is required, under a separate contract from his Consultancy – though recognising that the tender for such work may need to be competitive. Where more generally it may be helpful if the Consultant is able to carry out work directly is where a comparatively small project requires to be implemented.

Although the Measure defines the relationship in certain areas between the Consultant and the Cathedral Architect, it is not only the Architect with whom the Consultant needs to establish a good working relationship. The relationship with his employers, the members of the Chapter, is clearly of primary importance; but another key figure is often the Clerk of Works, and a separate architect is sometimes employed in relation to properties within the cathedral close. The Archaeological Consultant needs to have a good channel of communication to all these if he is not to go on site one day and find some work in hand of which he was unaware. Beyond the immediate circle of cathedral employees, the Consultant may also expect to be the link in any discussion of archaeological matters between the Dean and Chapter on the one hand, and on the other hand the Fabric Advisory Committee, the Cathedrals Fabric Commission, English Heritage and the Local Planning Authority.

Apart from advising the Dean and Chapter on any archaeological works, the Consultant also has a role in advising them on the compilation and archiving of archaeological records, and on the inventorying, storage and possible display of objects of archaeological interest. Here he will need to collaborate with other specialist staff Morris, R.K. 199if they are appointed at the particular cathedral in question: the Archivist, the Librarian and the Curator. He may also have a more general role in advising on publications of archaeological interest and in contributing from his particular perspective towards projects relating to education and interpretation for visitors. Education in the importance and relevance of archaeology is indeed especially important if the high profile given to archaeological matters in the Measure is not to come to be seen as a burden by those responsible for maintaining and funding the cathedral: archaeology still needs hard but tactful selling if it is to be seen as a positive asset and as a resource to be conserved willingly rather than reluctantly.

Addendum, September 1995

This paper was written in 1990. Subsequently the *Care of Cathedrals Measure* did indeed come into operation on 1st March 1991, together with the *Care of Cathedrals Rules 1990*. The *Care of Cathedrals (Supplementary Provisions) Measure 1994* came into operation on 1st July 1994 and provided for enforcement procedures. A party who considers that there has been an infraction of the main Measure, in respect of works carried out without due approval, may make representations to the diocesan bishop. The bishop may then initiate enforcement proceedings using his own visitatorial powers, backed up by the ecclesiastical court of the provincial vicar general.

Account should also be taken of the *Ecclesiastical Exemption (Listed Buildings and Conservation Areas) Order1994*, made pursuant to the *Planning (Listed Buildings and Conservation Areas) Act 1990*. This for the first time defines precisely the extent of the buildings within a cathedral precinct which are exempted from listed building control. Copies of the relevant maps showing the area of exemption designated by the Secretary of State may be consulted at the offices of the CFCE, the local planning authority or the cathedral in question. Discussions are in process with government to seek clarificationalso of the exemption from scheduled monument control.

The CFCE itself has produced a series of Guidance Notes offering guidance in the interpretationof the various aspects of the Measure, including its relationship to other planning procedures. Especial attention should be drawn her to *Guidance Note 5, Cathedrals and Archaeology: a Guide to Good Management* (November 1994) which in particular relates the Measure procedures to the government's *Planning Policy Guidance 16* and to English Heritage's *Management of Archaeological Projects* (2nd edition).

It is anticipated that in the quinquennium1995 - 2000 the General Synod will establish a review group to assess the working of the Measure and bring forward proposals for modification of any points of detail that have been problematic. It is not intended, however, to reconsider the fundamental principals of the legislation.

Finally, note should be taken of the coming into being of an Association of Cathedrals Archaeologists, formed in 1995 and arising out of a series of annual symposia for cathedral archaeologists, organized by the CFCE since the Measure came into operation.